KT-153-856

PENGUIN REFERENCE BOOKS

THE PENGUIN
DICTIONARY OF COMPUTERS

Anthony Chandor was educated at Epsom College, and New College, Oxford. A Fellow of the British Computer Society, he has been a member of the Council of the Society and, since its inception, a member of the Examinations Board for professional examinations. In over twenty years of systems and computer management experience, he has twice been appointed by the United Nations as data processing adviser. He is currently Managing Director of INSAC International Ltd, and is the author of *A Short Introduction to Computers*, *Computers as a Career*, *Choosing and Keeping Computer Staff* and, with Graham and Williamson, *Practical Systems Analysis*.

John Graham entered the computer industry in 1959 and in addition to his wide experience in systems, programming and data processing consultancy, he also has considerable experience of management in the data processing industry. He is currently a director of a major British software organization. A Member of the British Computer Society, he is the author of *Systems Analysis in Business* and *Making Computers Pay*.

Robin Williamson was educated at Tonbridge School and Magdalen College, Oxford. He entered the computer industry in 1963, has been a systems and programming manager responsible for major computer projects and has regularly lectured on systems analysis and development. He spent some time in New York as manager of ICL Dataskil's USA operations and currently holds a senior position with a leading software house.

THE PENGUIN
DICTIONARY OF
COMPUTERS

ANTHONY CHANDOR

WITH

JOHN GRAHAM

ROBIN WILLIAMSON

Second Edition

PENGUIN BOOKS

Penguin Books Ltd, Harmondsworth, Middlesex, England
Penguin Books, 625 Madison Avenue, New York, New York 10022, U.S.A.
Penguin Books Australia Ltd, Ringwood, Victoria, Australia
Penguin Books Canada Ltd, 2801 John Street, Markham, Ontario, Canada L3R 1B4
Penguin Books (N.Z.) Ltd, 182–190 Wairau Road, Auckland 10, New Zealand

—

First published 1970
Reprinted 1970, 1972, 1973, 1974, 1975
Second edition 1977
Reprinted 1977, 1978, 1979, 1980, 1981 (twice)

—

—

Typeset, printed and bound in Great Britain by
Hazell Watson & Viney Ltd,
Aylesbury, Bucks
Set in Linotype Times Roman

PREFACE

Every day more and more of us find that computers have become part of our daily background: magazines we read have been typeset by computers, architects have designed our houses with the help of computers, our payslips are printed by computers, we pay bills prepared by computers, using cheques marked with computer symbols, and the payments result in bank statements prepared by computers. Even more directly associated with the machines are those who use them in their day-to-day work – scientists and storekeepers, clerks and directors, soldiers and sailors, accountants and engineers – besides the growing numbers of computer personnel who are responsible for making the machines do the work. Each of us, whether layman, computer user or computer technician, will have problems with computer terminology from time to time, and it is the purpose of this book to provide a ready means of solving these problems.

Requirements of the Book

Since the early 1950s, when computers first began to be used commercially, many hundreds of everyday words have been given new meanings, and words which had a peaceful existence on their own in ordinary English dictionaries have been joined together in the computer world to make phrases which are quite unintelligible to anyone unaware of their specialist meaning. For example, neither *crippled leap-frog test* nor *graceful degradation* includes an unfamiliar word but both phrases have a specific technical meaning. In addition to the 'plain English' words, there are, of course, numbers of purely technical words which need defining in simple terms. This book provides a glossary giving as much information as possible, and the overriding aim has been helpfulness rather than deftness or lexicographical terseness. It is designed to satisfy both the layman whose association with computers is still only indirect and the technical reader already familiar with many of the terms but searching for a definition of a word used in a branch of computer technology he has not yet mastered.

To cater for these main categories of reader the following primary guide-lines are necessary:

For the layman:

Basic words must be explained in simple English and not in terms of each other.

Basic concepts must be explained at some length if necessary.

Advanced words must be extensively cross-referenced to make it possible to follow a word through a series of entries.

For the technical user:

Specialist words and jargon in common use must be included as well as the more generally recognized terms.

Some subjects (such as *Law and Computers* and *Audit of Computer Systems*) must be given a more discursive treatment than the conventional entries.

Structure of the Book

To meet these requirements the book has been organized in the following way. First there is a general article called *Introduction to Computers* for all readers to whom the subject of computers is entirely new. This explains very simply what computers are and how they are used, and sets the background for the rest of the book. It is followed by conventional dictionary entries for technical words and phrases, and widely used jargon expressions. The power and pervasiveness of the acronym are also recognized and those in common use (such as *P E R T* and *A L G O L*) are included. Interspersed with the definitions, in the same alphabetical sequence, are seventy general articles dealing concisely with a specific topic which requires more generous treatment than can be given in a conventional definition. Each topic has been selected to satisfy the requirements of the different categories of reader and is written at an appropriate technical level. For example, the article on *Programming* is written in simple language for the layman, as it is unlikely that an experienced programmer would need to refer to so general a heading. The article on *Information Retrieval Techniques*, however, is written for the informed reader, as it is improbable that a complete beginner will be looking up this subject.

Not all the articles are on strictly technical subjects. In the same way that, for example, an accountant may use this book to refer to the article on *Systems Analysis*, a computer professional may wish to inform himself generally on some aspect of accounting for which a computer is to be used – perhaps *Discounted Cash Flow* or *Budgetary Control*. Several such activities in which computers are commonly used are described in the book, and they are there to provide a background reference for the young computer technician. Similarly certain subjects related to the use of computers are described, such as *Allocation, Forecasting* and *Model Building*.

At the end of this preface, on page 11, there is a list of the general articles indicating the category of reader for whom the article is intended. Those shown as suitable for the man-in-the-street provide a background of information as simply as possible, and assume no prior knowledge other than that obtained from the *Introduction to Computers* on page 15. The articles shown as 'technical' will provide useful information for those starting a career in computers, for scientists and engineers using computers directly in their daily work, and, it is hoped, may provide agreeable browsing for computer personnel who are already established.

There is detailed cross-referencing throughout the book, and in any definition all those words themselves defined elsewhere in the book are printed in italics the first time they are used. In general the natural lead word of a phrase is taken to be the master word even if it is an adjective qualifying a noun – for example, *buffered computer* appears under the letter B and *overflow bucket* under O. With some terms it is not easy to see which the 'natural' lead word is, and for these a cross-reference is given under the appropriate words: for example, *machine-spoilt work time* appears under the letter M but there is also a reference from *work time, machine-spoilt*. Each definition is given in an attempt to explain the actual usage rather than to suggest any standard; various admirable attempts have been made to bring order to the anarchistic plethora of overlapping and conflicting usages of technical terms, but the terms are still used with a variety of meanings in different contexts and this book therefore explains each term with no attempt to give 'preferred' definitions only. The entry under *background processing* is not untypical: three different meanings and two of them directly contradictory, but all three in general use. Where appropriate the definitions include synonyms, antonyms, directly related words and, where this would help to expand the definition, a reference to one of the general articles.

Haslemere, 1970   ANTHONY CHANDOR

PREFACE TO THE SECOND EDITION

THE vigour and dynamism of the computer industry continues to be reflected in its words and phrases and the pace of growth of the industry is still matched by the speed at which new phrases become established. Men and women associated with computers are as quick to adopt new phrases to describe new techniques and advances in technology as they are ingenious in inventing the processes which require such labels. It has been pleasantly noticeable during the years since the compilation of the first edition of this Dictionary that, in general, it is the imaginative phrase which establishes itself rather than its pedestrian equivalent: such words as 'de-updating' still emerge, but phrases like 'deadly embrace', 'menu selection' and 'slave store' find swift acceptance; computer people would clearly rather use a compelling phrase than mangle an already tortured word. One notable failure has been an improvement on the somewhat sinister phrase 'computer people' (the even less agreeable 'liveware' having been mercifully rejected). Perhaps a user of this dictionary has already observed the use of a suitable phrase? Over the past few years I have been most grateful for suggestions for inclusion of new words from readers all over the world, and look forward to receiving many more. If one such suggestion allows a replacement for 'computer people' without leading inexorably to 'informatician' a great advance will have been made!

Haslemere, 1977   ANTHONY CHANDOR

ACKNOWLEDGEMENTS

THE help received from many individuals and organizations is most gratefully acknowledged. It is not possible to make particular acknowledgement except to those whose contribution was substantial; many thanks, therefore, to:

T. Hugh Beech	G. J. Mansell
R. R. Campbell	David Rogers
H. J. P. Garland	J. Wale
Rudi Malir	W. J. Woodward

and to the following organizations:
American Standards Association Incorporated; British Standards Institute; Business Equipment Manufacturers Association; Control Data Corporation; General Electric Company; G E C Computers and Automation Ltd; Honeywell Electronic Data Processing Division; I B M; International Computers Ltd; R C A Electronic Data Processing; The National Cash Register Company Ltd; U N I V A C – Division of the Sperry Rand Corporation.

We should like in particular to thank International Computers Limited for making time available on one of their 1900 series computers so that many of the tasks of putting this book together were accomplished efficiently with minimum effort.

LIST OF GENERAL ARTICLES

As explained in the preface, the following topics are dealt with at greater length than conventional definitions. They are grouped below according to whether they are more suitable for the layman or the technical reader and, except for *Introduction to Computers*, appear in the main text within the alphabetical sequence.

Articles for the layman

Introduction to Computers

Analog computers
Central processors
Computer personnel
Data processing department
  organization
Digital computers

Hybrid computers
Input devices
Output devices
Paper tape
Programming
Punched cards
Storage devices
Systems analysis

Articles for the technical reader

ALGOL
Allocation
Auditing computer systems

BASIC
Boolean algebra
Budgetary control

Character recognition
Check digits
COBOL
Communications devices
Control totals
Cost analysis systems
Critical Path Method

Data base management systems
Data preparation
Data processing standards
Debugging

Decision tables
Discounted cash flow
Documentation – systems
Documentation – programming
Dump and restart

Evaluating a new system
Executive programs
Extrapolation

Feasibility studies
Flowcharting
Forecasting
FORTRAN

Information retrieval techniques
Installation of computers
Instruction formats
Inventory control
Iteration

A NOTE ON SPELLING

THROUGHOUT this book, a programme of events is distinguished from a computer program by the convenient – and generally recognized – difference in spelling, and a similar distinction between analogue and analog computer and disc and magnetic disk has been adopted.

See references are denoted by an arrow: ◊
See also references are denoted by a double arrow: ◈

INTRODUCTION TO COMPUTERS

The purpose of a computer

A computer is a tool. A tool operates by taking raw material and converting it into a product by means of a device which performs a process. The process is determined by people. To take an analogy from everyday life: a blunt pencil (raw material) is converted into a sharp pencil (product) by means of a penknife performing the process of sharpening, as determined by a school boy. The device – the penknife – can of course be turned to several other uses, such as extracting stones from horses' hooves, or carving initials on a desk. But its scope is basically limited to one type of process and one type of material.

In all essentials, computers are tools, and in describing them we can consider each of the functions of any tool: the raw material, the product, the device, the process and the people.

The raw material

First, the raw material: facts (or *data*). A fact is a thing or event known to exist or have happened: something which can be described in precise, measurable terms. A fact may be an amount of £13 as written on a cheque; a line on an architect's plan; a measurement in a scientific experiment; a membership number; an address; an item on an invoice; a forecast in a plan. An individual fact, on its own, does nothing more than provide the single piece of information it represents.

The product

The product that a computer generates from this raw material is *information*. By the relation of facts of the same type or different types, something useful is obtained. In isolation, a cheque for £13 is of little interest to the bank manager: related to an overdraft of £88 and an agreed maximum of £100 for Mr Smith, the isolated fact becomes informative, with unfortunate consequences for Mr Smith. The single line on the architect's drawing is meaningless: related to all the other lines on the drawing it plays a part as representing an outside wall, or a room divider or a drain. The single

15

experimental measurement may be insignificant: related to hundreds of other measurements, the fact may become crucial in the proof of a scientific theory. The process carried out by the computer is the converting of isolated facts into information by relating them to each other. This is a process with which we are all familiar in daily life – figuring out how much has been spent on a shopping spree by jotting down facts, isolated purchases, and adding them up to form a grand total. Looking up an address in a street atlas is, again, the conversion of an isolated fact, an address, into information: the relationship of the address to a locality, and thus to a way of getting there. We are also familiar with tools used to process facts: the cash register, the adding machine, the library catalogue, the slide rule, even a dictionary, all are used to process facts into information.

The device: distinguishing features

How does the computer compare with other information-processing tools? The three main distinguishing features of a computer are speed, capacity and versatility. An example of speed: an average person might take about a minute to add up ten 7-digit numbers. In the same time, some computers could have added up 1,000 million or more numbers. Further, the average man would feel some unease about the accuracy of his addition of 1,000 million numbers: the computer sum would be correct. An example of storage capacity: the contents of a hundred volumes of the London telephone directory could be accommodated in one typical storage unit: in one second, 15,000 entries could be looked up. Examples of versatility: the same computer could be used to print bank statements; draw perspective drawings from outline sketches; calculate betting odds; calculate satellite orbits; match aspiring lovers; calculate population statistics. There are few fields of human activity in which the computer cannot be applied.

Instructions

The computer achieves such prodigious feats not because of any superhuman powers of intelligence, but because it is able to carry out a few extremely simple operations accurately and very quickly. We are all familiar with the principle of doing something complex by performing a set of simple instructions: a knitting pattern tells one how to make a garment by following a set of simple stitches; a do-it-yourself construction kit works in the same way. Just as the knitting pattern instructions consist of a few basic steps written in a special code (K1, P1 means knit one stitch, purl one stitch) so the computer has a repertoire of basic operations which it can carry out on data. These operations can be loosely grouped into control operations, which enable the computer to operate various devices which feed data into it for processing, and which accept results after processing; arithmetic operations, enabling the computer to add and subtract, and thus multiply and divide as well; and logical operations, which enable the computer to select different sets of instructions as a result of tests made on items of data.

Hardware

Hardware is the term given to all the electronic and mechanical gadgetry which together forms a computer system, as distinct from the sets of instructions which are used to operate them. A computer system consists of three basic types of machine. First, there is that part of the system which can perform operations as a result of instructions. This part is known as the *central processor*. Second, the unit used to store the raw material on which the processor is to set to work: this is known simply as a *storage device*, although the term *memory* is also used, as an analogy in human terms. Finally, there are devices (a) to place data into storage and (b) to extract the finished product from the system. These are known collectively as *input devices* and *output devices*. A computer is thus a collective noun used for a group of devices: a central processor, storage, input and output devices. In fact, the picture is not quite as clear-cut as this. Central processors contain a special type of storage device known as high-speed or *immediate access store*. The power and speed of a computer depends on the amount of this storage available, since all instructions are held in this storage device, as well as that part of the data which is being immediately affected by the instructions. As high-speed store is expensive (for example, it can consist of elaborately interwoven strands of wire and tiny rings of magnetized material known as *cores*), large quantities of data are held on *backing stores* which are cheaper, but from which it takes longer to extract individual items of data. Basic data still has to be placed into the backing store, so a common sequence of events is for this raw material to be put onto a backing store in one operation, and then be processed from the backing store before becoming the final product. Indeed, several stages of processing may take place, the intermediate results of each being transcribed to backing store, before the final product is available.

The central processor is usually placed in one box or cabinet, and input, output and storage devices each in their own boxes; for this reason the latter are all collectively known as *peripheral units*. Nowadays a computer system is much like a child's construction kit in that the user can buy the 'Mark 1' version and then improve his kit by buying new peripheral units and plugging them into his system. Or he can keep his peripheral units and change the central processor for a bigger and faster one. 'Bigger' will mean a larger immediate access store with the ability to hold larger and more complex sets of instructions; 'Faster' will mean that the instructions themselves will be carried out more quickly.

Types of computer

What we have described so far has been mostly concerned with computers used for commercial applications, and also by scientists and engineers engaged in the processing of large numbers of mathematical calculations. This sort of computer is known as a *digital computer*. It works on data held as a large number of distinct items, and operates in a series of steps or instructions. But 'raw material' or unprocessed data is not always in the form of individual and separate items – cheques, bills, bookings. In some cases this raw material is something which lasts over a length of time and changes its value over that time. For example, the speed of a car over a journey is in a sense an item of data, which lasts as long as the journey takes, and varies continuously over that journey. We may need to process this data item to obtain information, for example to detect a speed in excess of 70 m.p.h. and slow down. We are all familiar with a machine which does just this: the car speedometer displays the speed at any time, and by watching this we can control our vehicle. *Analog computers* are a type of computer which can accept data as a quantity varying over a length of time, rather than as a series of distinct items each with a unique value. Analog computers are used for scientific purposes, to measure the results of experiments, or to simulate processes which can be described in terms of quantities varying according to known rules over lengths of time. They are also used for process control of industrial operations, constantly measuring some varying quantity, for example voltage or gas pressure, and causing operations such as switching off circuits or opening valves when the quantity being measured reaches pre-determined values. *Hybrid computers* are yet another type of machine, combining some of the properties of both digital and analog computers. A varying input accepted by the analog computer can be converted into a series of distinct values which can then be processed by the digital part of the machine. Digital processing is usually faster and more sophisticated than the processing which can be done by analog machines, so *hybrid* processing gives the advantages of both types of device.

Processing – programs

We have said that the computer is a tool, and the job it does is processing facts to obtain information. But the same could be said of adding machines, cash registers and a number of other accounting and calculating machines. The great difference between a computer and other information-producing equipment is versatility: unlike the other machines, which in general perform one fixed type of operation, the computer's operations can be varied without limit. How does this happen? We have already explained how the computer performs a complex task by a series of relatively simple steps, and how the heart of the machine is a *central processor* in which the instructions are stored and obeyed. The storage unit of the processor can be likened to a large filing cabinet, with quantities of empty files or pockets each with a reference number. To start things off, one instruction is placed in each 'pocket'. In the computer system this is done by means of an input device 'reading' the set of instructions or program. The computer is then directed to start working. The first instruction is extracted from the first pocket and whatever this instruction says is obeyed. Then the next instruction is extracted from the next pocket, and so on until the sequence of instructions is completed. Data which is to be processed is placed in pockets in the same way; one instruction might be to fill up a number of pockets with data; another might be to empty pockets containing results. In the computer's processor, pockets or *storage locations* hold *characters, words* or *bytes*; they are the smallest unit of information with which the machine can operate. If we were to go to any storage location and extract its contents, we could not tell whether the 'number' was an instruction, a data item or the *address* of another storage location, for these are all held in exactly the same way in store. Since instructions are thus the same sort of thing to the computer as numbers, they can be *modified*. This means that once a program of instructions is placed in store, it can be changed by its own action: a program of instructions can thus be made to react to each problem it has to face, and this enables extremely sophisticated and complex operations to be performed. However, there is one difficulty – and it is a very significant one. The computer can only do what it is told: it slavishly obeys each instruction it extracts from successive storage locations, without any discrimination: it cannot say to itself 'that doesn't seem sensible', or 'I wonder what that means': it just obeys. So instructions must be carefully worked out to make sure that in no circumstances will the computer be asked to do anything illogical. Therefore, when a computer issues a final demand for payment of a bill for £0, it is not the machine that has done something stupid: it is correctly obeying a stupid instruction. The illogicality has been caused by the human operator who has failed to foresee the situation and give the computer appropriate instructions. The art of *programming* is thus an exacting one, for every combination of circumstance must be considered by the programmer and taken care of by an appropriate set of instructions.

Software

We have described the term 'hardware' already: it refers to all the machinery, electronic or mechanical, which together makes up a computer. Programs can be produced by individual computer users to perform specific jobs in which the user alone is interested. But many types of problem are more general, and programs written to solve one instance of a general problem may be used to perform the same job for others faced with similar problems; these programs are known as '*software*'. In particular, manufacturers of computers spend large sums of money on developing this sort of software. A computer is obviously much more useful to a user if it comes with a number of ready-made programs which can be put to use at once: also the user is saved the time and expense involved in working out the programs for himself. This sort of software covers a great range of programs, from quite short and simple routines (for example programs to work out taxation for payroll users) to large and sophisticated programs (such as those for *critical path method* analysis used in scheduling complex production programs).

Languages

Some of the most important pieces of software provided by manufacturers are computer *languages*. Instructions in the form operated on by the internal circuitry of a processor consist of a numeric code. Instructions operate on items of data stored with the program in the processor, and each item has its own 'pocket' or storage location, again identified by a number. Programs stored in the processor are thus a combination of numbers making up instructions and storage locations. To work out the numerical equivalents for all the instructions in a program is a tedious and difficult task, requiring great attention to detail and the obeying of exacting rules. But computers themselves are very good at tedious and repetitive tasks, obeying exacting rules. So programming can be simplified by inventing a way for instructions to be written out in a form more easily comprehensible to the user, and making the computer itself translate this into the numbers and codes which are required to use the program on the computer. For example, the programmer can write 'SUBTRACT TAX FROM PAY'; this is then translated for him into the computer code, say 100 326 475, which is then used by the machine to perform the specified calculation. The nearer the language used by the programmer to the code used by the machine, the lower the 'level' of the language. High level languages are what is known as *problem orientated*, that is, they are designed to simplify the writing of instructions for certain types of problem, either commercial or scientific.

People

We have attempted to explain the concept of a computer as a device (*hardware*) using a process (*software*) to turn a raw material into information. But none of this can be achieved without human control over this powerful tool. Perhaps the most exacting task is that which falls on the *systems analyst*. He has to consult his client, the potential user of the machine, to establish the problem to be solved. He must then examine in detail existing procedures: when he has understood exactly what is required, he must design a complete solution to the problem, covering not only computer procedures, but all associated operations, clerical and other. He has to decide what product he is trying to produce: what sort of *information* his system is designed to extract. He decides the raw material required to obtain this, and devises the procedures by which this 'raw data' is collected, fed to the computer, processed and finally dispersed to those who are to use it. He must be skilled not only in analysing a problem and devising a solution, but in communicating his solution to the client or management specifying the requirements, to the users of the information, to those involved in collecting raw data and distributing information and to the other computer professionals involved in the development of the computer side of the system.

There are two associated groups of people: programmers and operators. *Programmers* obtain from the analyst detailed descriptions or specifications of individual jobs which the computer has to perform to make up the overall system. Each such job will require a program to be stored in the computer to perform the tasks. The programmer is responsible for preparing the detailed instructions, and making sure that his program is correct and will in fact perform the required job accurately. Computer *operators* are responsible for the day-to-day operation of programs once these have been specified by the analyst and written by the programmer. They load programs into the processor, check the operation of the various peripheral units and make sure that the correct raw data is read into the computer when required and that the finished product, the information output, is returned to its correct destination.

The future

As the information explosion multiplies day by day, so the enormous problem of keeping this explosion under control becomes more and more acute. Computers, with their ability to process great quantities of facts at vast speeds, are the only means we have of creating some sort of order out of apparent chaos. Computers will give management the information they need to make correct decisions; politicians the facts on which to base policy decisions; research workers the details of results obtained by others in specific fields; architects up-to-date information about available materials and designs; doctors case histories of patients with specified symptoms; lawyers precedents; airline pilots flight plans. The list is endless, and it is endless just because we are continually devising new tasks for the computer and developing computers to perform them.

A

aberration A defect in the electronic lens system of a *cathode ray tube*.

abnormal termination *Termination* which takes place when an error condition is detected by hardware, indicating that a particular series of actions previously initiated cannot be completed correctly.

abort Refers to a situation in which some activity previously initiated is abandoned deliberately on recognition of an error condition. Usually implies that the activity is terminated in a controlled manner.

absolute address The actual *address*[2] of a *location* in *store* expressed in terms of the *machine code* numbering system.

Also known as actual address, direct address, machine address, real address, specific address.

absolute addressing To *address*[3] *locations* in *store* by their *absolute addresses*.

absolute code A programming code using *absolute addresses* and *operators*.

Also known as actual code, direct code, one level code and specific code.

absolute coding Program *instructions* which have been written in *absolute code*, and do not require further processing before being intelligible to the computer.

Also known as basic coding, specific coding.

absolute error The magnitude of deviation of a computed result irrespective of sign.

absolute value computer A computer in which data is processed in its absolute form, all variables maintaining their full values; contrasted with *incremental computer* in which changes in the variables are processed as well as the values of the variables themselves.

acceleration time The time which elapses between the interpretation of an *instruction* to a *peripheral unit* to *read* or *write*, and the moment when transfer of information from the unit to *store* or vice versa could begin; e.g. the time taken to accelerate the *tape transport* on a *magnetic tape* unit.

access Used as a verb describing 1. the process of obtaining data

23

from a *peripheral unit* or retrieving it from a *storage device*; 2. the process involved in obtaining an *instruction* from *memory* and obeying it.

access arm A device used to position the reading and writing mechanisms of a *storage device*.

access control register A *register* used to record the *access level* allocated to an active procedure. Part of the protection system built into a computer to ensure that interference does not occur between different software modules.

access level Within many computer systems there are a number of levels at which control mechanisms (*hardware* and *software*) may exist to prevent interference between modules of software. These access levels are numbered to represent different degrees of *security* – for example, the highest levels of security would be applied to check attempts to initiate routines in the *kernel* of an *operating system* which would be responsible for coordination of activities in the total hardware/software system.

access method Describes the way in which data in a file is retrieved for processing; e.g. a *direct access storage* system can contact files which are accessed in a number of different ways – *serial access, random access,* and *selective sequential access.* ◊ general article on *Updating and file maintenance.*

access permission A response given to an attempt to initiate a software routine, when access control mechanisms have determined that the attempt has correct status and satisfies predetermined security checks. ◊ *access right.*

access right Refers to the status granted to particular *users* of a system, indicating the method of *access* permitted, e.g. *read* a *file* only, or *write* to a file.

access, simultaneous Synonymous with *parallel access.*

access time The time taken to retrieve data from a *storage device* or to obtain data from a *peripheral unit*; measured from the instant of executing an *instruction* to call for the data to the moment when the data is stored in the specified *location.*

accountable time The time in which a computer system is available to users, and excludes time when the computer is switched off; undergoing scheduled or unscheduled maintenance; or closed down because of external factors.

accounting journal A journal maintained as a file by an *operating system* to record events relating to various jobs which are active in the computer and to provide a basis for subsequent analysis in order to assess charges to users.

accounting machine   Used to describe *keyboard* machines which prepare accounting records, but more specifically to describe a *punched card tabulator* capable of reading cards and producing lists and totals.

accumulator   Originally used to describe an electronic device performing arithmetic on *operands*; usually a part of the *arithmetic unit* consisting of a special register and associated circuitry. Now used frequently to refer to any *store* location in which arithmetic results are created. The implication is that an accumulator stores one value and on receipt of a second value it creates and stores the sum of these values.

accumulator register   Synonymous with *accumulator*.

accuracy   The size of error or range of error, the degree of conformity to a rule. High accuracy implies small error, but accuracy is contrasted with precision, e.g. three places of decimals properly computed are less precise but more accurate than four places of decimals containing an error.

A C dump   The removal of all alternating current from a system or part of a system; this may be intentional or accidental.

acknowledgement   A reply given to messages or signals within a computer system where an immediate response to initiate other actions is not required.

acoustic delay line   A *delay line* containing a medium which reacts to the propagation of sound waves.
Also known as sonic delay line.

acoustic memory   Synonymous with *acoustic store*.

acoustic store   A *regenerative store* using an *acoustic delay line*.
Also known as acoustic memory. ✧ *delay line store*.

acronym   A group of letters formed from the initial letters of the words in a name or phrase, e.g. F O R T R A N from F O Rmula T R A Nslator. Sometimes any appropriate letters are chosen, e.g. the word *bit* comes from *binary* dig*it*, and all too often the acronym is thought of first and a tortuous phrase is invented to fit it.

action period   The time during which data stored in a *Williams tube store* may be read or new data may be written to the store.

active element   1. That part of a computer system capable of performing operations. 2. A circuit receiving energy from a source other than a main input signal.

activity   1. In P E R T and *critical path method* an activity is the representation on the network of an actual task consuming time and resources necessary for progress from one *event* to another. Where interdependencies consume neither time nor resources they may be shown as activities, which may also represent waiting periods and transfers of information as well as actual jobs to be performed. 2. An indication that a *record* in a *file* has moved or been referred to.

activity ratio The ratio of the number of *records* which have moved in a *file* being updated to the total number of records in that file.

actual address Synonymous with *absolute address*.

actual code Synonymous with *absolute code*.

actual decimal point A decimal point which appears as a printed character on a *print-out* and for which an actual *location* has been allowed in *store*. Contrasted with *assumed decimal point*.

actual instruction Synonymous with *effective instruction*.

adaptive control system A control system which continuously monitors its own behaviour and, by adjusting its *parameters*, is able to suit itself to a changing environment.

addend One of the *operands* used in performing the function of addition. A distinction is usually drawn between the addend and its counterpart the *augend*. The addend is added to the augend to form a *sum*, in such a manner that the augend is replaced by the sum and the addend remains in its original form.

adder A device performing the function of addition using digital signals. It receives three inputs representing *addend, augend* and a *carry* digit; and will provide two outputs representing the sum and a carry digit.

It is also known as digital adder, and is sometimes referred to as a full adder to distinguish it from *half adder*.

adder, binary half ◊ *binary half adder*.

adder-subtracter A device which acts as either an *adder* or a *subtracter*.

addition An arithmetic operation in which two *operands* – the *addend* and *augend* – are added to form a *sum*.

additional characters Synonymous with *special characters*.

addition record When a *file* is being updated a *record* added to the file, as opposed to one which amends an existing record, is known as an addition record.

addition table In computers which use *table look-up* techniques for addition, the area of *memory* holding the table of numbers to be used is known as the addition table.

addition without carry Synonymous with *exclusive-or operation*.

address 1. That part of an *instruction* which specifies the location of an *operand*. 2. The identification of the position of a *location* in *store*. 3. Used as a verb, meaning to indicate a specific location. ✧ *real address, physical address, virtual address*.

address computation An operation on the *address* part of a *program instruction*. Related to *arithmetic address*.

address, direct Synonymous with *absolute address*.

address format The way in which the *address* part of an *instruction* is arranged.

address generation A technique used to retrieve *records* from a randomly stored *direct access file*.

address, indirect ✧ *indirect addressing*.

addressing An *address* is that part of an *instruction* which specifies the location of an *operand*. Each *word* or *byte* of *store* is allocated a number which is part of the coding system used by the *program controller* to perform operations on data; by specifying the number of a particular word as part of a program instruction, access is obtained to the operand stored within the word. To simplify the *assembly* of large programs a system of *relative addressing* is often used, in which the programmer does not use the *absolute addresses* which form the *machine code*. Instead addresses are specified relative to a *base address* [2] which is added to the *relative address* during assembly of the program or when the program is *loaded*. Thus *segments* of a program can be written independently by different programmers each using relative addresses. When programs are written in a programming language names are allocated to operands and these names, sometimes referred to as *symbolic addresses*, are used to specify the operands to be processed by particular instructions.

address, instruction The *address* of a *location* containing an *instruction*.

addressless instruction format Synonymous with *zero address instruction format*.

address, machine Synonymous with *absolute address*.

address mapping Conversion of data used to represent the physical location of *fields* or *records* and the process by which records or *blocks* of information are assigned to *storage* locations. For example, the translation of a *virtual address* to an *absolute address* or *real address*.

address modification The process of changing the *address* part of an *instruction* by means of a *modifier*, so that the instruction will operate upon a different *operand* each time the *routine* containing the instruction is performed. ✧ *instruction modification, program modification*.

address, multi- ⋄ *multiple address.*

address, one ⋄ *one address instruction.*

address, one-plus-one ⋄ *one-plus-one address.*

address part The part of an *instruction* in which is given the *location* of an *operand.*

address, real ⋄ *real address.*

address register A *register* in which an *address* is stored.

address, specific Synonymous with *absolute address.*

address, three ⋄ *three address instruction.*

address track A *track* on a *storage device* (e.g. on a *magnetic drum*) which contains *addresses* to facilitate *access* to data stored on other tracks.

address translation slave store A *hardware* entity used to assist in the translation of *addresses,* e.g. a *virtual address* to a *real address.*

address, variable Synonymous with *indexed address.*

address, virtual ⋄ *virtual address.*

address, zero level Synonymous with *immediate address.*

add-subtract time The time required by a computer to add or subtract, exclusive of the *read time* or *write time.*

add time The time required by a computer to perform one addition, exclusive of the *read time* or *write time.*

A D P Acronym for *automatic data processing.*

advance feed tape *Paper tape* in which the leading edge of the *feed holes* is in line with the leading edge of the (larger) character holes, thus making it possible to distinguish between the front end and the tail end of a piece of perforated tape. Contrasts with *centre feed tape.*

after-look journalizing In a system in which extensive recovery facilities are needed to safeguard against system failure, a journal is made of amendments to files. This term signifies that an entry is made to the journal after each change made to the file concerned. ⋄ *before-look journalizing.*

agenda A set of operations which form a procedure for solving a problem. In *linear programming,* a group of programs used to manipulate a problem matrix.

agendum call card In *linear programming,* a *punched card* containing one item of an *agenda* used to manipulate a problem matrix.

A L G O L ALGOL is an acronym for A L G Orithmic Language. It is a *problem oriented high level* programming *language* for mathematical and scientific use, in which the *source program* provides a means of defining *algorithms* as a series of statements and declarations having a general resemblance to algebraic formulae and English sentences.

An ALGOL program consists of *data items, statements* and *declarations*, organized in a program structure in which statements are combined to form compound statements and blocks.

Every data item processed in an ALGOL program is termed a variable, and is assigned a general name or identifier by the programmer. Groups of similar items of data can be processed as *arrays*, individual items within the *array* being identified by means of the identifier of the array followed by a *subscript*.

Every operation a program is to perform is represented as a statement. Statements may be assignment statements or conditional statements. An assignment statement has the form 'Variable := Arithmetic Expression' where the symbol ': =' means 'becomes', and the arithmetic expression includes variables, numbers and a series of standard functions, combined by the *operators* $+$, $-$, $\times$, $/$, $\uparrow$ (*exponentiation*). An example of an assignment statement is

$$x := (-b + \text{sqrt}(b\uparrow2 - 4 \times a \times c))/(2 \times a)$$

Any statement may be labelled by an identifier, which may be used subsequently as a reference for a branch statement. Conditional statements are used to express branches if specified conditions are satisfied. 'For statements' are used in the construction of *loops*. ALGOL also includes facilities for logical or *Boolean operations*. Certain variables can be declared as capable of taking only the values 'true' or 'false', and such variables can appear in statements containing the logical operators 'and', 'or', 'not', 'implies' or 'equivalent'.

Declarations are used in ALGOL to provide the compiler with information about quantities appearing in the remainder of the program. The 'type declaration' is used to specify whether a variable is an *integer* (a whole number falling within a range determined by the capacity of the computer being used), a 'real number' (a number expressed in *floating point representation*) or a 'Boolean variable' (capable of taking the values 'true' or 'false'). An 'array declaration' specifies not only the type of the elements but the range of *subscripts*, e.g. integer array Table [1:12, 1:15], which specifies storage for 12×15 integer elements, referred to as Table [1, 1] to Table [12, 15]. The 'procedure declaration' permits the programmer to give a series of statements an identifier, and to use this series of statements as a *subroutine* merely by quoting this identifier.

29

The structure of an A L G O L program consists of a series of consecutive statements separated by semi-colons. A series of statements may be combined to form a compound statement by enclosing the statement between the statement parentheses 'begin' and 'end'. A block has the form of a compound statement but contains at least one declaration. A complete program will normally consist of a number of blocks. This block structure of A L G O L is of great value because it permits parts of a program to be written by different programmers with no risk of duplication of identifiers; and it permits the compiler to produce an efficient and economical program by sharing storage between separate blocks. This is equivalent to the use of *segments* and *overlays* in other languages.

A L G O L was originally known as I A L or International Algebraic Language, and was developed in Europe at the same time as *F O R T R A N* was being developed in the United States.

algorithm A series of instructions or procedural steps for the solution of a specific problem.

algorithmic Pertaining to a method of problem-solving by a fixed procedure; ⋄ *algorithm*. Contrasted with *heuristic approach*.

algorithm translation A translation from one language to another by means of an *algorithm*.

allocate As a result of an action performed by an operator, a *program instruction*, or automatically by an *executive program*, to place a *peripheral unit* or *memory* area under the control of a program. The *hardware* allocated may be *released* and made available to some other program, in contrast to the situation where hardware is *assigned* to a program for a whole *run*. ⋄ *storage allocation*.

allocation Any planning needs, above everything else, to allocate the available resources to provide the best possible result, but before the resources can be allocated the meaning of 'best possible result' must be established, and it will be necessary to devise some criterion to judge the economic effect of each complete set of such allocations. In most business applications this criterion will be either total profit or total cost and the objective is to find the allocation which will maximize or minimize these respectively. Of course adjustments will have to be made for appreciation of investment and depreciation of inventory, but even so the problem would basically be a simple one if each resource could be examined independently. Unfortunately this is invariably not the case: the allocation of a resource limits the allocation of some or all of the other resources. If we decide to develop a new product, then this will require some of our manpower to be scheduled into this activity, which will in turn affect our recruitment campaigns, etc. The problems now become very complex since out of the many possible allocations the 'best' allocation of resources is not immediately obvious.

Methods of mathematical programming have been designed to solve such allocation problems. Mathematical programming can be considered in two separate categories: the treatment of linear forms, and the treatment of non-linear forms. In the linear category the objective (e.g. total profit) must be a linear function of the variables (cost per item, etc.); i.e. for each unit being considered the other variables must have fixed profit, cost, etc. If one costs £1, two must cost £2 and three £3. In the non-linear category this restriction is much weaker, the relationship between cost per unit and number of units, etc., need only be expressable as a function.

allocation, dynamic storage ◊ *dynamic allocation (of memory).*

all-purpose computer Synonymous with *general purpose computer.*

alphabetic Pertaining to a *character set* or a field of data in which the coded characters relate to letters of the alphabet only. As this is sometimes loosely used to include symbols, such as / @ $ £, it is as well to qualify the term when using it.

alphabetic code A system of coding data by the use of combinations of letters to represent items of information, either as abbreviations or *mnemonics.* ◊ *alphabetic.*

alphabetic string A *string*[2] in which the characters belong to an *alphabetic* set.

alphameric code Synonymous with *alphanumeric code.*

alphanumeric code Pertaining to a *character set* or *field* of data in which the coded characters may represent numerals or letters of the alphabet. In its strictest sense does not contain coded characters relating to symbols such as / @ $ £.

alteration Synonymous with *inclusive-or operation.*

alteration switch A *switch*[3] in which the path selected can be determined either manually or by *program.* Related to *indicator.*[2]

alternative denial Synonymous with *not-and operation.*

A L U Acronym for *arithmetic and logic unit.*

ambiguity error An error occurring in the reading of a number when its digital representation is changing: imprecise synchronization may, for example, cause the number 399 to be read as 499 when it was in fact passing to 400. ◊ *guard signal.*

amendment file Synonymous with *change file.*

amendment record Synonymous with *change record.*

amendment tape Synonymous with *change tape*.

amplifier A device which is capable of accepting an *input* signal in wave form and of delivering a magnified signal of the current or voltage applied to it.

amplifier, D C ◊ *directly coupled amplifier*.

amplifier, inverting Synonymous with *sign-reversing amplifier*.

amplifier, sign-changing Synonymous with *sign-reversing amplifier*.

amplitude The magnitude of a variable, usually its maximum value whether or not it varies with time.

analog The representation and measurement of the performance or behaviour of a *system* by continuously variable physical entities such as currents, voltages, etc. ◊ general article on *Analog Computers*. Contrasted with *digital*.

analog adder A device which provides one output variable which is a weighted sum of two input variables.

analog channel A channel, such as a *voice channel*, on which the data transmitted can be of any value between fixed limits defined by the channel.

analog computers Analog computers are machines designed to perform arithmetical functions upon numbers, where the numbers are represented by some physical quantity. For example, in mechanical analog computers the numbers are often represented by the physical dimensions of the members forming the various functional units, for instance by the angular rotation of shafts or gear wheels. In electrical analog machines voltages are used to represent the input variables.

Essentially an analog computer must be able to accept inputs which vary with respect to time, and directly apply these inputs to various devices within the computer which perform the computing operations of addition, subtraction, multiplication, division, integration and function generation. The output from the system may be in the form of a graph produced by a plotting pen, or a trace on a cathode-ray tube, and again the output signals might be used directly to control the operation of some other machine or process.

The computing units of analog computers are able to respond immediately to the changes which they detect in the input variables, and the connexion of these various units in a particular fashion can cause an analog computer to perform very complex arithmetical functions at high speed while the actual process under study is in operation. This ability to operate in *real time* mode means that analog computers have many applications in the scientific and industrial fields in simulating various physical systems or automatically controlling industrial processes. They are widely used for research into design problems, particularly where the solution is required speedily without difficult setting-up problems.

Analog computers do not have the ability of digital computers to store data in large quantities, nor do they have the comprehensive logical facilities afforded by programming digital machines. And although the arithmetic functions performed by the computing units are more complex in analog machines than in the digital systems, the cost of the hardware required to provide a high degree of accuracy in an analog machine is often prohibitive.

Some analog machines are designed for specific applications, but most electrical and electronic analog computers provide a number of different computing devices which can be connected together via a plugboard to provide different methods of operation for specified problems.

⋄ *digital computers* and *hybrid computers*.

analog/digital converter A unit which converts output signals from an *analog computer* into *digital* representation for use in a digital computing system.

analog network A circuit representing physical variables in such a way that mathematical relationships can be shown directly by examining measurable quantities continuously.

analog representation A representation of a variable by a physical quantity (such as voltage) whose magnitude is directly proportional to the variable.

analogue ⋄ *analog*.

analyser A *program* which analyses other programs submitted to it, summarizing references to *locations* in *store* and following the sequences of *branch instructions*. Such a program is an aid to *debugging*.

analyser, digital differential ⋄ *digital differential analyser*.

analyser, electronic differential ⋄ *electronic differential analyser*.

analyser, mechanical differential ⋄ *mechanical differential analyser*.

analysis The study of a concept or *system* by breaking it down to the separate elements that form the whole structure in order to determine the functional relationship between these elements. Contrasted with *synthesis*.

analysis, systems ⋄ *systems analysis*.

analyst, systems ⋄ general article on *Computer Personnel*.

analytical function generator A *function generator* in which the *function* [2] is a physical law.

Also known as natural law function generator, natural function generator.

and circuit Synonymous with *and element*.

and element A *logic element* operating with *binary digits* which provides one output signal from two input signals according to the following rules:

Input		Output
1	0	0
1	1	1
0	1	0
0	0	0

Thus a 1 digit is obtained as output only if two 1 digits are present as coincident input signals. See also *Boolean algebra*.

Also known as and gate, coincidence gate.

and gate Synonymous with *and element*.

and operation A logical operation applied to two *operands* which will produce a result depending on the *bit patterns* of the operands and according to the following rules for each bit position:

Operands		Result
p	q	r
1	0	0
1	1	1
0	1	0
0	0	0

For example, operating upon the following 6-bit operands,

$$p=110110$$
$$q=011010$$
$$r=010010$$

Also known as conjunction, logical product, intersection, meet operation. ✧ *Boolean algebra*.

anticoincidence circuit Synonymous with *anticoincidence element*.

anticoincidence element A *logic element* operating with *binary digits* which provides one output signal from two input signals according to the following rules:

Input		Output
1	0	1
1	1	0
0	1	1
0	0	0

Thus a 1 digit is obtained as output only if two differing input signals are received. ✧ *Boolean algebra.*

anticoincidence operation Synonymous with *exclusive-or operation.*

aperture plate A small part of a piece of ferromagnetic material constituting a *magnetic cell.*

application The particular kind of problem to which *data processing* techniques are applied; applications are usually referred to as being either 'computational', i.e. requiring considerable computing capacity, or 'data processing', i.e. where data handling capacity is of greatest importance.

application package A *program* or *suite of programs* designed to perform a specific type of work (e.g. payroll, sales ledger, or storm sewer analysis). The package may contain a number of functions pertaining to the field of application, but individual users can select functions required and vary their *input* and *output* requirements by using *parameters.*

application program A *program* forming part of a user's job and written by the user, as distinct from programs forming part of the general purpose *software* used to manage the operation of the total computer system.

application system A system designed to perform a particular task; a term used to distinguish a user's system from the various compiling systems and systems management software with which an *application* will co-exist within the computer.

application virtual machine Relates to a user's system operating in a computer system which is able to provide a *virtual machine environment.* Each application is allocated certain *hardware* and *software* resources, so that to the user his particular *application* appears to be operating within a computer system dedicated to his task. Each user job is, therefore, said to occupy a virtual machine.

arbitrarily sectioned file A *file* which has been organized in a simple manner to allow for the addition and removal of *sections* automatically.

arbitrary function generator Synonymous with *general purpose function generator*.

architectural protection Relates to the *hardware* and *software* facilities built into a computer system by the manufacturer to provide for the security of processes and data handled within the system. For example, facilities intended to prevent one user *application program* from interfering with others with which it may co-exist.

architecture The design of a computer and the way in which *hardware* and *software* interact to provide basic facilities and levels of performance. Computer manufacturers design computers to meet the needs of particular segments of the market and any particular model is designed to meet some or all of a number of design objectives. The architecture of the machine relates to the way in which hardware and software are constructed to achieve the objectives of the design. (Examples of design objectives: speed of throughput, resilience to system failure, cost, protection and security of user applications, ease of maintenance, ability to control several applications at once, orientation to specific types of work.)

archived file A *file* which has been *stored* on some backing medium (e.g. *magnetic tape*) and not held permanently *on-line* to the *main store*. The file will not appear in the *operating system*'s catalogue of current files, but can be reconstituted should the need arise. Archiving provides a cheaper method of storing data not required frequently, and the removal of files of this type from the *filestore* can greatly improve the efficiency of a computer system.

archiving The process of creating and maintaining *archived files* within a computer system – one of the functions which will be performed by an *operating system* under the control of the operations staff.

area Any part of *memory* assigned to hold data of a specified type. Such assignation may be at the programmer's discretion or determined by *hardware*.

area, common storage ◊ *common area*.

area search The scanning of a large group of *records* to select those of a major category or class for further processing.

area, working ◊ *work area*.

argument 1. A variable used to reference a table – the *key* which specifies the *location* of a particular item. 2. Synonymous with the *fixed point part* of a number in *floating point representation*. 3. A variable factor the value of which determines the value of a function.

arithmetic address An *address* obtained by performing an arithmetic operation on another address. Related to *address computation*.

arithmetical instruction An *instruction* which specifies an arith-metic operation upon data, e.g. addition or multiplication. Arith-metical instructions form a subset of the machine *instruction set* to be considered separately from *logical instructions*.

arithmetical operation An operation performed using the arith-metic instructions, e.g. addition, subtraction, multiplication and division. Performed upon numerical *operands* and yielding a numerical result according to the rules for arithmetic. ⟡ *logical operations*.

arithmetical shift To multiply or divide a numerical *operand* ac-cording to the number base inherent in the structure of the word holding the number. For example, if a number is stored in *decimal notation* as in a *character oriented* word, a *left shift* of n places has the effect of multiplying by 10^n. Similarly, a *right shift* has the effect of dividing by the appropriate power of ten. With numbers stored in *binary notation* a left shift has the effect of multiplying by 2^n and conversely, a right shift of dividing by 2^n. Contrasted with *logical shift*.

arithmetic and logic unit The *hardware unit* of a *central processor* which deals with arithmetical and logical operations.

arithmetic check The verification of an arithmetical process by means of a further arithmetical process, e.g. multiplying 33 by 18 to produce an arithmetic check of the result of 18 multiplied by 33.

arithmetic, floating-decimal ◊ *floating point arithmetic*.

arithmetic instruction ◊ *arithmetical instruction*.

arithmetic, multi-length ◊ *multiple-length arithmetic*.

arithmetic operation ◊ *arithmetical operation*.

arithmetic organ Synonymous with *arithmetic unit*.

arithmetic overflow ◊ *overflow*.

arithmetic register A *register*, usually part of the *arithmetic unit*, constructed for containing the *operands* and results of arithmetic functions on data.

arithmetic shift ◊ *arithmetical shift*.

arithmetic unit A unit within a computer performing *arithmetical operations* on *operands*; may also perform *arithmetic shifts, logical shifts* and other *logical operations* on data.
Also known as arithmetic organ. ⟡ *arithmetic and logic unit, arith-metic register*.

array An arrangement of items of data each identified by a *key* or *subscript*. Constructed in such a way that a *program* can examine the array in order to extract data relevant to a particular key or subscript. The dimension of an array is the number of subscripts necessary to identify an item; e.g., if an array consists of the days of the year, the array is one-dimensional if any day is identified by its number, e.g. 32 for 1 February, and 2-dimensional if identified by day and month, e.g. (1, 2) for 1 February.

artificial intelligence A term used to describe the use of computers in such a way that they perform operations analagous to the human abilities of learning and decision taking.

ASCII Acronym for American Standard Code for Information Interchange.

ASR Acronym for *automatic send-receive set*.

assemble To put a *program* through the process of *assembly* by means of an *assembly program*.

assembler Synonymous with *assembly program*.

assembly The operation on a *symbolic language program* which produces a complete program in *machine language*. Basically, assembly consists of (*a*) the translation of symbolic operation codes and *addresses* to machine language form, and (*b*) the grouping of the resultant machine language program from its constituent parts, e.g. the inclusion of *library software*, consolidation of program *segments*, adjustments to *links*, etc. ⬦ *compiler*, from which it is distinguished by the fact that assembly produces machine *instructions* on a one-for-one basis from relative instructions, while compiling usually produces many machine instructions from one *pseudo instruction*. ⬦ general article on *Languages*.

assembly language Any *symbolic language* used for programming which must go through an *assembly* in order to be converted into the *machine code* required for operation on a computer.

assembly list A list which may be produced during *assembly* to show the details of the *symbolic language* and the corresponding details of the *machine language* form created by assembly. The comparison of the two languages is particularly useful for any *debugging* which may be necessary.

assembly program The *program* which operates on a *symbolic language* program to produce a *machine language* program in the process of *assembly*.
Also known as assembler, assembly routine.

assembly routine Synonymous with *assembly program*.

assembly system ⬦ *assembly*.

assembly unit Part of a *program* capable of being incorporated into a larger program by the process of *assembly*, e.g. a *subroutine* forming part of the *library facilities* of the system.

assign To reserve a part of a computing system (usually a *peripheral unit*) for a specific purpose. This reservation is normally permanent for the duration of a *program*. Contrasted with *allocate*.

associative memory Synonymous with *associative store*.

associative store A *store* whose *locations* are identified by their content rather than by their specific *address*.
Also known as associative memory, content-addressed storage, parallel search storage.

assumed decimal point The position where a decimal point would appear when decimal fractions are printed or stored continuously with their *integral* part. Contrasted with *actual decimal point*.

asynchronous computer A computer which operates on a method of *asynchronous working*.

asynchronous working Mode of operation for a machine in which the completion of one operation initiates another. Contrasted with a machine in which operations are synchronized to a schedule provided by a clocking device (*synchronous working*).

asyndetic Omitting *connectives*.

attended time Time during which the computer is attended for serviceable operation (*up time*) or out of service for maintenance or engineering work.

attentuate To cause the reduction in amplitude of a signal.

attenuation The difference in amplitude between a signal at transmission and at reception.
Also known as loss.

atto- Prefix denoting one million-million-millionth or 10^{-18}.

audio Used to describe frequencies capable of being heard by the human ear, i.e. between 15 cycles and 20,000 cycles per second.

audio response unit Pre-recorded responses held in a digitally coded form on a computer *storage device* can be linked by an audio response unit to a telephone network to provide audible responses to inquiries.

audit of computer systems Ever since the earliest commercial *punched card* systems the *audit trail* has been in danger and auditors, both internal and external, have come to feel that much of their job lies in defending the trail from the possible ravages of *systems analysts* and programmers. This has been particularly so with the development of large *direct access memory* systems, and it has become quite clear that a very close liaison between auditors and *data processing* staff is essential. The difficulty arises in ensuring that good intentions about liaison do not deteriorate into the sudden realization that a *source document* can no longer be traced through to its final home in the company's financial statements.

The first step is usually to ensure that no *systems definition* may be passed for *programming* or implementation until it has been formally approved by both internal and external auditors. (Systems definitions usually have to be signed off by other authorities such as the user departments, operating authority, etc., and the formal addition of the auditors to this cycle presents no problems). Approval must also, of course, be given to any amendments to the system that are made later, and although it can be a tedious business getting approval for every small amendment to a new system, anarchy will prevail if this is not made a firm rule.

Even the regular approval of new systems is not the whole answer to ensuring that oversight or over-sophistication do not destroy the audit trail: anyone who has been given a three-inch thick systems definition and asked to approve it will appreciate that a prior knowledge of the design and workings of the system is invaluable in checking a definition for flaws. Auditors can acquire this by being present regularly at the design stage of a new system, and many companies now make it a rule that representatives of the auditors discuss new systems with analysts on a once-a-week basis. This ensures at least that the completed definition is not entirely new ground, and also allows the auditor to suggest amendments to the system before such amendments involve a laborious re-writing and re-drawing of a large part of the definition.

Having made sure that a new system has adequate controls and that the audit trail is satisfactory, the auditor now needs to consider methods of ensuring that the systems he has approved are the systems which are in fact operating. The main check here will be on the *programs*, and it is usual for auditors to maintain a copy of each program (perhaps in a locked cabinet in the *tape library*) and to compare these programs on a regular basis with those which are actually being used. The auditor must also constantly satisfy himself that adequate disciplines are being maintained in all the data processing areas – programming, *data preparation, work assembly*, operating and control – and his best chance of making sure that the disciplines he watches are indeed adequate is to ask for written standards of procedure against which he can check actual procedure.

So far we have outlined only an extra burden for the auditor, but computer systems can also be of great benefit to him and the more familiar an auditor becomes with computers the more readily he will call for special audit programs. Such programs might select particular transactions for a manual audit, either on a random basis or on an exception rating, i.e. all transactions which exceed a certain norm; or information obtained by audit staff at remote centres can be processed and compared with *master records*, saving audit time and increasing its breadth of operation. Again, details of transactions can be reframed and analysed in ways designed by the auditor, perhaps as part of the regular system so that special audit runs are made at the end of each job.

The computer can be a great help to an auditor, but it is clear that this is possible only when the auditor is to some extent familiar with the abilities – and requirements – of a computer. Regular discussion with the data processing personnel should give him this familiarity, and a once-a-week check on the design of new systems is perhaps the most satisfactory way of achieving this.

audit trail A record of processes and events relating to a specific record, transaction, or *file*. In a computer system the trail will be stored as a file and is created during the routine processing of data as a separate activity, thus allowing the system to be audited or subsequent reconstitution of files. ◊ general article on *Audit of Computer Systems*.

augend One of the *operands* employed in addition, used specifically to denote the operand that is replaced by the *sum* on completion of the operation. ◊ *addend*.

augment To increase a quantity in order to bring it to a required value.

augmenter A quantity added to another in order to bring it to a required value; an augmenter may be either positive or negative.

auto-abstract ◊ *automatic abstract*.

autocode Synonymous with *basic language*. ◊ *Languages*.

automatic abstract Key words selected from a document and arranged in an order meaningful to human beings; the selection and arranging is carried out automatically in accordance with certain criteria *programmed* previously.

automatically cleared failure A failure which is corrected by the system itself, e.g. a *parity* failure which has been overcome by retransmission of the data *blocks* concerned.

automatically corrected error An error which is detected and corrected by a system without the aid of an operator. Relates to the data handled by a system and is not necessarily caused by a failure of *hardware* or *software*.

automatic carriage A control device on, for example, typewriters and automatic *key punches*, which can control automatically the spacing, skipping, feeding and ejecting of paper, cards, preprinted forms, etc.

automatic check Any facility, *software* or *hardware*, for automatically performing a check for the absence of specific errors. Sometimes contrasted with *programmed check* and used only in the sense of *hardware check*.

automatic coding Any technique using a computer to assist in the clerical work of programming.
Also known as automatic programming. ◊ *relative coding, symbolic coding.*

automatic data processing Used for any form of processing performed by automatic equipment. Sometimes used more specifically for work performed by electro-mechanical equipment (e.g. *punched card* machines) as contrasted with *data processing* performed on electronic computers, known as *electronic data processing.*

automatic dictionary In *information retrieval* systems, an automatic dictionary substitutes codes for words and phrases. In a language translating system it provides a word-for-word substitution from one language to another. ◊ *dictionary.*

automatic error correction A technique which makes use of *error detecting codes* and *error correcting codes* and (usually) automatic re-transmission. Errors in transmission are automatically corrected.

automatic exchange A transmission exchange in which communication between terminals is effected without intervention from operators.

automatic feed punch Synonymous with *automatic punch.*

automatic hardware dump A *dump* arising from a system error and used to provide information for diagnostic purposes, e.g. concerning the internal state of the *instruction code* processes. The information will be dumped to a medium which is conveniently analysed by the maintenance staff.
Also known as hard dump, hardware dump.

automatic interrupt An interruption to a *program* caused by a *hardware* device or *executive program*, acting on some event occurring independently of the interrupted program.
Also known as automatic program interrupt.

automatic message switching centre ◊ *switching centre.*

automatic paper tape punch Synonymous with *automatic tape punch.*

automatic program interrupt Synonymous with *automatic interrupt.*

automatic programming Synonymous with *automatic coding.*

automatic punch   A *key punch* in which *punched cards* are passed through the machine automatically. Contrasted with *hand punch*. Also known as automatic feed punch.

automatic restart   A *restart* effected automatically by an *operating system* without reference to the computer operators.

automatics   The theory of *automation*.

automatic send-receive set   A *teletypewriter* which both receives and transmits.

automatic stop   A computer may be programmed to stop when an *automatic check* detects an error; the halt is then known as an automatic stop.

automatic switching centre   ◊ *switching centre*.

automatic tape punch   A *tape punch* activated automatically by signals transmitted from a *central processor* or over some *data transmission* circuit.

automatic verifier   A *punched card* machine used for *card verifying*.

automation   The automatic implementation of a process; the control of a process by the use of automatic devices.

automonitor   A *program* which causes a computer to keep a record of its own processing operations. ◊ article on *Debugging*.

autopolling   Referring to a party-line transmission circuit; each station is allowed to transmit according to a predetermined arrangement. ◊ *poll*.

auxiliary equipment   Data processing equipment not *on line* to the *central processor*. For example, a *punched card tabulator* which may be used for balancing to provide *control totals*. Associated with *off-line equipment*.

auxiliary store   Synonymous with *backing store*.

availability ratio   Synonymous with *operating ratio*.

available machine time   Synonymous with *available time*.[1]

available time   1. The time during which a computer is not under maintenance and has the power switched on and is otherwise ready for use. 2. The amount of time a computer is available to a particular user.

B

backgrounding ◊ *background processing.*

background job A *job* in an *operating system* which has a lower priority than jobs being run simultaneously which involve any *on-line* activity. ◊ *background processing*[1].

background processing 1. In a *multi-access* system, processing which does not make use of *on-line* facilities. 2. High priority processing which takes precedence (as a result of *program interrupts*) over *foreground processing*. 3. Low priority processing over which foreground processing takes precedence. Note: as definitions 2 and 3 are directly contradictory and definition 1 has a related but different meaning, this phrase should be used with caution.
Also known as backgrounding.

background program A *program* which requires *background processing.*

background reflectance In *optical character recognition*, the degree of reflection caused by those areas around an inked character.

backing store A store of larger *capacity* but slower *access time* than the *main memory* or *immediate access store* of a computer.
Also known as bulk store, auxiliary store, secondary store.

backspace In *sequential processing, punching* or typing: to move backward one unit at a time.

backup A facility intended to provide a service in the event of loss of service from some other resource; any resource necessary for effective *recovery.*

backup storage A section of *storage* not normally available to users but used within a computer system under the control of system management *software* to provide security copies of certain classes of file.

backward recovery A mode of system *recovery* in which transactions previously applied to a *file* are processed to reinstate the file to an earlier condition.

badge reader A *data collection* device (used, for example, in *in-plant* data communications systems) capable of reading data recorded as holes in prepunched cards or plastic badges. Sometimes these devices are also fitted with keys so that data can be entered manually.

balanced error When all values in an *error range* have an equal probability and the maximum and minimum values in the range are equal in value and opposite in sign, then the range has a balanced error.

balance error In *analog* computing, an error voltage which occurs at output of analog adders and is a multiple of the *drift error*.

band 1. A group of magnetic *tracks* on a *magnetic drum* or *magnetic disk store*. 2. A range of frequencies between two defined limits.

bar-code scanner An *optical character reader* which can automatically read data from documents bearing characters formed with a special bar code. The characters are translated into *digital* signals which may be entered directly into a *central processor* or recorded in some data medium such as *paper tape*.

barrel printer A *printer* in which all the characters for printing are placed round the surface of a cylinder (the barrel), the entire *character* set being placed round the cylinder at each *print position*. *Print hammers* opposite each print position can be activated by the computer, striking the paper and bringing it in contact with a continuous ink ribbon between the paper and the surface of the barrel. The barrel rotates at high speed, the appropriate character being selected as it reaches a position immediately opposite the print hammers. ✧ *on-the-fly printer*.

base 1. Synonymous with *radix*. 2. ✧ *data base*.

base address 1. In *address modification*, an address to which a *modifier* is added in order to obtain a variable *operand* address. 2. During the *assembly* or *loading* of a *program*, an address added to the address component of each *instruction* in order to obtain *absolute addresses*. ✧ *addressing*.

base notation Synonymous with *radix notation*.

base number A quantity which specifies a system of representation for numbers. ✧ *radix*.

BASIC is a *high level programming language* principally designed for developing programs in *conversational mode*, in an *online programming* environment. The name is an acronym for Beginner's All-purpose Symbolic Instruction Code.

In a conversational system each element of the program is input in sequence directly to the computer, which carries out elementary checking and validation of each step before the next one is input. **BASIC** is designed to simplify conversational programming by avoiding any complications of structure or format, and providing extensive diagnostic facilities as an aid to *debugging* and error correction. The B A S I C language contains two main parts, the *source language* statements themselves, which are the instructions forming the actual program, and system commands, which allow the user to control the use of the B A S I C *compiling* system.

The *source language* facilities are comparable with *F O R T R A N* (see general article on that language) with additional facilities for handling data transfers to and from files and powerful *matrix* handling facilities.

The particular feature of B A S I C is the ability it allows the user to interact with the program while it is being *executed*. The basic element of a program is the 'line', which consists of a *statement* of the source language identified by a unique line number. Line numbers define the logical sequence of statements within the program and act as *labels*[2]. Since the sequence in which statements are executed depends on their line number, the order in which they are input by the user is immaterial. This means that insertions and corrections can be input without the need to copy out the whole program, provided the correct line number sequence is maintained.

Examples of source language statements used in B A S I C may be found in the article on *F O R T R A N*.

System commands allow the user to use the control and editing facilities of the language.

Editing facilities allow the user to delete parts of a program, or add parts of a different program without typing in all the statements line by line. Facilities also allow the user to output all or part of any program onto a terminal.

File maintenance facilities allow the user to set up and maintain files of program statements which can be retrieved and executed or combined into other programs.

Instant calculation facilities allow the user to perform any arithmetic function available within the source language without creating and compiling a program in order to do so.

Examples of system commands in B A S I C are:

R U N   execute a program held in a B A S I C work file
D E L E T E   remove a program from a work file
L I S T   print a listing of a program on an output device
T Y P E   execute the arithmetic function following this command (e.g. T Y P E S Q R T for executing the square root function)

HELP   print an analysis of an error condition to assist in *debugging*.

basic coding   Synonymous with *absolute coding*.

basic instruction   In *instruction modification* the basic instruction is the *instruction* form which is modified to obtain the instruction actually obeyed.

Also known as presumptive instruction or unmodified instruction.

basic language   Synonymous with *low level language*. But ↷ BASIC.

basic linkage   A *linkage* which is standard for a given *routine* or *program* and is used repeatedly following the same rules each time.

basic mode   A communications line control procedure based on the International Standards Organization 7-bit code. Interactive processing between a *terminal* and its *main frame* processor.

batch   A collection of *transactions*, in the form, for example, of *source documents*, *punched cards* or a group of *records* on some *magnetic storage device*. Any group of records processed as a single unit, e.g. a *block*.

batching   Synonymous with *blocking*.

batch job   A *job* run in *batch processing mode*.

batch mode   ↷ *batch processing mode*.

batch processing   A method of processing data in which *transactions* are collected and prepared for input to the computer for processing as a single unit. There may be some delay between the occurrence of original events and the eventual processing of the transactions. Contrasted with *real time* processing in which transactions are dealt with as they arise and are automatically applied to files held in a *direct access storage device*.

batch processing mode   In *real time* systems there is usually some aspect of the *data processing* work that does not require to be handled on a real time basis. *Transactions* falling in this category may be batched on a daily/weekly/monthly basis and be accepted into the system for processing against *sequential* files. Thus, at certain periods of relatively low activity, a real time system may operate in batch processing mode; alternatively *batch processing* jobs may form *background processing* [3] work to real time operations in a *multiprogramming* environment.

batch total   A total developed by adding certain *fields* of a series of *records*, *source documents*, or *punched cards*, in order to provide a check that all records are present at successive stages of processing. The total may be a meaningful accumulation of a quantity or value field, or it may be a *hash total*.

baud A unit used to measure the speed of transmission in a telegraph or telephone channel. Named after Baudot, a pioneer of telegraphic communication, the unit was originally equivalent to twice the number of morse code dots transmitted continuously per second. At one time baud was often used as a synonym for bits per second and this was reasonable when in single-state signalling the modulation rate (expressed in bauds) and the data signalling rate (expressed in bits per second) had the same value. With multi-state signalling the modulation rate and data signalling rate cannot have the same value and it is therefore dangerous not to distinguish between bauds and bits per second.

B C D Acronym for *binary coded decimal.*

bead In a program a small *module* which performs a specific function. Beads are usually written and tested individually and then strung together and tested in groups sometimes known as *threads.* In this way programs can be written and tested in a modular way and this provides a sound method for controlling the development of complex programs. ✧ general article on *Modular Programming.*

beam store Any magnetic *storage device* in which electron beams are used to activate storage cells; e.g. a *cathode ray tube* store.

beat A unit of time related to the execution of an instruction in the *program controller* of a *central processor.* For example, in a two-beat machine one beat may be required to interpret the instruction and set up the necessary circuits to perform the specified operation, while a further beat is required to perform the function.

before-look journalizing Relates to a system in which entries in a *log* or journal are made before each attempt to update a *record* on a *file.* Thus the status of the file can be reconstructed should *recovery* be needed. (Contrast with *after-look journalizing.*)

beginning of file label A *record* at the beginning of a *file* which provides identification of the file, and information about the boundaries, and perhaps method of organization, of the file.

beginning of file section label A *record* identifying a specific section of a file and providing information about its physical limits.

beginning of volume label A label at the beginning of a unit of magnetic storage (e.g. *magnetic tape* or *disk*) which provides identification of that specific unit and its contents.

beginning of information marker An area of reflective material on a *magnetic tape* which indicates the beginning of the recording area. ✧ *load point.*

benchmark A task to be performed in a computer system, designed to measure the performance of the system under certain conditions or to evaluate its effectiveness in performing certain classes of work. Benchmarking is a method used by some purchasers to evaluate the proposals for the supply of *hardware* and/or *software*.

benchmark problem A particular calculation used to measure the performance of different machines or *programs*. ◊ *benchmark*.

bias 1. An error range having an average value not equal to zero; contrasted with *balanced error*. 2. A voltage applied to an electrical component to control the operating characteristics of a circuit.

bias testing A test used to check the operation of equipment, in which the operating characteristics are changed to reduce the safety margin of the various circuits against faults. ◊ *marginal testing*.

bi-conditional operation Synonymous with *equivalence operation*.

billi A prefix denoting one thousand million or 10^9, synonymous with *giga*.

bimag core A magnetic storage *core* having two states of magnetization.

binary Pertaining to a pair. As in the *binary notation* system in which only the digits 0 and 1 are used.

binary arithmetic operation Any *arithmetical operation* in which the *operands* are *binary numbers*.

binary Boolean operation Synonymous with *dyadic Boolean operation*.

binary cell A storage element able to represent one *binary digit*.

binary chop Synonymous with *dichotomizing search*.

binary code A *code* in which *characters* are represented by groups of *binary digits*. For example, a common coding system employs 6-bit groups to represent different characters and allows for up to 64 separate characters to be represented, each by a unique *bit pattern*.

binary-coded character A *character* represented by a *binary code*.

binary coded decimal notation A method of using groups of *binary digits* to represent decimal numbers, with each digit position of a decimal number being allocated four *bits*.

binary coded decimal representation ◊ *binary coded decimal notation*.

binary coded digit Any numeral represented by a coded group of *binary digits*. For example, the use of four *bits* to represent a *decimal digit*, or the use of three bits to represent a digit in the *octal* scale of notation.

binary counter A *counter* able to accumulate numbers recorded in the *binary* scale of notation.

binary digit A digit in *binary notation*; i.e. either 1 or 0. Generally abbreviated as *bit*.

binary dump A *dump* of the contents of *memory* in *binary* form onto some external medium such as *magnetic tape* or *paper tape*.

binary half adder A *half adder* operating with digits representing *binary* signals, capable of receiving two inputs and of delivering two outputs.

binary image An exact representation in *store* of each hole in a *punched card* or *paper tapes* as distinct from the character represented by a combination of holes.

binary incremental representation A form of *incremental representation* in which the value of an increment is represented by one *binary digit*, after being rounded to either plus one or minus one.

Input		Output	
Augend	Addend	Sum	Carry
1	0	1	0
1	1	0	1
0	1	1	0
0	0	0	0

binary notation A *positional notation system* for representing numbers in which the *radix* for each *digit position* is two. In this system numbers are represented by the two digits 0 and 1. In the same way that in the normal decimal system a displacement of one digit position to the left means the digit is multiplied by a factor of 10, so in the binary system displacement means multiplication by 2. Thus the binary number '10' represents two, while '100' represents four.

binary number Any number represented in *binary notation*.

binary numeral One of the two digits 0 and 1 used for representing numbers in *binary notation*.

binary operation A term used to refer to any *operation* using two *operands*; i.e. a dyadic operation. This term is, however, also used to mean any operation involving the use of operands in binary form – a *binary arithmetic operation*.

binary pair Synonymous with *bistable circuit*.

binary point The binary point performs the same function in the *binary notation* system as the decimal point in the decimal system, i.e. it separates the integral from the fractional part of a number.

binary representation ◊ *binary notation*.

binary search Synonymous with *dichotomizing search*.

binary-to-decimal conversion Conversion of a number represented in the *binary notation* to its equivalent decimal notation. A *routine* to perform this conversion automatically.

binary variable   A *variable* which can have one of two values (0 or 1).
Also known as two-valued variable.

bionics   The study of the functions and characteristics of living systems in relation to the development of *hardware* designed to operate in a similar manner.

bipolar   An input signal is defined as bipolar if different logical states are represented by signals of different electrical voltage polarity. Contrasted with *unipolar*.

biquinary code   The representation of a number (n) by a pair of numbers (x, y) where n=x+y and x=0 or 5, y=0, 1, 2, 3 or 4. The pair may be represented in a *binary* code using the following table:

Decimal	Biquinary	Binary Representation
0	0 + 0	0 000
1	0 + 1	0 001
2	0 + 2	0 010
3	0 + 3	0 011
4	0 + 4	0 100
5	5 + 0	1 000
6	5 + 1	1 001
7	5 + 2	1 010
8	5 + 3	1 011
9	5 + 4	1 100

bistable   Capable of assuming either one or two stable states. ◇ *flip-flop*.

bistable circuit   A circuit which can be triggered to adopt one of two stable states.
Also known as binary pair, bistable trigger circuit, trigger pair.

bistable magnetic core   A *magnetic core* which can adopt one of two states of magnetization.

bistable trigger circuit   Synonymous with *bistable circuit*.

bit   An abbreviation of *bi*nary digi*t*, one of the two digits (0 and 1) used in *binary notation*. The term is extended to the actual representation of a binary digit in different forms, e.g. an element of *core storage*, a magnetized spot on a recording surface, a pulse in an electronic circuit.

bit, check   A binary *check digit*.

bit density The number of *bits* stored per unit of length or area.

bite An alternative spelling for *byte*.

bit location An element of *store* capable of storing one *bit*.

bit pattern A sequence of *bits*. Bit patterns may be used to represent *characters* in a *binary code*.

bit position The *digit position* of a *bit* in a *word*, referenced as the first, second, third, etc., position from the least significant bit.

bit rate Relating to the speed of a device, e.g. the speed with which *binary digits* can be transferred over a communications channel. May be measured in *bits per second* or *bauds*.

bit, sign A *binary sign digit*.

bit string A continuous sequence of *binary digits* to represent data in coded form, in which each *bit* has significance according to its position in the *string*[2] and its relation to other members of that string.

bit track A term sometimes used to refer to a physical track on a *disk* or a *drum*, along which a *read/write head* reads or records data serially as successive *binary digits*. Compare with *byte track* or *logical track*.

blank A blank character in the repertoire of an automatic *data processing* code; e.g. in a computer's internal *machine code* or in a *paper tape code*. Not necessarily indicated by an empty position on the medium; e.g., in internal *memory* a blank character usually has a specific *bit pattern* in the same way as any other numeric or alphabetic character.

Also known as space character.

blank form Synonymous with *blank medium*.

blank medium The representation of a *blank* by means of an empty position on the medium concerned; e.g. the absence of punching in a *card column* or in a *row* position on *paper tape*.

Also known as blank form.

blank tape The representation of *blanks* on *paper tape* indicated by the presence of *sprocket holes* only in the *row* positions concerned.

blast A term sometimes used in relation to *dynamic storage allocation*; to *release* external or internal *memory* areas so that they become available for re-allocation to other *programs*.

bleed Related to the printing of characters for *optical character recognition*; the flow of ink beyond the specified limits of printed characters.

block A group of *records* or *words* treated as a logical unit of data; e.g., data is transferred between *memory* and *peripheral units* as individual blocks. Blocks may be fixed in length or may be of variable size.

block copy To copy a file from one medium to another without changing its contents. ⋫ *block transfer.*

block diagram The diagrammatic representation of any system (e.g. a computer *program*, an electrical circuit) in which logical units of the system are represented by labelled rectangles or *boxes* and the relationship between units is shown by means of connecting lines. ⋫ general article on *Flowcharts.*

block header *Words* or *bytes* at the beginning of a *block*, used to describe the organization of the *file* and the relationship between blocks.

block ignore character A character associated with a particular *block* to indicate that the block contains errors; e.g. errors stemming from *data preparation.*

blocking The grouping of individual *records* into *blocks*, usually to achieve a greater efficiency for *input/output* operations, by reducing the number of *read* or *write* operations required. Also known as batching.

blocking factor The maximum number of *records* of a given size which can be accommodated in a single *block.*

block, input ⋫ *input area.*

block length The size of a *block*, measured in the number of *characters, words* or *records* it contains. In certain cases, blocks may be restricted to a minimum and/or maximum length, by either *hardware* or *software* requirements.

block list A printed representation of a *file*, or print of a file, in which *records* and *fields* are listed in the sequence in which they appear with just enough reformatting to make the information understandable. Used, for example, as a diagnostic aid.

block mark A special character used to indicate the end of a block. Employed particularly for systems in which *variable blocks* are used.

block, output ⋫ *output area.*

block sort Particularly related to sorting with *punched card sorters*; the file to be processed is sorted first in the highest digit position of the *key*, thus reducing the operation to a number of smaller sorting operations which can be done independently, and the separate sections are then joined.

block transfer The movement of data as *blocks* rather than as individual *records*; e.g., in internal *memory* transfers or in transfers between a *central processor* and its *peripheral units.*

bobbin core A type of *magnetic core* formed by winding a length of ferro-magnetic tape around a bobbin.

Boolean algebra Boolean algebra (named after the mathematician George Boole, 1815–64) uses algebraic notation to express logical relationships in the same way that conventional algebra is used to express mathematical relationships. In conventional algebra, an expression such as $p+q=r$ is a general expression consisting of variables p, q and r, which can take numbers as values, and symbols standing for mathematical operations such as addition. In Boolean algebra the same sorts of expression are used, but the variables do not stand for numbers but for statements, e.g. 'the cat is on the mat', and the logical operations which relate such statements, e.g. 'or', 'and'.

The relevance of Boolean algebra to the logic of computers lies in a simplification of the system in which the values of the variables are restricted to the two possible 'truth values' of a statement, i.e. 'true' and 'false'. These values may be represented by the digits 0 and 1, thus enabling the logic of Boolean algebra to be applied to the *binary* logic of computers. The truth value of a complex logical statement made up of variables and the relations between them depends on the *truth table* of each variable and the logical relationships between them. Basic logical relationships or operations are defined by means of truth tables which give the 'truth value' of the expression for all combinations of values for the constituent variables. An example of a Boolean operation holding between two *operands* is the *and operation* (also known as the logical product, conjunction, intersection or meet). This can be represented symbolically as p & q, p.q, pq, Kpq. The truth table for the result r of the *and* operation on the operands p,q is given below:

Operands		Result
p	q	r
1	0	0
0	0	0
0	1	0
1	1	1

This can be interpreted as meaning that the operation *and* results in the truth value 1 only if both operands have this value, but is 0 if any one of the variables has this value. Boolean operations on two operands are known as *dyadic Boolean operations*. Truth tables for the following dyadic operations can be found under their appropriate article: *inclusive-or operation, exclusive-or operation, equivalence operation, not-and operation, nor operation, conditional implication operation, not-if-then operation*. Two Boolean operations are known as *complementary operations* if the result of one is the opposite or negation of the result of the other; e.g. the or operation is complementary to the nor operation. Two Boolean operations are known as *dual operations* if the truth table of one can be transformed into the truth table of the other by negating each value in the table; e.g., the or operation is the dual of the and operation.

In general, a Boolean operation is an operation in which the result of giving each of a set of variables one of two values is itself one of two values. Since the internal states of a digital computer can only have one of two values, circuits can be designed to simulate the Boolean operations. These devices are known as *logic elements*, or *gates*. For example, the *and element* corresponds to the Boolean and operation, and is a logic element which produces an output signal of 1 only if all its input signals are also 1. The use of logic elements is fundamental to the operations by the digital computer: all the operations available to the programmer are ultimately executed by means of some combination of signals passing through logic elements.

Boolean calculus Synonymous with *Boolean algebra*.

Boolean complementation Synonymous with *negation*.

Boolean connective A *connective* used to connect the *operands* in a statement of a *Boolean operation*, indicating the type of operation concerned.

Boolean logic Synonymous with *Boolean algebra*.

Boolean operation An *operation* which operates in accordance with the rules of *Boolean algebra*.

Boolean operation, dyadic ◊ *dyadic Boolean operation*.

Boolean operation table A table which indicates, for a particular *Boolean operation*, the values that will result for particular combinations of *bits* in the *operands*. When the values are interpreted as true or false, known as a *truth table*. ◊ *Boolean algebra*.

bootstrap The technique of *loading* a *program* into a computer by means of certain preliminary *instructions* which in turn call in instructions to read programs and data. Since the preliminary instructions are usually set manually or pre-set and called into action by the use of a special *console* switch or message from a console typewriter, the machine does not quite 'pick itself up by its own bootstraps'.

bootstrap input program   ⟡ *bootstrap.*

bootstrap routine, tape   ⟡ *tape bootstrap routine.*

border-punched card   Synonymous with *margin-punched card.*

borrow   A carry signal which arises in *subtraction* when the difference between digits is less than zero.

box   A *flowchart symbol* used to represent a logical unit of a system or *program.* ⟡ general article on *Flowcharting.*

box, connexion   ⟡ *connexion box.*

branch   A departure from (or to depart from) the normal sequence of *program* steps. This is caused by a *branch instruction* which can be *conditional* (i.e. dependent on some previous state or condition in the program) or *unconditional* (i.e. always occurring regardless of previous conditions). A branch of a program consists of a sequence of instructions between branch instructions.

Also known as jump. ⟡ general article on *Programming.*

branching   ⟡ *branch.*

branch instruction   A *program* is normally performed by obeying a series of *instructions* stored in successive *locations* of *memory.* This sequence of operation can be altered by special *branch* instructions which can direct the *program controller* to execute a specific series of instructions. Thus, the program can be considered as consisting of several branches which are entered according to branch instructions written into the program itself. A branch instruction specifies the address of the next instruction to be performed; sometimes a branch will be mandatory but often it may or may not be performed according to conditions occurring during execution of the program.

Also known as control transfer instruction, discrimination instruction, jump instruction. ⟡ *unconditional branch instruction, conditional branch, switch.*[3]

branchpoint   The point in a *program* where a *branch* takes place. Related to *switch*[3] and contrasted with *break point.*

breadboard   A mock-up or experimental model of any device.

breakdown   A failure of *hardware* or *software* requiring the attention of an engineer or technical support specialist.

breakpoint   A point in a *program* where the normal sequence of operations is interrupted by external intervention (e.g. by an operator signal) or by a *monitor routine* used in *debugging.* The normal sequence is resumed after the interruption has served its purpose, e.g. after visual checking, printing out. Contrasted with *branch-*

point, which is an internal interruption in the sequence of events due to a *branch instruction* within the program.

breakpoint instruction A *program instruction* located at a *breakpoint* which will cause the program to take action on recognizing an external intervention (e.g. an operator's signal) or transfer control to a *monitor routine* in *debugging* operations.

breakpoint symbol A symbol used in *programming* to indicate a *breakpoint* at a specific *instruction*.

bridge limiter A device used in *analog* machines to prevent a variable from exceeding specified limits.

bridgeware *Hardware* or *software* aids used to transcribe *programs* and *data files* written for a particular type of computer into the format necessary for operation on another type of computer. ◊ general article on *Transition*.

bridging The process of converting systems written for a particular type of computer into an appropriate format and structure to be run on another type. ◊ general article on *Transition*.

broadband A *band* [2] covering a wide range of frequencies, usually greater than those required for voice communications.

brush An electrical conductor used in some systems as a means of sensing the presence of a hole in a *punched card*.

brush compare check On some *punched card* reading and card punching machines a check is performed by means of *brushes* at different *brush stations*; the information read by one set of brushes is compared in a brush compare check with the information read by the other set.

brush station The location of *brushes* in a *punched card* reading or card punching machine using the brush sensing method of establishing the presence of a hole in a punched card.

brute-force approach An attempt to apply computer techniques to the solution of problems which cannot be solved by a precise mathematical or logical approach.

bucket In *direct access storage* a bucket is a unit of storage as distinct from the data contained in the unit. The data is *accessed* by reference to the bucket in which it is located.

budgetary control Budgetary control is a system used by management in which targets (budgets) are set and actual performance compared with them. The purpose is to establish where, how and why actual results are diverging from the budget and what action is needed to achieve the budget. Computers are often used for recording and reporting the information required in a budgetary control system, and a brief summary is therefore given here.

The main steps in operating a budgetary control system are: (i) The objectives of the organization and their relative importance are determined. For example, the importance of volume of orders as against profit from orders might be decided. In a normal trading business the key budgets are orders, revenue, production, manpower, capital expenditure, cash flow, profit and return on capital employed. (ii) A total budget is drawn up which would result in the achievement of the objectives. Certain of the resources available may be insufficient to attain the budget. Perhaps skilled labour is limited; or money. It is then clear that some definite action is needed to make the budget achievable. Perhaps a training programme needs to be set up; or financing arrangements made. This stage stimulates forward planning. (iii) The detailed budgets are set and each manager should be involved so that he fully accepts his own budget. Budgets should only include those items for which a manager has been given authority. (iv) Many of the individual budgets are interdependent and therefore have to be compatible so that the total budget is a realistic whole. For example, the sales manager's budget for revenue is dependent upon the production manager producing enough goods and at the right times. (v) There should now be a reliable total budget built up from the individual budgets to which each manager is committed. (vi) The actual results are recorded in the same form as the budget, compared with it and variances from the budget established. (vii) The causes of variances are analysed and reported to the appropriate levels of management. Each manager has to explain his variance and either to justify it or take action to remedy it.

The frequency of reporting will differ according to need and to the ability to take immediate action; e.g., cash may be reported daily whereas manpower may be monthly.

Attention is concentrated on the exceptions from the required results.

Budgets may be set for any length of time but if taken too far ahead become less reliable. They are often set annually, and should not be revised too frequently because there is then a danger of their becoming forecasts of expectations rather than targets for achievement.

Budgets may be fixed amount or flexible according to level of activity; e.g., a salesman's budget for entertainment may be a fixed sum or a percentage on orders taken, i.e. flexible. Flexible budgets are more complex but often give more useful information than fixed budgets.

The advantages of the system are that it provides: (i) definition of objectives; (ii) anticipation and planning; (iii) personal involvement of all levels of management; (iv) delegation of controllable items; (v) coordination of activities; (vi) concentration on exceptions; (vii) a basis for corrective action.

Budgetary control encourages management to anticipate as well as concentrating attention on those results which are deviating from the budget. Both of these effects are vital pillars in the structure of management control.

budgeting In computing, the process of allocating resources to a particular development activity in order to constrain the resources utilized for the project. For example, restrictions may be placed upon *programmers* to limit the amount of *main store, backing store*, and *peripherals* utilized by their *programs* as a policy to promote operational efficiency in the installation.

buffer Synonymous with *buffer store*.

buffer amplifier An amplifier used to isolate a signal source (e.g. an oscillator) from another circuit being driven by that source. This prevents the driving circuit from being affected by the characteristics of the driven circuit.

buffer, double ◊ *double buffering*.

buffered computer A computer in which *buffer stores* are provided to match the speed of the *peripheral units* to the higher speed of a *central processor*.

buffered input/output Relating to the use of *input/output buffers* to increase efficiency when data is transmitted to and from a *central processor*.

buffer store Generally used as a means of temporarily storing data when information is being transmitted from one unit to another; e.g. between a *central processor* and its input/output *peripheral units*. The purpose of a buffer is to compensate for the different speeds at which the units can handle data. Sometimes a *buffer* may be a permanent feature of a peripheral unit (e.g. as in a buffered *printer*) and in other systems *internal memory* areas may be assigned temporarily to act as buffers for particular units.

bug Any mistake or malfunction of a computer *program* or system. ◊ general article on *debugging*.

built-in check Synonymous with *hardware check*.

bulk storage Synonymous with *backing store*.

bulk store Synonymous with *backing store*.

burst 1. To separate sheets of continuous *stationery* by means of a *burster*. 2. The transmission of a group of *records* in a *store*, leaving an interval to allow *access* to the store for other requirements (cf. a burst of machine-gun fire).

burster   A device used *off-line* in a computer system to separate individual forms in a set of continuous *stationery* produced as output from a *printer*.

burst mode   A mode of data transfer between a *central processor* and a *peripheral unit* in which a signal from the peripheral unit causes the central processor to receive data until the peripheral unit signals that a transfer has been completed. ✧ *burst*.[2]

bus   Synonymous with *highway*.

bus driver, output   ✧ *output bus driver*.

byte   A set of *binary digits* considered as a unit; usually a subdivision of a *word*.
Also spelt bite.

byte mode   A mode of data transfer between a *central processor* and a *peripheral unit* in which the unit of transfer is a single *byte* at a time.

byte track   A number of *tracks* on the surface of a *disk* or *drum*, along which *read/write heads* move in parallel to read or record data representing a unit of information (e.g. *byte*). Compare with *bit track*; synonymous with *logical track*.

C

calculating punch A *calculator* equipped with a *card reader* and a *card punch*. Data to be processed is input on *punched cards* and, after a sequence of arithmetical calculations, results may be punched into specified *fields* of the same cards or on other cards.

calculator A *data processing* machine designed to perform arithmetic (e.g. addition, subtraction and multiplication) and a limited range of *logical operations* on data. For example, a *punched card* machine capable of processing data input on punched cards and of generating results on punched cards. Some early calculators were able to follow a simple step-by-step *program* but were not usually able to *modify* their own programs.

calendar time The total time available in a given working period, e.g. $6 \times 24 = 144$ hours in a working week of 6 days.

call A *branch* to a *closed subroutine*.

call direction code A special code, used in telegraph networks, transmitted to an outlying terminal to switch on automatically the teleprinter equipment at the terminal.

calling sequence The set of *program instructions* whose purpose is to set up initial conditions necessary before a *call* is made to a *subroutine*. Also the instructions within a subroutine used to provide the *link* with the main program.

call instruction An *instruction* which causes the *program control unit* to *branch* to a *subroutine*. The call instruction may also specify *parameters* required on entry to the *subroutine*.

capacitor store A type of storage unit commonly used in early *punched card calculators*, in which each *bit* of information was represented by a capacitor.

capacity 1. The number of *words* or *characters* that can be contained in a particular *storage device*. 2. The upper and lower limits of numbers which can be processed in a *register*.

capstan On a magnetic *tape transport*, a shaft on which a reel of *magnetic tape* is mounted and which drives the tape past the *read/write head*.

card ◊ *punched card*.

card back The unprinted side of a *punched card*; the obverse of the *card face*.

card bed Synonymous with *card track*.

card code The combination of holes in a *punched card* used to represent letters of the alphabet, numerals or special symbols.

card column The lines of a *punched card* parallel to the short edge of the card. Each column is treated as a unit for the purpose of punching and holes in one column represent a specific character. Contrasted with *card row*. (Some systems divide the columns in two, upper and lower, or allow punching in between the rows in a column thus making each column do the work of two.)

card, edge-punched ⋄ *margin-punched card*.

card, eighty-column ⋄ *eighty-column card* and *punched card*.

card face The printed side of a *punched card*; the side uppermost when the first *card column* punched is on the left-hand side. The obverse of the *card back*. Cards are usually made with one corner cut, so that, when cards are grouped in a *pack*, it is possible to ensure that all are facing the same way.

Also known as face.[2]

card feed A mechanism which moves *punched cards* one at a time into the sensing, reading or punching mechanism of a machine.

card field A group of consecutive *card columns* in a *punched card* containing a unit of information. For example, columns 6 to 9 might contain a four-figure staff number: these columns make up the staff number field.

card fluff When *punch knives* cut holes in *punched cards*, the edges of the holes are not always clean and the slightly burred effect – card fluff – can cause mis-feeding or mis-reading later.

card format A description of the contents of a *punched card*, usually provided as part of a *systems definition* or *program specification*.

card hopper A device for holding *punched cards* and making them available as required to a *card feed* mechanism, e.g. on a *card reader* or *card punch*.

Also known as input magazine. Contrasted with *card stacker*.

card image An exact representation in *store* of each character in a *punched card*, as distinct from the *binary image* representation.

card jam Synonymous with *card wreck*.

card leading edge The edge of a *punched card* which leads when the card is transported along a *card track*. Contrasted with *trailing edge*.

card loader   A routine used to *load* a *program* from *punched cards* into *store*.

card, margin-notched   ◊ *edge-notched card.*

card, ninety-column   ◊ *ninety-column card* and *punched card.*

card punch   A machine which causes holes to be punched in *punched cards*, thus allowing data to be stored and later conveyed to other machines which can read or sense the holes. A card punch can be *on-line* (when holes are punched as a result of signals from a *central processor*) or *off-line* (when holes are punched as a result of operator action). ◊ *automatic punch, hand punch.*

card punch buffer   Before a *punched card* is punched by an *on-line card punch*, the data is transmitted to the card punch *buffer store*. If for any reason the card punch is unable to punch the data in the buffer, e.g. because the input *hopper* is empty and there are no blank cards, the card punch will become inoperative and the data will remain in the buffer.

card punch, duplicating   Synonymous with *reproducer.*

card punching   The punching of holes into *punched cards*. The holes have particular significance according to the code being used, and the punching allows the data to be stored and later conveyed to other machines which can read or sense the holes. This is one of the basic methods of preparing data for input to a computer system. Contrasted with *paper tape punching* and *character recognition.* ◊ the general article on *Data Preparation.*

card reader   A machine for reading information represented by holes in a *punched card* and converting it into another form for processing by a computer. ◊ general article on *Input Devices.*

card reproducer   A machine which reads a *punched card* and punches a copy of the card. The machine can be set to reproduce a specified number of copies from one card, and to copy only selected parts of the original card. A card reproducer is not a computer *peripheral unit* but a 'conventional' data processing machine.

card row   A line of *punching positions* on a *punched card* parallel to the long edge of the card. There are, for example, twelve rows on a normal 80-column card. Contrasted with *card column.*

card stacker   An *output device* for holding *punched cards* (stacking them in a *pack*) after they have passed through, for example, a *card reader* or *card punch*. Contrasted with *card hopper.*

card systems   Computer systems which have no input *peripheral unit* other than a *card reader*, and no output peripheral unit other than a *card punch* and a *printer*. Such systems do not have a *backing store*.

card-to-card In *data transmission*, the operation of transmitting data on *punched cards* to a remote terminal where the data is reproduced onto other punched cards.

card-to-magnetic-tape converter A device which reads batches of data from *punched cards* and writes them as logical *records* on to *magnetic tape* ready for subsequent processing. This type of equipment was designed to permit data *input* and *validation* to be undertaken without monopolizing the *central processor* of the main configuration. Such devices are less necessary when comprehensive *time sharing* and *multiprogramming* facilities are available.

card-to-tape 1. The operation of converting data on *punched cards* to *paper tape*, performed on *card-to-tape converters*. 2. A routine for transferring data on punched cards to *magnetic tape* on a computer by means of a special *program*; the program may also *edit* and verify the data at the time of transcription.

card-to-tape converter A device used for converting from one unit of storage (*punched cards*) to another (*paper tape*). The data contained in the punched cards is read, converted into the new character code and punched into paper tape. ⟡ *card-to-magnetic-tape converter.*

card track That part of a *punched card* machine which transports cards through the various *reading stations* and/or *punching stations*, from the input *hopper* to the *stacker*.
Also known as card bed.

card trailing edge The edge of a *punched card* which trails when a card is transported along a *card track*. Contrasted with *leading edge*.

card, verge-perforated Synonymous with *margin-punched card*.

card verifier A *punched card* machine used for *card verifying*.

card verifying Checking the accuracy of punching in *punched cards*. This is usually carried out by placing the *punched cards* in a device similar to the *card punch* (a *card verifier*) which has keys similar to those of the card punch. The operator (not the one who did the original punching) reads the *source documents* and depresses the verifier keys; if these correspond with the original punching the card is accepted as valid, but if there is a discrepancy the keyboard locks and the card is rejected. In some systems the original holes are altered (e.g. round holes ovalized) and the *pack* of cards is then passed through an automatic verifier which rejects all holes without an altered shape. Most systems, however, depend on the fact that one operator keys original punching and another keys what should be the same information into the same cards. ⟡ general article on *Data Preparation*.

card wreck A fault condition that occurs when one or more *punched cards* become jammed along the *card track* of a punched card machine. Also known as card jam.

carriage return The operation causing an *automatic carriage* to be returned so that the next character is printed or punched at a pre-set left-hand margin.

carriage tape Synonymous with *control tape*.

carrier system A system which allows several independent communications signals to share the same circuit.

carry The digit added to the next high digit position when the sum of the digits in the lower position exceeds the radix or number base.

carry, addition without Synonymous with *exclusive-or operation*.

carry-complete signal A signal developed by an *adder* to indicate that all arithmetic carries relevant to a particular operation have been generated. ◊ *carry*.

carry, ripple-through Synonymous with *high-speed carry*.

carry, standing-on-nines Synonymous with *high-speed carry*.

carry time A system required to add a *carry* into the next higher digit position.

cascade control A system of automatic control in which control units are organized in sequence so that each unit controls its successor and is in turn controlled by its predecessor.

cascaded carry A *carry* into a digit position resulting in a carry out of the same digit position; uses the normal adding circuit, unlike a *high-speed carry*.

casting-out-nines A particular form of *modulo n check* in which *n* is equal to nine.

catalogue A file of named objects used or handled within a system. For example, in an *operating system*, the catalogue may contain details of devices, users, and files currently maintained and allocated.

category This term is sometimes used to describe a group of *direct access disks* or *volumes* containing a given set of information. For example, *files* used for *program* development work may be placed in a particular category.

category storage A section of the *filestore* used by an *operating system* containing a number of *categories*.

catena A series of items recorded in a *chained list*.

catenate To arrange a series of items in a *catena* or *chained list*.

cathode follower A form of *buffer amplifier* in which a thermionic valve is used, and in which the potential of the cathode follows that of the grid.

cathode ray tube An electronic tube in which a beam of electrons can be controlled and directed by an electronic lens so as to produce a visible *display* of information on the surface of the tube or to *store* data in the form of an energized portion of the tube's surface. Abbreviated as C R T.

cathode ray tube visual display unit A *visual display unit* in which a *cathode ray tube* is used as the medium for the output of data for visual inspection.

cell 1. The smallest unit of a *store* capable of storing a single bit. 2. An area of storage used to *extend* or *reduce* the size of a *dynamic buffer*.

cellar Synonymous with *push down store*.

cell, static magnetic ◊ *magnetic cell*.

center ◊ *centre* for all entries.

central control unit Synonymous with *program controller*, but sometimes used specifically to denote a unit which has control over one, or more, subordinate *control units* operating in the same system.

centralized data processing The grouping of all data processing requirements of an organization at a single *data processing centre*.

central processing unit Synonymous with *central processor*.

central processors The central processor is the nerve centre of any *digital* computer system, since it coordinates and controls the activities of all the other units and performs all the arithmetic and logical processes to be applied to data. All program *instructions* to be executed must be held within the central processor, and all data to be processed must first be *loaded* into this unit. It is convenient to consider the central processor as three separate *hardware* sections: *internal memory, arithmetic unit* and a control section.

This article concentrates mainly on the latter, the role of the other two sections being defined in more detail elsewhere in this book. The functions of the control section are more difficult to classify since they embrace a wide range of activities analogous to the central nervous system of a human being. It is, however, possible to distinguish the *program control unit* as a primary member. This unit, also known as the *program controller*, examines one by one the individual instructions in the user's program, interprets each instruction and causes the various circuits to be activated to perform the functions specified. Essentially these functions involve the selection of required *operands* from internal memory, and the activation of the arithmetic unit to perform the specified operation on these operands.

Internal memory consists of a series of magnetic storage devices, e.g. *magnetic cores*, organized to hold data or program instructions in a series of *locations* as either *words* or *characters*. In many computing systems the internal memory is stored within the cabinet housing the other sections of the central processor, but in large systems separate cabinets may be used to contain sections of internal memory. Nevertheless the memory can always be considered as part of the central processing unit.

The arithmetic unit consists of a series of special *registers* and circuits which are able to perform arithmetic and logical operations upon one or more operands selected from memory. For example, the arithmetic operations of addition, subtraction, multiplication and division may be performed, as well as various *shift* operations and comparisons including the *logical operations*, 'or', 'and', 'not', etc.

The control section has many complex functions to perform but to simplify the situation we will first consider the basic instruction cycle within the central processor. First the program control unit will select an instruction from memory and will store it within one of a number of special *control registers*. Here the instruction is decoded to ascertain the particular arithmetic or logical operation to be performed, and to ascertain the memory locations involved. Then the instruction is executed, causing the required operands to be selected from the specified memory locations and to be routed via the arithmetic unit and back again to the same or some other specified memory locations. The time required to perform an instruction is usually considered in two phases – the time to select the instruction and the time required to execute it. During the execute phase the arithmetic unit operates under the aegis of the program control unit to perform the required arithmetic or logical process on the selected operands.

The cycle is repeated for each instruction in the program: call an instruction, decode and execute the instruction, call an instruction, and so on. Each complete cycle is performed at high speed and takes place as a series of discrete pulses; e.g., during the execute phase the various digits of the operands are often handled one after the other as individual digit pulses. The control section has the function of generating the basic timing pulses to control the activities of the many circuits operating within the system to ensure that each instruction occupies a predetermined period, referred to as the *instruction time.* Futhermore the individual stages during the instruction time must be completed to a basic schedule governed by the timing pulses.

Thus it can be seen that the control section of the central processor coordinates the activities of the other sections, but it must also control the operation of *peripheral units*. In most computing systems the number of locations available within internal memory are comparatively few and data must be stored in some other peripheral unit (e.g. on a *magnetic disk*) until required for processing. Sometimes it is also necessary to write a program as a number of separate *segments*, each of which are called into memory as and when required.

Peripheral units are generally activated by instructions written in the user's program, often organized to call for data to be processed in *blocks*, so that the program control unit must decode *read* and *write* instructions in the user's program in order to initiate transfers to and from the central processor.

Once the program control unit has initiated a read or write operation the control section must continue to monitor the operation to ensure that it is satisfactorily completed. For example, *parity* errors or peripheral failures may be encountered and it is then necessary to provide a signal to the user's program and perhaps to the operating *console* to ensure that the situation can be corrected. Communications between the computer operator and the central processor are also handled via the control section. This aspect of the control function is often referred to as *input/output control*.

The function of the control section does not cease at this point, for in most systems nowadays some degree of *time sharing* is incorporated and it is necessary for the control section to coordinate several concurrent peripheral operations while data is processed internally within the central processor. The extension of this technique into the field of *real time* data processing implies also that the central processor must be able to receive *interruptions* from distant terminals at any moment in time; here the control section has very complex functions to perform in coordinating the receipt and transmission of data over perhaps several communications channels. In this sort of situation specialized communications control units often have to be connected to the central processor and in any highly developed time sharing system some kind of *executive program* is usually necessary. Such programs are stored permanently in internal memory and can effectively be considered as part of the hardware of the central processor, since as well as providing an economic and flexible control over concurrent operations they perform many of the routine functions otherwise done by hardware in more conventional systems – for example the complete coordination of all input/output control functions and the handling of all communications between the operator and the computer.

central terminal A *hardware* unit which coordinates communications between a computer and a number of outlying terminals. It may receive messages at random from the terminals, store them until they can be handled by the *central processor* and then return them to the terminal concerned.

centre, automatic switching ◊ *switching centre.*

centre-feed tape *Paper tape* with *feed holes* aligned exactly with the centres of the character holes. Contrasts with *advance feed tape.*

centre, semi-automatic switching ◊ *switching centre.*

centre, torn-tape switching ◊ *switching centre.*

chad The piece of paper removed when a code hole is punched in *paper tape* or a *punched card.*

chadded tape *Paper tape* punched in such a way that the *chads* are only partially removed and remain attached to the tape.

chadless tape *Paper tape* with the *chads* completely removed.

chain 1. A *routine* consisting of *segments*, each of which uses in turn the output from the previous segment as input. 2. A set of items organized as a *chained list.*

chain code A sequential arrangement of *words* in which adjacent words are linked by the rule that each word is derived from its neighbour by displacing the *bits* one position left or right, dropping the leading bit and inserting a bit at the end, so that a given word does not recur until the cycle is complete.

chained list A set of data ordered in such a way that each item contains an *address* to locate the next item in the set. The items may be stored in any sequence, and may be retrieved by a *chaining search.*

chained record A *file* of *records* in which the records are arranged in a random manner in *memory* or *backing store* but are linked by means of a control *field* in each record which gives the *address* of the next record in the series. The first such record is known as the *home record.*

chaining search A method of searching a set of data organized as a *chained list.* An initial *key* is transformed to obtain the *address* of a *location* which may contain a direct reference to the item required or may indicate another item in the chain. The search continues through the chain until the required item is located or until the chain is completed.

chain printer A high-speed *printer* in which the type is carried past the paper by the links of a continuous chain.

change dump A *print-out* or other output of all *locations* which have changed since a previous event (usually another change dump). Used in *debugging*.

change file A collection of *change records* used in *batch processing* to update a *master file*.
Also known as amendment file, transaction file.

change, intermediate control ◊ *intermediate control change.*

change, major control ◊ *major control change.*

change, minor control ◊ *minor control change.*

change of control A logical break in the sequence of *records* being processed which may initiate some predetermined action (e.g. the printing of *control totals*) before the next group of records is processed. ◊ *comparing control change.* 'Change of control' is sometimes also used for *transfer of control.*

change record A *record* whose function is to change information in a corresponding *master record*.
Also known as amendment record, transaction record.

change, step ◊ *step change.*

change tape Synonymous with *transaction tape*.

channel 1. A path along which information flows. When all elements of a digit are sent in parallel, a channel is made up of parallel paths. 2. A *paper tape* channel is a longitudinal row in which code holes may be punched in paper tape. 3. The part of a *store* accessible to a reading station.

channel, paper tape ◊ *channel* [2].

channel, peripheral interface ◊ *interface.*

channel status table A table maintained by an *executive program* to indicate the status of the various *peripheral unit interface channels*, so that control can be exercised over input/output operations.

channel-to-channel connexion The transfer of data between computers by means of connecting appropriate *channels* from each system.

chapter A self-contained section of a *program*, synonymous with *segment*.

character One of a set of symbols in a *data processing* system used to denote, for example, the numerals 0–9, the letters of the alphabet, punctuation marks, etc. Each character is represented by a unique code of *bits*, holes in *punched cards*, holes in *paper tape*, etc.

character-at-a-time printer A *printer* which creates each line of print by consecutively printing each *character* from left to right along the line; e.g. a teleprinter or electric typewriter used as an output device.

Also known as character printer. Contrasted with *line printer*.

character code The specific combination of elements (*bits*, holes in *punched cards*, etc.) used to represent *characters* in any system.

character code, forbidden ◊ *forbidden character code*.

character crowding ◊ *pack*².

character density The number of characters that can be stored per unit of length, e.g. on *magnetic tape*. (◊ *packing density*.)

character emitter An *emitter* which outputs a *character* at timed intervals.

character, erase ◊ *ignore character*.

character fill To fill a number of specified storage *locations* by repeatedly inserting a nominated *character*; e.g., to indicate an error condition.

character, functional ◊ *control character*.

characteristic An alternative for *exponent*, when reference is made to *floating point representation*. The characteristic is the signed integer which serves to indicate the position of the *radix point* for the *fixed point part* of the number.

characteristic overflow A condition arising when *floating point arithmetic* is used if an attempt is made to develop a *characteristic* greater than an upper limit specified for the particular *hardware* or *software* system employed.

characteristic underflow A condition that arises when *floating point arithmetic* is used if an attempt is made to develop a *characteristic* less than some specified lower limit for the particular *hardware* or *software* system employed.

character modifier A constant used in *address modification* to reference the *location* of a specific character.

character oriented Pertaining to a computer in which individual character *locations* can be *addressed* rather than *words*. Each *operand* in *memory* is addressed by specifying the first and last character location, thus permitting *variable length* operands to be used.

character printer Synonymous with *character-at-a-time printer*.

character reader A device which can convert characters input in a form legible to human beings into machine language. ◊ *magnetic ink character reader, optical character reader* and general article on *Input Devices*.

character reader, magnetic ink ◊ *magnetic ink character reader.*
character reader, optical ◊ *optical character reader.*
character recognition Human beings are taught to recognize patterns from an early age. In the first year of life a baby can be induced to make more or less consistent vocal responses to pictures, for example saying 'dog' whenever it is shown a picture of one. Later, children are taught to identify letters and numbers and subsequently to read and perform arithmetic. When children grow up some of them may spend their lives manipulating letters and numbers, recognizing patterns quite automatically.

The ideal *data processing* system is one in which data is captured at source and processed as soon as possible, and it would therefore be very desirable for machines to recognize symbols and numbers directly in the same formats as those used by human beings in their everyday social and commercial activities.

At present the patterns that most computers can recognize (i.e. holes in *paper tape* or *punched cards*) are not conveniently read by human beings. Similarly, data originating from people is not usually input directly into the computer. Data handling, therefore, is typified by a conversion process from 'human' format to computer format. This operation is usually performed manually, i.e. human operators read *source documents* and operate *keyboard* machines which punch the information in coded form into paper tape or cards. The cost of this method of data conversion is frequently as much as the actual cost of processing it. Moreover key punching slows down the processing cycle and the human element involved brings with it the risk of error. For this reason much effort has been devoted to devising an alternative method of presenting data to the computer.

The objective here is to enable the computer to read source documents directly, thus eliminating the punching stage. The problem of converting a pattern on an input document into electronic signals suitable for processing by a computer is one of pattern recognition.

It is necessary to strike a balance between a pattern convenient for people to read and one that is convenient for the computer. There are two main systems for automatically recognizing printed characters: *optical character recognition* (O C R) and *magnetic ink character recognition* (M I C R). In the former, characters are printed in conventional type formats, usually in black ink on a white surface, and the characters are scanned by measuring their optical reflectivity when subject to illumination. In MICR systems however, characters are printed in a highly stylized format using an ink impregnated with magnetizable particles. When M I C R documents are read the ink is magnetized before the characters are presented to a *read head*. The output signals generated are governed by the magnetized particles passing the head and for any character are proportional to the vertical projection of the character. *Mark reading* is also a form of character recognition and it is common to find mark reading and optical character recognition used within the same system. Despite the fundamental differences in these systems, the equipment utilized in each case contains similar types of unit. There is always a scanner, which reads characters and converts them into electronic signals, and this unit is associated with a normalizing unit, which examines each signal to improve its quality without changing its basic characteristics.

The signal thus generated is then examined to determine the basic properties of the character and a decision mechanism is used to analyse these properties and identify the character concerned. If the decision mechanism is unable to identify the character unambiguously then the character is rejected.

The ability of machines to recognize characters printed in a format easily recognizable to human beings has great advantages in reducing the task of *data collection* and thereby speeding up the flow of data in a system. Costs for *data preparation* can be considerably reduced and improvements in accuracy can often be achieved as compared with more conventional methods.

The development of character recognition systems has taken place in many different organizations and has led to a wide number of special type founts being developed. As improvements have been made in techniques of character recognition some degree of standardization has been evident but there are still many differing founts in use. In the field of M I C R there has tended to be less variation and two founts, known as E13B and CMC7, are more or less accepted as standard on an international basis. In O C R systems there are more variations although the International Standards Organization has proposed two standard founts known as O C R'A' and O C R'B'.

In some respects there appears to be less flexibility in M I C R founts than in O C R. The M I C R system requires that characters should be printed in a highly stylized format and with a high degree of accuracy, but this system of recognition relies on the magnetized particles forming each character and is not therefore so vulnerable as O C R systems are when handling damaged and folded documents, or with documents that have been soiled or have overwritten characters. O C R systems require less stylized formats and the characters can often be printed by the use of conventional machines such as typewriters; this aspect allows for cheapness and flexibility in establishing data collection points. In both systems characters to be read must be printed in certain specified areas of the documents with a fairly high standard of print registration.

M I C R has been used for cheques in banking throughout the world. M I C R sorter/readers are used to sort automatically the cheques in clearing houses for distribution to various branches, the cheques being preprinted with a branch code. The cheque number and customer's account number are also preprinted, and at a later stage the amount of the transaction can be added using an M I C R *encoder*. Details from such cheques can be read automatically into a computer *memory* to update subscribers' accounts.

O C R documents have been used as *turn-around documents* in hire-purchase accounting and similar applications, each customer being issued with a book of vouchers preprinted with the amount due for each payment in the hire contract. In some credit card *applications* customers are given a plastic ticket which is embossed with their own account number; this card has to be presented at point of sale to act as a plate in printing a record of the transaction. The record is then used to provide automatic input to O C R equipment.

O C R equipment is often used in gas and electricity accounting; a common system is to combine mark reading and character recognition techniques to enable meter reading staff to input details of consumption from turn-around documents, the actual consumption figures being entered as marks on preprinted areas of the forms.

Character recognition techniques are used with great advantage where large numbers of transactions in a fairly regular format are involved. They are best suited to applications where only a limited number of variable characters have to be entered, and in this context provide a speedy and accurate method for recording data.

character, redundant ◊ *check character*.

character repertoire The range of *characters* available in a particular code, or, for example, on each *print member* of a *line printer*. Related to *character set*.

character set The set of *characters* forming a particular group or code accepted as valid by a particular computer and not *illegal characters*. For example, a 64-character machine code might consist of the ten numerals (0 to 9), twenty-six alphabetic characters (A to Z) and 28 *special characters* including *blank*.

character string A one-dimensional *array* of *characters* in *memory* or some other storage medium.

character subset A selection of characters from a *character set*; e.g., the subset that embraces alphabetic characters only.

chart Any diagram used as an aid in analysing or solving a problem when developing a system or *program*, or when documenting any system or procedure. ◊ *flowcharting*.

chart, systems ◊ *systems flowchart*.

check Any operation performed to test the validity or accuracy of an *operand* or result; e.g., to test for the presence or absence of certain specified conditions. *Data processing* requires both machine checks and clerical checks in order to verify the accuracy of data handling and the correctness of machine operations. Machine checks may be especially *programmed* or may be performed automatically by *hardware*.

check bit A *binary check digit*.

check character A *character* forming one of a group of characters, the value of which is dependent on the other members of the group. Its sole function is to act as a check on the other characters when data is stored or transferred, and it is redundant in so far as its information content is concerned. ◊ general article on *Check Digits*.

check digits In most *data processing* applications it is necessary to ascribe numbers, or codes, to people or objects in order to process data about them. People are given staff numbers; spare parts are given numbers; almost everything, for data processing purposes, is given a number.

At some stage in the data processing these numbers are handled by people to whom they are meaningless. Although part number 24573986 may mean a washer to an engineer, and customer number 25679467 may mean Peter Smith & Co. of Brighton to a salesman, they are meaningless to a punchgirl or to a clerk and the possibility of transcription errors looms large. Although by *verification* of punching (◊ *Data Preparation*) many errors may be removed, it is still probable that if one punchgirl read a 'bad' 3 for an 8 another might also, and the error will slip through the checking stage.

In many applications such errors are not important; the probability of them occurring is small and the effort to recover from them when they do is not great. If we are selling nuts and bolts in threes and fours it is not too terrible if, through such an error, we reduce the stock of the wrong nut by three when we stock thousands of them. On the other hand it would be embarrassing if, because a mispunching went undetected, we charged the wrong customer for an oil tanker!

In applications where the risk of errors must be reduced to a minimum, check digits, generated by the machine performing the data processing, are often used. In a computer installation the extra processing time needed to take care of check digits is negligible.

A check digit is simply one or more digits added to a number; one method of calculating the digit is by finding the remainder when the original number is divided by a fixed number. Thus if we are using the number 7 to generate check digits, instead of 127 we would write 1271, the 1 being the remainder when 127 is divided by 7; instead of 324 we would write 3242, 2 being the remainder when 324 is divided by 7. These remainders are calculated by the machine when the system is initiated, and thereafter remain as part of the number, the machine checking that the remainder given is correct each time the number is processed.

The use of check digits reduces considerably the probability of an undetected error. If the probability of an error escaping the verification stage is one in a thousand, then the addition of a two-digit check digit will reduce the probability of an undetected error to, at most, one in a million.

The choice of method used to generate the check digits is not material. Several well-known techniques are available and choice will depend on the particular application requirements.

Before the decision is taken whether or not to use check digits in a data processing system, a study should be launched to find the incident rate of undetected errors and their effect; if it is found that the incidence rate is too high for tolerance the use of check digits will considerably reduce it.

check indicator A method of showing that a check has failed. The indicator may be a *hardware* indicator, causing a *console* display or an internal *switch* to be set which may be tested by *program*; or it may be a programmed indicator causing an error message to be printed.

checking program A *program* which diagnoses errors in other programs by identifying, in the format of the various *instructions*, mistakes resulting from incorrect coding or mispunching. Used in *debugging*.

checking routine Synonymous with *checking program*.

check, marginal ⬦ *marginal testing*.

check number Synonymous with *check digit*.

checkout routine Synonymous with *debugging aid routine*.

checkpoint A point in a *program* at which details concerning the state of the program are recorded to assist in *recovery* should it be subsequently necessary. ◊ *dump and restart*.

checkpoint dump The process of recording details in the progress of a job to allow for the possible need for *recovery* after a failure. ◊ *dump and restart, checkpoint*.

checkpointing The practice of writing a *program* in such a way that it automatically *dumps* information at frequent intervals throughout a job, to enable the job to be restarted in the event of a *failure*. ◊ *dump and restart, checkpoint*.

check problem A problem with a known solution used to check that a *program* or machine is working correctly.

check, redundant ◊ *redundancy check*.

check register A *register* used to store input data temporarily before it is compared with the same data input at a different time or by a different path. A form of *transfer check*.

check row A *row* (or rows) on *paper tape*, forming part of an item *field* on the tape and attached to the field to act as a *check symbol*, permitting a *summation check* to be made for that item when the tape is used as input to a computer.

check sum A *sum* generated using individual digits of a number and employed as part of a *summation check*. Sometimes used as a synonym for *hash total*.

check symbol A digit or digits generated for a particular item of data by performing an *arithmetic check* on the item. These digits are then attached to the item and accompany it through various stages of processing so that the *check* can be repeated to validate the item at each stage.

check total Synonymous with *control total*.

check word A *word* appended to a *block* of *records*, and containing data generated for that block, to act as a *check symbol* when the block is transferred from one *location* to another.

chip tray A small receptacle positioned beneath the *punching station* of a *card punch* or *tape punch* to collect pieces punched from the *punched cards* or *paper tape*.

chopper A device for interrupting a current or a beam of light to produce a pulsating signal. Sometimes done to achieve timing pulses, as for example in a photo-electric cam. In the case of a continuous current signal a chopper *amplifier* is often used in order to amplify the signal in the presence of *noise*.

chopper-stabilized amplifier A device which includes a *modulator*, an a.c. coupled *amplifier* and a *demodulator*, to stabilize fluctuations in a circuit. The modulator acts as a *chopper*.

circuit, and ◇ *and element.*

circuit, duplex ◇ *duplex channel.*

circuit, half-duplex ◇ *half-duplex channel.*

circuit noise level A measure of the disturbance in a *data transmission* circuit, usually expressed as a ratio of the *noise* measured in a circuit in relation to some chosen reference level.

circuit, simplex ◇ *simplex channel.*

circular shift Synonymous with *logical shift.*

circulating register A *register* in which digits can be shifted around in circular fashion, in such a way that digits removed from *locations* at one end of the register are automatically inserted at the other end.

clear To replace data in a *storage device* with some standard *character*, e.g. zero or *blank*. Contrasted with *hold*.

clear band In relation to *optical character recognition*, any area on a document which must be kept free of printing.

clock Any electronic device which provides pulses at fixed intervals to monitor, measure or synchronize other circuits or units operating within the same system. For example, a device to measure the frequency of a circuit or to measure the time used for particular activities.

Also known as clock signal generator.

clock pulses Electronic pulses which are used to control the timing of all circuits within a machine. The pulses are emitted repetitively from a *master clock* to synchronize the operations carried out by the machine.

A clock pulse is also known as a clock signal.

clock rate The frequency at which pulses are emitted from a *clock*.

clock signal Synonymous with *clock pulses.*

clock signal generator Synonymous with *clock.*

clock track A track on a magnetic recording medium which provides *clock pulses* to control *read* and *write* operations.

closed loop 1. A continuous *loop* in a *program* from which there is no exit except by operator intervention or by action on the part of some *executive program* monitoring the operation of the *program* concerned. A closed loop is usually an error, and may be signalled by a *hoot stop*. 2. Referring to a system in which there is no human intervention and in which the output from the system is fed back to adjust the input. For example, in certain *process control* applications in which the computer is able to set switches, valves, etc., to control directly the process concerned.

closed shop Describing a method for running a computer installation, particularly with regard to the testing and running of *programs* under development. The programming staff are not allowed to be in attendance when their programs are run on the computer but are supplied with their results and with reports generated by *diagnostic programs*, including *memory prints, file prints,* etc. The objective of the closed shop system is to minimize the computer time spent in *debugging* programs and to ensure that only specialized operating staff are allowed to run the machine. Contrast with *open shop method.* ⇨ the general article on *Remote Testing.*

closed subroutine A *subroutine* which generates a re-entry point for returning to the *main program* according to conditions established on entry to the subroutine. Contrasted with *open subroutine.*

cluster, tape Synonymous with *magnetic tape group.*

clutch point On *card punches* and *card readers* the movement of cards along the *card track* is initiated by engaging a clutch which transmits the drive to the card transport mechanism. The clutch can often only be engaged at one, or more, fixed points in the feed cycle – these are known as clutch points. Some mechanisms, however, have asynchronous clutches which allow the feed mechanism to be activated at any instant.

coalesce To create a single *file* from two or more files.

COBOL COBOL is an acronym for COmmon Business Oriented Language. It is an internationally accepted programming *language* developed for general commercial use, originally under the sponsorship of the American Department of Defence. C O B O L is a *problem oriented high level language* in which the *source program* is written using statements in English of a standard but readable form.

A C O B O L program is written in four divisions; these are: Identification Division; Environment Division; Data Division; Procedure Division.

The Identification Division contains descriptive information that identifies the program being compiled.

The Environment Division deals with the specification of the computer to be used for operating the object program (the *object computer*), including such information as the size of *memory*, the number of *tape decks, printers* and other peripheral devices that will be used; a description of the computer to be used for compiling the source program (the *source computer*) is also given.

The Data Division is used to allocate identifying names or *labels* to all units of data on which operations are to be performed. All input and output *files* are defined and associated with the *peripheral units* to be used for input and output. *Records* and *fields* within the files are described, as are all *constants* used by the program and any *working store* required.

The Procedure Division gives the step-by-step *instructions* necessary to solve the problem. These steps are specified by means of instructions expressed in stylized but meaningful English statements which can be recognized by the *compiler* and translated into a sequence of *machine code* instructions capable of being used by the computer to solve the problem. These statements are compounded of (i) *reserved words* which have a special significance, enabling the compiler to generate the appropriate machine instructions for the particular operation required, and (ii) identifying labels used by the programmer to reference units of data described in the Data Division, or used to identify other sections of the Procedure Division. The following statements are given as examples:

ADD OVERTIME TO NORMAL-HOURS

In this example, ADD ... TO ... are reserved words instructing the compiler to generate the machine coding necessary to perform addition, and OVERTIME and NORMAL-HOURS will be labels defined in the Data Division to refer to units of data.

READ INPUT-A AT END GO TO FINAL

Here READ causes the compiler to produce the coding necessary to activate an input device; AT END GO TO produces a *branch instruction* when the last item on the input device is recognized; INPUT-A will be the name given by the programmer to a particular input file, described in the Data Division and there associated with its peripheral device; and FINAL will refer to the name given by the programmer to another section of the Procedure Division in which is specified the action to be taken when all items have been accepted from the input device.

Other examples of COBOL statements are:

WRITE LINE-3 AFTER ADVANCING 2
    LINES
IF STOCK LESS THAN MINIMUM GO TO
    REORDER
MOVE SPACES TO LINE-4

Development of C O B O L is coordinated by a body known as C O D A S Y L, an acronym for C Onference on D Ata S Ystems Languages. C O B O L *compilers* supplied by manufacturers do not always provide all the facilities of full C O B O L, so it is possible that programs written with a particular compiler in mind will not be acceptable to another compiler with a slightly different subset of facilities. In general terms, the advantages of using C O B O L are that it is relatively simple to learn, and programs can be quickly written and tested; programmers can easily understand programs not written by themselves, and thus associated documentation can be simplified; and programs can be used on other machines, within the limitations noted above. Disadvantages are (i) the relative inefficiency of the resulting object program as compared with a program written in *machine code* or a machine oriented language and (ii) the lack of flexibility imposed by the restrictions on the type of instructions and methods for performing operations inherent in a highly standardized language. ⇨ the general article on *Languages*.

code 1. The representation of data or *instructions* in symbolic form; sometimes used as a synonym for *instruction*. 2. To convert data or instructions into this form.

code, alphameric Synonymous with *alphanumeric code*.

code area An area of *main storage* containing, at a particular moment, executable *code* representing processing *instructions*, as distinct from areas containing only data.

code, binary ⇨ *binary code* and *binary notation*.

code, column-binary ⇨ *column-binary*.

code, computer Synonymous with *machine code*.

code, cyclic Synonymous with *Gray code*.

coded decimal A notation in which each decimal digit is separately represented in coded form, e.g. by the *binary notation* of the digit. ⇨ *binary coded decimal notation*.

code, direct Synonymous with *absolute code*.

code-directing characters Characters attached to a message to indicate the routing and destination of that message.

coded stop Synonymous with *programmed halt*.

code elements The basic elements from which a code is constructed; e.g. the individual *bits* that make up a 6-bit *character code*.

code, error checking ⇨ *error checking code*.

code, error correcting ⇨ *error correcting code*.

code, error detecting ⇨ *error detecting code*.

code holes Holes punched in *paper tape* or *punched cards* to record data.

code line A *program instruction* in written form.

code, macro ⟡ *macro instruction*.

code, micro ⟡ *micro instruction*.

code, minimum latency Synonymous with *minimum access code*.

code, mnemonic operation ⟡ *mnemonic operation codes*.

code, numeric The representation of data as coded groups of *bits* to denote numerals; e.g. in *binary-coded decimal* format. Contrast with *alphabetic code*.

code, one-level ⟡ *absolute code*.

code, optimum ⟡ *minimum access code*.

code position Any part of a data medium into which a code may be inserted; e.g. a *row* on a piece of punched *paper tape*.

coder A person who writes computer *instructions* from *flowcharts* prepared by others, as distinct from a *programmer*, who prepares the flowcharts as well as *coding* from them.

code segment An area of *storage*, representing a subdivision of the storage allocated to a *process*, and containing executable *instructions*. Other segments forming part of the process include *data segments* and *dump segments*.

code, self-checking ⟡ *error detecting code*.

code, single-address ⟡ *single-address instruction*.

code, specific Synonymous with *absolute code*.

code, symbolic Synonymous with *symbolic instruction*.

coding The writing of *instructions* for a computer. Coding is part of the activity of *programming*.

coding check A check performed to ascertain whether a *routine* contains errors. Usually performed initially by following the logic of the routine on paper using test data. ⟡ *dry running*.

coding sheet A form on which computer *instructions* are written before being transferred to an input medium, e.g. *punched cards*.

coding, specific Synonymous with *absolute coding*.

coefficient Synonymous with *fixed point part*.

coincidence element Synonymous with *equivalence element*.

coincidence gate Synonymous with *and element*.

collate To produce a single ordered *file* from two or more files which are in the same ordered sequence. Synonymous with *merge*, although collate is more usually used when the files are *punched card* files.

collator A machine for merging two *punched card files* (which have been sorted into the same sequence) into a single file, which will be in the same sequence. Cards which match may also be separated from those which do not match; thus a collator may also be used for card selection.

Also known as *interpolator*.

collector   A *software module* used in *compiling*; collates various compiled *program* modules into a form suitable for *loading* onto the computer system for subsequent *execution*.

column   ⋄ *card column*.

column binary   A method for representing *binary numbers* on *punched cards*; consecutive *punching positions* on each *card column* are considered as consecutive digits in a binary number. Contrasted with *row binary*.

column binary code   ⋄ *column binary*.

column 1 leading   The way in which *punched cards* are placed in the feed *hopper* of some punched card machines; i.e. with a short edge leading and with column 1 read first.

column split   The facility on a *punched card* machine for reading two parts of a *column* as two separate codes or characters.

C O M.   Acronym for computer output on microfilm.

combined head   Synonymous with *read/write head*.

combined read/write head   Synonymous with *read/write head*.

command   Synonymous with *instruction*.

command chain   Part of a *process* which can be *executed* independently as a sequence of *input/output instructions*.

comment   Written notes which can be included in the coding of computer *instructions* in order to clarify the procedures, but which have no effect on the computer itself, i.e. are not translated into *machine language*.

Also known as narrative.

commercial data processing   *Data processing* concerned with or controlling a commercial application; e.g. *inventory control*, payroll. Contrasted with *industrial data processing, scientific data processing*.

commercial language   A *language* designed for the writing of *programs* for commercial applications such as payroll, invoicing. ⋫ *C O B O L*.

commission   To instal a computer to the point where it is capable of successful operation. Commissioning may precede a *customer acceptance test*.

common area   An *area* of *store* which can be used by more than one *program*, or more than one *segment* or *routine* of the same program. ⋫ *multiprogramming* and *overlay*.

common business oriented language   ⋄ *C O B O L*.

common language   The representation of data in a form intelligible to the many different units of a *data processing system*, so that information can be transferred between parts of the system.

common storage area   ◊ *common area*.

common target machine   A *target machine* is a machine represented by some, or all, of the resources in a computer installation, and is a particular set of resources intended for an *application*: for example, a hypothetical machine in a *virtual machine environment*. The common target machine represents the full potential machine available from a particular *hardware/software* system. ◊ *compiler target machine*.

communication channel   A channel for transmitting data between distant points; e.g., to connect a remote data station to a central computer system.

communication devices   The collection of data from remote locations for centralized processing has long been necessary in both business and scientific organizations. This need has increased as more powerful and expensive computer systems have been installed and as applications based on centralized *on-line* files have been developed. This process has led to the development of many types of communications device to suit the varying needs of users in terms of the volume and speed of transmission required.

In the earlier stages of the development of data transmission there was a tendency to use existing forms of equipment to transmit data, for example, the teleprinter and associated *paper tape* machines were used to transmit data over conventional telegraph circuits. Such a system usually requires that data is prepared and input as paper tape at one terminal, and is transmitted to a central location where a duplicate tape is punched automatically to be taken by hand to a *paper tape reader* for loading into the computer. This type of system has many disadvantages: the speed of transmission is only about 50 *bits* per second, the handling of paper tape at the sending and receiving terminals limits the system to *batch processing* applications and introduces time delays which are unacceptable for many systems, and the lack of inbuilt error detection and correction facilities is a severe restraint – a single bit transposed could generate very significant errors in subsequent processing.

In meeting these problems equipment has been developed to meet the following needs: (i) to allow for the capture of original data by automatic *data collection* techniques at distant stations; (ii) to transmit the data automatically at high speeed (say 2,000 bits per second) to a central computer; (iii) to check all transmissions to detect and automatically reject or correct transmission errors; (iv) to accept

84

data at the central location and to present it directly to the computer for processing, e.g. against *files* maintained there, if necessary using a *multiplexor* to enable the central computer to control perhaps a hundred or more *communication channels*; (v) to enable the central computer to prepare data for transmission back to the terminal; and (vi) to enable data to be displayed or recorded at the distant terminal.

Of course not every system requires all these needs to be satisfied: some systems may control only a few communication channels, some or all of which may be required to operate in batch processing mode only; and again volumes may be such that a fairly low speed of transmission may be suitable in some off-peak period.

In straightforward data collection systems devices such as *card readers, paper tape readers, badge readers* and *keyboard* machines may be available at distant locations. These units can be connected to a communication channel by special transmission units designed to *interface* the appropriate data collection device to the particular channel used.

In remote inquiry systems the remote stations will also include output devices such as *page printers, visual display units, card punches, paper tape punches*, etc. Thus an inquiry transmitted to the central computer can be processed and a reply is automatically transferred back to the terminal. (Airline reservation systems provide an example of this.) In inquiry systems the distant terminals are connected to their communication channels by transmit/receive data terminal units.

In large organizations a data processing capability may be required at several decentralized locations, even though a large degree of centralized data processing is maintained. Depending upon the volume of traffic and the type of application, such a situation could give rise to high speed links directly from one computer to another, or more conventional transmission techniques, e.g. from *magnetic tape* at one terminal to magnetic tape at another.

At the centralized location the computer can simply accept input in the form of some input medium such as *punched cards*, magnetic tape or paper tape, but this type of input would not be suitable for *real time* inquiry applications, and instead some form of high speed link might be required. Here a special transmission control unit, perhaps incorporating a *multiplexing* facility, is used to connect the computer to the various communication circuits. Such systems often require very complex *software/hardware* facilities to accept and transmit data to and from a large number of channels on a *time-sharing* basis.

85

In order to achieve the advances listed above there has been a considerable development in data transmission techniques, improving both the speed of transmission and the facilities for error detection and correction.

The limitations of distortion and attenuation in circuits, particularly over long distances, make for slow transmission speeds by conventional telegraph methods. However by transmitting a modulated carrier wave much higher speeds can be obtained depending upon the quality (e.g. band width) of the transmission circuit used. Switched public telephone circuits may offer transmission rates in the order of 200 to 600 bits per seconds. Private speech quality circuits can allow between 1,200 bits and 2,000 bits per second. These speeds will vary for different communication authorities. A wide range of *buffer* units, *modulators* and *demodulators* are manufactured to suit the various circuits in use, modulation techniques and transmission speeds required.

Error detection and correction techniques rely for the most part upon the use of a *redundancy code*. For example, *parity* checks may be applied to each *character* at the receiving terminal. Another method, known sometimes as a *loop check*, requires data to be transmitted in blocks, which when received are sent back to the transmitting terminal via a special return circuit for comparison with the data originally transmitted. If a transfer is incorrect the block is then retransmitted until a 'correct' transfer is signalled. Using re-transmission techniques an error rate better than a single error in 10^7 characters can be achieved.

communication link Synonymous with *communication channel*, but sometimes used to include *data terminal* equipment.

communications line control procedure A particular procedure used in a communications network to control signals from a particular class of device or method of transmission.

communications link controller A *hardware* device containing *software* or *microprograms*, and designed to interfere between a *main frame* system and a communications network. May contain various buffers for a wide range of line speeds and for different *communications line control procedures*.

commutator pulse One of a group of pulses used to set the limits of a *digit period*.
Also known as P-pulse (abbreviation of position pulse).

comparator A device for comparing two items and producing a signal dependent on the result of the comparison. This may be used to compare two different items or two versions of the same item in order to check data transference.

compare To determine the relationship between two data items and to signal the result. This may be any one of the possibilities 'equal to', 'greater than', 'less than'. The result may be signalled by setting an *indicator* or by a *conditional branch*. Also used in *file processing* to refer to comparing the contents of two or more *files* in order to check for similarities or discrepancies in data.

comparing control change A change in the value of *control fields* in a *record* which causes defined actions to take place, e.g. the production of totals on a *punched card tabulator*. Also known as *control break*, control change.

compatibility Compatibility is said to exist between two computers if *programs* can be run on both without alteration. A computer is said to be 'upwards compatible' with another if a program written on the first can be run on the second, but not vice versa.

compatibility, equipment ◊ *compatibility*.

compilation The process of using a *compiler* to create an *object program* from a *source language*.

compilation time The time at which a *program* is *compiled*; contrasted with *run time*.

compile To create an *object program* by means of a *compiler*.

compiled module format An intermediate format used in the process of *program compilation*, usually created prior to the consolidation or collection of program *modules* into the final form ready for *loading*.

compiler A complex *program* which converts computer *instructions* written in a *source language* into *machine code*. The resulting *object program* can then be read and acted upon by the computer. In order to produce the object program the compiler (a) translates each language *statement* into its *machine code* equivalent, (b) incorporates into the object program any *library subroutines* requested by the user, (c) supplies the interconnecting links between the parts of the programs. A compiler is distinguished from an *assembly program* by the fact that a compiler usually generates more than one machine code instruction for each source statement, whereas an *assembly* language is one-for-one with machine code. ◊ *Languages*.

compiler diagnostics Relating to the facilities incorporated in a *compiler* to detect, and indicate to the user, errors in *source programs*. Such routines provide the programmer with listings both in the *source language* and *machine code* form, these listings being accompanied by error messages and references to potential sources of error in the program.

compiler manager *Software* which controls the *compilation* process – usually part of the *operating system.*

compiler target machine The machine potentially available from a specific *hardware/software* system, for which a *compiler* is capable of generating *programs*. Most applications will run in a subset of the total resources available and each application therefore has its own *target machine.* ✧ *common target machine.*

compiling system A collection of *software modules* forming part of an *operating system*, used to convert *source language* into *object code*. The compiling process may consist of several stages including *compilation, collection* and *loading.* ✧ *compiler.*

complement A number which is derived from another by one of two rules: (i) subtract each digit from one less than the *radix* or number base (e.g. 9 for the decimal system), then add one to the result; (ii) the same as (i), but do not add one to the result. Method (i) is known as the *radix or noughts* or *true complement.* 770 is the true complement of 230 in the decimal system. Method (ii) is known as the *diminished radix complement, radix-minus-one complement* or, in the decimal system, *nines complement*, and in the binary system, *ones complement.* 769 is the nines complement of 230, 010 is the ones complement of the binary number 101. The complement of a number is frequently used in computers to represent the negative of a number, and the act of making a number negative is known as *complementing.*

complementary operation A *Boolean operation* which has a result which is the *negation* of the result of another operation is said to be a complementary operation to the other, e.g. the *or operation* is complementary to the *nor operation.* Contrasted with *dual operation.*

complementing The method of producing the negative of a number by obtaining its *complement.* Contrasted with *negation.*

complete carry The result when a *carry* arising from the addition of carries is allowed to generate a carry. Contrasted with *partial carry.*

complete operation The complete implementation of a computer *instruction*, involving the *accessing* of the instruction and associated *operands*, obeying the instruction and placing the results in *store.*

complete routine A *routine*, usually supplied by the computer manufacturer, which does not need any user modification before use.

compute mode The operating mode for an *analog computer* in which the input signals are connected directly to the computing units to develop a solution. Contrasted with *hold mode* and *reset mode*.

computer Any machine which can accept *data* in a prescribed form, process the data and supply the results of the processing in a specified format as information or as signals to control automatically some further machine or process. The term is used generally for any kind of computing device, the three main categories being *digital computers, analog computers* and *hybrid computers*; there is a general article on each of these. There is also a general article under the heading *Introduction to Computers* at the beginning of this book.

computer, analogue ◊ *analog computer.*

computer, all-purpose Synonymous with *general-purpose computer.*

computer applications A general term for the uses to which a computer may be put. ◊ *application package.*

computer code Synonymous with *machine code.*

computer, digital ◊ *digital computer*, also *computer.*

computer efficiency A measure of the reliability of a computer. Various definitions of efficiency will be found under *serviceability ratio, operating ratio* and *utilization ratio.*

computer instruction ◊ *instruction*, and general article on *Instruction Formats.*

computer operation ◊ *operation* [2].

computer, parallel ◊ *simultaneous computer.*

computer personnel The general article on *Data Processing Department Organization* shows the kinds of task which have to be undertaken in a data processing department and the staff levels at which they are usually carried out. As indicated in the article, these levels are by no means mandatory and usually the allocation of jobs depends very much on the people available. This article will look at some of the qualities ideally found in each of the prototype jobs in an ideal installation and will give some indication of the sort of things those concerned with the installation will be called upon to do. The jobs described are Data Processing Department Manager, Systems Analyst, Programmer, Senior Systems Analyst, Chief Programmer, Computer Operator, Tape Librarian, Punch Operator, Control Clerk, Operations Manager.

First, the manager of the department: although it is certainly true that he requires technical ability and practical data processing experience it should not be forgotten that he is primarily a manager and that without the qualities associated with management – clear,

89

energetic thinking, tenacity, tact, imagination and ability to control – he will never be able to run a data processing department. Added to these qualities must be certain specialist ones such as the technical competence to control staff with specialized skills; the ability to absorb technical writings so that he can advise his superiors of new developments in data processing relevant to their problems; and a general receptiveness to new ideas. As with managers of most other departments, his best asset will be the ability to remain unruffled in all circumstances.

The systems analyst's job must begin and end in communication, although, as will be seen in the general article on *Systems Analysis*, the design stage of his job requires maturity and imagination. The ability to communicate is all-important, however, and this must include conversational ability (i.e. being able to mix with people) and the ability to express himself on paper. He must be able to work methodically and precisely (errors of fact or of omission can be extremely expensive) and must ally a creative imagination with a willingness to undertake considerable drudgery at times. Since he is nearly always working with other people rather than alone, it is a great help if he is generally likeable, but it is even more important that he should be determined to get things right and then be able to put them on paper.

The programmer must be able to reason logically and clearly and must have the patience and tenacity to see his way through to the end of a problem. He must be able to cope with routine work and, when the chance of doing something clever but perhaps unpractical appears, must be able to curb himself if, in the end, the best answer is the simple and straightforward one. It is by no means necessary to be a mathematician (unless, of course, the programming work involves some of the techniques of *operational research* or the computation of statistics) but the usual qualities of mathematicians are found in programmers; these are the ability to reason logically, a precise awareness of detail and the self-discipline to work within prescribed standards. As will be seen from the general articles on *Programming* and *Documentation – Programs* the programmer must also be able to work well in a team and must be able to work in an orderly way, documenting his work carefully.

Leading the systems analysts and programmers are the senior systems analyst and chief programmer who are 'technical management' rather than 'line management', i.e. they are experienced technicians themselves, able to undertake the work, at any level, of those they lead, and able to control in detail the work of their teams.

Since both systems analysts and programmers are often called upon to reduce large work loads in a short time, the senior systems analyst and chief programmer must also both be able to maintain a good team spirit amongst those they lead.

General responsibility for the day-to-day efficiency of the computer and ancillary machines will rest with the operations manager who will manage the computer operators, the data control staff, the librarians and the data preparation staff. This may easily add up to forty or more people and the operations manager must be a skilled manager as well as technician. He is closer to the output of the installation than anyone else, and since this will inevitably result in crises at times, it will often be his task to make the best possible use of limited means. Perhaps the best qualities for an operations manager are resourcefulness and good humour.

One of the most important things he has to do is to ensure a high standard of computer operating, and the computer operators he trains must have a considerable interest in the job and be willing to accept responsibility. *Operating systems* are helping to solve the problem of finding computer operators able to handle routine work and yet with enough mental alertness to cope with *multiprogramming* machines, but any operator still needs to be sufficiently self-reliant to take on responsibility for very expensive equipment, which, when badly operated, can become even more expensive as lost minutes cost money.

Librarians and work assemblers are needed to control the storage, issue and control of all *magnetic tapes, paper tape* and *punched card files*, and, as these jobs usually call for a monitoring of the work flow into and out of the computer room, they require a considerable organizing ability and some technical knowledge of programming and operating.

Punch operators, *verifier* operators and ancillary machine operators (e.g. reproducers, balancing *tabulators*) all need to be accurate, able to work under pressure and have a sense of responsibility. This last will depend largely on the machine room supervisor, who will have to be ready at all times to cope with unexpectedly large punching loads or other sudden re-arrangements of work.

In general the data processing department needs to work very closely as a team: the systems analyst is as dependent on good operating as the operator is on good operating instructions, and the work of both can be set back by poor punching. Perhaps the most important quality for all new members of the department is that they should be well liked by the others.

computer program ◊ *program.*

computer, stored program ◊ *stored program computer,* also *computer.*

computer system A *central processor* and associated *peripheral units,* which are or can be *on-line* to the processor, form a computer system. Also known as *configuration.*

computer word ◊ *word.*

computing amplifier An amplifier in which the output voltage is related by *negative feedback* to the input voltage.
Also known as operational amplifier.

conceptual modelling A method of problem-solving whereby a *mathematical model* is constructed to suit the results obtained from an experiment; the model is used to conduct further experiments to ascertain whether the model is correct. ◊ the general article on *Model Building.*

concurrent conversion The simultaneous running of *conversion programs* with normal programs ◊ *multiprogramming.*

concurrent processing Synonymous with *multiprogramming.*

condensing routine A *routine* for transferring an *object program* from *memory* or a *storage device* onto *punched cards* in such a way that the maximum number of *instructions* possible is contained on each card.

conditional branch instruction A *branch instruction* which will transfer control to another *program* instruction if, and only if, some specified condition is satisfied; e.g., if a nominated item of data is zero or less than zero. If the specified condition is not satisfied the program proceeds directly to the next instruction.
Also known as conditional transfer or conditional jump. Contrasted with *unconditional branch instruction.*

conditional breakpoint A *breakpoint* at which the particular sequence of *instructions* to be followed after the external instruction has occurred may be varied by setting specified conditions.

conditional breakpoint instruction A *breakpoint instruction* which acts, after the external intervention has occurred, as a *conditional branch* by which alternative courses of action may be entered.

conditional implication operation A Boolean *operation* in which the *result* for the values of the *operands* p and q is given by the table:

Operands		Result
p	q	r
0	0	1
1	0	0
0	1	1
1	1	1

Also known as if-then operation, implication, inclusion, material implication.

conditional jump Synonymous with conditional branch.

conditional stop instruction An *instruction* which can cause a *program* to be stopped if some given condition is detected. For example, the program may be required to stop if it finds that a *console switch* has been set by the operator.

conditional transfer Synonymous with *conditional branch instruction*.

conditional transfer of control To *transfer control* to another part of a *program* by means of a *conditional branch*, i.e. depending upon certain specified criteria.

configuration The general term given to a *computer system*, usually used to indicate the physical units of the system.

configuration block A collection of *hardware* devices which respond to a particular type of *command* given by the operator when configuring the computer for operation. ⟡ *configuration state*.

configuration state Relates to the status of a device in a computer *configuration* and indicates its availability for allocation to an *application*, e.g. configured-in – available for use, configured-out – available for certain privileged users, configured-off – not available.

configuration table A table maintained in a computer by the *operating system* to signify the status of individual units of the system. ⟡ *configuration state*.

configured-in ⟡ *configuration state*.

configured-off ⟡ *configuration state*.

configured-out ⟡ *configuration state*.

conjunction Synonymous with *and operation*.

connection box ⟡ *connexion box*.

connective A symbol representing an *operation* between two *operands* which is written between the operands, e.g. the symbol used to represent the *logical connective* 'and', written P & V in order to relate the variables P, V.

93

connector 1. A symbol used in *flowcharting* to indicate the connexion between different points on a flowchart. 2. A mechanical means of allowing the connexion or separation of one or more electrical circuits.

connexion box A mechanical device used in some *punched card* machines for controlling operations by means of variable linkages. The mechanical equivalent of a *plugboard*.

connexion (of a node) A link between an *application program* and a resource (e.g. a *peripheral* device) established under control of an *operating system* and represented by entry in the *catalogue*.

consistency check 1. A check performed by *program* to ensure that a *record*, or *transaction*, does not contain contradictory data. 2. A check performed to ensure that a result is *accurate*, achieved by using alternative techniques to derive answers which are then compared.

console The unit of a computer used for all manual communication with the computer. The console provides a display of information from the computer, either through a typewriter or by means of display lamps, and provides a means for the operator to put messages into the computer, again either through a typewriter or by the depression of switches.

console, data station ◊ *data station console*.

console display register A special *register* into which data can be loaded by program, or under operator control, to allow data to be displayed by a visual indicator on the *console*.

console switch A *switch* which can be set from an *operator's console*, enabling a *program* to alter its actions according to the setting it detects.

console typewriter A unit of the *console* whereby the computer can display messages to the operator and the operator can input instructions to the computer. Console typewriter messages may be of two types: messages informing the operator of actions required, e.g. *tape decks* needing attention, paper running low on the *printer*, and messages output from a running *program* giving information on the progress of the *run*, e.g. the printing of *control totals*.

constant area The part of store *allocated* by a *program* used to hold *constants*.

constants In a *program* constants are items of data which remain unchanged for each *run*, e.g. page headings or numerical constants required for calculations, such as the constant 12 required for dividing dozens to obtain units.

construct A statement in a *source program* which will produce a predetermined effect when executed.

container file Synonymous with *controlling file*.

content The content of a *location* in *store* is the data held in the location.

content-addressed storage Synonymous with *associative store*.

contention The condition which arises when using *multiplexor channel time sharing*, and more than one unit attempts to transmit at the same time.

continuous stationery A continuous supply of paper consisting of perhaps several hundred individual sheets separated by perforations and folded to form a pack. The stationery is designed for automatic feeding through the print unit of a *line printer* and sprocket holes are punched for this purpose in the margins of each sheet.

contrast In *optical character recognition* (OCR), the difference in colour or intensity between the character and its background.

control The function of interpreting and acting upon *instructions*, or performing required operations when certain specific conditions occur.

control break A *key change* which occurs in a *control data* [1] field. This term is more commonly used in connexion with computer *report program* whereas comparing *control change* is used in *punched card* terminology.

control card 1. A *punched card* containing data required for control purposes, e.g. *control totals*. 2. Also used as a synonym for *parameter card*.

control change ⋄ *comparing control change*.

control change, intermediate ⋄ *intermediate control change*.

control change, major ⋄ *major control change*.

control change, minor ⋄ *minor control change*.

control character A character whose function is to initiate controlling operations over *peripheral units*, e.g. a paper-feed control character will specify the amount of paper to be passed through a *printer* before the next line is printed.
Also known as functional character.

control circuits The circuits in a computer's *control unit* used to carry out the operations initiated by the computer *instructions*.

control computer A computer used in *process control* where the process under control feeds signals to the control computer, which in turn sends signals back which directly control the operation of the process.

control counter   A synonym for *control register*.

control data   1. Pertaining to *records* which bear *keys* or information of certain significance in *batching* and sequencing the records. For example, in *punched card* practice and in *electronic data processing* a group of records might need to be sorted into order according to data in three separate *fields* of each record; the first field might specify C O U N T Y, the second T O W N and the third S T R E E T. The first field would be the *major control data*, the second *intermediate control data* and the third *minor control data*. 2. Information used to influence the operation of a *routine*, either by selecting it or by modifying it. In this sense, associated with *parameter*.

control field   A *field* within a *record* where *control data* is held. The presence or absence or change in value of the contents of the control field will cause specified *operations* or *routines* to occur.

control, flow   ◊ *job flow control*.

control holes   Punchings in a *punched card* which indicate how further data in the card is to be treated in the machine. Also known as function holes, designation holes or control punchings.

control, input/output traffic   ◊ *input/output traffic control*.

control language   In an *operating system*, the set of *commands* available to the user for the organization and control of the *programs* and *resources* available in the computer system. Also known as *job control language* (J C L), *system control language* (S C L).

control language interpreter   A *software* routine which is used to *read*, *interpret* and *execute* statements written in a *control language*. Usually part of an *operating system*.

controlling file   A section of *storage* which occupies a number of complete *cylinders* on a *magnetic disk*, and which can be expanded or contracted in size to contain a number of *files*. Synonymous with *container file*.

control loop   Synonymous with *control tape*.

control mark   Synonymous with *tape mark*.

control-message display   A device which displays control information (e.g. information on the operation of a given *program* as it is being run), in plain language. A *console typewriter* is an example of a control-message display.

control, numerical   ◊ *numeric control*.

control panel   1. A panel on a computer *console* containing manual switches used for direct communication with the *central processor*. 2. Also used for the unit containing engineers' controls. 3. In *punched card* machines, control panel is synonymous with *plug-board*.

control punchings Synonymous with *control holes*.

control register A *register* whose function is to contain the *address* of the next *instruction* in the sequence of operations. The term is also used for the register which holds the address of the current instruction, normally known as the instruction register.

Also known as control counter.

control sequence The normal order in which *instructions* are acted on in a computer. A *transfer of control* is said to occur when a *branch instruction* alters the normal sequence.

control stack A *hardware* mechanism consisting of a number of *storage locations*, and used to provide procedural control over processes within the computer, to assist in the *dynamic allocation* of work space, and to perform arithmetic. It is an *architectural* feature of some computer models and provides an efficient means of calling procedures and ease of implementation of *re-entrant code*.

control statement In a *high level programming language* in which the expression *statement* is used to refer to an *instruction*, a control statement is a *directive* to the program used to cause actions to take place according to specified conditions. The expression is also used for directives present in a *source program* which control the operation of the *compiler* without affecting the resulting *object program*, e.g. directions for a page change on the *printout* of the *source language* during compilation.

control tape A closed *loop* of punched *paper tape* or plastic tape used to control the operation of printing devices.

Also known as paper tape loop, carriage tape, control loop.

control total A total established for a *file* or group of *records* during a specific operation (e.g. a computer *run*) to check that the processing operation has been applied to all records. The total may be significant in itself, as for example a total of a value *field*, but ⬦ *hash total*.

Also known as check total. ⬦ general article on *Control Totals*.

control totals Control totals are used during the processing of data as a check upon accuracy. Their purpose is to ensure that the processing has been done correctly without having to check each individual item.

Where many documents or *punched cards* are being handled during a series of clerical or mechanical processing operations there is always risk of loss or error. If a total of the results is taken after processing and this agrees with the control total of the data before it was processed, considerable detailed checking can be avoided.

In addition, where documents are being sent from one person to another they can be supported by the control total. By totalling the documents and comparing them with the control total supplied, the recipient can be sure that he has received all the documents sent to him.

As an illustration, a system for recording suppliers' invoices can be considered. The clerk receiving the invoices would check them for price, etc., put them into batches and produce batch control totals of the amount payable and number of invoices. The control totals might be produced on a manual add-listing machine.

Each batch of invoices together with a slip giving the batch control total would be sent to the punching section. A punched card would be produced for each invoice and the cards listed on a *tabulator*. The batch totals on the list would be checked with the batch control slips. It would then be certain that the invoice values had been punched correctly and that no invoices or cards had been mislaid. This certainty will have been achieved without any detailed checking.

Where any errors occur then a comparison of the batch totals indicates immediately the incorrect batch. If the number of documents in each batch is kept to a manageable quantity then the number which have to be checked, in the case of an error, is minimal. Errors can be found quickly.

Control totals are an extremely useful device as a total check on the processing of data and one which avoids checking each item in detail.

control transfer The departure from the normal sequence of *program instructions* which occurs when a *branch instruction* is obeyed.

control transfer instruction Synonymous with *branch instruction*.

control unit That part of computer *hardware* which accesses *instructions* in sequence, interprets them and initiates the appropriate operation required. ◊ *central control unit, program controller*.

control unit, peripheral ◊ *peripheral control unit*.

control word A *word* in *store* which contains information used for control purposes. These purposes depend on the type of control involved. In a *subroutine* the control word acts as a *parameter* directing the specific action required; the control word associated with data *blocks* may contain information about the size of the block or the type of data held in the block.

conventional In describing *punched card* equipment, used to distinguish *tabulators, sorters, collators,* etc., from *computers.* Coined at a time when computers were unconventional.

conversational compiler A *compiler* which uses the *conversational mode* of computer operation in which the user enters each *source language statement* in turn to the computer, which immediately checks its validity and informs the user if he can proceed or must correct a mistake.

conversational mode A method of operation in which the user is in direct communication with the computer and is able to obtain immediate response to his input messages. Also known as interactive mode.

conversion 1. The process of transcribing a *file* from one format to another on to the same or a different *storage* medium – *file conversion.* 2. The process of converting a *source program* from one *dialect* of a language to another (e.g. when converting programs written for a specific range of computers to another range) – *program conversion.*

conversion equipment Equipment used for performing data conversion without involving a *processor*, e.g. a *card-to-tape converter.* Such devices are known as *converters.*

conversion program 1. A computer *program* designed to perform data *conversion.* 2. A computer program designed to convert programs written for one computer system into programs capable of being run on a different system. ⟡ *simulator routine.*

converter ⟡ *conversion equipment.*

coordinate store Synonymous with *matrix store.*

copy To reproduce data from one *storage device* to another, or another part of the same store, without altering the original data.

CORAL A *high-level language* for *real-time applications.*

cordless plug A *plug* with connectors incorporating no flexible part.

core, core store The term used to refer to the *main store* or *main memory* of a computer, and was derived from the fact that such storage devices were made up of small ferrite cores capable of holding a magnetic charge. (⟡ *core storage*). In many modern computers the main store is no longer composed of cores and the term is not therefore entirely apposite.

core dump Transferring the contents of *core storage* to an *output device*, e.g. a *line printer* or *paper tape punch.* Synonymous with *memory dump*, although strictly should only be used for memory composed of *cores.*

core memory A computer *memory* or *store* composed of *magnetic cores*.

core memory resident A *routine* which is retained permanently in *core storage*.

core storage A type of *memory* composed of magnetic *cores*, in which data is held in *binary* form by means of the property of cores of retaining a positive or negative charge. The pattern of charges serves to represent the coded data.

corner cut A corner from a *punched card* to enable all cards in a *pack* to be stacked the same way round before being fed to a machine.

correction, automatic error ◊ *automatic error correction*.

corrective maintenance Work required to correct a machine fault; maintenance in addition to *routine maintenance*.

corruption The mutilation of *data* or *code* caused by a failure of *hardware* or *software* or an error in an *application program*.

cost analysis The purpose of cost analysis is to ascertain the cost of production of any job, process or service in an industrial or commercial organization. If standard costs or budgets have been previously set up, deviations from the norm can be brought to the attention of management. The routine tasks of sorting and manipulating data involved in cost analysis, and the subsequent tabulation of data and production of summary reports have been undertaken by computers for many years, and an outline of the main factors of such systems is given below.

Systems of cost analysis are designed by cost accountants; basically their purpose is to break down the total expenditure involved in production, administration and marketing into a number of subdivisions. For example factory costs may be broken down into direct labour costs, direct material costs and overheads. Direct costs are those which are completely incurred in the production of a certain unit. Overheads include indirect items which cannot readily be assigned to any particular process, such as rent, rates and insurance.

Once costs have been broken down the cost analysis data processing cycle consists of the generation of records (for example on *punched cards*) each of which represents a unit of expenditure under some cost subdivision. As well as cost each record will specify an account chargeable, usually a job or department.

For example, a simple form of cost analysis system might involve the generation of the following types of punched card: labour card; stores card; purchases card and expense card.

Each of these card types would contain at a minimum the following *fields*: date, record type number, job or account number and quantity. (Other fields might be included if the cost analysis system were part of a large data processing system.) Thus a labour card would have information punched into it recording the date, a man number, a job or account number and the hours worked by that man during the period concerned. The stores and purchases cards record quantities of direct materials issued to jobs, a stores card being generated if the material comes from stock, and a purchases card if material is bought from outside. The last card, expenses, records incidental costs such as packing or delivery.

Data recorded in these punched cards might be written to *magnetic tape* under a computer system, and processed in various ways. First of all the data would be *sorted* into some useful sequence, for example job number, within cost type. Then the quantity fields in the records would need to be converted into monetary costs. For example, labour cost would be found by multiplying hours worked by a rate for the job. Then the data might be re-sorted to cost type within job number, and passed against a work-in-progress file *updating* it to give the latest cost position. *Printouts* might be required at stages during the computer run, to agree *control totals* and to summarize information for management.

It is likely that a cost analysis system implemented on a computer would be more sophisticated than that described above, which is intended to illustrate only the basic principles. For example, the power of a computer makes it possible to set up an integrated *production control* system of which costing would be a small part. Again it is likely that a *standard costing* technique would be embodied in the data processing cycle to enable management to compare actual with expected results.

count A cumulative total of the number of times a specified event occurs, e.g. a count of lines printed or *records* read. A count is also used in *programming* to mean a total of the number of times a particular *instruction* or *routine* is performed, and is used for control purposes, determining the operation of the process concerned.

counter Any device used to accumulate totals. For example, an electro-mechanical device on a *punched card* machine, or in a *digital computer* a *memory* location or *register* used as an *accumulator* or to record a number of repeated *loops* in a *program*.

counter, control ◊ *control register.*

counter, program address ◊ *program address counter.*

C P M 1. Acronym for *critical path method.* 2. Acronym for *cards per minute.*

C P S Acronym for character-per-second or cycles-per-second.

C P U Central processing unit. ◊ *Central Processors* (general article).

creation A term in *file processing* referring to initial *data collection,* and the organization of this *raw data* into a *file.*

crippled leap-frog test A variation of *leap-frog testing* in which the test arithmetic is performed on only one part of *store,* not on different *locations.*

crippled mode A machine operates in crippled mode when certain parts are not working, but the system is still able to operate at reduced capacity. Related to *graceful degradation.*

criterion A *constant* used in decision-taking as the standard against which variable data is compared to determine action to be taken.

critical path method (C P M) This is a technique used in planning, scheduling and controlling major industrial, technical or commercial projects. An alternative term for C P M is *P E R T* (*Project Evaluation and Review Technique*). Originally slightly different in concept, the two terms are now interchangeable, and both are referred to as *network planning.* C P M is useful in conjunction with projects which require the combination of varying amounts of different resources at different times and which involve a large number of interrelated events and activities.

The first stage in planning a project using C P M techniques is the drawing up of a network, a special type of chart made up of circles and arrows. Each circle represents an *event,* i.e. something that happens at a particular point in time. The circles are joined up by arrows which represent *activities,* i.e. jobs of work that are spread over a period of time. An event cannot occur until all the activities leading up to it have taken place.

A network will always start with an event, for example 'Authorization of Project', and will always end with one, for example 'Product Launched'. In between the first and last events there will be a number of intermediate events, each preceded and followed by one or more activities. Thus any intermediate event will be dependent on the completion of certain activities and will itself control the start date of later activities.

Each activity on a network is given a time estimate which represents the time that activity is expected to take. A common convention for networks is that time flows from left to right. Each event is given a number, later events having a higher number than earlier events. It is not necessary to number events in sequence however, and gaps in sequence are often left to facilitate later insertions on a network.

Sometimes it is not possible to give an accurate estimate of the likely duration of activities. In these circumstances it is usual to specify three time estimates; optimistic, pessimistic and most likely. Another peculiarity of activities is that no actual work need be done in the time allotted to them. Awaiting delivery of a component is an example of this sort of activity. It is also possible for an activity to take up no time at all. Although this appears to be a negation of common sense, activities of zero duration are a convention used to simplify the drawing of networks. Activities which require no resources and/or no time are known as dummy activities.

The drawing up of a network is a useful discipline because it causes the designer to consider the interrelationship between the various activities. The real value of a network, however, lies in the use that can be made of it in scheduling and controlling projects. First of all it is possible to process a network in order to establish how long the project is likely to take from start to finish. This is known as isolating the critical path.

The critical path of a network is determined by considering each event in turn and calculating the earliest possible time at which the event can occur. If an event depends on several activities the earliest time is determined by the activity which takes longest to finish. Thus the critical path is the sequence of interconnected events and activities which will require the longest time to accomplish. The sum of all the time estimates of the activities on the critical path will be the shortest time in which a project can be completed.

The characteristic of events and activities on a critical path is that if any of the time estimates are not met, the completion date of the project will be affected. Conversely time estimates not on the critical path can change (within limits) without affecting the overall completion date. The degree to which a time estimate is free to change is known as the degree of *float*. The total float of any activity is the maximum time that can possibly be made available for its completion minus the duration of the activity. Any expansion or movement in an activity in excess of its total float will change the critical path and increase the overall project time. Deliberate use can be made of knowledge of float times in order to divert resources from non-critical activities and concentrate them on activities on the critical path. It should be stressed that the critical path in a network can never possess float.

Critical path techniques enable a project to be controlled as well as scheduled. Control will obviously need to be tightest for events which lie on the critical path. The technique used is to insert actual performance times on the network, which is then re-analysed to see the effects of the work done. This will enable management to take action on anything which is likely to jeopardize the future progress of the project. It is evident that any slipping on a critical activity will delay completion of the project. To correct this, it may be possible to transfer resources from non-critical activities.

Critical path analysis is usually thought to be a technique associated with electronic computers. This need not necessarily be the case, but when a project involves more than a few hundred activities, or any additional operation apart from simple scheduling is required, it is probably essential to use a computer in order to cope with the volume of calculation. Most computer manufacturers offer C P M or P E R T packages as part of their standard *software*, and these programs can be run either on the user's own computer or by computer bureaux which sell computer time. As well as the analysis of the critical path, the computer can also handle problems associated with re-allocation of resources, and the effect of resource *allocation* can be immediately tested by *simulation*.

The main features of a computer C P M or P E R T system may be summarized as follows:

(a) The handling of events and activities and their changing values.

(b) The ability to interrelate networks of different levels.

(c) The ability to accept progress data and to produce progress reports.

(d) The ability to determine the critical path through a network.

cross-check The checking of the result of a routine or calculation by obtaining the result by different methods and comparing.

cross compiler A *compiler* used on one computer system to provide *object code* in accordance with the format needed to run on a different type of computer.

cross talk The appearance of signals from one telephone circuit on another circuit, causing interference.

crowd Synonymous with *pack* [2].

C R T Acronym for *cathode ray tube*.

cryogenics The study of the operating characteristics of electronic devices at temperatures approaching absolute zero.

current instruction register A special *register* in which *instructions* are stored so that they can be executed under the aegis of the *program controller*.

customer acceptance test A test designed by, or on behalf of, an organization purchasing a computer system to test the performance, facilities, and reliability of the system. May include tests of *hardware* and *software*, and perhaps *application* systems developed for the customer. Usually such a test takes place on the customer site after the computer has been *commissioned*.

customizing The modification of a standard *hardware* or *software* product to meet the needs of a specific *user*.

cybernetics The study of the theory of control systems with particular regard to the comparisons between machines and the nervous system of animals and men.

cycle 1. A sequence of operations performed repetitively in the same order. 2. The time required to complete a given set of operations.

cycle count A count of the number of times a given cycle has been performed, or a count of the number of repetitions still required.

cycle index counter A *counter* used to count the number of times that a given cycle of *program instructions* has been performed. The cycle index counter can be examined at any selected time to ascertain the number of repetitions still required in a *loop*.

cycle reset Setting the *cycle count* to its initial value or some other selected value.

cycle shift ◇ *cyclic shift*.

cycle, store ◇ *storage cycle*.

cycle time The time taken to complete a *cycle* of operations. Store cycle time is the minimum time required to retrieve an item of data from *store*.

cyclic code Synonymous with *Gray code*.

cyclic redundancy check A check carried out on a *storage device* or in a *communication* circuit to detect errors. ◇ *summation check*.

cyclic shift A *shift* in which a *string* of *characters* or *bits* is treated as if it were a *closed loop*, so that data from one end of the string is re-entered at the other end. For example, if the string 123456 is given a cyclic shift of two places to the right the result will be 561234.

Also known as cycle shift.

cyclic store A *storage device* in which the storage medium is arranged in such a way that access to individual *locations* can be obtained at only fixed points in a basic cycle; e.g. a *magnetic drum*.

cylinder Synonymous with *seek area*.

D

dagger operation Synonymous with *nor operation*.

damping The decreasing of unwanted oscillation or wave motion.

data A general expression used to describe any group of *operands* or *factors* consisting of numbers, alphabetic characters or symbols which denote any conditions, value or state, e.g. all values and descriptive data operated on by a computer *program* but not the program itself. The word data is used as a collective noun and is usually accompanied by a singular verb: 'data are' may be pedantically correct but is awkward to say and therefore awkward to understand. Data is sometimes contrasted with *information*, which is said to result from the processing of data, so that information derives from the assembly, analysis or summarizing of data into a meaningful form.

data acquisition control system Relating to a *computer system* in which high speed data channels are used to connect a central computer to distant locations. Essentially a system designed to operate in *real-time* applications, receiving data from a number of remote stations, and transmitting data to them under *program control*. The *data collection devices* within such a system may cater for both *analog* and *digital* forms of data *input* and *output*.

data adapter unit A unit designed to allow a *central processor* to be connected to a number of data *communications channels*; for example, for connexion to distant terminals over telegraph channels or to a number of local *in-plant data collection* points.

data administrator A person responsible for control of data within an organization implementing a *data management* system. He is responsible for the design of data structures, and for ensuring standards of accuracy and mutual integrity within the computer system and in the organizational environment. ◊ general article on *Data Base Management Systems*.

data analysis display unit Relating to the facilities offered by *cathode ray tube visual display units* for an *on-line* analysis of data.

data area An area of *store* containing *data* rather than *executable code* forming part of the system *software* or *application program*.

data bank A comprehensive *file* of *data*, usually stored on a *direct* *access storage device*. Data stored in a data bank is usually available to a large number of users by means of remote terminals, and is often updated by means of a *real-time* system.

data base A file of data so structured that appropriate applications draw from the file and update it but do not themselves constrain the file design or its content. A file which is not designed to satisfy a specific, limited application.

data base management systems Computer users have increasingly accepted the concept that the various sub-systems of an organization should be integrated to form a total system (sometimes referred to as I.M.I.S. – Integrated Management Information System). Thus all users of data within the organization share common records of information and the information available to staff and management at every level is drawn from the same source, providing mutually consistent levels of accuracy to all users. This concept constitutes an ideal condition which has seldom been achieved in practice, there being two major requirements which militate against complete success: i) Large complex organizations find it difficult to organize the control of basic operational data since this demands standards of accuracy and quality spanning departmental boundaries and requires extensive coordination outside the needs and objectives of individual departments. ii) The *software* systems required to manage the data within the computer system are complex and demand large investments from both computer manufacturers and user organizations. Such systems have the general title of Data Base Management Systems.

Some organizations have achieved a degree of success by integrating the various sub-systems which constitute a major part of their business activity. The boundaries of such systems usually have to be restricted to groups of systems with a major operational significance. This article seeks to describe the general nature of such systems and the characteristics of the software needed.

The first concept which characterizes the nature of data base systems is that data should be recorded once only, and be shared by the various sub-systems and users of the system. Thus to eliminate the duplication of data it must be structured and organized to include the requirements of all users. Information should not be recorded in local files designed for specific applications.

The data base concept is also strengthened when data is captured and recorded in the data base at the time when events in the organization give rise to the transactions concerned. Thus there is a trend towards *real time* processing. Although this ideal takes time to evolve within an organization, the objective is to ensure that files are updated as events occur and the computer is able to communicate relevant information to people in many different places at the same time, thus overcoming problems of communication in large organizations. The data base system needs to ensure that data is accurate and available to users who need it, but also needs to protect the *security* and confidentiality of information.

Thus the Data Base Management Systems (D.M.S.) which manage the information must be able to insure that files are accessed concurrently and yet be protected from corruption. A high degree of *resilience* is necessary to handle breakdowns which might destroy the mutual consistency and accuracy of data.

The gradual development of a data base system requires the originators of data to be responsible for its accuracy, and it is usually accepted that a *data base administrator* should be appointed to monitor the quality of data and to be responsible for the development and organization of the files. ◊ *data administrator*.

An essential feature of a D.M.S. system is to enable application programs to operate against a background of changing file structures; this is achieved by providing independence of methods of file access from the application program logic. The appropriate record access mechanism is allocated to programs at *run time* (e.g. the program need not know whether a file is *sequentially* or *randomly* organized). The method of file access is not the only feature to be handled in this way. The structure of records will change in the evolution of a data base, and routines are necessary in the D.M.S. to mask out unwanted *fields* automatically. Thus the data base can be developed without the need to *recompile* individual programs which were previously written to address records according to an earlier form of file organization.

This concept is described by a number of different terms. For example the term *data independence* is used; and also the term *transparency*, which relates to the notion that the D.M.S. provides each application program with a specific view of the data base structure relevant to the application concerned. This facility is usually made available in D.M.S. by a Data Description Language (D.D.L.). At any time there is only one complete description for the total data base but there may be many sub-descriptions which delineate data structures for specific application programs. The complete description of the data base is referred to as a *schema* whereas the sub-descriptions are known as *sub-schema*. The D.D.L. facilities enable the data base administrator to describe the physical extent of the data base as it is *mapped* onto the hardware – it defines also all data elements, records and all logical relationships between records, and the sub-schema enables the data administrator to name the fields, records, and logical sets which he wishes to make available to individual applications.

A D.M.S. system usually provides *data dictionary* facilities, giving a variety of reports to the data base administrator to assist in the control of the data base.

In some cases, the records stored in a data base are not organized into files in the form conventionally associated with free-standing applications. The reason for avoiding conventional structures is that they do not provide methods of access suitable for all possible uses of the data base. It is preferable to store data as a number of networks which permit many complex logical relationships between data elements to be expressed. This ability to support such logical relationships is one of the factors to be considered in evaluating the effectiveness of a particular D.M.S. The logical relationships are usually described as *sets*, and there are often options for describing the order of member records within a set. For example a record may be a member of a number of sets, and at the same time be the owner of one or more sets of records. A record will, however, appear only once in the data base as a prime location to be updated by transactions which relate to it.

The members of a set are automatically linked in forward or reverse directions by pointers enabling a chain of records to be processed in a desired direction.

As previously described, an application programmer can gain access to records in the data base only by means of a sub-schema. The sub-schema is provided to the application in its working storage area in response to statements written in the data manipulation language (D.M.L.). The D.M.L. is the language used to describe processes to be performed upon data by application programs. In many D.M.S. the D.M.L. is provided as an extension of the *C O B O L* language. The D.M.L. provides facilities to store, delete and modify records; to insert and remove records from sets; to find and get records by key and/or according to set relationships.

A D.M.S. system must provide privacy facilities to prevent users from gaining access to data elements or records which they are not authorized to examine. The same facilities may be used to prevent users from updating or deleting data elements, which they may otherwise examine.

Although in some D.M.S., records may be stored in the form of conventional files, the individual application program may still regard the records as being organized into particular files. For example, allowing a file to be accessed by a variety of keys enabling each user to view the data as a file with a desired field as the key. This is sometimes referred to as the *alternate key* facility.

Where records in a data base have to be accessed in more than one hierarchical grouping then the more complex facilities described earlier are needed. The logical sets available in such systems are sometimes referred to as owner coupled sets. Almost all D.M.S. systems have been developed by computer manufacturers, or *software* houses – the skills and investment required to develop such large general purpose systems is usually beyond the scope of individual computer-using organizations.

data capture ◊ *data collection* 2.

data carrier A general term referring to a medium for recording data, e.g. *paper tape, magnetic tape*, etc.

data carrier store Describing any form of *data storage* in which the storage medium is external to the computer. For example, both *magnetic tape* and *paper tape* can be used to store data, and they must be loaded on to a *peripheral unit* before the data can be *accessed* for automatic processing. Contrasted with *inherent store*.

data cell drive Sometimes used in reference to a *direct access storage* device, particularly where a number of such devices are connected to a single *central processor*. Thus, each device or data cell drive represents a module of storage within the total storage capacity of the system, perhaps running into billions of characters of information.

data channel multiplexor A device, usually associated with a central computer, servicing a number of *communications channels*, any of which may be transmitting or receiving data from the computer. The communications channels may operate at varying speeds according to the needs of the system, but the *multiplexor* will operate at a much higher speed to service these channels successively one *character* at a time.

data collection 1. The process of capturing *raw data* for use within a *computer system*. Also known as *data gathering*. Related to *file creation*. 2. In modern business systems the term is often used to imply the *capture* of information at the instant of a transaction occurring. For example, requiring the use of *data transmission equipment* to connect distant locations with a central computer where the transactions are recorded and processed.

data collection and analysis Related to a system in which a number of *data collection* points are connected directly to a *central processor*, so that data can be collected and automatically analysed as events arise. Such techniques may be used in both *real time* commercial systems and in industrial *process control* applications.

data communications Synonymous with *data transmission*. Concerning the use of communications equipment to transfer coded data by telephone, telegraph or radio communications circuits. (◊ the general article on *Communications Devices*.)

data communications exchange A special *hardware unit* that connects a control unit of a *central processor* to a communications network. Used in *real time* applications where data is to be transmitted and received simultaneously over several *communications channels* perhaps operating in many different modes.

data communication terminal A distant or *in-plant* terminal at which *input* and *output devices* may be stationed and connected via a *channel* to some central computer system. For example, *paper tape readers* and *punches* are often used for communication with a *central processor* from distant locations. When the terminal equipment is not being used for *data transmission* it can often be used for *data preparation* and editing in an *off-line mode*.

data control Related to the control of data entering or leaving a data processing system. For example, in *batch processing* applications input documents may be collected and vetted to ensure that they have been correctly coded and batched.

data conversion ◊ *conversion*.

data conversion language A language used to describe the data structures of *files* to be transcribed under the operation of a file *conversion* routine.

data delimiter Synonymous with *separator*.

data description The specification of an element of data in a *source program* written in accordance with the rules for a particular programming *language*. For example, an entry describing a *data-name* as written in the *data division* of a *C O B O L* program. The description specifies the *data name*, the length in characters, whether the item is numeric, alphabetic or alphanumeric, and the *data level* of the element in relation to others.

data description language A language used in a *data base management system* to describe the structure of *records*, *data elements*, *files* and their relationships.

data description library A *record* composed of accumulated data definitions in a *data management system*, and representing a definition of the entire *data base*. Used by the *data administrator* to control and manage the system.

data display unit A term sometimes used when referring to a *visual display unit* in which data stored in *memory* can be selected and displayed as characters or graphs upon a screen. Sometimes a *data display unit* may incorporate a *light pen* to enable graphs to be modified by a user under *program control*.

data division ◊ *C O B O L*.

data element Any item of data which for a given situation may be considered as a unit, e.g. *field, record*.

data format A description of the way data is held in a *file* or *record*, e.g. whether it is in *character form*, is a *binary* number, etc.

data gathering Synonymous with *data collection*.

data handling equipment In the broadest sense any equipment used to process data, but more specifically equipment used in *automatic data processing systems*.

data item A unit of data within an *application* system, one of the logical elements contained in a *record* and describing a particular attribute (e.g. name, address, age). May require a number of *characters*, *words*, *bytes*, or perhaps just a single *bit* to represent the entity concerned.

data level Relating to the rank of a particular *data element* in relation to other elements specified as part of the same *record* in a *source language*. For example, in the *data division* of a *C O B O L* program each data element is described, and that description includes a reference number which specifies for the C O B O L *compiler* the relationship between that element and other elements in the same hierarchy.

data link A communications circuit in which data may be transferred in a coded format amenable to automatic *data processing* equipment.

data management The process of handling data in a controlled environment; including the control of data having complex relationships by various system management routines without loss of integrity and without interference to other processes within the total system. ◊ general article on *Data Base Management Systems*.

data management utility system A *data management* system based on a number of parameter-driven routines each of which perform some common data processing facility such as *updating, sorting, editing*.

data manipulation language In a *data base management system* a procedural language used to define the processes required by users when processing data.

data matrix An array of values stored as a series of rows and columns representing variables and the values they may take.

data-names In writing a *program* in a programming *language*, items of data are allocated data-names which are specified as part of the *source program*. These names are used as *operands* in the source program *instructions* and replace the *addresses* of the items of data that they represent. When the source program is compiled the *compiler* will usually allocate *relative addresses* to these items of data and will substitute the appropriate relative addresses as operands in instructions which quote the data-names. When the *object program* is finally loaded, the *loading routine* will allocate an *absolute address* to each relative address and thereby each data-name originally specified in the source program will relate to a specific address in the *memory* at *run* time. ✧ *addressing*.

data net A *data communications exchange* for controlling the transfer of messages to and from remote terminals and a central computer.

data phone A device which permits data to be transferred over a telephone channel.

data plotter A device designed to give a visual display, usually in the form of a graph on paper, by plotting the course of coordinates. Also known as *X-Y plotter*.

data preparation One of the main limitations of any electronic *data processing* system lies in the initial preparation of the information to be processed. The data preparation stage must be carefully organized to ensure that all transactions entering a system are correctly transcribed into some medium suitable for input to a computer, and this transcription process is inherently slow. *Punched cards* and punched *paper tape* are two common input media, and in each case it is usually necessary to punch information from the documents representing the original transactions, in order to record these transactions as *characters* represented by holes in the cards or paper tape. In certain situations it is possible to obtain punched tape or cards as a by-product of the process which records the initial transaction, but this is not always possible.

The transcription of data into cards or paper tape is achieved by an operator using a *keypunch*. The operator reads the original documents and enters the characters that she reads onto a *keyboard*, and the activation of the keyboard energizes an electromagnetic or mechanical punching unit to punch appropriate holes

113

into the input medium. The process has several potential sources of error: for example, entries on the original document may be illegible or ambiguous, the operator may read a character incorrectly or depress the wrong key, the punch unit itself may fail. To reduce the possibility of errors remaining undetected it is usual to have a further checking stage known as *verification*. For example, in the preparation of punched cards a further operator takes the original documents and the cards previously punched from them and feeds the cards again through a *verifier*. The cards to be verified and the *source documents* are kept in their original sequence, and the verifier operator repeats the keystrokes made by the original punch operator. However, on this occasion no holes are punched into the cards but a sensing operation takes place to ascertain whether the holes previously recorded in each column agree with the keystrokes. If there is disagreement at any point the keyboard becomes temporarily inoperable and a warning lamp is lighted.

The verifier operator may then repeat the operation for that column and if disagreement still occurs she must examine the card and the original documents to ascertain the nature of the error. If the original card was incorrectly punched, the card is taken from the batch and is repunched and verified again.

Verification of paper tape follows a similar principle. In one method two tapes are produced by different operators working from the same source documents and these tapes are compared automatically by a machine which compares them character by character and automatically generates a third tape. In the event of a disagreement between the original tapes the machine stops and an operator has a facility for keying in the correct character. It is preferable to check automatically the *parity* of characters on this third tape when it is punched in order to safeguard against punch failures.

Another method of paper tape verification is the so-called two-tape method. Here only one original tape is produced and this is passed with the original documents to the operator of a paper tape verifier. The machine has a keyboard, a reading unit and a punch unit. The verifier operator enters data onto the keyboard from the original documents and this is compared with the original tape, which is fed through the reading unit. If the keystrokes agree with the characters punched in the original tape, signals are automatically transferred to the punch unit where a second, verified, tape is produced. If there is a disagreement between the keystroke and the corresponding character in the first tape the machine is temporarily halted and a signal lamp is illuminated to warn the verifier operator.

The operator may then examine the original documents before entering the correct character directly into the output tape.

The methods of verification described above are designed to ensure that data is rigorously checked before input to a computer. It is axiomatic that poor results will be generated if the input data is incorrect, but not all data needs to be subject to such rigid checks. For example, some paper tape preparation devices are designed to provide checks on batches of data by providing batch totals for certain specified quantity *fields* only. The batches are generally fairly small and a printed copy of the items punched has to be produced so that each item can be checked if the batches do not agree with the previously generated totals. This type of preparation would be suitable only for certain kinds of work where errors in certain fields were relatively unimportant. In some survey work, for example, errors in data preparation could be allowed for in the presentation of the final results, and to some extent they may be considered to cancel out in effect.

All the methods of data preparation described above are suitable only where data is processed in batches, but many applications require more advanced *data collection* techniques. The potential of modern *digital computers* is severely restricted where such delays are experienced in getting data into a system. The logical development is towards the elimination of the process of data preparation and in some applications this has been achieved, but in many other applications it is not practical or desirable.

The development of techniques for the automatic recognition of preprinted characters by machines has led to some improved concepts in data collection. These techniques are described in more detail under the heading *character recognition*, but some details are given here. The essential principle involved is that the original transaction document is used as input to the computer system. Machines are available which can read documents bearing either magnetized-ink characters or special characters for *optical recognition*; these machines can be connected directly to a *central processor* to facilitate the automatic transcription of the data from the documents on to a storage medium such as a *magnetic disk*. These techniques are suitable for many applications involving large volumes of data to a fairly standard format; for example the use of magnetized-ink characters on bank cheques. They are particularly suitable where *turnaround documents* can be used and where the details to be entered for each transaction involve relatively few items of data. Gas, electricity and hire purchase accounting are examples.

The development of *real time* data processing applications requires data collection devices to be held permanently *on line* to the central processor via some form of data transmission or *in-plant* communications network. Here *interrogating typewriters, cathode ray tube visual display units, key-to-disk* units and other keyboard input devices come to prominence. The data preparation limitations can be virtually eliminated as far as the recording of transactions is concerned, and the system can be designed to respond immediately to each transaction as it arises.

In all forms of data preparation it is usually preferable to allow the computer to perform a range of validity checks on every item of data as it is transcribed from the input medium. In this way it is possible to ensure that each record entering the system conforms to a prescribed pattern in the number and type of characters in specified fields, and in the logical relationship between fields for certain transaction types. These types of check are even more important in real time applications.

In *batch-processing* applications it is also necessary to maintain *control totals* throughout the stages of preparation and transcription to ensure that individual transactions or complete batches are not lost.

Generally, all data preparation is concerned with accuracy of transcription or transmission, and the eventual integrity of data depends very largely on this initial accuracy.

data processing The operations performed on *data*, usually by automatic equipment, in order to derive information or to achieve order among *files*. A data processing system may incorporate clerical functions and ancillary machine operations as well as all arithmetic and logical operations performed by a computer.

data processing, automatic ◊ *automatic data processing.*

data processing centre The general term used when referring to the offices or buildings in which automatic data processing equipment is installed, including the equipment itself and all the programming, operating and systems staff necessary to run the centre. It is common to find such a unit organized as a single management group providing a service to the company or organization within which it operates.

data processing department organization A great deal has been written about organizational structure in data processing departments, but what is not always recognized is something far more important than the titles of the members of the department: the question of whether all the functions which should be carried out are being carried out. The charts on pages 118 and 119 show the main functions and it is possible to draw up an organizational structure to suit any organization – and indeed any personalities in an organization – by ensuring that the different functions are covered. The functions are shown on different levels of responsibility as a guide only: it is quite possible for one man to fulfil functions on several different levels. The charts on pages 122 and 123 show two standard organizational structures. These structures are variable, but act as a useful guide-line for the brief outlines of jobs given below. Remarks on the qualities needed for each job are given in the general article on *Computer Personnel*.

The data processing manager is the centre of the organization, and on his imagination, determination and flexibility will depend much of the success of the department. He is responsible for deciding policy within the department and ensuring that the systems analysts, programmers and computer operations staff are all working towards the same end (and this is by no means automatic!). He should have a clearly defined position in the company, preferably one with an immediate contact at policy-making level. This is not only because he will need to influence policy, but also because one of his most important functions is communication: he must constantly ensure that the service his department offers is well known throughout the company, and he must encourage initiative in utilizing these services.

The systems analysts design systems and procedures (including documenting them) and implement them throughout the company. Sometimes such systems will be restricted to those which utilize, either directly or indirectly, computer time or *punched card* machine time and in this case *organization and methods* staff or *operational research* staff are employed in another department. More usually, O and M and OR activities are considered to be part of the data processing activities of the company. In the design stage, systems analysts will be as much concerned with people as with machines, and before any system can be approved for implementation it must be fully documented (◊ general article on *Documentation – Systems*).

The functions of the *programmers* are to prepare, test and document computer programs from written specifications prepared by the systems analysts, and include amending existing programs to meet changing requirements. Further information on programming strategy, tactics and design are given in the general article on *Programming*, and this is supplemented by the general article on *Docu-*

| Senior Management | Policy | Company organization | Budget setting | Objective setting | Senior personnel selection |

| Line Management | Communications | Application selection | Budget control | Resource planning |
| | Personnel training | Physical planning |

	Systems Analysis	*Programming*	*Operations*	*General*
Junior Line Management	Budget control	Budget control	Budget control	Documentation and standards
	Resource allocation	Resource allocation	Resource allocation	Data administration
	Personnel	Personnel	Personnel	
	Training	Training	Control	
	System selection	Program strategy	Statistics and reporting	
	User contact		Training	

	Systems Analysis	Programming	Operations
Technical Management	Supervision Feasibility studies Systems specification Maintenance Standards writing Clerical	Supervision Program organization Maintenance Standards writing Clerical	Scheduling – operations – data control – data preparation Supervision Clerical
Staff	Informal training Analysis and design Implementation	Informal training Programming and testing	*Operations* Work assembly Computer operating Data control Data preparation Informal training Library *General* Stock control Typing and copying
Trainees	Undergoing training		

Functions of a Data Processing Department

mentation – Programming. After the program has been *coded, desk-checked*, tested and documented it will be ready for productive *runs*, and may be passed to the computer operations staff for running as required.

The computer operations staff are responsible for the day-to-day running of the data processing equipment, which may include data control and editing, data preparation and computer operating. *Data control* and *editing* functions include the following: ensuring work progresses satisfactorily by supervising the passage of a job through the department according to work schedules; receiving and preparing clean '*raw data*' from other departments for the data preparation section; ensuring the enforcement of *control total* and error procedures and checking them; collecting and preparing all input data, and issuing programs and operating instructions for the jobs to be run by the computer operating section; controlling the issue of all programs and current files which are held in a *magnetic tape* or *punched card library* : ensuring that output is dispatched to the correct addresses; and filing input data after use.

Data preparation includes the following functions: preparing actual computer input by recording raw data received from the data control section in a computer input medium (e.g. punched cards or paper tape or by direct input such as *key-to-disc*); preparing computer programs for input by recording a program (supplied by the programmers) in a computer input medium; arranging the computer input in a prescribed manner; updating master card files, etc., as instructed by the data control section.

Computer operating includes the following functions: operating equipment in the computer area, processing data as instructed and supplied by the data control section; and maintaining log-books giving details of machine utilization.

Many data processing department managers have found that a service section can relieve a great deal of the load of non-productive work from other sections. Among tasks which can be handled by such a section are maintenance of standards manuals and organization manuals, control of documents including technical literature and records of *file layouts*, card layouts, etc; the organization of training; internal communications; and administration such as ordering new desks, recording absence and holidays and controlling stationery usage.

The task of *data administrator*, controlling the integrity of data and the design of data structures, is identified as a specific post in installations utilizing *data base management* techniques.

data processing, electronic ⋄ *electronic data processing.*

data processing standards There are probably no data processing managers who do not readily accept the need for standard procedures in their departments, but there are far too many who will ruefully admit that many of their present difficulties are directly attributable to the fact that, in the early stages, getting on with the job seemed more important than writing out standards and since that time they have been too busy extricating themselves from the troubles this caused to do anything about it. It cannot be stressed too strongly that the most important thing about any data processing standard is that it shall exist; so long as there *is* a standard it doesn't matter too much if it is the best or not. Standards should embrace the activities of systems analysis, programming, operating and clerical procedures, and in general serve the following functions. (i) Communication: a successful data processing installation depends so much on successful communication (from systems analyst to programmer and to operating staff, for example, and between data processing staff and user departments) that a standard form of presentation and terminology helps to prevent ambiguity. Standard forms of *documentation* will also help to ensure that documents are complete and that necessary steps in, for example, *systems design* have been taken. Later, when modification of the system becomes necessary, standard documentation will allow easy access to the relevant section. (ii) Control: performance of specialist functions such as systems analysis and programming requires to be carefully controlled, and standards of work and method ensure that work reaches a prescribed quality and allows management to assess progress against timetables. It is also helpful to be able to assign clear responsibilities to staff. (iii) Continuity: if all work is prepared to a given standard, prepared by a standard method and documented in a standard way, then the bugbear of complete dependence on individuals is avoided. Sometimes complete systems have been thrown overboard because, when the time came to amend them, it was found that the original designer had left and no one could make head or tail of the notes he had left behind. Further notes are given in the general articles on *Documentation.*

data processor A general term for any machine capable of processing data; e.g. a *punched card tabulator,* a *computer.*

data purification The process of validating and correcting data to reduce the number of errors entering a data processing system.

data record A *record* containing a unit of data for processing by a computer *program.*

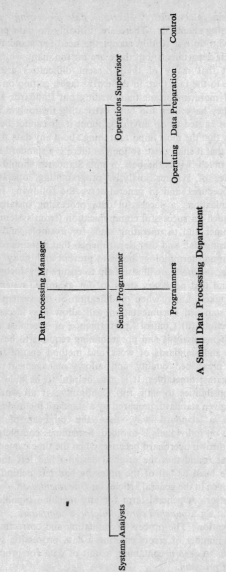

A Small Data Processing Department

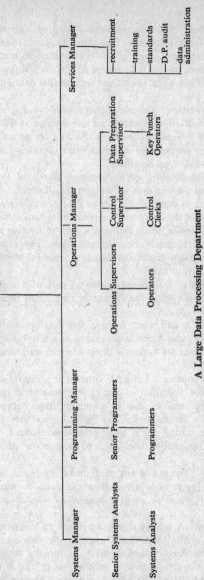

A Large Data Processing Department

Data Processing Manager
- Systems Manager
  - Senior Systems Analysts
    - Systems Analysts
- Programming Manager
  - Senior Programmers
    - Programmers
- Operations Manager
  - Operations Supervisors
    - Operators
  - Control Supervisor
    - Control Clerks
  - Data Preparation Supervisor
    - Key Punch Operators
- Services Manager
  - recruitment
  - training
  - standards
  - D.P. audit
  - data administration

data reduction The selection and *editing* of *operands* to derive facts from large volumes of *raw data*. To summarize information for subsequent processing or for presentation to management.

data reduction, on-line To accept data from a source directly *on-line* to a computer and to *edit* and arrange that data into an ordered format.

data representation The use of characters (i.e. numerals, letters and special symbols) to represent values and descriptive data. In a digital computer all *program instructions* and data are recorded as electrical impulses arranged in a coded form (⋄ *binary notation* and *binary-coded decimal notation*).

data retrieval ⋄ *retrieval, Information Retrieval Techniques.*

data segment A sub-unit of the *storage* allocated to a particular *process*, used to contain *data* rather than *executable program code* forming part of the *application program* or system *software*.

data set A device which connects a *data processing* machine to a telephone or telegraph communication line. For example, a *telephone data set* converts *digital* signals to tones for transmission over a speech quality circuit.

data statements *Statements* written as part of a *source program* to identify and specify the format of data items used in the program.

data station A unit which incorporates data processing *input* and *output devices* and which is connected to a telephone or telegraph circuit by a *data set* to permit direct communication with a central computer.

data station console A *console* situated at a distant *data terminal* to control the operation of the various *input* and *output devices* located there, and to control communication between the *data station* and a central computer. Generally includes a *data set* to connect the station to a communications channel, and circuits to handle automatic detection and correction of transmission errors.

data storage The use of any medium for storing data; but implying a capability to store large volumes of data, immediately *on-line* to a *central processor* as in a *magnetic drum*, or *magnetic disk* store.

data terminal A remote station employed to transmit and receive data from a central computer. ⋄ *data communication terminal.*

data transmission Pertaining to the automatic transfer of data from one computer system to another, or to and from a central computer and distant *data collection* points. The data may be transferred by special equipment using either telegraph or telephone circuits, or by radio link. The speed of transmission is largely governed by the characteristics of the data transmission line or channels. (⋄ the general article on *Communication Devices*.)

data unit   A group of one or more characters which are related in such a way that they form a whole. Similar to (but not always synonymous with) *field*.

data word   Any unit of *data* stored in a single *word* of a storage medium.

D C amplifier   Abbreviation for *directly coupled amplifier* or *direct current amplifier*.

D C F   Acronym for *discounted cash flow*.

D D A   Acronym for *digital differential analyser*.

D D L   Acronym for *data description language*.

dead halt   ⋄ *drop dead halt*.

deadly embrace   A condition which arises when all processes active at the same time within a computer become suspended while competing for the same resources. The condition is such that no one process can be continued without external intervention to remove a process from the system, allowing others to be reactivated.

dead time   A period of time allowed between two related events in order to avoid overlap or mutual interference.

dead zone unit   A device used on an *analog computer* to give a constant output signal over a predetermined range of an input variable.

debatable time   A term used in the keeping of computer usage statistics. It is usual to consider machine time under various headings for purposes of evaluating performance of the machine room, and debatable time is time that cannot be directly attributed to some other classification; e.g., where time is lost and there is no information to indicate whether it is due to, say, a programming error or an operator fault.

deblocking   To extract *records* from a *block* of data so that the individual records can be processed.

debugging   Debugging is the technique of detecting, diagnosing and correcting errors (also known as bugs) which may occur in *programs* or systems (both *hardware* and *software*).

The two main types of program error that can occur are logic errors and syntax errors. The former are the result of incorrect appreciation of the problem, and the latter the result of incorrect *coding* of the program. An example of an error in logic would be the attempt to calculate average speed by dividing fuel consumption

125

by time taken, instead of distance travelled by time taken. The calculation would be performed correctly by program, but the result would be incorrect. An example of a syntax error would be writing the *instruction* DOV TIME, DIST where DIV, referring to the operation 'divide', should have been written instead of DOV, which is meaningless and would not be operated on by the computer.

Errors are detected by observing that programs do not produce the results expected from them, or by the failure of a program written in a *symbolic language* to *compile* correctly. Detecting errors by means of observing results involves testing programs with samples of data which the program would expect to be presented with in normal running. The nature of this data would be predetermined and the results expected from the program calculated by the programmer or systems analyst concerned, and compared with the actual results obtained. Test data of this sort is presented to the program either directly in the form expected in normal running, or by means of simulated input conditions, for example, by storing data with the program and altering the data input instructions to *access* the data directly from *store* rather than from an *input device*. As well as testing programs by means of *test data*, testing of all conditions expected in normal running must also be carried out, for example, all conditions causing a program to print messages requiring operator action, such as loading paper on a *printer*, must be simulated. Any failure of a program to achieve expected results, or any unexpected halt occurring within a program, will require error diagnosis, as described below.

Programs written in a symbolic language require *compilation*, or translation into the *machine language* understood by the processor. The process of compilation enables syntax errors involving incorrect handling of the symbolic language to be detected. Most compilers reject incorrectly used statements, and print some indication of the type of error. However, errors in logic cannot usually be detected by compilers: any correctly formed statement will be translated, even if the instruction will cause the program to perform a calculation incorrectly.

Once an error has been detected, either through incorrect results from test data or simulated operating conditions, or through an unexpected halt, or through compilation errors, the cause of the error must be diagnosed. Various methods of error diagnosis may be used. A *dry run* may be performed on the program *flowchart* or compilation listing. This involves the programmer in performing each step of the program as if he were the computer, checking and recording the action of each instruction or flowchart step. Instead of performing the computer's actions himself, the programmer may use a trace or diagnostic routine which performs the program on the computer in the normal way, but at the same time provides a printed record of the action taken by each instruction. Simpler versions of such a routine provide printed information about selected types of instruction. Other aids to diagnosing the causes of errors include prints of portions of internal store at various stages during the operation of a program, enabling the programmer to check the progress of the program. Prints may also be obtained of the contents of *backing store*, e.g. *magnetic tapes* or *magnetic disks*.

Errors of syntax detected by compilers are usually recorded by the compiler, and the type of error identified. Normally programs which have caused compilation errors cannot be run, and the errors must be corrected before the program can be tested.

Once the cause of an error has been detected, a correction must be applied to the program. Programs may be corrected by several different methods. The incorrect instruction may be altered directly if the program exists in machine code on an external medium such as *punched cards*. If the program is written in a symbolic language, the *source code* must be corrected and the program recompiled. Correcting source codes may be done directly by removing incorrect *statements* and substituting correct ones if the program is on a suitable medium such as punched cards, or corrections may be applied by using source code maintenance routines. Another technique for correcting programs is to apply a *patch*. This consists of deleting the incorrect instruction and substituting a *branch* to a section of coding correcting the error. Corrections may also be applied to a program at *run* time by directly altering the program after it has been loaded into store. However in most cases the best method of correcting errors is by amending incorrect coding at source, at the same time ensuring that all documentation supporting the program is kept up to date.

Debugging is not confined solely to programs. The term is also applied to the process of testing the performance of hardware systems, and also to the testing of a complete data processing system. In the latter case the system may be tested for flaws by means of *pilot systems* or *parallel runs*.

⇨ general articles on *Documentation, Flowcharting, Remote Testing*.

debugging aid routine Any *routine* used by programmers when testing *programs*. For example, a *diagnostic routine* or any routine for producing a *memory print*, a *tape print*, etc. Also known as checkout routine.

debug on-line 1. To test and correct errors in a *program*, using only certain sections of the *hardware* in a *multiprogramming* computer, thus allowing the *central processor* to continue to process other routines which may be *loaded* in *memory* at the same time. 2. To detect and correct errors on a program from a *remote console* in a *multi-access* system.

decade A group of ten storage *locations*. For example, a *magnetic drum* might consist of a number of storage *tracks* each consisting of 200 words, the tracks being divided into twenty decades as the minimum unit of *access*.

decay time The time taken for a voltage to decrease to one-tenth of its original value.

deceleration time Pertaining to a *storage device* which requires the storage medium to be physically moved for *reading* or *writing* to take place. For example, using *magnetic tape*, the time required from the completion of a reading or writing operation to the moment when the tape is stopped.

decentralized data processing The organization of data processing activity within an organization so that computing equipment is deployed at several widespread branches to serve the operational needs of individual management groups.

decibel One tenth of a bel; a unit of measurement of signal loss or gain in a transmission circuit. The unit is often used to express intensities of sound.

decimal An integer represented by a single character in the range 0–9. The term is also used when referring to a *bit pattern* representing such a character.

decimal, binary coded ⋄ *binary coded decimal notation.*

decimal notation The system of writing numbers in which successive digit positions are represented by successive powers of radix 10. In computers decimal numbers are usually represented by *binary digits* arranged in groups of four, each group corresponding to a digit of a decimal number. ⋄ *binary coded decimal notation.*

decimal notation, coded ⋄ *binary coded decimal notation.*

decimal numeral A number represented in *decimal notation;* i.e. one using the *decimal* digits from the range 0, 1, 2, 3, 4, 5, 6, 7, 8 and 9.

decimal point The *radix point* used to separate the integral and fractional parts of a decimal number.

decimal representation, binary coded ◊ *binary coded decimal notation*.

decision An operation performed by a computer to choose between alternative courses of action. Usually made by comparing the relative magnitude of two specified *operands*, a *branch instruction* being used to select the required path according to the result obtained.

decision box A *flowchart symbol* used to represent a *decision* or *branch* in the sequence of *program instructions*. ◊ general article on *Flowcharting*.

decision instruction Any *instruction* which discriminates between the relative value of two specified *operands*. Usually a *branch instruction* which will branch conditionally; e.g. when one operand is greater than another.

decision plan A method for making managerial decisions according to rules developed to cover certain specified events or conditions. Not necessarily involving the use of *data processing* equipment, but generally concerned with the *exception principle system* of reporting.

decision table A method for presenting the relationship between certain variables in order to specify the required action when various conditions are present. These tables may be used to assist in developing solutions to problems, or to display the relationship between various phenomena when documenting a *system* or *program*. Some programming *languages* have been written to make use of *decision tables* when a problem is specified. ◊ general article on *Decision Tables*.

decision tables In the general articles on *Programming* and *Documentation – Programs*, the processes of problem description and problem solution are outlined, and in the general article on *Flowcharting* a method of problem analysis is shown. The documentation of programs before, during and after they have been written is often a combination of English narrative and program flowcharts, but these alone are not always complete, easy to understand or capable of being easily altered to allow for system changes. Another method of logic analysis and presentation – sometimes supplementary to narrative and flowcharts, sometimes able to replace them altogether – is the use of decision tables.

Ordinary tables are a familiar way of recording data in a standardized format; they are called decision tables when they are based on an 'if ... then' presentation. For example, if I am at railway station A and I wish to go to station D, I might expect to scan two or three lists of destinations (A to B, A to C, etc.) until my eye lit on A to D, showing me which platform to go to. The choice and necessary action could be presented like this:

A to B	Yes	No	No	No
A to C	No	Yes	No	No
A to D	No	No	Yes	No
A to E	No	No	No	Yes
Go to Platform 1	X	—	—	—
Go to Platform 2	—	X	—	—
Go to Platform 3	—	—	X	—
Go to Platform 4	—	—	—	X

It will be seen that I must go to platform 3 for the A to D train, and that the problem has been represented in a tabular form rather than as a continuous flowchart. Each condition is shown, together with the appropriate result. The table has been drawn as four main blocks.

1	2
3	4

Block 1 (known as the 'condition stub') answers the question 'What are the conditions?' Block 2 (known as the 'condition entry') answers the question 'What values do the conditions have?' Block 3 (known as the 'action stub') answers the question 'What actions occur when a condition is fulfilled?' Block 4 (known as the 'action entry') answers the question 'What values do these actions have?'

This structure is the basis for all decision tables, and even extremely complex problems can be reduced to this format. The condition entry and action entry together make a further element, the 'decision rule', which is illustrated in the example below. If we are outlining the credit control rules for a business, we might describe them as 'If the credit is good, approve an order; if previous payment history has been favourable, approve the order; if neither credit nor previous history is good, a special clearance must be obtained before the order is approved. Otherwise, no approval is

	Rule 1	Rule 2	Rule 3	Rule 4
Credit good	Y	—	N	N
Payment history good	—	Y	N	N
Special clearance obtained	—	—	Y	N
Approve order	X	X	X	—
Do not approve order	—	—	—	X

to be given to an order'. This credit control procedure is represented by a decision table with four decision rules, as shown above.

In the condition entry, Y=yes, N=no, —=not significant.

In the action entry X=perform this action, —=do not perform this action.

The table shown above is a simple example of a 'limited entry' decision table, where all questions can be answered Y, N or —. There are also 'extended entry' tables (where only part of the condition or action is shown in the appropriate stub, e.g. where a condition entry might be 'less than 50' rather than Yes or No) and 'mixed entry' tables (a combination of limited entry and mixed entry).

An example of a mixed entry table, showing also how control is passed from one table to another, is given below:

	Rule 1	Rule 2	Rule 3
Security available	Y	N	N
Credit allowed	—	£100	£100
Special clearance	—	Y	N
Pass	X	X	—
Return to customer	—	—	X
Go to table no.	4	6	7

It will be seen that, as complex problems can be considered and solved by the use of these tables, they can be an extremely powerful tool for both *systems analyst* and *programmer*, particularly when it is remembered that pre-processor *languages* exist for converting decision tables to *source language* statements (e.g. C O B O L) for the production of an *object program* via an ordinary *compiler*.

It is true that the use of decision tables sometimes tempts systems analysts and programmers to identify in too much detail all the possible eventualities and to cater for them individually (which makes large programs) instead of by a general action; but this is probably outweighed by the overall advantages of the use of decision tables, which may be summarized as follows: (i) they ensure that the user makes a clear and complete statement of the problem; (ii) they provide an efficient means of communication between management, systems analyst and programmer; (iii) they ensure that program descriptions are structured in modules for ease of programming; (iv) alterations and additions can easily be made (and, incidentally, the re-drawing of flowcharts by systems analysts is unnecessary since fair copies can be made by typists); (v) decision tables provide a standard format, and deviations from the standard are immediately apparent; (vi) computer programs can be automatically created from tables.

deck 1. A collection or *pack* of *punched cards* belonging to a specific card *file*. 2. Also used as an abbreviation for *magnetic tape deck*.

deck, tape ◊ *magnetic tape deck*.

declaration Synonymous with *declarative statement*.

declarative macro instruction *Instructions* used as a part of an *assembly language* to instruct the *compiler* (or *assembly program*) to perform some action or take note of some condition. When a declarative macro is used it does not result in any subsequent action by the *object program*. Contrasted with *imperative macro instructions* and *macro instructions*, by which object program instructions are generated.

declarative statement An *instruction* written as part of a *source program* to specify for the *compiler* the format, size and nature of *data elements* and constants used as *operands* in the program. Also known as declaration.

decode To alter data from one coded format back to an original format. To translate coded characters to a form more intelligible to human beings or for a further stage of processing.

decoder A device used to alter data from one coded form to another. A *matrix* of devices capable of selecting one or more *output* channels in response to a combination of *input* signals. Contrasted with *encoder*.

decollator A device used *off-line* in a computer system to separate multi-part sets of continuous stationery produced as output from a *printer*.

decrement A quantity or value used to decrease the magnitude of a variable.

defect A fault in *hardware* or *software* liable to cause processing *failures* in a computer system.

defective Describes a *hardware* or *software* unit which is in such condition that it is likely to cause processing *failures* in a computer system.

deferred addressing A form of *indirect addressing* in which several references are necessary before the desired address is found, the successive references being controlled by some pre-set *counter*.

degradation Referring to the operation of a computer system, to provide a lower level of service in the face of failures in certain areas of the equipment. ✧ *graceful degradation*.

delay device, digit ✧ *digit delay device*.

delayed updating A method of *updating* a *record* or set of records in which *fields* in the records are not amended until all alterations related to a specific transaction (or set of transactions) have been processed.

delay element, digit ✧ *digit delay element*.

delay line A transmission line (or circuit) in which signals are deliberately delayed to achieve some specific purpose.

delay line, acoustic ✧ *acoustic delay line*.

delay line, magneto-strictive acoustic ✧ *magneto-strictive acoustic delay line*.

delay line, mercury ✧ *mercury delay line*.

delay line, quartz ✧ *quartz delay line*.

delay line register A *register* in which data is stored by continually re-circulating a signal.

delay line, sonic ✧ *acoustic delay line*.

delay line store A device which stores information by continually regenerating a signal. The output from the device is transferred via a *delay line* and is re-input. Thus, data in the store is allowed to circulate without alteration until such time as it is no longer required, whereupon the regenerating loop is interrupted.

delay unit ✧ *transport delay unit*.

delete 1. Any operation to eliminate a *record* or group of records from a *file*. 2. To remove a *program* from the *memory* of a computer, e.g. at the end of a *run*.

deleted representation Related to *paper tape codes*; the use of a code superimposed upon any other character code to delete the character concerned. An *ignore* character, for example, consists of all code holes and when recorded upon any other previously punched character it effectively deletes that character.

deletion record A *change record* which will cause one or more existing records on a *master file* to be deleted.

delimit To specify the bounds of a certain related group of *characters*, by means of special characters not otherwise members of the group.

demand processing Refers to a system in which *data* is processed virtually as soon as it is received; i.e. it is not necessary to *store* large quantities of *raw data*.

Also known as in-line processing, immediate processing.

demand reading (or writing) A technique for performing *input* (or *output*) *operations* in which *blocks* of data are transferred to or from the *central processor* as required for processing. No specific arrangements are made for storing input or output data in *buffer areas* to enable operations to take place in parallel.

demand writing ◊ *demand reading (or writing)*.

demodifier An element of data used to reinstate a *basic instruction* to its original value. ◊ *program modification*.

demodulator A terminal unit to a *data transmission* link: capable of receiving a modulated carrier wave and of recreating the signal originally transmitted by removing the carrier wave. ◊ *modulation*.

denial, alternative ◊ *not-and operation*.

denial, joint ◊ *nor operation*.

dependent In a data structure, a data item, or set of data items, belonging to a nominal point or *node*, or said to be dependent upon that point.

deposit To preserve the contents of an *area* of *memory* by *writing* to a *backing store*: ◊ *dump*.

description A significant *element* of data used to identify a *record* in which it appears.

description, problem ◊ *problem definition*.

designating device, independent sector ◊ *independent sector designating device*.

designation 1. Special punching in a specific *card column* of a *punched card*, to indicate that the card is of a certain type. 2. Coded information forming part of a computer *record* to indicate the class of record and thus to determine the processing to be applied to it.

designation holes Synonymous with *control holes*.

design, logical ◊ *logic design*.

desk checking Synonymous with *dry running*.

destination file A term sometimes used to refer to a *file* that receives *output* data from a particular *run*.

destination warning marker Synonymous with *end of tape marker*.

destruction (of a node) The removal of a nominated point (or *node*) in a data structure, from a *catalogue* describing that structure (when the catalogue is used to control the selection of individual data items or sets).

destructive addition An operation in which two *operands*, *addend* and *augend*, are added to form a *sum* which appears in the *location* originally occupied by the augend.

destructive reading An operation in which data is taken from a *location* to a specified destination in such a way that the data in the original location is lost or mutilated.

DETAB (DETAB X, DETAB 65) A programming *language* which is based on *C O B O L* but enables the user to specify problems in the form of *decision tables*.

detachable plugboard A *plugboard* which can be removed by the operator and exchanged for another; thus enabling the set-up to be changed for each *run*, without *connexions* having to be unplugged.

detail file Synonymous with *transaction file*.

detail flowchart ⋄ the general article on *Flowcharting*.

detected error An error in a system which is detected, but not automatically corrected, before the output from the system is produced.

de-updating Part of a *recovery procedure*. A method of re-creating an earlier version of a *file* by replacing *records* which have been recently updated by versions of those same records which have been preserved from an earlier stage.

device control character A character used in *paper tape codes* to control the operation of *data processing* or telecommunications equipment. When transmitted, or incorporated in any way in a *record* or *message*, it does not form part of the information conveyed.

devices, input/output ⋄ the general articles on *Input Devices*, *Output Devices*.

D F G Acronym for *diode function generator*.

diagnosis Locating errors in *software*, or failures in *hardware*. ⋄ the general article on *Debugging*.

diagnostic check Synonymous with *diagnostic test*.

diagnostic program Synonymous with *diagnostic routine*.

diagnostic routine A *program* written to trace errors in other programs or to locate the cause of a machine breakdown. Usually written as a *general purpose program*, and may be supplied to the computer user as part of the *software* available with the machine. ⋄ the general article on *Debugging*.

diagnostic test The use of a special *program* in order to identify and isolate faults or sources of potential failure in the *hardware* of a computer.

Also known as diagnostic check. ◊ the general article on *Debugging*.

diagram, logical ◊ *logic diagram*.

dichotomizing search A method of searching a *table* of items in order to locate an item with a specific *key* value. The method relies upon the items in the table being in some known sequence; e.g., in ascending sequence by key value. The technique involves comparing the key required with a key midway in the table; one half of the table is then rejected according to whether the result shows the required key to be greater or lesser than the key selected from the table. This process is repeated, continually dividing the remainder of the table in half until the desired record is located.

Also known as binary search, binary chop.

dictionary A translation table used to specify the size and format of *operands* in a *file*, each *record* type and *field* type being identified by a *data-name*. Used, for example, in standard *file-processing programs* to enable the user to specify the size and structure of any particular file to be processed.

Also known as directory.

dictionary, automatic ◊ *automatic dictionary*.

difference The result obtained in the arithmetic *operation* of *subtraction*.

difference, symmetric Synonymous with *exclusive-or* operation.

differential amplifier A circuit which will produce an output signal derived from the difference between two input signals.

differential analyser An *analog computer* which employs connected *integrators* to solve differential equations.

differential analyser, digital ◊ *digital differential analyser*.

differential gear A device used in mechanical *analog computers* in which two input variables and one output variable are represented by angles of rotation of shafts. The output variable may be the *sum* or *difference* of the two input variables.

differentiating amplifier A *computing amplifier* used in electronic *analog computers*. ◊ *differentiator*.

differentiator A device, used on *analog computers*, having one input variable and one output variable which is proportional to the differential of the input with respect to time.

digit A component of an item of data – a character position in an *operand* which may assume one of several values. For example, the number 991 comprises three digits but is composed of two types of character.

digital Referring to the use of discrete signals to represent data in the form of numbers or characters. Most forms of *digital representation* in *data processing* are based upon the use of *binary numbers*, sets of *binary digits* being grouped together to represent numbers in some other *radix* when required; e.g., ◊ *binary coded decimal notation*. In a similar way sets of binary digits can be grouped to represent alphabetic characters and symbols in coded form. Contrasted with *analog*. ◊ the general article on *Digital Computers*.

digital adder ◊ *adder*.

digital/analog converter A unit which converts *digital* signals into a continuous electrical signal suitable for input to an *analog computer*.

digital clock 1. A timing device which controls operations within a computer. 2. Also used to describe a clock which records physical conditions and routine events that must be logged as part of the computer's operation.

digital computers A digital computer is a machine capable of performing operations on data represented in digital or number form; i.e., the data is represented as a series of discrete elements arranged in a coded form to represent numbers. The devices used for recording or manipulating the numbers usually contain a series of individual *elements* [2], one for each position in the number, and each element is capable of adopting any one of a number of stable states according to the base of notation required in each position. In most electronic digital computers the method of number representation is based on the system of *binary notation* and each element in any series must be capable of representing either of the *bits* (*binary digits*) 0 or 1. Sometimes sets of bits are grouped to represent numerals in other scales of notation and such sets are referred to as *binary coded digits*.

The individual operations performed by a digital computer are very simple arithmetic or logical processes involving the manipulation of the bits in *words* or *characters* of information. The great power of any digital computer rests in the ability to *store* large volumes of data and to perform these various functions at extremely high speed; e.g., two ten digit numbers can be added together in a few *microseconds*.

The binary notation system is most widely used because of the convenience in constructing logic circuits and *storage devices* capable of handling data in this form. For example, a magnetic *core store* unit consists of perhaps several thousand individual magnetic cores each of which can be energized in either of two ways to represent the binary digits 0 or 1. If these cells are grouped to form words or binary coded characters, information can be stored for processing in units of specified size. In the same way, digital data can be recorded as a series of magnetized spots on, for example, *magnetic tape* or a *magnetic disk*.

Arithmetic and logic circuits for processing data in binary form are constructed from simple basic units designed to perform the operations of *Boolean algebra*: 'and', 'or', 'not', etc. These simple units are used as building blocks in constructing the complex logic and control circuits required.

It can be seen that the processes performed by a digital computer are essentially simple. These operations can be performed at extremely high speeds and with a high degree of coordination between the different functional units of the *hardware* system, and this ability means that digital computers can undertake highly complex tasks.

Although digital computers are sometimes constructed for specialized tasks, the term is almost universally applied to mean a *general purpose computer* in which the operations to be performed are specified by means of a stored *program*. The *instructions* are stored within *memory* as data, and can be modified under control of the program itself to perform different processes as required (◊ *Program Modification*). Some of the earlier digital computing devices were developed from *punched card* machines and the program was set up by means of connexions on a *plugboard*; machines in this category are generally referred to as calculators, rather than computers.

An electronic digital computer generally consists of *input devices*; a *central processor* containing memory, arithmetic units and a control section; *backing storage*; and *output devices*. ◊ the general articles entitled *Analog Computers* and *Hybrid Computers*.

digital differential analyser A digital computing device which has special circuits in-built to perform the mathematical process of integration.

digital divider A device used in *digital computers* which accepts signals representing a *dividend* and *divisor* and generates a *quotient* and *remainder*.

digital incremental plotter An *output device* which is capable of accepting signals transmitted from a computer and which can plot graphs to show statistical trends and other graphical solutions to problems. Digital signals from a *central processor* are employed to activate a plotting pen and a plotting drum which carries the paper. The plotting action results from step motions of the drum and/or pen, giving steps in the XY plane on the paper.

digital integrator An integrating device in which digital signals are used to represent increments in input variables *x* and *y* and an output variable *z*.

digital multiplier A device used in *digital computers* to perform *multiplication*. It accepts two signals representing the *multiplicand* and *multiplier* and generates the representation of their *product*.

digital representation The use of discrete impulses arranged in some coded format to represent data in the form of numbers or *characters*. To record a value or quantity by means of *digits*.

digital subtractor A device operating with digital *operands* to perform the function of *subtraction*; capable of accepting two input signals representing numbers, and of generating an output signal representing their *difference*.

digit compression Describing any system for condensing the size of items of data in order to reduce the size of a *file*. Special *programming* techniques may be used to *pack* data into a lesser number of characters or digits and to *unpack* the data for subsequent processing.

digit delay device A logic device for delaying digit signals; e.g., to achieve the effect of a *carry* from one digit position to another in arithmetic circuits.

digit delay element A *logic element* which accepts a single digital input signal, and which produces an output signal delayed by one *digit period*.

digit emitter On a *punched card tabulator* or *calculator*, a device to emit signals at various points in the time cycle of the machine. The pulses emitted are used to initiate specified actions at corresponding moments during the machine cycle.

digit emitter, selective ◊ *selective digit emitter.*

digit filter A device used on *punched card* equipment to detect the presence of a particular *designation* in a specified *card column*.

digitize To convert an *analog* representation, e.g. a voltage, to a *digital* form of representation.

digitizer A device which can convert a physical quantity (i.e. an *analog* measurement) into coded character form.

digit period The time interval for each consecutive digital signal in a series, determined by the basic *pulse repetition frequency* of the particular computer.

digit place   Synonymous with *digit position*.

digit plane   The *magnetic cores* forming the *memory* of a computer are usually assembled in the form of a three-dimensional array. The term digit plane refers to the plane containing elements for a particular *digit position*; i.e., the first digit of each *word* will appear in the same plane, the second digit in another and so on.

digit position   In *positional notation* the particular position of each digit in a number. The digit positions are usually numbered from the lowest significant digit of the number. For example, in a system using twelve-bit *binary representation*, the individual positions will be referenced as follows:

$$11\ 10\ 9\ 8\ 7\ 6\ 5\ 4\ 3\ 2\ 1\ 0$$

Also known as digit place.

digit pulse   A pulse used to drive a number of *core storage* elements, all corresponding to a particular *digit position* in a number of *words*.

digit selector   A selecting device on a *punched card* machine which can be activated by *designations* punched into the cards thus calling for a particular series of operations to be performed according to the card type.

digits, equivalent binary   ⟡ *equivalent binary digits*.

digit time   The time interval corresponding to a specific digit signal in a series.

diminished radix complement   A number derived by subtracting each digit of some specified number from one less than the equivalent *radix*. *Complements* are used in many data processing machines as a means of representing negative values. ⟡ *nines complement* and *ones complement*.

diode   A device used to permit current flow in one direction only, and thus used as a switching device to control current flow in an associated circuit. Originally used to describe a thermionic valve with only two plates (cathode and anode); nowadays diodes are constructed of germanium or silicon crystals.

direct access storage   A *backing store* device in which the *access time* to retrieve items of data is constant, relatively short and independent of the *location* previously *addressed*; i.e., a *device* in which the mode of access is not *serial* as it is with *magnetic tape*. A more detailed examination of direct access storage is given in the general article on *Storage Devices* and the principles of direct access updating are given in the general article on *Updating*.

direct address   Synonymous with *absolute address*.

direct allocation Contrasted with *dynamic allocation*; a system in which the specific *peripheral units* and *storage locations* allocated to a *program* are defined at the time the program is written.

direct code Synonymous with *absolute code*.

direct coding Program *instructions* written using the actual instruction codes and *addresses* employed in the computer's *machine code*.

direct control Relating to a system in which one machine is controlled by another master machine; i.e., the master machine exerts direct control over the other.

direct current amplifier Synonymous with *directly coupled amplifier*.

direct display A *visual display unit* used to display data in graphical or character form direct from *memory*.

direct insert subroutine A term sometimes used when referring to a *subroutine* written as part of a *main program*.

direct instruction Any *instruction* which directly *addresses* an *operand* on which the specified *operation* is to be performed.

directive A statement written as part of a *source program* to instruct or direct the *compiler* in performing the translation to *machine code*. A directive is not usually translated into *object program* instructions. Also known as *control statement*.

directly coupled amplifier An amplifier for magnifying direct voltages, usually employing some form of resistive coupling between stages.
Also known as direct current amplifier.

director An integral part of an *operating system* which has direct control over the allocation of internal resources of the computer, and is usually responsible for the *programs* within the system. For example, control over *virtual machines*.

directory Synonymous with *dictionary*.

direct serial file organization A method of *file* organization on a *direct access* device in which the individual *records* can be selected for processing by number, and *updated* in situ on the device without affecting other records.

dirigible linkage A system of mechanical connectors used in mechanical *analog computers* as part of multiplication and division units.

disable To override or suppress some *hardware* or *software* feature; e.g., to suppress an *interrupt* facility.

disc ◊ *magnetic disk*.

discounted cash flow Discounted cash flow (D C F) is a method for the financial analysis of capital projects. Although its use in this context under this name has spread only in recent years, the principle is essentially the same as underlies the calculation of redemption yields on gilt-edged stocks and the actuarial valuation of pension and life assurance funds.

The data required for D C F calculations are estimates of the amount and timing of all the various cash inflows and outflows associated with the project throughout its estimated life (not forgetting investment grants, tax charges and tax reliefs which the project will generate). No differentiation is made between capital and revenue items and no attention is paid to accounting artifices such as book depreciation or book profit. There are two main ways of applying D C F techniques to such data. In one version the operator, at a standard predetermined rate of interest, discounts each item of inflow and outflow to produce the equivalent flow at a convenient standard datum point of time such as the date at which the first sum of money is to be spent. From the sum of the total discounted values of the inflows, the operator subtracts the sum of the discounted values of the outflows, to obtain the 'net present value' (N P V) of the project. Only if the N P V turns out to be positive will the project earn its keep in the sense that the (varying) amount of cash tied up in it from time to time will be earning more than the rate of interest used for the discounting process.

In the other common version of D C F analysis, the above process is carried out at several rates of interest until, by trial and error and finally interpolating between two adjacent rates, a rate of interest is found at which the N P V is zero. This rate, known as the D C F yield, is the effective rate being earned on the varying amounts of money invested in the project throughout its life. In general, projects with high yields will be preferred to those with low yields but special considerations apply if one project is more risky than another or if the commission of one project excludes the possibility of carrying out another. In the latter case, the amounts of money invested and the time in which the money is invested at the D C F yield may be more important than that yield itself. It would be foolish to embark on a project yielding 15% for one year on £1,000 if by so doing one were prevented from carrying out another project which would yield 14% per annum for 10 years on £10,000, if alternative uses of money were only expected to earn 10%.

Subject to such special features, one may stipulate a cut-off rate of D C F yield, and accept or reject projects according to whether or not the D C F yield exceeds this rate. If the rate chosen were the same as the standard rate of interest used in the N P V version, the two variants would produce the same criterion. This assumes, as is generally the case, that the D C F yield is unique; an objection to D C F yield is that if the cash outflows interleave in time with the inflows, instead of falling exclusively after them, it may be possible for there to be either two D C F yield solutions or none. This phenomenon, which rarely occurs in practice, can be avoided by an extension of the method known as the 'extended yield' method.

The cut-off rate of yield, or standard rate of interest for discounting in N P V version, should be chosen as representing the effective after-tax cost of capital. Ideally this should have regard to how far an individual project can be financed from debt, i.e., relatively cheaply, and how far it must rely on equity capital, either in the form of plough-back earnings or a new equity issue, which is more expensive since equity money has to be obtained in competition with the equity market in general, from which investors expect to receive over the years (by way of dividend and capital appreciation) considerably greater net-of-tax returns than fixed interest investors, to compensate for their added risk. Rates of the order of 8–12% are typically considered appropriate, but the particular company's balance between debt and equity finance and special risk features of the industry or of the project should be taken into account.

With the aid of interest tables, which give the present value of £1 receivable or payable at any future year, for discounting the future cash flows back to the starting date, the various N P Vs required for D C F analysis can be easily calculated by hand; alternatively they lend themselves well to computer operation, and this will be preferred where a large number of analyses are required. There has been considerable controversy on the respective merits of the D C F yield and the N P V at a standard rate of interest; if the former is calculated, the production of the latter involves little extra effort (or programming) and there is much to be said for producing both figures as a matter of routine.

A frequent objection to D C F analysis is that it demands forecasts of cash inflows and outflows many years ahead and that these may be in serious error. However, these uncertainties with regard to the future *are* inevitably reflected in the yield which will be obtained in the event, and it is indeed a virtue of the method, rather than a vice, that it focuses attention on the forecasting problem instead of pushing it under the carpet. By contrast, more commonly used methods such as the 'payback period' (under which the amount of profit expected after the investment has been recouped is completely ignored) or the 'accountants' return on capital' (the ratio of average book profit after depreciation to the initial or average capital invested) can give seriously misleading results, in particular because they ignore the increasingly important effect of different types of tax allowance and their timing.

discrimination instruction   Synonymous with *branch instruction*.

disjunction   Synonymous with *inclusive-or operation*.

disk   ◊ *magnetic disk*.

disk file   ◊ *magnetic disk file*.

disk file controller   A *hardware* device which is concerned with addressing a number of *magnetic disk* units and controlling the transfer of data between these units and the *main store*.

disk store, magnetic   ◊ *magnetic disk*.

disperse   To distribute *items* of data extracted from an *input record* to several *locations* in one or more *output records*.

dispersed intelligence   Describes any system in which programmable processing units (perhaps operated by *microprograms*) are used to perform *application* or *system control* functions remote from the *main frame*. The remote units are connected to the main frame which performs the major central application functions.

dispersion   Synonymous with *not-and operation*.

display   Any operation in which a message or selected data is output to the operator/user for visual inspection. For example, data may be output as a printed report, or in graphical or character form on a *cathode ray tube visual display unit*.

display console   A unit which can be used to interrogate *files* or *areas* of *memory* in order to display *data* being currently processed or stored in a computer. A display console may be equipped with a *cathode ray tube visual display unit* to enable data to be presented in graphical or character form. Such a unit may also be equipped with a *light pen* to enable the user to change the information displayed under *program control*.

display console, message   ◊ *message display console*.

display control   An *interface* unit used to connect a number of *visual display units* to a *central processor*.

display, data analysis   ◊ *data analysis display unit*.

display, inquiry and subscriber   ◊ *inquiry and subscriber display*.

display tube   ◊ *cathode ray tube visual display unit*.

distance   Synonymous with *exclusive-or operation*.   ◊ *signal distance*.

distance, hamming   ◊ *signal distance*.

diversity   Synonymous with *exclusive-or operation*.

dividend An *operand* used in *division*. The dividend is divided by the *divisor* to produce the *quotient* and *remainder*.

divider A device which performs the arithmetic function of *division*.

division An arithmetic operation in which one *operand*, the *dividend*, is divided by another, the *divisor*, to produce the *quotient* and a *remainder*.

division subroutine A *subroutine* written specifically to perform the arithmetic operation of *division*. Usually achieved by an *algorithm* which basically performs repetitive *subtraction*.

divisor An operand used in *division* – the divisor is divided into the *dividend* to produce the *quotient* and *remainder*.

document Any form or voucher containing details of some *transaction*.

documentation – programming A fully tested working computer *program* typically exists as a pattern of flux changes on a magnetic recording medium capable of being loaded into a computer *store* and obeyed. The program may be capable of successfully fulfilling the task it has been designed for, but it will be impossible to use it unless enough people understand the *input* necessary for the program, the types of processing it performs, the output it produces and the way in which the computer must be operated to meet the requirements of the *programmer*. Some form of documentation must accompany a program otherwise it is useless.

Apart from assisting the everyday running of a computer program, documentation serves the following purposes. It enables the work of one programmer to be continued by another if the first programmer leaves. It makes it easier to amend existing programs. It enables programs to be converted to a new machine. It serves as a record of work done and enables the relative performance of programmers to be assessed.

A somewhat idealized picture of the way in which programmers document their work during the production of a program is as follows. Having studied the specification of the program in terms of input data formats, *file formats* and *printout* formats, the programmer produces an outline *flowchart* which shows in general terms the work the program is to do. A flowchart consists of a number of symbols, representing processing stages, linked by arrows which show the flow of control. Once the general logic of the program has been mapped out in *decision tables* or the outline flowchart a more detailed flowchart is produced and here the processes indicated by the symbols cover fewer steps, perhaps only a few program *instructions.* Finally the program is written down on *coding* sheets, punched, *compiled*, tested and incorporated in a working *library* of programs. Compilation will usually produce a listing of the *source program*, which is a valuable item of documentation, and the programmers themselves are responsible for the production of *operating instructions* for the live running of the program.

Documentation produced in this way, as a by-product of program development, is unlikely to be completely satisfactory. First of all the final program will rarely bear much resemblance to the programmer's first ideas on the subject since it is inevitable that errors will be found during program testing. Program testing is a particularly arduous time during program development and the programmer is unlikely to have the time or the inclination to update his preliminary flowcharts as each error is discovered. Here the source listing is much more important, since a new listing will be produced after each round of *debugging* and recompilation.

Probably the best practical method is for the programmer, after ensuring that the program is completely error-free, to produce a completely up-to-date detailed flowchart, possibly with an accompanying explanatory text, and detailed operating instructions. These, together with the latest listing of the source program, form the backbone of the documentation for the program. Input, output and file formats should all be preserved, perhaps on pre-printed forms, unless they are built in to the source program, as in *C O B O L*. The original coding sheets should be amended in the light of errors discovered and carefully preserved, and if the library version of the program were accidentally destroyed, the program could be re-punched from the coding sheets.

All the items of documentation mentioned above should be preserved in a special file, and it should not now be necessary to alter the program or its documentation until a system change requires a program change; since any change to the system should involve acceptance by all appropriate authorities (◊ *Documentation – Systems*) the program documentation should at all times represent precisely the program for a current, fully approved system. A great deal of time and money has been spent by people trying to work out what sort of program they had got on their hands after a year or two of 'minor', undocumented, alterations.

documentation – systems There is no general standard for the document which must be produced by the systems analyst to mark the end of his task in explaining to the *programmer* what is to be programmed. Luckily, though, the job must be done in some form or other (unlike *program documentation*, which is sometimes forgotten) and there are certain things the programmer cannot do without. If possible, the systems analyst will try to think of the specification he produces as something which will do a good deal more than merely tell the programmer what to write, and for this reason the document is often called a *systems definition*: it contains information for those who commissioned the work (a brief outline of the system, with a note on the benefits to be obtained and an introduction schedule); it provides a handbook for those who are going to use the system when the programs are operational (detailed instructions on *paper flow*, coding required, how the output is to be filed), which will include points which may have already been discussed in detail but which need to be set out in a permanent record; and finally it gives the details of the programming requirements, including all *test packs* and expected outputs from the tests.

The analyst should remember that his systems definition will have failed if he has to discuss anything with the programmer once the definition has been handed over, and he will be wise to work to a check-list of the headings he may have to deal with. Various attempts have been made to devise standard forms on which the systems definition must be prepared, but, because space has to be found for so many things which may have no relevance for one system and yet be vital for another, none of these forms is entirely successful. The definition itself falls into two clear parts, however: the systems description in words (to be read by those who need to know the outlines, but who will probably not take very kindly to being presented with a few yards of flowchart); and the program specification in detail. Most systems will include something under each of the following chapter headings in these two parts:

> (a) Authorization
> Definition of terms
> Aims of the system
> Summary of the system
> Benefits
> Planning and introduction schedule
> Equipment utilization
> Change-over procedure
> Clerical procedures
> (b) *Source document* specification
> *Printout* specifications

> *File* specifications
> *Decision tables*
> Systems test data
> Program descriptions

Even though the two halves of the definition are quite distinct, they should never be issued separately, one half for the general reader and one for the programmer. In particular, no definition should ever be passed for programming before being officially accepted by the line managers involved in using the system and by the appropriate *audit* and accounting authorities.

documentation book A collection of all the *documentation* relevant to a particular *program* or *system*.

document, original ◊ *source document*.

docuterm A *data-name* used to designate a *data element* and to indicate the content of that element. Specifically assigned to assist in subsequent *retrieval*.

do nothing instruction An *instruction* which performs no action during the operation of a *program*. Sometimes used to allow for future changes to the program but more often used to complete a set of instructions where the *machine code* system requires instructions to be written in complete groups.
Also known as dummy instruction, null instruction.

dope vector Associated with the processing of *array* structures, and used in *mapping* data stored in a linear medium on to a multi–dimensional structure; a collection of information used as parameters to an algorithm which provides this function.

dot printer An output *printer* in which individual characters are formed by a matrix of wires or styluses.

double buffering The use of two areas of *memory* as *buffer stores* during *input/output* operations involving a particular *peripheral unit*. For example, if data from an input unit is loaded first into one buffer and then into the other, the unit can be driven at its maximum input speed: while the input loads one buffer the *central processor* can process the data in the other.

double-ended amplifier Synonymous with *push-pull amplifier*.

double-length number A number stored in two *words* in *memory* for use in *double-precision arithmetic*.

double-precision arithmetic Relating to arithmetic operations performed with *operands* which each occupy two *words*, allowing greater accuracy to be obtained in the result.

double-precision hardware Special arithmetic units designed to permit greater accuracy in arithmetic results, by allowing a *programmer* to perform arithmetic operations using *double-length numbers* as *operands*. Double-precision hardware may also allow *floating point arithmetic* to be undertaken.

double-precision number Synonymous with *double-length number*.

double-pulse reading A technique for recording *binary digits* in a *magnetic cell*, in which each cell incorporates two regions that can be magnetized in opposite directions. For example, a cell containing a negative followed by a positive region may be used to represent a digit 0, whereas a positive followed by a negative region may represent 1.

double punching A term used to describe the condition where two holes appear in the same *card column* of a *punched card*. More specifically used to denote a punching error in a column of a numeric *field*; with numeric punching it is usual to punch only one position of each card column.

double tape mark A physical indicator consisting of two *tape marks* used to indicate the end of a *volume* or *file*.

down time The period during which a machine is inoperable due to a machine fault.

drift A change in the output of a circuit (e.g. an amplifier) which takes place very slowly. Usually caused by voltage fluctuations or changes in environmental conditions. Circuits can be designed to include correction for drift and are used in *analog computers* to eliminate the errors which would otherwise arise.

drift-corrected amplifier A device used in *analog computers* – a type of amplifier that includes circuits designed to reduce *drift*.

drift error In *analog computers*, an error incurred in a computing device because of *drift*.

drive 1. A general term for any device which physically transports some recording medium, e.g. a *tape transport*. 2. Also applied to any circuit which generates pulses for operating some electro-magnetic device, e.g. a *print member*.

drive, data cell ▷*data cell drive*.

drive, magnetic tape ▷ *tape transport*.

drive pulse In a *core store*, a pulse applied to a storage element to induce a corresponding magnetizing force.

drive winding A coil of wire (known as drive wire) inductively coupled to a *magnetic cell*.

drive wire ▷ *drive winding*.

drop dead halt A *halt* which may be deliberately *programmed* or may be the result of a logical error in programming (e.g. division

by zero) but from which, in either case, there is no recovery.
Also known as a dead halt.

drop, false ◊ *false retrieval.*

drop-in The accidental generation of unwanted *bits* during *reading* from or *writing* to a magnetic *storage device*. Contrasted with *drop-out*.

drop-out A failure when *reading* or *writing* to a magnetic *storage device*. A loss of digits due to some fault condition during a *reading* or *writing* operation. Contrasted with *drop-in*.

drum ◊ *magnetic drum.*

drum mark A special *character* used to signify the termination of a group of characters on a recording *track* of a *magnetic drum*.

dry running Checking the logic and coding of a *program* from a *flowchart* and written *instructions*, using paper to record the results of each step of the operation before actually running the program on the computer.
Also known as *desk checking*. ◊ the general article on *Debugging*.

dual operation A *Boolean operation* whose *truth table* can be obtained from another operation by reversing the value of each element in the table is said to be a dual operation to the other, e.g. the *or operation* is dual to the *and operation*. Contrasted with *complementary operation*.

dual recording In a system which is required to provide *security* and *resilience* to *failure*, two copies of *master files* may be made by updating them at the same time as transactions are received. This method is not to be confused with the method of copying master files at intervals in a job.

ducol punched card system A system in which numbers in the range 0 to 99 are punched as two holes in the *lower curtate* of a single *card column*. The absence of *overpunching* indicates that the higher value digit is the tens digit, whereas the presence of 10 (Y) overpunching denotes that the lower value digit is the tens digit. An 11(X) overpunching is used to denote that a single hole is to be treated as two digits; e.g. 33, 22, 55, etc.

dummy Any feature included in a *routine* to satisfy some logical or structural requirement, but which in a particular circumstance is not used. For example, a *subroutine* may be incorporated in a routine to satisfy some general *software* requirement; in certain applications the programmer may not wish to use the facilities offered by this routine, and may need to write a dummy routine which, as soon as it is entered, will cause an *exit* to the programmer's *main program*.

dummy instruction Synonymous with *do-nothing instruction*.

dump To *write* an area of *memory* to a *peripheral unit*. ◊ *dumping*.

dump and restart When a computer *run* has been terminated at a point earlier than its completion (because of a machine failure, for example) dump and restart techniques ensure that the run can be restarted without the need to go back to the beginning. Various techniques can be used to achieve this, but all conform to a basic pattern: at various points within the *programs* making up the run *dump points* will be present; when the program reaches a dump point, the state of the *memory* and the state of all *peripheral units* is *dumped*. This will involve *writing* memory onto a suitable peripheral, e.g. *magnetic tape* or *paper tape*, and printing or punching details of the point reached by all peripheral units. Normally the program will continue to run after recording the dump details until it reaches the next dump point, when the new state of the program is dumped.

If a program is terminated for any reason – because of machine failure or because the machine is required for other jobs – the operator records the last dump point reached and preserves the dump information produced at that point. When it is required to restart the program, the memory dump is read into *store*, returning it to the state it was in when the dump took place. The operator resets the peripheral units to the condition required by the dump point for example, places unread *punched cards* in the *card reader*) and the program can be restarted at the point immediately after the last dump point occurring before the stoppage.

Manufacturers or users usually write special dump and restart routines which automatically record and restore the peripheral and store information. The technique is particularly useful for inclusion in long or complex jobs where much time might be wasted if the whole job had to be run from the beginning. The selection of suitable dump points is at the discretion of the *programmer* or *systems analyst*: these points may occur at fixed time intervals or at recognized points within a run, e.g. when it is necessary to change *reels* in *multi-reel file* working.

dump check A check performed to verify the accuracy of a *dump*; e.g., by creating *control totals* and/or *hash totals* during *dumping* and to check these totals when the data is re-entered into *memory*.

dump cracking Used to describe the job performance by programmers or engineers in diagnosing faults in *application programs* or in *system management software*. The process entails visually scanning and analysing lists dumped by the computer at the time of the failure, and showing the internal contents of the computer at the time the process failed.

dumping A technique used during the running of a *program* to ensure, in the event of a machine failure or some other interruption of the job, that the program can be resumed without the need to start again from the beginning. This precaution is particularly advisable for long runs using slow *input/output peripheral units*. The technique involves periodically *writing* the program and its data, with the contents of *work areas*, to a *backing store*. The program will incorporate *restart* procedures to enable the program to be resumed from the last *dump point* in the event of an interruption. ✧ general article on *Dump and Restart*.

dump point A point in a *program* at which it is advisable to *write* the program and its data to a *backing store*, as a safeguard against machine failure. Dump points may be chosen to effect dumping at specific time intervals (e.g. every twenty minutes) or at predetermined events in the running of the program.

Also known as check point. ✧ *dumping* and general article on *Dump and Restart*.

dump, storage Synonymous with *memory dump*.

duodecimal number system A *number system* in which each digit position has a *radix* of twelve.

duplex A system which allows transmission in both directions simultaneously; compare with *simplex* and *half-duplex*.

duplex channel A *channel* allowing simultaneous transmission in both directions.

duplex computer system An *on-line* configuration in which two computer systems are employed, one acting as a standby to safeguard against the failure of the other.

duplex console In *on-line* computer systems, a *console* which can be switched to control two computers so that one or the other may be connected on line.

duplexing Any system of *data transmission* which permits simultaneous two-way transmission between terminals.

duplicate To copy data from one *location* within *store* to another, without losing or mutilating the data in its original form.

duplicated records *Records* which are exact copies of other records and which are retained to safeguard against the loss or mutilation of the original records. (But ✧ *duplicate record*.)

duplicate record An unwanted *record* occurring in a *file* and having the same *key* as another record in the same file. (But ◊ *duplicated records*.)

duplicating card punch Synonymous with *reproducer*.

duplication An exact copy of a *file* or group of *records*; e.g., a copy of a *paper tape, pack* of *punched cards* or *reel* of *magnetic tape*.

duplication check A check that requires a particular calculation to be performed twice, using a different method on each occasion, the two *results* being compared. A form of *arithmetic check*.

dyadic Boolean operation A *Boolean operation* where the result is determined by the *bit patterns* of two *operands* and the *truth table* of the *operator*.
Also known as binary Boolean operation.

dyadic operation An *operation* utilizing two *operands*. Also known as *binary operation*.

dynamic allocation 1. A method adopted on *multiprogramming* computers for assigning *main store* and *peripheral units* to a *program*. Usually performed under control of an *executive program*, and designed to permit complete flexibility in the *loading* of programs dependent upon the peripherals and storage available at any one time. As each program is compiled a series of statements, sometimes known as a *request slip*, is generated indicating the requirements of the particular program. Before the program is loaded the *executive program* reads the request slip and ascertains whether the program can be accepted. If it can, the executive program allocates the appropriate peripherals and main storage to the program. The essence of the system is that the *programmer* need not specify the particular peripherals he requires, but only the type of peripheral and thereafter he uses *symbolic names* to address the units in the program. At *run time* the executive program allocates specific units of the desired type to the program. 2. An extension of the allocation system described in 1 above, concerns the assigning of *magnetic tape files* to a program. Here, the programmer specifies, by means of the *header labels*, the particular tape files processed by his program. The operator can then load these files on to any of the available *tape decks* at run time. When a program requires to open a particular file the executive program searches all unallocated decks to find a tape with the appropriate label. When it does so, the deck is allocated to the program. ◊ *multiprogramming*.

dynamic allocation (of memory) The system used in *multiprogramming* whereby an *executive program* allocates areas of *memory* to a *program* as and when the program is loaded. In such a system several programs may be operating in memory at the same time. Before any program can be accepted into the system the executive program has to check that sufficient *main storage* is available for running the program. This mode of operation requires that all programs must be written using *symbolic addresses*, and *absolute addresses* are automatically generated only when a particular program has been accepted and is being loaded into *memory*. At any time during the operation of programs the executive program may re-assign areas of memory to achieve a more efficient utilization of storage *locations*; this activity will usually take place when one program is completed, whereupon the executive program will attempt to create the largest possible free area of contiguous storage locations. ⬦ *multiprogramming*.

dynamic buffering A technique used in handling messages entering a system or process in which messages may be of variable length and frequency. The *storage* area allocated as a buffer to receive messages is extended or contracted by adding or removing units of storage while messages are arriving.

dynamic check A check performed on the operation of an *analog* device and on the *set-up* of a problem, by comparing results obtained in the *compute mode* with some previously computed values. Also known as dynamic test.

dynamic dump A *dump* carried out during the execution of a *program*.

dynamic error An error incurred in an *analog* device resulting from an inadequate frequency response of the equipment.

dynamicizer A *logic element* which converts a set of *digits* represented by the spatial arrangement of *bits* in *store* into a sequence of signals occurring in time. Contrasted with *staticizer*.

dynamic memory Synonymous with *dynamic store*.

dynamic memory relocation Relating to a characteristic of *multiprogramming* computers, in which *memory* areas are automatically allocated and re-allocated to *programs* as and when any program is *loaded* or deleted from memory. ⬦ *dynamic allocation (of memory)*.

dynamic stop The use of a *branch instruction* to create a *program loop* which is in turn used to signify an error condition.

dynamic storage allocation ⬦ *dynamic allocation (of memory)*.

dynamic store 1. Pertaining to a *regenerative store* in which information is retained by continually circulating a signal (⬦ *delay line store*). Essentially a store in which information can be obtained at fixed intervals in a cycle. Also known as dynamic memory.

2. Sometimes used to denote any form of storage using a moving magnetic medium.

dynamic subroutine A *subroutine* which requires *parameters* to specify the particular action to be performed each time it is entered. Contrasted with *static subroutine*.

dynamic test Synonymous with *dynamic check*.

E

E 13 B   A type fount used for *character recognition machines*.

E A M   Acronym for *electrical accounting machines*.

E B R   Acronym for *electron beam recording*.

eccles jordan circuit   Synonymous with *flip-flop*.

echo check   A *check* on the accuracy of *data transmission* in which the data transmitted is returned to the point from which it was sent and compared with the original data.

econometrics   Applying the techniques of the empirical sciences in order to establish significant relationships in economic and statistical data, and to use these relationships as a basis for predictions. The use of computers in econometrics lies mainly in their ability to analyse large volumes of data, and also to construct and test economic and *mathematical models*.

edge, card leading   ◊ *leading edge.*

edge, card trailing   ◊ *trailing edge.*

edge-notched card   A card containing holes in one or more edges used in a simple mechanical search technique: each hole position is given a coded significance and for particular cards the holes are turned into notches by the removal of the part of the card between hole and edge. Particular cards may now be mechanically selected by the insertion of a long needle in a hole position and the raising of the card *pack* to allow notched cards to remain unraised while unwanted cards remain in the main pack on the needle.

Also known as margin-notched card. Contrasts with *margin-punched card.*

edge-punched card   ◊ *margin-punched card.*

edit   To arrange data into the format required for subsequent processing. Editing may involve deletion of data not required, conversion of *fields* to a machine format (e.g., *value fields* converted to *binary*) and preparation of data for subsequent output, e.g., *zero-suppression*.

E D P   Acronym for *electronic data processing*.

E D P M   Acronym for *electronic data processing machine*.

E D S   Acronym for *exchangeable disk store*.

effective address   An *address* actually used by the computer for executing an *instruction*, as opposed to the address written in the *program*. This is normally the result of *instruction modification*, and refers to the address after modification has taken place.

effective instruction The *instruction* performed as the result of altering a *basic instruction* during *program modification*. Also known as actual instruction.

effective time Time during which a computer is being used for work which produces useful results. This includes *productive time*, *program development time* and time used for demonstrations, training, *housekeeping*, etc. (*incidentals time*). Does not include time spent on operating delays and *idle time*. Related to *serviceable time*, contrasted with *ineffective time*.

efficiency ◊ *serviceability*.

eighty-column card A *punched card* with eighty vertical *card columns*.

either-or operation Synonymous with *inclusive-or operation*.

elapsed time The total apparent time taken by a process, as measured by the time between the apparent beginning and the apparent end of the process. This may well be longer than the actual time taken by the process itself. ◊ *real-time clock*.

electrical accounting machine Any electro-mechanical device used in *data processing*, other than computer equipment. Such devices include *tabulators, calculators, balancers*, etc.

electron beam recording A method of utilizing an electron beam to write computer-generated data direct to microfilm.

electronic Related to the branch of science concerned with the behaviour of electrons. A device is termed electronic if it depends mainly for its operation on the use of thermionic valves, vacuum or gas tubes, or solid state devices such as transistors.

electronic calculating punch A device which reads data from a *punched card*, performs a sequence of arithmetic calculations on the data and punches the result into another punched card.

electronic data processing *Data processing* performed by *electronic* machines; the methods and techniques associated with such processing. The term is usually contrasted with *automatic data processing*, which does not involve electronic machines.

electronic data processing machine Any machine or device used in *data processing* which uses *electronic* circuitry either wholly or mainly in order to perform arithmetic and logical operations.

electronic differential analyser An *analog computer* designed for solving differential equations.

electronic switch A *switch* [1] which makes use of an *electronic* circuit, enabling the switching action to take place at high speed.

electrostatic printer A printing device in which the parts of paper which are to be printed are electrostatically charged, and attract a fine dust which is then fused to the paper by the application of heat to form the printed character.

electrostatic storage A *storage device* which uses the presence of an electrostatic charge to represent data, e.g. the surface of a *cathode ray tube*.

element 1. A member of a collection of items which cannot itself be subdivided into any constituent parts which may themselves be considered as members of the collection, e.g. the elements of a computer *word* are *bits*, while the elements of a *record* may be *words*. 2. A circuit which can be considered as a single entity in so far as it performs a unique function, can be combined with other elements to perform more complex functions, but cannot itself be divided into individual components. ◊ *logic element*.

elementary item A *C O B O L* expression for an item of data which contains no subsidiary items.

element, combinational logic ◊ *combinational logic element*.

element, digit delay ◊ *digit delay element*.

element, equivalent-to ◊ *equivalence element*.

element, logical ◊ *logic element*.

element, nand ◊ *not-and element*.

element, non-equivalence ◊ *exclusive-or element*.

element, non-equivalent-(to) ◊ *exclusive-or element*.

element, not ◊ *negator*.

eleven position ◊ *Y-position* and *X-position*.

eleven punch ◊ *Y-punch* and *X-punch*.

else rule In a set of operations depending on certain specified conditions being satisfied, the else rule defines the operations to be carried out if none of the specifically described conditions occurs.

emitter A device in *punched card* machines for generating signals in order to simulate the presence of holes not actually punched.

emitter pulse One of a set of *pulses* which, in *punched card equipment*, define a particular *row* within the *columns* of a card. ◊ *selective digit emitter*.

emitter, selective digit ◊ *selective digit emitter*.

empty medium A *medium* which has been prepared to accept information by having some preliminary data recorded in it, e.g. *feed holes* punched in *paper tape*, *magnetic tape* with *header labels* already written. Contrasted with *virgin medium*. ◊ *data carrier*.

emulated executive A form of *emulation* in which *software* is used to represent an *executive program* of a different computer type.

emulation   The process of using a computer to operate on data and code produced for a different computer type; special *hardware* and *software* are used to represent the computer for which the work was originally implemented. ◊ *Transition*.

emulator   A *hardware* device (but sometimes *software* is used) designed as part of a particular range of computers, but used to run jobs originally prepared for another range of computers. For example, used as *bridging* from one *generation* of computers to another generation. ◊ *Transition*.

enable pulse   A *digit pulse* which together with a *write pulse* is sufficiently strong to alter the state of a *magnetic core*, but which is not of sufficient strength to do so on its own.

enabling signal   A *signal* which allows an *operation* already set up to take place.

encode   To represent data in digital form as a series of impulses denoting *characters* or *symbols*. To facilitate *automatic processing* by the arrangement of facts into a coded form suitable for subsequent processing.

encoder   1. A device which converts signals into a coded digital format suitable for a particular processing stage. Contrasted with *decoder*. 2. A *keyboard* operated machine for printing characters onto documents in the stylized form necessary for subsequent reading by *character recognition* equipment.

end-around carry   A *carry* generated in the *most significant character* position which causes a carry into the *least significant character* position.

end-around shift   Synonymous with *logical shift*.

end mark   A *code* used to signal that the end of an item of information has been reached.

end of data marker   A *character* or *code* which indicates that the end of all data held on a particular *storage unit* (e.g. a *reel* of *magnetic tape*) has been reached. This should not be confused with *end of file marker*.

end of field marker   An additional *data element* which indicates that the end of a *field* (usually a *variable length* field) has been reached. Also known as *flag*.

end of file indicator   Synonymous with *end of file marker*.

end of file marker   A *marker* which can be recognized by *hardware* as well as *software*, which indicates that the end of a *file* has been reached.
Also known as end of file indicator or end of file spot.

end of file routine A *routine*, either provided by a *housekeeping package* or user-written, which provides the special processing required when the last *record* of a *file* of data has been reached. This may involve checking *control totals* and *counts*.

end of file spot Synonymous with *end of file marker*.

end of first file section label A *record* used to define the end of first *section* of a *serial file* stored on *magnetic tape*.

end-of-job card A *punched card* (placed at the end of a *pack* of cards used as input to a *job*) which informs the *program* that the job has been completed and usually initiates some form of further action such as starting the next job.

end-of-message A *character* or *code* which indicates that the end of a message has been reached.

end of record word A *word* which terminates a *record*, usually in a special format so that the end of the record can be identified.

end of run The completion of a *program* or programs forming a *run*, usually signalled by a *message* or *indicator* [2] from the program.

end of run routine A *routine* provided by the programmer to deal with various *housekeeping* operations before a *run* is terminated, e.g. *rewinding* tapes, printing *control totals*.

end of tape marker A *tape mark* which indicates the physical end of a *reel* of *magnetic tape*, usually by means of a strip of reflective material attached to the tape.
Also known as destination warning marker.

end of tape routine A *routine*, either provided by a *housekeeping package*, or written by a user, which provides the special processing required when the last *record* on a *reel* of *magnetic tape* has been reached. This may involve such operations as checking *control totals* and *counts*, and opening *continuation reels* if required.

end printing A type of *interpreting* of data on *punched cards* in which the printing occurs across the end of the card.

endwise feed A *card feed* designed to accept *punched cards* placed in the *hopper* so that one of the ends of the card enters the *card track* first. Contrasted with *sideways feed*.

engineering time, scheduled ◊ *scheduled engineering time*.

engineer's journal A *file* designed to receive information from a computer system providing the maintenance staff with details of the use of the system, thus assisting in diagnosis of faults and analysis of computer utilization.

enquiry ◊ *inquiry*.

entry 1. The *address* of the first *instruction* in a *program* to be obeyed; also the first instruction of a *subroutine*. 2. A unit of information, either *input* or *output;* an item of data in a list or table. Also used for *statement* in a *source language.*

entry block Part of *store* into which an *entry* [2] or unit of information is placed on *input.*

entry condition A condition which must be specified before a *program* or a *routine* is entered. Entry conditions may include *parameter*-specified values for the *operands* to be used by the routine, the setting of *switches* to the state expected of them when first tested, and in the case of *subroutines* will include the *link* information giving the *address* of the instruction in the main routine to which the subroutine is to *exit.*

Also known as initial condition.

entry instruction The *instruction* obeyed when *entry* [1] is first made to a *routine.* Some routines may have several *entry points,* and depending upon conditions at the time of entry one of these points will be entered.

entry, keyboard ◇ *keyboard entry and inquiry.*

entry point The first *instruction* in a *routine* or *program* to be obeyed. A routine or program may have several entry points corresponding to different *entry conditions* or operations to be performed.

enveloped file A *file* containing information established on one type of computer, but provided with special *labels* enabling it to be *catalogued* and handled on a different type of computer.

E O F Acronym for *end of file.*

E O R Acronym for *end of run.*

equality circuit Synonymous with *equality unit.*

equality unit A device which can accept as *input* two numbers and generate an *output signal* of 1 if these numbers are equal and 0 if they are unequal.

equal zero indicator An *indicator* which is set if the result of a calculation or test is zero, and which can be tested by a *branch instruction.*

equipment compatibility ◇ *compatibility.* The situation in which *programs* and data are interchangeable between different types of equipment.

equipment, data transmission ◇ *data transmission equipment.*

equipment, electronic data processing ◇ *electronic data processing machine.*

equipment failure Any *hardware* fault that prevents the completion of a job.

equipment, input ◇ *Input Devices.*

161

equipment, on-line ⋄ *on-line.*

equipment, output ⋄ *Output Devices.*

equipment, peripheral ⋄ *peripheral units.*

equivalence A logical relationship in which two statements are said to be equivalent if they are both true or both false. ⋄ *logic*, also *Boolean algebra.*

equivalence element A *logic element* in which the relationship between two *binary input signals* and a single binary *output signal* is defined by the *equivalence operation*. In effect, the element produces an output signal of 1 when the two input signals are the same and 0 when they differ.

Also known as equivalent-to element, coincidence element.

equivalence operation A *Boolean operation* on two *operands* (p and q), the *result* (r) being given by the table below.

operands		result
p	q	r
1	1	1
1	0	0
0	1	0
0	0	1

This operation is also known as match, bi-conditional, if and only if operation.

equivalent binary digits The number of *bits* necessary to represent each member of a set of characteristics by a unique *binary number*, e.g. in order to represent each letter of the alphabet (i.e. 26 elements) five bits are necessary, since 26 in binary notation is 11010.

equivalent-to element Synonymous with *equivalence element.*

erasable storage A medium of *store* which can be used repeatedly because new information *overwrites* or erases information previously occupying its *location*. Examples are *magnetic tape, magnetic drum.*

erase The replacing of *data* in a medium of *store* with some uniform code representing null data. This may be zeros or space characters, or some suitable code.

erase character Synonymous with *ignore character.*

erase head The device on a *tape transport* which erases data before new data is written (⋄ *write*) to the tape.

error Any condition in which the expected results of an operation are not achieved. Errors may be of two main types, *software* or *program* errors and *hardware* errors. The former are errors in the writing or specification of programs and system, and the latter are caused by the malfunctioning of equipment.

error character Synonymous with *ignore character*.

error checking code A general term for all *error detecting codes* and *error correcting codes*.

error code The identification of a particular *error* by means of a *character* or *code*. The error code can be printed out as information that an error has occurred or can be associated with the erroneous item of data in *store* so that the data may be ignored or dealt with in a specific manner when subsequently processed.

error correcting code An *error detecting code* designed so that it is in some cases possible to recognize not only that an error has occurred, but also what the correct code should have been. An example will be found under *Hamming code*.

error correction routine A *routine* designed to detect and correct errors on *files* of data.

error detecting code A *code* in which the representation of each *character* is constructed according to specific rules. Certain combinations of the elements out of which the set of characters is constructed will not conform to these rules; such combinations are known as *forbidden characters* and can be recognized and rejected as errors if they occur in a message.

Also known as self-checking code. An example will be found under *Hamming code*.

error detection routine A *routine* designed to check data items for validity and to detect errors. ✧ *validity checking*.

error diagnostics The checking of *source language statements* for errors during *compilation* and the printing of error messages identifying the errors made.

error interrupts An *interrupt* which occurs as a result of a *program* or *hardware* error, causing a message to be printed indicating the error condition, and the *suspension* of the program in which the error has occurred.

error list A list produced by a *compiler* indicating incorrect or invalid *instructions* in a *source program*.

error message A *message* output by *program* indicating the incidence and type of *error* which has occurred.

error range The range of values for an item of data which will cause an *error* condition if the item falls within the range.

error rate In *data transmission*, the ratio of the total number of transmission *errors* to the total volume of data transmitted.

error report A list of error conditions generated during the execution of a particular *program*; e.g., errors caused by incorrect or unmatched data.

error routine A *routine* which is entered whenever an *error* is detected. An error routine may output an *error message*, attempt to correct the error, repeat the process which caused it or perform any other required action.

error tape A *magnetic tape* onto which *errors* are written for subsequent listing and analysis.

escape character A *character* which indicates that the following character belongs to a different *character set* from the preceding characters.

evaluating a new system The last step in the design of any new system should always be an attempt to evaluate it in comparison with the system it will be replacing, and management should ensure that no new system is implemented until such an evaluation has been made: too many systems have been introduced on a wave of enthusiasm and followed closely by a trough of depression as expense and effort rise to keep the system operating. The two systems should be compared under two main headings, cost and information availability.

In order to evaluate a system's cost it will be necessary to establish a breakdown, for each area affected by the system, of the wages and salaries, equipment, supplies and overheads. It should always be possible to do this fairly accurately both for the new system and the old one, and a comparison of the respective costs can then be made. Since likely savings in the future will be a key point (the introduction of new equipment probably being a heavy initial expense) it is often useful to indicate a date when the installation costs of the new system will have been covered by savings. It is also important to realize that the replacement of several low-paid staff by fewer but better-paid staff is not necessarily a saving.

In considering information availability and quality it is essential to relate it to the need for readily available and better quality information. An inexperienced systems analyst will always try to justify an expensive system on the grounds that it provides information that was never obtainable before and that this may result in a saving of thousands, but such claims should always be very carefully examined; above all it must be clear that a system which results in the handling of mountains of irrelevant data by highly-paid executives will probably result in a loss rather than a saving.

Evaluation of a new system may well result in the eradication of unnecessary information rather than its proliferation. In any event it will have involved a careful assessment of the disadvantages of the system which will have been salutary for all concerned.

even parity check A *parity check* in which the number of ones (or zeros) in a group of *binary digits* is expected to be even. Contrasted with *odd parity check*.

event 1. Any occurrence which affects an item on a *file* of data, e.g. a purchase, sale, issue, etc. 2. In *PERT* an event is a defined occurrence which terminates one *activity* and commences another. ◊ general article on *Critical Path Method*. 3 A signal generated by *hardware* or *software* indicating to the *operating system* a recognizable condition, e.g. hardware failure, or completion of an internal activity.

except gate Synonymous with *exclusive-or element*.

exception principle system A computer system designed so that normally only situations deviating from expected standards are reported, while results falling within expected limits are not reported.

exception reporting Related to an *information system* in which the *exception principle system* is used.

excess fifty A *binary code* in which a number n is represented by the binary equivalent of $n + 50$.

excess-three code A *binary code* in which a number n is represented by the binary equivalent of $n + 3$.

exchange In a *transaction processing* system, a message received by the *T.P. program* in the *main frame* and the response given by the program to the originating *terminal* constitute an exchange. An exchange may provoke further messages which in total constitute a complete *transaction*.

exchangeable disk store A *backing store* device in which *magnetic disks* are loaded into a *disk transport* mechanism as a unit; e.g. as a capsule containing say six disks. A capsule can be replaced by an operator during operation of the computer and individual capsules containing particular *files* can be retained in a *library* until required for use with a particular *program* or *suite* of programs.

exchange, remote computing system ◊ *remote computing system exchange*.

exclusive-or element A *logic element* in which the relationship between the two *binary* input signals and the single binary output signal is defined by the *exclusive-or operation*.
Also known as except gate.

exclusive-or operation A *logical operation* applied to two *oper-*

execute

ands, which will produce a result depending on the *bit patterns* of the operands and according to the following rules for each bit position.

Operands		Result
p	q	r
0	0	0
1	0	1
0	1	1
1	1	0

For example, operating on the following 6-bit operands

$$p = 110110$$
$$q = 011010$$
$$r = 101100$$

⊘ *Boolean algebra.*
Also known as anticoincidence operation, distance, diversity, exjunction, non-equivalence operation, symmetric difference.

execute To perform the operations specified by a *routine* or *instruction*. Also to cause a specified instruction to be performed by some external action, e.g. setting a *switch* from a *console*. ⊘ *execution.*

execute cycle Synonymous with *execute phase.*

execute phase That part of a *control cycle* in which an *instruction*, having been *accessed*, is performed.
Also known as execute cycle, execution cycle.

execution The *execution* of a *program* occurs when its compiled *object code* is run in the computer to perform its intended *application* function.

execution cycle Synonymous with *execute phase.*

execution time The time taken to complete the cycle of events required to perform an *instruction*.

executive program An executive program, or executive system, usually consists of a number of complex *routines* which reside wholly or partly in the *main memory* of a computer in order to monitor and supervise certain basic control functions. In *time sharing* computers the executive program is usually considered as part of the computer's *hardware*, since the equipment cannot generally be operated without such a program. An executive program might for example be employed to control the following functions: to handle and interpret all control messages and signals received from, or transmitted to, the *operator's console*; monitor and supervise the *time sharing* system to ensure that *peripheral units* can be simultaneously operated in an *asynchronous* manner, thus permitting all parts of the *hardware* system to be employed with maximum efficiency; and to control the simultaneous operation of several programs within a *multiprogramming* environment, including automatically switching control between one program and another, according to specified priorities, and to permit automatic *interrupts* to service *peripheral* units and other events.

Within a multiprogramming system an executive program should also control the *dynamic allocation* of peripheral units and areas of memory to programs, including automatically reallocating programs during processing in order to optimize the availability of memory for further programs. Protection against interference between programs is another common feature of executive programs, and also the automatic logging of program times and console *events*.

In some systems the executive control functions extend to the automatic control of communications circuits to handle simultaneous *input* and *output signals* on many different lines. In large computer systems the executive functions also include provision for *graceful degradation* in the event of equipment failures. In addition an executive system may control the automatic running of programs presented to the system as a set of jobs, thus relieving the operating staff of the problem of organizing schedules.

The functions outlined above are generally provided through a close interaction of hardware facilities in the computer with the routines of the executive system.

Executive programs are also known as supervising systems, *monitor systems* and *operating systems*.

executive system Synonymous with *executive program*.

exit The last *instruction* in a *routine* or *program*, usually a *branch* from the routine into another part of the program or into a control routine.

exjunction Synonymous with *exclusive-or operation*. ♢ *Boolean algebra*.

exponent The power to which a quantity is raised; e.g., in the expression 2^{23} the exponent is 23. ♢ *characteristic, floating point representation*.

expression The symbolic representation of a mathematical or logical statement, e.g. $A+B$, P/Q, O R(A AND B) (C AND D).

extended basic mode   *Basic mode* is a class of *interactive* processing between a *terminal* and its *main frame* processor. Extended basic mode provides additional functions allowing the basic mode and the transfer of bulk data.

extended time scale   Synonymous with *slow time scale*.

exterior label   A written or typed identification on the outside of a *reel* of *magnetic tape*, contrasted with *tape label*.

external delays time   In accounting for the effective utilization of a computer system one classifies time lost according to various factors. External delays time is time lost because of circumstances outside the reasonable control of the user or manufacturer, e.g. power failure.

external memory   Synonymous with *external store*.

external store   A *backing store* which is under the control of, but not necessarily permanently connected to, a *central processor*, and which can hold data or *programs* in a form acceptable to it, e.g. *magnetic tape, direct access store*.
Also known as external memory.

extract   To remove a selected part from an item or set of items of information.

extract instruction   An *instruction* which will place selected parts of an item of information into a specified *location*. ⟡ *masking*.

extractor   Synonymous with *mask*.

extrapolation   Extrapolation is the name given to the process of deducing a value greater or less than all given values of a function or graph assuming that a projection of the function or graph would continue to satisfy the same relationships as the part whose values are known. In everyday life almost everyone extrapolates; at a very early age we answer such questions as 'If two eggs cost five pence how much do a dozen eggs cost?' Most of us will quite happily have given the answer of 30p although now in later life we might not be surprised to find that a shop might well sell eggs at two for 5p and 28p a dozen. Here an important point emerges; we have extrapolated assuming the same conditions to hold as held in the values given. There is no statistical evidence to justify this; it is made as a basic assumption to our manner of dealing with the problem.

One of the simplest, and possibly most commonly used, methods of extrapolating is by 'regression techniques'. Regression technique assumes that the relationship between a variable and one, or several, other variables is linear. In the former case it is called 'simple' regression, in the latter 'multiple' regression. In both cases the treatment is the same in that we take a set of 'points' on a graph and find the straight line which gives the best 'fit' to these points. This line is called the 'regression line'; further points may be read off from the line either in the interval for which points are known or before or after that interval.

There are various techniques for finding the best fit of a curve, but an adequate description of these is not possible here. The 'least squares' method is frequently used although there are differing ways of applying this.

In order to extrapolate from a set of observed values one must first ensure that to the best of one's knowledge one has chosen variables which are at least to some extent reasonably well related; it would be pointless trying to correlate time taken to sort a *file* of *magnetic tape records* to the number of records without first ensuring that the same number of *tape decks* were always being used, and that the record size was always constant. Having made sure that one's assumptions are, as far as one can tell, reasonable, one must also remember that results obtained are, at best, a guide to actual future observations, an indication of a trend which may assist in the forecast of a future result.

F

face 1. In *optical character recognition*, the term used to distinguish character sets with different relative dimensions. 2. Of a *punched card*, that side which bears the printing: synonymous with *card face*.

face down feed Describes the attitude in which a *punched card* is placed in a *hopper* and moved along a *card track*; the *card face* of a punched card is that side which bears the printing. Contrasted with *face up feed*.

face up feed Describes the attitude in which a *punched card* is placed in a *hopper* and moved along a *card track*; the *card face* of a punched card is that side which bears the printing. Contrasted with *face down feed*.

facsimile The process of scanning any fixed graphite material so that the image is converted into electric signals which are transmitted and used at a receiving station to produce a recorded likeness of the original.

Also known as fax.

facsimile posting The process of transferring a line of information from one group of records to another, e.g. from a listing of transactions prepared on an accounting machine to a ledger.

facsimile telegraph A telegraph system for the transmission of pictures, maps, diagrams, etc.

factor A *data element* which is one of the *operands* in an *arithmetical operation*.

fail safe Relating to a system which is able to close itself down in a controlled manner in the event of a serious *failure*. ⟡ *fail soft*.

fail soft Synonymous with *fail safe*, but perhaps a more pertinent phrase in view of the characteristic way in which *fail soft* systems are able to mitigate the effects of serious *failure*. The object is to terminate the system or reduce it to a low level of activity without loss or disruption of data, until the failure can be corrected.

failure Any disruption of a computer system caused by a defect in the *hardware* or system *software*. Failures can be of several types and have different levels of seriousness.

failure logging The automatic recording of those machine faults which can be detected by *program*, giving rise to corrective procedures, e.g. the repeating of attempts to *read* or *write magnetic tape*.

failure rate A measure of the number of *failures* occurring in a specific period of time. The time period may be expressed as hours of serviceable time, or over a longer period of weeks or months of calendar time. To appreciate the significance of the failure rate, it is necessary to classify types of failure and the time period concerned.

failure recovery The re-establishment of system service following a *failure*. It may imply correction of the failure, but perhaps allows the service to be resumed after the system has been *reconfigured* to avoid the faulty condition.

false drop Synonymous with *false retrieval.*

false error A condition arising when the system signals an *error* condition but no error in fact exists.

false retrieval In *information retrieval*, an error in specifying the criteria for selection causing an unwanted item of data to be selected.
Also known as false drop.

fast-access storage *Store* with relatively rapid *access time*; whether or not a particular storage device is described as fast depends on the relative speeds of other devices in the system.

fast time scale. When the *time scale factor* in an *analog* computer is less than one, the operation is said to be on a fast time scale. Contrasted with *slow time scale.*

fault The failure of any physical component (*hardware* or *software*) of a system to operate in an expected manner.

fault time Synonymous with *down time.*

feasibility studies A feasibility study is research into the possibility of developing a solution to a problem. In computer terms this may mean placing an order for the appropriate *configuration* and the research may be primarily an appraisal of the current situation of *hardware* and *software*, leading to the choice of equipment. It may also be an assessment of whether a particular area of a company's activities should utilize a computer already used by the company. Some comments on this type of study are given at the end of this article.

The *raison d'être* of the feasibility study should be that there is reasonable doubt whether the problem is capable of solution within an acceptable time-scale and budget, or at the very least whether solution A or B is the better one. Any study which begins on firmer ground is not a feasibility study, it is phase one of an actual project. Probably over ninety per cent of systems design is imitative and the feasibility of the proposals is self-evident; however, the economic benefits may be more apparent than real; the originator of a real feasibility study should be moved by a vision of Utopia, on the other hand he should place a limit on the time and resources that may be expended before a return on the investment must be achieved.

An early example of a well-conducted computer feasibility study was the banks' preparation for automation through M I C R encoding of documents. Computer typesetting is another application which grew from a whole series of feasibility studies. *Information retrieval* has been the subject of numerous investigations, for instance the world's police forces have tried for years to perfect a system for the automatic indexing and retrieval of fingerprints.

Nowadays it is customary for some form of feasibility study to be carried out for every large project which affects the national interest: for example a conversion to the metric system. Even though the estimates of cost and benefits are sometimes wide of the mark such studies are an essential feature of the democratic process, providing an opportunity for debate and allowing priorities to establish themselves. The computer has become an essential tool in conducting these feasibility studies, both through the analysis of survey data and through *simulation* techniques.

As indicated earlier, feasibility studies are also made to establish whether a computer should be used in solving some particular problem. It is very important that such a study be made as crisply and tidily as possible, and it often helps if the study is carried out within a formal framework. For example, a representative of the problem area should be formally appointed to work with the man (often a systems analyst) conducting the study, and terms of reference should include a statement of the nature and type of application to be studied, the objectives and expected duration of the study, and a clear identification of the areas to be investigated. Those conducting the study will generally examine permanent records within the problem area; interview staff handling the work; observe and measure the work; summarize the facts to provide a broad statement of requirements of a new system; consider possible solutions; and provide an estimate of the cost of completing a full systems investigation. This information should provide those who called for the study with enough information to decide whether or not the project is feasible.

feed To cause data to be entered into a computer for processing; a device for so doing.

feedback The use of information produced at one stage in a series of operations as input at another stage. In *cybernetics* feedback is the method by which the result of a *controlling* operation is used as part of the data on which the next controlling operation is based, enabling a system to monitor its own actions and take self-correcting steps.

feed holes Holes punched in paper or card to enable it to be driven by sprockets. The holes have no significance in themselves but are also sometimes used for indexing in, for example, *paper tape* (where other driving techniques are used instead of the sprocket wheel). Also known as *sprocket holes*.

feed pitch The distance between *feed holes*.

feed track That *track* of a *paper track* which contains the *feed holes*.

femto- Prefix denoting one thousand million-millionth or 10^{-15}.

ferrite core A small piece of ring-shaped magnetic material, capable of receiving and holding an electromagnetic charge, used in *core store*.

field A subdivision of a *record* containing a unit of information. For example, a payroll record might have the following fields: clock number, gross pay, deductions, net pay.

field length The size of a *field*, in terms of the units in which the *record* is composed, e.g. on a *punched card* record, field length is measured in *card columns*, and on a *magnetic tape* record the field length may be measured in *characters* or *words*.

file An organized collection of *records*. The relationship between records on a file may be that of common purpose, format or data source, and the records may or may not be *sequenced*.

file conversion The process of converting *data files* from one format to another; e.g. manually-kept records to *punched card* files, or files created on a magnetic medium for use on one type of computer to files for use on a computer of a different type.

file extent A contiguous group of *tracks* on a particular *file volume*; usually representing a *section* of a file.

file identification A *code* devised to identify a *file*. The purpose of file identification is to ensure that no confusion arises between files containing different data, and to provide a means by which *programs reading* and *writing* files may check that the correct files are input and output. The method of file identification varies and depends on the type of file and medium of *store* being used. ◊ *file label, tape label.*

file label A type of *file identification* in which a file has as its first *record* or *block* a set of *characters* unique to the file. Information in the file label may consist of a description of the file content, the file *generation number* and, if the file is on *magnetic tape*, the *reel number*, and date written to tape. Also known as *header label.*

file layout A description of the organization of the contents of a *file*, usually part of a *systems definition* or *program specification.*

file maintenance Modifying the contents of a *file* by adding, deleting or correcting *records*. Maintenance is distinguished from *updating*: a file is *updated* in order to reflect real changes in the *events* recorded on the file; maintenance is performed in order to make sure that the file contents do in fact accurately record the required data.

file name The set of *alphanumeric characters* used to identify and describe a *file* in a *file label.*

file, on-line central ◊ *on-line central file.*

file organization Relates to the way in which *data elements* and/or *records* are mapped on to the physical *storage* medium used for a particular *file*. The file organization method may impose a particular method of file access, e.g. *index sequential, serial*, or *random* access.

file print A *printout* of the contents of a *file* stored on some *storage device*, usually for the purpose of aiding *debugging.*

file processing File processing involves all operations connected with the creation and use of *files*. These operations include: *creation, validation, comparing, collating, sorting* and *merging.*

file protection The prevention of accidental *overwriting* of data *files* before they are released for use. File protection can be by *hardware*, e.g., through the use of *file protection rings* on *magnetic tape*, or by causing a *program* to check *file labels.*

file protection ring A detachable ring which can be fitted to the hub of a *magnetic reel* to indicate the status of the reel. In some computer systems *write permit* rings are used; e.g., the computer *hardware* is designed so that data cannot be written to a tape *file* unless the ring is fitted. Alternatively the system may use *write-inhibit rings*, in which case data cannot be written to the tape if the ring is fitted. Thus the ring is used to protect a data file by ensuring that an operator does not load a file to a *tape deck* in a situation which will allow it to be overwritten.

file recovery A procedure which occurs following a system *failure*

174

which has interrupted *file processing*. It implies that the content of the file is brought to an accurate condition consistent with the valid *transactions* received to date, and that the status of the file is such that processing can be resumed without loss of accuracy.

file reconstitution The process of recreating a *file* which has been corrupted or damaged, usually involving the *updating* of a previous *generation* of the file with a file of previous *transactions* which have been retained for the purpose.

file section A part of a *file* occupying certain consecutive physical locations on a *disk volume* or on *magnetic tape*.

file set A collection of *files* related to one another and stored consecutively on a *magnetic disk volume*.

files, shared ◊ *shared files system*.

filestore In an *operating system* the *files* required in the total environment may be stored on *backing store* in an organized *library* under the management of the operating system. The backing store resources allocated for this purpose may include *exchangeable disk volumes*, *magnetic tapes*, etc. The files needed *on-line* at a particular time are held on disks and referred to as being a *high level filestore*. Files held on disk or tape but not on-line are in *low level filestore*.

file tidying An operation carried out on a *filestore* by an *operating system*, to remove various minor inconsistencies which are derived from previous errors. The purpose is to avoid lengthy operations to *reconstitute* files which have been affected by such errors, and use is made of data stored temporarily after previous incidents.

film ◊ *thin-film memory*.

film optical sensing device A device which converts data recorded on film into a form acceptable to a computer by optical scanning of the film.

film reader Any device capable of transcribing data recorded on film into a form acceptable to a computer.

film recorder An *output device* which transcribes data from a computer onto a photographic file.

filter Synonymous with *mask*.

final result A result created at the completion of a *routine* or *subroutine*; essentially a result presented to the user at the completion of a major processing operation. Contrasted with *intermediate result*.

fine index A secondary *index* used to supplement a main index or *gross index* when the latter is not sufficiently detailed to distinguish between all items being indexed.

first generation computer A machine which uses thermionic valves. Compare *second generation* and *third generation*.

first item list Synonymous with *group indication*.

first-level address An *address* which gives the *location* of the item referenced directly, without modification.

first remove subroutine A *subroutine* which is entered directly from a main *program* and which *exits* back to that program.

fixed block length *Blocks* of data have a constant number of *words* or *characters* in a system with a fixed block length requirement. This requirement may be due to the *hardware* limitations of a machine, or be determined by *program*. Contrasted with *variable block*.

fixed field The organization of *fields* in *records* so that the fields containing similar information in each record are located in the same relative position within the record and are the same length. Contrasted with *variable field*.

fixed form coding The coding of *source languages* in such a way that each part of the *instruction* (*label, operation code, operand, narrative*) appears in a *fixed field* on the *punched card* or *paper tape record* used as the method of *input* for the instruction.

fixed length record *Records* whose size in *words* or *characters* is constant. This may be because of *hardware* requirements, or be due to specific *programming*. Contrasted with *variable length*.

fixed placement file A *file* which may be expanded or controlled, but which has been allocated a fixed location in the *filestore*. This is done to ensure its availability in *high level filestore*, and to prevent *roll out* to *low level filestore*.

fixed point arithmetic The performing of arithmetical calculations without regard to the position of the *radix point*, treating the numbers as integers for the purpose of calculation. The relative position of the point has to be controlled during calculations.

fixed point part In *floating point representation* a number is represented by the product of the fixed point part and the *index* raised to the power of the *exponent*.
Also known as fractional part, coefficient.

fixed point representation A method of *number representation* in which a number is represented by a single set of digits, the value of the number depending on the position of the digits. In the case of fractional numbers the position of the *radix point* (e.g. decimal point in the decimal system) is located at a fixed predetermined position. ⟡ *positional notation, floating point representation*.

fixed radix notation The representation of quantities where all positions have the same *radix* of notation.

fixed word length A system of organizing a *store* where each computer *word* is composed of a fixed number of *characters* or *bits*.

flag An additional piece of information added to a *data* item which gives information about the data item itself, e.g. an error flag will indicate that the data item has given rise to an error condition. The term is also used to refer to *end of field* and *end of data markers*.

flag event A condition occurring in a *program* which causes a *flag* to be set.

flip-flop A device or circuit which assumes one of two possible states (0 or 1); the nature of the state is reversed on receipt of an *input signal*.
Also known as one shot multivibrator, eccles jordan circuit.

float To add the *origin* to all *relative addresses* in a *program*, thus determining the area of *memory* occupied by the program.

float factor Synonymous with *origin*.

floating address Synonymous with *relative address*.

floating point arithmetic Arithmetical calculations based on *floating point numbers*. In floating point arithmetic the position of the decimal point does not depend on the relative position of the digits in the numbers as in *fixed point arithmetic*, since the two parts of the floating point number determine the absolute value of the number. The use of floating point arithmetic means that numbers can be stored more economically and in wider ranges of magnitudes, and calculations can be performed to consistent relative degrees of accuracy.

floating point number A number expressed using *floating point representation*.

floating point package *Software* provided with a computer system to enable the computer to perform *floating point arithmetic*.

floating point radix In *floating point representation* a number n is represented by two numbers a and b where $n = a.r^b$. The radix is the particular value of r used in the representation.

floating point representation A method of *number representation* in which a number is represented by two sets of *digits*, known as the *fixed point part* and the *exponent* or *characteristic*. If a number n is represented by a fixed point part a and an exponent b, then $n = a.r^b$, where r is the *radix* or *base* of the number system, e.g. 10 for the decimal system, 2 for the *binary* system. Contrasted with *fixed point representation*.

flow A sequence of *events*, usually represented by a *flowchart*.

flowchart The diagrammatic representation of a sequence of events, usually drawn with conventional symbols representing different types of events and their interconnexion. ◊ *flowchart sym-*

177

bols, *systems flowchart*, *program flowchart* and general article on *flowcharting*.

Also known as flow diagram.

flowcharting Flowcharting is a technique for representing a succession of events in symbolic form. The 'events' recorded in a flowchart may represent a variety of activities, but in general a particular flowchart will record the interconnexion between events of the same type. In *data processing*, flowcharts may be divided broadly into *systems flowcharts* and *program flowcharts*.

Systems Flowcharts: The object of systems flowcharts is to show diagrammatically the logical relationship between successive events in a data processing system. The main types of 'event' in a systems flowchart will be the clerical and manual procedures involved, *data collection* and *data preparation*, and the computer *runs* involved. The flowcharts will identify the various procedures involved, showing their interconnexion and the overall design of the system.

Program Flowcharts: The object of a program flowchart is to show diagrammatically the logical relationship between successive steps in a computer program. Flowcharting a computer program may involve a number of different levels of complexity, but at least two levels are usually prepared, outline flowcharts and detail flowcharts.

The purpose of an outline flowchart is: (i) to help the conversion of a program specification into a sequential statement of operations; (ii) to guide the further development of the program; (iii) to ensure that no *input* or *output* record is overlooked, and that all requirements of the program specification are met. In order to achieve this an outline flowchart must show: (i) all input and output functions; (ii) how each type of record will be processed; (iii) how the program will be divided into *segments* and *routines*; (iv) all *entry points* and *halts*.

The purpose of a detail flowchart is: (i) to interpret the detailed program specification; (ii) to define the programming techniques to be used; (iii) to provide clear directions for *coding;* (iv) to make the coded program more intelligible. A detailed flowchart will be used as the basis for coding the program, either in a *high level language* or in *machine code*. Thus the level of detail must be sufficient for unambiguous coding. This will vary according to the language to be used and the complexity of the program: the most detailed level of flowcharting will have a symbol representing each individually coded *instruction*. However, it is usually sufficient to represent a sequence of instructions forming a logical unit of the program by means of a single symbol.

Symbols: flowcharting symbols usually conform to some standard set in which each symbol has a specific meaning. Internationally and nationally accepted standards have been designed, such as the European Computer Manufacturers' Association standard and the American Standards Association standard, but local peculiarities prevail in almost any installation. For this reason great care (and often great resourcefulness) is needed in reading the flowcharts of anyone whose personal whims are not publicly accepted: considering that the flowchart is a major tool in the science of communication, it can sometimes be strangely uncommunicative. Among the symbols defined will be symbols representing the following functions:

Flowlines   Flowlines show the *transfer of control* from one operation to another.

Process   A symbol to represent any kind of processing function.

Decision   A symbol which represents a decision or switching type of operation that determines which of a number of alternative paths is to be followed.

Connector   A symbol to represent an entry to or exit from another part of the flowchart. It is used to indicate a transfer of control that cannot be conveniently shown by a flowline (e.g. because the flowchart continues on another page).

Terminal   A symbol representing a terminal point in a flowchart (e.g. start, stop, halt or *interrupt*).

Other special symbols are used to represent subroutines, input/output functions and different types of *peripheral unit* and sources of input and types of output.

The techniques of flowcharting are often complementary to those of using *decision tables*, on which there is a general article.

flowchart symbols Conventional diagrammatic representations of different events which are shown on a *flowchart*.

flow diagram Synonymous with *flowchart*.

flow direction The method adopted to distinguish between antecedent and successor event on a *flowchart*. This may be by means of arrows or by the convention that *flowlines* connecting antecedent to successor flow from top to bottom and left to right of a page.

flowline A line drawn on a *flowchart* connecting an antecedent event to a successor event. ◊ *flow direction*.

179

flow-process diagram   Synonymous with *systems flowchart*.

fluid logic   The simulating of logical operations by means of varying the flow and pressure in a fluid – either gas or liquid. Fluid logic is used to control the operations of *pneumatic computers*.

forbidden character code   An *error detecting code* in which certain combinations of *bits* are not permitted and known as forbidden characters.

force   To intervene in the operation of a computer *program* by *executing* a *branch instruction* transferring control to another part of the *routine*. Forcing is usually carried out in order to bypass an error condition which has caused the program to come to a *halt*, or to terminate a *run* by forcing *entry* to the *end of run routine*.

forced checkpoint   An operation instigated by an operator to cause the status of a job to be recorded on *backing store*, so that the job can be restarted at a later occasion. Usually done in an emergency situation to relieve the load on the computer so that corrective action can be taken. ◊ *checkpoint*.

forecasting   The problem of planning for the future is met in many situations, and in endeavouring to make the best possible plan some assumption or forecast of future conditions has to be made. The best forecast will be based on the projection and analysis of past results viewed in the light of experience. There have developed, in recent years, several statistical methods of making forecasts mathematically based on past performance, and whereas no one can pretend that these methods will always give an exact forecast there can be little doubt that the correct use of such methods can greatly improve planning.

The use of the digital computer commercially has greatly increased the value of statistical forecasting methods, for when used together they enable many forecasts to be made very quickly, where once armies of statisticians would have been needed. Such methods are of great value in such areas as market planning, *inventory control*, personnel planning, etc., where often forecasts of many items have to be made.

There are so many variants of different forecasting methods that it is impossible to discuss them all here. Instead we shall mention their common principles and give a few examples. In any forecasting system our first concern must be to obtain consistently expressed past results. Having ensured that they are so expressed, we study our past results under three headings:

(i) Seasonal Variation: Is there any periodicity to the sales level? Is the seasonal pattern changing? Are there any variable seasonal effects which we can categorize explicitly, e.g. those due to holidays.

(ii) Trends: Is there evidence of a regular change between successive results? Does this appear to be a 'long' trend or a 'short' trend? Are there any symptoms which indicate that a new trend is likely?

(iii) How large is the effect of any random variation? If there is a large random variation we must remember this when quoting our forecast.

One of the most widely used methods of forecasting, in one form or another, is that of exponential smoothing. In its simplest form exponential smoothing is a means of dealing with item (iii) by computing a moving average. In carrying out this operation the square of the sum of successive errors is minimized. By a little more sophistication we can extend exponential smoothing to calculate a linear trend as well, and also to calculate any seasonal effects. R. G. Brown has developed multiple exponential smoothing, which can be adapted to give forecasts where almost any type of trend is being experienced. The problem here is in monitoring such a system. The basic idea in exponential smoothing is that of taking a moving average by adding to our last forecast a fraction of the difference between our last forecast and the observed result. By successively applying this technique we are able to find an 'average of an average' which can be made to give a trend.

Another method in use at the present time is that of Box and Jenkins. Developed as a method of *process control*, it can be shown to be equivalent to exponential smoothing in its developed form. The forecast is made by taking this month's known result and adjusting it in the light of the difference of the last two forecast errors to date. Any seasonal effects must be removed before this calculation is applied, but the method requires very little storage of information and therefore lends itself to use on the digital computer.

Of course there is no definitive forecasting system. One method may be best for one application where another may perform better in a different application. Before any method can be used a study of past data has to be made so that the best values of weighting factors can be made. Any method has to be adapted to suit the peculiar requirements of a particular system. The accuracy required and the cost of achieving this accuracy must be considered, for inevitably the more sophisticated our forecasting method becomes the more it will cost. Very often the simple method will give good enough results for the purpose required, and the expense of introducing a more sophisticated method is not justified by the small increase in accuracy that would be obtained.

Finally, no forecast will give an exact answer except by chance. All our forecast can do is to show us a region where the true answer will lie. If this region is small we can make firm plans; if it is large we must make flexible ones. At least we shall be working with relevant knowledge rather than on inspired guesswork.

foregrounding ◊ *foreground processing.*

foreground processing 1. In a *multi-access system,* processing which is making use of *on-line facilities.* 2. High priority processing which takes precedence (as a result of *interrupts*) over *background processing.* 3. Low priority processing over which background processing takes precedence.

As definitions 2 and 3 are directly contradictory and definition 1 has a related but different meaning, this phrase should be used with caution.

Also known as foregrounding.

foreground program A *program* which requires *foreground processing.*

format The predetermined arrangement of data, e.g. the layout of a printed document, the arrangement of the parts of a computer *instruction,* the arrangement of data in a *record.* ◊ *data format, record format, print format, card format.*

format effectors Synonymous with *layout characters.*

form feed The mechanical system of positioning *continuous stationery* in a printing device.

form feed character A character punched in a *paper tape control loop* used on some printing devices for the control of *form feed.*

form stop A device which automatically stops a *printer* when the paper has run out.

FORTRAN FORTRAN is an acronym for FORmula TRANslation. It is a *problem oriented high level programming language* for scientific and mathematical use, in which the *source program* is written using a combination of algebraic formulae and English statements of a standard but readable form.

A FORTRAN program consists of data items, executable statements and non-executable statements. The program is structured in *segments,* which consist of a master segment and optional function segments and *subroutines.*

Data items in FORTRAN are either variables or constants, and are assigned *alphanumeric* names by the programmer. Groups of similar items of data can be processed as *arrays,* or tables of data, in which case the individual items are defined by their position or reference within the array by naming the array followed by one or more *subscripts*. Data items in FORTRAN may take the following forms:

Integer   A whole number value falling within a range determined by the capacity of the computer being used.

Real   A number expressed in *floating point representation* accurate to a number of significant digits, the range again dependent on the capabilities of the particular machine being used.

Complex A complex number in which two real numbers are used to express the real and imaginary parts.

Logical A quantity which can only take two values, true or false. (◊ article on *Boolean Algebra*.)

Text   Character information, which is not used for mathematical operations.

The actual operations of the program are expressed by means of 'executable statements'. These can take two basic forms, 'assign statements' and 'control statements'. An assign statement takes the form Variable=Expression. The expression may be either arithmetic or logical. An arithmetic expression can include variables, elements, form arrays, constants and a variety of standard functions, which are combined by arithmetic operators, e.g. $+$, $-$, $*$ (multiplication), $/$ (division), $**$ (exponentiation). A logical expression is similar but can include the operations AND, NOT, OR, the logical operators. An example of an arithmetic assignment statement would be:

$$ROOT=(-B+SQRT(B**2-4*A*C)) \ / \ (2*A)$$

In more usual mathematical notation this expression would be written

$$\frac{-b+\sqrt{b^2-4ac}}{2a}$$

The word ROOT, and the letters A, B, C represent variables, and SQRT the function provided for calculating square roots. The compiler recognizes these symbols and translates them into appropriate machine code.

An example of a logical assignment statement would be:

$$BOOL=A. OR. B$$

In this expression the variable B O O L would be given the value true or false according to the truth values of the variables A and B and the *truth table* defined by the Boolean operator O R.

Each statement can be preceded by a numeric label, permitting reference to the statement by means of control statements. Control statements enable the program to *branch* to other statements and enable *loops* to be constructed. Branches may also be constructed which are conditional on the results of arithmetic or logical operations. Examples of control statements are:

G O T O 25

This statement is an unconditional branch to statement number 25.

D O 24 I=J, K, L

This statement calls for the repeated execution of succeeding statements up to and including that labelled 24. At the first repetition I is set to equal J, at the second to J + L, at the third to J + 2L, and so on until the next value would be greater than K, at which point the loop is terminated.

I F (A. L T.B. AND C. G T. D) GO TO 19

This statement causes a branch to statement numbered 19 if A is less than B and C is greater than D.

While executable statements specify the operations the program is to perform, 'non-executable statements' merely provide the *compiler* with information. An example is

C O M P L E X R O O T 1, R O O T 2, A N S

which indicates to the compiler that storage is required for three complex variables with labels as specified.

A F O R T R A N program consists of one or more *segments*, of which there is one and only one master segment, and, optionally, function and subroutine segments.

A function segment is used where the same form of function is required several times in a program. The statements describing the operation required to calculate the result of using the function are named and written once, and whenever the function is required in the program it is only necessary to give the function name and a list of parameters to replace the 'dummy' variables used in the function segment.

A subroutine is similar to a function segment except that it may provide more than one result, and must be specifically called by a separate statement, in contrast to a function, which itself may form part of an expression. Input and output in a F O R T R A N program is performed by means of statements which identify the peripheral unit to be used and the external format of the list of items to be input or output.

forward compatibility standards Standards adopted to ensure that *programs* developed for one range of equipment can be utilized on a further range of equipment which will replace the present installation. ◊ General article on *Transition*.

foundation virtual machine A *virtual machine* established in a *virtual machine environment* to initialize the system, i.e. to enable the system to be *loaded* or reloaded.

fount-change character A *character* punched in *paper tape* used to control a printing device, causing the device to alter the type fount being used.

four address instruction A computer *instruction* whose *address* part consists of four addresses, usually two *operand* addresses, the address of the destination of the result of the operation, and the address of the next instruction to be performed.

four-wire channel A circuit capable of transmitting and receiving simultaneously by using two separate and distinct paths in each direction.

fractional part Synonymous with *fixed point part*.

fragmentation ◊ *virtual storage*.

frame A transverse section of *magnetic tape* or *paper tape* consisting of one *bit* position for each tape *track*. For paper tape the term *row* is also used for frame.

free field The organization of data in a *storage* medium so that an item of data, or *field*, may be located anywhere within the medium as opposed to *fixed field* organization in which the relative position of a field determines the nature of its contents.

free-standing display A *display* unit apart from the main operating *console*, intended to assist in the efficient operation of a computer system by providing *prompts* to operators handling *peripheral units*.

frequency The rate of repetition of a periodically recurring signal, usually measured in cycles per second (cps) kilocycles per second (1kcs=1,000cps) or megacycles per second (1mcs=1,000kcs).

frequency band The range within which the *frequency* of a signal may be allowed to vary.

full adder ◊ *adder.*

full duplex Transmission circuits in which messages may be transmitted in both directions at the same time.

function 1. That part of a computer *instruction* which specifies the operation to be performed. 2. The expression in mathematical symbols of the relationship between variables, e.g., the expression a + b = c may be said to be a function of the variables, a, b, c.

functional character Synonymous with *control character.*

functional design The detailed specification of the interrelationship between the working elements of a system, taking into account both *logic design* and the equipment used in the system.

functional diagram The diagrammatic representation of a *functional design* in which conventional symbols are used to represent the specific elements of *logic design* and equipment.

functional unit A series of *elements*[2] which together perform a single computer *operation*, e.g. multiplication or addition.

function code The part of a computer *instruction* that specifies the operation to be performed.

function generator A unit of an *analog computer* which can accept one or more input variables and which will provide an output variable based on some mathematical *function.*[2]

function holes Synonymous with *control holes.*

function polling A method of *polling* in which a device requiring to be serviced not only provides a signal indicating a need for service, but also signifies the type of service required.

function table In *table look-up* techniques, the function table consists of two or more sets of information arranged so that an item in one set provides a cross-reference to items in the other sets.

future labels *Labels* used in *instructions* in a *program* written in a programming language (◊ *languages*); they refer to *locations* to which a *compiler* or *assembly program* has not yet allocated *absolute addresses.*

G

gain The ratio of output signal from a circuit to the original input signal.

gang punch 1. A *punched card* machine having a single *card track* incorporating a *reading station* and a *punching station*, each with a position for each *card column*. The machine is used to reproduce information from a single card at the beginning of a pack into all subsequent cards of the pack. Cards are fed one after another along the card track and information originally punched into the leading card is read at the reading station and transferred to the punching station for punching into the following card; and so on. 2. Used as a verb, meaning to punch the same information, e.g. a date, into a group of cards by pre-setting the information so that the punching is automatic for each card.

gap Synonymous with *interblock gap*.

gap digit A *digit* present in a *word* which does not form part of the information conveyed by the word, e.g. a *parity bit*.

gap scatter The deviation from correct alignment of the magnetic *read heads* for the several parallel *tracks* on a *magnetic tape*.

garbage Meaningless data present in any *storage device*. The data may be meaningless because of errors or it may be data left in store by a previous unrelated job.

gate In general, an electronic *switch*.[1] Used in *data processing* to refer to an electronic circuit which may have more than one *input signal* but only one *output* signal. In this sense used synonymously with *logic element*.

gate, and Synonymous with *and element*.

gate, coincidence Synonymous with *and element*.

gate, nor Synonymous with *nor element*.

gate, one Synonymous with *or element*.

gate, or Synonymous with *or element*.

gathering, data ◊ *data collection*.

gather write The ability to write a *block* of data composed of logical *records* from non-contiguous areas of *store*. ◊ *scatter read*.

general peripheral controller A *hardware* unit, containing a *pro-*

cessor which controls the transfer of data to and from a range of *peripheral units* and *main store*; usually operates under the control of commands set up by the main *order code processor*.

general purpose computer A computer capable of operating on different *programs* for the solution of a wide variety of problems, as opposed to a *special purpose computer* specifically designed for solving problems of a particular type.

Also known as all-purpose computer.

general purpose function generator A *function generator* which is not specifically designed for a particular type of function, but which can be adapted to generate different functions.

Also known as arbitrary function generator.

general purpose program A *program* designed to perform some standard operation, e.g. *sorting* or one of the *file processing* functions. The specific requirements for any *run* of the programs are provided by means of *parameters* which describe the requirements of the run. A general purpose program is similar to a *generator*, but differs in that it normally requires parameters each time it is run, whereas a generator produces a specific program which can subsequently be used without parameters.

generate To use a *generator* to produce a specificized version of a *general purpose program*.

generated address An *address* developed by *instructions* within a *program* for subsequent use by that program.

Also known as *synthetic address*.

generating program Synonymous with *generator*.

generating routine Synonymous with *generator*.

generation number A number forming part of the *file label* on a *reel* of *magnetic tape*, which serves to identify the age of the file. Each time amendment data is applied to a magnetic tape file an entirely new copy of the file is created containing all the valid amendments. This new reel will bear the same *file name* as the original reel that was amended; the two will however be different generations of the same file and as such will bear different generation numbers. ⇨ *grandfather tape*.

generator A *routine* which will produce a *program* to perform a specific version of some general operation by completing a predetermined framework with the details required for the particular application. A generator is similar to a *compiler* in that source *statements* are converted into a program, but differs from it in that only programs of a specific type are produced, e.g. *sort generator, report generator*.

Also known as program generator, generating routine, generating program. Compare with *general purpose program*.

generator, analytical function   ◊ *analytical function generator*.

generator, arbitrary function   ◊ *general purpose function generator*.

generator, diode function   ◊ *diode function generator*.

generator, general purpose function   ◊ *general purpose function generator*.

generator, manual word   ◊ *manual word unit*.

generator, natural function   Synonymous with *analytical function generator*.

generator, natural law function   Synonymous with *analytical function generator*.

generator, number   ◊ *number generation*.

generator, output routine   ◊ *output routine generator*.

generator, program   ◊ *generator*.

generator, random number   ◊ *random number generator*.

generator, report program   ◊ *report program generator*.

generator, sorting routine   ◊ *sort generator*.

generator, tapped potentiometer function   ◊ *tapped potentiometer function generator*.

gibberish total   A total accumulated for control purposes when handling *records* by the addition of specific fields of each record, although the total itself has no particular intelligence or meaning. For example, an accumulation of indicative data such as customer's account number. ◊ *hash total*.

giga-   A prefix denoting one thousand million or 10^9, synonymous with *billi*.

gigo   Acronym for 'garbage *in*, garbage *out*'; the principle that the results produced from unreliable data are equally unreliable.

graceful degradation   Related to machine breakdowns on computers; the ability to undergo graceful degradation ensures that failure of certain parts does not cause complete breakdown, but allows limited operation. ◊ *resilience*.
Also known as operating in crippled mode.

grandfather tape   It is normal practice when updating a *magnetic tape file* to retain the original copy of the file thus enabling the file to be reconstituted in the event of any permanent loss or damage to the current file. It is usual to keep at least three generations of a tape file, referred to as 'grandfather', 'father' and 'son'. The generation is identified by means of the *generation number*.

graphical display   A specialized *display* unit, commonly using a *light pen*, to present graphical information to a computer user.

graphic panel In *process control*, a device which displays the state of the process in the form of illuminated light, dials, etc.

graphic solution A solution to a problem provided by means of graphs or diagrams rather than printed figures.

graph plotter ◊ *plotter*.

graunch An unplanned error.

gray code A code in which the binary representation of the numbers 0—9 are given in the following table:

Decimal	Gray	Decimal	Gray
0	0000	5	0111
1	0001	6	0101
2	0011	7	0100
3	0010	8	1100
4	0110	9	1101

Also known as cyclic code.

grid In *optical character recognition*, a scale for measuring characters by means of a network of parallel lines at right angles to each other and a fixed distance apart.

gross index The first of a pair of indices used to locate *records* in *store*. The gross *index* is used to give a reference in the second or *fine index*, which acts as a supplement.

group 1. A specified sequence of storage *locations* used to contain a particular *record* (or records). 2. The data stored within such locations. 3. A set of records in a *sorted file* which have the same *key* value.

group code A *systematic error checking code* used to check the validity of a group of *characters* transferred between two *terminals*.

grouped records Several *records* contained in a single group in which the *key* of one record is used to identify the group.

group indication Relating to a practice commonly adopted when printing a *totals only* tabulation on a *punched card tabulator*. A special device is used to list descriptive information from the first card of each group; this information would normally be common to the whole group of cards and is therefore referred to as group indicative data.

Also known as *first item list*. The device used is known as an independent sector designating device on some machines.

group mark A special *character* used to indicate the end of a

190

group of characters in *store*, the group itself usually being a logical record to be *addressed* and processed as a unit of data.

Also known as group marker.

group marker Synonymous with *group mark*.

group polling A method of *polling* which enables a number of devices within a given set to respond to a single inquiry.

group printing In a *report program*, the information printed out for a *group* of *records* when a *key change* occurs.

guard band A frequency band left unused between two *channels* of a *data transmission* device, usually to prevent interference between channels.

guard signal A signal used to permit the output signals from a *digitizer* to be read only at moments when the signals are not susceptible to *ambiguity error*.

guide edge The edge of *paper tape* used when the tape is lined up for automatic handling by a *paper tape reader* or *paper tape punch*.

guide margin The distance measured between the *guide edge* of a *paper tape* and the centre line of the first *track* of holes punched parallel to this edge.

gulp A group of *binary digits* consisting of several *bytes*.

half adder A device forming part of an *adder* capable of receiving two inputs, i.e. *augend* plus either *addend* or *carry*, and of delivering two outputs, *sum* and *carry*.

half adder, binary ◊ *binary half adder*.

half-duplex A system (e.g. telegraph) capable of working in either direction but not in both directions simultaneously.

half-duplex channel A *channel* providing for transmission in both directions but not simultaneously.

half subtracter A device forming part of a *subtracter* capable of receiving two inputs, i.e., *minuend* and *subtrahend* or *carry*, and of delivering two outputs, *difference* and a digit to be borrowed. Also known as *one-digit subtracter*.

halt The situation which occurs when the sequence of operations in a *program* comes to a stop. This can be due to a *halt instruction* being encountered or due to some *unexpected halt* or *interrupt*. The program can usually continue after a halt unless it is a *drop dead halt*.

halt, dead ◊ *drop dead halt*.

halt, drop dead ◊ *drop dead halt*.

halt instruction A machine *instruction* to stop a *program*.
Also known as stop code, stop instruction.

hamming code An *error checking code* (named after its inventor) in which each character has a minimum Hamming distance (◊ *signal distance*) from every other *character* in the code. An example of a Hamming code using four ternary digits with minimum distance of 3 would be:

    0000   0112   0221   1011   1120   1202   2022   2101   2210

It should be noted that this particular example is an *error correcting code* as well as an *error detecting code*. For example, the combination 0120 is detected as an error since it does not obey the rule for construction, and may be corrected to 1120 as it differs from this in only one respect.

hamming distance Synonymous with *signal distance*.

hand feed punch Synonymous with *hand punch*.

hand punch 1. A device which causes holes to be punched in *punched cards* as a direct result of pressure on a key of a *keyboard*; it has no automatic facilities. Contrasted with *automatic punch*. 2. As for 1, but related to *paper tape* not punched cards.

hang-up   Synonymous with *unexpected halt*.

hard copy   A document in a form suitable for human beings to read produced at the same time as information is produced in a language suitable for a machine.

hard dump   Synonymous with *automatic hardware dump*.

hardware   The physical units making up a computer system – the apparatus as opposed to the *programs*. Contrasted with *software*.

hardware availability ratio   A ratio used to measure the availability of a computer system to provide productive work. The availability ratio is normally expressed as the ratio of difference between *accountable time* and *down time* to accountable time. Down time usually includes *corrective maintenance* and *recovery time*. Also known as *hardware serviceability ratio*.

hardware check   A *check* which is performed by *hardware* in order to detect errors in the transmission of data within a computer, e.g. *parity check* performed by hardware.
Also known as built-in check, automatic check. Contrasted with *programmed check*.

hardware dump   Synonymous with *automatic hardware dump*.

hardware dump area   An area of *storage* used to record the internal state of an *order code processor* after the occurrence of a system *failure* (e.g. *parity error*) which cannot be automatically corrected.

hardware recovery   Relating to the ability of a system to recover automatically from a *failure* and re-establish the current workload to enable processing to continue in a controlled manner. Recovery may be affected by either *hardware* or *software*, and in many cases a combination of both.

hardware serviceability ratio   Synonymous with *hardware availability ratio*.

hash   Meaningless or unwanted information present, for example, in *store*, or written to *magnetic tape* in order to comply with *hardware* requirements on minimum *block length*. ◊ *hash total*.

hashed random file organization   A method of *file organization* on a *direct access device*, in which the *address* used to select or *write records* to a file is determined by applying an *algorithm* to the record key. ◊ general article on *Updating and File Maintenance*.

hash total   An addition of values in a particular *field* or area of a *file* where the total has no indicative significance but is used for control purposes, e.g. a total of staff personnel numbers. Also known as *check sum*. Associated with *batch total, gibberish total*.

head An electromagnet used to read, record or erase polarized spots on a magnetic medium such as *magnetic tape, magnetic disk* or *magnetic drum*. Examples are *read head, write head, read/write head*.

head, combined read/write ◊ *read/write head*.

head, combined ◊ *read/write head*.

header A set of data placed at the head of one or more sets of data, e.g. a *record* at the beginning of a *file*, and containing an *identifier* for the following sets. Sometimes the header will contain *control data* or data common to the following sets.

header label A *block* of data at the beginning of a *magnetic tape file* containing descriptive information to identify the file. Examples of data on a header label are: *file name, reel number, file generation number, retention period*, and the date when the data was written to tape. When a file is *opened* this data is checked by the *program* to ensure that the correct file is being processed; and also, if the tape is to be used for writing, to check that the *retention period* has been exceeded.
Also known as *file label*.

head gap The distance between a *read* or *write head* and the surface of the recording medium (*magnetic tape, magnetic drum, magnetic disk*, etc.).

head, playback ◊ *read head*.

head, reading ◊ *read head*.

head, record ◊ *write head*.

head, writing ◊ *write head*.

hesitation A short automatic suspension of a main *program* in order to carry out all or part of another operation, e.g. a fast transfer of data to or from a *peripheral unit*.

heuristic approach An exploratory approach to a problem which uses successive evaluations of trial and error to arrive at a final result. Contrasted with *algorithmic approach*.

heuristic program A *program* which solves a problem by a method of trial and error in which the success of each attempt at solution is assessed and used to improve the subsequent attempts until a solution acceptable within defined limits is reached.

heuristics The methodology of solving a problem by trial and error, evaluating each step towards a final result.

hexadecimal notation A notation of numbers to the base or *radix* of sixteen. The ten decimal digits 0 to 9 are used, and in addition six more digits, usually a, b, c, d, e and f, to represent ten, eleven, twelve, thirteen, fourteen and fifteen as single characters.

high level filestore   A type of *filestore* used in an *operating system* to hold *physical files* needed *on-line*. The medium typically used is *magnetic disc* or *magnetic drum*.

high level language   A *language* in which each *instruction or statement* corresponds to several *machine code* instructions. High level languages allow users to write in a notation with which they are familiar (e.g. F O R T R A N in a mathematical notation, C O B O L in English) rather than a language oriented to the machine code of a computer. Contrasted with *low level language*. ◊ *Languages*.

high level recovery   *Recovery* from a *hardware/software failure* by use of resources and information not directly associated with the cause of failure; e.g. use of a *back up file* to effect recovery rather than use of further attempts to execute a *block transfer* from a device.

high order   The more significant figure or figures in a number expressed in positional notation, e.g., in the numeric representation of sixteen as 16, the 1 is of a higher order than the 6, since it represents tens rather than units. In describing a *binary word*, therefore, reference can be made to the high order *bits*.

high performance equipment   Equipment which produces output signals of sufficiently high quality to permit these signals to be transmitted on telephone or teleprinter circuits.

high-speed carry   A *carry* into a column which results in a carry out of that column, bypassing the normal adding circuit when the new carry is generated.
Also known as a ripple-through carry or, where appropriate, *standing-on-nines carry*. When, in contrast, the normal adding circuit is used in such a case, it is called a cascaded carry.

highway   A major route along which signals travel from one of several sources to one of several destinations.
Also known as *trunk* or bus.

highway width   Relates to the capacity of a *highway* to transfer data simultaneously, the greater the width the faster the throughput. For example, a highway which is four *bytes* wide, has the capacity to transfer four bytes at a time.

hit   A *record* which satisfies specified identifying criteria; e.g. in an *information retrieval* system; or, during *updating*, a *change record* which corresponds with a *master record*.

hit-on-the-fly printer   Synonymous with *on-the-fly printer*.

195

hit on the line A momentary open circuit on a *teletypewriter* loop.

hold To preserve data in one *storage device* after transferring it to another storage device or another *location* in the same device. Contrasted with *clear*.

hold facility A method of interrupting the operation of an *analog computer* without altering the values of the variables at the time of interruption, so that the computation can continue when the interruption ceases.

holding beam A wide spray of electrons used for regenerating: electrons which have dissipated after being stored on the surface of a *cathode ray tube* can be regenerated by a holding beam.

holding gun The source of a stream of electrons which make a *holding beam*.

hold mode The operating mode for an *analog computer* in which the *hold facility* is used. Contrasted with *compute mode*.

holes, designation ◊ *control holes*.

holes, function ◊ *control holes*.

hole site Each specific area on a *punched card* or *paper tape* in which a hole may be punched, e.g. on an 80-*column*, 12-*row card* there are 960 hole sites. The presence or absence of a hole in a hole site can itself be significant in representing *binary numbers* (◊ *column binary, row binary*).

holes, sprocket ◊ *feed holes*.

Hollerith card A *punched card* in which information is punched using the *Hollerith code*.

Hollerith code A *punched card code* invented by Dr Herman Hollerith in 1888 in which the top three positions in a *card column* have a *zoning* significance so that a combination of a hole in the top position (known as Y-*position*) plus a hole in the fourth position would have a different significance from a combination of a hole punched in the second position (known as X-*position*) plus a hole in the fourth position. The third position (known as 0) gives another zone and it is thus possible to code all twenty-six alphabetic characters and the ten numerals 0–9 in the twelve *punching positions* of a card.

homeostasis The state of a system where input and output are exactly balanced, producing no change; steadiness.

home record The first *record* in a *file* in which the *chained record* system of file organization is used.

hoot stop A *closed loop* producing an audible signal, generally used to indicate an error or for operating convenience.

hopper A device which holds *punched cards* and presents them to a feed mechanism for reading or punching.

horizontal feed Where a *punched card* is placed in a *hopper*, enters and traverses the *card track*, all in a horizontal position. Contrasted with *vertical feed*.

horizontal flowcharting A technique for recording the movement of paper in an organization; distinguished from ordinary *flowcharting* by the fact that the movement of a recording medium is charted rather than the information it records. One line is used for each form, *punched card* or other medium, and the movement of each type (shown by standardized symbols for e.g., 'data added', 'handled' and 'filed') is recorded from the time it is first used to the time it is destroyed.

housekeeping *Routines* within a *program* which are not directly concerned with the solution of the problem. Housekeeping functions include the setting of *entry conditions, clearing* areas of *store* if the program expects these to be set to some initial condition, performing any standard preliminary operations required by *input* or *output devices* (e.g. writing *header labels* to *magnetic tape*), performing standard *input/output routines*, e.g. the *blocking* of *records* on to magnetic tape.

housekeeping operation An operation performed by a computer in connexion with *housekeeping* requirements.

housekeeping run A *run* to maintain the structure of a *file* (or files), e.g., to add new *records* and to delete or amend existing records.

hub 1. The hole in the middle of a *reel* of *magnetic tape* which fits over the *capstan* when the reel is mounted on a *tape deck*. 2. The socket on a *plugboard* into which a *plug* is inserted.

hunting An unstable condition resulting from a continuous attempt by an automatically controlled *closed loop*[2] to find a state of equilibrium. The system will usually include a method of measuring deviation from a predetermined standard and a method of ensuring that the difference between the standard and the measured state tends to zero except for 'hunting' oscillations.

hybrid ▷ general article on *Hybrid Computers*.

hybrid computers The term hybrid computer is frequently used to refer to any mixed computer system in which *analog* and *digital* computing devices are combined. A more strict definition requires that a digital and analog computer be interconnected via a *hybrid interface*, or that analog units be integrated as part of the *central processor* of a digital computer and have direct input/output facilities. Hybrid machines are in fact designed to perform specific tasks and it is probably for this reason that many forms exist. The basic objective of any such system is to obtain for the user the best properties of the two computing philosophies.

In analog systems data is handled in continuous form (e.g. input can be a continuous voltage lying in a specified range) and this permits true *real time* operation. Such systems can perform mathematical operations such as integration with speed and ease, and have great potential for tackling *on-line simulation* exercises, *model building* and *forecasting*. On the other hand they are not as accurate as digital computers, and have a very limited form of *memory* and less developed logical processes than digital computers. Analog machines are programmed by using a plugboard to interconnect various *hardware* devices, and this type of arrangement is inherently less flexible than the digital machine, which has the advantage of having both *program* and data recorded in the same memory medium.

The digital computer scores on account of its large memory capacity and the ease with which logical procedures can be set up, but whereas it is more accurate than the analog machine, it can perform the more complex mathematical functions by iterative routines only (see *iteration*).

In a hybrid system the digital and analog computers are interconnected in such a way that data can be transferred between them via *analog-to-digital converters*, and *digital-to-analog converters*. The digital unit is able to exert control over the analog computer by means of *instructions* stored in the digital memory. These instructions can control the operation mode of the hardware units in the analog section, while the analog machine can interrupt the digital computer to initiate input/output operations. This type of system combines the properties of the true analog system with the accuracy, reliability, memory capacity and programming flexibility of the digital system.

Hybrid machines are generally used in scientific applications or in controlling industrial processes; in both situations the user is able to exploit the machine's ability to process both discrete and continuous data, using accurate digital *subroutines* where necessary and the analog machine's fast integration functions.

hybrid interface A channel for connecting a *digital computer* to an *analog computer*. Digital signals are transmitted in serial mode by the digital machine and have to be converted and transmitted to the various operating units in the analog machine as simultaneous signals. On the other hand data collected as a set of simultaneous readings from the analog units must be digitized and transmitted in serial mode to the digital computer. Both control signals and data may be transferred through the interface system. ◊ the general article on *Hybrid Computers*.

I

I A L Acronym of *International Algebraic Language*, which developed into *A L G O L*.

identification A label consisting of a coded name that serves to identify any unit of data; e.g. a *file name*. ✧ *file identification*.

identification division One of the four divisions of a *C O B O L program*. In the identification division the programmer provides descriptive information that identifies the program being *compiled*. ✧ the general article on *C O B O L*.

identifier A *label* which identifies a *file* of data held on an *input* or *output device*, or identifies a particular *location* in *store*. ✧ *file identification*.

identity element A logical element, operating with *binary* signals, which provides one output signal from two input signals. The output signal will be 1 if, and only if, the two input signals are alike; i.e. both inputs are 1 or both 0. ✧ *Boolean algebra*.

identity unit A device with several *binary input signals* and a single *binary output signal* which has the value 1 if all the input signals are identical, and 0 if they differ. An identity unit with only two input signals is also known as an *equivalence element*.

idle time The time during which a data processing machine remains inactive even though switched on and otherwise in an operable condition.

I D P Acronym of *Integrated Data Processing*.

if and only if operation Synonymous with *equivalence operation*.

if-then operation Synonymous with *conditional implication operation*.

ignore Synonymous with *ignore character*.

ignore character A *character* used to cause some action to be inhibited, or a character that is itself ignored.
Also known as erase character and error character.

illegal character A group of *bits*, holes or other units used to represent any of the symbols in the *character set* of the system. ✧ *forbidden character code*.

image An exact copy of an area of *store* located in another part of store or in a different storage medium. ✧ *binary image, card image*.

IMIS Acronym of integrated *management information system*.

immediate access Pertaining to a *store* in which information can be retrieved without significant delay; e.g. retrieval of information from a storage device by directly *addressing* the unit of data required.

immediate access store A *storage device* in which the access to data can be achieved without significant delay. Originally used to emphasize the advantages of *ferrite core* stores as against other magnetic storage devices in which the medium has to be physically moved past a *read head* to obtain data. The *access time* in the former case might be measured in *microseconds* whereas in the second it might be measured in *milliseconds*. Now commonly called *memory* or *store*. ⬦ the general article on *Storage Devices*.

immediate address The *address* in an *instruction* which operates on its own address component.
Also known as zero-level address.

immediate processing Synonymous with *demand processing*.

imperative macro instructions Macro instructions which result in the creation of *object program* instructions; as distinct from *declarative macro instructions*, which tell the *compiler* to perform some particular action.

imperative statements *Instructions*, in a *source language program*, which are converted into the actual *machine language* instructions of an *object program*.

implementation 1. Of a system – the process of conducting a systems project including the initial investigation and design followed by *programming, program testing, pilot running, parallel running*, live operation and review of the live system. 2. Also the implementation of a computer installation, including choosing the *hardware* and *applications* to be tackled, preparing the site and accommodation, selecting and training staff, as well as the activities mentioned in 1 above for each systems project.

implication Synonymous with *conditional implication operation*.

implication, material Synonymous with *conditional implication operation*.

implication operation, conditional ⬦ *conditional implication operation*.

impulse An electrical signal the duration of which is short compared with the time scale under consideration.

incident A *failure* which requires activity by an operator to correct or remove the jobs concerned.

incidentals time Time during which a computer is being used effectively, but not for productive *runs* or *program* development.

Incidentals time could be spent on demonstrations, training, etc. ⟡ *effective time, serviceable time.*

inclusion Synonymous with *conditional implication operation.*

inclusive-or operation A *logical operation* applied to two *operands* which will produce a result depending on the *bit patterns* of the operands and according to the following rules for each *bit position*:

Operands		Result
p	q	r
0	0	0
1	0	1
0	1	1
1	1	1

For example, operating on the following 6-bit operands,

$$p = 110110$$
$$q = 011010$$

$$r = 111110$$

Also known as disjunction, logical sum, or operation. ⟡ *Boolean algebra.*

incomplete program A *program* which consists of a basic framework of *instructions* designed to perform some general type of operation, but which cannot be run until the specific requirements of a particular version of the operation are supplied to the program either by *parameters* or by *own coding.*

incomplete routine Synonymous with *incomplete program.*

inconsistency A data condition detected by *software*, in which the data concerned is found to contain contradictory statements.

increment A quantity which is added to another quantity.

incremental computer A computer designed to process changes in variables; for example a *digital differential analyser*. Contrasted with *absolute value computer.*

incremental display Synonymous with *cathode ray tube visual display unit*; a device employed to convert *digital data* into character or graphical form.

incremental dump A method of *dumping* in which data is preserved for *security* purposes, by regularly *writing* away small amounts of data at frequent intervals. For example, used to preserve the contents of *filestore.*

incremental plotter A unit providing output from a computer in the form of continuous curves or points plotted, along with information in character form, under control of a *program*.

incremental representation A method of representing variables used in *incremental computers*, in which changes in variables rather than the variables themselves are represented.

incremental representation, binary ◊ *binary incremental representation*.

incremental representation, ternary ◊ *ternary incremental representation*.

independent sector designating device A device used for *group indication*.

index 1. A table of references, held in *memory* in some *key* sequence, which may be *addressed* to obtain the addresses of other items of data, for example items in a *file* on some *backing store*. 2. A number used to select a particular item from an *array* of items in *memory*. ◊ *indexing*.

indexed address An *address modified* by the contents of an *index word*.

Also known as variable address.

indexing 1. A method used to retrieve information from a *table* in *memory* or a *file* on a *direct access store*. For example, on a direct access device a file may be organized in such a way that one part contains an *index* which serves to locate items in other parts of the file. 2. The *modification* of an *instruction* by the contents of an *index word*.

index point A reference point during the cycle of operation of any *punched card machine* in which cards are transported by the action of rotating shafts. An index point may, for example, correspond to the moment when a *card column* or a row of *punching positions* on a card is opposite the *reading* or *punching station*.

index positions Synonymous with *punching positions*.

index register In some computers *program modification* is performed automatically and indeed it may be always used to *address* certain *locations* within *memory*. In such machines there will be at least one index register which will contain a *modifier* to enable data to be indirectly addressed. Each program *instruction* must therefore refer to an index register when addressing locations in store. Sometimes known as a *modifier register*.

index sequential access method The technique of *accessing records* held on a *file* in *index sequential file organization*.

index sequential file A *file* in which *records* are subject to *index sequential file organization.*

index sequential file organization A type of *file organization* for *files* on a *direct access storage* device in which the *address* of a *record* on a *physical file* is identified by reference to an *index* [1] which contains the record *key.*

index word During *program modification* an index word may be used to contain a *modifier* which will be added to a *basic instruction* when it is executed. An index word may, for example, be used to *address* data stored in a *table* in *memory*. ✧ *index register.*

indicator 1. A lamp or display device on a *peripheral unit* or a *console.* 2. A device which can be set when a specified condition occurs (e.g. when a calculation has produced a negative result) and which may be tested by *program* to initiate an appropriate course of action. Related to *alteration switch.*

indicator chart A chart used by a programmer during the *logical design* and *coding* of a *program* to record details about the use of *indicators* in the program. Part of program *documentation.*

indicator, end of file ✧ *end of file marker.*

indicator, sign check ✧ *sign check indicator.*

indirect addressing A *programming* technique in which the *address* part of an *instruction* refers to another *location* which contains another address. This further address may specify an *operand* or yet another address.

Also known as multi-level addressing.

indirect control The relationship between two units in which one controls the other by some sequence of events involving manual intervention. The unit being controlled is *off-line* to the controlling unit.

inductive potential divider An auto-transformer with a toroidal winding and one, or more, adjustable sliders. Used on electro-mechanical *analog computers.*

industrial data processing *Data processing* concerned with or controlling some industrial process, as distinct from *commercial data processing* or *scientific data processing.*

ineffective time Time during which a machine is serviceable (✧ *serviceable time*) but effective use of the machine is not made, due to *operating delays* or *idle time.* Contrasted with *effective time.*

infix notation A notation for representing *logical operations* in which the *operator* is written between the *operands*, e.g. A&B where & represents the operation 'and'. Contrasted with *prefix notation.*

information Sometimes the following distinction is made between *information* and *data*: information results from the processing of data, i.e. information is derived from the assembly, analysis or summarizing of data into a meaningful form.

information bits In a signal carried in coded form, information bits are *characters* or *digits* which are *data* and which can be processed to provide *information* subsequently; the term does not include digits which may be required for *control* purposes by *hardware* or *software*.

information channel The *hardware* used in a *data transmission* link between two terminals. Including *modulator, demodulator* and any *error detection* equipment required. A channel may involve transmission by telegraph or telephone lines or by a radio link.

information – feedback system A control system used in message transmission, in which information received at a terminal is retransmitted to the sending terminal for automatic checking.

information flow analysis The study of an organization or system in which analytical techniques are used to ascertain information about the origin and routing of documentation and to ascertain the requirements and uses of the *data elements* at each stage.

information, loss of Synonymous with *walk-down*.

information processing The processing of data to derive meaningful results as *information*. Generally used as a synonym for *data processing*.

information requirements The results required from any series of data processing operations; e.g. the information required by management as output from a system.

information retrieval A branch of computing technology related to the storage and categorization of large quantities of information and the automatic retrieval of specific items from the *files* and indexes maintained. Essentially incorporating the ability to retrieve items with relatively short *access time* and the ability to add additional information to the files as it arises. Usually requiring a *direct access store* with *on-line interrogation units*. ✧ the general article *Information Retrieval Techniques*.

information retrieval techniques Information Retrieval is the phrase used generally to describe the problems of recovering, from collections of data, those particular items of information which are required at a particular time for a particular purpose. Information retrieval is basically a problem of communication: communication between the originator of information and the individual requiring to use the information. What is required is a method for providing the closest possible coincidence between the description of the subject by the user and the description of the information produced by the originator. Thus a third element appears in the line of communication between these two: the process of classifying or indexing the information. A common information retrieval system is a library. The user *accesses* the individual books he requires via a catalogue organized in such a way that he can formulate a request, find a reference to the book and then locate the book on the library shelves.

Information retrieval involves basically the following sequence of events: (i) Information coming into the system is analysed and given some form of classification. (ii) The information is stored in an ordered manner (not necessarily corresponding to the classification made at stage (i)). (iii) The user translates his requirement for information into a classification by a process analogous to that made for original information. (iv) A search of the store is made for an item with a classification corresponding to that made by the user. This step may be divided into two, the first stage being a search through an index to the classifications, which will give a reference to the location of the item in the store. (v) When a match or *hit* is obtained, the item of information is extracted from the store.

It can be seen from this general outline that the events correspond generally to normal experience of searching for information, for example in libraries, catalogues of merchandise, office filing systems, trade directories, reference book indexes. These techniques have been adopted and extended, utilizing the great speeds and storage facilities of computers to provide rapid access to increasingly large and diverse collections of information. There are an almost infinite number of possible approaches to the problems of information retrieval: this article can only attempt to describe in general terms some of the approaches made to solving the problems posed by each of the steps described above.

The problem of information retrieval starts, in fact, with that of storing information. Two possibilities are open: either the information entering the system can be stored separately from the index used to reference it (as happens in a library) or the index and the information can be stored together (as happens in an office filing system). In computer applications, the choice depends on the amount and type of computer *storage devices* available and the type of information being dealt with. A computer system used, for example, to provide an information retrieval system for accessing technical literature would normally be of the first type, the actual information items being stored apart from the index. A system of personnel records, however, might be of the second type, a complete computer record being created and stored for each individual together with identifying and classifying information. The development of storage devices with differing capacities and *access time* means that in some systems the information may be held on one type of device while the index to be searched is on another. Other developments, particularly in the field of miniaturization of original documents through microfilming, enable physical copies of the documents to be stored with some form of coded representation of reference information. *Punched card* systems have been developed by which microfilmed documents may be inserted within a card on which reference information is punched. By using mechanical devices, selected cards may be retrieved and the associated document obtained. Extensions of this principle to computers involve associating microfilms with magnetic recording surfaces – either tape or cards – which can be coded and read by computers. Other developments are the recording of televised images of original documents on video tape, and associating the video image with identifying information which can be read by the computer. A different approach is the development of devices which can read printed documents automatically, and convert them into computer format.

Indexing information within a system makes possible the correlation of requests for information with relevant items of information stored by the system. There are many possible indexing schemes, but basically there are two types of approach to the problem. Each item of information may be given an identifying *key*, which in the case of systems separating the information from the index will act as the cross-reference from the index to the item. As well as this key, selected attributes possessed by the information will be coded in some form and associated with the identifying key. For example, in a system of personnel records, the identifying information may be a staff number, followed by a series of codes isolating such attributes as experience, qualifications, marital status, occupation code. In addition, if the system is one which incorporates information together with reference tables, there may be non-coded details such as the individual's name and address, job title, etc. An alternative approach is that of inverse filing. In this system each individual item is again given an identification code. Selected attributes are chosen, and a list of all possible combinations of attributes is made. Against each combination of attributes is placed the identifying key of all items of information having that combination. This system is used, for example, in assisting police forces to identify criminals from fingerprints. Any fingerprint may have several different attributes. Lists are made of all combinations of these attributes, and any known criminal having any combination of attributes is listed against the combination. Thus by studying any fingerprint, identifying its attributes and comparing them with the files, the police can find a list of all criminals whose prints have the same combination of attributes. The more precise this classification can be the smaller will be the short list obtained; ideally, the coding of attributes should be sufficiently detailed to identify a single individual.

The choice of which system to adopt depends again on the type of information being considered, and also on the sort of questions expected. Inverse filing can only be used if the type of inquiry will always be limited precisely to a given combination of attributes, since adding new attributes or revising the codes used is a difficult and complex activity. The alternative system is more generally used when flexibility of approach is required, since any combination of different attributes can be specified, and extension of attributes merely involves adding another code to each item of information without necessarily altering any of the codes already used.

Most storage devices are used in information retrieval systems, both for storing of indexes and for storing information. The type of device chosen will depend on the type of file organization adopted (*inverted files* or *serial files*) and on the amount of data to be stored. *Magnetic tape* is usually used for serial files, which require each record to be examined in turn when any search for information is made. If, however, the description of required attributes can be used to generate an *address* where the corresponding information is required, as for example in an inverted file, then *direct access* storage devices may be chosen. The great capacities of direct access devices may also be utilized for files which contain large quantities of information. These files may be held serially, and individual items located by first searching a magnetic tape containing index information only, the relevant items being accessed directly from the storage device by means of an address found on the index tape. Another factor relevant to the choice between types of storage device is the expected usage of the system. The time taken to read through a long magnetic tape file may not be justified if the normal expected 'hit rate' (the ratio of items satisfying the given inquiry to the total of items examined) is low.

Performance characteristics of an information retrieval system can be measured in terms of completeness, relevance, specificity and response time. 'Completeness' refers to the number of items which could be relevant to the user's inquiry that are in fact retrieved by the system. This will normally depend on the accuracy and efficiency of the coding and indexing system adopted. 'Relevance' is the inverse of completeness: it is a measure of the number of items retrieved by the system which do in fact conform to the needs of the user. 'Specificity' is a term which refers to the degree of generality of the information retrieved. These first three characteristics depend on the system design. The fourth item, 'response time', is a measure of the time taken to retrieve an item of information from store, and depends also on the *hardware* involved.

One of the major items of applications *software* provided by most manufacturers is software concerned with aspects of information retrieval. This software can assist a user at all the stages of setting up and using such a system. Indexing can be assisted by means of such routines as K W I C (key word in context) indexes, which provide lists of items of information sequenced by specific words or codes, each word or code appearing in the sequence in its appropriate location. Files of information can be subjected to statistical analysis to determine the frequency of occurrence of attributes, thus isolating factors for further identification. Routines can assist in setting up and maintaining files on tape and direct access devices. On the problem of specifying requests to a computer file, software exists which enables a user to relate different combinations of attributes by means of Boolean operators (A N D, O R) and logical relations (equal to, greater than, less than, etc.). More specialized software may be provided for specific information retrieval problems, such as library cataloguing, indexing of technical literature and personnel record systems.

information separator An *indicator* which is used to separate *fields* or items of information within a *record*, particularly a *variable length record*.

information system A general term to denote all the operations and procedures involved in a *data processing* system; i.e. including all clerical operations and communication methods used within the organization concerned.

information theory The theory concerned with the rate of information transmission over a communications network; related to the type of transmission channel employed. The theory was a result of the study of the ways of sending messages, particularly telephony, and relates to the least number of decisions necessary to identify any message in a given set of messages. ⟡ *Probability Theory*.

information word A collection of *characters* representing information from a *store*, and handled by *hardware* or *software* as a complete unit. ⟡ *word*.

inherent store A *store* forming part of the *hardware* of a computer system. Contrasted with *data carrier store*.

inherited error 1. An error in a result or intermediate result, attributed to some previous stage of processing. For example, in *single-step operation*, an error carried through from a previous step. 2. An error arising initially from the inability to measure values with sufficient *accuracy*.

inhibit To prevent a particular signal from occurring, or to prevent a particular operation from being performed.

inhibiting signal A signal which prevents an operation from being performed.

inhibit pulse A *pulse* applied to a *ferrite core* to oppose a corresponding *write pulse* and thus prevent the cell from assuming a set condition.

initial condition Synonymous with *entry condition*.

initial condition mode Synonymous with *reset mode*.

initial instructions A *routine* stored within a computer to facilitate the *loading* of *programs*.

Also known as initial orders.

initialization A process performed at the beginning of a *program* or *subroutine* to ensure that all *indicators* and *constants* are set to prescribed conditions and values before the routine is obeyed.

initialize ⟡ *initialization*.

initial orders Synonymous with *initial instructions*.

initiate Synonymous with *trigger*.[2]

ink bleed The flow of ink by capillary action beyond the prescribed area of characters when characters are being printed for *optical character recognition*. Such action can prevent the character from being recognized when it is subsequently *read*.

ink ribbon A continuous ribbon of ink, used, for example, when printing from a computer *line printer* or a *punched card tabulator*. In the case of a computer line printer a typical ribbon is sixteen inches wide and several feet long, and is fed vertically through the print unit while the printer is operating; a typical tabulator ribbon is only half an inch wide and is fed laterally across the print unit.

ink smudge The condition in which ink appears outside the prescribed area of a printed character. In *optical character recognition* this condition can prevent the character from being recognized during reading.

ink squeezeout The displacement of ink from the centre of a character when characters are printed for *optical character recognition*.

in-line coding A collection of *program instructions* written as part of the *main path* of a *routine*.

in-line processing Synonymous with *demand processing*.

in-line subroutine A *subroutine* the *coding* of which must be repeated each time it is required, in contrast to a subroutine which can be entered from the main *program* each time it is required.

in-plant Abbreviation of inside plant; a term used in *data transmission* to denote a communication system operating within a central office or factory.

in-plant system Relating to a communications system for handling data automatically within a particular building or group of buildings, e.g. a factory. ✧ *input station*.

input The process of transferring *data*, or *program instructions*, into *memory* from some *peripheral unit*. Sometimes used to denote the data itself, sometimes to denote the signal applied to a circuit or device. Also used as a verb.

input area An area within *memory* reserved for data input from a *peripheral unit* or *backing store*. The data once received may be *edited* and distributed to *work areas* for processing.
Also known as input block.

input block Synonymous with *input area*.

input buffer ✧ *input / output buffers*.

input devices Within the *central processor* of any computer, information can be processed at very high speeds, but before the central processor can be set to work, the data and *programs* must be entered into the computer *memory*. This is done by means of input devices which provide a vehicle for communication between the computer and the people who are concerned with its operation.

Some form of intermediate coding is required to bridge the gap between the language of human beings and the internal *machine code* language of the computer: human beings are able to recognize and understand the relationships between numerals, characters and symbols, whereas within the internal store of a computer the various electronic circuits are able to respond to patterns of electrical impulses. There are often various stages of translation between the original character representation used by human beings and the

211

internal code of the computer, *punched cards* being a good example: initially, during the course of a commercial procedure, a clerk may enter details of a transaction on to an original document (e.g. an order form). A copy of this form will be dispatched to the *data preparation* centre where an operator using an *automatic keypunch* will punch the information into a card in accordance with a standard punching code. This card may then be checked by a further operator using a *punched card verifier*, and in this way the initial stages are completed and an item of data is represented as holes punched into a card. The cards representing a particular series of transactions will eventually be *batched* together and input to the computer via a *card reader*, which will read the cards and translate the information into a series of coded impulses which can be transferred to the central processor and be stored in the computer memory. Card readers generally consist of a *card hopper* into which the cards are initially loaded, and a card track which transports the cards past a *reading head*. The reading head is often a photo-electric sensing device which is able to detect the holes in each *card column* and generate appropriate coded signals. After a card has been read it is deposited in a *stacker*. (Some card readers have two or more stackers to permit cards to be outsorted according to whether they are read successfully or not.) The speed of card reading varies from one machine to another but an average would be in the region of 1,000 cards per minute.

Paper tape is an input medium similar to punched cards and generally involves all the stages described above. First the data is punched into paper tape by means of a keyboard-operated tape punch, then it may be verified, and finally it is read into memory by a paper tape reader which may operate at about 1,000 characters per second.

Paper tape readers and card readers are fairly reliable devices and are designed to input large batches of data, but although, as mechanical devices, it can be said that they operate at high speed, they nevertheless limit the operation of computer routines in which processing is carried out at electronic speeds.

Other devices, such as *key-to-disk units*, allow data to be written direct from data station keyboards to a magnetic medium without the need for the intermediate process of producing punched cards or paper tape.

There are various programming and systems techniques which can be used to mitigate the limitations of these input devices, including the use of *input buffers* which permit peripheral units to be operated continuously at high speed, and also the use of *time-sharing* techniques to enable the computer to perform other functions whilst waiting for input from a slow peripheral. With the development of *on-line* storage systems and *multiprogramming* a further range of input devices comes to the fore; these are devices which are permanently connected to the computer but which are situated at distant terminals to record transactions as they occur. Here it is not so much the speed of the device which counts, but the fact that the complete system is able to deal with the transactions as they arise, and it is then mainly a question of considering the economics of the number and type of input devices required in order to deal with the volume of transactions to be handled at each transaction point.

Another characteristic of these on-line input devices is that they frequently incorporate features to permit two-way communication; for example, electric typewriters or teleprinters can be connected via communications circuits to a computer. These connexions may be over long distances or may be part of an *in-plant* system. Here the operator may enter data directly into the system by typing on a keyboard and the computer may reply by causing a message to be printed directly at the inquiry terminal. One of the limiting factors here is that the operator may make mistakes in keying in the inquiry or data, and usually a comprehensive set of *validity checks* must be performed by the computer to detect such errors. Since such a system deals essentially with transactions as they arise errors are often detected immediately in the natural course of performing the transaction.

Where there is a danger that incorrect data may be input, much of the descriptive information relevant to any transaction can be input by means of some medium which allows certain elements of data to be prerecorded. For example in some in-plant systems operatives may be given prepunched cards or plastic tickets which contain standard information such as job number, or employee number. Various simple card-reading devices can be located in the plant to record events that occur, and it is only necessary for the operative to insert the prepunched card and supply the variable data required for each transaction. The input devices will read this prerecorded data directly into the computer system and the operative can at the same time set up variable data by means of a keyboard, a dial, or a series of switches. Items such as date and time can often be generated automatically as each event is recorded.

Character recognition systems provide similar features; here it is often a question of prerecording data as characters on documents for *optical character recognition* or *magnetic ink character recognition*. These documents may be issued to be returned eventually to the system with the variable data added. For example, in electricity billing, documents may be printed with optical characters giving descriptive data for each customer. They are given to meter readers who add marks indicating details of electricity consumed since the last reading. The documents are eventually batched and an optical character reader is used to read the information on the documents directly into the computer system. Bank cheques preprinted with magnetic-ink characters are a further example of this type of system. Although these character recognition systems do not provide a direct on-line input to the computer they do allow data to be captured more accurately, speedily and economically than other more conventional systems.

To return to on-line input/output systems, it is important to note that *visual display units* have many applications as input devices in *real time* systems. These units, which can be used for remote in-plant inquiry stations, usually have keyboards to enable transactions or inquiries to be input directly into the central computer, and have *cathode ray tube display* units to enable results to be presented to the inquirer.

Most of the input systems described above are designed to reduce the time required to get data into the computer for processing and to try to eliminate many of the stages necessary in more conventional systems. Graphical display units probably provide more potential than the other systems, and particularly noteworthy are the developments being made in the use of *light pens* (devices which enable data to be input into memory directly as drawings or graphs). The initial input of data is still a comparative limitation in most computing systems and it is to be expected that considerable efforts will be made to develop improved techniques.

input instruction code An *instruction set* forming part of some automatic input *language* designed to simplify the programmer's task in writing an *input routine*.

input limited Pertaining to a *program* in which the overall processing time is limited by the speed of an input unit; i.e. during the course of the program processing is delayed to await the input of further items for processing. ⇔ *output limited* and *processor limited*.

input loading The electrical load placed on units supplying a signal to the input of a device.

input log 1. A manual record prepared by an *operator* of all data input to a computer. 2. Within an *operating system* a *file* containing a record of all *messages* input to a system with the objective of allowing a *restart* to identify incompleted messages. ✧ *log*².

input magazine Synonymous with *card hopper*.

input/output buffers Areas of *memory* assigned to receive data transmitted to or from a *peripheral unit*. The use of buffer areas enables a number of peripheral units to be activated simultaneously at full speed while data is processed within the *central processor*. On earlier machines, areas of storage were often allocated permanently for this purpose, but it is now usual to permit the programmer to specify the *locations* required according to the characteristics of his *program*.

input/output channel A *communication channel* for transmitting data to and from a central computer.

input/output control The *hardware/software* system which controls the interaction between a *central processor* and its *peripheral units*. Usually different modes of control are available according to the type of peripheral unit and the speed of transfer.

input/output control systems *Software*, usually supplied by the computer manufacturer, designed to control the performance of *input* and *output operations*, including such activities as error checking, *record* batching, writing of *labels*, etc.

input/output devices ◊ general articles on *Input Devices, Output Devices*.

input/output interrupt A break in processing during which a *central processor* may transmit or receive a unit of data to or from a *peripheral unit*. ◊ *interrupt*.

input/output interrupt identification The act of ascertaining the cause of an *input/output interrupt*, including identifying the *channel*¹ and type of *peripheral unit* causing the interrupt, and the status of the peripheral unit.

input/output interrupt indicators *Indicators* which are set when an *input/output interrupt* occurs.

input/output library A collection of *programs* or *routines*, usually developed by computer manufacturers for users of their equipment. Part of a library of standard routines but denoting specifically those designed to control the operation of *peripheral units*. Such routines relieve the programmer of the task of writing standard routines common to a whole range of problems.

input/output limited Pertaining to a *program* in which the overall processing time is governed by the speed of *input/output peripheral units*; i.e. processing is delayed from time to time during the program whilst data is transferred to or from the *central processor*. Contrasted with *processor limited*.

input/output referencing A method by which specific *input* or *output devices* can be referenced by means of a symbolic name within a *program*, the actual device allocated to the program being determined at *run* time.

input/output routines *Routines* specifically designed to simplify the *programming* of standard operations involving *input/output* equipment, e.g. the *blocking* of *records*, use of *input/output buffers*.

input/output switching Relating to a technique in which *peripheral units* are allocated more than one *channel*[1] for communicating with a *central processor*. Thus if access to a peripheral is required the connexion may be made through any available channel, so that during the course of one *program* several channels may be used to service a particular peripheral.

input/output traffic control This term is sometimes used to denote the *hardware/software* facilities which coordinate the activities of a *central processor* and its *peripheral units*. The function of this controlling feature is to permit the simultaneous operation of several *input/output devices* while data is being processed in the central processor.

input/output trunks *Interface* channels between a *processor* and its *peripheral units*. The number of peripherals connected to a processor depends on the number of trunks available.

input/output unit ⋄ *input device, output device.*

input program Synonymous with *input routine*.

input record 1. A *record* read into *memory* from an *input device* during a *run*. 2. The current record stored in an *input area* ready for processing.

input register A *register* designed to accept data from a *peripheral unit* at relatively slow speed and to supply this data to the *central processor* at higher speed as a series of units.

input routine That part of a *program* which controls and monitors the transfer of data from some external medium to an *input area* in *memory*.

input section 1. That section of a *program* which controls the *input* of data from external devices to *memory*. 2. The area of a *store* reserved for the receipt of input data.

input stacker A *magazine* fitted to a *punched card* machine in which cards are placed prior to reading or punching. Note : the term *stacker* is also used in some cases to refer to the receptacle in which cards are automatically stacked after reading or punching.

input station In an *in-plant* communications system input stations may be situated at various locations within a building to enable personnel to *input data* directly into the systems as *transactions* or events occur. This enables files to be immediately updated, and if necessary exception reports (◊ *exception principle system*) can be generated immediately for management.

input storage An area of *memory* assigned to the task of holding *data* input from a *peripheral unit*.
Also known as *input area*, input block.

input unit Any *peripheral unit* which provides input to the *central processor* of a computer, e.g. a *card reader*, *paper tape reader*. ◊ general article on *Input Devices*.

input unit, manual ◊ *manual input unit*.

inquiry and communications systems Pertaining to computer systems in which central files are maintained from data input from various sources using *data transmission* equipment or *in-plant* networks. Inquiries may be *addressed* into the system from remote stations, immediately producing response from the central system.

inquiry and subscriber display A *visual display unit* designed for operation as a remote *interrogation unit* for a *real time* data processing system. Capable of displaying information requested by the subscriber who keys in his inquiry on a *keyboard*.

inquiry display terminal A device which consists of a *keyboard* and a *cathode ray tube* display unit. Inquiries are specified to the computer by means of messages typed on the keyboard, and results are displayed on the cathode ray tube.

inquiry, remote ◊ *remote inquiry, real time*.

inquiry station A terminal from which a *remote inquiry* may be transmitted to a central computing system.

inquiry unit Any device used to transmit an inquiry into a central computing system.

inscribe To rewrite data on a document in a form capable of being read by a *character recognition* device, e.g. the printing of the amount of a cheque in *magnetic ink* characters on the original cheque.

inside-plant ◊ *in-plant system*.

installation 1. The installation of a computer including the preparation of the site and all services required; ◊ general article on *Installation of Computers*. 2. A place where there is a computer.

installation of computers It would be wrong to consider the process of installing a computer as the installation of the equipment

217

alone; more properly one should consider the development of all the resources necessary for the *data processing centre* as a whole, including the *hardware*, *software*, the buildings, air conditioning equipment, office furniture and specialized cabinets and furniture for storing and handling *input/output media*. The recruitment and training of new staff and the education of existing personnel must also be an integral part of any installation plan, and careful thought must be given to the timing of these activities. In this present article consideration is given mainly to those aspects referred to as the 'environment'.

The computer itself should be housed in an air-conditioned area which must include an engineer's room, and a room or area set aside for storing magnetic media – e.g. *magnetic tapes* and *magnetic disks*. Adjacent to the computer room there should be an area for *data preparation* equipment, *work assembly*, an output dispatch area, and possibly further storage areas for non-magnetic materials – *punched cards, paper tape, stationery*, etc. There must be general office accommodation for computer operations staff and also for programmers, systems analysts, etc., but these latter need not be adjacent to the computer room.

The computer site plan should always be developed in consultation with the computer manufacturer's staff. It is most important to provide sufficient space and to site units in such a way that space is available to meet operating and servicing requirements. The floor of the computer room must be designed to bear the weight of the equipment, and generally a false floor is required to house cables and perhaps air conditioning ducts. The ceiling must be constructed to house air conditioning ducts and the height should permit a suitable air flow. The whole fabric of the computer room should be designed to minimize dust and to reduce the general noise level. The power requirements are important for the whole installation, and one of the first steps must be to test the main power supply to see if it meets the requirements specified for the equipment; for example a voltage regulator might be needed. Lighting within the computer room should be bright and evenly distributed.

The humidity and temperature of the computer room must be controlled strictly within limits laid down for the equipment. The air-conditioning plant installed for this purpose must also include an air-infiltration system to ensure that particles are removed from the air to a specified efficiency.

Computers are not potential fire risks in themselves, but there is a vital need to provide equipment for automatic fire detection, alarm systems and fire extinguishing equipment in the installation. Particular regard should be given to special furniture for the protection of magnetic recording media containing data files.

The cost of constructing these environmental conditions is often considerable, particularly where new structures have to be built to house the computer. It is therefore important to ensure that there is plenty of capacity for later expansion, not merely in terms of physical space required, but also in such expensive facilities as the air-conditioning plant.

The whole process of installation must be scheduled so that the various activities can be dovetailed to meet the final delivery date for the computer hardware, and to meet the various intermediate dates for the arrival of staff and ancilliary equipment.

installation processing control A system for automatically scheduling the handling and processing of *jobs* within a computer installation in order to reduce time spent in setting up jobs and to deal automatically with job priorities.

installation tape number A unique reference number given to a *reel* of *magnetic tape* to identify it. Differentiated from the tape manufacturer's reference number.

installation time Time during which a computer is being installed, commissioned and tested before being handed over to a customer. ◊ general article on *Installation of Computers*.

instruction That part of a computer *program* which tells the computer what function to perform at that *stage*. Instructions are usually examined by a special unit, sometimes known as a *program controller*, which interprets each instruction and initiates the actions specified. An instruction consists of a series of characters subdivided into groups which represent coded commands to the computer. An *operation* such as add or subtract may be specified, along with one or more *addresses* which specify the *locations* of *operands* to be used at that step; for a more detailed description of this, ◊ *Instruction Format*.

Also known as command, order. ◊ the general article on *Programming*.

instruction, actual ◊ *effective instruction*.

instruction address The *address* of a *location* containing an *instruction*.

instruction address register A *register* which forms part of the *program controller*, and which stores the *addresses* of *instructions* in order to control the retrieval of the instructions from *memory* during the operation of a program.

instruction area The area of *memory* used to store *program instructions*.

instruction, arithmetic ◊ *arithmetical instruction*.

instruction code The set of symbols and characters forming the rules of a particular computer code or *programming language*. Also known as order code, *machine code, instruction set, function code, operation code*.

instruction, conditional branch ◊ *conditional branch*.

instruction, conditional stop ◊ *conditional stop instruction*.

instruction, control transfer Synonymous with *branch instruction*.

instruction counter A device that indicates the *location* of the next *instruction* to be obeyed in a *program*. Usually part of, or associated with, the *program controller*.

instruction, discrimination Synonymous with *branch instruction*.

instruction, dummy Synonymous with *do nothing instruction*.

instruction format Different types of *program instructions* may be prepared in different formats. To illustrate the term, a *word oriented* machine will be considered first. An instruction is usually required to fit within the basic *word-length* of the computer, allowing instructions to be processed as individual units. An instruction consists of a series of digits subdivided into groups, each group having a certain functional significance within the *machine code* system of the particular computer, and the way in which the various digits are allocated to represent specific functions is referred to as the instruction format. As a minimum an instruction must contain digits to represent the *function* to be performed, and two other groups to represent the *addresses* of *operands*. Thus for example, a machine having a word-length of 24 *binary digits* might have an instruction format as follows:

4 bits	10 bits	10 bits
Function Code	Operand 1	Operand 2

This simple example would only allow up to 16 unique *bit* combinations to represent different function codes (e.g. *add, subtract, logical shift*, etc.) and would permit operations capable of addressing operands stored in *memory locations* up to word number 1,023 only.

This type of system is referred to as a two-address format, and the implication is that the result of any *arithmetic operation* will always replace one of the original operands. To avoid this a three-address format could have been adopted by specifying a third location address to be used for the result, but in general this practice is not adopted since it requires the machine to have a long basic word-length. As an alternative, a format known as the one-and-a-half address format is often adopted. In this situation one of the operands must always be moved to one of a series of special *registers* before being subject to any arithmetic process, thus the program instruction specifies a function code, a memory address for one operand and a register address for the other operand. The result is usually formed in the specified register. Thus the registers are used as *work areas* and are not required to store any particular operand for more than a few program steps, and the original operands are retained in memory if required. As only 8 or 12 registers may be required, a few digits only are needed to represent the register address in the instruction format. Some instruction formats also enable the programmer to specify an *index word* which may contain a *modifier* for the memory address specified in the instruction. On a computer with this facility the technique of *program modification* is much simplified from the programmer's point of view, and also the machine code system can address memory locations far in excess of the maximum number given by the operand field of the instruction (◊ *indirect addressing*).

A sample of an instruction format incorporating the features mentioned is given below:

7 bits	3 bits	12 bits	2 bits
Function code	Register	Operand	Index register
Can specify any of over 120 separate functions	Can address any one of 8 registers	Can address locations up to word 4095	Can address one of three index registers for indirect addressing

Another format is the four-address instruction in which the programmer is able to specify two operand addresses, the address of the result and the address of the next instruction to be performed.

So far only word machines have been mentioned, but the same principles apply to *character oriented* machines, except that groups of characters are used to represent functional elements rather than binary digits as in the example above. One of the features of character machines is the ability to specify *variable length* operands; for example, it is possible to specify an operand of one character only, or any number of characters up to the full size of the memory unit. The usual practice in the character machine is to specify the address of the first and last character locations of the required operand, or else the address of the first location and the number of characters in the operand.

Some instructions perform operations upon one operand and these will specify one address only. However, it is often necessary to include additional information in the instruction format; for example, a *shift instruction* requires an indication of the number of places to be shifted, a *conditional branch instruction* may require an indication of the tests to be applied to an operand. A brief study of the *instruction set* of any particular machine will reveal other examples.

To summarize: the instruction format is part of the basic machine code of the computer, and it specifies the way in which the digits or characters are allocated to represent the functional codes of the computer's instruction set.

instruction format, one-plus-one   ◊ *one-plus-one address.*

instruction format, zero address   ◊ *zero address instruction format.*

instruction, machine code   ◊ *machine code.*

instruction modification   Changing the value of some parts of an *instruction*, so that the next time the modified instruction is obeyed it will perform a different *operation*. Since an instruction is held within the computer as a set of digits, *modification* is performed by treating the instruction as though it were an item of *data* and performing an appropriate *arithmetic* or *logical operation* on it. ◊ *address modification* and general articles on *Programming* and *Program Modification.*

instruction, multiple address   ◊ *multiple address.*

instruction, no-op   ◊ *no-operation instruction.*

instruction, null   Synonymous with *do nothing instruction.*

instruction register   A control unit register in which the address of the current instruction is stored.
Also known as *control register* and program address counter.

instruction repertoire   Synonymous with *instruction set.*

instruction set   The repertoire of commands available as the *language* of a particular computer or *programming* system.
Also known as *instruction code, machine code* and *order code.*

instruction, table look-up ◊ *table look-up instruction.*

instruction time The time taken to *staticize* an *instruction* within the *instruction registers* of a computer, plus the time required to execute the instruction.

instruction, unconditional branch ◊ *unconditional branch instruction.*

instruction, unconditional control transfer Synonymous with *unconditional branch instruction.*

instruction, unconditional jump Synonymous with *unconditional branch instruction.*

instruction, waste Synonymous with *do nothing instruction.*

instruction word A computer *word* containing an *instruction.* An *instruction format* is usually designed to fit within the basic *word length* of a computer. Thus instructions may be moved and manipulated like any other items of data stored in *memory.*

instruction, zero address ◊ *zero address instruction format.*

integer A whole number, i.e. one that does not contain a fractional component.

integral Pertaining to that part of a *mixed number* which is to the left of the decimal point.

integrated circuit A circuit in which all the components are chemically formed upon a single piece of semiconductor material. Computers using integrated circuits are said to be *third generation*, as contrasted with *first generation* machines using thermionic valves and *second generation* machines using transistors.

integrated data processing A concept which implies that all systems within an organization are considered as sub-systems of a larger system which embraces all *data processing* requirements within that organization. In this way the systems are dovetailed to achieve, as far as possible, continuous and automatic processing with the elimination of unnecessary duplications, particularly seeking to reduce the number of entry points for *raw data.*

integrated management information system ◊ *management information system.*

integrator 1. ◊ *integrator (computing unit).* 2. Synonymous with *digital integrator.*

integrator (computing unit) 1. A device which has two *input* variables (x and y) and one *output* variable (z), the value of z being proportional to the integral of y with respect to x. 2. A device with one input and one output variable, the value of the output variable being proportional to the integral of the input variable with respect to elapsed time.

223

integrity An attribute of a set of *data* signifying that the data is self-consistent (e.g. a *hash total* check has proved *valid*) and consistent with the information system the data is representing (e.g. a *validity check* has proved valid).

intelligence The ability of a system or device to improve its capability by repeated performance of a particular problem.

intelligent terminal A *terminal* which within its *hardware* contains logic circuits capable of retaining a *program* enabling the terminal to undertake some *processing* of data independently of the *processor* to which the terminal is connected.

interactive batch job A *background job* run under an *operating system* in *batch mode*, which is initiated and monitored from a *terminal* operating in a *M A C* mode by means of *messages* or *output* to a terminal, and which can accept *input* from the terminal.

interactive display Any *display* which allows the user to *input* data in response to the information displayed.

interactive mode Synonymous with *conversational mode*.

interblock A *hardware* device or *software* feature which will prevent interference between one part of a computing system and another. For example, in *multiprogramming*, to prevent one *program* from violating the *memory* area allocated to another.

interblock gap The distance between *blocks* of *records* on *magnetic tape*. The gap is originally created during the period in which the tape is slowing down at the end of a *write* operation. During subsequent passes of the *reel* during *reading* from the tape, the tape may be stopped and accelerated to full speed in this distance. Two gap lengths commonly in use are 0.75 inches and 0.56 inches. Also known as *interblock space*.

interblock space Synonymous with *interblock gap*.

interchangeable type bar Relating to a certain type of *punched card tabulator* in which special *type bars* can be exchanged by the operator to permit the printing of *special characters* or *symbols* for any particular job.

intercycle A cycle of operation, on a *punched card tabulator*, in which card feeding is suspended and *control totals* are created and printed.

interface This term is used to refer to the *channels* and associated control circuitry providing the connexion between a *central processor* and its *peripheral units*. It may be used more generally to refer to the connexion between any two units. ✧ *standard interface*.

interface channel ✧ *interface*.

interface routines Linking *routines* between one system and another.

interference The presence of unwanted signals in a communications circuit.

interfix A method used in *information retrieval* systems to describe the relation between *key words* in *records*, in such a way that inquiries are satisfied without ambiguity.

interior label A *label* written to the beginning of a *magnetic tape* in order to identify its contents. Contrasted with *exterior label*, which refers to a written or typed identifying label placed on the outside of a *reel* of magnetic tape.

interlace A method of assigning *addresses* to *store locations* on a *magnetic drum* so that locations in separated physical positions can be *accessed* with reduced average *access time*.

interleaved carbon set A *stationery* set, used for printing results from a computer, in which additional copies of the *output* are obtained by means of carbon sheets interleaved among the stationery.

interleaving A technique sometimes used in *multiprogramming*, in which *segments* of one *program* are inserted in another program to allow the effective execution of both programs simultaneously.

interlude A *routine* or *program* designed to perform minor preliminary operations usually of a *housekeeping* type, before the main routine is entered. The area occupied by the interlude may be *overwritten* after it has performed its operations.

intermediate control A level of control established when *intermediate totals* are produced on a *punched card tabulator* (as distinct from major totals and minor totals). ◊ *comparing control change.*

intermediate control change A change in the value of an *intermediate control* initiating some predetermined action.

intermediate control data ◊ *control data.*

intermediate result The *result* of an *operation* obtained in the course of a *program* or *subroutine* which is itself used again as an *operand* in further operations before the *final result* is obtained.

intermediate storage A medium of *store* used for holding working figures or for storing totals temporarily until required. Also known as *work area.*

intermediate total A total produced at an *intermediate control change*, i.e. resulting from a change of control data at neither the most nor the least significant level.

internally stored program A *routine* stored within a computer *memory* rather than on a *backing store* or some other external medium.

internal memory Synonymous with *internal store*.

internal store A term used generally as a synonym for *immediate access store*; specifically a store forming part of the *main memory* of a computer as distinct from a *backing store*.

internal timer An electronic *timer* which provides the facility of monitoring or logging events at predetermined intervals.

international algebraic language An early form of the language which developed into *A L G O L*.

interpolator Synonymous with *collator*.

interpret To print information by means of a *punched card interpreter* onto a *punched card* from the *code* punched in the card.

interpreter 1. ◊ *punched card interpreter*. 2. Synonymous with *interpretive routine*.

interpreter, punched card ◊ *punched card interpreter*.

interpreter, transfer ◊ *transfer interpreter* and *punched card interpreter*.

interpretive code A form of *pseudocode* for use with an *interpretive routine*.

interpretive programming The writing of *programs* in a *source language* which is subsequently *executed* by means of an *interpretive routine*.

interpretive routine A *routine* which translates *pseudocode instructions* into *machine code instructions* during the live operation of the routine; i.e. the pseudo-instructions are translated by subroutines into machine code instructions which are immediately used to process data.

interpretive trace program A *trace program* which is also an *interpretive program*, i.e. translates each *symbolic instruction* into its equivalent *machine code* before executing it and recording its result.

interrecord gap The distance between *records* on a *magnetic tape*, where records have been written singly as *blocks*. In such a case, synonymous with *interblock gap*.

interrogating typewriter A typewriter connected to a *central processor* for the purpose of communicating with a *program* in *main memory*; e.g. capable of inserting data into the program or of receiving output from the program. Contrasted with *console typewriter*.

interrupt A break in a *program* or *routine* caused by an external source, which requires that control should pass temporarily to another routine; e.g. to monitor an *event* which may be proceeding in parallel to take action as a direct result of an event which has taken place. The interrupt is made so that the original routine can be resumed from the point at which the break occurred.

interrupt event An *event* [1] which causes immediate entry into a predetermined *procedure*.

interruption ◊ *interrupt*.

interrupt mask A method of ignoring an *interrupt* when it occurs and postponing action required until some later point in time.

interrupt mode Synonymous with *hold mode*.

interrupt signal The *signal* which is generated in order to cause an *interrupt* to occur.

interrupt trap A *switch* [1] under *program* control which prevents or allows a corresponding *interrupt* according to its setting.

intersection Synonymous with *and operation*.

interstage punching Punching which takes place between the normal *punching positions* on a *punched card*. Used in a punched card system in which each *card column* contains the equivalent of two columns of information. The equipment processing such cards *senses* in the normal stages and the interstage positions of each column, and treats these positions as separate columns; thus, an 80-column card would contain 160 columns of information.

intersystem communications The ability of two or more computer systems to share *peripheral units* and to intercommunicate by means of common *input* and *output channels* or by direct linking of *central processors*.

inventory control In most industries it is the practice to hold stocks to meet demands, for there are few occasions where demand and supply are matched closely enough to make this unnecessary. Even when stocks are held, temporary shortages are often experienced, due perhaps to a sudden rise in demand or delay in production.

The theory of inventory control, or 'stock control' as it is often called, is applicable to all types of stockholding and aims to strike a balance between costs of turnover, shortages, stockholding and administration. The earliest developments in this field were shortly after the 1914–18 war, and in the 1950s this was expanded into a powerful science. General commercial use of the computer means that stocks, shortages, etc., can be recorded accurately and many savings thereby obtained. Although many systems using a computer are operational, providing a variety of output including orders, invoices and shortage reports, most of them which use cost-optimal control rules have the control levels fed in as data rather than being computed by the machine.

There are four main costs associated with an inventory control system: (i) the value of stock turnover; (ii) the cost of shortages; (iii) the cost of stockholding; (iv) the cost of operating the system.

The value of stock throughput is the total value of material received by a stores system. Although the control of stock throughput can be achieved to some extent by pricing and quality decisions, it is not readily controlled by an inventory control system which regards throughput as dependent on needs which arise from outside the system.

The cost of shortages is often difficult to estimate, since it involves such intangibles as loss of future sales, etc. Often the approach used is to opt for a particular service level which is decided as a matter of policy, often based on forecast costs of maintaining that level.

The cost of stockholding is the cost of storage space plus the cost of tied-up capital, and can also include the cost of deterioration and scrapping. Stockholding affects shortages directly; the more stock held, the fewer the shortages.

The operating costs of the system cover the cost of ordering and receiving material and keeping records, and exclude the cost of shortages and stockholding.

The role of an inventory control system is to measure the effect of reprovisioning decisions in terms of physical effects (number of shortages, volume of stock) and to translate this into cost effects. By suitably manipulating the provisioning *model* to give lower total costs the optimum provisioning policy can be obtained. There have been two main streams of approach here. The first concentrates on a study of mathematical methods of optimizing total system costs, while the second studies methods of predicting demand (◊ *forecasting*). The full inventory control system should aim to forecast demand and from this forecast calculate those quantities which will give best results in terms of total costs. Such calculations would include optimum order quantities, buffer stocks, etc., relevant to service levels and stock holdings.

inversion 1. The process of creating an *inverted file* from a *file* organized in some different way. 2. Synonymous with *negation*.

inverted file A form of *file organization* in which each separate characteristic which may apply to a particular item has attached to it an identifying *key* indicating each item having that characteristic. For example, if one of the characteristics in a personnel record file is 'salary in the range £3,000–£3,250' this item would be followed by the identifying key of all personnel having this characteristic. Inverted files are used mainly for *information retrieval*.

inverter A *logic element* having one *binary* input signal and performing the logical function of *negation*.

inverting amplifier Synonymous with *sign-reversing amplifier*.

invigilator A device which checks the performance of a *control unit* and generates a signal if the response to control action does not conform to specified limits.

invisible failure A *failure* of either *hardware* or *software* which has no noticeable effect on the operation of a system.

I/O Abbreviation for *input/output*, as in I/O routine.

I P O T Acronym of *inductive potential divider*.

irrecoverable error An *error* from which no *recovery* is possible.

irreversible magnetic process A change of magnetic flux within a magnetic material which persists after the magnetic field causing the change has been removed. Contrasted with *reversible magnetic process*.

irreversible process Synonymous with *irreversible magnetic process*.

I S A M Acronym for *index sequential access method*.

isolated locations *Locations* of *store* which are protected by some *hardware* device which prevents them from being *addressed* by the user's *program* and safeguards their contents from accidental mutilation.

item advance A method for operating successively upon a group of items in *memory*.

item design The designing of a *record* or *file* in order to achieve efficient processing or efficient *input/output* operations. For example, the *packing* of several items into one *word* may significantly reduce the overall time for a *program* by reducing the input/output time, but this might be offset by the need to unpack the items into individual words for internal processing. Similar considerations may apply when items are stored in, say, *character* or *binary* form.

item of data Any data treated as a unit within a program or process, e.g. a single *operand* or an entry in a *table*.

item size The number of *characters* or *digits* in an *item of data*.

iteration A single cycle of operations from an *iterative routine*. Iterative methods of obtaining approximate solutions to various types of equation are most suitable for use by digital computer. If an iterative process can be set up, the computer, by virtue of its ability to perform simple calculations quickly, can produce an answer of any desired accuracy. The prerequisites for an iterative process are: (i) a starting point or a guess. (ii) an iterative step.

Suppose, for instance, we want to find the square root of a number, then if we take as our starting point the integer which gives the nearest answer, and define our iterative process to be:

$$x_n = \frac{x_{n-1}^2 + a}{2x_{n-1}},$$

where a is the number whose square root is required, we will successively get better and better answers (i.e. we will produce a series of numbers which converge to $\sqrt{a}$. Take for instance the square root of 2.

If we start with $x_1 = 1$ we get:

$$x_2 = 1 \cdot 5$$
$$x_3 = 1 \cdot 417$$
$$x_4 = 1 \cdot 414$$

So that with only three steps we have reached a very good approximation. Of course we need not have started as close to the answer as 1. Suppose we had started with $x_1 = 50$, then we would get:

$$x_2 = 50$$
$$x_3 = 25 \cdot 02$$
$$x_4 = 12 \cdot 54$$
$$x_5 = 6 \cdot 36$$
$$x_6 = 3 \cdot 34$$
$$x_7 = 1 \cdot 97$$
$$x_8 = 1 \cdot 499$$
$$x_9 = 1 \cdot 418$$
$$x_{10} = 1 \cdot 414$$

As we might have expected then, the better guess one takes as a starting point the less steps one has to make. Usually a compromise has to be made between making a good guess and having a large number of steps. If we wanted to find the square root of a number which we knew lay between 0 and 10,000 we might well take 50 as a starting point rather than search for a closer one.

The iterative process may be continued until any desired accuracy is reached. In terms of a *program* this merely requires the insertion of a test routine to test how much more accurate each step is making the solution. If the value of our x changes only by one part in 1,000 at a particular step, then our solution will be within at least one part in 100 of the exact solution.

A very simple iterative process has been cited here: there are many extremely useful and sometimes sophisticated iterative processes for solving various types of equation. The example was, in fact, an application of Newton's Method, which may be applied to many types of equation.

It would be wrong to suggest that all equations can be solved by iterative methods. Where such methods can be used, however, the digital computer proves invaluable in removing the tedium of repetitive calculation.

iterative process A process for calculating a result by performing a series of steps repeatedly, and in which successive approximations are made until the desired result is obtained. ◊ *Iteration.*

iterative routine A *program* which achieves a result by repeatedly performing a series of operations until some specified condition is obtained. ◊ *Iteration.*

J

jack A connecting device used for terminating the wiring of a circuit, to which access is obtained by inserting a *plug*. Otherwise known as *socket*, or, in *punched card* machines, *hub*.[2]

jack panel Synonymous with *plugboard*.

jam A machine fault which prevents *punched cards* from feeding through a machine and causes a piling up of cards on the *card track*.

Also known as wreck.

J C L Acronym of *Job Control Language*.

jitter Instability of a signal for a brief period; applied particularly to signals on a *cathode ray tube*.

job A unit of work for a computer, usually consisting of several *runs*.

job control language A *language* associated with an *operating system* which enables the user to express to the system the requirements for the control of the *jobs* within the system. ⇕ *job control program, control language*.

job control program A *program* which accepts *statements* written in a *job control language* and interprets these into *instructions* that control the course of a *job* in an *operating system*, e.g. *programs* to be *run*, *files* to be *loaded*.

job control, stacked ⇕ *sequential-stacked job control*.

job flow control Control over the sequence of *jobs* being *processed* on a computer, in order to maximize the efficient use of *peripheral units* and *central processor* time. Job flow control may be performed manually, e.g. by a work controller, or by means of an *operating system*.

job oriented terminal A data terminal designed to allow data to be transmitted to a computer directly from the data source, e.g. a cash register designed to produce *paper tape* which can be fed directly to a computer.

job restart ⇕ *restart*.

job stream A group of *jobs* run consecutively in a processing system, generally under the control of a *scheduling* system.

joggle Before a *pack* of *punched cards* is placed in a *hopper* the cards should be aligned to help trouble-free feeding. The agitating of the cards is called joggling.

join   Synonymous with *inclusive-or operation*.

joint denial   Synonymous with *nor operation*.

journal   A *file* containing *messages* within an *operating system* so that information is available both for *restarts* and for historical analysis of the functioning of the system.

jump   Synonymous with *branch*.

jump, conditional   Synonymous with *conditional branch*.

jumper   A length of electrical conductor used temporarily to complete a circuit or to bypass an existing circuit.

jump instruction   Synonymous with *branch instruction*.

jump, unconditional   Synonymous with *unconditional branch instruction*.

justification   ◊ *justify*.

justify   1. To adjust the positions of words arranged for printing so that either left-hand or right-hand margins or both are regular. 2. By extension of 1, to shift an item in a *register* so that the most or least significant digit is at the corresponding end of the register.

K

k An abbreviation for *kilo*, used to denote a thousand.

K C S An abbreviation for a thousand *characters* per second.

kernel In a *virtual machine* a set of *procedures* controlling real *resources*.

key 1. A digit or digits used to locate or identify a *record*, but not necessarily attached to the record. ◊ *argument, subscript*. 2. A marked lever or button on a *keyboard* depressed manually and used for entering a *character*.

keyboard A device for encoding *characters* by the depression of *keys*.[2] This causes the selected code to be generated by, for example, the punching of holes in a *punched card*.

keyboard computer A computer which receives *input* direct from a *keyboard*.

keyboard entry and inquiry The use by an operator of a *keyboard* to provide a computer with information and to establish what is stored in any specified *location*.

keyboard inquiry ◊ *keyboard entry and inquiry*.

keyboard lockout An interlock on a *keyboard* on a *data transmission* circuit which prevents data from being transmitted while the transmitter of another station on the same circuit is in operation.

keyboard punch Synonymous with *key punch*.

key change When a *file* of *records* which have been *sorted* into a sequence defined by *keys* is being read, e.g. by a *report program*, a key change occurs when an *input record* has a key different from its immediate predecessor. ◊ *control break*.

key-driven Pertaining to devices which require operators to depress a *key*[2] in order to translate a character into a form which a machine can recognize; e.g. a *key punch*.

keying-error rate The ratio of incorrectly keyed signals to the total number of signals keyed. The term is usually (but not necessarily) used in a *data transmission* context.

key, load ◊ *load key*.

key punch A *keyboard*-operated machine used for punching data manually into *punched cards* or *paper tape*. ◊ *card punch, tape punch*.

234

key-to-disk unit A *data preparation* device which allows data to be written direct from a punch station keyboard to a *magnetic disk* without having to go through the intermediate stage of producing *punched cards* or *paper tape*.

key verify To use a *punched card verifier*. ◊ *card verifying*.

keyword In *information retrieval* systems, the significant word in a phrase: used for the significant word in a title which describes a document. For example, in the title 'The Practice of Philately' the word 'philately' is the keyword, the other three having no significance on their own.

kilo A prefix signifying one thousand.

kilobaud A measure of *data transmission* speed; a thousand *bits* per second.

kilocycle A thousand cycles, especially a thousand cycles a second (◊ *megacycle, gigacycle* and *teracycle*).

kilomega A prefix with a significance of 10^9. Synonymous with *billi* and *giga*.

kilomegacycle 10^9 cycles per second. Also known as gigacycle, billicycle.

L

label 1. A group of *characters* used as a *symbol* to identify an item of data, an *area* of *memory*, a *record* or a *file* (◊ *header label*). 2. A label assigned to a particular *instruction* step in a *source program* to identify that step as an *entry point* in the coding or to enable that step to be used as a reference point for entry to the *routine* or *subroutine* in which it appears.

label group A collection of *labels*[1] held in an *operating system*, usually of the same type.

label identifier A set of *characters* held within a *label*[1] used to identify the type of item labelled.

label (magnetic tape) ◊ *header label*.

label record A *record* used to identify a *file* recorded on some magnetic storage medium such as *magnetic tape*. ◊ *header label*.

label set A collection of *labels*[1] with the same *label identifier*.

label, tape ◊ *header label*.

laced card A *punched card* in which all, or nearly all, *card* columns have been punched and wherein several holes appear in each column. Generally used for testing purposes or to signify the end of a card *file*.

language, programming ◊ *languages*.

languages In order to communicate with each other, men use language: in the same way, 'languages' of one sort or another are used in order to communicate instructions and commands to a computer. The unique feature which distinguishes a computer from other man-made tools and devices is its versatility in dealing with vastly different problems. This means that some very versatile method of communicating these enormously varied problems has to be devised. This article describes in outline the development and use of the concept of computer languages.

A computer performs its various functions by means of a *program* of *instructions*. In the form in which they are actually operated on by the computer's *central processor* these instructions consist of a series of numbers or a coded pattern of digits. The general article on *Instruction Format* describes in detail the various types of representation used for instructions in the form they take when

236

present in the computer's central processor. In this form, the instructions are said to be in *machine code*. When computers were in an early stage of development, all programs had to be written in this basic machine code. This was the only 'language' of communication available for the programmer.

However, machine code as a means of communication has many drawbacks. The various numeric operation codes have no obvious relationship to their function. *Addresses* of *store locations* used by the programmer have to be carefully noted and their numeric values used when the area is referred to. Similarly, the programmer has to keep careful note of the numeric addresses of each program instruction, so that *branches* and *loops* may address the correct branch points. If the programmer has to make any alteration in his program which alters the numeric addresses of any locations, all other references to these locations must be checked and changed. This complexity and need for constant checking means that a machine code program, particularly a long and complicated one, is difficult to write and prone to many errors.

It became obvious that a great deal of the work involved in checking and cross checking when writing a machine code program was purely mechanical. The first step in the development of computer languages came when it was realized that much of the detailed checking of addresses, locations, branches and so on can be done by a computer program. Languages were devised in which numeric operation codes were replaced with mnemonic codes, such as A D D, S U B, M P Y. Store locations are referred to by *labels* or alphanumeric codes, which can be remembered more readily than numbers. A program called an *assembler* or *compiler* is used to convert the program as written by the programmer into a machine code equivalent known as the *object program*. Since the assembler program allocates actual numeric values to addresses referred to by labels in the original or *source program*, the programmer is relieved of the burden of remembering the actual address of locations or instructions. Further, if he alters his program in its 'source' form, when it is assembled again addresses will be automatically adjusted wherever they occur.

These basic languages, where the program as written by the programmer is similar to the machine code version, when each instruction has a corresponding machine code equivalent but the use of mnemonics and labels relieves the programmer of 'clerical' effort, are known as *low level* or *basic* programming languages or *autocodes*. Such languages have been refined, and many sophistications added, such as facilities for creating and using *macro instructions*, the incorporation of *library subroutines* at *compilation time*, the use of *packages* to handle *input* and *output routines*. However, all such basic languages are closely allied to the machine code into which the source program can alternatively be converted. While they are relatively easy to use, their use has drawbacks. Programs written in a basic language can normally only be used on a particular machine or range of machines (a restriction which applies even more to machine code programs themselves). Further, since the languages are closely linked to machine code, a program is not related in any way to the problem it is designed to solve, so that anyone looking at a program will have little indication of what the program is trying to do.

The first problem, that of intercommunication between different types of machines, was brought into prominence by the U S Department of Defence, which found itself faced with massive investment in a large number of different types of computer. In order to overcome this problem, a language was devised for which all suppliers of equipment had to provide compilers rendering programs written in this language capable of being run on any computer. This language was designed to make the writing of commercial programs simpler, and was called *C O B O L* (Common Business Oriented Language). Other *high level languages* which have been developed for scientific and mathematical purposes include *A L G O L* and *F O R T R A N*. Features which high level languages have in common are the fact that they are *problem oriented* rather than machine oriented (that is, designed not with a particular machine code in mind but rather so as to make the solving of a specific type of problem simpler) and also the fact that compilers exist for converting the languages into the machine code of different types of machine.

Higher level languages differ from lower level languages in that the *instructions* in a high level language take the form of fairly complex *statements*. On compilation a high level statement will generally be translated into several machine code instructions. With low level languages, each instruction generally is equivalent to a single machine code instruction. The object program produced from a high level language is thus normally rather more cumbersome and hence longer than that produced from a low level language, since the programmer has less detailed control over the specific machine code instructions his program generates and less control over the organization of the object program as it appears in store.

Generally, a program written in a high level language makes some sort of 'sense' and can be read and understood by someone who has not 'learned' the language. In the case of a commercial language, the program resembles a highly artificial but still recognizable English; in the case of a scientific language, the resemblance will be to mathematical notation.

However, the fact that these languages have this generality which enables them to be understood by people does not mean that they are automatically capable of being understood by all computers. It is still necessary for a compiler to be written for each machine on which the program is to be run. Thus high level languages only become general if manufacturers can agree on their features and provide the appropriate compilers.

The fact that generality of use of high level languages is only as good as the compilers supplied by manufacturers has led to the situation where large numbers of 'dialects' of the various common high level languages have emerged. It is usually the case that when a compiler for a specific machine is being written, certain features of the language have to be omitted or modified because of the difficulty of translating them into a specific machine code. Thus although in theory a general language is common to all machines, in practice only some subset of the language will apply to all machines. In fact, with the development of more powerful computers, the efficiency and capacity of compilers has improved, so that this common 'subset' is increasing for most languages.

However, the ideal situation in which a universal language would allow complete communication between all machines is still hardly nearer realization than in the ordinary world of human communication. The problem still remains to devise a language which is sufficiently general for all purposes, but which can be 'understood' by anybody, and be sufficiently simple for the production of compilers for identical versions on all types of machine. An attempt to achieve generality has been made in the development of the language *PL/1*, which combines features from commercial languages (C O B O L) and mathematical languages (F O R T R A N). The problem of producing standard compilers and avoiding different 'subsets' has been met in P L/1 by making the language *modular*. The language has been defined in a series of units, each specifying a related but independent set of features. Thus the user need only use the particular set of features needed for his program, and a compiler will provide for as many of these modules or units as required. However, any language which attempts to do

239

everything inevitably has its critics, and criticism of PL/1 has been made on the grounds that it is cumbersome, and that it is difficult to produce compilers which will create efficient object programs.

Another approach to the problem of generality and intercommunication between computers is the attempt to develop a common machine code. The object of this is to standardize the internal instruction formats for all machines. Thus, any object program could run on any machine. Compilers would still be needed to translate high level languages into this machine code, but, since compilers themselves would be written in the common machine code, a single compiler would suffice for each language, thus making the problems of 'dialects' disappear.

All these solutions have been based on the assumption that the ideal state to aim at is for all programmers to be able to write all programs in the same language, which can then be compiled and run on all machines. Another approach, however, is to develop problem oriented languages even further. This means that, for example, in order to write payroll programs, a special 'payroll language' is devised; similarly an 'inventory control' language, 'structural analysis' languages or 'matrix analysis' languages can be developed. Each such highly specialized language requires a compiler, and special high level languages have been developed specifically for the production of compilers: a language for producing other languages.

In fact, high level problem oriented languages approach the field of applications software: for example applying *parameters* to a highly sophisticated application such as a *PERT* package could be said to be writing a program in a high level language designed to perform network analysis programs.

Languages are the medium by which man communicates problems to the computer and the easier this communication can be made the wider will be the application of computers; the problem of ideal communication has still to be solved, although much progress has been made.

In a general article it is not possible to describe in detail all the various types of language and the details of the methods used to translate languages into the machine code understood by the computer. Details of the languages *ALGOL, BASIC, COBOL, FORTRAN* and *PL/1* will be found under those headings. The reader will also find useful information under *Programming, compiler, assembler, Instruction Format.*

The following notes describe in outline some of the common features of languages and the processes of converting them into machine code.

A program written in any language other than machine code requires conversion to machine code before it can be run. This applies equally to basic languages and higher level languages. Programs used to convert programs written in a high level language (known as source programs) into a lower level language (known as the object program) are known variously as assemblers, compilers and *generators*. The term generator is used specifically for the conversion of highly problem-oriented languages used for producing such programs as *reports* and *sorts*. Assembler and compiler are often used synonymously, although assembler usually refers to the process of converting basic languages into machine code, where each language instruction has a corresponding single machine code equivalent. A compiler is a program which converts higher level languages into a lower level language – either machine code or a basic language. A compiler will normally generate several low level instructions for each source language statement. Assemblers and compilers, as well as providing a method for communicating the instructions which form the program, also allow the programmer to perform additional functions. Storage areas used by the program can be defined and allocated, and the programmer can define and store any *constants* needed by his program. In addition, compilers enable the programmer to incorporate *subroutines* from a *program library* held on *backing store*, and enable the programmer to define and use macro instructions. Compilers usually allow the programmer to incorporate statements which direct the compiler to take some action but have no effect on the program (e.g. directives to include *trace* routines within the program). Compilers and assemblers will usually print out their actions on a *printer*, giving the programmer a listing of the source program together with details of the generated object program. Such listing may, at the programmer's option, include comments or *narrative* to explain what the program is doing: these statements have no effect on the object program.

latency ◊ *waiting time.*

lattice file A *file* within an *operating system* within which individual *records* can have more than one *owner*, and also themselves are *owners* of more than one record.

law and computers Early fears of the inadmissibility of evidence based on magnetically recorded data have proved groundless. Any loss of data by *overwriting* or other electronic hazards would have no greater significance in law than the loss of documents in a fire. Also the need to print out records held on a magnetic medium may be compared with the translation of evidence gathered in a foreign country. Although a computer system may dispense with intermediate records, the validity of its *output* can be established by circumstantial evidence obtained by a re-run of the *programs* with proven *input* data. In a vital case it may also be desirable to call an expert witness to give evidence that the installation is efficiently conducted and that the information it provides can be relied on in a commercial environment.

There is, however, some danger from actions in tort. The directors of a company should ensure, when they delegate responsibility for customer relations to an unthinking computer, that fail-safe *exception reporting* has been incorporated in the programs and procedures. Thus, in Burnett *v.* Westminster Bank Limited (1965) the bank was held liable for damages when its computer system (which relied on the *magnetic ink character recognition* encoding on cheques) failed to detect that the customer had altered the account details in manuscript.

A company providing computing services for others might also be liable for damages, for example, in the event of an incorrect engineering calculation resulting in the collapse of a structure. On the other hand, negligence could be held against a company which failed to employ a computer in a situation where similar enterprises had established their value in maintaining safety limits.

Whatever litigation may arise, a company's interests will be protected best when a meticulous control is maintained over its data processing operations, through the enforcement of proper *data processing standards*. All activities should be logged immediately and accurately, recording *batch* sequence numbers, the total number of items processed, *control totals* and other matters relevant to data security. *Operating systems* should be operator-proof. There should be automatic checks on the *validity* of data, e.g. correct codes, logical situations, quantitative limits. A reliable *dump and restart* procedure should be used. Output should be identified by program-generated *header* and *trailer labels* giving time and date, description, page numbers, data record count and control or *hash totals*. Environmental records should be equally thorough in respect of atmospheric conditions, maintenance schedules, the logging of *down time*, fault reports, and operators' duty rosters. There should always be two people on duty when operational jobs are being run.

All these precautions will substantiate the evidence of an 'expert witness' if the need should arise.

layout character A character appearing amongst data on *paper tape* for the purpose of controlling the way in which the data is printed or otherwise treated in some subsequent processing operation.

Also known as format effector.

leader 1. A length of unpunched paper that precedes the data recorded on a reel of *paper tape*. Usually containing *feed holes* only. 2. A *record* that precedes a group of records and which identifies the group or provides data common to the group.

leading edge Pertaining to a *punched card* – the edge that first enters the *card track* of a punched card machine. Contrasted with *trailing edge*.

leading end The end of a piece of *paper tape* that first enters a *paper tape reader*; i.e. the end at which the first character of a message appears.

leapfrog test A test performed by a *program* which is in *memory* and which performs tests on different *locations* and then transfers itself to another *memory area* to continue the tests on other locations.

leased line A communications circuit reserved permanently for a particular user; i.e. not a switched circuit for servicing different users.

least significant character The character in the extreme right-hand position of a group of *significant characters* in *positional notation*.

left justified Descriptive of any item of data which is stored in such a way that it occupies consecutive *locations* starting at the left-hand end of the area allocated to it. Thus empty locations may appear consecutively at the right-hand end if the item requires less positions than have been allowed.

left shift A *shift* operation in which the digits of a *word* are displaced to the left. In an *arithmetical* shift this has the effect of multiplication.

leg A *path* in a *routine* or *subroutine*.

length The numbers of *bits* or *characters* forming any *word, record* or other unit of data.

length, fixed ◊ *fixed length record*.

length, variable ◊ *variable field*.

letter A character of the alphabet. Contrasted with *symbol* in a *character set*.

librarian 1. The person who controls the library in which all *magnetic files* and *programs* are kept, issues *data files* and maintains records of tape usage, including details of current *file generations* and their associated *reel numbers.* May also assemble tapes ready for running a job and issue all associated materials and *operating instructions.* 2. A synonym for *librarian program.*

librarian program A *program* forming a part of the *operating system* of a particular computer. The program maintains a complete library of all the *routines* and *subroutines* required by the user including programs developed for the user's applications, *compilers, service routines,* and any special *packages* or subroutines developed by the user or the computer manufacturer. Programs can be deleted, added or modified by the librarian program under the user's control. The complete library is stored on a *backing store* (e.g. a *disk file*) so that required routines can be called into *memory* as necessary.

library facilities The facilities provided by a *program library,* but more specifically relating to the library of *routines* developed by computer manufacturers for users of their equipment. These routines and *subroutines* are generally available on a *backing store* and can be directly compiled into the user's *object program* by the *instructions* written in the user's *source program.*

library program A program available in the *program library.*

library routine A *routine* in the *program library.*

library software All *programs* and *routines* forming part of the *library facilities* of a computer system.

library subroutine A *subroutine* in the *program library.*

library tape A *magnetic tape* containing the *library software* of a computer system.

library, tape ◊ *magnetic tape library.*

light pen A highly sensitive photo-electric device used as an adjunct to a *cathode ray tube* display unit. The operator can pass the pen over the surface of the cathode ray tube screen to detect images displayed on the screen. The light pen can also be used to activate a computer to change or modify images it has caused to be displayed, in accordance with movements made by the operator and under *program* control.

limited integrator An *integrator*[1] in which two input signals are integrated as long as the corresponding output signal does not exceed specified limits. ◊ *integrator (computing unit).*

limiter A device used to limit the power of an electrical signal to some predetermined maximum value.

line, acoustic delay ◊ *acoustic delay line.*

linear equation An equation in which both sides are linear functions of the variables. The equation may be expressed in the form $l(a, b, c, \ldots) = k$, where l is a linear function and k is a constant.

linear optimization Synonymous with *linear programming.*

linear program A mathematical technique used in *operational research* to solve problems in which it is required to find an optimum solution involving the combination of many variables; a procedure for ascertaining the minimum or maximum linear function of variables subject to constraints in the form of linear inequalities. ◊ general article on *Linear Programming.*

linear programming Linear programming is a section of mathematical programming which has proved extremely valuable in many fields, particularly that of allocation problems (◊ *Allocation*).

Linear programming problems are those in which: (i) the objective can be expressed as the maximization or minimization of a linear function of the variables i.e. the variables have fixed costs, profits, etc. per unit of the items; and (ii) the objective function described in (i) is restricted by a set of constraints which may also be expressed as linear functions of the variables. Putting this less formally, linear programming enables us to maximize or minimize a function which is the sum of multiples of several variables subject to constraints upon these variables; these constraints can themselves be written as sums of multiples of the variables.

To illustrate the use of linear programming we shall consider a very simple example, for clarity. Suppose we wish to make a diet for pigs, and we want the diet to cost as little as possible, but to contain definite minimum quantities of various vitamins, using certain basic foods. We consider one unit by weight of this food, say one pound. We want to minimize the total cost so we need to know the cost of each food per ounce. Our constraints are that the diet must contain certain minimal quantities of various vitamins, and since the vitamin content of each food will depend on its weight this can be expressed linearly. Thus we will need to know: (i) the cost of each food per ounce; (ii) the vitamin content per ounce of each food. We can then write:

Total cost = a × (cost of first food) + b × (cost of second food), etc.
Content of vitamin 1 = a × (vitamin 1 content of first food) + b × (vitamin 1 content of second food), etc.
Content of vitamin 2 = a × (vitamin 2 content of first food) + b × (vitamin 2 content of second food), etc.

Total weight = 16 ounces = a + b + c, etc.

where a, b, c, etc. are the amounts of each food.

Use of linear programming will then find for us the values of a, b, c, etc., which will give us the minimum vitamin content defined and minimize the total cost.

Perhaps linear programming has become so popular because its results can be readily shown to be economically valuable and that it can be very easily used with a digital computer.

There are several techniques for the solution of linear programming problems, perhaps the most common of which is the simplex technique.

linear unit A unit used in an *analog computer* in which the change in output, due to any change in one of two or more input variables, is proportional only to the change in that input and is not dependent upon the values of the other prevailing inputs.

line-at-a-time printer Synonymous with *line printer*.

line-feed code A control character which is used to specify the number of lines of paper to be passed through a *printer* between each line of print.

line (in display) A horizontal row of *character* positions forming part of a *display* on a *visual display unit*.

line, magneto-strictive delay ◊ *magneto-strictive acoustic delay line*.

line, mercury delay ◊ *mercury delay line*.

line, nickel delay ◊ *nickel delay line*.

line noise *Noise* [2] generated in a *data transmission* line.

line printer A *printer* which prints out results from a computer one line at a time (◊ general article on *Output Devices*).

line, quartz delay ◊ *quartz delay line*.

line, sonic delay ◊ *acoustic delay line*.

link A *branch instruction*, or an *address* in such an instruction, that is used specifically to *exit* from a *subroutine* in order to return to some desired point in a *main program*.

linkage A connexion between mechanical members used in a mechanical *analog computer* to perform some arithmetic function. For example mechanical multiplication units can be made based on the geometry of similar triangles.

linked subroutine A *subroutine* which is not stored in the *main path* of a *program*, but which is entered via a *branch instruction* from the *main routine* and which executes a branch instruction to return control subsequently to the main routine.

list 1. Any printing operation in which a series of *records* on a *file*, or in *memory*, are printed one after another. 2. When processing *punched cards* on a *tabulator*, to print details from every card being processed rather than *totals only*.

list, first item Synonymous with *group indication*.

literal operands *Operands*, usually in *source language instruction*, which specify precisely the value of a *constant* rather than an *address* in which the constant is stored. This technique enables the coding to be written more concisely than if the constant had been allocated a *data-name*.

liveware A word deliberately coined to contrast with *hardware* and *software* meaning the personnel associated with all aspects of a computer, e.g. *operators, programmers, systems analysts*.

load 1. To load a data medium on to an *input unit*; e.g. a *reel* of *magnetic tape* on to a *tape deck* or *punched cards* into the *hopper* of a *card reader*. 2. To read data or *program instructions* into *memory*.

load-and-go Descriptive of a type of automatic coding in which the user's *source program* is automatically translated into *machine code* and stored in the *central processor* ready to be performed. Thus it is never necessary to create the *object program* on any external medium.

loader Synonymous with *loading routine*.

loading program Synonymous with *loading routine*.

loading routine A *routine* existing permanently in *memory* to enable any *program* to be loaded into memory from an external medium.

Also known as loader, loading program, load program.

load key A hand-operated switch used on earlier computers to activate circuits for reading data or a *program* into *memory*.

load point A physical marker at the beginning of a *reel* of *magnetic tape*, which is detected by *hardware* to ensure that the reel is correctly positioned when the tape is first *loaded*, or after it has been rewound.

load program Synonymous with *loading routine*.

local system library A *program library* containing standard *software* available to a particular computer system.

location Any place in a computer *store* capable of containing a unit of information. Usually expressed in terms of the basic unit of storage employed in a particular computer system; e.g. a *word* is a location in a *word oriented* storage unit, and a *character* in a *character oriented* machine. The position of a location in store is identified by its *address*[2].

location counter A value used within a *subroutine* for *addressing* a series of *locations*; the value being modified by *program* to address a separate location on each occasion the subroutine is used.

lock In an *operating system* a method by which a *process* is given exclusive use of a *resource*.

locked down A condition in which an *area* of *virtual store* remains in a fixed position in *main store*.

locking of files A process by which different *virtual machines* are prevented from simultaneously *accessing* a *file*.

lock-out 1. To inhibit the activation of a *hardware* unit or a *routine*; e.g., where the action would otherwise have coincided with some uncompleted operation utilizing the same areas of *memory*. 2. A device used to safeguard against an attempted reference to a routine or area of equipment currently in use. 3. The status of a *process* which is waiting to obtain a *lock* in order to give exclusive use of a *resource*.

log 1. To record a series of events. 2. A record of a particular series of events; e.g. a maintenance engineer's log, operator's log, console log.

logger Any device which records events over a period of time.

logic The science dealing with the formal principles of reasoning; in electronic data processing, the principles observed in the design of a computer system or of any particular unit. Pertaining to the relationships between elements in the unit concerned, without consideration of the *hardware* necessary to implement this design.

logical A term used in the context of *operating systems* to describe entities (*files, resources*) as they appear to a *user*, in contrast to *physical* files etc., which are the actual entities as they exist. Logical entities are derived from physical entities by means of operating system software. Associated with *virtual machine environment*.

logical comparison The operation performed when two *operands* or *keys* are examined to decide whether they are equal in value or to ascertain their relative size one to another.

logical connectives The words that connect statements and which enable the truth or falsity of the statements thus created to be ascertained from the individual statements and the logical meanings of the connectives. ⬦ *logical operator* and *Boolean algebra*.

logical decision A choice between alternatives made by reference to some specified conditions. For example, alternative paths might be available in a *routine* and the selection of the required path might be made according to whether an *intermediate result* were, say, negative or positive.

logical design ◊ *logic design.*

logical diagram ◊ *logic diagram.*

logical element ◊ *logic element.*

logical flowchart ◊ *logic flowchart.*

logical instruction Any *instruction* which specifies one of the *logical operations* (e.g. an *and* instruction). Used in the widest sense to embrace those instructions that are not *arithmetical instructions*, e.g. *comparing, shifting* or *branching* instructions.

logical multiply A *logical operation* involving the use of the *logical operator* known as *and operating.* ◊ *Boolean algebra.*

logical operation 1. Any operation involving the use of the *logical operators* 'and', 'not', 'or', 'nand', etc. 2. In a computer, any operation in which the result in each digit position is dependent only upon the values of the corresponding digit positions in the *operand* or operands concerned, i.e. no *carries* take place. 3. Sometimes used to refer to any processing operation not involving arithmetic, e.g. *shifting.*

logical operator A word or symbol representing some logical function to be applied to one or more associated *operands*. It may appear in front of the operand, as in the *monadic* operation known as *negation*, but in *dyadic* operations it appears between operands and is often known as a *logical connective.* ◊ *Boolean algebra.*

logical product Synonymous with *and operation.*

logical record A *record* containing all the *fields* necessary to represent some transaction or to present some specific collection of facts. The length and structure of the record is expressed in regard to the information that it must convey, rather than to satisfy any limitations imposed by the medium of *store.*

logical shift A *shift operation* in which *digits* in a *word* are moved left or right in circular fashion, so that digits pushed out at one end of the word are re-introduced at the other.
Also known as circular shift, end-around shift and non-arithmetic shift. Contrasted with *arithmetical shift.*

logical sum Synonymous with *inclusive-or operation.*

logical symbol A symbol used to represent one of the *logical operators* such as 'and', 'or', 'not', 'nand', etc.

logical track A group of *physical tracks* which can be *addressed* as a single entity.

logical unit Of data, a group of *characters, digits* or *fields* which, as a group, represent some *transaction* or any other unit of information.

logic chart ◊ *logic flowchart.*

logic design A description of the working of a computer or any associated unit, in which the functional parts of the system are represented by *logical symbols*. A specification of the mode of operation without consideration of the physical components required.

Also known as logical design.

logic diagram A representation of the design of any device or system in which graphic symbols are used to represent the *logic elements* and their relationships.

Also known as logical diagram.

logic element A device used to perform some specific *logical operation*; e.g. an *and element, or element, not element*, etc. A small unit, part of a system consisting of several logic elements each performing some logical function such as 'and', 'or', 'not', 'nor', 'nand', etc. ◊ general article on *Boolean algebra*.

Also known as *gate*, logical element.

logic flowchart 1. A chart representing a system of *logical elements* and their relationships within the overall design of a system or *hardware* unit. 2. The representation of the various logical steps in any *program* or *routine* by means of a standard set of symbols. A *flowchart* produced before detailed *coding* for the solution of a particular problem. ◊ *flowcharting*.

Also known as logical flowchart.

logic shift ◊ *logical shift*.

logic symbol ◊ *logical symbol*.

longitudinal check A type of *parity check* performed on a group of *characters* or *bits*. For example, where a number of characters are transmitted as a *block*, a parity check is usually performed on each character, but in addition it is often desirable to treat each bit position within the successive characters of the group as being a further unit for checking purposes. To this end, a *parity character* is generated and transmitted as the last character of the group, thus achieving either *odd* or *even parity* for each longitudinal bit formation.

longitudinal-mode delay line A *magneto-strictive delay line* in which the mode of operation depends on longitudinal vibrations in some magneto-strictive material.

look-up A programming technique enabling an item of data to be selected from an *array* or *table* in which the item is identified by a *key*.

look-up table An *array* of data so organized that it can be searched by a *routine* to retrieve information related to specified *keys*.

loop 1. A series of *instructions* which are performed repeatedly until some specified condition is satisfied, whereupon a *branch instruction* is obeyed to exit from the loop. ✧ general article on *Programming*. 2. Sometimes also used as a synonym for *control tape* or *control loop*.

loop checking A method sometimes used to check the accuracy of *data* transmitted over a *data-link*; signals received at one terminal are returned to the transmitting terminal for comparison with the original informaion.

loop stop A *loop* that is entered to stop a *program*, usually when some specific condition occurs requiring action by the operator.

loosely coupled twin A system in which two *processors* are used with *switches* to enable them to use common *peripheral units*; each processor has its own *operating system* and it is not possible for them to operate simultaneously sharing *data* and *code*. Such a system provides switching to aid in system *resilience* in the event of *hardware failure*.

loss Synonymous with *attenuation*.

loss of information Synonymous with *walk down*.

lower curtate Certain *punching positions* of a *card column* (usually those without *zone* significance) grouped at the bottom of a *punched card*. Contrasted with *upper curtate*.

low level filestore A type of *filestore* used in an *operating system* to hold *physical files* not needed *on line*. Typically the medium used is *magnetic tape*, and the user cannot access such files directly.

low level language A *language* in which each *instruction* has a single corresponding *machine code* equivalent.
Also known as basic language. Contrasted with *high level language*.

low order Descriptive of the significance attached to certain *characters* or *digits* in a number. For example, the two low order positions of the decimal number 38654 are those occupied by the numerals 5 and 4.

low-order position The right-hand or least significant position of a number or *word*.

L P Acronym for *linear programming*.

L P M Acronym for lines per minute, as used to describe the output speed of a *line printer* (e.g. 1,000 lpm).

M

M A C Acronym for *multi-access* computing. ⟡ *M A C mode.*

M A C background job A *background job* run under an *operating system* in *batch mode*, either as an *interactive batch job* or as an ordinary *batch job* (in which the status of the job is determined through a terminal). ⟡ *M A C mode.*

machine address Synonymous with *absolute address.*

machine code The coding system adopted in the design of a computer to represent the *instruction repertoire* of the computer. The various operations that can be performed are represented by numeric *function codes* and all *store locations* are allocated numbers to enable the *data* stored in such locations to be *addressed.*
Also known as computer code, *instruction code, instruction set,* order code.

machine cycle Pertaining generally to a *punched card* machine in which operations are performed during a complete cycle of the *card feed* mechanism and wherein a card is fed to be read or punched. Applicable to any machine in which a cyclic pattern of events exists, particularly electro-mechanical units in which operations are initiated by rotating shafts.

machine error An error in the results of automatic processing which can be attributed to a machine malfunction rather than to a *software* or operating fault.

machine independent Used to describe a *program* or procedure which is expressed without regard to any particular *machine coding* system. The procedure is designed in terms of the logical requirements of the problem.

machine instruction An *instruction* written in terms of a computer's *machine code*; i.e. one which can be obeyed directly by the machine without translation.

machine instruction code Synonymous with *machine code.*

machine interruption A break in the processing of a *program* caused by some event detected by the computer *hardware*. For example, some automatic checking operation may reveal a *parity error.*

machine language In its strictest sense refers to *instructions* written in *machine code* which can be immediately obeyed by a computer without translation. Used more loosely to refer to any *symbolic instructions* which are written for execution by a computer system.

machine language code ◊ *machine code.*

machine learning The ability of a machine to improve its performance with repeated experience of particular problems; i.e. *artificial intelligence.*

machine logic The design of a computer in respect of the way in which its various elements are interactive. Relating to the methods employed in the machine to solve problems rather than to the actual components used or any circuit values.

machine operation A predetermined group of activities which a machine is built to perform, e.g. *addition.*

machine operator The person who loads *programs* and data into a computer or who manipulates the *console* controls to achieve the running of a program or *suite* of programs.

machine processible form Describing any data arranged in some medium which can be accepted and processed by an *automatic data processing* machine.

machine run A complete *routine*, or set of interlinked routines, which would normally be executed on a computer without major intervention. Sometimes an operator may have to take specific action in the event of certain error conditions but otherwise a run would not require any additional set-up procedures following the initial *loading* operations for the job.

machine script Any data represented in *machine code* form.

machines, electrical accounting ◊ *electrical accounting machines.*

machine sensible Related to data recorded in such a way that it can be sensed or read by an *automatic data processing* machine.

machine-spoilt work time Time spent in processing data where the results contain *errors* because of a machine fault. Essentially, wasted time where the results are useless and in which all or part of the job will need to be re-run.

machine word A physical location in *memory*, which may be *addressed* as a single unit but which will contain a predetermined standard number of *characters* or *digit positions.* The *word* is the standard unit of transfer for all computers having *fixed word-length*, and usually operations are performed in *parallel mode* when performing any specified function; i.e. all digit positions are processed simultaneously. This method may be contrasted with that of *character oriented* computers in which operands can be of *variable length* and can consist of a *string* of characters as specified by the programmer for any particular *instruction*. In this latter method most processes are performed in *serial mode* on one character after another.

M A C mode A method of using an *operating system* in which *jobs* are submitted from *remote terminals* and are then carried out in *conversational mode*. M A C is an acronym for *multi-access* computing.

macro 1. An abbreviation for *macro instruction*. 2. In an *operating system*, used for the name of a set of operating system *control language* statements which can be activated collectively by giving the macro name.

macro assembly program An *assembly program* in which concise *instruction* statements are used to generate procedures containing several *machine code* instructions for each source statement. Such an assembler may also permit the *segmentation* of large programs and facilities for tracing programming errors.

macro code Synonymous with *macro instruction*.

macro-coding The use of *macro instructions* in the writing of a program. Contrasted with *micro-coding*.

macro flow chart A chart used in designing the logic of a particular routine, in which the various *segments* and *subroutines* of a program are represented by blocks. No attempt is made in such a chart to specify detailed programming tactics, this being the province of the programmer.

macro instruction A single *instruction* written as part of a *source language*, which when compiled into a *machine code* program will generate several machine code instructions.
Also known as programmed instruction, macro, macro code.

macro-programming The *programming* of a problem in which all statements are written in terms of *macro instructions*; usually where some *assembly system* or *package* is available to perform translation of the macro instructions into *machine code*.

M A C sub-system Part of an *operating system* which controls work submitted in *M A C mode*.

magazine 1. An input *hopper* which holds *punched cards* and presents them to a feed mechanism for reading or punching. 2. A device forming part of a *magnetic card file* which holds *magnetic cards* and presents them for reading or selection.

magnetic card A card having a magnetizable surface upon which data is recorded by the energizing of certain parts of the surface, thus providing a storage medium.

magnetic card file A *direct access storage device* in which individual *buckets* of data are stored upon *magnetic cards* held in one or more *magazines*[2]. The cards, once addressed, are selected from the magazine and transported at high speed past a *read/write head*.

magnetic cell   A storage *cell* in which the two possible values of one *binary digit* are represented by different magnetic flux patterns. A magnetic cell may consist of one or more storage *cores*, or of a small part of a larger piece of perforated ferromagnetic material known as an aperture plate.

Also known as a static magnetic cell because the means of setting and sensing the contents are stationary with respect to the magnetic material.

magnetic cell, static   Synonymous with *magnetic cell*.

magnetic character   ◊ *magnetized ink character*.

magnetic core   A small ring of ferromagnetic material which may be polarized by electric currents applied to wires wrapped around it. The magnetic core is thus capable of assuming two states and may be used as a switching device, or as a storage medium. These devices have been used extensively for the *memory* of computers; e.g. a single magnetic core being used to represent a single *binary digit* of some item of information represented in a numerical code.

magnetic core storage   A large array of *magnetic cores* arranged in *matrices* to form the *memory* of a computer. Each individual core is capable of assuming two states and some cores may be assigned as storage *locations* for information to be held in *binary coded form*, whereas others may perform *switching* or *gating* functions.

magnetic disk   A storage device consisting of a number of flat circular plates each coated on both surfaces with some magnetizable material. A number of *tracks*[1] are available on each surface and data is read from or written to these tracks by means of *read/write heads*. There may be several heads to each surface, a particular head being allocated a specific area (or *sector*) on the disk. (◊ *random access*.)

magnetic disk file   A *file* of data held on a *magnetic disk*.

magnetic drum   A storage device consisting of a cylinder coated with magnetizable material; the cylinder is continuously rotated past a series of *read/write heads* which are arranged to coincide with recording *tracks* on the surface of the cylinder. *Binary coded* data can be recorded serially upon any track as the drum rotates, and data can be read from or written to any one of the tracks by switching from one *read/write head* to another.

magnetic film store   ◊ *thin-film memory*.

magnetic head   An electromagnet used to read, record or erase polarized spots on a magnetic medium such as *magnetic tape, magnetic disk* or *magnetic drum*. Examples are *read head, write head* and *read/write head*.

magnetic ink   Ink containing particles of magnetizable material, which can be energized to facilitate automatic reading of printed characters. ◇ *magnetic ink character recognition*.

magnetic ink character reader   A *character reader* which reads characters printed in magnetized metallic ink by using *magnetic ink character recognition* techniques.

magnetic ink character recognition   The technology related to the recording of information on documents by means of *magnetized ink characters* and the automatic recognition of such characters by means of machines. ◇ *magnetic ink document sorter/reader* and *Character Recognition*.

magnetic ink document reader   A device which reads specified fields of *magnetized ink characters* from documents and translates the information read into a coded format, usually for direct insertion into an *input area* of a computer's *core storage*.

magnetic ink document sorter/reader   A machine capable of reading information from documents containing *magnetized ink characters* and of sorting the documents into order according to the digits recorded in a specified *field*.

magnetic memory   Pertaining to any *storage device* which operates using principles of electro-magnetism.

magnetic store   Synonymous with *magnetic memory*.

magnetic tape   Magnetic tape is the commonest form of *backing store* used for computers. It is usually in the form of a continuous strip of plastic material which is coated with a magnetic oxide on which data may be recorded as a series of magnetized spots. The general dimensions of the tape vary somewhat from one system to another, but ½in. tape is probably most common and is ½in. wide and may be approximately 2,400 feet in length. Magnetic tape is wound on a *reel* usually of 10½in. diameter.

A *magnetic tape deck* must be used in order to record data on to a reel of magnetic tape. A deck consists basically of a drive mechanism capable of driving two tape reels at very high speed so that tape is wound from one reel on to another. As the tape is transported between the two reels it passes a *read/write head* which is used either to read from the tape or to write to it.

With ½in. tape data is recorded in seven *channels* which run lengthwise along the tape, and seven *bits* are therefore available across the width of the tape. Of these seven bits, six are used to form a coded *character*, whilst the other is used as a *parity* bit. In this way data is recorded as a series of sequential tape characters which are grouped to form the basic *records* of information required.

These records may be written singly as *blocks* of data on tape, but generally it is more efficient to group a predetermined number of records into each block. A block is a physical unit of data written to or read from tape as a single operation. Each block is separated by an *interblock gap* which is a small area of unrecorded tape about ½in. in length.

Although data is recorded in most systems as a series of tape characters this does not necessarily imply that all data must be recorded in character form. *Binary numbers* may be recorded directly on magnetic tape by the technique of regarding any number of sequential 6-bit tape characters as a contiguous set of binary digits.

The capacity of a reel of magnetic tape is initially dependent on the density of the recorded signals on the tape. A number of *recording densities* are currently in use, and generally the higher the density, in terms of tape characters per inch, the higher the cost of the magnetic tape system. A typical recording density is 556 characters per inch, and it will be seen that at this density the speed for transferring data between a reel of tape and *memory* can be very high. This in turn depends on the speed of the tape drive mechanism, but for example with a density of 556 characters per inch and a tape speed of 75 inches per second the rate of transfer is 41,700 characters per second.

The actual capacity of any particular reel is dependent on the way in which blocks of data are organized: the shorter the tape blocks the more interblock gaps are incurred. A full reel containing blocks 400 characters in length would, at 556 characters per inch, permit a total capacity of 7·84 million characters.

The physical beginning and end of tape are distinguished by strips of reflective material which are automatically detected by hardware.

The important thing to note about magnetic tape is that it is a serial medium, i.e. all data must be organized into sequential files. To update the information on a tape file it is necessary to read records from the file as a series of blocks and place them in turn in memory. Amendment records in the same sequence are read into memory at the same time as a series of blocks, so that amendments can be applied consecutively to the records from the original file. An entirely new file is created on another reel of magnetic tape,

257

still in the original sequence, but this time containing all details relevant to the latest amendments. Thus at least two *generations* of the same file may exist but only one will be current at any particular time.

The operations controlling magnetic tape are initiated by instructions executed in the *central processor*. The main instructions are those which write to tape, read from tape or rewind tape. A read or write instruction is required for each block of data read from or written to the tape. A rewind instruction may be called at any time to wind the tape back to the *load point*. Other operations available in some tape systems include: read reverse, which enables a tape to be read backwards; write *tape mark*, which causes a special character to be written to tape; skip to next tape mark, which enables the tape to be moved without reading until a special tape mark character is detected; and backspace tape, which causes the tape to be moved backwards one block.

The use of the parity bits previously mentioned enables the computer to detect any errors that may arise when reading or writing. When a character is written to tape a parity bit is generated to complete the 7-bit character as it is recorded. The parity bit is computed automatically to make the number of 1 bits in the character equal to an even number (in some systems odd parity is used: ⋄ *parity checking*). When the tape is read on some subsequent occasion a check is again performed on each character to ensure that the parity is even.

In many systems the tape decks are equipped with recording heads that enable the computer to read each character immediately it has been written. It is then possible to check not only that the correct parity has been maintained but also to check that the actual *bit pattern* detected for that character on the tape is the same as the original bit pattern in memory.

Whenever an error is detected during a write operation the computer automatically rewrites the block concerned; during a read operation the computer will try again to read the block. Where the error is caused by some transient condition this will often prove successful and the job may be continued. Persistent errors will usually mean that the reel of tape is damaged or that there is a tape deck malfunction. It is always necessary to safeguard against tape failure by retaining a previous generation of every master file plus the associated amendment records so that the current generation can be re-created if necessary.

Tape failure can be caused by dust particles or by damage to the oxide coating. A proper system of air conditioning is required in the machine room, and also in any *magnetic tape library*, so that dust and dirt are avoided. Proper maintenance of the tape decks and correct handling of tape reels by operators are also necessary. All this might lead one to suspect that magnetic tape is a very sensitive medium for storing data but in any well-run installation tape failures are comparatively rare.

It is clear from the foregoing that considerable care is taken by computer equipment manufacturers and by computer users to safeguard the physical condition of reels of magnetic tape. It is also necessary to safeguard the information forming data files on the magnetic tapes to ensure that the data is not inadvertently *overwritten*. To this purpose each tape file starts with a *header label* which identifies the file name, generation number and the retention period. The *tape serial number* is also recorded as part of this label as well as the reel number, the latter being important where more than one reel is necessary for a particular file. When a tape file is opened to be read the header label is checked by program to ensure that the correct file has been loaded; on the other hand when a reel is opened as a write tape the retention period is checked to make sure that important data is not being overwritten.

In a program which processes tape files there are many operations that are common to any tape processing job. In order to simplify matters for users it is customary for computer manufacturers to supply *housekeeping packages*, which are designed to perform many of the routine functions concerned with magnetic tape processing. The user is able to write his tape processing requirements using *macro instructions* which will call into operation standard routines perhaps consisting of many instructions.

An indication of the relative advantages and disadvantages of direct access equipment compared with magnetic tape is given under *Direct Access Storage*.

magnetic tape deck A complete *tape transport* and its associated *read/write heads*, capable of either reading from or writing to a *magnetic tape file*.
Also known as deck [2], *tape deck* and magnetic tape unit.

magnetic tape drive Synonymous with *tape transport*.

magnetic tape file Used in the strictest sense to refer to a *reel* of *magnetic tape* containing *records* of information arranged in an ordered sequence; loosely used to refer to any *scratch tape* or *work tape* used in some intermediate processing.

magnetic tape group A set of *magnetic tape decks* built into a single cabinet, each deck capable of independent operation but sometimes arranged to share one or more *interface channels* for communication with a *central processor*.

Also known as cluster or tape cluster.

magnetic tape-head   That part of a *magnetic tape deck* which reads or writes information to the tape. Some tape decks have a single *read/write head* but others have separate heads for reading and writing; these are known as two gap heads. The heads are positioned so that reading takes place immediately after writing thus enabling a *parity check* to be made after the data has been recorded on the tape. If a machine malfunction causes the data to be incorrectly recorded this will be detected and the *block* will be rewritten.

magnetic tape librarian   The person who stores *magnetic tape files* ready for use on a computer; he is usually responsible for maintaining clerical or mechanical records showing the use and availability of tape *reels* [3] and is responsible for issuing correct files to operators. In some installations the tape usage records may themselves be maintained on a tape file by a special *program*.

magnetic tape library   The physical location in which *magnetic tape files* are stored, or the tapes themselves including all necessary clerical or mechanical records maintained to administrate the allocation and handling of tape *reels* [3]. ⟡ *magnetic tape librarian*.

magnetic tape parity   An automatic checking technique used when *reading* or *writing* data to *magnetic tape*. As each tape *character* is transferred to the tape a *parity bit* is generated and added to the character. Each character written is read back, to check that the writing operation for that character has been correctly executed. In addition a complete parity character is written to the end of each tape *block* and this is used to check parity for the whole block. A *parity check* guards against the loss of *information bits* during the transfer of information from tape to *memory* and vice versa.

magnetic tape plotting system   A system in which data recorded on *magnetic tape* is used to develop an X-Y plot for the purpose of controlling a *digital incremental plotter*.

magnetic tape reader   A device for sensing data recorded as a series of magnetized spots on *magnetic tape*. ⟡ general article on *Magnetic Tape*.

magnetic tape unit   Synonymous with *magnetic tape deck*.

magnetic thin film   ⟡ *thin-film memory*.

magnetic wire store   A storage device in which data is recorded on a thin moving wire by an electro-magnetic *read/write head*.

magnetized ink character   A character printed on a document by means of ink which is impregnated with a magnetizable material. The characters are in a stylized format to allow automatic recognition by machines (*magnetic ink character recognition*), while at the same time remaining readable by human beings. Machines which recognize such characters are usually fitted with a head which magnetizes the ink before the characters are presented to the reading head.

magneto-strictive acoustic delay line An *acoustic delay line* in which certain materials exhibiting the *magneto-strictive effect* are used to convert electrical signals to sonic waves and vice versa.

magneto-strictive effect An effect observed in certain materials when they are magnetized; certain physical strains are apparent, the mechanical stresses being approximately proportional to the square of the applied magnetic field. Such materials have applications where electrical signals are to be converted into sonic waves.

magnitude Of a number, the absolute value of the number irrespective of its sign.

main frame Originally implied the main framework of a central processing unit on which the arithmetic unit and associated logic circuits were mounted, but now used colloquially to refer to the *central processor* itself.

main memory The internal *memory* of a computer, i.e. the *immediate access store*, as distinct from any *backing store* that may be available as part of the computer system.

main path The main course followed during the execution of a *routine* as distinct from the various alternative routes that may be entered according to conditions occurring during execution of the routine, perhaps dependent on the data being processed.

main program The central part of a *program* which usually transfers control to other *subroutines* according to the nature of the data being processed or dependent on conditions arising during the operation of the program. The central framework on which the various sections or subroutines are mounted.

main routine Synonymous with *main program*.

main storage The *store* from which *instructions* are executed; usually the fastest store of a computer.
Also known as primary storage.

main store The principal fast or *immediate access store* of a machine. *Core store* is one form of main store.

main store quota In an *operating system* the area of *main store* made available by the *scheduling system* to a process when it is *rolled in.*

maintenance The efficiency of any computer installation is dependent on the effective maintenance of both *hardware* and *software*. Various categories of maintenance of hardware may be recognized, all aimed at reducing *down time* and maximizing the serviceable time for running of *programs; preventive maintenance, routine maintenance* and *scheduled maintenance* are terms used to imply work performed to prevent failures, undertaken according to a pre-arranged timetable, whereas *corrective maintenance* is work required to correct a machine fault. These and other categories are useful classifications for collecting statistics about the efficiency of a particular computer or *peripheral* device. Software maintenance is the work required to keep *programs* up to date, e.g. to make them more efficient or otherwise amend them in accordance with changing circumstances affecting the user. It is usually necessary to see that programming effort is clearly scheduled for this task separately from any time scheduled for the development of new programs.

maintenance contract Many computer manufacturers have a standard contract which allows the user the benefit of a resident service engineer or of periodic visits from a member of the manufacturer's service staff. The contract usually guarantees the user certain hours of *preventive maintenance* work throughout the duration of the contract, and may also specify a timetable for this work during which time the user must allow access to the equipment.

maintenance, file ◊ *file maintenance.*

maintenance of programs ◊ *maintenance.*

maintenance routine A *routine* specifically designed to assist a service engineer in performing routine *preventive maintenance.*

maintenance, scheduled ◊ *routine maintenance.*

major Describing the relative significance of a *key* or *control data* [1] stored in a computer *record* or in a *punched card.*

major control change On a *punched card tabulator*, the action of suspending *card feeding* and initiating *major control cycles* as a result of detecting a difference in major *control data* between one card and the next. ◊ *comparing control change.*

major control cycles On a *punched card tabulator*, a series of control cycles that are automatically initiated during the processing of a file of punched cards as a result of detecting a change of major *control data.*

major control data ◊ *control data.*

major cycle 1. The time between the recurrence of a given digit in a *cyclic store*. 2. One of the *control cycles* initiated in a *punched* *card tabulator* on a change of major *control data*. 3. A complete revolution of the storage medium in a *dynamic store*.

majority element   A *logic element* which has several *input* signals and which can be switched to provide an *output* signal only if a majority of the *weighted input signals* are present. ◊ *threshold element*.

malfunction routine   A *routine* designed to trace a fault in a computer's *hardware* or to assist in diagnosing an error in a *program*.

management information system   A system which may perform routine commercial processing functions, but which is designed so that much processing will also produce information that will be presented to management, including top management, to assist in decision making. The implication is that the results will be produced speedily, perhaps requiring *real time* processing, to enable management to ascertain the progress of the organization in terms of satisfying its major objectives.

manipulated variable   An *operand* which may be altered by *program* in order to control the operation of a *routine* in which the operand is used as a *parameter*.

mantissa   Strictly the fractional part of a logarithm; but also used to refer to the *fixed point part* of any *floating point* number (◊ *floating point arithmetic*). It can be misleading to use this word in the latter context and the term fixed point part is usually preferred.

manual control   Relating to a *program* or system in which some aspect of the work is controlled by the computer operator from the computer *console*.

manual input   The entry of data into a system or *program* directly, by the use of a *keyboard* device.

manual input unit   Any device which allows an operator to inject data into a system directly without the use of some intermediate medium such as *punched cards* or *paper tape*. For example, the entry of data into *memory* by means of a *console typewriter*.

manual operation   Any *data processing* operation performed without the use of automatic equipment; e.g. the pulling of documents or *punched cards* from a file.

manual (operations)   The status of a *peripheral unit* when it is *off-line* and hence cannot be controlled by an *operating system*.

manual word generator   A device by means of which an operator can set up a *word* of information for direct entry into *memory*. Also known as manual word unit.

manual word unit   Synonymous with *manual word generator*.

marginal checking   ◊ *marginal testing*.

marginal cost   The amount by which the cost of any operation is altered as a result of a change in the number of units handled or processed.

marginal testing   A test performed on equipment to diagnose some intermittent fault or to see whether the equipment is able to operate within specified operating tolerances. For example, the output of a power unit may be restricted to ascertain the effect on circuits of a reduction in power supply.

Also known as marginal checking. ⬦ *bias testing*.

margin-notched card   Synonymous with *edge-notched card*.

margin-punched card   A card which is punched with holes in a comparatively narrow strip along one edge of the card, leaving the centre free for written information. The punching *code* often resembles the type of punching used in 5, 6 or 7 *track paper tape*.

Also known as edge-punched card, border-punched card, verge-perforated card. Contrasts with *edge-notched card*.

mark   1. A *character* used to identify the end of a set of data, e.g. *tape mark, group marks*. Also known as marker. 2. In *telegraphic communication*, a positive pulse representing an element in a *character code*.

mark, control   ⬦ *tape mark* [1].

marker   Synonymous with *mark*.

mark hold   In telegraphic circuits, a steady signal transmitted to signify that no information is being transferred. The first element of any message would be a *space signal* of opposite polarity to the mark; thereafter the characters transferred would consist of a coded series of marks and spaces each of comparatively short duration.

mark reading   Synonymous with *mark scanning*. ⬦ *Character Recognition*.

mark scanning   A process in which marks made in predetermined positions on documents are read optically and interpreted as *digits* or *characters* for direct entry into a computer, or for punching into some other medium. The documents are preprinted to enable entries to be made in specified locations; the layout of the documents can be designed to enable the user to code information in a required manner. The marks may be made with any material provided there is a clear optical contrast with the paper. Contrasted with *mark sensing*.

Also known as mark reading. ⬦ *Character Recognition*.

mark scanning document   A document specially printed with reference columns to enable marks to be made for subsequent reading by a *mark scanning* device.

mark sense cards *Punched cards* divided into *card columns* to facilitate *mark sensing*. Mark sense columns are usually the width of two or three normal punching columns.

mark sensing The automatic sensing of marks made with some conductive material on predetermined positions of a *punched card*. The marks are made, usually with a graphite pencil lead, in columns to represent digits, in much the same way as holes in *card columns* represent digits. These marks are sensed electrically and as a result holes are punched in corresponding *punching positions* of predetermined card columns, either on the same, or another, card.

mark-space multiplier A *multiplier* [2] used in *analog computers* wherein an input voltage is used to regulate the *mark-to-space ratio* of a square wave. Another input voltage controls the amplitude of the wave, and the output signal is then operated upon by a smoothing circuit to develop a product which is represented as an average value of the signal.

mark-to-space ratio A ratio of the duration of the positive and negative cycles of a square wave. A mark is a positive cycle and a space is a negative cycle.

mask A pattern of *characters* or *bits* devised so as to alter or isolate specific *bit positions* present in another *bit pattern*. A mask is usually one of the *operands* in a *Boolean operation*.
Also known as extractor, filter. ✆ *masking*.

masking The technique of using a *mask* to operate on the *bit pattern* of some other *operand*, in order to alter or isolate certain *bit positions*. Usually involves the use of one or more Boolean operations such as *and operation, or operation*.

mask register A *register* used specifically for *masking*; i.e. to determine which portions of *operands* are to be tested under the aegis of some *logical operation*.

mass data Data in such volume that it cannot be stored in *memory* at one time, e.g. data stored on a *magnetic disk file*.

mass storage Some *backing storage* medium of large capacity directly *on-line* to a *central processor*. For example, a large *magnetic disk file*.
Also known as bulk storage.

master card A *punched card* holding any fixed information about a group of cards or a whole card file, usually appearing as the first or last card of the group.

master clock A device which generates clocking signals to synchronize the operation of a machine. In an electronic computer, a device which generates clock pulses to maintain the basic time frequency of the electronic circuits.

master control routine 1. A *routine* which forms part of a *program* consisting of a series of subroutines. The master control routine controls the linking of the other subroutines and may call the various *segments* of the program into *memory* as required. 2. Also used to describe a program which controls the operation of a *hardware system*, for example assigning *peripheral units* and controlling operator activities; but ◊ *executive program*.

master console A *console* exercising overall control over a computer system.

master data Those *data elements* of a *record* which seldom change; e.g. descriptive data such as personnel number, stock item number.

master file A *file* of reference data which is changed relatively infrequently but which is used to provide data for a system on a routine basis; e.g. a cross reference index. 2. A current, fully updated file to which *change records* of new transactions are applied.

master instruction tape A *magnetic tape* which maintains all the *routines* required for a particular *suite* of *programs*.

master library tape A *reel* of *magnetic tape* which contains all the *programs* and major *subroutines* required in a particular data processing centre. During operation of the computer this tape may remain permanently *loaded* on a *magnetic tape deck*: at the beginning of any *run* the computer operator calls into *memory* the particular program required.
Also known as master program file.

master operating station An *operating station* which contains a *console* by means of which overall control of a computer system can be exercised.

master program file Synonymous with *master library tape*.

master record In a *magnetic tape* system, the latest version of any particular *record* carried forward to the next processing *run*. Contrasted with *change record*.

master/slave system A system in which a large central computer is connected to one or more *satellite processors*. The central or master computer has control over the other machines, usually via direct control over the input and output operations. The computers in the system may be assigned special tasks under control of the master computer such as the transmission and receipt of data to or from some external source, the assembly and editing of data for processing or the processing of data to obtain desired results.

master tape A *magnetic tape* containing data that must not be *overwritten*; for example a tape containing a *master file*, or current transaction data.

match Synonymous with *equivalence operation*.

matching The technique of comparing the *keys* of two *records* to select items for a particular stage of processing or to reject invalid records.

material implication Synonymous with *conditional implication operation*.

mathematical analysis The study of the relationship between numbers and the operations performed on them, including the concepts of algebra and arithmetic.

mathematical check A check performed to verify a result achieved by some arithmetic operation. The use of alternative methods to obtain results using given *operands*; e.g. $(A \times B) \div C = (B \div C)\ A$.

mathematical logic The use of mathematical concepts, including the adoption of a symbolic notation, in order to represent valid argument without the attendent inaccuracy and ambiguity of ordinary language.

mathematical model A representation of some process or problem in mathematical form in which equations are used to simulate the behaviour of the process or system represented. Usually enables a range of alternative actions to be simulated in order to ascertain the optimum conditions under which the system would be operated to achieve, or most nearly achieve, its objectives. ◊ general article on *Model Building*.

mathematical subroutine A *subroutine* written to perform some mathematical function; e.g. square root, sine, tangent, etc.

matrix 1. A rectangular array of numbers that may be operated on using prescribed rules involving mathematical operations such as addition, multiplication, etc. The term has become more loosely applied in data processing to any table of items. 2. Sometimes used to refer to an array of circuit elements; e.g. diodes in a conversion matrix for generating one set of coded signals from another.

matrix printer Synonymous with *stylus printer*.

matrix store A *store* in which a particular *location* or circuit element is addressed by the use of coordinates.
Also known as coordinate store.

mean repair time In a given time period, the ratio of time spent in *corrective maintenance* of a unit to the number of unit *failures*.

mean time between failures In a given time period, the ratio of the total time in the period to the number of *failures* in the period.

mean time to repair Synonymous with *mean repair time*.

medium As, for example, in input medium, the particular material in which data is recorded for the purpose of input to *memory*. Examples of input media are *punched cards, paper tape, magnetic tape, magnetic ink* documents or documents bearing characters for *optical character recognition*.

meet operation Synonymous with *and operation*.

mega- A million; as in 10 megacycles per second, meaning 10 million cycles per second.

megabit Pertaining to a *store*, a million *binary digits*.

memory This term is usually reserved for describing the *internal store* of a computer, i.e. the *immediate access store*. In its strictest sense it refers to the storage *locations* that can be immediately addressed by the *program controller* of the *central processor*, rather than to any *backing store* medium such as *magnetic tape, magnetic disk* or *magnetic drum storage*. However, these backing stores are sometimes referred to as *memory units*, as in *disk-file memory*, in which case the internal storage would be referred to as *main memory*.

Also known as immediate access storage, *store, core store*, main store.

memory, acoustic ◊ *acoustic store*.

memory address register A *register* used in the addressing of *operands* in other *locations* of *store*. The *address* component of each *instruction* is stored in a memory address register while the instruction is executed.

memory, associative ◊ *associative store*.

memory buffer register A special *register* through which all data entering or leaving *memory* must pass. Thus the register acts as a *buffer store* to facilitate transfers of data to and from the memory and *peripheral units*.

memory capacity The number of units of data that can be stored in *memory*, expressed in terms of the number of *locations* available; examples are 32,000 24-bit *words*, 1 million *binary digits*, 120,000 6-bit *characters*.

memory core ◊ *ferrite core*.

memory cycle 1. The complete sequence of operations required to insert or extract a unit of data from *memory*. 2. The time taken to perform a complete sequence of operations.

memory dump An operation to output the contents of all or some of the *locations* in *memory* by printing out or writing to some *backing store medium*. Printing out is usually adopted when a *program* is being tested or an attempt is being made to diagnose some *software* error, but memory dumps are also made as a precaution against machine malfunction.

Also known as storage dump. ◊ the general articles on *Dump and Restart* and *Debugging*.

memory, dynamic ◊ *dynamic store.*

memory, external ◊ *external store.*

memory fill A technique used to bring to notice the fact that a *program* is trying to derive *instructions* from forbidden *locations* or *registers*. The registers concerned are filled with predetermined characters which signal an error condition if addressed.

memory guard A *hardware* or *software* device which prevents a program from *addressing* specified *locations* in *internal store.*

memory, internal Synonymous with *internal store* ◊ *memory.*

memory overlays The utilization of *memory* by various sections or *segments* of a *program*; e.g. where the program is of such size that it cannot conveniently be held in its entirety in *main memory* at any one time. Thus at any instant the memory locations will be occupied by segments which in turn may be *overwritten* by other segments as the functions performed by these segments are required.

memory, permanent ◊ *non-volatile memory.*

memory power The efficiency of a particular *memory* design in respect of its rate of processing; e.g. a *store* may be said to have a cycle speed of one *microsecond*.

memory print The output of the contents of *memory locations* to a *printer*. ◊ *memory dump.*

memory protect A feature of *multiprogramming* computers, in which a *hardware* device is used to protect each *program*, and its data, from being mutilated by any other program that may be operating in the system at the same time.

memory, random access Synonymous with *direct access storage.*

memory, rapid-access ◊ *rapid-access loop.*

memory, thin-film ◊ *thin-film store.*

memory unit Synonymous with *backing store*. ◊ *memory.*

menu selection A method of using a *terminal* to *display* a list of optional facilities which can be chosen by the *user* in order to carry out different functions in a system.

mercury delay line An *acoustic delay line* in which mercury is used to recirculate sonic signals.

mercury memory A storage device in which information is retained by recirculating signals in a *mercury delay line*.

merge An operation performed on two, or more, ordered sets of *records* to create a single set or *file*. The two original sets must first be arranged into the same sequence by *sorting* on a common *key*. This operation may be performed on *punched cards* by a *collator*, or on any ordered file of records held in *memory* or on a *backing store* medium.

message 1. Any combination of *characters* and *symbols* designed to communicate information from one point to another. For example, a set of *records* transmitted over a *data link* between one computer and another, or an *error message* displayed on a computer *console* to draw the operator's attention to some specific machine or *program* error. 2. *Data* input to a *transaction processing* system through a *terminal* for processing. A message together with the *reply* it generates constitutes an *exchange*. A set of *exchanges* constitute a *transaction*.

message display console A *console* unit fitted with a *visual display tube* to permit data to be displayed in character form. When this is fitted to a *central processor*, data stored in *memory* can be selected and displayed as a page. For example, twenty lines each of 80 character positions might be displayed, using a full *character repertoire* of 64 characters.

message exchange A *hardware* device forming part of a *data link*, which performs certain routine switching functions to relieve the computer of these tasks.

message queuing In a *data communications* system, a technique for controlling the way in which messages are handled. Messages may be accepted by a central computer and be temporarily stored until they are processed or routed to some further destination. Such a system is essential where messages may arise at random and possibly overload the system at any instant.

message routing A function performed by *hardware* or *software* in a *data communications* system: messages received in a central computer are examined and routed to the destination required.

message switching system A *data communications* system in which a central computer is used to service several distant terminals, receiving *messages* from them and storing them until they can be retransmitted to some desired destination.

method study The use of certain techniques for recording and examining existing and proposed methods of working in order to improve them. ◊ *Time Study.*

MICR Acronym for *magnetic ink character recognition.*

micro- A prefix denoting one millionth (10^{-6}), as in *microsecond.*

micro code Synonymous with *micro instruction.*

micro-coding The process of simulating a program *instruction* not normally part of an *instruction set* by means of a series of simple program steps. A section of micro-coding forms a *macro instruction.* Contrasted with *macro-coding.*

micro instruction An *instruction* at *machine code* level which directly controls the functioning of *hardware* independently of *operating system* or *application software.* Also known as micro code.

microprogram A set of *micro instructions* which together define a specific *hardware* function independently of *application software* or *operating system* control. For example a microprogram may be used to effect *code conversion* or *data input.*

microsecond One millionth of a second.

microwave Pertaining to *data communications* systems in which ultra high-frequency waveforms are used to transmit voice or data messages.

middleware Computer manufacturer's *software* which has been tailored to the particular needs of an installation.

milli- A prefix meaning one thousandth (10^{-3}), as in *millivolt, millisecond,* etc.

millisecond One thousandth of a second.

millivolt One thousandth of a volt.

minimum access code A coding system which minimizes the time needed to retrieve any required unit of data from a *storage device.* Also known as minimum latency code, minimum delay code, optimum code.

minimum access coding The technique of *programming* computers so as to reduce *access time* to a minimum. ◊ *minimum access code.*
Also known as minimum delay coding, optimum coding.

minimum delay code Synonymous with *minimum access code.*

minimum delay coding Synonymous with *minimum access coding.*

minimum latency code Synonymous with *minimum access code.*

minor control change On a *punched card tabulator* the action of suspending card feeding and initiating *minor cycles* as a result of detecting the difference in minor *control data* between one card and the rest. ◊ *comparing control change.*

minor control data ◊ *control data.*

minor cycle 1. On a *punched card tabulator*, a cycle of machine operations occurring during a *minor control change.* 2. In any *storage device*, the interval between corresponding positions of successive *words.*

minuend One of the *operands* used in subtraction, the quantity from which another quantity is subtracted.

minus zone The *character* or *digit position* displaying the algebraic sign of an *operand.*

misfeed A failure to feed a *punched card* from the *hopper* of a punched card device. Usually caused by damaged cards or by *card fluff* at the entrance to the *card track.*

MIT Acronym for *master instruction tape.*

mixed base notation The representation of quantities where any two or more adjacent *digit positions* have a different *radix* of notation.
Also known as mixed radix notation.

mixed number A number consisting of an *integral* part and a *fractional* part; e.g. 10·52 is a decimal mixed number.

mixed radix notation ◊ *mixed base notation.*

mnemonic A *label* chosen so as to be associated in some way with the item to which it refers, e.g. the *fields* in a payroll *record* might be given labels G R O S S, N E T, T A X, etc. ◊ *mnemonic operation codes.*

mnemonic operation codes In *symbolic programming languages*, the *operation code* forming part of each *instruction* is represented by some symbolic code easier for the programmer to remember than the numeric code forming part of the basic *machine code.* For example, the operation *multiplication* might be represented as M U L T.

mode A particular method of operation for a *hardware* or *software* device; for example, a particular unit might be capable of operating in, say, *binary mode* or *character mode.* For further examples, ◊ *burst mode, byte mode, conversational mode.*

model A representation of a system, device or process in a mathematical form ◊ *mathematical model, Model Building.*

model building Many computer systems, and most *operational research*, can be regarded as comprising the formulation and studying of models of real life situations. In this sense a model is a representation of a situation. Loosely the model may be many things, from a profit and loss account representing a business situation to a weather chart representing the meteorological situation. More strictly we use the word 'model' in the operational research sense to mean a model expressed in terms which can be analysed, usually by mathematical methods, or, if not analysed directly, can be studied by *simulation* techniques.

The aim of building a model is to include in it only those features of the situation which are important to it. The model builder must consider, at the formulation stage, what features he is to include. It is easier to investigate the model than the situation it represents (which may not even exist), although generally speaking, the more features that are included the more difficult the subsequent analysis will be. The amount of detail included should give both meaningful results and ease of analysis.

The simplest models will yield results directly, the more complicated will need complex techniques to handle them. In the simple case the analyst may find he has only to solve a series of simultaneous equations, or optimize some variables, perhaps by *linear programming* techniques. In the more complex he may have to resort to sampling theory, using perhaps Monte Carlo Methods, or operational gaming. The engineer (and others) may often find that the *analog computers* can be of help.

A *digital computer* is often essential in analysing a model. Simulation studies are made much more easily, allowing larger samples to be taken. Particularly when the analysis has to be repeated regularly (e.g. in reflecting market demand for a product) the digital computer achieves something that would be impossible without it. However the use of a computer can present its own problems. The *programming* of a computer for simulation studies is not an easy task, although the introduction of new *languages* is making this easier. Also the ability of a computer to handle large samples does not replace the necessity for the model builder to provide a model which corresponds closely to the real situation. Sampling errors are, of course, unavoidable, but there are many techniques for detecting and measuring them.

The construction of a mathematical model of a situation is nearly always worthwhile, since it can only add to the understanding of that situation; it must be remembered, however, that a model is literally only a model, and the more detailed the model becomes the more difficult will become subsequent analysis.

modem An acronym for modulator/demodulator. A device which enables *data* to be transmitted over long distances without error. ◊ *modulation* and general article on *Communication Devices*.

modification The technique of altering *instructions* and *addresses*

273

in a *program* by treating them as data and applying *arithmetical* and *logical operations* to them. ◊ general article on *Program Modification*.

modifier An item of data used to alter a *program instruction* so that the instruction, sometimes referred to as a *basic instruction*, can be used repetitively to execute a different operation on each occasion, e.g. the *operand address* may be modified to operate upon successive items in an *array* of date. ◊ *Program Modification*, *address modification*.

modifier register A *register* into which a *modifier* can be loaded in order to effect the *modification* of a *basic instruction*. Also known as *index register*.

modify To apply the technique of *modification*. ◊ the general article on *Program Modification*.

modular A method of constructing a *hardware* or *software* system using standard compatible units. In this way a wide range of *configurations* can be built up with combinations of the standard units.

modularity The condition exhibited by any *hardware* or *software* system that permits the subsequent expansion of the system by the addition of standard *modular* units.

modular programming Modular programming is a technique used in *programming* which simplifies the tasks of developing and maintaining large *suites* of programs. The objective of modular programming methods is to achieve two main goals: speed and efficiency of *debugging* and ease of *maintenance* of the programs in a suite.

The basis of modular programming techniques is to divide each program at the planning stage into a number of logical parts or *modules*[2]. Each module corresponds to a particular program function and can be treated as a separate entity. A number of different programs may in practice share certain common modules. Each individual module is relatively simple to specify, write and test. Changing requirements can be met by simply changing existing modules or adding new modules to the system.

Modular programming techniques have been powerfully extended by means of modular program testing software, sometimes known as a *testbed*. A testbed is a software system which allows the user to test individual modules independently of the overall context of the program of which they are subdivisions. *Test data* needed for the program is supplied to the testbed and fed automatically to modules being tested. Where modules require to pass data to or from other modules not yet developed, the testbed can simulate the presence of these modules for testing purposes. A testing system for program modules may also have available other programming aids such as keeping records of the progress of testing, providing detailed diagnostic information, automatic generation of test data. A further feature is the ability of the user to choose different *languages* for different modules, for example mixing *C O B O L, F O R T R A N* and possibly a *low level language* within a single program. The testbed software would co-ordinate the *object code* generated for the complete program regardless of the *source code* used for each module.

modulation   A technique used in radio, telegraphic and telephonic communication systems, in which data signals are used to modify either the amplitude or frequency of a carrier wave by means of *modems* (modulator/demodulators). The carrier wave is of a suitable frequency for transmitting over a specified channel, and therefore carries with it the data signals which normally would not be capable of transmission over the circuit concerned.

modulation code   A coded signal used to modulate the frequency or *amplitude* of a carrier wave. ◊ *modulation.*

modulator   A device which superimposes a data signal on a carrier wave according to a predetermined method. ◊ *modulation.*

modulator/demodulator   ◊ *modem* and *modulation.*

module   1. A *hardware* device or *software* item which, as a standard unit, forms part of a *modular system.* 2. The term is used more specifically for a self-contained subset of a *program* and in this sense is related to *segment.* ◊ general article on *Modular Programming.* 3. In an *operating system,* the unit of a *process,* consisting of a number of *areas* including *code* areas and *data* areas, which can be held as a single entity in a *filestore.*

module key   A *key* used to identify and access an area in a *module* in *filestore.*

modulo   An *arithmetical operation* in which the *result* is the remainder after the first *operand* is divided by the second, e.g. 27 modulo $4 = 3$.

modulo n check   A method for checking the validity of a numeric *operand,* in which the number is divided by n to produce a remainder (◊ *modulo*). The remainder then accompanies the result as a *check digit* and subsequently the number may again be divided by n and the remainder is compared with the previously calculated check digit. When $n = 9$, known as *casting-out-nines.*

modulo 2 sum   Synonymous with *inclusive-or operation.*

monadic operation A processing operation performed upon one *operand*.

monitor Any device which examines the status of a system to indicate any deviation from some prescribed operational conditions. For example, a device which examines the characteristics of a signal in a communications channel.

monitor display A *display* on a *terminal* which is for information only and is not an *interactive display*.

monitor routine 1. Any *routine* which observes the progress of work in a computer system. 2. More specifically, a routine designed to supervise and control the operation of *programs* in the computer, performing the functions of an *executive program*. 3. A routine used to provide diagnostic information on the progress of a program for the purpose of *debugging*.

monitor system A collection of *routines* stored permanently in *memory* which control the operation of users' *programs* and coordinate the various *hardware* and *software* activities. Synonymous with *executive program*. Such a system controls the allocation of *store* and *peripheral units* to programs, the loading and scheduling of programs, *time sharing* of *input/output* operations, and *multiprogramming*.

monostable device A device which has only one stable state. For example, a monostable trigger can be activated to assume momentarily an unstable condition but it will immediately resume its stable state.

most significant character The character in the extreme left-hand position of a group of significant *characters* in *positional representation*.

M T B F Acronym for *mean time between failures*.

M T T R Acronym for *mean time to repair*. ◊ *mean repair time*.

multi-access A multi-access system is one that allows a number of people to perform the interactive role usually associated with an *operator's console*. The access points (which may be a few only or hundreds in number) are generally linked to the *central processor* by switched *data transmission* lines rather than by direct cabling as with most types of *on-line peripheral unit*. The remote terminals may range from simple devices like cash registers, perhaps with an automatic input mechanism for reading pre-coded data, through *console typewriters* and *visual display units* to complete *satellite processors*. There are two main categories of multi-access system: one operates with a single complex of *programs* and the other allows the processing of as many diverse programs as there are terminals.

Systems which employ multi-access terminals in support of a common series of tasks are mainly *real time* applications, such as airline seat reservation, banking, stock exchange dealing, crime detection and weather forecasting. Essentially, multi-access is used to facilitate communications. The remote stations transmit data to the central processor for *updating* large central files held on *direct access storage devices*; and the same network is used to send back status reports to the terminals, such as the number of seats available on a given flight or the name and address registered under a vehicle licence number.

Multi-access, *multiprogramming* systems have been installed by many universities and research institutes to make a powerful computing facility available to the greatest possible number of students and researchers. The technique provides the benefit of *open shop* problem-solving without consequent dispersal of the budget for *hardware*. Numerous consoles can be used simultaneously, each programmer conducting his work in *conversational mode* so that his experiment can be completed in one sitting, avoiding the difficulty of scheduling *debugging time*. A *response time* of a few seconds can be given to each terminal because human intervention is an inherently slow process. This level of service is sufficient to make each user feel that he has the machine to himself.

Both types of multi-access system rely on the art of *time sharing*. A different degree of sophistication is required for different applications, for example a critical real time system should be *modular* to permit *graceful degradation* rather than catastrophic failure, and a multi-user system must incorporate *memory protection*. It may be necessary to charge users pro rata for the service, requiring adequate logging of time and peripheral usage by the central *operating system*.

Considerable developments may be expected in multi-access and time sharing systems, leading to the establishment of *data banks* for various spheres of activity. Thus insurance brokers, travel agents, doctors and lawyers may be able to share systems which will provide background information and do their clerical work, with access by telephone circuits.

multi-address instruction An *instruction* which specifies the *address* of more than one *operand*. ⟡ *Instruction Format*.

multi-aspect search A search conducted on a series of items using various logical combinations of the elements within each item to identify and select the items required. ⟡ *Information Retrieval*.

multi-cycle feeding A system used on *punched card tabulators* in

277

which several lines of print can be obtained from a single card. The card is *read* repeatedly on several consecutive machine cycles and on each occasion certain specified *fields* (e.g. name, street, town, etc.) are read until all the lines required have been printed.

Synonymous with multi-read feeding.

multi-length arithmetic ◊ *multiple-length arithmetic.*

multi-level addressing Synonymous with *indirect addressing.*

multiple address Pertaining to *instructions* which specify the *addresses* of more than one *store location.* For example, some computers have *instruction formats* which enable two or three *operands* to be specified as part of one instruction.

multiple-address code Pertaining to an *instruction format* that requires the programmer to specify the *address* of more than one *operand* at any one *instruction.*

multiple connector A symbol used in *flowcharting* to indicate the confluence of several *flowlines.*

multiple-length arithmetic Arithmetic performed using two or more machine *words* to *store* each *operand,* usually to achieve greater precision in the result, e.g. by storing a decimal function in two words, one holding the *integer* and another the fractional part. Arithmetic involving the generation of a result which requires to be stored in two or more words.

Also known as multi-length arithmetic. ◊ *double-precision arithmetic* and *triple-length working.*

multiple-length number In a *word oriented memory,* any *operand* which exceeds the capacity of one word.

multiple-length working Any processing in which two or more *words* are used to *store* a number.

multiple punching In *punched card* practice, the punching of more than two holes in any single *card column.*

multiple recording Where more than one copy of a *file* is maintained, and *updated* simultaneously *on-line* to a processor. The objective of multiple recording is to minimize the chances of losing a current file. ◊ *redundancy*[4].

multiplex 1. A multiplex system involves the transfer of data from several comparatively slow-speed *storage devices* over a series of channels to a fast central storage device which continually scans and accepts data from each channel in turn. The fast storage device is able to service the channels without any part of the system being delayed. 2. To transmit a number of messages concurrently over the same circuit.

multiplex data terminal A terminal unit at which two or more *input/output* devices may be stationed and which acts as a modulator/demodulator (◊ *modem*) to accept and transfer signals between the input/output units and a data channel.

multiplexer ◊ *multiplexor*.

multiplexing 1. The simultaneous transmission of several messages over a single communications channel, usually by modulating a carrier wave in such a way that separate signals are transmitted using particular frequencies within the full bandwidth of the channel. 2. Pertaining to any system in which a single device is used for many purposes.

multiplexor A communications control device which enables a *central processor* to be connected to a large number of different communications *channels*, any or all of which may be transferring data to or from the processor. The multiplexor operates at high speed to service each channel in turn *character* by character, and interrupts the processor to place each character into *memory*. Control data is transferred to and from the central processor to identify each character, and this allows input messages to be assembled in memory for processing or retransmission.

multiplexor channel A *channel* allowing the interleaving of many simultaneous transmissions in both directions.

multiplexor-channel time sharing A system whereby a number of terminal units may be connected to the same communications *channel* so that effectively a number of independent channels exist over the same circuit. Each unit is able to transmit data *characters* over the circuit accompanied by identifying characters, and by the use of *time sharing* techniques the terminal units can all use the channel concurrently.

multiplexor, data channel ◊ *data channel multiplexor*.

multiplicand One of the factors used in *multiplication*: a quantity which is multiplied by another.

multiplication The arithmetic process in which a result (the *product*) is obtained from two factors, the *multiplicand* and the *multiplier*. In most digital computers the result is obtained as an accumulation of the *multiplicand* repeated according to the value of the *multiplier*; but this basic method is usually adapted to reduce the number of steps involved. ◊ *multiplication table*.

multiplication table In some computers the process of multiplication is performed indirectly by looking up values in a table stored permanently within the *memory*. The table is referred to as the multiplication table.

multiplication time The time required to multiply a specified pair of *operands*.

multiplier 1. One of the factors used in *multiplication*; that number which is used to multiply another. 2. A *hardware* unit capable of performing multiplication.

multiplier register A *register* used to hold the *multiplier* while *multiplication* is being performed.

multi-precision arithmetic The use of two or more *words* for any *operand* in an arithmetic process, where undesired inaccuracy would have resulted if a single word had been used.

multiprocessor A *central processor* containing two or more independent arithmetic units and their associated *control logic*.

multiprocessor interleaving A technique for allocating *memory* areas to the different processors within a *multiprocessor system*. The *store* is subdivided into *modules* which are referenced as even or odd, and the *addressing* structure for the *locations* within any module remains as in the standard *machine code*. In this way a number of modules are allocated to each processor to avoid interaction between *programs* being run simultaneously.

multiprocessor system Two or more *processors* capable of driving the same *applications* and providing extra processing power and/or *resilience* in the total system. In a fully effective multiprocessor system the *main store* (i.e. *data* and *code*) must be shareable between processors and no one processor inherently has a dominant relationship to the others. All processors operate under the control of one *operating system*, which automatically switches work from any processor which is faulty, and will ensure that work is distributed to ensure rational loading of the processor. ⟡ *loosely coupled twin* and *tightly coupled twin*. Contrasted with *multiprogramming* system, in which a single processing unit is used on a *time sharing* basis to operate several *programs* independently.

multiprogramming There is an extreme difference in the speeds at which a computer handles its internal operations (performing calculations on data in its *central processor*) and the speeds at which even the fastest *peripheral units* used for input and output of data operate. In the time taken to print one line on a *printer* working at 1,200 lines per minute, a processor could perhaps perform something of the order of ten thousand additions. Few *programs* would in fact perform anything like as many operations between printing successive lines of print, or performing any other peripheral operation, and this means that during the operation of a program which makes fairly frequent use of a peripheral device there will be long periods of time (long, that is, in relation to the internal speeds of the computer, something like several thousandths of a second) during which the processor is idle, waiting for a peripheral transfer to finish before it can continue by performing the next set of internal operations.

To help redress the balance, *time sharing* techniques have been developed which enable a single program using more than one peripheral unit to continue processing while several of the units under its control continue their respective actions. However, there will still be periods of time when the processor remains idle, and in any event peripheral units not used by the program during time sharing cannot be used at all, since they need a program to 'drive' them.

Multiprogramming is a technique developed in order to utilize a computer more efficiently by enabling the processor to spend a greater proportion of its time in action and by making more use of all available peripheral units. The basic principle of multiprogramming is that more than one program can be present in *memory* at the same time, and share the available processor time and peripheral units. Each program is written as a completely independent unit, as if it were being produced for a single-program machine, and each program uses peripheral units allotted to it for the duration of a *run*. With several programs sharing the computer the best use is made of the central processor time, whilst all the programs concerned also make more practical and extensive use of the available peripheral units. For example, a program to read data from *paper tape* and transcribe it to *magnetic tape* will only require the use of the central processor for a very small fraction of the program running time, the remainder representing peripheral transfer time during which other programs in the system can use the central processor. Benefits to be gained from this concept of multiprogramming include the elimination of *off-line* equipment to transcribe data onto a faster medium for input since while this activity is proceeding, using limited numbers of peripheral units and little processing time, other more productive programs can use the remaining peripherals and processor time.

In order to achieve multiprogramming, several problems must be overcome. Obviously, if more than one program is present in memory at the same time, there must be no danger of one program interfering with another. Interference could involve *overwriting* another program's *area*, or attempting to use a peripheral unit at the same time as another program. In order to achieve optimum utilization of processor time and of peripheral units, some method of allotting priorities between the programs sharing the computer must be made. Further, in order to enable programs of different sizes to be *loaded* into the computer at different times, as and when store space becomes available because of programs finishing, the method of loading programs and sharing memory between them must be as flexible as possible. These various objectives are achieved by a combination of *hardware* and *software*. Different multiprogramming systems adopt different combinations of these two methods; in a short article it is not possible to describe all types of system. One typical approach combines a system of hardware checks to prevent one program from interfering with another's area, and an *executive program* to control peripheral sharing and the operations concerned with loading and communicating with programs.

The method by which the executive program controls the sharing of processor time between programs and the operation of peripheral transfers can be described in outline as follows. When a program requires a peripheral transfer to be carried out, it obeys an instruction which transfers control to the executive program. The executive program then initiates the transfer, and returns control to the program just left. This program may proceed until it requires to use the information being read in by the transfer or the area from which data is being transferred. At this point the program will obey an instruction which suspends the program from further operation until the peripheral transfer is completed. Control is then transferred to the executive program. At this stage the order of priorities allotted to the programs present in the computer is consulted by the executive program, which looks for the program of highest priority that can now proceed because it is not held up for a peripheral unit. This program is entered to make use of processor time which would otherwise be wasted. When the transfer relating to the first program is complete an automatic *interrupt* occurs, and, assuming that the first program had higher priority, the executive program suspends the current one and re-enters the first one. As a general principle, programs that are *peripheral limited* (i.e. those which use very little processor time compared to the time they spend on peripheral transfers) will be given a higher priority than those which are *processor limited* (i.e. those which use a relatively large amount of processor time). Written at the beginning of each program is descriptive data which includes the program's priority number. This number is entered by the programmer, but to allow flexibility when several programs are being run simultaneously, it is also possible

282

for the operator to alter the priority at any time during the run. Another technique used to achieve multiprogramming is *interleaving*. In this method, *segmented* programs are used, and segments of one program are inserted between segments of another program so that control is constantly switched from one program to another as each segment is completed. Using this technique the programmer will segment his program in such a way that processing and peripheral transfers occur in different segments; he must also know with which programs interleaving is to take place, so that as control alternates between segments, one program is performing a peripheral transfer while a processing segment of another program is being executed.

A further refinement of multiprogramming systems is the use of sophisticated *operating systems*, in which the functions of an executive program are extended to cover more comprehensive control over the scheduling of many programs and associated data files through the system.

multi-read feeding A system for reading cards on a *punched card tabulator*, in which the card passes a *sensing station*, and consecutive machine cycles take place to enable different data to be read on each occasion, e.g. name, street, town, etc. each held in a different *field*. Also known as *multi-cycle feeding*.

multi-reel file A *file* of data stored on *magnetic tape* which exceeds the capacity of one *reel* of magnetic tape and is therefore stored on two or more reels.

multistation Relating to any communications network in which several data terminals are involved. ◊ *data transmission*.

multivibrator A type of oscillator which is used to generate non-sinusoidal waveforms.

mylar A trade name used for polyester film which is often coated with magnetizable particles for use as a magnetic storage medium.

N

nand element Synonymous with *not-and* element.

nand operation Synonymous with *not-and operation*.

nano- Prefix denoting one thousand-millionth or 10^{-9}.

narrative Statements included in the *coding* of a *program* to serve as explanatory documentation of the coded procedures. Such statements are not translated into program *instructions*, but serve as useful aids during the *debugging* or amending of a program. Also known as *comment*.

natural function generator Synonymous with *analytical function generator*.

natural law function generator Synonymous with *analytical function generator*.

negation An operation performed upon a single *operand* in which the result produced has reverse significance in each *digit position*; e.g. a *bit pattern p*:   010110

would appear as *r*: 101001

This is contrasted with *complementing*, which is a method for obtaining the negative of a number, whereas negation does not have this effect, merely reversing the bit value of each *bit position* in a word.

Also known as Boolean complementation, inversion, not operation.

negative indication Relating to the practice of specifying negative *fields* on a *punched card*, e.g. by an *overpunching* in the most significant *card column* of the *field*. It is not essential to use a position within the field itself and any column of the card could be assigned to receive a negative indication.

negator A *logic element* which has one *binary* input signal and which provides a single binary output signal of reverse significance. That is, if a 1 *bit* is used as input, a zero bit is produced as output, and vice versa. Also known as *not element*.

neither-nor operation Synonymous with *nor operation*.

nesting Pertaining to a *routine* or *subroutine* which contains a structure similar to itself. For example, a *loop* of *instructions* which may contain another loop and so on perhaps down through several levels.

nesting loops A programming technique in which a *loop* of *instructions* contains another loop, which may in turn contain another, and so on.

nesting store A *store* comprising several *locations* only one of vhich may receive data from or transmit data to the associated equipment. Thus data entering the store is pushed down from location to location as though moving through several levels.

nesting subroutines A series of *subroutines* arranged at different levels, i.e. one written within another. Thus, *entry* [1] to a lower level subroutine can be achieved via any of the other high-level subroutines, and in each case facilities are incorporated to generate an appropriate *branch* to *exit* back to the *calling* subroutine.

network Relating to any system that represents a series of points and their interconnexions, e.g. an electricity supply network. ⟡ general article on *Critical Path Method*. Relates also to *data transmission* systems.

network analog An *analog* device for studying *networks*, in which electrical circuits are used to represent the physical phenomena under study.

network analyser A *simulator* designed to study *networks*.

network analysis ⟡ general article on *Critical Path Method*.

nexus A point in a system at which interconnexions occur.

nickel delay line An *acoustic delay line* in which nickel is used to recirculate sonic signals.

nine-edge leading The manner in which cards are placed in the feed *hopper* of some *punched card* machines. The cards are fed broadside so that the *row* of 9-digits is read first then the row of 8-digits and so on through to the *X-position*. Contrasts with, for example, *column 1 leading*.

nines complement Related to a method used in some computers and *accounting machines* to represent negative values. The number itself is represented by the result obtained when subtracting each digit from a digit one less than the *radix*. For example, the five-digit decimal number $-18,764$ would be represented as 81235
i.e.   99999
    -18764
    81235

Some type of sign indicator is used when this technique is adopted, in order to distinguish between complements and positive numbers. Complements are converted to the correct representation before output. In a *binary notation* a *ones-complement* could be used to achieve the same effect.

ninety-column card A *punched card* which has 90 columnar positions in any of which holes may be punched to represent a character.

no-address instruction An *instruction* that does not require to specify an *address* in *memory*.

node An expression used in the context of *data base management systems* to define the location of information about an object, e.g. *file*, *record*, *user*.

noise 1. Any disturbance affecting the characteristics of a signal, e.g. random variations in voltage, current or frequency. 2. Errors in data generated by disturbance in a circuit, particularly in a *data transmission* circuit.

noise digit A digit, usually zero, generated during the *normalizing*[2] of a *floating point number*, and inserted during a *left shift* operation into the *fixed point part*.

noisy mode The method of operation adopted when *normalizing* a *floating point number*, in which digits, other than zero, are generated as part of the *fixed point part*.

non-accountable time Time during which a system is not available to the *user*, either because it is switched off or is unavailable for reasons beyond the user's or the supplier's control, e.g. in a power failure.

non-arithmetic shift Synonymous with logical shift.

non-destructive read Reading information from a *location* or *register* in *memory* in such a way that the data is retained undamaged in the source *location*.

non-equivalence operation Synonymous with *exclusive-or operation*.

non-erasable store Any medium of *store* of which the contents cannot be erased during processing, e.g. *punched cards*, *paper tape*, a photographic store.

non-numeric character Any *character* that is not a numeral, e.g. alphabetic characters or symbols.

non-print code Relating to telegraphic communications: a code which will initiate functions on a teleprinter without printing taking place.

non-reproducing codes In relation to *paper tape*, special codes punched into the tape to cause a *hardware* unit to perform specific functions when the tape is read. The codes are not punched into any resultant output tape.

non-resident routine Any *routine* which does not reside permanently in *memory*. Contrasted with *resident routine*.

non-volatile memory A medium of *store* in which the contents are not mutilated when the power is switched off and are available when power is restored. Also known as *permanent memory*. Contrasted with *volatile memory*.

no-operation instruction Synonymous with *do nothing instruction*.

no-op instruction Synonymous with *do nothing instruction*.

nor circuit A digital circuit which produces an output signal only when two corresponding input signals are absent.

nor element A *logic element* operating with *binary digits* which provides an output signal according to the following rules applied to two input signals:

Input		Output
1	0	0
1	1	0
0	1	0
0	0	1

Thus a 1 digit is obtained as an output only if neither of the two input signals is 1.

Also known as nor gate.

nor gate Synonymous with *nor element*.

normalize 1. In mathematics, to multiply a quantity within an expression by a numeric coefficient so that an associated quantity can be made equal to a specified value. 2. In programming, using *floating point numbers* to adjust the *fixed point part* of a number so that the fixed point part is within a prescribed range.

normal range A prescribed range of values established for the results obtained from a system or routine. Any results falling outside the limits of this range are presented to management or are subject to further analysis.

normal stage punching Relating to a *punched card* system in which *interstage punching* is used, and describing the data punched as holes in the usual *punching positions* of a card.

nor operation A *logical operation* applied to two *operands* which will produce a result depending on the *bit pattern* of the operands according to the following rules:

Operands		Result
p	q	r
1	0	0
0	1	0
1	1	0
0	0	1

For example, operating on the following 6-bit operands.

$$p = 110110$$
$$q = 011010$$
$$\overline{r = 000001}$$

Also known as dagger operation, joint denial. ✧ *Boolean algebra*

not A *logical operator* with the property that if a condition p is true, then the not of p is false, and if p is false then the not of p is true. ✧ *Boolean algebra*.

not-and A *logical operation* with the property that if p is a statement, q is a statement and r is a statement, then p.q.r ... is true if at least one statement is false; and p.q.r ... is false if all the statements are true. ✧ *Boolean algebra*.

not-and element A *logic element* operating with binary signals which will produce an output signal representing 1 when any of its corresponding input signals represent zero.

not-and operation A *logical operation* applied to at least two *operands* which will produce a result according to the *bit patterns* of the operands, thus:

Operands		Result
p	q	r
0	1	1
1	0	1
1	1	0
0	0	1

For example, operating on the two following 6-bit operands:

$$p = 110110$$
$$q = 011010$$
$$\overline{r = 101101}$$

Also known as nand operation, not-both operation, alternative denial, dispersion. ✧ *Boolean algebra*.

notation, binary ✧ *binary notation*.

notation, binary-coded decimal ✧ *binary-coded decimal notation*.

notation, coded decimal ✧ *binary-coded decimal notation*.

notation, mixed radix ✧ *mixed base notation*.

not-both operation Synonymous with *not-and operation*.

not circuit A circuit which provides an output signal of reverse phase or polarity from the original input signal.

not-element Synonymous with *negator*.

not operation Synonymous with *negation*.

nought output signal The signal obtained when a *read* pulse is applied to a *magnetic cell* which is in the condition representing zero.

noughts complement Synonymous with *radix complement*.

nought state Synonymous with *zero condition*.

n-plus-one address instruction An *instruction* containing an *address* plus one address which specifies the *location* of the next instruction to be obeyed.

null instruction Synonymous with *do nothing instruction*.

number cruncher A name given to machines with great computational power, where the accent is on the ability to handle large figures rather than to process large amounts of data in the form of, for example, invoices.

number generator Used as a synonym for *manual word generator*; a device which can be set by a computer operator to cause a *parameter* or *constant* to be entered into a predetermined *memory location*. This sort of device has been largely superseded by *console typewriters* and other keyboard *input units*.

number representation 1. Any method in which symbols are used to represent numbers, e.g. the use of digits 0 and 1 arranged in groups to represent *binary* numbers. 2. The use of coded impulses, or other signals, to represent numeric data.

number system Any system for representing numeric values or quantities. For example, the decimal system utilizes ten digits, 0 to 9; these digits may be arranged in groups, the contribution of each digit being made according to the value of the digit and the significance of its position in the group.

numeral One of a set of digits that may be used in a particular system of *number representation*.

numerical analysis The study of mathematical methods for solving problems numerically and ascertaining the bounds of errors in the results.

numerical control ◊ *numeric control*.

numerical tape A tape containing punched holes to represent numbers; usually made of paper, or sometimes of plastic, and used to input instructions to a numerically controlled (N/C) machine (for example, to control an automatic milling and drilling machine). (◊ *numeric control*.) These tapes may be generated automatically by means of a computer *program*, which significantly reduces the time spent by planning engineers in developing the detailed instructions required to set up the numerically controlled machine.

numeric character   Any character used as a digit in the representation of numbers; e.g. in decimal notation one of the characters 0 to 9.

numeric coding   Any system of coding which uses numerals only.

numeric control   Pertaining to the control of machinery, particularly machine tools, by means of numerical instructions. Computers have been used extensively in this field to provide programming *languages* for automatically generating numerical lists. These lists are *compiled* from simple *source language statements* written by planning and production engineering staff.

Also known as numerical control.

numeric data   Any *field* of characters which contains numeric digits only.

numeric punching   On a *punched card*, data represented by the punching of single holes in each *column* of a *field*. *Alphabetic* characters and other symbols may be punched, for example, as two holes per column.

O

O and M ◊ *organization and methods.*

object computer The computer on which an *object program* is designed to be run, as opposed to the computer used to *compile* the program. ◊ *compiler.*

object configuration The system *configuration* necessary for running an *object program*, which may be applied on a different configuration.

object language The *language* or set of coded *instructions* into which a *source language* is translated by means of a *compiler*. The object language is usually but not necessarily a *machine language* directly understandable by a computer; some *high level languages* are translated initially into a lower level object language which requires further translation before it is converted into machine language.

object machine Synonymous with *object computer.*

object program A program in *object language* produced by translating the program written in the *source language* through the use of a *compiler*. The object program will normally be in a *machine code* capable of being directly understood by the computer and thus in the form required for running. When some *high level languages* are in use the object program may itself need further translation before it is in a form understandable by the computer.

observation matrix ◊ *data matrix.*

O C R Acronym for *optical character recognition.*

octal digit A *digit* in the *octal notation* system, i.e. one of the digits 0, 1, 2, 3, 4, 5, 6, 7.

octal notation The *number system* using eight as a base or *radix*. The octal system uses the digits 0, 1, 2, 3, 4, 5, 6, 7, and each digit position represents a power of eight, thus the octal number 107 represents $1.8^2 + 0.8^1 + 7.8^0 = 71$ in decimal. Octal notation is sometimes used as a shorthand way of representing a *string* of *bits*. For example, the string 001000111 can be considered as being formed by the three *binary coded* octal numbers 001 000 111, i.e. 1 0 7. Thus the string 001000111 can be represented as 'octal' 107, sometimes indicated merely as $\#$ 107.

odd-even check A form of *parity check* in which an extra *bit* is added to a *word or character*; this bit has the value 1 or 0 depending on whether the number of 1 bits in the word or character is odd or even. The value of the parity bit is recalculated whenever the data is transferred, and compared with the value of the original bit as a check on the accuracy of the transfer. In the case of odd parity, the parity bit is 1 if the number of 1 bits is even, 0 if odd; in the case of even parity the parity bit is 0 if the number of 1 bits is even, 1 if odd.

odd parity check A *parity check* in which the number of ones (or zeros) in a group of *binary digits* is expected to be odd. Contrasted with *even parity check*.

off-line A part of a computer system is off-line if it is not under the control of the *central processor*. ◊ *off-line processing.*

off-line equipment Devices which are used in conjunction with a computer system but which are at no time connected to the *central processor*.

off-line processing Performing some part of a data processing system on equipment not directly connected to the *central processor*, and thus not under *program* control. For example, *punched cards* may be transcribed to *paper tape* by means of an off-line *card-to-tape* [1] machine and the tape subsequently processed *on-line* by the computer.

off-line storage A *storage device* not under the direct control of a *central processor*. A *reel* of *magnetic tape* not *on-line* but placed in a *library* may be considered an example of off-line storage.

off-line unit Synonymous with *off-line equipment.*

off-line working Synonymous with *off-line processing.*

off punch To punch a *punched card* in such a way that the holes are not aligned with the *punching positions*. This means that when the card is subsequently *read* the reading mechanism may not be able to sense the presence of the holes.

O L R T Acronym for on-line *real time* operation.

one address instruction An *instruction format* which makes use of one *address part* involving one *location* of *store* only.

one condition The state of a unit of *store* when it is representing the value 1.

one digit adder Synonymous with *half adder.*

one digit subtracter Synonymous with *half subtracter.*

one element Synonymous with *or element.*

one-for-one A form of *compiler* in which one *machine code instruction* is generated for each *source instruction*.

one gate   Synonymous with *or element*.

one level address   Synonymous with *absolute address*.

one level code   Synonymous with *absolute code*.

one level store   A concept used in a *virtual machine environment* to describe a storage system which appears to the user as a single directly accessible *store* while in fact being made up of a number of different *hardware* devices, e.g. *core*, *disk*.

one level subroutine   A *subroutine* which is complete in itself, i.e. does not use any other subroutines during its operation.

one output signal   The form of signal produced by a unit of *store* in a *one condition* when a *read pulse* is applied to it.

one-over-one address format   Synonymous with *one-plus-one address instruction format*.

one-plus-one address   An *address format* in which each *instruction* includes one *operation* and two addresses, one showing the *location* containing the data to be operated on and the other showing the location containing the next instruction. (The purpose of the second address is indicated by the phrase *plus-one*: a two-plus-one address, for example, has three addresses, one containing the location of the next instruction.)

ones complement   The term used to describe the *radix minus one complement* applied to *binary notation*. ⬦ *complement, nines complement*.

one shot circuit   Synonymous with *single shot circuit*.

one shot multivibrator   Synonymous with *flip-flop*.

one shot operation   Synonymous with *single step operation*.

one state   Synonymous with *one condition*.

one to one assembler   An *assembly program* which translates each *source language statement* onto a single *machine language instruction*.
Also known as one to one translator.

one to one translator   Synonymous with *one to one assembler*.

one to zero ratio   The ratio of the magnitude or amplitude at a particular instant of time of a *one output signal* to a *zero output signal*.

on-line   A part of a *computer system* is on-line if it is directly under the control of the *central processor*. Contrasted with *off-line*.

on-line central file   A *file* of data present on a *storage device* which is *on-line*, and can be used in *real time* or *direct access* applications as a continually available data source.

on-line data reduction   The processing of information as soon

293

as it is transmitted from source to a computer system. ✧ *real time.*

on-line equipment Those devices which form part of a computer system and which may be placed under the direct control of a *central processor.*

on-line processing *Data processing* in which all operations are performed by equipment directly under the control of a central *processor.* Contrasted with *off-line processing.*

on-line programming A method of *programming* by which the programmer inputs program *statements* directly to the computer by means of a *terminal.* Program statements are checked for validity as they are input, and the programmer controls the *compilation* and *execution* of the program by means of commands from the terminal. ✧ *B A S I C, conversational mode.*

on-line real time operation (O L R T) ✧ *real time.*

on-line storage A *store* under the direct control of a *central processor.*

on-line typewriter An *input/output* typewriter under the control of a *central processor* and thus under *program* control. An on-line typewriter may be used as a form of *peripheral unit,* as an *interrogating typewriter* or as a *console typewriter.*

on-line unit ✧ *on-line equipment.*

on-line working ✧ *on-line processing.*

on-the-fly printer A type of high-speed *line printer* in which all the characters in the *character set* are engraved on the surface of a rapidly rotating *print barrel,* and are printed by means of hammers which strike the paper as the appropriate character position on the barrel is in position relative to the paper.
Also known as hit-on-the-fly printer.

op code Abbreviation for *operation code.*

open ended A *program* or system so designed that it can be extended in scope or sophistication without alteration to those parts already in existence.

opening a file This process is performed by manufacturer's *software* and consists basically of identifying the *file* and checking the *header label* against details supplied in the user's *program* to ensure that the file can be used for the purpose defined by the program. For example, if a *magnetic tape file* is to be used as an output tape the *retention period* must be exceeded and a *write permit ring* must be present. To open a magnetic tape as an input file the correct file name and file *generation number* must be present.

open loop A control system in which corrective action is not automatic, but depends on external intervention as a result of displayed information.

open routine A *routine* inserted into a larger routine without the *calling sequence* and *link* associated with a *subroutine*.

open shop The organization of a *data processing* installation so that any suitably qualified individual has access to the machines. Contrasted with *closed shop* in which only specialist staff have access. In particular, open shop implies that *programmers* may test *programs* on a computer rather than by *remote testing*.

open subroutine A *subroutine* which has to be reinserted into the main sequence of *instructions* each time it is required, rather than merely requiring a *link* to a sequence of instructions held in a separate part of the *program*. Contrasted with *closed subroutine*.

operand The item in an *operation* from which the *result* is obtained by means of defined actions.

operating delays Time lost as a direct result of mistakes or inefficiency in operating a *data processing* installation, as contrasted with delays due to other causes such as *repair time, machine-spoilt work time, fault, program* errors, data errors.

operating display A *terminal* or *video* display reserved for the use of *operators*. ✧ *operating station.*

operating instructions A step-by-step description of the activities to be performed by an *operator* in running a particular *program* or *suite* of programs. Usually provided by a programmer or systems analyst as part of the program *documentation*.

operating ratio A measure of the time that a particular system (usually a combination of *hardware* and *software*) is able to provide a service. The measure is derived as a percentage of the time available, excluding *down time*, to the total time that the machine is switched on. (Down time may include time lost due to *failure*, scheduled maintenance, unscheduled maintenance, time waiting for engineering staff.) The operating ratio may or may not include time required to establish the service once failures have been corrected. Thus it is necessary to specify whether the operating ratio includes *recovery time* or not.
Also known as availability ratio.

operating station A *console* or set of consoles which is used by an *operator*[2] to control all or part of a data processing system.

operating systems An operating system can be properly defined as those procedures which control the *resources* within a *data processing* installation. Resources include *hardware, programs, data* and *operators*, and control is by manual procedures or *soft-*

ware. Generally, however, an operating system is defined as a program which supervises the running of other programs. Operating systems were unknown in *first generation* computers, the programs standing alone within the computer. In about 1955–6 several large U.S. companies began to develop operating systems to suit their individual requirements. These were on *second generation* machines and while effective to a certain extent they are more important in that the manufacturers realized this field required serious investigation. With *multiprogramming* being so much a part of *third generation* machines an operating system became almost a necessity and a lower level version of this type of program exists in the *executive program* of the third generation computers.

In practice the operating system supervises the programs, controlling the input and output functions of each program and passing control from one program to the next. Human action is still required for the physical loading of magnetic media and punched cards on to the respective units but all human intervention or decision-making at the end of each program is by-passed. The operator loads as many programs and relative data files as the *configuration* will allow.

Control language instructions are fed in, often by punched card or paper tape, and the machine is started by the operator. By referring to the control instructions the operating system selects the first program and data files to be processed. During processing the operator unloads each *peripheral unit* as it is released and loads further data files, etc. At the end of the processing of the first program all control information for that program is printed out, e.g. files used, record counts, time charged, etc. and control is given to the next program for processing. The main object is to keep the operator *loading* the units in advance of the program requiring them, using the processing time for one job as the set-up time for another. Before one series of programs and control instructions comes to an end the operator loads the programs, data, etc. for the next, thus avoiding, if possible, a machine halt. An important additional function of an operating system is job *scheduling*. Jobs are loaded and the time when a job must be completed is given to the operating system together with relevant data on the size of the files, etc. The time may vary between a few minutes and days. At intervals – say 10 seconds – the operating system interrupts the job being processed to review the timings on other jobs. It selects the job which is least advanced according to the time schedule and processes it until it is interrupted and the jobs are again reviewed.

By continuing in this manner the jobs are produced when and as they are required and central processor time is fully utilized. Obviously jobs can be advanced or retarded by altering their scheduled time for completion. In ways like this an operating system can increase the efficiency of an installation, and such increases grow more and more necessary as computer users recognize the difficulties encountered by human operators in controlling the varying input and output requirements of a big machine which may be running, at the same time, a complex mix of *batch* and *on line processing* as well as controlling a network of *communication devices* and the activity of a number of *remote processors*.

operation 1. A defined action by which a *result* is obtained from an *operand*. 2. An action defined by a single computer *instruction*. 3. An action defined by a single *logic element*.

operational amplifier Synonymous with *computing amplifier*.

operational research Operational Research first became recognized as a separate field of study just before the Second World War, and its use spread rapidly in the armed services. Since then operational research has become widely used in industry and commerce, where the adoption of quantitive techniques in management has been shown to be universally successful.

The aims of the operational research scientist are principally to quantify a problem in statistical or mathematical terms and to use these methods to find a solution, or a better solution, to the problem. In this respect operational research is the leading applied science. Since the aims of the systems analyst or programmer are at least in the first part identical to this, the two will often be found working together.

Thirty years ago the term 'management science' was unknown. Nowadays terms like economic re-order quantity are common and the art of decision making is becoming a science of interpreting data: it is here that operational research has an important role.

There are two main methods of analysis used by the operational research worker. The first is that of handling complex information in order to reach a decision, *linear programming* and *critical path method* (or *PERT*) being two examples of techniques using this analysis. The second deals with those problems where difficulty arises because of uncertainty; information is available as probability distributions or frequencies of past events. Here such techniques as *forecasting* and *simulation* have been developed.

Techniques in operational research often involve statistical and mathematical methods and are frequently viewed with suspicion by line management. Here lies one of the major problems of the day. Not until management science is fully accepted as an essential part of management can the full value of operational research, and with it often the value of a computer, be realized.

Some of the techniques of operational research are discussed under the following headings: *simulation, queuing theory, critical path method (PERT), linear programming, forecasting, extrapolation, iteration, allocation.*

operation, biconditional ◊ *equivalence operation.*

operation, binary (Boolean) ◊ *dyadic Boolean operation.*

operation code The *code* which specifies the particular *operation* to be performed.

operation cycle The part of a *machine cycle* during which an *instruction* is executed.

operation, dagger Synonymous with *nor operation.*

operation decoder A circuit which interprets the *operation* part of an *instruction* and switches to the circuits required for its execution.

operation, dyadic Boolean ◊ *dyadic Boolean operation.*

operation, either-or ◊ *inclusive-or operation.*

operation, meet ◊ *and operation.*

operation, nand ◊ *not-and operation.*

operation, neither-nor ◊ *nor operation.*

operation, non-equivalence ◊ *exclusive-or operation.*

operation, not-both ◊ *not-and operation.*

operation, one shot ◊ *single step operation.*

operation, or ◊ *inclusive-or operation.*

operation part The part of an *instruction* which contains the specification of the particular *operation* [2] to be performed. The *operation code* will be contained in the operation part of the instruction.

operation register A *register* in which the *operation code* is stored during the *operation cycle.*

operation, single shot Synonymous with *single step operation.*

operations research ◊ *operational research.*

operation, step by step Synonymous with *single step operation.*

operation time The time required to complete the *operation cycle* for a particular *operation.*

operation, unary Synonymous with *monadic operation.*

operator 1. In an *operation*, an operator defines the action to be performed on the *operand* to obtain the *result*. ◊ *operators.* 2. A person who operates a machine. ◊ general article on *Computer Personnel.*

operator command A *message* input to an *operating system* by an *operator*[2] at his own instigation in contrast to a message input in response to a message generated by the operating system itself.

operator name In an *operating system*, the name used by an *operator*[2] to identify himself to the operating system through an *operating station*, thus enabling him to input *operator's control language* commands and receive *prompts*.

operator part The part of an *instruction* in which the *operator* is specified.

operators Characters which designate different operations, e.g. $+$, $-$, $\times$, etc.

operator's console A *console* used by the computer *operator* in order to control the operation of the *programs* and *peripheral units*, and to receive information about their functioning. The console may include a panel of switches and warning lights, and/or a *console typewriter*.

operator's control language *Control language* commands designed for use by an *operator*[2].

operator's control panel An *operator's console* which consists of a panel of switches and lights.

optical bar-code reader A device which reads by optical means information which has been coded by making marks on documents with pencil, ink or other means. ✧ *mark sensing*.

optical character reader A device which uses *optical character recognition* to read information into a computer system; a character reader which reads characters by analysis of their configuration.

optical character recognition The identification of printed characters by means of light sensing devices. ✧ the general articles on *Character Recognition* and *Input Devices*.

optical scanner A device which analyses the light patterns made by printed characters and converts the pattern into a signal which can be processed by a computer.

optical type fount A special fount designed for use with *optical character recognition* devices which is also easily read by people.

optimization The design or modification of a system or *program* in order to make it achieve maximum efficiency. The particular type of efficiency sought after in optimization depends on the requirement specified: examples are time, cost, storage capacity.

optimum code Synonymous with *minimum access code*.

optimum coding Synonymous with *minimum access coding*.

optimum programming The production of optimized *programs*. ✧ *optimization, minimum access code, linear programming*.

optional stop instruction An *instruction* which will halt the *program* if certain conditions are satisfied.

O R Acronym for *operational research*.

or circuit Synonymous with *or element*.

order 1. Synonymous with *instruction*. 2. As a verb, synonymous with *sequence*[2].

order code Synonymous with *instruction code*. ◊ *order code processor*.

order code processor Part of a large computer system whose function is to select *low level language instructions* from *main store*, carry them out and return the results to main store. In addition the order code processor may initiate *input* and *output* instructions and respond to *interrupts*.

ordered serial file A *serial file* whose *records* have a *key* and which are *sorted* on that key so that the *physical* and *logical* sequences are the same.

orders, initial Synonymous with *initial instructions*.

order structure Synonymous with *instruction format*.

or element A logic element operating with *binary* digits, and providing an output signal according to the following rules applied to two input signals.

Input		Output
1	0	1
1	1	1
0	1	1
0	0	0

Thus a 1 digit is provided as an output if any one (or more) of the input signals are 1.

Also known as one gate, one element, or circuit, or gate. ◊ *Boolean algebra*.

organization and methods The activities, often known as O and M, involved in a specialist view of the organization, management, methods of control and general procedures of any undertaking. A systematic review is carried out, as opposed to the general duties of any administrator with overall responsibilities for such procedures. Sometimes O and M staff are included in a *data processing* organization.

or gate Synonymous with *or element*.

origin The *absolute address* of the start of any area of *store* to

300

which reference is made when *indirect addressing* techniques are used to locate items in the storage area. The term is also applied to the absolute address of the beginning of the *program* area in store. (This is not necessarily the first instruction to be processed.) Also known as *base address*[1], *float factor*.

original document   Synonymous with *source document*.

or operation   Synonymous with *inclusive-or operation*.

out device   Synonymous with *output device*.

outline flowchart   ◊ the general article on *Flowcharting*.

out of line coding   Part of the *instructions* of a *routine*, but stored in another part of the *program storage*. ◊ *patch*, for example.

out of service time   Time during which a computer cannot be used for running *programs* for any reason. This may be due to the development of a fault in the machine or because the machine is undergoing *routine maintenance*, etc.

out-plant system   A *data processing* system which uses remote *data transmission* terminals for transmission of information to a central computer. Contrasted with *in-plant system*.

output   1. Results produced by a computer. 2. To transfer information from a *central processor* to an *output device*. Computer output may take many different forms, including *printout, punched card, punched paper tape, visual display*.

output area   A part of *store* from which data is transferred to an *output device*.
Also known as output block, output section.

output block   Synonymous with *output area*.

output buffer   ◊ *input/output buffers*.

output bus driver   A device for amplifying output signals.

output devices   All the data and *programs* within a computer are stored as electrical impulses in a coded form according to the *machine code* system of the particular computer. When data is held in this form it cannot be readily understood by human beings and therefore output units are employed to transcribe this data into information that can be used by human beings as and when they require it. There are various types of unit designed to present information in a particular manner or to deliver it at appropriate speed. For the most part output units will deliver information in *character* form to be examined visually by the user, but sometimes output data is required for subsequent entry to another data processing machine and is therefore output in some other coded medium (e.g. on *paper tape* or *magnetic tape*).

The commonest types of output unit are *line printers*. These are generally electro-mechanical devices which print complete lines of print, up to 160 characters in width, at speeds from about 300 to 2,000 lines per minute. There are also *page printers* which operate using *xerographic* printing techniques or the result of *electron beam recording*.

Of the electro-mechanical printers we can distinguish two classes, *barrel printers* and *chain printers*. Both rely on a similar principle – type characters are driven continuously at high speed, and print hammers are energized by electronic signals to strike the paper and an ink ribbon against the moving type at precise instants. The electronic circuitry in the line printer and the *central processor* is designed to transcribe the data in the output area of the internal store into a series of timing pulses which will activate the hammers.

Line printers of this type are used mainly to print out the results of calculations and they can be programmed to print on preprinted stationery, for example, to produce invoices or statements. The individual pages are part of a continuous sheet and are marked out by folds and perforations across the sheet at intervals according to the required form depth. The stationery is supplied as a pack and a complete set may consist of several sheets with interleaved carbon paper to produce additional copies. After being printed, these stationery sets can be split up into single sheets by means of *de-collators* and *bursters*.

Most line printers have a repertoire of about 64 separate characters, any of which may be printed at any of the *print positions* across the page. This repertoire normally includes all twenty-six capital letters of the alphabet, the numerals 0 to 9, and a range of special symbols.

Punched card or paper tape output is achieved by *card punches* and *paper tape punches* designed to respond automatically by signals transmitted from the central processor. Speeds of output vary from about 100 to 400 cards per minute in the case of cards, and for paper tape from 25 to 110 characters per second. Output in this form is often used to record data which will be processed further by other equipment. Where output data is in relatively small quantities (e.g. *error reports* from programs) an output device of this type may be preferred, particularly where the alternative would tie up a line printer for a whole *run*.

Magnetic tape decks or *magnetic disk stores* may be used for both input and output, but are not usually considered as either input or output units: rather as *backing stores*. ◊ *Storage Devices*.

Typewriters are often used as input/output units, particularly as *interrogating typewriters* to interrogate programs to ascertain conditions regarding the status of the programs or data being processed. They are also used specifically as *console typewriters* in which they satisfy the need for communication between the operator and a supervisory or *executive program.*

The operator is able to enter data (e.g. run *parameters*) or inquiries directly from the *keyboard* and may receive information typed automatically on the typewriter. Thus where a device such as a console typewriter is used, the output on the stationery forms a complete operating log for all the jobs that have been run.

Other types of output unit include *visual display units* which can present information in character form, but will also display data as drawings or graphs. These units incorporate either a *graph plotter* or a *cathode ray tube* and associated control electronics. For drawings shown on a cathode ray tube the computer has to calculate the coordinates of every spot forming the picture to be portrayed. Characters can be more simply formed by passing the cathode ray through a mask which creates the appropriate character shape and the beam is then deflected to display the character on the desired part of the screen. The more complex the output pattern, the more complex the program to control the cathode ray tube.

Some graphical display units incorporate facilities to input data. For example, some models have keyboards that enable queries to be input in coded form to a control program which will in turn select and display the required answer in a matter of microseconds. When such an input/output device is used in conjunction with a *direct access store*, inquiries can be satisfied from files on a random basis.

Some display units can be used as input units by means of a special stylus known as a *light pen*. In such a system graphs, shapes and other pictorial data can be entered into the *memory* of the computer by passing the light pen across the screen. The position of the pen is detected by magnetic devices which with associated circuitry instruct the computer to form a corresponding drawing in memory. Thus drawings can be created, displayed and amended. This type of input/output system, in conjunction with the keyboard input mentioned above, opens great potential for applications in the fields of science, education and engineering. Where large volumes of data are to be produced and distributed, use is often made of computer output microfilm with consequent savings in storage space and distribution costs.

303

output program A *program* written specifically for the transcription of data to an *output device*.

output punch 1. An *output device* which transcribes information onto *paper tape*. 2. An output device which transcribes information onto *punched cards*.

output record 1. A *record written* (◊ *write*) to an *output device*. 2. The current record stored in the *output area* before being *output*[2].

output routine A *routine* which performs all the processing associated with the transcription of data to an *output device*. This processing may include placing the information in the *output area*, *editing*, converting information from internal format to external format and providing control information to the output device.

output routine generator A *generator* which will produce an *output routine* to given specifications.

output section Synonymous with *output area*.

output table Synonymous with *plotting board*.

output unit ◊ *output device*.

overall availability ratio ◊ *operating ratio*.

overall serviceability ratio ◊ *serviceability, ratio*.

overflow The generation of a quantity as a *result* of an arithmetic operation which is too large to be contained in the result *location*. The term is also used to describe the actual amount of the *excess*. Contrasted with *underflow*. ◊ *overflow records*.

overflow bucket A *bucket* used to accommodate *overflow records* in a *direct access file*.

overflow records *Records* which cannot be accommodated in assigned areas of a *direct access* file and which must be stored in another area from which they can be retrieved by means of a reference stored in place of the records in their original assigned area.

overlay A technique in which, during the operation of a lengthy *program*, the same area of *store* is used to contain successively different parts of the program. Each part of the program that is to share the same overlay area is held on some form of *backing store* and read into the area by means of a control program. Communication between different overlays is usually through use of a *common area*. ◊ *programming, segment*.

overpunch A hole punched in a *zone* position of a *punched card* used for *designation* purposes, e.g. to indicate whether a *field* is positive or negative.

overwrite To place information in a *location* and destroy the information previously contained there.

own coding The addition of user-written *coding* to a standard *software routine* in order to extend its capabilities, to cover special conditions.

owner A *user* or *process* which has overriding control over *resources* or *data*. ✧ *ownership*.

ownership A relationship between the elements within an *operating system* indicating that the *owner* has overriding control over the object owned. e.g. a *process* owns a data item if it has the right to access and alter the data and to transfer this right to another process; a user owns a *resource* if he has overriding control over the resource.

P

pack 1. A collection of *punched cards* having something in common, e.g. a data pack or a *program* pack. Also known as deck [1]. 2. To place more than one item of information into a single unit of *store* in order to conserve storage space. In this sense, also known as crowd; contrasted with *unpack*.

package A generalized *program* written for a major application in such a way that a user's particular problems of data or organization will not make the package any less useful. Examples might be a *production control* package, a payroll package, an *inventory management* package. ◊ *Software*.

packing density A measure of the capacity of a *medium* of *store*, usually given as the number of storage units per unit length of recording surface.

padding The adding of blanks or non-significant characters to the end of a *record* or *block* in order to make it up to some fixed size. This technique is employed when *fixed length records* or *fixed blocks* are being used, to enable units which do not contain enough significant data to be processed.

page 1. A concept used in *virtual storage* to refer to the subdivisions of large sets of data into smaller units which can be more economically located within the *physical storage* available to a system. 2. A full screen of data displayed on a *video* or *terminal*.

page-at-a-time printer Synonymous with *page printer*.

paged segment A *segment* occupying more than one *page* [1].

page printer A *printer* for which the character pattern for a complete page is determined before printing. Contrasted with *line printer*. Also known as page-at-a-time printer.

page turning The process by which the *pages* [2] displayed on a *video* are successively replaced.

paging The method in *virtual storage* whereby *physical storage* is allocated to the *pages* [1] which makes up a set of data.

pair, binary Synonymous with *bistable circuit*.

pair, trigger Synonymous with *bistable circuit*.

panel, patch Synonymous with *plugboard*.

paper advance mechanism That part of a *printer* which moves the paper past the printing positions. The mechanism may be under computer control, enabling the number of lines advanced to be determined by *program*.

paper low condition A warning condition indicating that the supply of *continuous stationery* on a *printer* is about to run out.

paper tape Punched paper tape has been used as an *input/output* medium since the earliest developments of electronic *digital computers*. To some extent it was used initially simply because 5-track paper tape was already in use to meet the requirements of the telegraph service, and *paper tape readers* and *paper tape punches* were adapted for use as input/output units. Subsequently much specialized development work has taken place to produce paper tape systems specifically to meet the demands for high speed computer input and for *data transmission*. As an input medium it is now probably rivalled only by *punched cards*.

Each *character* is recorded as a single *row* of holes across the width of the tape; a further hole, known as a *sprocket hole*, also appears in each row and is used to feed the tape mechanically in slow speed readers, or, on high speed machines, to act as a *clock pulse* when the tape is read by a photo-electric head. Paper tape is normally in reels approximately 1,000 ft in length and one inch in width, the individual character rows being punched into the tape 10 to the inch. Paper tape may have either 5, 6, 7 or 8 data holes in each row, and is referred to as 5-track tape, 6-track tape, 7-track tape or 8-track tape. Several different tape codes remain in use today but a great deal of work has been done to standardize the character sets and to specify the particular coding structure for 5, 6, 7 and 8-track codes. Bodies such as the British Standards Institute and the American Standards Association have cooperated with the International Standards Organization and standard codes have been recommended. For data processing purposes the 5-track code has little appeal, since there is not sufficient coding capacity for the full range of characters and special symbols needed. It is common practice to use an 8-track code, based upon I S O recommendations; this allows each character to be represented by seven data *bits* plus one *parity bit*, the seven data bits providing sufficient unique code combinations to represent 128 alphanumeric characters and symbols.

Paper tape has the advantage that it is a compact medium, less bulky than punched cards. It is comparatively cheap to produce and easy to transport. It can be read at a speed of 1,000 characters per second without difficulty, and can often be prepared as a by-product of some other machine operation; e.g. from a cash register or adding machine. The punching and verifying of punched tape from original documents is similar to the operation for cards, some details being given in the general article on *Data Preparation*.

There are some disadvantages in using paper tape but these are not really significant where the tape is used simply as an input medium for *raw data* or transactions. The most significant disadvantage lies in the fact that one *error character* in a tape may mean that the tape must be repunched, but provided that individual tapes are generated for batches of transactions with suitable batch *control totals*, this problem does not represent a severe constraint. Input programs can be written to check and validate individual batches of transactions on paper tape; these batches can be presented to the computer in any sequence, and this allows invalid batches to be rejected and re-input at a later stage. Typical validity checks at the input stage might include checking to see that *fields* conform to specified maximum and minimum values, that decimal places are in correct positions, that specified fields contain alphabetic characters and other fields numeric only, and so on.

As a computer output medium paper tape is particularly useful for small volumes of data; e.g. summaries or error reports which can be printed *off-line* on a teleprinter or typewriter. Paper tape can also be produced for subsequent transmission over a *data link* or can even provide a numerical list for controlling an automatic machine tool. The speeds of paper tape output punches range from 25 to 300 characters per second.

Paper tapes usually have to be wound into reels so that they can be easily stored, handled and fed into *paper tape readers*. Some readers and punches are equipped with automatic winding attachments, although there is a possibility of damage to tapes if the units get out of adjustment; in any case they usually wind tapes directly fed from the machine, and therefore wind the *leading end* towards the centre of the spool. Manually operated winding devices are more popular and are surprisingly efficient in spooling paper tape. The usual practice is to allow the tape to fall into a bin until it is expended, whereupon the operator takes the *trailing end* and winds the tape manually onto a spool.

Damaged tapes can be repaired by the use of simple tape *splicers* which can be employed to join independent lengths of paper tape or to insert corrections. The nature of error and the type of data will govern the extent to which splicing may be employed.

paper tape channel   ◊ *channel* [2].

paper tape code   A *code* consisting of a pattern of holes punched across a strip of *paper tape*. Codes are determined by the number of *tracks* [2] on the paper tape, the most usual being 5-track, 7-track and 8-track codes.

paper tape loop Synonymous with *control loop*.

paper tape punch Synonymous with *tape punch*.

paper tape punching The punching of holes into *paper tape* whereby the pattern of holes form a *code* for recording information. One of the basic methods of *data preparation* for *input* to a computer.

paper tape reader A device which translates the information punched in code on *paper tape* into *machine language* and transmits the data into a *central processor*.

paper tape reproducer A device which can automatically produce a copy of a punched *paper tape*.

Also known as a reperforator.

paper tape verifier A machine for checking that the holes punched in *paper tape* represent the data on the original documents. ◊ general article on *Data Preparation*.

paper throw Movement of paper through a *printer*, other than the advance of paper for printing, at a speed greater than that of single line spacing.

parallel Dealing with all the elements of an item of information simultaneously. Contrasted with *serial*.

parallel access Synonymous with *simultaneous access*.

parallel allocation A method of allocating *controlled files* in such a way that each file is allocated the same *tracks* in each *cylinder* of the *controlling file*.

parallel computer Synonymous with *simultaneous computer*.

parallel feed Synonymous with *sideways feed*.

parallel running A method of testing new procedures by operating both the new system and the one it is designed to replace together for a period of time; the results produced by the new system can be compared for accuracy with those produced by the old.

parallel search storage Synonymous with *associative store*.

parallel storage A *storage device* in which the time required to *access* any item within the store is the same as the time required to access any other item in store.

parallel transfer A method of data *transfer* [1] in which each element of a unit of data is transferred simultaneously.

parameter A quantity or item of information which is used in a *subroutine, routine, program, adaptive control system* or mathematical calculation, and which can be given a different value each time the process is repeated. Also known as *control data*[2].

parameter card A *punched card* on which the value of a *parameter* required by a *program* may be punched and subsequently read. Also known as *control card*[2].

parameter word A *word* of *store* in which the *parameter* for a *routine* is placed.

parity bit 1. A check *bit* whose value (0 or 1) depends on whether the sum of 1 bits in the word being checked is odd or even. If the total number of 1 bits, including the parity bit, is even, the word is known as having *even parity*; if the number is odd, it has *odd parity*. 2. A bit added to a group of bits to make the sum of bits (including the parity bit) always even or always odd, e.g. with a set of six bits 010110 a parity bit of 1 is needed to give the set even parity, and a bit of 0 is needed to give the set odd parity.

parity check A check made when data is *transferred* which consists in adding up the *bits* in a unit of data, calculating the *parity bit* required and checking the calculated parity bit with the parity bit transferred with the data item. This form of check will normally be performed automatically by *hardware*.

parity check, even ⋄ *parity check*.

parity check, odd ⋄ *parity check*.

parity error An *error* caused by incorrect parity detected as a result of a *parity check*.

partial carry A technique used in *parallel* addition in which a *carry* is temporarily stored instead of being added in immediately. Contrasted with *complete carry*.

partial system failure ⋄ *system failure*.

pass 1. The passage of *magnetic tape* past the *read heads*. 2. A single execution of a *loop*.

password A group of *characters* which on input to a computer from a *terminal* give the *user* access to information and allow the user defined control over the information. ⋄ general article on *Security*.

patch A group of *instructions* added to a *routine* to correct a mistake. The patch is usually placed as *out of line coding* and is entered by means of an *unconditional branch* from the part of the routine being altered.

patchboard Synonymous with *plugboard*.

patchcord A connector with a flexible part used to connect the sockets of a *plugboard*. In *punched card* usage, synonymous with *plug*.

Also known as patchplug, plugwire. Contrasted with *cordless plug*, where there is no flexible part.

patch panel   Synonymous with *plugboard*.

patchplug   Synonymous with *patchcord*.

path   The logical sequence of *instructions* in a computer *program*. (But ⟡ *critical path*.)

pattern-sensitive fault   A *fault* caused by the recognition of some specified pattern of data.

P C M   Acronym for 1. *punched card* machine; 2. *pulse code* modulation.

pecker   The sensing device in a mechanical *paper tape reader*.

perforated tape   Synonymous with *paper tape*.

perforation rate   The rate at which holes can be punched into *paper tape* with a *tape punch*.

perforator   A hand-operated *tape punch* for punching *paper tape*. Also known as *keyboard* perforator.

perforator, keyboard   ⟡ *perforator*.

performance monitoring journal   ⟡ *journal*.

period, scan   Synonymous with *regeneration period*.

peripheral   Used as a noun, for *peripheral unit*.

peripheral buffers   Small elements of *store* forming part of a *peripheral unit* used for storing data before transmission to a *central processor*, or receipt from the central processor before transcription to the *output medium*. ⟡ *input/output buffer*.

peripheral controller   That part of a system whose function is to control data transfer to or from *peripheral units* of different types.

peripheral control unit   A device which acts as the link between a *peripheral unit* and a *central processor* and which interprets and acts on instructions from the processor.

peripheral device   ⟡ *peripheral unit*.

peripheral equipment   Synonymous with *peripheral units*.

peripheral interface channel   A *channel*[1] which provides the connecting path for information to flow between a *peripheral unit* and a *processor*. ⟡ *standard interface*.

peripheral limited   A system is known as peripheral limited when the overall processing time is dictated by the speed of the *peripheral units* rather than the speed of the *central processor*. Contrasted with *processor limited*.

peripheral manager interface   Part of a *kernel* which controls *input* and *output* requirements.

peripheral processor   In a *data processing* system making use of more than one *processor*, a peripheral processor is a processor operating under the control of another processor. Usually the peripheral processor will control all *input/output* functions of the system, providing a flow of data to and from the processor.

peripheral prompt A *message* initiated by an *operating system* to inform the *operator* of the state of a particular *peripheral* unit, or the need to *load* a *file*. ✧ *prompt*.

peripheral transfer The transfer of a unit of data between a *peripheral unit* and a *central processor* or between peripheral units.

peripheral units Machines which can be operated under computer control. Peripheral equipment consists of *input devices, output devices* and *storage devices*. For examples of peripheral equipment ◇: *card punch, card reader, magnetic disk, magnetic drum, magnetic tape, paper tape, tape reader, tape punch*. ✧ general articles on *Input Devices, Output Devices* and *Storage Devices*.

permanent memory Synonymous with *non-volatile memory*.

personnel records The recording of data concerning personnel is a common computer application. Personnel records may be kept both in order to produce a payroll and to provide a record of information about employees which can be used by management for a variety of planning and administrative functions. The type of information recorded and the method in which it is coded and stored depends largely on the ultimate use to which the data is to be put.

If records are kept purely for payroll purposes then information will be confined to the financial details relevant to each employee together with data necessary for payment, such as details of hours worked, absence, rates of pay, etc. Tax calculations in payroll applications are usually performed by means of *software packages* provided for the purpose by the manufacturer or user. The medium for storing personnel records used primarily for payroll purposes will normally be one suited to regular *sequential processing* in which each *record* is processed at every *run*. This will as a rule be *magnetic tape*, or possibly *punched cards* or *paper tape*, depending on volumes of data.

Personnel records can provide a more detailed source of information about employees. Additional data about each person can include information on qualifications and experience, administrative details such as department, address, medical details, etc. The actual data recorded will depend on the applications envisaged for the information, but in all cases some system of coding information, so that retrieval and analysis may be simplified, must be devised. Where a file of personnel records is going to be used extensively for *information retrieval*, e.g. searching for personnel satisfying given conditions, the file organization will depend on the retrieval techniques to be adopted. If frequent interrogation of the file is expected, each interrogation producing a limited number of *hits*, a *direct access* storage device would normally be used, using random storage methods. The use of *inverted file* structures is used in some applications, e.g. in the recording of fingerprint details on criminal files.

Updating methods will depend on the particular application, but the *turn-round document* technique is particularly suited to updating personnel records of employees.

PERT Acronym for Project Evaluation and Review Technique. ◊ the general article on *Critical Path Method*.

physical A term used in the context of *operating systems* to describe actual existing entities (*files*, *resources*), in contrast to *logical*.

physical address ◊ *address*.

physical data independence Where a *file structure* or the *physical medium* on which a *file* is held, may be changed without affecting the *application software* using the data.

physical file In an *operating system* refers to a *file* contained on a specific physical *storage* medium, e.g. a specific *magnetic tape* or *disk*. A file in an operating system may be contained on a number of different *physical files*.

physical file copy A copy of a *physical file* on the same or different *medium*.

physical file report A list in readable form of the contents of a *physical file*.

physical track The path along which a single *read/write head* on a *disk* or *drum* moves. Synonymous with *track*[1] and used in *operating systems*. ◊ *logical track*.

pico- Prefix denoting one million-millionth or 10^{-12}.

picture A set of information which is available for *display* on a *video* or *terminal*. Because of the physical limitations of the screen on a specific device the picture may consist of a number of *pages*[2].

pilot system A method of testing new procedures by processing a representative sample of data from the operations to be covered by the new system, either by sampling historical data or taking a sample from current operations. ◊ *parallel running*.

pinboard A form of *plugboard* in which the interconnexions are made by cordless *plugs* in the form of pins.

ping-pong A programming technique for processing *multi-reel files* which uses two *magnetic tape* units, switching between them until the whole file is processed, the successive reels being placed on alternate units.

pipelining The overlapping of the *execution* of several *instructions* in an *order code processor* at the same time. Each instruction is usually executed as a number of cycles which must be performed in sequence. Pipelining enables several instructions to be performed by the execution of different cycles on different instructions simultaneously.

P L/1 P L/1 (Programming Language 1) is a programming *language* developed with the intention of combining features of commercial languages (such as *C O B O L*) and scientific languages (such as *A L G O L*). Commercial applications with their emphasis on efficient handling of large volumes of data have led to the development of languages with sophisticated *input/output* facilities; scientific problems with their emphasis on rapid definitions and description of complex problems have led to the development of highly sophisticated *algorithmic* languages while neglecting the data handling aspects. P L/1 aims at combining the problem-solving facility of scientific languages with the data-handling capabilities of commercial languages, in order to meet the needs of increasingly mathematical commercial analysis and increasingly large volumes of data being processed by scientific routines. Among the more important features of P L/1 are the following:

(i) The language is *modular* in structure. This means that the user need only master the set of facilities necessary for his programming needs. More complex problems can use more extensive *subsets* of the language.

(ii) The language has a 'default' feature by which every error or unspecified option is given a valid interpretation, thus minimizing the effects of programming errors.

(iii) The language structure is 'free form'. No special documents are needed for *coding*, since the significance of each statement depends on its own format and not on its position within a fixed framework.

An example of P L/1 is given below; it is a routine designed to read the maximum and minimum temperature for every day of the week, and calculate and print the average temperature for each day of the week.

WEATHER: PROCEDURE
DECLARE MAXDAY (7); MINDAY (7); AVER-

AGE (7); READ LIST ((MAXDAY (I), MINDAY
(I)) I=1 TO 7); AVERAGE=(MAXDAY+MINDAY)
/2; WRITE ((MAXDAY (I), MINDAY (I), AVER-
AGE (II)) I=1 TO 7) (2F(5),F(8,1), SPACE); END
WEATHER;

place In *positional notation*, a *digit position* within an ordered
set of digits corresponding to a given power of the *radix* or *base* of
the number system.

plant To place the *result* of an *operation* of a *routine* in a *location*
where it will be used at a later stage in the *program*.

platen A solid, usually cylindrical, backing used in certain printing devices to form a base for a striking mechanism.

playback head Synonymous with *read head*.

plot To draw a line connecting the points on a graph.

plotter A device which automatically draws a graph.

plotter, digital incremental ◊ *digital incremental plotter*.

plotter, x–y Synonymous with *data plotter*.

plotting board A *plotter* which acts as an *output device* giving
graphical representation to the results of computer operations.
Also known as plotting table, output table.

plotting table Synonymous with *plotting board*.

plug A device, usually consisting of a flexible cord with a metal
pin at each end, used to connect the sockets of a *plugboard*.
Also known as patchcord, patchplug, plugwire. Where there is no
flexible cord, the plug is known as a cordless plug.

plugboard A device for controlling the operation of certain types
of *data processing* machine by means of a removable board with
terminals which may be connected in different patterns by the use
of plugs fitting into sockets on the board. The specific action required for the machine is determined by the particular interconnexions made; these may be changed at any time to alter the
functioning of the machine.
Also known as patch panel, patchboard, control panel[3], problem
board, jack panel.

plugging chart A printed chart representing the sockets on a
plugboard. It is used for planning interconnexions of sockets which
will enable a machine to perform its required function.

plug-in unit A self-contained circuit assembly which forms part
of a more complex whole but which can be removed and replaced
as a unit.

plugwire Synonymous with *plug*.

pneumatic computer A computer in which signals are transmitted and information stored by means of the flow and varying of pressure in a fluid – either gas or a liquid. ⟡ *fluid logic.*

pocket Synonym for *stacker*, usually used in connexion with a *sorter.*

point, fixed ⟡ *fixed point arithmetic.*

point, floating ⟡ *floating point arithmetic.*

point mode display A method of displaying data as dots plotted on the tube surface of a *cathode ray tube visual display unit.*

Polish notation A form of notation in *Boolean algebra* in which all the *operators* in a statement precede all the variables.

poll A technique used in *data transmission* whereby several *terminals* share *communication channels*, the particular channel chosen for a given terminal being determined by testing each channel in order to find a free one available for transmission, or locate a channel on which incoming data is present. Also used for the technique of calling for transmissions from remote terminals by signal from a central terminal. Polling is a method used for avoiding *contention.*

portability A characteristic of *code* or *data* which can be used on more than one system.

positional notation A form of *number representation* in which a given number is represented by a set of digits in such a way that both the position of the digit within the set as well as its value is of significance. The normal decimal system of number representation is an example of a positional notation in which each position in the set of digits represents an increase by a factor of ten on the preceding place. ⟡ *binary notation.*

positional representation Synonymous with *positional notation.*

post To update a *record* with information.

posting interpreter Synonymous with *transfer interpreter.* ⟡ *punched card interpreter.*

post-mortem dump A *dump* which takes place after a *program* has finished, usually to give information during *debugging.*

post-mortem program ⟡ *post-mortem routine.*

post-mortem routine A *routine* which is used to provide information about the functioning of a *program* after the program has finished. ⟡ *debugging, diagnostic routine.*

post-mortem time ⟡ *system recovery time.*

P-pulse Synonymous with *commutator pulse.*

precision, double ⟡ *double-precision arithmetic.*

pre-edit The technique of having a preliminary *editing* run on *input* data before the data is used for further processing.

prefix notation A type of notation in which a complex *expression* consisting of several *operators* and associated *operands* is formed without the use of brackets, the scope of the operators being determined by their relative positions. ✧ *Polish notation.*

pre-read head A *read head* placed in such a position near another read head that it may be used to read *records* before they pass under the second head.

preset parameter A *parameter* whose value is fixed before a *routine* is run. ✧ *program parameter.*

presort 1. The first *pass*[1] of a *sort program*[2]. The sorting of data on *off-line equipment* before processing it on a computer.

pre-store The placing of data in a special part of *store* before entering a *routine* to process the data.

presumptive address A quantity which appears in the *address part* of a *quasi instruction* and acts as an *origin* for subsequent *address modification.* ✧ *base address.*

presumptive instruction Synonymous with *basic instruction.*

preventive maintenance *Maintenance* carried out with the intention of preventing the occurrence of faults, i.e. regular maintenance as opposed to 'fire-brigade' maintenance.

P R F Acronym for pulse repetition frequency. ✧ *pulse repetition rate.*

primary storage Synonymous with *main storage.*

primitive file In an *operating system* a term used for a set of *physical files*, possibly on different devices, which are handled as a single entity by the operating system.

print bar A type of *print member.*

print barrel A drum on the surface of which are engraved all the *characters* used by an *on-the-fly printer.* The barrel is rotated rapidly and characters are printed by hammers which strike the paper as the appropriate character is in position relative to the paper.

printer An *output device* which converts data into printed form.

printer, hit-on-the-fly Synonymous with *on-the-fly printer.*

printer, line-at-a-time Synonymous with *line printer.*

printer, matrix Synonymous with *stylus printer.*

printer, wire Synonymous with *stylus printer.*

printer, xerographic ✧ *xerographic printer.*

print format A desciption of the way information is to be printed on a *printer*, usually provided as part of a *program specification.*

print hammer The device on certain types of *printer* which is activated in order to force paper into contact with the *character* to be printed.

print member The mechanism in a *printer* responsible for the form of the printed character.

printout A general term for the output from a *printer*; printed pages produced by a printer.

printout, memory ◊ *memory print*.

print position The position on a *printer* at which a *character* may be printed. The positions are usually numbered 1 to n (where n is the maximum number of characters which can be accommodated on a line) starting from the left-hand edge of the line.

print totals only To print totals pertaining to a batch of input data, as contrasted with *list* [2] which involves the printing of details from each individual record in the batch.

print wheel In a *wheel printer*, a wheel which has around its rim the type for the characters available for printing. The wheel is moved to bring the appropriate character into position for printing.

priority indicator In *data transmission*, a code used to indicate the relative importance of a message, and hence the order of transmission of the message.

priority processing A system used in *multiprogramming* for determining the sequence in which different *programs* are processed.

privacy The concept of restricted *access* to *data* and *information* held within a computer system. ◊ general article on *Security*.

private volume A category of *filestore* where the *user* has direct control over the placing of his *files* and can restrict the ability of other users to place files in his *volumes*.

privilege The rights of a *user* to make use of facilities within a system, e.g. his right to have *access* to certain *files*.

probability The assessment of probabilities of events is one of the spheres where the *digital computer* can prove to be an extremely useful tool. Probability calculations are often long and tedious and by their nature repetitive; such calculations may be performed with ease with the aid of a computer.

The term 'probability' is given a precise meaning. The probability of an event is defined to be the quotient formed by dividing the number of ways the event can happen by the number of possible happenings. If we take the simple example of tossing a coin, the probability of throwing a tail is $\frac{1}{2}$, since a tail can be thrown in only one way, whereas there are two possible results of a throw, namely a head or a tail. Thus,

$$\text{Probability} = \frac{\text{Number of successful results}}{\text{Number of possible results}}.$$

Many readers will be familiar with comparing 'odds' of events (usually connected with horses). The odds of an event may be obtained directly from the probability. In our previous example the odds of throwing a tail are 1:1 or evens; if the probability of an event is the quotient p/q then the odds of that event are $p:q-p$; or, putting this another way, if the probability of an event is P the odds are $1:1/P-1$.

i.e. Odds = Number of successful results: Number of unsuccessful results.

The value of the probability as calculated above can lie between 0 and 1 corresponding to odds of 0:1 and 1:0. A probability of 0 represents the impossible; that of 1 the unavoidable. A probability of greater than $\frac{1}{2}$ is more likely to happen than not; that of less than $\frac{1}{2}$ is more likely not to happen.

In calculating probabilities care has to be taken to choose a 'random variable', and to distinguish between connected and unconnected events. The following two examples set out the differences:

(i)　　A boy is chosen at random and found to come from a family with two children. What is the probability that the other is a boy?

Answer: $\frac{1}{2}$. The other child can be either a boy or a girl, the fact that the first child was a boy does not affect this.

(ii)　 A certain family with two children is known to contain a boy. What is the probability that it contains two boys?

Answer: $\frac{1}{3}$. Writing down all possible families with two children:

First child	Second child
Boy	Boy
Boy	Girl
Girl	Boy
Girl	Girl

Of these four possibilities, three satisfy our initial condition that the family shall contain a boy, and one that the family will consist of two boys. Thus the probability is $\frac{1}{3}$.

Where an event consists of a combination of two independent events the probability of the compound event is calculated by multiplying together the two independent probabilities. Thus the probability that two consecutive throws of a coin will both be heads, for example, is obtained by multiplying the probability of a head by the probability of a head to give $\frac{1}{2} \times \frac{1}{2} = \frac{1}{4}$. Note that this is the same as the probability of two tails, or head–tail, or tail–head, but that the probability of throwing one head and one tail (with no ordering conditions) in two throws is $\frac{1}{2}$.

Probability theory often turns up rather unexpected answers, and an assessment of probabilities is nearly always worth while when examining possible behaviour or comparing differing systems.

problem board Synonymous with *plugboard*.

problem definition A method of presenting a problem for computer solution in a formal and logical manner.
Also known as problem description. ◊ the general articles on *Documentation* and *Programming*.

problem description Synonymous with *problem definition*.

problem oriented language A *program language* designed for handling problems in certain broad application types related to e.g. mathematical, scientific or engineering systems, or to business systems. Essentially a language which enables the user to write *statements* in a form with which he is familiar, say in mathematical notation or English. Examples of mathematical languages are *A L G O L*, *F O R T R A N*, and of a business language, *C O B O L*.

procedure 1. The sequence of steps required in order to solve a problem. 2. More specifically, used to describe a section of *code*[1] which acts as a *subroutine* within an *operating system*.

procedure analysis ◊ *systems analysis*.

procedure oriented language A *program language* designed to make the expression of problem-solving procedures simple to use.

process 1. A general term for any computer operation on data. 2. More specifically, is used in connection with an *operating system* to refer to a set of user *programs*, system *software* and *data* brought together by the operating system in order to carry out a specific job.

process chart Synonymous with *systems flowchart*.

process control The use of computers (usually *analog computers* or *hybrid computers*) for controlling directly the operation of physical processes, e.g. the use of computers in the automatic control of chemical and electrical plant.

process image Within an *operating system*, used for the totality formed by a particular *program* together with any system *software* utilized to carry out the program.

processing, automatic data ◊ *automatic data processing*.

processing, centralized data ◊ *centralized data processing*.

processing, conversational ◊ *conversational mode.*
processing, electronic data ◊ *electronic data processing.*
processing, in-line Synonymous with *demand processing.*
processing, integrated data ◊ *integrated data processing.*
process, irreversible ◊ *irreversible magnetic process.*
process limited Synonymous with *processor limited.*
processor A general term for any device capable of carrying out operations on data. Sometimes used as a synonym for *central processor.*
processor error interrupt The interruption of a *program* because of the failure of a *parity check* in the transfer of information within the *central processor.*
processor limited A system in which the overall processing time is dictated by the speed of the *central processor* rather than the speed of the *peripheral equipment.* Also known as process limited. Contrasted with *peripheral limited.*
process, reversible ◊ *reversible magnetic process.*
process state The state which a *process* has reached during the course of its *execution.*
product The result of multiplying two *factors*, the *multiplicand* and the *multiplier.*
production control The purpose of production control is to enable a manufacturing organization to meet all orders placed by customers within a reasonable time. Computerized production control will often increase business by means of an improvement in delivery dates. Other benefits are a reduction of capital tied up in stock, reduction in labour costs and improved utilization of plant.

The starting point for a production control cycle is a sales forecast. Typically a company will have firm orders for a short period in the future, tentative orders in the medium term and intelligent anticipation (perhaps based on *extrapolation* of past trends) will have to be used for the long term. The length of these time periods will be specific to particular industries and production problems. Given a sales forecast as *input*, a computer can break down the products demanded into their constituent main units, assemblies, sub-assemblies, etc., down to piece parts and raw materials. Processing of this information is in two stages: (a) calculation of gross requirement of each constituent element of each product; and (b) calculation of net requirements of each constituent element taking into account work-in-progress and stock levels.

Finally the net requirements must be converted into economic manufacturing batches and orders to outside suppliers.

It is obvious that an integral part of a production control system must be a system of *inventory control*, because without a knowledge of stock levels it is impossible to establish net requirements for parts and raw materials. The basic objective of inventory control is to maintain stocks at the lowest levels that are compatible with the economics of production. There are two conflicting requirements here. On the one hand the cost of stockholding increases with the quantity of stock held and, on the other, the lower the stock levels the longer the turn-round time on orders tends to be. The break-even point for each stock level is most likely to be achieved using a computer system.

Input to the computer will be details of items received into, returned to and issued from stores. These items will be used to keep up to date a master stock file which can be processed for reports and queries. The computer can also carry out automatic re-order point control on stock levels and signal unusual circumstances (for example, exceptional demand and non-moving stocks).

Breakdown and inventory control are reasonably straightforward applications to put on a computer. Having ascertained the production requirements in terms of components and raw materials reached, however, the next stage is to plan the flow of work on the factory floor. This is also amenable to computer control but is a more challenging project to design and implement.

The final output from the breakdown analysis is a list of manufacturing batches, which will be necessary to meet the required production. This information can be used to plan plant loading, showing the effect of the work load on production centres and enabling management to make decisions: for example, on the need for increased plant capacity and labour force or on the possibility of subcontracting. The role of the computer is to tabulate the load in hours for a given time period, on each production centre.

Computer analysis of plant loading can be made more sophisticated in various ways. For example, the computer can load demand against appropriate time periods, starting at the required completion date and working backwards, and printing out the potential overload/underload on each shop in each time period.

Once any imbalances between load and capacity have been smoothed, it becomes possible to plan the workload through machine and assembly shops so as to optimize use of plant. This procedure involves several operations, among them maintenance of a work-in-progress file which reflects the current state of all jobs, the printing of works documentation (such as route lists and departmental schedules) and progress control. Progress control is achieved by analysis of the work-in-progress file and the printout of details of jobs behind schedule.

production run   A normal operational *run* of a system. Contrasted with *parallel run, pilot run, test run.*

productive time   Time spent by a computer system in processing *production runs* during which no machine faults occur.

product, logical   Synonymous with *and operation.*

program   A set of *instructions* composed for solving a given problem by computer. ◊ the general article on *Programming.*

program address counter   Synonymous with *instruction register.*

program cards   *Punched cards* containing *program instructions*, either in *machine language* or *source language*, often with one card used for each instruction.

program compatibility   The situation in which two different computers can accept and operate on the same *program* or programs written in the same *machine language* or *source language.*

program compilation   ◊ *compiler.*

program control   Any device operating on-line to a *central processor* is said to be under program control.

program controller   The unit in a *central processor* which controls the execution of the computer *instructions* and their sequence of operation.
Also known as program control unit.

program control unit   Synonymous with *program controller.*

program counter   A *control unit register* in which the *address* of the next *instruction* to be performed is stored. Synonymous with *control register.*

program development time   The total time taken to produce a working computer *program*. This will include time taken in *compilation, testing* and *debugging.*

program, diagnostic   ◊ *diagnostic routine.*

program documentation   ◊ the general articles on *Documentation.*

program file   Synonymous with *program tape.*

program flowchart   A *flowchart* using *flowchart symbols* to represent the functions performed by a particular routine. ◊ the general article on *Flowcharting.*

program, general   ◊ *general purpose program.*

program generator   ◊ *generator.*

program generator, report   ◊ *report program generator.*

program instruction   ◊ *instruction.*

program, internally stored   ◊ *internally stored program.*

program language A *language* used for writing computer *programs.* ⟡ *Programming.*

program library 1. A collection of proven *routines* or *subroutines* used in a particular installation and consisting usually of *programs* developed by the user concerned and also by the computer manufacturer. The programs may exist in various media (e.g. *punched cards* or *paper tape*) but are generally maintained on *magnetic tape* or a *direct access file.* 2. An indexed book or volume of papers describing the routines and programs in the *program library* [1] with instructions to enable users to employ them for their specific tasks.

program maintenance The keeping of *programs* up to date both by correcting errors, and by altering programs according to changing requirements.

program, master control ⟡ *master control routine.*

programme ⟡ *program* for computer program.

programmed check A *check* performed by means of *program instructions.* Sometimes contrasted with an *automatic check* performed by *hardware.*

programmed dump A *memory dump* which occurs at specified points within a *program* as a result of instructions incorporated into the program. ⟡ *debugging.*

programmed halt A *halt* in a *program* due to the program encountering a *halt instruction* or an *interrupt.*
Also known as coded stop. Contrasted with *unexpected halt.*

programmed instruction Synonymous with *macro instruction.*

programmed switch ⟡ *switch* [3].

programme evaluation and review technique Also known as PERT. ⟡ general article on *Critical Path Method.*

programmer A person responsible for producing a working *program* from a *program specification.* ⟡ *Programming.*

programmer defined macro A *macro instruction* defined by a programmer for use in a specific *program*, in contrast with a predefined macro instruction which may form part of the *instruction set* of a given *language.*

programming Programming is the process by which a set of *instructions* is produced for a computer to make it perform specified activity. The activity can be anything from the solution of a mathematical problem to the production of a company payroll. The instructions ultimately obeyed by the computer are the numerical codes significant to the computer's *central processor.* Since a computer cannot reason, but is entirely dependent on instructions supplied to it by its all too human users, it cannot be expected to perform any task adequately unless the problem it is required to solve has been specified correctly in every detail and the instructions it is asked to obey define in complete detail each step of the solution. The main steps which have to be covered before a program is completed are: (i) Understand the problem, and plan the solution. (ii) Prepare a *flowchart* or *decision table* of the problem. (iii) Prepare the instructions in coded form. (iv) Test the program until it is performing correctly. (v) Prepare detailed documentation of the program and instructions on its operation. The amount of time spent on each of these steps, their relative importance and the techniques used depend largely on the type and complexity of the problem being programmed: but some attempt to implement each of these stages must be made for nearly every program.

Understanding the problem is of fundamental importance. In most cases the programmer will work from a detailed program specification prepared by a systems analyst. A detailed program specification will include descriptions of all input to be processed by the program, the processing required and details of all output from the program. The programmer must satisfy himself that all possible conditions have been specifically catered for, or that any conditions not specifically detailed can be adequately handled. Having satisfied himself of the adequacy of the specification of the problem, the programmer has next to consider the 'strategy' to be adopted in writing the program. Depending on the complexity of the problem, the capacity of the computer and the type of *language* to be used, the program may be written as a single entity or divided into sections or *segments*, each one covering a logically distinct part of the problem. For example, a program might be divided into a *housekeeping* segment in which the program is set to its *entry conditions*, an input segment which deals with reading and validating data input to the program, a processing segment which operates on the input data and an output segment which presents the results of the processing in the required format. Each of these segments can be considered as separate programs, possibly written by different programmers. Further, if the whole program cannot fit into *store* certain segments can become *overlays*.

Flowcharting the problem is the next step to be performed. The general article on this topic gives details of the techniques involved and the general article on *decision tables* is also of relevance here. The object of flowcharting is to produce a diagram showing the logical relationship between the various parts of the program. It is particularly important to maintain an overall outline flowchart of the whole problem when segmentation takes place to ensure that all parts of the program specification are taken care of. A flowchart will normally be independent of the type of computer to be used or the language the program is to be written in, although these factors must be borne in mind. In some cases however the restrictions on the language to be used will determine the logic of the program and hence the flowcharting, for example in the case of report programs in which a *report generator* will be used as the program language.

Coding the program follows the completion of flowcharts. The logical steps described in the flowchart are translated into instructions to the computer. These instructions will either be in *machine code*, i.e. the basic code of instructions understood by the processor, or in some form of *symbolic language*. The nature of programming languages is described in the article on *Languages*. The choice of language will depend on the complexity of the problem and the capacity and resources of the computer to be used. The more sophisticated and easier to use a language is, the less control a programmer will have over the final form of the *object program* operated on by the computer, and thus some loss of efficiency in running time or increase in size of program may occur. These penalties are counterbalanced by the speed of writing a program in a higher level language and the fact that fewer mistakes are likely.

Whatever language is used to write a program, the programmer must achieve the same basic end: to reproduce the logic of the program as shown in the flowchart as simply, economically and efficiently as possible. In a brief article it is not possible to describe in detail all the techniques used by programmers to achieve these aims; more information will be found under the following headings: *instruction, loop, program modification, switch, subroutine.*

It is most unusual for a program to work correctly the first time it is tested. Errors in a program are known as *bugs*, and the process of correcting these errors is described in the article on *debugging*. Errors are of two main types: errors due to incorrect use of the programming language and errors due to incorrect logic in the solution of the problem. Programs are tested with samples of the data normally expected to be input to the program and the results obtained compared with calculated results obtained manually from this test data. When the results obtained by the program match up to the expected results, and the programmer or systems analyst is satisfied that all possible conditions that the program is expected to meet with in normal operating circumstances have been simulated, the program may be said to be working correctly. However, a correct program is of little use unless it is supported by full *documentation*, and it is the duty of a programmer to ensure that this is maintained and supplied to any user of the program.

Documentation of a program is designed to fulfil two functions: to enable a user to operate the program correctly, and to enable another person to understand the program so that it may if necessary be modified or corrected by someone other than the programmer who first wrote it. Operating instructions include the following elements: a program description; set-up; running procedure; output disposal. Program documentation will include details of the program specification, flowcharts, coding and any *compilation* listings, and test results: a description of these requirements will be found in the general articles on *Documentation*.

programming, automatic ◊ *automatic coding.*

programming, heuristic ◊ *heuristic program.*

programming language ◊ *language.*

programming, micro ◊ *microcoding.*

program modification 1. The use of *modification* in a *program* by which *arithmetical* and *logical operations* are performed on *instructions and addresses* so as to alter their actions during the program (◊ general article below). 2. To modify a program by rewriting it or adding a *patch* so as to change the function of the program.

In the earliest programmed electronic accounting machines the *program* consisted of a fixed sequence of steps which was set up by plugged connexions on a *plugboard*. With the development of *core storage* for computers the program was stored in the computer's *memory* and was therefore available for processing in the same way as any other element of data held in the store. Thus it became possible for a computer program to perform operations on its own instructions so that the same basic instructions could be modified to carry out different processes on each occasion that they were performed. This ability is of considerable significance in programming; and the general principles of program modification apply to all *digital computers* regardless of the *instruction formats* employed.

The techniques of program modification are commonly used to modify the *address* component of an *instruction*, thus enabling the same instruction to be used for performing operations on different items of data in different store *locations*, or to determine which *branches* of the program are to be executed at some later stage in the program. This process is referred to as *address modification*. Another technique is to modify the operation code of an instruction in order to make the instruction perform a different function on each occasion it is executed.

As an example of the power and flexibility of program modification consider the techniques of *looping*. If a program could only perform a series of steps sequentially, the program to achieve a particular purpose might need to be very long and to include many repeated sections. However by modification of the instructions it is possible to repeat a sequence of instructions a specified number of times according to the nature of the data being processed. For example, a record in a file for a stock control application might show, for each item in the inventory, the item number followed by fifty-two quantity *fields* (stored in consecutive *words*) showing the demand for the particular item as collected each week over the preceding year. Assuming that it is necessary to generate the aggregate demand for each item during the year as a single total, it would be possible to write this simple process as fifty-two individual add instructions for each item, loading the contents of each of the fifty-two individual words into an *accumulator*, but this would be very wasteful, and a single basic instruction could be used of the form:

$$ADD \quad N \quad to \quad X$$

where N represents the address of an *operand* and X the address of an *accumulator*. When a new record is read into memory, the accumulator specified by X would be zeroized, N itself would be set equal to the address of the first quantity field, and another location C (to be used as a counter) would be set equal to 52. This part of modification is sometimes referred to as initialization.

The basic instruction is then performed to add the first week's demand into the accumulator X. Now modification takes place: the operand N is incremented so that it now represents the address of the second quantity field, and one is subtracted from C. The program then loops back to perform the basic instruction once more, this time to add the second week's demand into X. This process is repeated, incrementing the operand N and decrementing the counter C. When C reaches zero the operation for that stock item will have been completed and X will contain an aggregate of the fifty-two quantity fields. After the required information is stored away or printed a new input record will be obtained to *overwrite* the previous one in memory and the whole process is repeated. Such a

328

simple program might require about eight instructions instead of the fifty-two originally suggested and, as the modification would be carried out automatically, it would not interfere with the processing of data.

The technique of program modification is a basic tool in programming and is used in a variety of ways to reduce the number of instructions required to perform any particular series of operations. ⋄ *indexing*.

program overlay ⋄ *overlay*.

program parameter A *parameter* whose value is incorporated into a *routine* by means of *program instructions* after the *run* has commenced. Contrasted with *preset parameters*, which are incorporated into a routine before the run commences.

program register Synonymous with *instruction register*.

program segment ⋄ *segment*.

program-sensitive fault A *fault* which occurs as a result of some combination of *program instructions*.

program specification A comprehensive description of procedures for which a computer *program* is required. The program specification is used by a programmer in order to prepare a program. ⋄ *system definition*, and general articles on *Documentation* and *Programming*.

program step A single element of a *program*, usually a single *instruction*.

program storage The area of *store* in which a *program* is placed. On some systems this may be a specially reserved part of store, or may be specially protected to prevent accidental interference with the program.

program, supervisory ⋄ the general article on *Multiprogramming*.

program tape A *magnetic tape* or *paper tape* on which one or more *programs*, usually in *object program* format, are stored. When a particular program is required for running, it is read into the *main store* from the program tape.

Also known as program file.

program test A computer *run* designed to discover errors in the *program* being run. ⋄ *Debugging*.

program testing Checking a *program* (in order to establish that it is performing expected operations correctly and that all errors have been discovered) by running the program on a computer, usually with *test data*. ⋄ *Debugging, dry running, Remote Testing*.

program testing time Time spent on a computer in *program test-*

ing. Program testing time is part of the total *program development time.*

program, utility ◊ *service routines.*

prompt Any *message* given to an *operator* by an *operating system.*

prompt identifier A code or number displayed with a *prompt* in order to identify it uniquely.

proof total A *control total* which can also be used, in combination with others, to check the consistency of a group of totals, e.g. if a group of control totals consists of a gross total, deductions total and net total, proof totals will check that gross less deductions equals net.

propagated error An error which occurs in an operation and whose influence extends to other operations.

propagation time The time taken by an electrical impulse to travel between two given points.

protected location A *location* of *store* whose contents cannot be altered without some special procedure, thus preventing unplanned *modification* of the contents of the location.

protected record (or field) A *record* or *field* displayed on a *video* which cannot be *overwritten* by the *operator* but can be changed only by data sent from the processor.

protection The techniques of prevention of interference between units of *software* or areas of data within a *multiprocessing system.*

protection mechanism Means of carrying out *protection.*

proving Testing a machine in order to find out whether it is free of *faults*, usually by running a *test program.*

proving time Time spent on a machine in *proving.*

P R R Acronym of *pulse repetition rate.*

pseudocode A *code* in which *program instructions* are written, making use of symbolic representations of *operation codes* and *addresses*, and requiring translation into *machine code* by means of a *compiler* before the program can be run. ◊ *Languages, Programming.*

pseudo instruction An *instruction* composed of characters arranged in symbolic form, but not performed as an actual instruction in the running of the *program*, but used to control the conversion from *source language* to *object language*. An instruction input as data to an *assembly system* or a *compiler.*

pseudo off-lining Synonymous with *spooling.*

pseudo operation An *operation* which is not performed by means of *hardware*. Such an operation may be performed by means of a *macro instruction* or by means of special *software*.

pseudo-random sequence A set of numbers which is produced by a defined process but which can nevertheless be considered to be a set of *random numbers* for a given calculation.

pulse A sudden and relatively short electrical disturbance.

pulse code The representation of *digits* by means of sets of *pulses*.

pulse, P- ◊ *commutator pulse*.

pulse recording, double- ◊ *double-pulse recording*.

pulse repetition frequency A *pulse repetition rate* which is independent of the time interval over which it is measured.

pulse repetition rate The average number of *pulses* occurring in a unit of time.

pulse train A sequence of *pulses*.

punch 1. To make a hole in a *punched card* or piece of *paper tape*. 2. A device for making such a hole. ◊ *card punch, tape punch*.

punch, automatic feed ◊ *automatic punch*.

punch, automatic tape ◊ *automatic tape punch*.

punch card ◊ *punched card*.

punch, duplicating card Synonymous with *reproducer* [1].

punched card A punched card contains data represented in the form of punched holes which can be sensed by a variety of machines in order to carry out functions such as adding, subtracting, comparing, collating, printing. There are various shapes and sizes of card, the most common being an 80-column card which measures $7\frac{3}{8}$in. × $3\frac{1}{4}$in. and may be ·007in. or ·009in. thick. The columns are numbered from 1 to 80 from left to right along the face of the card and each vertical column is divided into 12 *punching positions*. Each column of a card is used to contain a numeric digit (represented by a single hole in a card column) or an alphabetic character or special symbol (represented by two, or more, holes in a single column). Examples of other cards in use are 21-column, 40-column, 45-column, 65-column, 90-column, and the holes may be round or rectangular. The principles of all are much as described below, as are the machines which use them, although of course different manufacturers' equipment differs in detail.

Of the twelve positions in each card column, nine are used to represent the numeric digits 1, 2, 3, 4, 5, 6, 7, 8 and 9, and the other three, known as zone positions, are designated as 0, 11 and 10. The 11 position is sometimes referred to as the X-position and the 10 position is also known as Y or 12. More annoyingly, the 11 position is as often known as the Y-position, and the 10 position as the

X-position, so communication on this subject is best handled with care.

Numeric digits are represented by punching in the appropriate position of each column from 0 to 9, whereas alphabetic characters or symbols are represented by punching a *zone* digit (0, 11 or 10) in combination with a numeric digit (1 to 9). By this means up to 48 individual characters can be encompassed within the card code. Some card codes permit three holes to be punched in the same card column in order to represent a further range of special symbols, e.g. to represent up to 64 individual characters.

Items of data are recorded by grouping consecutive card columns to form *fields*, the number of columns required depending upon the maximum length of the item concerned. Thus a numeric field consisting of four columns could be used to represent any decimal number up to the value 9999, the layout of a particular card being determined by the user according to the requirements of his application.

The holes are punched into the cards by a *keyboard* operated machine known as a *card punch*, sometimes referred to as a *key punch*, or *automatic key punch*. The operator simply depresses keys on the keyboard to cause holes to be punched column by column into the card. Two basic types of keyboard are available, a numeric keyboard or an alphabetic keyboard.

A numeric keyboard is operated with one hand; it has twelve keys corresponding to the *punching* positions of a card, plus a number of function keys, e.g. a space key. An alphabetic keyboard is very similar to a typewriter keyboard, except that on a punch the numerical keys are grouped to permit one-handed operation if required when entering numerical data.

A card punch usually consists of a hopper into which blank cards are placed, a *card track* along which the cards are fed column by column to be punched and a *stacker* into which the punched cards are finally ejected. The punch unit is positioned above the card track and is activated directly from the keyboard. Some card punches include facilities for automatically *gangpunching* information from one card to another, and some also include a simple print unit for printing characters along the top edge of the card.

When cards have been punched they must usually be checked to ensure that the punching operation has been completed correctly. A machine known as a *verifier* is used for this purpose. It is very similar to a card punch except that it has a reading unit instead of a punch unit and it has *comparator* circuits to compare entries made on the keyboard with information punched in corresponding card columns. The verifier operator therefore merely works from the original source documents repeating the keystrokes made by the original punch operator. If the comparator reveals a discrepancy the verifier operator checks again to see that she herself has not caused the error and if the original card is incorrect will reject it. All verified cards are usually notched automatically on one edge and may then be taken to further stages of processing. (⇔ *Data Preparation*.)

Punched cards can be used as direct input to a computer using a *card reader*, but there is also a wide range of punched card equipment available for processing data in punched card form. Some of these are described below.

Punched cards can be *sorted* into some desired sequence according to the information punched in specified fields; e.g., if a particular field of each card contains the employee number, the cards can be arranged into numerical sequence of employee number. A machine known as a *sorter* is used for this purpose. A sorter has twelve pockets which correspond to the twelve punching positions in a card column, plus a further pocket called a reject box which corresponds to a blank column. Each column of the required field is examined one column at a time, the cards being automatically sorted into the appropriate pockets according to the information appearing in the specified column. When sorting numerical fields one pass is required for each column of the field under examination. Alphabetic sorting however requires two examinations of each column. Sorters operate at speeds ranging from 400 to 1,200 cards per minute.

When two independent card files have been sorted into sequence they can be merged, using a machine known as a *collator*. The card files must each have identical control fields, e.g. both be sorted into the same *key* sequence. The collator is also able to outsort unmatched cards while the merging operation takes place, and to check the sequence of each of the two files.

Sometimes a complete duplicate set of cards must be produced, in which case a *reproducer* is used to read the original cards and punch another copy automatically.

A *tabulator*, or *accounting machine* as it is also known, can be used to produce printed reports of information contained in punched cards. These reports may list every item from each card or certain fields from specified cards only. Tabulators have facilities to perform addition and subtraction using electro-mechanical counters, and therefore totals can be accumulated and printed at the end of specified card groups and sometimes a reproducer or a *gangpunch* can be linked to a tabulator to punch summary cards. Thus the tabulator produces the end product of any punched card data processing activity: reports or commercial documents on preprinted *continuous stationery* such as cheques, invoices, statements, bills, etc.

These and other anciliary machines provide a wide range of processing functions for punched cards. Punched card machines are sometimes referred to as *unit record* equipment since each transaction within a system is represented by an individual punched card. *Electronic calculators* were a development of the earlier punched card systems and themselves led to some of the developments of the first computers. Calculators were principally developed to perform multiplication and division upon *operands* punched into card fields. Sometimes the result was punched into the same card and sometimes into another card.

Most 80-column punched card machines were programmed by plugged connexions on a *plugboard*. These plugboards became quite complex and unwieldy on the larger tabulators and calculators. The major development work for this type of equipment ceased in the late 1950s and the computer with its internally stored program gradually superseded punched card unit record systems. However, many such systems continue to be in use and punched cards themselves still form an important input/output medium for computers.

punched card duplicating Synonymous with gang punching. ◊ *gang punch*.

punched card, edge- Synonymous with *margin-punched card.*

punched card field A *field* of information present in a *punched card*.

punched card interpreter A machine capable of reading the holes punched in a *punched card* and causing the corresponding alphabetic and numeric characters to be printed on the same card or (on a *posting interpreter* or *transfer interpreter*) on the following card.

punched card system, ducol ◊ *ducol punched card system*.

punched card tabulator A machine which automatically feeds *punched cards*, reading data from them to be directly listed and/or accumulated for the printing of totals at the end of certain card *groups*.

punched card verifier A machine used to ensure that data punched into *punched cards* is the same as the data on the original documents from which it was punched. The process of manual punching from original documents is repeated and the machine recognizes any difference in key depression. ◊ general article on *Data Preparation*.

punched paper tape ◊ *punched tape* and general article on *Paper Tape*.

punched tape A tape of fixed width into which information can be recorded by means of a pattern of punched holes. Tape is normally of paper, approximately 0·004in. thick. The width of tape is referred to by the number of *tracks* or *channels* it holds, i.e. the number of holes which can be punched across it. The usual widths are 5-track ($\frac{11}{16}$in.) 6- or 7-track ($\frac{7}{8}$in.) and 8-track (1in.). Also known as *Paper Tape*, under which heading there is a general article.

punch, eleven ◊ *X-punch* and *Y-punch*.

punch, hand (card) ◊ *hand punch* [1].

punch, hand-feed Synonymous with *hand punch*.

punch, hand (paper tape) ◊ *hand punch* [2].

punching, normal stage ◊ *normal stage punching*.

punching positions The places on a *punched card* into which holes can be punched. A punching position lies at the intersection of a *row* and a *card column*.

punching rate The rate at which information can be punched in the form of holes in *punched cards* or *paper tape*. In the case of cards the rate is normally measured by the number of cards which can be punched per unit of time and in the case of paper tape by the number of *characters* per unit of time.

punchings, designation Synonymous with *control holes*.

punching station The position within a *card punch* at which a *punched card* is punched.

punching track The part of a *card punch* which moves the *punched card* through the machine.

punch, keyboard Synonymous with *key punch*.

punch knife The part of the mechanism of a *card punch* which makes the hole in a *punched card*.

punch position ◊ *punching positions*.

punch tape ◊ *paper tape*.

punch tape code ◊ *paper tape codes*.

punch, twelve ◊ *twelve punch* and *Y-punch*.

punch, zone ◊ *zone digit*.

punctuation bits *Bits* used in *variable field record* systems to indicate the beginning and end of items of information.

push down list A method of storing a list of items of information; as each new item is entered into the list it occupies the first location in the list, all the other items moving down one place in the list. Contrasted with *push up list*.

push down store A *store* which works on the principle of a *push down list*, so that as new items of data are added to the store, previous items are moved back, the latest item occupying the first *location* in the store. This arrangement of data can be performed either by *hardware* or by *program*.

Also known as cellar.

push-pull amplifier An amplifier in which the input signal is accepted simultaneously by two amplifying units which operate in opposite phase to produce two output voltages with opposite signs but of the same magnitude.

Also known as double-ended amplifier.

push up list A method of storing a list of items of information; each new item is entered into the list after the last item, so that the other items do not change their relative positions in the list. Contrasted with *push down list*.

Q

quanta Plural of *quantum*.

quantity, double-precision ⟡ *double-precision arithmetic*.

quantization Dividing the range of values of a variable into a finite number of distinct subdivisions or *quanta*.

quantizer A device for converting an *analog* quantity into its *digital* equivalent.

quantum One of the subdivisions made as a result of *quantization*.

quartz delay line A form of *acoustic delay line* in which quartz is used to recirculate sonic signals.

quasi instruction An item of data present in a *program* in *instruction format* but never in fact executed as an instruction.

queuing theory The application of probability theory to the study of delays or queues produced at servicing points.

QUICKTRAN QUICKTRAN is a subset of the programming language *FORTRAN*, designed primarily for use with *multi-access* systems. The basic program statements are compatible with FORTRAN, but the language is extended to include extensive facilities for controlling the *testing, debugging* and *operating* of programs. The use of special statements enable the user to *compile*, test and *run* a program from a *remote terminal*.

quinary Synonymous with *biquinary*.

quotient Part of the result produced by dividing one number by another; a *remainder* may also be produced. In a digital computer the precision given in respect of these two resulting *operands* is governed by the way in which the arithmetic process is performed. The precision depends on the way in which the programmer specifies the termination of the operation.

R

rack-up A method of presenting data on a *video* whereby each time the last line of the *screen* is filled, the first line is deleted and all lines move up one line, thus enabling a new line to be entered. Compare with *wrap round*.

radix The basis of a notation or number system, defining a number representational system by *positional representation*. In a decimal system the radix is 10, in an *octal* system the radix is 8, and in a *binary* system the radix is 2.
Also known as base.

radix complement The radix complement of a number is obtained by subtracting each digit of the number from one less than its *radix* and then adding 1 to the result obtained. (For example, the radix complement of the decimal number 171 is $999 - 171 + 1 = 829$.)
Also known as noughts complement and true complement.

radix complement, diminished ◊ *diminished radix complement*.

radix-minus-one complement Synonymous with *diminished radix complement*; usually a more explicit term is used, e.g. *nines complement* or *ones complement*.

radix notation A generic term embracing both *fixed radix notation* and *mixed base radix notation*. Also known as *base notation*.

radix point The location of the separation of the integral parts and the fractional part of a number expressed in a *radix notation*. This location is marked in the decimal system by the decimal point (a dot in English usage, a comma elsewhere).

R A M P S Acronym of *resource allocation in multi-project scheduling*.

random access storage A *storage* designed to give a constant (or almost constant) *access time* for any *location* addressed and regardless of the location previously addressed. ◊ the general article on *Storage Devices*.

random number generator 1. A *hardware* unit designed to produce *random numbers* in specified quantities. 2. A *program* designed to produce random numbers in specified quantities.

random numbers 1. A set of numbers produced entirely by chance. 2. A set of numbers which for a specific purpose may be assumed to be free from statistical bias, i.e. the numbers have no predetermined sequence. The set may be produced by chance, but may also be derived by means of an *algorithm* designed to produce numbers sufficiently random for any desired degree of statistical accuracy.

random number sequence ◊ *random numbers.*

range 1. The difference between the upper and lower limits of a function or quantity. 2. A family of *processors* with similar characteristics, differing in power and size but usually using a common *machine language.*

range independence A characteristic of *software* which can be processed on any machine in a given *range*[2].

rank To arrange in a given order of importance.

rapid-access loop A part of *store* with a faster *access time* than the rest of the storage medium.

rate, pulse repetition ◊ *pulse repetition rate.*

rate, residual error ◊ *residual error rate.*

raw data Data which has neither been subject to *data reduction* nor processed. It may be readable or converted to machine-sensible form (e.g. *punched cards*).

read To obtain data from one form of *store* (e.g. *punched cards*) and transfer it to another (e.g. the *main memory* of a computer). Contrasted with *write.*

read-around ratio The number of times information held in *electrostatic storage* at a specific spot can be referred to before the spillover of electrons causes data loss in the nearby spots. Data in the surrounding spots must be restored before this deterioration. (The term is now obsolete.)

reader A device designed to *read.*

reader, magnetic tape ◊ *magnetic tape reader.*

reader, paper tape ◊ *paper tape reader.*

read head An electromagnet used to read from a magnetic medium such as *magnetic tape, magnetic disk* or *magnetic drum.* Also known as reading head or playback head.

reading head Synonymous with *read head.*

reading station That part of a *card track* at which holes punched in a *punched card* are sensed; e.g. by means of a photo-electric head.

read-only storage A device which holds permanent data that cannot be altered by *program instructions.*

read-out To *read* from the *internal store* of a computer and transfer it to an *external store.*

read-punch unit An *input/output device* capable of both reading punched data and then punching computed results. If the unit is reading and punching *punched cards* (as opposed to *paper tape*) it may also segregate the newly punched cards from the ones previously input.

read rate Number of units of data (e.g. *characters, words, blocks, fields, cards*) capable of being *read* by an input reading device in a given unit of time.

read time The time interval between the instant the transfer from a *store* begins and the instant it is completed. The read time is therefore the *access time* less the *waiting time*.
Also known as transfer time; related to *write time*.

read while writing The reading (◊ *read*) into *store* of a *record* or group of records simultaneously with the writing (◊ *write*) from store of another record or group of records.

read/write channel A channel connecting a *peripheral unit* with a *central processor*.

read/write head An electromagnet used to read or write on a magnetic medium such as *magnetic tape, magnetic disk* or *magnetic drum*.

real address An *address* in *main store*; contrasted with *virtual address* from which the real address is obtained by reference to a table or by addition of a datum. Synonyms for real address include *direct address, absolute address* and *specific address*.

real file A collection of *records*, created from one or more *primitive files* by means of a *record access mechanism* in an *operating system*.

real store A term used in contrast to *virtual storage* to refer to a specific *hardware* storage device in use for a particular activity within an *operating system*.

real time Real time is an expression used to refer to any system in which the processing of data input to the system to obtain a result occurs virtually simultaneously with the event generating the data. Thus most process control systems operate in real time, since input data must be processed quickly enough to enable the results to be used as feedback information. In commercial data processing an example of a real time system is an airline booking system, in which each booking must be processed by the system immediately it is made so that a completely up-to-date picture of the actual state of affairs is maintained by the computer at all times. Real time systems normally require the use of *data communication* equipment to feed data into the system from remote terminal, *direct access storage devices* to store incoming data in large volumes and the use of *central processors* capable of *timesharing* the *programs* needed to validate data and control the input data, at the same time as using this data for the particular application required. Since the point of having a real time system is that the computer provides a picture of events as they occur such a system will also be associated with some form of *information retrieval* system, making use of equipment such as *visual display units, interrogating typewriters* or others forms of inquiry station.

real time clock A device which generates readable signals at regular intervals of time. Such a device is used in *real time* systems to calculate the actual or *elapsed* time which passes between the occurrence of two events, in contrast to the time, usually much shorter, taken by the computer to compute the time interval. Such a device is also used to control the operation of certain equipment in accordance with a defined time scale. In this sense also known as *clock, digital clock*.

recompile To repeat the process of *compilation* of a *program*, usually as a result of *debugging*, or in order to create a version of the program which will run on a different *range* of equipment.

reconfiguration Changing the availability or method of use of the component parts of a computer system, including the *operating system software* necessary to control the new *configuration*.

reconfiguration console ◊ *console*.

reconnexion The replacement of one *resource* by another, or the re-establishment of a resource which for any reason has been made inoperative.

reconstitution The restoration of a *file* to an earlier stage, e.g. as a result of a *dump and restart* procedure.

record access management ◊ *record access mechanism*.

record access mechanism Software within an *operating system* used to *access data* forming a particular *real file* by means of operations on the constituent *primitive files*.

record A unit of data representing a particular *transaction* or a basic element of a *file* consisting in turn of a number of interrelated *data elements*.

record blocking The practice of grouping *records* into data *blocks* which can be read and/or written to *magnetic tape* in one operation. This arrangement enables the tape to be read more efficiently and reduces the time required overall to read or write the file.

record count A total of the number of *records* in a file. Usually maintained and checked each time the file is *updated* to provide control information about the performance of a *program* or a specific computer *run*.

record format A description of the contents and organization of a *record*, usually part of a *program specification*.

record head Synonymous with *write head*.

record header A *data element* or *field* within a *record* set aside for information required by system *software*, but not available to the *user* of the record.

recording density Relating to the distance between the magnetized spots on a magnetic *storage device*. For example, on a *magnetic tape* the density of the *binary digits* recorded on the tape is measured in *bits* per inch. Sometimes, usually where coded characters are recorded as individual *rows* across the tape, the density may be expressed in characters per inch. The following are typical packing densities encountered on magnetic tape:

> 256 bits per inch, or 256 characters per inch;
> 512 bits per inch, or 512 characters per inch.

The speed at which data may be transferred to or from a tape is dependent upon the recording density and the speed of the *tape drive*. ⟡ *transfer rate*.

record list Information held on a *file* presented in readable format.

record, reference ⟡ *reference listing*.

record section Where a *record* is held in more than one *block*, that part of the record held in one block.

recovery Actions taken to restore a system to working order after a *failure*; depending on the type of failure, these actions may be taken by the *user*, the *operating system* or both.

recovery file A file holding details of all changes made in another file so as to enable *reconstitution* to take place in the event of *failure*.

red-tape operations Operations performed as part of a *routine*, but concerned mainly with the organization of the routine itself rather than with the processing of *data*. For example, to monitor the progress of *input/output* operations to ensure that data in input/output areas is not *overwritten* until it has been processed. The more general red-tape operations are known as *housekeeping*.

redundancy 1. The use of extra *characters* or *bits* which are attached to an item of data to provide a means for checking the accuracy of the data, as in *redundancy check*. For examples ⟡ *check digit* and *parity check*. 2. The recording of information by means of a bit pattern which is theoretically capable of distinguishing between a wider range of values than the information requires. 3. The availability of alternative means for performing a specific function. 4. The retention of more than one copy of a set of data to avoid the consequences of *failure*.

redundancy check Any checking operation which depends on extra *characters* or *bits* that are attached to *data* to permit the automatic detection of errors. The extra characters do not themselves contribute to the information content of the data, e.g. ⟡ *parity check*.

redundant character Synonymous with *check character*.

redundant check ⟡ *redundancy check*.

redundant code A code in which more *bits* are used than are strictly necessary for the information to be conveyed; e.g. a 7-bit *paper tape* code in which each character requires 6 *information bits* plus one *parity bit*.

reel 1. A roll of *paper tape* perhaps mounted on a cardboard or plastic former. 2. A flanged spool for holding a *magnetic tape*. 3. A general term to describe a magnetic tape and the spool upon which it is mounted. In this context it is common to refer to tapes by their *reel numbers*, when strictly the term *tape serial number* is intended.

reel number Where a file of data extends over more than one *reel* of *magnetic tape* each reel of the file is identified by a different reel number. If the file is sequenced the reel numbers will indicate the order in which the reels must be taken. ⟡ *tape serial number*. Also known as reel sequence number.

reel sequence number Synonymous with *reel number*.

re-entrant code Synonymous with *re-entrant procedure*.

re-entrant procedure A *procedure*[2] that may be entered before a previous activation of the same procedure has been completed, since no interference is caused between more than one activation. Also known as re-entrant code.

reference address An *address* used as a reference point for a group of *instructions* written to contain *relative addresses*. Thus, for example, an *absolute address* is obtained by adding a reference address to a relative address.

reference listing A list printed by a *compiler* to show *instructions* as they appear in the final *routine*, including details of *storage allocation*.

reference picture A *picture* which provides operations staff with information about their activities.

reference supply A voltage source used in an electrical *analog* *computer* as a unit by which other voltages can be measured.

reference time The time at which an electrical pulse used to initiate some action first reaches 10 per cent of its specified amplitude.

regeneration period The time that elapses while the screen of a *cathode ray tube* store is scanned by an electron beam to regenerate the charges on the surface of the screen.

regenerative reading A *read* operation involving the automatic *writing* of data back into the locations from which it is extracted.

regenerative store A type of storage unit in which signals representing data are constantly being regenerated so that information can be retained for as long as required. When some new item of data is loaded the regenerating circuit is automatically broken to permit the old data to be *overwritten*.

regenerative tracks On a *magnetic drum* these tracks are associated with the *read* and *write heads* and are arranged in such a manner that signals are regenerated during each drum revolution to retain data recorded on the drum. Thus each regenerative track and its *read/write heads* acts as a *regenerative store*.

regional address That part of an *address* which indicates that the address itself is from a specified set of addresses for a predetermined region of *memory*.

register A special *store location* generally having a capacity equivalent to the *word size* of the computer concerned and having specific properties for use during arithmetic and/or logical operations. For example, in some computers arithmetic operations can be performed only if at least one *operand* is stored in a special register. A computer may have several registers each of which is designed for a specific function.

register capacity The limiting values, upper and lower, of the quantities that may be processed by a *register*.

register, console display ◊ *console display register.*

register, control ◊ *control register.*

register, current instruction ◊ *current instruction register.*

register, delay line ◊ *delay line register.*

register dump ◊ *dump.*

register length The number of *characters* or *bits* that can be stored in a particular *register* within the *register capacity*.

register, memory buffer ◊ *memory buffer register.*

register, program ◊ *instruction register.*

register, sequence control ◊ *sequence control register.*

rejection Synonymous with *nor operation*.

relative address A number used in the *address* part of an *instruction* to specify a required *location* with respect to a *base address*. The *absolute address* is obtained by adding the *base address* to the relative address.

Also known as floating address.

relative addressing A system of *programming* in which *instructions* are written so that they do not refer directly to *absolute addresses* in *memory*; instead a *base address* is added to the address component of each instruction when the program is loaded in order to create numbers that refer to absolute *locations*. Thus a *subroutine* consisting of 20 instructions might be written to occupy 20 *words* commencing at a base address R, through $R+1$, $R+2 \ldots$ to $R+19$. If R were set equal to 1200 in *absolute coding* the *subroutine* would occupy words 1200 to 1219 in memory. This method enables a programmer to write a program in several independent sections or *segments* without having to consider the absolute addresses required.

relative code A *program* code in which *addresses* are specified in respect to some *base address* or one in which *symbolic addresses* are used.

relative coding Writing *program instructions* using the techniques of *relative addressing*.

relative error The ratio of an error in some computed result in respect to the quantitive value of the result. Contrast with *absolute error*.

relay amplifier A device used in an *analog* system for comparing two signals which incorporates an amplifier that drives a switch.

relay centre A *switching centre* in which message signals are received and automatically directed to one or more output circuits according to data contained in the message itself.

release As a result of an action performed by an operator, by a *program instruction* or automatically by an *executive program*, to release a *peripheral unit* or a *memory* area from the control of a particular program. The *hardware* released becomes available for allocation to some other *program*.

reliability The performance of a particular machine measured against some predetermined standard for operating without failure of the equipment, for example the ratio of *serviceable time* to serviceable time plus *down time*.

reload time Synonymous with *system recovery time*.

relocatable program A *program* coded in *relative code* in such a way that it can be stored and executed in any part of the *memory*.

Such a system requires some form of *executive program* to be stored in memory to allocate required storage areas and to ensure that all *instructions* are executed in respect to the current *base address* for the program. ⟡ *dynamic allocation*.

relocate The automatic *modification* of the *instructions* in a *program*, undertaken to permit the program to be *loaded* and executed in any specified *memory* area.

remainder Part of the result obtained from the arithmetic operation known as *division*; the *dividend* is divided by the *divisor* to give the *quotient* and the remainder.

remedial maintenance Maintenance work performed on equipment to repair some machine fault; classified as *fault time* or *down time* and not as part of *scheduled engineering time*.

remote calculator A *keyboard* device connected directly to a *central processor* via some *data link* to enable users at remote locations to present problems requiring calculation to the computer.

remote computing system A *hardware* configuration in which *remote consoles* are connected directly to a computer to enable users to have direct communication with the *central processor*. Users are able to *compile, test, debug* and execute their *programs* from these remote terminals. Proven programs are stored centrally on some *mass storage* device and can be called into *memory* as required. ⟡ *multi-access systems*.

remote computing system exchange A device that handles messages and data transmitted between a *central processor* and *remote consoles*. The exchange device enables a number of remote consoles to be operated simultaneously without mutual interference. It will receive characters transmitted from these terminals and form them into statements for transfer to *memory, results* and *messages* being returned to the appropriate terminal as required. ⟡ *multiplexor*.

remote computing system language A language used for communication with a central computing system from *remote consoles*. Such systems are usually installed to give scientists and engineers direct access to a computer for solving problems expressed in a *scientific computer language*: for example, *program statements* are often written in *FORTRAN*. However, it is also necessary for the language to incorporate operating statements; e.g. instructions to *test, debug*, change and execute programs. ⟡ *QUICKTRAN*.

remote computing system log A record of events occurring during the operation of *remote consoles*; it may be printed but is often recorded on some other output medium to enable analyses to be subsequently generated. The log may record the volume of traffic for individual terminals to facilitate financial charging or to demonstrate the efficiency of the remote system. It will record the types of error made, the numbers of *statements* used and volumes of data transferred.

remote console A terminal unit used in a *remote computing system*. A number of these distant consoles may be available, each equipped with facilities to send and receive data to and from the *central processor*. Connexion to the processor is usually made via a *remote computing system exchange*. Devices at the remote console might include *card readers, card punches, paper tape readers, paper tape punches, visual display units* and *line printers*. Usually a *keyboard* operated device such as an *on-line* electric typewriter or a *teleprinter* is available to permit direct communication with the central computing system.

remote data stations Remote *terminals* capable of sending data to, and receiving data from, a central computer. Communication may be by means of a telegraph circuit or a telephone voice quality line. Unlike a *remote console* in a *remote computing system*, a data station has no direct operating control over the central computer but acts as an automatic *data collection* point. Equipment at these stations may include *punched card* and *paper tape input/output devices* and perhaps a keyboard-operated unit. A data station also requires special data transmission units to connect the terminal to the communications channel and to perform *automatic error correction*.

remote data terminal Synonymous with *remote data station*.

remote debugging 1. In the strictest sense, the testing and correction of *programs* from a *remote console* as used in a *remote computing system*. 2. ◊ *Remote Testing*.

remote inquiry, real time Pertaining to a system in which distant terminals are connected to a *central processor* to enable users to interrogate the system and obtain information from data files. The terminals may be connected over outside *data transmission channels* or over some *inplant network*. Such a system requires that files are stored on a *mass storage* device with facilities for *direct access* to data.

remote job entry The input of data direct to a central computing system by means of a device remote from that system.

remote processing Related to a system in which data is transmitted as messages from distant stations to be processed by a central computer. For this type of system the central computer is usually equipped with an *executive program* or *operating system*, capable of

347

receiving random messages from distant points and of processing and transmitting data at unpredictable intervals. During periods of peak activity the executive program will store messages and establish priorities for processing them. Some form of *remote computing system exchange* will be used to handle messages passing to and from the *central processor*. But ✧ *remote processor*.

remote processor A *processor* which is located away from a computer's *central processor* and whose activities are under the overall control of the central processor's *operating system*.

remote testing Remote testing is a method for organizing the flow of work being processed through a computer system. Using this method, programmers do not accompany their *programs* when they are being tested on the computer, but supply the programs and associated *test data* with comprehensive instructions to be performed by the computer operators. The purpose of this technique is to speed the flow of work through a computer room and also to provide a useful discipline in the testing and *debugging* of programs. This discipline is necessarily a part of remote testing, since the programmer responsible for completing the instructions to the operator must consider all possible conditions which might arise during the operation of the program in order to provide comprehensive instructions. These instructions will include requests for any diagnostic aids required, such as *memory prints*, or prints of data on *backing stores*, and also contain details of all expected actions of the program, including messages requiring operator action. Being compelled to write down all actions required from the operators, the programmer has a detailed record of the actions taken at each test run: such instructions given verbally during in-attendance testing can easily be forgotten or overlooked. An installation in which testing is always remote is known as a *closed shop*. ✧ *Debugging*.

removable plugboard Synonymous with *detachable plugboard*.

reorganize To copy *data* into a new part of *filestore*, either because the user requires changes to the data format, or because the current *storage* structure has become inefficient (e.g. because the file contains dead *records*).

repair delay time Time lost due to the inability to repair equipment because of lack of test equipment, spare parts or service staff.

repair time Time spent on repairing equipment faults outside the time allocated to *routine maintenance* and *supplementary maintenance*.

repair time, mean ◊ *mean repair time* and *repair time*.

reperforator Synonymous with *paper tape reproducer*.

repertoire A range of *characters* or separate *codes* available in a particular system of coding. It is also common to refer to the *instruction repertoire* of a particular *program language* or *machine code*.

repetition frequency, pulse ◊ *pulse repetition frequency*.

repetition instruction An *instruction* that can cause an instruction, or group of instructions, to be repeated a specified number of times. Generally used in a *loop* to cause the required number of cycles to be executed. Often such instructions are made conditional on some other set of circumstances occurring in the *program*.

repetition rate, pulse ◊ *pulse repetition frequency*.

repetitive addressing A system adopted in some computers in which, under certain conditions, *instructions* can be written without the quoting of an *operand address*. The *program controller* automatically assumes that the address is that of the *location* addressed by the previous instruction.

repetitive operation Pertaining to *analog computers*, a technique in which a solution is generated successively using the same equations and *parameters*, in order to display the solution as a steady graph on a *visual display unit*.

replication The use of more than one identical *hardware* unit in a system in such a way that the units are interchangeable in the event of *failure*. A form of *redundancy*[3].

reply A *message* generated in response to an earlier message.

report A general term for any printed analysis of data produced by a computer. ◊ *report program*.

report generation The printing of information extracted from one or more computer *files* using the techniques associated with a *report generator*.

report generator A *generator* specially designed to produce *programs* which will print out information from any computer *files*, in which it is necessary for the user to specify the format of the files concerned plus the format and content of the printed report, along with any rules for creating totals, etc.

report program A *program* designed to print out an analysis of a data *file*. Usually the data will be in some sequence of *keys*, and the report will consist of totals or analyses performed for various groups of *records*, each analysis or total being produced when a key change occurs. Where key changes have different levels of significance they are known as *control breaks*.

report program generator A *general purpose program* that can generate other *report programs* to meet users' specific requirements for printing results, summaries, etc., for computer files.

representation, binary-coded decimal ◊ *binary-coded decimal representation.*

representation, binary incremental ◊ *binary incremental representation.*

representation, positional ◊ *positional notation.*

representation, ternary incremental ◊ *ternary incremental representation.*

reproducer A *punched card* machine capable of reading a *pack* of cards and transferring information to be automatically punched into another set of cards. Usually, a *plugboard* is used to control the format of the cards thus produced, so that the *fields* can, if required, be arranged in a format differing from the original cards. A standard model reproducer has two *card tracks* known as the reading track and the punching track.

Also known as reproducing punch.

reproducer, paper tape ◊ *paper tape reproducer.*

reproducing punch A synonym for *reproducer.*

request slip A statement of the requirements of *store* and *peripheral units* of a *program*. Used in conjunction with *dynamic allocation.*

rerouting Establishing a new *route* between two *resources* or between a *process* and a *resource*, in particular the route between *main store* and a *peripheral* resource.

rerun To repeat the execution of a *program*, usually as a result of an error condition.

rerun point A point in a *program* from which it is possible to *restart* following an error or a machine failure.

rerun time ◊ *systems recovery time.*

rescue dump A technique in which the contents of *memory* are periodically output to a *backing store*, so that the *data, intermediate results* and the *program* of *instructions* can be preserved as at a particular step. Thus, in the event of a subsequent machine failure the program can be constituted in *memory* to restart from the last rescue dump. ◊ general article on *Dump and Restart.*

research, operations ◊ *operational reseach.*

reservation The allocation of *memory* areas or *peripheral units* to a particular *program* in a *multiprogramming* computer.

reserve To assign a *memory area* and/or *peripheral units* to a particular *program* operating in a *multiprogramming system.*

reserved word In a *programming language*, a *data name* not available to the user because it has some specific significance to the *compiler*; or any *data name* or *label* which can be used only in a specific context.

reset 1. In *programming*, to set a *counter* to zero, or to return an *indicator* to some stable condition. 2. On a *punched card machine*, to zeroize a *counter*.

reset cycle To return a *cycle index counter* to its original value.

reset mode Pertaining to an *analog computer*, a state during which the initial conditions are applied to the system.
Also known as initial condition mode. Contrasted with *compute mode*.

reset pulse One of the pulses that control the state of a *storage cell*, specifically one that tends to restore a cell to the *zero condition*.

reshaping, signal ◊ *signal regeneration*.

resident routine A *routine* which exists permanently in *memory*; e.g. a *monitor routine* of an *executive program*. Contrast with *non-resident routine* which refers to a routine called into *memory* from an external *store*.

residual error An error generated during an experiment; i.e. the difference between an exact result calculated theoretically and one obtained empirically.

residual error rate In *data transmission*, the ratio of undetected or uncorrected errors incurred in transmitting a given volume of data.

residue check A check performed to verify an *arithmetical operation* in which each *operand* is divided by a number *n* which generates a remainder that accompanies the operand as a *check digit* in subsequent operations.

resilience The ability of a system to continue operating in the event of *failure* of part of it; in this event the system may be said to be operating in *crippled mode*.

resolution error An error derived from the limitations of an *analog* computing unit to respond to changes of less than a given increment.

resolver On an *analog computer*, a *function generator* the input variables of which are polar coordinates of a point, the output variables being Cartesian coordinates.

resolving potentiometer A potentiometer employed to operate as a *function generator*, in which the output variables are Cartesian coordinates of a point and the input variables are polar coordinates.

resource Any part of a computer system or *configuration* which can be considered as a separate unit for the purpose of allocation (◊ *allocate*) for the use of a specific *process*.

resource allocation in multi-project scheduling A system of *allocation* using a network analysis to assist in making the best use of resources which have to be stretched over a number of projects. Usually known by the acronym R A M P S.

response duration The interval between the *time origin* of a pulse and the time at which the pulse falls below a specified operating value.

response time The time required to answer an inquiry. For example, the time needed to transfer an inquiry from a terminal to a central computer and to receive a reply at that terminal. Includes the time required for transmission in each direction plus time for retrieving and processing data to meet the inquiry.

restart To return to a previous point in a *program* in order to begin again following an error or machine malfunction. During the processing of large *batches* of data a programmer may cater for various restarts at regular intervals in his program so that a job can be resumed following a failure without going back to the beginning of the data. A cold restart is a restart at an earlier *restart point*. A warm restart indicates the ability of a program to restart without having to return to a restart point. ◊ general article on *Dump and Restart*.

restart point A point in a *program* that allows the program to be re-entered in order to effect a *restart* following an error or machine failure.

restore To set a *counter, register, switch* or *indicator* to some previous value or condition.

result A quantity or value derived from some *arithmetical* or *logical operation* performed upon one or more *operands*. ◊ *final result* and *intermediate result*.

retained peripheral A *peripheral unit* which was previously used on one type or *range* of processors but is subsequently used on a different range of equipment.

retention period The length of time (measured in days/weeks/months) for which data on a *reel* of *magnetic tape* is to be preserved, i.e. before the tape may be *overwritten*. This information may be held on the *header label* of the reel, and is used to ensure data security.

retrieval The extraction of *data* from a *file* or files by searching for specified *keys* or *labels* contained in *records* stored on the file. Records may be selected according to logical relationships between *fields* and may be processed or summarized to produce the required information. ◊ *Information Retrieval Techniques.*

return address Synonymous with *link.*

return instruction An *instruction* performed to return to a main *routine* after the execution of a *subroutine.* The instruction is usually modified by a *link* which has been previously stored to ensure that the main routine is re-entered at a desired point.

return-to-bias recording A method of *return-to-reference recording* in which each storage cell is permanently energized to a predetermined bias condition.

return-to-reference recording A system for recording information in *magnetic cells,* in which each cell can be magnetized to represent the *binary digit* 1 by applying energy to alter the condition of the cell with respect to some predetermined reference condition. The reference condition may be the magnetization of a cell to a specified level or the absence of magnetization.

reversible counter A *counter* in which the value stored can be incremented or decremented according to a specified control signal.

reversible magnetic process A process whereby the flux within a magnetic material returns to its previous condition when the magnetic field is removed. Contrasted with *irreversible magnetic process.*

reversible process Synonymous with *reversible magnetic process.*

revolver track On a *magnetic drum,* a track which acts as a *regenerative store.* ◊ *regenerative track.*

rewind To reposition a *magnetic tape* to the *load point* (i.e. so that the tape is ready to *read* from the beginning).

rewrite To retain data in an area of *store* by recording it back in the *location* concerned after reading from that *location.*

right justified Describing an *item of data* which is stored in such a way that it occupies consecutive positions starting from the right-hand end of the *location* assigned. Thus, if an item should contain less *characters* than are allowed, the left-most positions will be blank.

right shift A *shift* operation in which digits of a *word* are displaced to the right. In *arithmetical shift* this has the effect of division.

ring ◊ *write permit ring, write inhibit ring.*

ring counter A series of interconnective storage elements arranged in a loop. Only one element at any moment in time can exhibit a specified condition, and as input signals are counted this condition is displayed by successive elements around the loop.

ring shift A *shift* operation in which digits expelled at one end of a register return automatically at the other end.

ripple-through carry Synonymous with *high-speed carry*.

rise time The time required for an electrical pulse to rise from one-tenth to nine-tenths of its final value.

R J E Acronym of *remote job entry*.

R J E mode A method of operating a computer system whereby *jobs* are submitted from *terminals*.

role indicator A code associated with a *keyword* to identify it as a noun, verb, or adjective, etc.

roll Synonymous with *spool*.

roll in 1. Activating a *process* in an *operating system* by bringing parts of the process successively into *main store*. 2. An action performed by an electro-mechanical *counter* on a *punched card tabulator*, in which the counter unit receives impulses representing numeric values read from a *card field* or emitted from another counter.

roll off The process by which a *primitive file* is copied from a specific *physical storage medium* or *volume* into *low level filestore*, *overwriting* any version of the file currently existing in filestore.

roll on The process of copying a *primitive file* from *low level filestore* into a specific type of *volume*.

roll out 1. Removing a *process* from *main store*. 2. An action performed by an electro-mechanical *counter* on a *punched card tabulator*, in which the counter emits electrical impulses representing the numeric value currently stored in that counter. The original value remains in the counter after the roll out function is completed.

round To alter the value of digits at the least significant end of a number, in order to allow for digits to be removed in *truncating* the number. ⋄ *rounding off*.

rounding error An error in a result that is attributable to *rounding off*.

rounding off The process of adjusting the *low order* digits of a number so as to reduce the effect of *truncation*. For example, a value equalling half the *radix* may be added to some specified *digit position* so that *carry* digits may be generated to increase the value in the next *highest significant position*. The number may then be truncated by ignoring the specified position and all succeeding positions.

route Synonymous with *channel*[1] but more commonly used in connexion with *operating system*.

routine Used as a synonym for *program*, but often used to mean part of a program. For example, a program may be said to consist of an *input routine*, a *main routine*, *error routines* and an *output routine*. This term may in fact be used to denote any major *software* procedure which performs some well-defined function in the operation of a *program* or system.

routine, assembly ◊ *assembly program*.

routine, checking ◊ *checking program*.

routine, closed ◊ *closed subroutine*.

routine, compiling ◊ *compiler*.

routine, debugging ◊ *debugging aid*.

routine, executive ◊ *executive program*.

routine, floating point ◊ *floating point package*.

routine, heuristic ◊ *heuristic program*.

routine, housekeeping ◊ *housekeeping*.

routine, interpreter ◊ *interpretive routine*.

routine maintenance Maintenance work carried out according to a schedule, usually as recommended by the equipment manufacturer, to prevent equipment failure; the work usually includes testing, repairing, replacing, cleaning and adjusting components.
Also known as scheduled maintenance. Contrasted with *corrective maintenance* and *supplementary maintenance*.

routine maintenance time Computer time assigned for performing *routine maintenance* work. Usually planned by the user well in advance, and often entailing a written agreement between the user and equipment manufacturer.

routine, master ◊ *master control*.

routine, object ◊ *object program*.

routine, open ◊ *open subroutine*.

routine, test ◊ *test program*.

routine, trace ◊ *trace program*.

routine, tracing ◊ *trace program*.

routine, translating ◊ *translator*.

routing Meaning *message routing* in a system in which a central computer is attached to a communications network to receive and direct messages to their required destinations.

routing indicator In *message routing* systems, a group of *characters* or digits forming part of a message and specifying a required destination.

row 1. A horizontal row in a *matrix*. 2. A row of holes punched across the width of *paper tape*; in this sense also known as *frame*. 3. Synonymous with *card row*.

row binary Relating to *punched cards*, a method of representing numbers by considering consecutive *punching positions* on each *row* of a card as consecutive digits in a *binary number*. Contrasted with *column binary*.

row binary code ◊ *row binary*.

row pitch The distance between the holes running lengthwise along a punched *paper tape*, measured from centre to centre of consecutive positions.

run The performance of one *program* or *routine*. Related particularly to *batch processing* applications, in which the beginning of a run is characterized by the operating functions necessary to *load* the program and its data, and the end of a run by operator activity to unload and then load a further program and files. Usually a number of runs are combined to form a *job*, or *suite* of runs.

run book An operating guide for assembling the necessary materials and data for running a job, including a complete set of *operating instructions* for a *run* or *suite* of runs.

run chart A *flowchart* showing a *run* or series of runs combined to form a single *job*. It indicates the files and data to be input and output and shows by means of standard *flowchart symbols* the various *peripheral units* required for each run. It is used, for example, as part of the *operating instructions* for a job, but is not suitable for showing the detailed procedure for a run. Contrasted with *logic flowchart*.

run diagram ◊ *run chart*.

run duration The time required to execute a particular *run*.

run locator routine A *routine* that locates a specified *program* on a *program tape*.

run, machine ◊ *run*.

running accumulator A storage unit consisting of a number of *registers* connected in such a way that data can be passed successively from one to another. Only one of the registers is able to accept data from, or transfer data, outside the system. Thus, as this register receives successive *words* of data they are pushed down into the other registers, and as it emits a *word* of data the other words move back up the system.

run phase Related to *program compilation*, and used to denote the period at which the compiled *object program* is first tested and run.

run time The time during or at which a *program* is *run*. Contrasted with *compilation time*.

S

sampling The process of recording the value of a *variable* at intervals of time.

sampling rate The ratio of measurements of recorded values to all the values available, e.g. if a variable is measured every millisecond the sampling rate is 1,000 measurements per second.

satellite processor A *processor* which is part of a larger *data processing* system and whose function is to process *runs* which are subsidiary to the main work of the system.

scale The process of altering a set of quantities by a fixed quantity so as to bring the values within the limits capable of being handled by the equipment or routines being used.

scale, extended time ⋄ *extended time scale.*

scale factor The quantity used in scaling by which the quantities being altered are multiplied or divided in order to bring them within the desired limits. ⋄ *scale.*

scale, fast time ⋄ *fast time scale.*

scale of two Synonymous with *binary notation.*

scale, slow time ⋄ *slow time scale.*

scaling factor Synonymous with *scale factor.*

scan 1. To examine every item in a list, or *record* in a *file*, usually as part of an *information retrieval* system in which each item is tested to see whether or not it satisfies certain conditions. 2. To test the condition of *communication links* or *input/output channels* in order to determine whether or not the channels are in use.

scanner A device which automatically carries out *sampling* and initiates required operations according to the values obtained.

scanning The action performed by a *scanner.*

scanning rate The rate at which a *scanner* samples.

scan period Synonymous with *regeneration period.*

scan rate In *process control*, the rate at which a quantity being controlled is checked.

scatter read The process of distributing data into several areas of *store* from a single *input record* or *block*. ⋄ *gather write.*

scheduled engineering time Time spent on installing and performing regular maintenance on a computer.

scheduled maintenance Synonymous with *routine maintenance.*

scheduling The organization of the sequence and priority in which *jobs* are to be run, and the allocation of *resources* to jobs. Scheduling may be done manually by operators or may be part of the function performed by an *operating system.*

schema A complete description of a *data base.*

scientific computer A computer used for *scientific data processing.*

scientific data processing *Data processing* for scientific purposes, usually requiring machines with great computational power rather than ability to handle large files of data in a backing store. Contrasted with *commercial data processing* and *industrial data processing.*

scientific language A *language* designed for the writing of mathematical or scientific *programs.* ⇗ *ALGOL, FORTRAN.*

scratch pad memory An area of *memory* reserved for intermediate results: a working area.

scratch tape Any *reel* of *magnetic tape* whose *header label* contains information indicating that the tape may be used for any purpose, i.e. a tape containing information that may now be *overwritten.* Contrasted with *master tape.* Compare also with *work tape.*

screen 1. The surface of a *cathode ray tube.* 2. In *information retrieval*, to make an initial selection from a set of data according to specified conditions.

screen mode A technique of operating a *video* by which pages of information are formatted for the device.

search To examine each item in a set in order to discover whether it satisfies specified conditions.

search time The average time required to identify an item of data satisfying a specified condition.

secondary storage Synonymous with *backing store.*

second generation computers Machines built with transistors, as opposed to *first generation* (thermionic valves) and *third generation* (*integrated circuits*).

second level address An *address* in a *computer instruction* which references a *location* in which the actual address of the required *operand* is to be found. Synonymous with *indirect address.*

second remove subroutine A *subroutine* which is entered from another subroutine; contrasted with a *first remove subroutine* which is entered from and exits to the *main program.*

section 1. Synonymous with *segment.* 2. A part of a *magnetic tape*, sometimes also used as a synonym for *block.*

section, input ▷ *input area.*
section, output ▷ *output area.*
sector A part of a *track* or *band* of a *magnetic disk* or *magnetic drum*; also used as a synonym for a *block* of data stored on a sector.
security Security in the context of computing is a large subject, and a short article necessarily is limited to considering a few major aspects of the subject.

Security implies protection from a risk. Computer installations are subject to three main types of risk: (i) Risk to *hardware* (ii) Risk to *software* (iii) Risk to *information.*

Hardware is subject to the whole range of physical risks which may effect any item of sophisticated electronic equipment. A properly organized installation will be protected against fire, flood, sabotage. This means devices to detect and report the occurrence of any physical disturbance of the computer's environment: fire detectors, burglar alarms and so on. Some physical dangers, however, are particular to computer systems. Adequate air conditioning and environment control is necessary to protect an installation against temperature, humidity and dust which go beyond the limits of tolerance specified by the manufacturers. This often means not only proper environmental control equipment but also proper staff discipline (no smoking, cleanliness, doors closed).

Software in a computer installation is a highly valuable and highly vulnerable asset. The library of user-developed and manufacturers' programs frequently has cost as much as the hardware to produce. Moreover, while a damaged item of equipment can be replaced relatively quickly, or borrowed at short notice from another user, destroyed or damaged software may require as many months of painstaking effort to recreate as were required for initial development. Security measures must therefore be taken to protect software from physical hazards, loss by fire, theft, etc. Most important, however, the user must take proper measures to enable software to be replaced if loss does in fact occur. An obvious precaution is to store alternative copies of all system software away from computer installations.

This procedure is not as simple as it sounds. Not only must copies be stored, the stored copies must be kept as up-to-date as the currently used versions. In addition all associated *documentation* must be stored with the machine readable versions of the software. This imposes a rigorous discipline on the installation's management in order to ensure proper updating and control procedures are maintained.

Information is the end-product of a computer system, and is perhaps the most valuable and most vulnerable part of any installation. The information held within the computer may well be crucial to the viability of the whole of an organization's operations. Loss of fundamental records, customer accounts, payroll, engineering records, laboratory results may totally destroy an organization. Fraudulent use of information may cost a company far more than a 'conventional' burglary or payroll raid. Industrial espionage may give commercial rivals an overwhelming competitive position.

The risks to which computer-held information is subject again can be divided between conventional risks and those specific to computer systems.

Fire, sabotage, theft can destroy records. To prevent this, proper access control and physical security must be maintained. Again, in order to minimize the results of loss of information, it is advisable to hold copies of vital files in a location remote from the computer itself. As for software, proper control is needed to make sure that security copies of data files are updated regularly.

A *generation number* system is one technique for preserving copies of files together with the data required to update files (see also *grandfather tape*). In very large systems, particularly those controlled by *operating systems*, standard software is provided which regularly *dumps* copies of master files for security purposes.

Information in a computer system is vulnerable to more subtle risks than the conventional physical risks referred to. Unauthorized modification of software may result in generating false information resulting in fraudulent gain. For example, false invoices may be generated and submitted for payment; tampering with payroll output may result in excessive payments. The incidence of computer fraud shows the greatest growth rate of any type of civil crime in the developed world, and as new security measures are adopted, new and more ingenious ways of manipulating computers are devised. A short article cannot hope to cover the variety of possible frauds and counter measures. Security lies fundamentally in the proper control of software, and in proper controls built into computer systems. In addition the user must take the usual care in selection and supervision of the staff he entrusts with these controls.

One method of controlling software is to preserve an 'audit copy' of all vulnerable software. This is a version of the software known, as far as possible, to be error free and 'honest', i.e. not perpetrating fraud. At random intervals the version of the program actually being used for the particular application can be removed and physically compared with the audit copy to ensure no unauthorized modifications have been made. Audit *test data* can be kept for the same purpose, run against a program, and results checked against standard test results to ensure that there has been no unauthorized change.

Auditing techniques have been widely extended and adopted to provide both internal and external auditors with a wide range of aids in auditing computer systems.

Such aids include audit software which enable auditors to call for sample data from computer files and selectively process samples against inquiry and report programs generated by the auditor himself. ($\diamond$ General article on *Audit of Computer Systems*). The incidence of large communication systems with extensive *on-line* inquiry facilities poses further security problems for computer based information.

Terminals enable a user both to examine and to modify data. Both these facilities can be abused either deliberately or accidently. Data protection is a major subject in its own right. Hardware devices enable terminals to be controlled physically through the use of physical controls: locks and keys to allow a user to use a terminal, or to restrict the use of a terminal to an input mode or output mode only. Software controls allow for highly complex access control by means of hierarchies of *passwords*. Software may be developed which examines passwords submitted through the terminal: files may be restricted to the owners of certain passwords only, and the level and type of information also may be controlled by passwords. The ability to update a *file, record* or even *field* may be restricted to certain passwords. In addition to unauthorized access and use by people, sophisticated *operating systems* and *data base* systems must be secure internally to prevent unauthorized interference of data by software operations. Operating systems and data base systems are concerned with the manipulation of data held within a computer system, and a hierarchy of software controls limits the operations which can be performed on different levels of file structure within such systems.

Security in a computer sense is thus concerned with the whole spectrum of risks and hazards to which all aspects of computers, hardware, software and information, are vulnerable. Techniques used to protect computers from such risks range from basic physical protection to complex computer based techniques for monitoring the computer's own functions.

see-saw circuit Synonymous with *sign-reversing amplifier*.

seek Synonymous with *search*.

seek area In a *direct access* store (e.g. a *magnetic disk file*), an area of storage assigned to hold specified *records* and chosen to permit rapid access to the records concerned in accordance with the physical characteristics of the device.
Also known as cylinder.

segment 1. To divide a long *program* into a series of shorter units (segments, also known as *chapters*). A program may be divided into segments for convenience of programming, all segments being present in *store* together when the program is run; or because the program is too long to be contained in store all at once, in which case segments are read in sequence. In this latter case, segments or groups of segments read into store together may be called *overlays*. ⟡ *Programming*, *common area*. 2. A fixed length part of a *track*.

segmented program A *program* written in separate *segments* or parts. Only one, or some, of the segments may fit into *memory* at any one time, and a main part of the program, remaining in memory, will call for other segments from a *backing store* as and when required, each new segment being used to *overlay* the preceding segments.

segment mark A *character* used to separate sections of a *tape file*.

segregating unit A *collator* used to select from a card file *punched cards* satisfying certain conditions.

select To make a choice between alternative courses of action as a result of a *test*.

selecting A method by which the transmission of information to remote *terminals* is controlled by carrying the *address* of the receiving terminal in the *block* being transmitted.

selection sequential access ⟡ *selective sequential*.

selective digit emitter A device in *punched card* machines which can simulate signals usually generated by particular punchings.

selective dump A *dump* of a limited area of *store*.

selective sequential A method of processing a *direct access sequential file* in such a way that selected *records* in the file are located by means of an index table and are presented to the processing *program* in *key* number sequence.

selective trace A *trace program* in which only specified *instruction* types or *store* areas are analysed. ⟡ *Debugging*.

selector A device which tests for the presence of specified conditions and initiates appropriate operations according to the result of the test.

selector channel Where several *peripheral units* are connected to a *central processor* by a single *channel*, the selector channel controls the transfer of data between each peripheral unit and the central processor.

self-checking code Synonymous with *error detecting code*.

self-checking number A number which has attached to it a *check digit* whose value depends on the values of the other digits in the number, enabling the number to be checked after being transferred between *peripheral devices* or between *locations* of store.

self-resetting loop A *loop* which contains *instructions* restoring all *locations* affecting the operation of the loop to their original condition as at entry to the loop.

self-triggering program A *program* which begins operating as soon as it has been placed in a *central processor*. ⟡ *trigger*.

semantic error An error in the selection of the correct *symbol* to represent a given idea or meaning, e.g. using the wrong *instruction format* for the *operation* required.

semantics The study of the relationship between symbols and their meaning.

semi-automatic switching centre ⟡ *switching centre*.

semiconductor A material whose conductivity at room temperature lies between that of metals and insulators, but increases at high temperatures and decreases at low ones. Semiconductors are used in *transistors*.

sense 1. To test the state of some part of *hardware*, especially the state of a *switch*[1] set either manually or in the course of the operation of a device. 2. Synonymous with *read*.

sense switch A *switch*[1] on an *operator's console*, which can set a *switch*[3] in a *program*, thus allowing the operator to determine which *branch* is selected in a program with alternative paths.

sensing station The position within a *punched card* machine at which a card is read, e.g. by means of sensing brushes.

sentinel A *character* which is used to indicate the occurrence of a specified condition, e.g. the physical end of a *magnetic tape*, or the end of a *variable length record* in *store*.

separator A *character* used to separate logical units of data, e.g. *fields, records*.
Also known as data delimiter.

sequence 1. To place a set of items into some defined order of the *keys* used to identify the items, e.g. to place a set of names into alphabetic sequence. Also known as order [2]. 2. Any set of items or instructions which have been placed in a defined order.

sequence check A check designed to ensure that an ordered set of items is in the expected *sequence* of *keys*.

sequence checking routine A routine which checks that a set of items expected to be in a defined *sequence* is in fact in the correct order.

sequence control register A *register* whose contents determine the next *instruction* to be performed.

sequence error An error detected by a *sequence checking routine*, i.e. an error arising because the arrangement of items in a set does not conform to some defined order.

sequence register Synonymous with *sequence control register*.

sequential access storage A *storage device* in which data can only be *accessed* in the sequence in which it is stored in the device, i.e. an item can only be processed after all the preceding items have been accessed. An example of sequential access storage is *magnetic tape*. ◊ *sequential processing*.

sequential control A method of computer operation in which *instructions* are stored in the order in which they are executed.

sequential processing Processing *records* in a data *file* according to some predetermined sequence of *keys*. This is contrasted with *serial processing* in which each record is processed in the order in which it is stored in a given *storage device*. The two expressions become synonymous when used for *magnetic tape* processing, in which records are held both in sequence and in series on the tape, but on *direct access* devices *sequential* and *serial* processing are distinct techniques : records processed serially may not be in a given sequence and in sequential work only selected records need be examined. ◊ *selective sequential*.

sequential-stacked job control A control system which ensures that jobs are performed in the sequence in which they are presented to the system.

serial To deal with items of information or *instructions* in sequence; contrasted with *parallel*.

serial access *Access* to *records* in a data file in the order in which they occur in a given storage device. ◊ *serial processing*.

serial feeding A method of feeding *punched cards* in which a card enters the *card track* with (for 80-column cards) column 1 or 80 leading. Contrasted with *sideways feed*.

serial processing Processing *records* in a data file in the order in which they occur in a given *storage device*. This is contrasted with *sequential processing* in which records are processed according to some predetermined sequence of *keys*. The two expressions become synonymous when used for *magnetic tape* processing in which records are held both in sequence and in series on the tape. However on *direct access* devices *sequential* and *serial* processing refer to distinct techniques.

serial transfer Transfer of data in which each unit of data being transferred travels in sequence. Contrasted with *parallel transfer*. It should be noted that serial and parallel transfers can occur together, e.g. a series of *words* may be transferred serially, although each *bit* within the word is transferred in parallel.

serviceability The reliability of equipment, based on some objective criterion. Various criteria for assessing serviceability are adopted, ◊ *serviceability ratio, utilization ratio, operating ratio*.

serviceability ratio The *ratio of serviceable* time to the sum of *serviceable time* and *down time*.

serviceable time The total time during which a machine is in a state where it can operate normally, including time when the machine is idle, but not time when it is unattended.

service bits *Bits* which are used in *data transmission* to convey signals monitoring the transmission itself (e.g. requesting repetition) rather than conveying information. Associated with *check bit*.

service programs Synonymous with *service routines*.

service routines *Routines* whose purpose is to perform all functions associated with the maintenance and operation of a computer and the preparation and correction of *programs*. Service routines are normally *general purpose programs*, and include *executive* routines, *compilers, generators* and *assemblers, debugging routines, diagnostic routines* for *hardware* checking, and general *input/output* routines.
Also known as utility routines, service programs, utility programs. ◊ general article on *Utility Programs*.

servo Synonymous with *servo-mechanism*.

servo-mechanism A powered device used to control operations which is activated by a difference in the actual and desired values of the quantity under control and acts so as to minimize the difference.

set 1. To place a desired value into a storage *location*. 2. To give a *bit* the value one. 3. A collection of items having some common property.

set pulse A pulse which has the property of *setting* a *bit*.

365

set up To prepare equipment for operation, e.g. to place paper in a *printer*, cards in a *card reader*, etc.

set up time Time taken during the running of a job in *set up* procedures.

several-for-one The association of several *machine language instructions* with a single *source language statement*.

shared files system A system in which more than one computer is able to *access* information stored on one *direct access storage device*.

shift To move the elements of a unit of information (*bits, digits, characters*) to the left or right. ⬦ *arithmetical shift, logical shift*.

shift, arithmetic ⬦ *arithmetical shift*.

shifting register Synonymous with *shift register*.

shift, non arithmetic ⬦ *non arithmetic shift*.

shift register A *register* in which the data stored can be subjected to a right or left *shift*.
Also known as shifting register.

shift, ring Synonymous with *circular shift*.

sideways feed A method of feeding *punched cards* in which a card is placed in the *hopper* in such a way that it enters the *card track* with one of its long edges leading. Contrasted with *serial feeding*.

sight check Checking that holes punched in two or more *punched cards* are identical by holding the cards together and looking through the pattern of holes.

sign An arithmetical symbol which distinguishes positive from negative quantities.

signal conditioning Modifying a signal so as to make it comprehensible to a particular device.

signal distance The number of corresponding *bit positions* which differ in two *binary words* of the same length, e.g. the signal distance between the two following 6-bit words is 3.

$$100101$$
$$001100$$

⬦ *Hamming distance* and *Hamming code*. The *exclusive-or operation* performed between two words will result in a word which corresponds to the signal distance. For this reason the operation is sometimes known as the *distance* operation.

signalling rate The rate at which signals are transmitted in a communications system; measured, for example, in *bits* per second.

signal normalization Synonymous with *signal standardization*.

signal, nought output ⬦ *nought output signal*.

signal, one output ◊ *one output signal.*

signal regeneration Restoring a signal to its original specification; a form of *signal standardization.*

Also known as signal reshaping.

signal reshaping Synonymous with *signal regeneration.*

signal standardization Using one signal to generate another which usually conforms to more stringent conditions.

Also known as signal normalization, standardization.

sign bit A *sign digit* composed of a single *bit.*

sign check indicator An *indicator* which can be set when the result of an arithmetic operation either changes sign, or is either positive or negative. Appropriate action can be taken according to the state of the indicator, thus providing a check on the sign when arithmetic calculations are performed.

sign-changing amplifier ◊ *sign-reversing amplifier.*

sign digit A *character*, normally at the end of a value *field* or *word*, used to indicate the algebraic sign of the value. For example, it is a convention to represent negative *binary* numbers as *true complements* of the corresponding positive numbers, thus, the left-hand character of the binary word indicates a positive value if set to 0 but a negative value if set to 1.

signed field A *field* containing a number which incorporates a *sign digit* indicating the *sign* of the number.

significance In *positional notation* the significance of a particular *digit position* in a number is the contribution to the total of a digit with the value 1 in that position; e.g. the significance of the italicized digit position in the following decimal number is 100: 1*4*59.

significant digits Those *digits* or *digit positions* in a number whose values are known and are relevant to the precision of the number, e.g. the number 123·4 has four significant digits, whereas the number 123 has three significant digits and the number 123,000, when known to be correct to the nearest thousand, also has three significant digits.

Also known as significant figures.

significant figures Synonymous with *significant digits.*

sign position The position in a number in which the *sign digit* or symbol is placed.

sign-reversing amplifier Pertaining to a device in which the output voltage has the same magnitude as the input voltage but is of opposite sign.

Also known as sign-changing amplifier, inverting amplifier.

simplex A communications system which allows transmission in one direction only. Compare with *duplex* and *half-duplex*.

simplex channel A communications *channel* which allows data to be transmitted in one direction only.

simulation The mathematical representation of problems allowing physical situations to be represented mathematically as a means of solving the problems created by the factors of the physical processes.

simulator A system, either *hardware* or *software*, designed to perform the *simulation* of some real process.

simulator routine An *interpretive routine* designed to enable *programs* written for one computer to run on a different computer.

simultaneity A feature by which certain *operations* in a *program* can be performed concurrently with others. This term is usually applied where separate *hardware* features are available to perform the separate tasks, but is sometimes, perhaps unwisely, used as a synonym for *timesharing* or *multiprogramming*.

simultaneous ◊ *simultaneity*.

simultaneous access Placing data into *store*, or retrieving data from store, by means of *parallel transfer* of all elements of the unit of data.

Also known as parallel access.

simultaneous computer A computer which contains a unit giving it *simultaneity* of operation.

Also known as parallel computer.

single address code Synonymous with *single address instruction*.

single address instruction An *instruction format* which contains only one *operand* address.

Also known as single address code.

single column pence coding A *punched card* code which enables the values 0 to 11 to be represented by a punching in a single *card column*.

single-ended amplifier An amplifier which develops only one output signal. Contrasted with a *double-ended amplifier*. ◊ *push-pull amplifier*.

single length The representation of numbers in *binary* form in such a way that the values of the numbers can be contained in a single *word*.

single shot circuit *Circuits* or *logic elements* arranged to perform *signal standardization* in order to convert an imprecise input *signal* into one which conforms to the requirements of a particular machine.

Also known as one shot circuit.

single shot operation Synonymous with *single step operation*.

single step operation A method of operating a computer in which the *instructions* in a *program* are performed one at a time in response to an engineer's or operator's intervention. Single step operation is usually performed during *debugging*.

Also known as step-by-step operation, single shot operation, one shot operation.

sizing Sizing is concerned with the evaluation of the resources and facilities needed to perform a data processing task, to achieve a specified service at a cost commensurate with the user's requirements. The service itself will require a number of aspects to be considered. For example, the work load required by the user's system may entail a given *throughput* of *transactions* in a specific time; the system may have to handle peaks of transactions at critical times; individual users of the system may require specific *response times* to be met. There can also be a requirement for *resilience* in the system and an overall *serviceability* requirement to be met. The user's functional needs must also be understood so that the complexity of the processing can be assessed.

A study of these aspects enables a statement of the end-user's work load to be formulated, against which the sizing exercise will determine the resources needed both to develop and run the required system operationally. The end result of a sizing study would normally include: a statement of the work load and its future growth; a statement of the *hardware resources* needed both initially and to cope with future growth; an outline description of the *software* resources needed (both existing software and bespoke software which needs to be developed); a statement of manpower resources needed to develop and maintain the system; a statement of expected throughput and resource levels; the spare capacity within the system; and the planned system *up time*.

A sizing study may be initiated in a number of situations; e.g. when a company issues a tender to purchase a new computer it is to be expected that the manufacturer's staff will size the project before submitting responses to the tender; a data processing department should size every major development which it undertakes; sizing techniques can also be used to review the operational efficiency of an installation or of a specific application.

The methodology used in a sizing study will depend on the degree of precision required, and on the availability of information and time to complete the study. In principle a sizing study

369

requires information in two basic categories – product information
and work load information.

With product information we are concerned with the performance ratings of hardware devices and the performance of existing
or planned software used by the system. Software performance entails measuring or evaluating *instruction* path lengths and calculating the performance to be expected in executing specific functions
on specified hardware.

Compiling work load information entails collecting up-to-date
data about the end-user's requirement, and this may be based
partially upon an assessment of his existing procedures and workload and upon future developments planned. Sometimes programs
have to be written to collect and analyse data from existing systems. In designing future systems one should also consider developing special routines known as instrumentation to collect data in an
organized way for future sizing activity.

The sizing technique used will be dependent on the quality of
the information available and the resources and time available to
carry out the exercise. A sizing exercise may embody the use of
analytical methods applied in the construction of hand-worked
models, or it may involve the use of parameter driven *simulation
models*. It is important not to use techniques which cannot be
supported by the quality of data, and it is also important to use
methods which allow for iteration easily and inexpensively to permit variations in work load and resources to be evaluated. It is
also important to be able to check results using a different
method.

The most common area for sizing activity is in the evaluation of
hardware and software configurations needed to perform a given
task or set of tasks. This is often done at a time when the full extent
of the ultimate system is not known. Thus it is important to continue to use sizing concepts throughout the development of projects from the time of their inception through to efficient and
effective live running. A study conducted after completion of a
systems definition will be based on better information than one
based upon an outline design or a functional specification. The
performance aspects of a system can obviously be better predicted
and controlled when detailed *program specifications* have been produced.

The sizing of a project will go through a change of emphasis as
the project develops. The initial sizing is done to match the work
load and the resources/facilities which are to be budgeted for the

project. At this stage, usually based upon a functional specification, a number of trade-offs can be made according to the findings of the sizing study; e.g. reducing systems functions in favour of performance or lower cost, increasing hardware in favour of improved system resilience or increased capacity for future growth. Obviously as one approaches the later stages of a project subsequent sizing activity provides a basis for tuning the design of the system to provide the performance and facilities originally planned.

There are a number of problems which can arise in sizing studies and, therefore, all projects must be managed with the principles, concept, and limitations of sizing in mind. Some of the problems are summarized below.

The requirements of a system are often changed by users during the development of a project. These are likely to invalidate initial sizing and imply the need for continual sizing studies throughout the project. There is also a tendency in project development to aim at achieving the timescales and facilities needed at the expense of software efficiency, thus resulting in dilution of original performance objectives. This must be monitored and performance targets and budgets maintained by reappraisal of sizing assumptions at key stages. The organizational environment may change during project development, thus presenting a different balance in the workload to that initially evaluated. Assumptions about the performance of hardware or software products may not be realized in practice, and this can affect the performance of the system in a major way.

The output from a sizing exercise is able to provide information permitting changes in the design and giving management the opportunity to exercise trade-offs in the best interest of the project and the organization. It is important, therefore, to budget for on-going sizing activity in a project, and to create within the data processing organization a responsibility for promoting and developing sizing disciplines. The objective of sizing is to provide a basis of decision for making trade-offs which balance the level of service, the facilities and their cost within a particular computing project or installation.

skeletal code An incomplete set of *instructions* forming part of a *general routine* and completed by means of *parameters*.

skip 1. A computer *instruction* in which no operation is performed other than a jump to the next instruction in sequence. 2. A device, on a *card punch*, enabling *columns* on a *punched card* on which no punching is required to travel rapidly under the *punch knives*.

skip-sequential access A method of *file access* in which each successive access requires a *record* with a *key* higher than that of the previous access.

slave store A *store* which compensates for the different speeds of operation of storage units which must interact. For example, a fast *pipeline* can be slowed because it is dependent upon access to a relatively slower *main store*. In such a case *instructions* and *operands* required by the pipeline will be transferred via a slave store which is designed to drive the pipeline at high speed.

slow time scale A *time scale* which is greater than the unit of time in the physical system being studied.

Also known as extended time scale. ⟡ *analog computer*.

smudge In *optical character recognition*, ink which appears outside the limits of the shape of the printed character.

snapshot dump A *dump* of selected parts of *store* which can occur at various points during the running of a *program*, usually for *debugging* purposes.

socket A device which terminates the permanent part of a circuit, into which a *plug* can be inserted to complete the circuit.

Also known as hub [2] (*punched card* machines) and jack (telecommunications).

soft dump Synonymous with *register dump*. ⟡ *dump*.

software In its most general form, software is a term used in contrast to *hardware* to refer to all *programs* which can be used on a particular computer system. More specifically, the term is applied to all those programs which in some way can assist all users of a particular type of computer to make the best use of their machine, as distinct from the specific programs written to solve the problems of any particular user. In this case, software is usually produced by the computer manufacturer, and indeed the importance of software is such that investment in its production is a major item in the development and marketing of computers. By intelligent use of available software the user of a computer can considerably reduce the effort that is required in devising a system and writing the programs required to implement it.

Software comes in all shapes and sizes; this article gives a brief description of the various types of software, from the simplest to the most complex. More information can be obtained by consulting the various main entries.

Subroutines are the smallest items of software normally provided by a manufacturer. These are usually routines devised to perform large numbers of routine calculations, for example, tax calculations, multiplication and division (if these functions cannot be performed by hardware), editing of data for input and output (e.g. inserting cheque protection symbols when printing sterling values). Subroutines to perform input and output operations also form part of this category of software: these are also called *packages* or *housekeeping routines.* Large numbers of these routines are supplied by manufacturers and they usually form part of a software *library* held on some form of *backing store.* Subroutines of this sort are not independent programs but will be incorporated by a user in his own programs when required.

Assemblers and *compilers* are programs used to convert programs written in a symbolic *language* into the machine code required by the computer.

Executive programs and *operating systems* are programs which are held permanently in store and are used to control the operations of other programs, particularly in *multiprogramming* systems.

Generators are programs which are similar in action to compilers and assemblers but only *object programs* of a particular type can be produced from them.

Utility programs are programs devised to perform some of the basic data handling operations, such as file conversion (e.g. transcribing a *punched card* file to *magnetic tape) sorting,* controlling the location of data in a *direct access* file. Utility programs are generally devised for each type of *peripheral unit.*

Debugging routines include programs for producing *printouts* of *memory* at various stages of a program, and also various forms of analysis of the progress of a program. Such programs are known as *trace* or *monitor* routines.

File processing programs are programs devised for performing operations on data *files,* such as editing, validation, comparing and *updating.*

The types of software so far described involve routines designed either to form part of a user's program or to assist generally in the utilization of a computer and associated peripheral devices. A further extension of the concept of software is the application package. This involves a set of programs designed to perform the routines associated with a particular example of a broad general system. Examples are payroll packages, *P E R T* packages, packages for the solution of transportation problems, *inventory management, production control,* etc. The user wishing to use a package of this type defines his own requirements by means of *parameters* which are employed by the programs in the system to produce the specific results required.

solid state computer   A computer constructed mainly from *solid state devices*.

solid state device   A device whose operation depends on the electronic properties of solid materials, e.g. *transistors, ferrite cores*.

sonic delay line   Synonymous with *acoustic delay line*.

sort   To arrange items of information into groups according to the identifying *keys* of each item. The items will be sequenced if the arrangement of the keys follows some predetermined order. ⟡ general article on *Sorting*.

sorter   A *punched card* machine which feeds cards into several *pockets* according to the punchings present in specified *card columns*.

sort generator   A *generator* in which the *object program* is designed to *sort* a set of items into a given sequence defined by the *parameters* specified to the generator.

sorting   Usually data which is to be processed requires to be ordered and presented in a predetermined *sequence*. The need for sorting arises after the data has been transcribed onto a computer *input medium*, e.g. *punched cards, magnetic tape*. The sorting of data after transcription may take place externally from the computer (*off-line* sorting) or internally on the computer (*on-line* sorting). Off-line sorting can be used only on data which is on a medium enabling each item of data to be handled separately, e.g. punched cards and documents printed with characters which can be read by some form of *character recognition* device.

All forms of sorting depend on the sequencing of items of data according to some ordering of a *key*. For example, in a telephone directory names are sorted in alphabetical order, the key being the subscriber's surname. An alternative sequence of the names in a directory is that of the street directory. In this case the key is the street and number of the house. If the streets are listed in alphabetical order and the occupiers in each street in the numerical order of their house number, we can say that two keys are being used: street name and house number. The items are listed in number within street sequence.

Off-line sorting is done by means of mechanical devices known as *sorters*. Basically these devices can sense the value of a particular *column* in a card or *mark* in a character recognition *field* and cause all items having the same value to be placed together in the same batch or *stacker*. In all off-line sorting the time taken to sequence a file of data depends largely on the size of the keys, since a separate pass through the machine is required for each digit in the key.

In on-line sorting, the principle of sequencing by means of an ordering of keys remains. Normally the record is handled together with its key although in some forms of sorting time is saved by removing the record from the key and sorting only the keys. The most common form of on-line sorting is *magnetic tape* sorting. Methods of tape sorting are variants of a method known as *merge* sorting. The merge sorting method is made up of two logical phases:

(i) A *string generation* phase in which data records are read from the unsorted input file, formed into groups which are in sequence, and written as ordered groups or *strings* onto other tapes.

(ii) A *string merging phase* in which one or more strings are merged or combined to form longer strings.

A phase of a sort is known as a *pass*. The maximum number of strings that may be merged together in one pass to form a single string is called the *way* of the sort. The various different methods of tape sorting, e.g. 'classical sorting', 'polyphase sorting', 'oscillating sorting', 'cascade sorting', differ in the techniques used in distributing the initial strings between the available magnetic *tape decks*. The particular sorting technique used for any application will depend on three main factors: the number and type of tape decks available, the amount of *storage* available for holding the data to be sorted and the time available for the sorting operation. It should be mentioned here that in contrast to off-line sorting, the size of the key in magnetic tape sorting does not have a significant effect on the overall sort time.

Most manufacturers supply *software* for performing sorts. This software consists of *sort routines* which operate on *parameters* supplied to the program at *run time*, specifying the keys, size of records, tape decks available, etc., and also *sort generators*, which are used to create specific sort programs for subsequent use.

Internal storage sorting is another method of sorting which does not require magnetic tape. In this method all records being sorted are present together in internal storage. The two basic techniques are 'exchange sorting' and 'extraction sorting'. An exchanging sort entails the sorting of complete records within the original data storage area, based on the comparison of the record keys and the movement of the records according to the result of the comparison. Different methods of comparing records may be adopted. One of the methods commonly used is the *dichotomizing search* or *binary chop*, in which the first key is compared with one half way through the group of data, then the second two keys of each half are compared, and so on until all the data has been covered. Further passes through the data are made, each time the distance between keys being compared being halved until finally each key is compared with the next. One of the most time-consuming features of an exchange sort is the transfer of complete records after a comparison. An extraction sort overcomes this difficulty by associating each key with the *address* of the record in store, then transferring the keys and associated addresses to another part of store in which they are sorted. After the sort is completed the associated addresses can be used to sequence the original records.

Sorting on other *storage devices* may make use of the same techniques as tape sorting, or internal sorting, depending on whether the storage device is used as a *backing store* or as a store of the same level as internal storage.

sorting needle A needle used to probe a *pack* of *punched cards* in order to establish that a particular punching is common to all cards in the pack.

sorting routine A *routine* which will arrange items of data into sequence according to the values contained within specified *fields* (*key words*) of the individual *records*. Various types of sorting routine are described in the general article on *Sorting*.

sorting routine generator Synonymous with *sort generator*.

source code ◊ *source language*.

source computer A computer which performs the *compilation* of a *source program*, contrasted with an *object computer*, which is the computer on which the *object program* will be run.

source document An original document from which data is prepared in a form acceptable to a computer.

source language A programming *language* which cannot be directly processed by the *hardware* of a computer but requires *compilation* into an *object program* consisting of *instructions* in a *machine language* which can be directly understood by the computer. Examples of such languages are *C O B O L, A L G O L, F O R T-R A N, PL/1.*

source machine Synonymous with *source computer*.

source module A unit of *source code* that can be *compiled* as a single unit.

source program A program written in a *source language*.

space character Synonymous with *blank*.

space suppression Inhibiting the normal movement of paper in a *printer* after a line of *characters* has been printed.

span The difference between the highest and lowest values in the *range* of values which a quantity can have.

spanned record A group of one or more *record sections* which together constitute a record but which span consecutive *blocks*.

special characters *Characters* in a *character set* which are neither letters nor numerals, e.g. !, ", /, @, £, etc.
Also known as additional characters, *symbols*.

special purpose computer A computer designed to solve problems of a restricted type. Contrasted with *general purpose computer*.

specific address Synonymous with *absolute address*.

specification A precise and detailed statement of requirements. The requirements may refer to the system being developed (◊ *system definition*), to a program (◊ *program specification*) or to the equipment required to operate a system.

specific code Synonymous with *absolute code*.

specific coding Synonymous with *absolute coding*.

specific program A *program* written in *absolute code*.

splicer A hand-operated device used to join together two pieces of *paper tape* in such a way that they can be satisfactorily *read* by a *paper tape reader*.

split-word operations *Operations* which can process part of a *word*, as distinct from the whole word, which is the normal unit of data on which operations are performed. ◊ *single-length* working, *double-precision arithmetic*.

spool Properly, the mounting for a roll of *paper tape*, but also used to describe a coiled length of paper tape. Also known as *reel*[1], roll.

spooling A method of achieving effective use of *hardware* during *input/output* operations by decoupling slow devices from the main process which requires the input/output.

spot carbon Carbon paper which is treated on selected parts of its surface only, so that only the required part of the printing is reproduced.

spot punch A punch, operated directly by hand, capable of making single holes in a *punched card* or *paper tape*.
Also known as unipunch.

sprocket holes 1. Holes punched in *paper tape* whose function is to drive the tape, or more usually to generate a signal used for indexing or timing the tape. Contrasted with *code holes*. Also known as *feed holes*. 2. Holes at the edges of *continuous stationery*, used by a *printer* to drive the stationery.

377

sprocket pulse In a *paper tape reader*, the pulse or signal generated by the reading of the *sprocket holes* on paper tape.

squeezeout In *optical character recognition*, printing in which the ink has gone to the edges of a character, making them appear darker than the centre of the character. ⟡ *smudge*.

stability In *optical character recognition*, the ability of inks to keep their colour when exposed to light or heat.

stable trigger circuit Synonymous with *toggle*.

stack An area of *store* reserved for the temporary storage of data, usually on *input* or before *output*. ⟡ *buffer*.

stacker A receptacle for holding *punched cards* after they have passed through a machine. Contrasted with *hopper*.

stacker, card ⟡ *stacker*.

standard costing Efficiency and profitability can be increased by the use of a system in which standards are set for performance and cost per unit: the actual results are compared with standards and the extent and reasons for variances are reported.

The system embraces many other techniques such as work measurement, methods study and *budgetary control*, and expresses the results in terms of performance and cost.

The steps in setting up a standard costing system are: (i) The standard unit of output is established. For example, a refrigerator factory might use a unit of a refrigerator, a brick works one ton of bricks or a haulier one ton-mile. (ii) The standard volume of output is established. Normally this will be slightly below the theoretical maximum capacity so as to allow for shortfalls. (iii) Costs of each department have to be assessed so as to arrive at the standard cost per unit at the standard volume of output. The standard cost per unit is made up of: direct materials; direct labour; indirect costs (overheads). (iv) The costs of those departments (cost centres) which only contribute indirectly to the output are divided over the direct cost centres. For example, part of the costs of a factory maintenance department (indirect) would be allocated to the metal cutting department (direct). The allocation is treated as an overhead on the direct cost centres. (v) The direct cost per unit is assessed by work measurement and methods study. Standard amounts of labour time and material content for each unit are set and the indirect overheads added to obtain the standard cost per unit. (vi) Some of the indirect costs vary with the volume of output and some are fixed. Costs have to be analysed into fixed and variable to establish what variances are due to the volume of output deviating from standard. (vii) Actual costs are recorded in the same way as the standards, and variances are calculated and the reasons for them identified. Because of the analysis done in setting the standards and recording the actuals, comprehensive information can be produced about the causes of variances. For example. it may be due to the volume of output, labour efficiency, materials wastage, price or labour rate changes. (viii) Standards need to be kept under constant review but should only be amended if there is permanent change. It will be seen that the advantages of standard costing in management control are: (*a*) work methods can be improved; (*b*) costs are reduced; (*c*) performance is judged; (*d*) variances are identified; (*e*) a basis for selling prices is provided.

standard form *Floating point representation* in which the *fixed point part* lies within a standard range of values chosen so that any given number can be represented by only one pair of numbers.

standard interface A *hardware* system providing standard logic circuits and *input/output channels* for the connexion of *peripheral units* to a *central processor*. Each peripheral is coupled to the processor via a standard multiway connector plug which carries all wiring for the necessary control signals and data flowing between the processor and the peripheral unit. In this way a standard processor can be fitted with any number and type of peripherals according to the number of channels provided on the processor itself, thus allowing for the later expansion of the system with minimal alteration of the *hardware*.

standardization 1. The process of replacing the *floating point representation* of a number by its *normalized* form. 2. A synonym for *signal standardization*.

standardize To replace the *floating point representation* of a number by its *normalized* form.

standards ◊ general article on *Data Processing Standards*.

standard subroutine A *subroutine*, designed to perform a function having application in more than one *program*, which can be incorporated into different programs as required. Standard subroutines are usually supplied by computer manufacturers and may be present on a *library tape*.

standing-on-nines carry Synonymous with *high-speed carry*.

start-stop time Synonymous with *acceleration time* and *deceleration time*.

statement A *source language instruction*. Also used for any expression which can be input to a *compiler*, including *narrative* statements and *directives* controlling the operation of the compilation. Statements usually result in several *machine code* instructions when compiled.

statement number A serial number given to each *statement* in a *program* written in a *source language*.

state, one Synonymous with *one condition*.

static dump A *dump* performed when a program reaches an *end of run* condition or some other recognizable stage within the *run*.

staticizer A *logic element* which converts information from a sequence of signals arriving one after the other in time to a corresponding representation of the information held permanently in *store*. Contrasted with *dynamicizer*.

static magnetic cell Synonymous with *magnetic cell*.

static store 1. A *store* in which each *location* has a fixed space, and access to information does not depend on the location being available at a specific time. Contrasted with a *cyclic store*. 2. A *store* which has no moving parts.

static subroutine A *subroutine* which always performs the same operation, i.e. which does not require *parameters* in order to alter its functioning. Contrasted with *dynamic subroutine*.

stationery Stationery is used in computer systems to record results produced on a *printer* or *typewriter*. Most printers make use of continuous forms, driven through the printer by means of sprocket holes at each edge. Pages are separated from each other by perforations. Form designs may be preprinted on each page, the computer supplying the variable information, e.g. invoice details. Multi-part sets of stationery enable several copies to be printed of each page, either by means of interleaved carbon paper or specially treated chemical surfaces. Computer stationery can be obtained in a variety of different form widths and depths, the maximum size depending on the capacity of the printer being used. Multi-part sets can be divided by means of a *decollator*, and individual pages separated from each other with a *burster*.

Stationery used on typewriters is usually in the form of a continuous roll of paper without separate page perforations.

status word A *word* which contains information about the condition of a *peripheral unit*. This information includes, for example, warning information when a peripheral needs attention (e.g. when the *paper low condition* is present on a *printer*) and is entered into the status word automatically by hardware.

step Synonymous with *instruction*.

step-by-step operation Synonymous with *single step operation*.

step change A change from one value to another as a single increment taking negligible time.

step counter A *counter* used to keep count of the steps in those *instructions* such as division and multiplication which involve a succession of separate operations.

stock control Synonymous with *Inventory Control*.

stop code Synonymous with *halt instruction*.

stop instruction Synonymous with *halt instruction*.

stop instruction, conditional ⟡ *conditional stop instruction*.

stop instruction, optional ⟡ *optional stop instruction*.

stop time Synonymous with *deceleration time*.

storage Synonymous with *store*.

storage allocation The process of allocating specific areas of *store* to specific types of *data*. Storage allocation is one of the functions which must be carried out during preparation of a *program*, and one of the operations performed by a *compiler* is to specify the areas allocated to the various types of data. But ⟡ *dynamic allocation (of memory)*.

storage allocation, dynamic ⟡ *dynamic allocation (of memory)*.

storage block Any area of *store*, usually set aside for some particular purpose, e.g. *input area, work area*.

storage, buffer ⟡ *buffer store*.

storage capacity The amount of information which can be held in *store*, usually expressed as the number of units of data (*words, characters*) which can be retained.

storage cell 1. The smallest physical element of a *store*, e.g. in a *core storage*, a single core. 2. That part of a store which can contain a single unit of data, e.g. a *bit* or *character*.

storage compacting A practice adopted on *multiprogramming* computers, in which *memory locations* are assigned to *programs* so that the largest possible area of contiguous locations remains available for any other programs that are to be run. Thus, when one program is finished the memory areas may be automatically reallocated. ⟡ *dynamic allocation (of memory)*.

storage, content-addressed ⟡ *associative store*.

storage cycle In a *cyclic store*, the interval between the times when any given *location* can be *accessed*.

storage density The number of units of data which can be stored per unit length or area of the storage medium, e.g. the number of *bits* per inch which can be stored in *magnetic tape*.

storage devices A modern *digital computer* consists of a number of storage devices which are used to store both *data* and *program instructions*. This storage may be considered in two categories: *main memory* and *backing store*. There are within these categories a variety of memory systems some details of which are given below; first of all we shall discuss main memory systems.

A computer program consists of a large number of individual instructions which are executed one by one to operate on data. An individual instruction may require only a few microseconds to complete its function, and this operation time must include the time needed to transfer the instruction from memory to the *program controller* and to interpret and execute the instruction, including extracting the required *operands* from memory and storing away the result. Thus it can be seen that the memory must allow for the storage of a large number of instructions and operands, which must be available as required, at high speed. Reliable storage systems of this type are very expensive, and in the past it has been usual to build only the main memory to meet this requirement, utilizing various backing store devices to provide mass storage facilities. The commonest form of main memory is *magnetic core storage*; currently it is not unusual to have a computer with a main memory capacity of a million or more *bits*, but the earlier computers had a capacity of perhaps only 80,000 bits in their main memory. This increase in memory size has been made possible mainly by improved techniques for constructing magnetic core storage units, and also because magnetic cores, and the various electronic components used in association with them, have been miniaturized.

The physical size of components is a very important factor in memory design, because in miniaturized circuits signals have to travel over very short distances and this enables high signal speeds to be obtained. For example, in some of the earlier core memories a core could be *switched* in about twenty microseconds whereas switching speeds of less than one microsecond are now quite common.

The earliest computers used thermionic valves and capacitors in the construction of the main memory and *logic circuits*. Such systems were expensive to manufacture and maintain, and the physical size of the components placed severe restrictions on the storage capacity and speed available. Also the power consumption of such memory units was high, and they required comprehensive cooling facilities.

The use of core stores for memory circuits and the spectacular advances in the manufacture of transistors brought about a rapid change in the development of computer memories. Core store memories, for example, were faster, smaller and more reliable than the earlier vacuum tube devices, and although they were expensive to construct in the early 1950s, they soon became cheaper as more efficient methods for assembling and testing them were developed. A magnetic core memory consists of thousands of tiny magnetic rings threaded upon a matrix of small wires and arranged into groups so that each group represents a unit of data, e.g. a *word* or a *character*. The wires themselves represent paths along which signals can be transmitted to energize individual cores so that they adopt a particular polarity. Each core represents a *binary digit* and the polarity of the core at any particular instant determines the value of the digit (i.e. 0 or 1). Magnetic cores are very small in size ranging from one twelfth down to one fiftieth of an inch in diameter, which makes it possible to construct large memories containing more than one million individual bits. The speed of the earlier magnetic core systems was such that two numbers of say ten decimal digits each could be added together in less than twenty microseconds, while in more recent times basic functions such as addition and subtraction can be executed in less than one microsecond.

The particular characteristics that make magnetic cores suitable for use as main memory can be summarized as follows: (i) *Access* to any word in the memory system is by a direct *addressing* technique in which each memory location has a numbered address. The addresses are represented and selected by means of electronic impulses and no physical movement of the storage medium is required. (ii) Access time is very short (say one microsecond) and is constant for any item of data stored in the memory. (iii) Reliability is high. (iv) Power consumption is low. (v) The components are small and a comparatively small unit can provide a large storage capacity.

Another storage medium exhibiting similar characteristics is the *thin-film memory*. This particular system has, perhaps, not yet achieved the potential claimed for it in the early 1950s but nonetheless it is widely used today. Thin-film memories rely upon many thousands of discrete storage elements deposited upon the surface of thin film, which in turn is usually mounted upon wires, glass rods or a sheet of glass. Each element can be magnetized in one of two directions to represent the binary digits 0 and 1, and they can be switched in a few *nanoseconds*. It was originally forecast that very large capacity thin-film memories would serve the needs for mass information storage and would replace many of the backing storage devices currently in use, but this prediction has not yet been realized.

Integrated circuit memories probably provide greatest potential. In this technology logic circuits and memory devices can be etched on little chips of silicon less than one tenth of an inch in size. Such a

383

chip might for example contain more than 100 bits of information, and these devices can be manufactured and tested comparatively cheaply.

The systems described above are sometimes described as *immediate access stores*, but more properly may be described as random access memories, since it is possible for any unit of data to be available on demand at a guaranteed access time of very short duration. However the requirements of most modern digital computers are such that it is uneconomic to consider storing all data and program instructions in such a medium. Computers are instead designed to provide a certain volume of such storage, with backing storage facilities to hold say 200 million or more characters. At any moment in time the main memory is used to hold current data and instructions, and other data and program *segments* may be called in as *blocks* from backing store as required.

Backing storage usually consists of magnetic storage media such as *magnetic tape, magnetic drum, magnetic card* or *magnetic disk* storage. These are all in the general category known as dynamic storage, because the storage medium has to be physically moved past a magnetic *read/write head* to obtain access to storage areas.

Magnetic tape is a *serial* store: data is recorded as individual characters along a length of tape and processing can be achieved only by sorting records into sequence so that each can be examined in turn (◊ the general article on Magnetic Tape).

A magnetic drum is a *cyclic* store; the drum is revolved continuously and data stored upon *tracks* around the periphery of the drum is available at fixed points in the basic cycle time. For example, if each track has a single read/write head the average access time for any unit of data is one half the time required to complete one drum revolution. A magnetic drum might have a total capacity of more than 200,000 words and it is possible to connect several drums to a central processor. Operating at about 7,000 revolutions per second a high speed drum might provide an average access time of a few milliseconds and have a transfer rate as high as ten million bits per second. In certain respects magnetic drums have some of the qualities possessed by magnetic core main memories; data need not be arranged in strict sequence and an item of data can be read from the drum without reference to the record last read. Of course the access time for data stored upon a drum is much longer than for a core memory, but high speed magnetic drums, with their mass storage capability, are very suitable for use in direct access applications. Direct access devices, such as magnetic drums or disk stores, are a compromise to obtain, at an economic cost, certain of the qualities exhibited by magnetic core memories. In general the access time for any particular record is measured in milliseconds rather than microseconds and in many cases the access time is not entirely independent of the location last addressed. However, the maximum access time is sufficiently short to permit them to be considered as truly direct access devices. With these storage units programs can be organized to process data as it arises, and during such processing transactions can be applied to many *files* in the same *run* without the need to sort transactions into a specific sequence.

A typical magnetic disk store consists of a number of rotating disks each coated upon both surfaces with a magnetizable material. Information is written to, or read from, the disk by a series of arms, one for each disk surface. Each arm contains one, or several, read/ write heads, and the arms can be positioned above certain areas of the corresponding disks according to instructions received from the central processor. Each disk surface usually contains a number of recording tracks and these may be further subdivided into sections or bands; the instructions from the central processor can cause the recording arms to be positioned to read or write from specified tracks. As with magnetic tape, information is generally recorded as a series of six-bit characters each with an associated *parity bit*. A device of this type might hold say 140 million six-bit characters, and access time to any chosen bit might vary between 20 to 100 milliseconds.

Direct access (or random access) backing stores are often rather complex to program, and although they provide great advantages for *real time* processing applications, they must still be considered as being an intermediate development in the evolution of mass memory immediate access systems.

In time we may expect a further breakthrough in the design and manufacture of integrated circuit techniques, or of thin-film memories, and the dependence upon backing store media may then be a thing of the past. The ability to build extremely large capacity main memory systems will probably lead to a concentration of computing power within organizations so that large centralized *data banks* can be maintained. This will, in turn, emphasize the need for commensurate developments in the field of *data transmission*.

storage, direct access   ◊ *direct access storage.*
storage, disk   ◊ *magnetic disk.*

storage, drum ◊ *magnetic drum.*

storage dump Synonymous with *memory dump.*

storage, dynamic ◊ *dynamic store.*

storage, erasable ◊ *erasable storage.*

storage, internal ◊ *internal store.*

storage location Synonymous with *location.*

storage, magnetic ◊ *magnetic memory.*

storage, magnetic core ◊ *magnetic core storage.*

storage, magnetic disk ◊ *magnetic disk.*

storage, magnetic drum ◊ *magnetic drum.*

storage, magnetic film ◊ *thin-film memory.*

storage, magnetic tape ◊ *magnetic tape.*

storage, main ◊ *main memory.*

storage, mercury ◊ *mercury memory.*

storage, non-erasable ◊ *non-erasable store.*

storage, parallel search ◊ *associative store.*

storage register A *register* located in *store.* Contrasted with, for example, an *instruction register* which is located in the *program controller.*

storage, secondary Synonymous with *backing store.*

storage, Williams tube ◊ *Williams tube storage.*

store 1. Any device or medium which is capable of receiving information and retaining it over a period of time, and allows it to be retrieved and used when required. ◊ general article on *Storage Devices.* 2. To place information into a storage device.

store, cathode ray tube ◊ *cathode ray tube.*

store, core ◊ *core storage.*

store cycle time The minimum time required to retrieve an item of data from *store.*

stored program A *program* which is wholly contained in *store,* and which is capable of being altered in store.

stored program computer Any computer which functions wholly or mainly with *instructions* which are held in *store,* and which can themselves be altered and manipulated in the same way as other data. The term computer now almost universally refers to stored program computer.

stored routine Synonymous with *stored program.*

store dump ◊ *dump.*

store, erasable ◊ *erasable storage.*

store, magnetic ◊ *magnetic memory.*

store, magnetic disk ◊ *magnetic disk.*

store, magnetic drum ◊ *magnetic drum.*

386

store, magnetic film   ◇ *thin-film memory.*
store, magnetic tape   ◇ *magnetic tape.*
store, magnetic wire   ◇ *magnetic wire store.*
store, non-volatile   ◇ *non-volatile memory.*
store, random access   ◇ *random access storage* and *direct access.*
store, secondary   Synonymous with *backing store.*
store, volatile   Synonymous with *volatile memory.*
store, Williams tube   ◇ *Williams tube storage.*
straight line coding   Avoiding the use of *loops* during the *coding* of a program by repeating a set of *instructions* instead of *branching* repeatedly to the same set. The purpose of straight line coding is to improve the speed of execution of the program, since the use of a loop is usually slower because of *instruction modification.* ◈ general article on *Programming.*
stream   A data *route* from a *resource* to a *controller.*
string   1. Any set of items which has been arranged into a *sequence* according to some specific order of *keys.* 2. Any set of consecutive *characters* or *digits* present in *store.*
string break   In *sorting,* a string break occurs when there are no more *records* with *keys* higher than the highest key so far written to the current output *string* [1].
string length   In *sorting,* the number of *records* in a *string* [1].
string manipulation   The process of manipulating *strings* [2] of *characters* in *store,* treating them as single units of data.
stunt box   Part of a teleprinter which decodes signals used to control the operation of the machine, as contrasted with the information to be printed.
style   In *optical character recognition,* the distinctive proportions of the characters which remain constant whatever the size of the character.
stylus input device   Synonymous with *light pen.*
stylus, light pen   ◇ *light pen.*
stylus printer   A *printer* in which each character takes the form of a pattern of dots produced by a stylus or number of styluses moving over the surface of the paper.
subprogram   ◇ general article on *multiprogramming.*
subroutine   Part of a *program* which performs a logical section of the overall function of the program and which is available whenever the particular set of *instructions* is required. The instructions forming the subroutine do not need to be repeated every time they are required, but can be entered by means of a *branch* from the *main program.* Subroutines may be written for a specific program or they

may be written in a general form to perform operations common to several programs. ⇨ general articles on *Subroutines* and *Programming*.

subroutine library   Any collection of *subroutines* which have been written for general application and can be incorporated in different *programs* when required.

subroutines   Subroutines are self-contained sections of a *program* which can be incorporated into a complete program. A subroutine can be entered from any point in the main program and is usually so constructed that, when the subroutine has been obeyed, a return *branch* is automatically made to the instruction immediately following the branch into the subroutine. The actions performed by the subroutine may be modified by the use of *parameters*. Parameters may be specified in the main program by setting values into certain reserved *locations* or by setting up *dummy instructions* in the program area immediately following the branch to the subroutine. Also, the subroutine may be modified to return to an instruction other than the one immediately after the branch to the subroutine.

There are two main reasons for using subroutines:

(i) Certain routines are of a general nature and are common to many programs. For example, calculations of mathematical functions such as square roots, routines associated with the control of *input* and *output devices*. This type of subroutine is generally provided by the manufacturer as part of the *software* supplied with the computer.

(ii) Certain sections of a particular program may be required at several different points in the main program. Storage space can be saved by making these sections into subroutines, thus storing them only once instead of storing them separately each time they are required. Subroutines of this type are written by the programmer at the same time as the main program.

The object of a subroutine is thus:

(i) To make programming easier and quicker by incorporating pre-programmed and pre-tested subroutines, or

(ii) To save storage space by writing a section or program only once, and branching to it only when it is required in the main program.

Where a program is written using a programming *language*, a common feature of many *compilers* is the facility for incorporating subroutines of the first type into the *object program* by means of *source language statements*. The usual method is to incorporate all subroutines, whether supplied by the manufacturer or developed by the user, on some form of backing store, e.g. a *magnetic tape*. The compiler then extracts the required subroutine from this medium when required by the source program. A collection of subroutines of this type is known as a *library* and a magnetic tape holding subroutines will be known as a *library tape*. However the terms library and library tape are also used for collections of *general purpose programs* and other items of software.

subscriber station In *data transmission*, the connexion provided for linking an outside location to a central office, including the connecting circuit and some circuit termination equipment, and sometimes also associated *input/output* equipment.

subscript A notation used to identify individual members of a set of items, usually by means of a number added to the name of the set, e.g. the members of the set of items named 'Invoices' could be given subscripts 1, 2, 3, etc., being identified as 'Invoice $_1$', 'Invoice $_2$', 'Invoice $_3$' etc. ⟡ *array*.

subset 1. Any identifiable group of items which themselves belong to a larger grouping. 2. A contraction of the words *subscriber set*; synonymous with *modem*.

subtracter A device performing the function of subtraction using digital signals. It receives three inputs representing *minuend, subtrahend* and a *carry* digit, and provides two outputs representing the *difference* and a *carry*.

subtracter-adder ⟡ *adder-subtracter*.

subtraction An arithmetic operation in which one operand – the *subtrahend* – is subtracted from another – the *minuend* – to form the *difference*.

subtrahend In *subtraction*, the subtrahend is subtracted from the *minuend* to give the *difference*.

suite (of programs) A number of interrelated *programs* run one after the other as an operational job.

sum In *addition*, the *addend* and the *augend* are added to obtain the sum.

sumcheck To carry out a check using *checksums*.

sum-check digit A *check digit* produced by a *summation check*.

summary A *report* which omits details from each *record* processed but provides information derived from such details.

summary card A *punched card* containing totals and descriptive data resulting from an associated group of detail cards.

summary punch A *card punch*, directly under the control of a *tabulator*, used for punching *summary cards* from data processed by the tabulator.

summary punching Punching *summary* information from a *report* prepared by a *tabulator* or other machine onto *punched cards*, which can then be processed at a later time, either as additional data or as totals carried forward from one run to another.

summation check A *check* performed on a group of *digits* which consists of adding up all the digits in the set and comparing the result with a previously computed total. If *overflow* is ignored on performing the summation, so that the result is always a single digit, this digit can be used as a *check digit,* and is then known as a *sum-check digit.*

sum, modulo 2 ◊ *modulo 2 sum.*

supervising system ◊ *executive program.*

supervisor ◊ *supervisory program.*

supervisory control A *control system* in which information about the processes under control is provided at a central location but controlling action is taken by an operator.

supervisory program A master program permanently resident in the memory of a computer to control *time sharing, input/output* and *multiprogramming* functions. Usually considered as an integral part of the computer and often classified as being part of the *hardware* of the system. ◊ *executive program.*

supplementary maintenance Maintenance work which is not *routine maintenance* or *corrective maintenance,* usually undertaken in order to improve reliability of the equipment by minor modifications.

supplementary maintenance time Time spent on *supplementary maintenance.*

suppression Preventing the printing of certain selected *characters* when specified conditions occur. ◊ *zero suppression.*

switch 1. Any device for opening, closing or directing an electric circuit. 2. To alter the state of a *bit* from 1 to 0 or 0 to 1. 3. In *programming,* a *branch instruction* which selects one of a number of alternative paths; the particular path chosen is determined by the setting of the switch, i.e. by the *modification* of the branch instruction or by giving a specified value, either manually or by *program,* to a *location* which is tested by the instruction.

switched-message network A *data transmission* system in which data can be communicated between any users of the network. The *TELEX* system is an example of a switched-message network.

switching centre In *data transmission,* the location where incoming messages are directed to their correct destinations. Switching may be automatic, in which case the routing is done without operator intervention, or semi-automatic or manual, involving some degree of operator intervention. In a *torn-tape* switching centre, operators tear off *paper tape* arriving on a receiving *paper tape punch* and transfer the piece of tape to a transmitting *paper tape reader*.

switching, message ◊ *message switching system.*

symbol Any character, set of characters or figure conventionally or arbitrarily accepted as representing some quantity, process, instruction, data item or any other object, relationship or operation.

symbolic address The form an *address* takes in a *source language*, in which it can be represented by an arbitrary *label* chosen by the programmer. The address is translated into an *absolute address* when the program is *compiled*.

symbolic assembly-language listing A *printout*, which may be produced at the time a *source program* is *compiled*, which gives the *source language statements* together with the corresponding *machine coding* generated.

symbolic assembly system An automatic programming system embodying the use of an *assembly language* and an *assembly routine*.

symbolic code Synonymous with *symbolic instruction*.

symbolic coding Writing a program in a *source language*.

symbolic debugging A method of *debugging* in which certain *source language* statements can be *compiled* together with a *source program* containing known errors in order to correct the errors.

symbolic instruction An *instruction* in *source language* form.

symbolic language A programming *language* in which *instruction codes, data items* and *peripheral units* may be assigned *symbolic addresses*. Synonymous with *source language* and contrasted with *machine code*.

symbolic name A *label* used in *programs* written in a *source language* to reference *data elements, instructions, peripheral units*, etc. Symbolic names often make use of *mnemonic codes*.

symbolic programming Writing a program in a *source language*.

symbol table A *table* containing *symbols* and their interpretation.

symmetric difference Synonymous with *exclusive-or operation*.

synchronizer A *storage device* which acts as a *buffer* to counteract the effects of transmitting data between devices which operate at different rates.

synchronous computer A *computer* in which the timing of all operations is controlled by equally spaced signals from a *clock*.

synchronous working Performing a sequence of operations under the control of a cycle of equally spaced signals from a *clock*. Contrasted with *asynchronous working*.

syntax The rules which govern the structure of language statements; in particular, the rules for forming *statements* in a *source language* correctly.

synthesis The combination of separate things or concepts to form a complex whole. Contrasted with *analysis*.

synthetic address Synonymous with *generated address*.

synthetic language Synonymous with *source language*.

system Any group of objects related or interacting so as to form a unit. In *data processing* the objects which are interrelated will be individuals and machines, the purpose of their interacting being to achieve certain defined ends concerned with the manipulation of information, e.g. to produce a payroll. System can also be used to refer specifically to a particular interrelated collection of machines (in this sense, the term *configuration* is also used). ⋫ general article on *Systems Analysis*.

systematic error checking code A form of *error-detecting code* in which a valid *character* consists of the minimum number of *digits* required to identify the character, together with a *check digit* designed to maintain the minimum *signal distance* between characters as required by an error-detecting code. ⋫ *Hamming code*.

system chart Synonymous with *systems flowchart*.

system checks Checks which monitor the performance of a system, e.g. *control totals*, *record counts* and *hash* totals.

system control language ◇ *control language*.

system, ducol punched card ◇ *ducol punched card system*.

system failure ◇ *failure*.

system generation Use of a set of utility *programs*, including the *updating* and *maintenance* of system *libraries*.

system, hybrid computer ◇ *hybrid computer system*.

system, information ◇ *information system*.

system, information retrieval ◇ *information retrieval*.

system, management information ◇ *management information system*.

system, real time ◇ *real time*.

system reliability The ability of a *hardware* system to achieve its defined objectives. ◇ *reliability*.

systems analysis Systems analysis as an activity existed long before computers were invented: the art of analysing methods of doing things and designing and implementing new and better methods has been applied ever since mankind organized itself into social groups. Out of this organizing activity have developed the modern sciences of organization and methods, work study, systems engineering and other associated techniques.

The advent of computers has produced a new and powerful tool, capable of handling huge amounts of information at enormous speed. Systems analysis is the name given to the technique of determining how best to put this powerful and expensive tool to work.

This article gives a brief description of some of the aspects of systems analysis. The range of activities which come under this concept, however, is not clearly defined. Some of the activities described may be performed by an individual employed as a systems analyst: others may be considered to be more appropriate to a *programmer* or to an O & M expert. Nevertheless, the activities described are all concerned with using a computer efficiently and profitably: this is the ultimate aim of systems analysis.

The work of a systems analyst can be likened to that of an architect. In designing a building the architect must first of all determine in consultation with his client what the building is for: teaching, nursing, family living, etc. He must analyse the activities to be performed in the building: eating, sleeping, cooking, etc. He must then determine the physical limitations within which his design must come: costs, materials, dates. He then designs a solution to the problem: this solution must be communicated to the user, to the builder, to the contractor, to his clients. Once the design is approved, he must monitor progress on the building and alter designs if requirements change (although he will hope to have to do as little of this as possible). Finally, when the building is complete, he must satisfy himself that it conforms to his design and to the client's requirements. He can then have the satisfaction of seeing his design realized, and performing the function for which it was created.

This is only a rough analogy: but it illustrates the main functions of systems analysis: (i) definition of the problem; (ii) investigation of the working of existing systems; (iii) analysis of the results of the investigation so as to help determine the requirements of a new system; (iv) design of a new system that is practical and efficient and makes the best use of available *hardware* and *software;* (v) communication of the new system to all parties concerned; (vi) assistance in implementation of the new system and its maintenance thereafter.

Each of these functions will form part of the analysis of any particular system: however, the relative importance of each step and the responsibility for undertaking it may vary considerably from system to system. The following remarks outline briefly the methods adopted at each stage.

(i) Definition of the problem: Before embarking on a systems project a clear statement and understanding of the problem must be made: otherwise, the answer produced will not meet the needs that it is supposed to and the whole project may well prove to be abortive. Thus the first important task of a systems analyst is to obtain a definition of the problem. The subject of the project, and its boundaries, as well as the objectives and hoped-for benefits must be specified as precisely as possible in a written systems project assignment. This will be the result of cooperation between the 'clients' or users of the proposed new system and the staff to be involved in the design of the new system.

(ii) Investigation of the working of existing systems: This stage can be divided into an interim survey, followed by a full scale systems investigation.

The purpose of an interim survey is to provide a guide from which to estimate the time needed for a full scale investigation and the resources required to carry the investigation out. The interim survey will normally cover the following points: volume of work; staff involved; time involved; costs of present system. The interim survey will not propose solutions but obtain facts highlighting areas for further investigation and defining the extent of the problem.

A full scale systems investigation can continue indefinitely: it is thus essential to plan such an investigation carefully, breaking it down into a series of separate projects. One approach to the problem is the systems project teams. The investigation is planned as a series of tasks, each of which is given to a team to solve. The team is given precise terms of reference and a limit is set on the time for completion. Team members are taken from those closely involved in the subject under investigation, as well as systems specialists. In assigning tasks and breaking down a detailed investigation into separate projects it is essential to determine what facts are to be looked for, so that unnecessary detail is not included. *Documentation* of the results of the investigation is essential, and several techniques are available, such as systems *flowcharting, horizontal flowcharts* and *decision tables.* In carrying out a systems investigation it is not sufficient merely to record what is formally laid down in company rules or other documents as being the situation: neither is the correct picture necessarily obtained from what any individual says the situation is. The real situation must be discovered by patient observation and discussion. From the results of the investigation can be determined the best way of meeting the real needs of the system.

(iii) Analysis of results: Once the detailed systems investigation described above has been completed, the results obtained must be analysed so as to determine the weak points of the system investigated and the relation between the existing situation and the overall objectives of the new system. This stage attempts to produce answers to the following questions: Is the present system doing what it is supposed to do, in the time allowed, with the required accuracy and at reasonable cost? Is the organization of the system adequate to its task, and is the staff adequate? Are the documents used and produced necessary and are they efficiently designed? On the basis of answers to questions of this type the new system can be designed more effectively.

(iv) Design of new system: The designing of a new system is a creative function and, as such, difficult to define in detail. However, in designing a new system some of the following activities normally take place: *a.* Re-appraise the original terms of reference of the investigation in the light of results so far obtained; *b.* Reflect again on the results of the analysis of the existing system, particularly any weak points and any unexpected discoveries. *c.* Determine precisely what output will be required from the new system and how it will be used. *d.* Determine the *data items* required in order to produce the required output. *e.* Decide on the medium and format of all *input* and *output files*, taking into account hardware and software availability and timing requirements. *f.* Devise efficient methods for processing input to obtain output, making use of software available and defining any special programs required. *g.* Devise an efficient method of *data collection*. This is particularly important, since the results produced by the system depend on how accurate, complete and up-to-date the raw data input to the system is. *h.* Define in detail all the clerical procedures and documentation (e.g. *turn around documents, source documents*) required at the data capture stage. *i.* Decide how the system is to cope with changes and modifications. No systems design is perfect, nor can an analyst predict completely the requirements of any system in the future. Thus as much flexibility as possible must be incorporated into all parts of the system. This can be done using general purpose software (e.g. applications software, file processing programs) or by specifying programs which can be modified by means of variables input from *parameters*.

(v) Documentation: The general articles on *Documentation* describe the documentation which must accompany any new system. Such documentation is essential: *a.* As a record of agreement on all decisions. *b.* As a method of communication between the analyst and the programmers responsible for preparing all programs required. *c.* As a method of communication between the analyst and those responsible for operating the system, both the user and the specialist data processing personnel. The documentation should be signed as agreed by the users, the programming staff and also representatives of company auditors and accountants.

(vi) Implementation: Before a new system is finally operational, several stages of testing must take place. The first step is the detailed testing of individual programs, for which the systems analyst will provide *test data* and schedules of expected results.

Once the individual programs of the system have been proved correct against test data, the system as a whole must be tested, to ensure that all procedures, both manual, off-line and on-line are working as planned. This form of test requires some simulation of the 'real life' situation. This can be achieved on a limited basis by means of a pilot scheme, where one small but representative area of the system is used to test the new procedures before these are extended to other areas. This may be sufficient test of procedures: but in some cases, full *parallel running* will be required. This means that the new procedures are operated at the same time as the procedures they are designed to replace. The results obtained by the two systems are compared and the old system dispensed with when the new one is operating successfully.

The pilot scheme and parallel run steps are also used to try out the provisions made for auditing and controlling the operations of the new system, so that control is established over the full implementation of the system.

A major function of implementing a new system is ensuring that all documentation is accurate and up to date. And modifications made to a system in the light of testing or operational experience must pass through the same acceptance and audit procedures as the original system. The analyst must ensure that this documentation is maintained accurately and is always up to date.

(vii) Conclusions: This article has discussed in general terms some of the activities involved in systems analysis. Great emphasis is laid on the necessity for the analysis of a system to be complete and thorough. However, too great a rigidity in a system can prove fatal to its ultimate effectiveness. Any worthwhile system must be capable of being changed without involving a complete revision of all that has gone before. With the increasing availability of general purpose application-oriented software the task of the analyst is considerably eased. By definition, general purpose software is designed to be used in a large number of related applications which differ in detail. Thus a system making use of such software will be more flexible than one using specially devised routines. Software is designed to be modified, whereas single-purpose routines generally will do one job only, and cannot easily be modified. Thus the task of a systems analyst is as much to forecast how the system and its requirements will change, as it is to define the specific requirements of the system at a fixed point in time. Developments in software by which the user is able to interrogate a computer, and control the input and output from it directly, mean that the systems analyst will be less an intermediary between a user and the mysterious world of the computer, and more a teacher, explaining how to use and control a powerful tool in the simplest and most efficient manner.

systems analyst ◊ general article on *Computer Personnel*.

systems definition The document produced by a systems analyst which defines in detail the system he has designed. This document explains all clerical procedures and includes *program* specifications. Also known as systems specification. ◊ the general articles on *Documentation – Systems* and *Systems Analysis*.

systems design The investigation and recording of existing *systems* and the design of new systems. ◊ general article on *Systems Analysis*.

systems flowchart A *flowchart* in which the *flowchart symbols* represent specific clerical, *data preparation* and computer procedures which are combined in *systems design*.
Also known as flow-process diagram, process chart. Contrasted with *program flowchart*. ◊ general article on *Flowcharting*.

systems recovery time The period spent on recovery. Also known as *rerun time*.

systems, inquiry and communications ◊ *inquiry and communications systems*.

systems specification Synonymous with *systems definition*.

system structure ◊ general article on *Systems Analysis*.

system, time-sharing monitor ◊ *time-sharing monitor system*.

T

table An *array* of data in *memory*, or on some other storage medium, which is so organized that individual items may be retrieved by the specifying of *keys* stored as part of each item. Sometimes items may be located by specifying their position in the table.

table look-at The process whereby items in a *table* are obtained by calculation. That is, an *algorithm* is used to locate the position of the item in the table, rather than employ a search as in *table look-up*.

table look-up 1. A method of obtaining a function value from a *function table* corresponding to a specified *argument*. 2. Any method of searching a *table* to locate items relevant to a specified *key*.

table look-up instruction A *basic instruction* which may be modified to refer to data arranged in a *table*. An instruction used to search for an item containing a nominated *key*.

tabular language A system for specifying programming requirements in terms of *decision tables*, in which the tables fulfil the role of a *problem-oriented programming language*.

tabulate 1. The accumulation of totals for groups of items, each group consisting of items bearing a common *key*. 2. On a *punched card tabulator*, the printing of totals for groups of cards, each line of totals being initiated by a change of *control data* between the end of one group and the beginning of the next.

tabulation 1. A printed report produced on a *punched card tabulator* consisting of *totals only*. 2. The automatic movement of the carriage of a typewriter or teleprinter through a series of specified positions in a succession of print lines.

tabulation character A *character* forming part of some data to be printed but which is not itself printed and instead is used to control the format of the printed output, e.g. to cause a throw to the next line; or, on a teleprinter, to initiate the *carriage return* function. A member of the set of characters known as *format effectors*.

tabulator A machine which automatically feeds *punched cards*, reading data from them to be directly *listed* and/or accumulated for the printing of totals at the end of certain card *groups*.

tag 1. A collection of *characters* or *digits* attached to a *record* as a means of identification. 2. A short *record* inserted in a location of a *direct access file* to retrieve an *overflow record*. The tag usually consists of the *key* for the *overflow record* plus the current *address* of that *record*. 3. A perforated price tag which is attached to goods and which can be removed at point of sale and used in an *automatic processing* system.

tag converting unit A machine for reading *tags*[3] and for punching the data thus sensed into some other medium such as *punched cards* or *paper tape*. Some tag readers provide for direct input to computer *memory*.

tag format The layout and design of a *record* used as a *tag*[2] to locate an *overflow bucket*.

takedown The process of removing *magnetic tapes, punched cards, paper tape* and *printouts* from *peripherals* at the end of a computer *run* or suite of runs. To clear the equipment ready for *loading* the next job.

takedown time The time required to complete a *takedown* operation.

tally A printed list of figures produced on an adding machine.

tally reader A machine that can read data as printed characters from a *tally* list; e.g. by means of *optical character recognition*.

tandem system A system in which two *hardware* units are used to fulfil some processing operation. For example, some processing applications require the use of two *processors*, one acting as a slave performing routine processing operations under the control of the master processor.

tank Sometimes used as a colloquialism for *mercury delay line*.

tape A continuous strip of material for recording data, e.g. *paper tape* or *magnetic tape*.

tape alternation A process, achieved under *program* control or by operator intervention, whereby a program can be made to switch from one *tape deck* to another to minimize the time delay in changing from one *reel* to another when processing a *multi-reel file*.

tape bootstrap routine A *bootstrap* routine present in the first *block* of a *program tape*. When the routine is read into *store* it reads specified programs from the tape: it may also contain other *utility programs*.

tape, chadded paper ◊ *chadded tape*.

tape, chadless paper ◊ *chadless tape*.

tape cluster Synonymous with *magnetic tape group*.

tape code, paper ◊ *paper tape code*.

tape comparator A machine that automatically compares two *paper tapes* which have been prepared from identical *source documents*. The tapes are compared *character* by character and the machine stops if a discrepancy is detected; if no errors are detected the initial preparation is assumed to have been correctly completed. In most systems of this sort a third tape is automatically produced as the comparison takes place. In the event of a discrepancy the operator can enter correct characters from a *keyboard*.

tape controlled carriage An *automatic carriage* which is activated under the control of a loop of paper or mylar plastic into which holes have been punched to provide a *program* for automatically feeding the stationery.

tape core A *magnetic core* which is constructed using a length of ferromagnetic tape wound as a spiral.

tape deck A device consisting of a *tape transport mechanism* for handling *magnetic tape*, along with an associated *read head* and *write head*. Sometimes a single tape deck is mounted in a free-standing unit, a number of which may be connected to a *central processor*. More often a number of decks, say four or six, are mounted in a single unit known as a *tape group*.

tape drive Used loosely as a synonym for a *magnetic tape deck*, but more accurately refers to the *tape transport mechanism* only. Also used to describe the mechanism that feeds *paper tape* in an automatic *paper tape punch* or *paper tape reader*.

tape feed A mechanism forming part of a *paper tape reader* or *paper tape punch*. That part of the machine which can feed *paper tape* to be read or punched.

tape file Synonymous with *magnetic tape file*; a series of *records* arranged sequentially on *magnetic tape*.

tape group A single unit containing two or more *tape decks*. Also known as cluster. ◊ *magnetic tape group*.

tape labels Special *records* appearing at the beginning and end of a *reel* of *magnetic tape* to provide details about the *file* of *records* stored on the tape. ◊ *header label* and *trailer label*.

tape library ◊ *magnetic tape library*.

tape mark 1. A special *character* recorded on a *file* of *magnetic tape* in order to subdivide the file into sections. A tape mark is usually followed by a *record* providing descriptive data concerning the particular section of the file. Also known as control mark. 2. A special character that indicates the physical end of a *reel* of tape. In this sense, also known as *end of tape marker*.

tape, master instruction ◊ *master instruction tape*.

tape, perforated ◊ *punched tape*.

tape plotting system A system for driving a *digital incremental plotter* from data recorded on *magnetic tape* or *paper tape*.

tape processing simultaneity Pertaining to a *time sharing system* in which several *magnetic tape decks* may be activated to *read* or *write* data at the same time while continuing to process data in the *central processor*. ⋄ *time sharing*.

tape punch A device for punching holes in *paper tape*; the term is generally used to denote a *keyboard* operated unit. Contrasted with *automatic tape punch* which refers to a unit that can be connected to a *central processor* or any communications circuit to punch data received from a channel.

Also known as paper tape punch.

tape punch, automatic ⋄ *automatic tape punch*.

tape, punched ⋄ *paper tape*.

tape reader A device which reads *data* recorded as holes punched in *paper tape*.

tape reader, magnetic ⋄ *magnetic tape reader*.

tape reproducer A device used to copy data from one length of *paper tape* to another. It may also incorporate facilities to enable the operator to interrupt this process in order to insert new data from a *keyboard* on to the tape thus produced.

tape serial number An identification number, usually recorded on a tape *header label*, which is allotted to a new *magnetic tape* and remains unchanged through the life of the tape even though all other identifying information (e.g. *file name, reel number*) may change.

tape sort A computer operation in which a *file* of data held on *magnetic tape* is sorted into sequence according to a *key* contained in each *record* of the file. ⋄ the general article on *Sorting*.

tape splicer ⋄ *splicer*.

tape station Synonymous with *magnetic tape deck*.

tape thickness The least of the cross-sectional dimensions of a piece of *paper tape* or *magnetic tape*. Contrasted with *tape width*.

tape transport 1. The mechanism that drives a *reel* of *magnetic tape* past the *read* and *write* heads on a *tape deck*. Also known as magnetic tape drive. 2. A mechanism for driving *paper tape* through a *punching station* or *sensing station*.

tape transport mechanism Part of a *magnetic tape deck*; the mechanism that drives and controls the movement of *magnetic tape* past a *read* or *write* head.

tape unit Usually means a single *magnetic tape deck* and its associated control circuitry, but sometimes used as a synonym for *magnetic tape group* to mean two or more tape decks housed in a single cabinet.

tape verifier A device for checking the accuracy of data punched into *paper tape*. In one *data preparation* system the operator enters data from *source documents* to a *keyboard*, and the device automatically compares the *data* with holes previously punched into a paper tape by another operator. ◊ *Data Preparation*.

tape width A piece of *paper tape* or *magnetic tape* has two cross-sectional dimensions: the greater of these is the tape width (the other being the *tape thickness*).

tape wound core A *magnetic core* made from a coil of ferro-magnetic tape.

tapped potentiometer function generator A device, used on *analog computers* for generating functions of one variable, in which the input variable sets the angular position of a potentiometer shaft. A number of taps along the potentiometer are positioned to represent the table of values for the function.

target computer The specification of the particular system required for running a particular *object program*. Also known as target machine.

target configuration Same as *target computer*, but referring to the particular combination of *peripheral units* and the number of *memory locations* needed to run a particular *object program*.

target language Synonymous with *object language*.

target machine Synonymous with *target computer*.

target phase During *compilation*, the phase at which the *object program* is first run.

target program Synonymous with *object program*.

teaching machines Traditional teaching methods rely on teachers and textbooks and both have their drawbacks: in a typical class-room or lecture, a teacher stands in front of a number of pupils and talks; this can be a one-way process with information being transmitted but with little indication of how well it is being received (particularly if the number of pupils is large). Often the teaching rate will be too fast for some students, who will become confused, and too slow for others, who will become bored.

The use of textbooks also has deficiencies. Like the lecturer, the textbook can make little provision for response on the part of the student. However, response is considered to play a vital role in learning, with the corollary that poor response should be immediately picked up so that remedial action can be taken.

Teaching machines have the following features:

(a) There is continuous and active response to each unit of information presented, e.g. questions are asked before the student moves on to new material.

(b) There is immediate feedback to the student's responses, e.g. he is told whether his answers were right or wrong.

(c) The student can work at his own pace and teaching material presented can be varied to suit individual capabilities.

A teaching machine consists of two elements, the *program* and the *hardware*. The program is of particular importance, since this is what does the teaching. Hardware used may range from interactive *on-line* computers to sheets of paper printed and bound in a special way (i.e. a special sort of book).

Computer teaching programs may be one of three varieties: linear programs, branching programs or a mixture of both.

All programs consist of a number of frames which present a unit of information and request a response from the student.

Linear programs are based on the operant theory of learning propounded by Professor Skinner of Harvard. The typical unit of information consists of one or two sentences followed by a sentence containing blanks. The student's response consists of filling in the blanks with words, phrases or numbers. This is known as a constructed response. Once the student has made his response the right answer is revealed to him. Progress through the program is linear in the sense that one frame follows another in sequence, although there may be some provision for skipping some frames for able students, or going back to earlier frames for revision.

Branching programs have rather larger units of information, perhaps two or three paragraphs. Having read the frame the student responds by answering a multiple choice question. According to the answer he gives the student branches to another part of the program. The main path of a branching program is the path that a student follows if he always answers questions correctly. Branches off the main path are provided to give remedial teaching to those who answer questions incorrectly. Thus different students may see different sequences of information.

It is impossible to describe the whole range of teaching machines here, but the basic elements of most teaching machines can be outlined as a storage unit to hold the program, a display mechanism and a response panel.

Programs can be stored on rolls of paper or strips of card, the frames being displayed at a window. Alternatively slides, film strips or microfilm can be used. Some machines incorporate a soundtrack with individual earphones for the student. The response mechanism may be a write-in window (particularly with linear programs), push-buttons, typewriters or a microphone.

It is possible to use a computer as a teaching machine. The way to make this economically feasible is to use a very large *time sharing* computer, with massive *backing* storage, capable of serving a large number of *on-line consoles* simultaneously. The student sits at a console (which may be a two-way typewriter or a *visual display unit*), receives instructions from the computer and types back a response. Interaction between student and machine is controlled by a computer program (probably of the type known as an *operating system*), but the textual material for display would probably be called in from *backing store* rather than reside permanently in *memory*. In this way a large number of pupils can receive what amounts to individual attention from a teaching machine which has a particular eye for their problems and which is never impatient or forced to leave one pupil behind for the benefit of the others.

telecommunication The transmission and reception of data over radio circuits or transmission lines by means of electromagnetic signals.

telegraphic communication Communication by means of signals in an on/off mode. For example, the earliest telegraph systems were operated by a manual key which interrupted current in a circuit to produce audible clicks for a distant operator. This technique was developed and the teleprinter (and associated equipment) emerged as the principal device for this form of communication. In this system the teleprinter is able to generate and respond to coded signals in which combinations of on/off pulses are used to represent numeric or alphabetic characters. Modern *multiplexing* techniques have largely invalidated the earlier distinction between telegraphic and *telephonic communication*. ✧ *data transmission*.

telemeter Equipment for recording and transmitting measurements as data to a distant location by electromagnetic waves.

telemetering The recording and transmitting of measurements and data by electromagnetic means and the reception of such data at a distant point.

telephone data set A unit used to connect a *data terminal* to a telephone circuit, e.g. to transmit data from the terminal to a processing centre. A telephone data set converts signals from the terminal into a form suitable for transmission over a telephone circuit, and vice versa.

telephonic communication A method of communication in which signals are transmitted by electrical tones of different frequency over a *communications link*. In relation to *electronic data processing* this form of communication permits data to be transmitted at very high speed, and by the use of *multiplexing* techniques several signals can be transmitted over a single channel. ◊ *data transmission*.

teleprinter A device resembling a typewriter which can be connected to a *communications link* to receive or transmit data from and to a distant point. Incoming signals may be received on a print unit forming part of the teleprinter, and on some machines the incoming signals may also be automatically recorded on *paper tape*. Outgoing messages may be entered on a *keyboard* and, on some teleprinters, may be transmitted automatically by the passing of a message tape through a paper tape reading unit. Teleprinters are sometimes used for direct *input/output* to a *central processor*.

teleprocessing A term registered by I B M used to describe systems in which remote locations are connected to a central computer by *data transmission* circuits. For example, to facilitate the direct *on-line* control of industrial processes or of commercial systems.

Teletype The trademark of the Teletype Corporation of the U S A, often used generally when referring to equipment or systems of *telegraphic communication*.

teletype grade A grade of circuit suitable for the transmission of signals for *telegraphic communication*.

teletype input/output unit A telegraphic terminal device specifically used for connexion to a central computer; e.g. a *teleprinter* used as an *input/output* unit.

teletypewriter A telegraphic terminal device, resembling a typewriter, used to transmit and receive messages in a telegraphic communications system. ◊ *teleprinter*.

telex An automatic exchange service provided for communication between subscribers using telegraphic equipment such as *teleprinters*.

temporary storage *Storage locations* which have been reserved, during the operation of a particular *program*, for storing *intermediate results*.

ten position ◊ *X-position*.

tens complement A number produced by subtracting from nine each digit of a number whose *radix* is ten and then adding one to the *least significant position*. For example, the tens complement of 291 is 709. ◊ *radix complement*.

teracycle   One million *megacycles*.

terminal   Any point at which *data* may be input to or output from a *data communications* system. Also known as *data terminal*.

terminal, data communication   ◊ *data communication terminal*.

terminal, job-oriented   ◊ *job-oriented data terminal*.

terminal, multiplex-data   ◊ *multiplex-data terminal*.

terminal symbol   A symbol on punched *paper tape* to indicate the end of a *record* or some other unit of information.

terminal user   A person using a *terminal*. Also known as transactor.

termination   Conclusion of a series of actions. See also *abnormal termination*.

ternary   Pertaining to three. The ternary system of *number representation* uses the three *digits* 0, 1 and 2 to represent numbers expressed using a base or *radix* of 3. For example the number 5 is represented as 12.

ternary incremental representation   Pertaining to *digital integrators*; a method of *incremental representation* in which increment values are rounded off as either $+1$, -1 or zero.

test   To examine an element of data or an *indicator* to ascertain whether some predetermined condition is satisfied.

testbed   A *software* system designed to simplify the testing of *programs* by providing *test data* and diagnostic information. ◊ general article on *Modular Programming*.

test, crippled leapfrog   ◊ *crippled leapfrog test*.

test data   Sample data, covering as many likely and unlikely combinations as reasonable, prepared as input to test a *program*. Expected results are also prepared and compared with the results produced by the computer.

testing envelope   *Software* which provides an environment for the testing of a *program* or a *program module*. ◊ general article on *Modular Programming*.

test pack   A *pack* of *punched cards* containing both *program* and *test data* for a *test run*.

test program   A *program* designed to check the correct functioning of the *hardware* units of a computer. It may also identify particular kinds of fault, but ◊ *diagnostic program*.

test routine   ◊ *test program*.

test run   A test, performed to check that a particular *program* is operating correctly, in which *test data* is used to generate results for comparison with expected answers.

text   The information element of any message, excluding those *characters* or *bits* required to facilitate the transmission of the message.

thin-film memory An *internal storage* medium consisting of a thin layer (a few millionths of an inch thick) of magnetic substance deposited on a plate of non-magnetizable material such as glass. The film can be polarized for the representation of *digital* information, enabling data to be written or retrieved at speeds measured in *nanoseconds*. This type of *memory* has the characteristics necessary for miniaturized components which can operate at very fast processing speeds. ◊ general article on *Storage Devices*.

text editor *Software* which allows the location and modification of the *data* in a *file*.

third generation computers Machines built with *integrated circuits*. Related to *first generation* and *second generation*.

thread A group of *beads*.

three address instruction An *instruction* in which three *addresses* are specified as part of the *instruction format*. When arithmetic operations are performed, one *location* will be used to contain the *result*, the other two containing *operands* to be used in the process.

three-input adder A *logic element* employed for performing *addition* using *digital* input signals. It will accept three input signals (representing digits of *addend, augend* and *carry*) and will produce two output signals, representing a *carry digit* and a digit for the *sum*.

three-input subtracter A *logic element* used for performing subtraction with *digital signals*. It will accept three input signals (*minuend, subtrahend* and *borrow*) and will produce two output signals representing a digit to be borrowed in the next *digit position* and a digit for the *difference*.

three-level subroutine A *subroutine* in which entry is made to a second, lower level, subroutine, from which a further entry is made to a third level.

threshold A specified value established to control the output from a *threshold element*.

threshold element A *logic element* having one output signal but several input signals, each given a specified weight. The output signal is dependent on the input signals being greater or less than some given value, known as the *threshold*. For example, in a *majority element*, if all n inputs are weighted as 1, the output is dependent on threshold equal to $(n+1) \div 2$.

throughput The productivity of a machine, system or procedure, measured in some terms meaningful to the process under consideration. For example, a payroll system may deal with 100 employee records per minute; an *information retrieval* system might handle 10,000 inquiries per hour.

tie-line A leased communications channel operating between two private branch exchanges.

tightly coupled twin One of two *processors* using separate *operating systems* but able to share *data* and *code* via an inter-processor *buffer* and to control access to *backing store* without mutual interference. Contrasted with *loosely coupled twin*.

time-derived channel A channel obtained by *multiplexing* several signals over a single channel, in such a way that each signal is separated from any other by time.

time-division multiplexing A system whereby a channel is made available to a number of terminal devices each occupying the channel for the transmission of *data* for short periods at regular intervals. The effect is such that all terminals appear to transmit simultaneously over one channel. ✧ *time sharing*.

time division multiplier An *analog* unit used for multiplication, in which there are two input variables and a single output. One input variable is used to control the amplitude of a square wave, while the other variable controls the *mark-to-space ratio* of the wave form. The output voltage is smoothed to derive the average value of the output as a product. Same as *mark-space multiplier*.

time, fault ✧ *down time*.

time, latency ✧ *waiting time*.

time, machine-spoilt ✧ *machine-spoilt work time*.

time, mean repair ✧ *mean repair time*.

time-of-day clock An electronic device which registers the time in hours, minutes and seconds over a 24-hour cycle, and which will transmit a signal to the *central processor* on request so that events can be logged. ✧ *timer clock*.

time origin A reference point during the generation of a pulse, i.e. the point at which the pulse reaches a certain percentage, usually ten per cent, of its full amplitude. All subsequent events related to that pulse are measured over time with respect to the time origin. ✧ *reference time*.

time, program development ✧ *program development time*.

time, program testing ✧ *program testing time*.

timer An automatic timing device that provides clock signals within a *central processor*, for example, to register *elapsed time* for an event in millisecond increments. ✧ *timer clock*.

timer clock An electronic device used for timing events that occur during the operation of a computer system. Situated in the *central processor*, it can provide data for charging out computer time, monitor operations to detect looping and similar error conditions and provide time in hours and minutes for maintaining an operating log.

time, routine maintenance ◊ *routine maintenance time.*

time scale (factor) The ratio between the time for an event as simulated with an *analog device* and the actual duration of time for the event in the physical system under study. ◊ *slow time scale* and *fast time scale.*

time, scheduled engineering ◊ *scheduled engineering time.*

time series Data transmitted as a series of discrete elements distributed over time. Quantitative values are assigned to specific instants in the time series.

time shared input/output system A computer system in which independent *peripheral units* may be activated simultaneously under control of the *central processor* which shares its time in accepting or transmitting data to the peripheral units. At the same time the central processor may continue to process data internally by *time sharing* one or more *programs.*

time shared system Any system in which *hardware* is used more efficiently by using *time sharing* techniques to facilitate concurrent operations. For example, in a *multiprogramming computer*, several *programs* may be processed concurrently by switching from one to another in a fixed sequence to permit a certain number of *instructions* to be performed on each occasion. In some systems programs are given priorities before being loaded into the *central processor*, so that a program of highest priority is activated continuously until it is held up, say, for data from a *peripheral unit*, whereupon the program with next highest priority is activated.

time sharing A system in which a particular device is used for two or more concurrent operations. Thus the device operates momentarily to fulfil one purpose then another, returns to the first, and so on in succession until the operations are completed. This activity is performed at high speed according to a strict sequence, each independent operation being executed as a series of finite steps.

time sharing dynamic allocator An *executive program* which controls the activation of independent programs in a *multiprogramming* or *time sharing* system. This type of program also allocates storage *areas* and *peripheral units* to any program entering the system, and when a program is deleted it re-allocates storage for the remaining programs to ensure that the largest possible area of contiguous locations remains available for another program.

time sharing monitor system An *executive program* consisting of a number of routines which coordinate the operation of a *time sharing* computer, including the automatic switching from one program to another in a *multiprogramming* system and the control of all input/output operations so that several *peripheral units* may be operated concurrently while data is processed in the *central processor.*

time slicing Synonymous with *time sharing.*

time, start ⋄ *acceleration time.*

time study When the optimum method of performing an operation has been determined through method study the work content of that operation may be established by work measurement, which essentially determines the time required to carry out the operation to a specified standard of performance by a qualified worker. This enables standards of machine utilization and labour performance to be set. These standards have a number of applications: determining the manning necessary; providing the proper basis for incentive schemes; planning and controlling production; and establishing selling prices and delivery promises.

The main techniques of work measurement are time study, synthesis (from standard data, such as predetermined motion time standards) and analytical estimating. Time study is generally appropriate only for repetition work and differs from the other two in that the time for an operation is determined by means of direct observations. An accurate specification of the operation must be recorded, including the method to be used and all relevant conditions. The operation is broken down into its constituent elements and times for each are obtained with a stopwatch.

These recorded times by themselves are not sufficient as a measure of the work content of the operation. It is necessary to take account of the effectiveness of the speed and effort employed, and to give this a numerical value by mentally comparing it with a standard of effectiveness. This process is known as rating, and the standard rate of working (usually taken as 100 rating) is defined as that corresponding to the average rate at which qualified workers will naturally work on the operation, providing they know and adhere to the specified method and provided they are motivated to apply themselves to their work. A basic (or normalized) time can thus be obtained for each element:

$$\text{basic time} = \text{observed time} \times \frac{\text{observed rating}}{\text{standard rating}}.$$

This basic time is independent of the operator observed and is a genuine measure of the work content.

The basic time accounts only for the productive part of the work cycle, and allowances must be added for non-productive time. A process allowance is necessary if the operator is forced to be idle during part of the cycle owing to unbalanced work of men and machines; a rest allowance is given for recovery from the physical and mental stresses that may be involved; a synchronization allowance, to compensate for natural interference of men and/or machines; and a contingency allowance, to cover any irregular small delays whose precise measurement is uneconomic.

Careful assessment of the value for each allowance is made in the light of the work and conditions involved. The addition of these values to the basic time gives the standard (or allowed) time for the operation.

time, supplementary maintenance ◊ *supplementary maintenance time*.

timing considerations The economics of designing a *file* or a system expressed in terms of the machine time or the overall *throughput* speed for a *run* or series of runs.

timing error An error made in designing a *program*; e.g. one in which, when designing the program, the programmer has under-estimated the time allotted for an *input/output* operation, as a consequence of which unnecessary delays are incurred during processing.

T L U Acronym for *table look-up*.

toggle A circuit or device which must always assume one of two stable states. ◊ *flip-flop*.

toggle switch A manually operated switch which can be set to either of two positions.

torn-tape *Paper tape* which has been torn from a *paper tape punch* on receipt at a *switching centre* so that it can be taken to a transmitting *paper tape reader*.

torn-tape switching centre ◊ *switching centre*.

torsional mode delay line A *delay line* in which mechanical vibrations are propagated by subjecting a material to torsion, with the object of introducing a specific delay in the transmission of a signal.

totals only To print a report using a *punched card tabulator*, or a computer *printer*, in such a manner that for specified groups of cards or input *records* totals only are printed; i.e. data from the individual records is not listed directly but is accumulated and printed when a *control change* takes place.

total system A complete system of clerical and computer procedures embracing all the main activities of a particular company or organization. An integrated network of sub-systems comprising all the data processing activities of an organization.

total time The total time available for utilization of a particular computer installation, including all *attended time* and *unattended time*.

total transfer A method for accumulating minor, intermediate and major *control totals* (◊ *control data*) when preparing printed results on a *punched card* tabulator. The minor total is accumulated directly from a card *field* and higher levels of totals are created by accumulating from minor to intermediate, and from intermediate to major totals.

T P Abbreviation for *transaction processing*.

trace program A *diagnostic program* used to check and locate errors in other programs. The output from the trace program may consist of selected *instructions* from the program being checked, as well as results obtained during the operation of the instructions.

trace routine Synonymous with *trace program*.

trace statement A statement available as part of the *source coding* for certain *programming languages*, enabling specified *segments* of a *source program* to be checked at the *source language* level.

track 1. A channel on a *magnetic memory* device for recording data, e.g. the tracks on a *magnetic disk*. 2. One of the longitudinal channels for recording data as holes punched in *paper tape*, e.g. *6-track tape*.

track labels Special *records* used to identify *tracks* on a *magnetic storage* medium; e.g. on a *magnetic card file* a card/track number might be used as a label at the beginning of each track of each card.

track pitch The physical measurement separating two adjacent *tracks*; e.g. on *paper tape* or *magnetic tape*.

track, reading ◊ *card track*.

trailer label A special *record* appearing at the end of a *file* stored on *magnetic tape* or other magnetic recording medium. It serves to identify the end of the file and usually provides certain *control data* related to that file, e.g. number of records.

trailer record A *record* which immediately follows an associated group of records, and which contains totals and other *control data* relevant to the group.

trailing edge Pertaining to a *punched card* – the edge that last enters the *card track* of a punched card machine. Contrasted with *leading edge*.

trailing end Relating to *paper tape*, the logical end of a length of tape, i.e. the end at which the last *record* occurs for that particular batch. Contrasts with *leading end*.

transacter A device which can be linked to a computer system to permit a number of data sources to be coupled with the system. For example, a number of input stations could be connected to a *central processor* via a transacter to provide a *real time data collection* capability within a factory.

transaction 1. Any event which requires a *record* to be generated for processing in a data processing system. Also refers to the record itself. 2. A set of exchanges between a *terminal user* and a computer system, including the processing of these exchanges which may also involve the *updating* of *files*.

transaction data A collection of *characters* or *digits*, representing one or more events, which requires to be accepted into a data processing system to *update* a *master file* or to generate results. In a *real time* system such data may arise at random and must be dealt with as it occurs; in a *batch processing* system transactions are batched to form groups which are sorted and applied to the *master files* at predetermined periods.

transaction file Synonymous with *change file*.

transaction processing The activation of a *central processor* by messages from remote locations, and its response to those locations. ◊ *transaction* [2].

transaction record Synonymous with *change record*.

transaction tape A *magnetic tape* or length of *paper tape* containing a *transaction file*.
Also known as amendment tape, *change tape*.

transactor Synonymous with *terminal user*.

transceiver A terminal unit which can both transmit and receive information from a *data transmission* circuit. Data is transmitted by a device which reads *punched cards* to send information to line, and information received from line is also punched into cards.

transcribe To copy from one medium to another, e.g. from *punched cards* to *paper tape*, or from *paper tape* to *magnetic tape*. This type of operation can be achieved by special *off-line* equipment or by a computer *program*.

transcriber A device used to transfer information from one medium to another, e.g. from *paper tape* to *punched cards*.

transducer A device that converts energy from one form to another. For example, in an *acoustic delay line* electrical energy is converted to sound energy.

transfer 1. As in a *transfer operation*, i.e. an operation to copy data from one part of *memory* to another. Effected by a *program instruction* which specifies the memory *locations* required. 2. To *transfer control* from one part of a *routine* to another, or to transfer control from one routine to another, by means of a *branch instruction*. 3. To transfer data to memory from a *peripheral unit* and vice versa – a *peripheral transfer*.

transfer card When a *program* has been loaded into a computer by means of *punched cards*, a transfer card executes the entrance into the program after loading.

transfer check A *parity check* performed to verify the accuracy of a *transfer operation*.

transfer control A *branch instruction* is said to transfer control from one part of a *program* to another part, i.e. the *program controller* jumps from one set of instructions to another. In a *multiprogramming* computer an *executive program* transfers control from one program to another according to specified priorities for the completion of programs. A transfer of control is sometimes referred to as *change of control* but must be distinguished from *comparing control change*.

transfer function A mathematical expression which specifies the relationship between two phenomena existing at different points in time or space in a particular system.

transfer instruction 1. An *instruction* which copies data from one part of *memory* to another. 2. A *branch instruction* to *transfer control* from one part of a *program* to another.

transfer instruction, condition control Synonymous with *conditional branch*.

transfer instruction, control Synonymous with *branch instruction*.

transfer instruction, unconditional control Synonymous with *unconditional branch instruction*.

transfer interpreter A *punched card interpreter* which reads information from a *punched card* and prints the information on to the same card or on to a following card.
Also known as posting interpreter.

transfer of control ◊ *transfer control*.

transfer of control, conditional ◊ *conditional transfer of control*.

transfer operation An operation in which data is moved from one area of *memory* to another, or from one medium of *store* to another.

transfer rate The rate at which data may be transferred between a *peripheral unit* and the *main memory* of a computer. Dependent upon the speed and operational mode of the *peripheral* and upon the speed of the memory. On *magnetic tape* the maximum transfer rate is governed by the speed of the *tape drive* and the *packing density* of the information recorded on the tape. For example, with a packing density of 256 characters per inch and a tape speed of 7 feet per second, the maximum transfer rate is 21,504 characters per second. Hence the expression *21kch/s tape decks*.

transfer time Synonymous with *read time*.

transfer, unconditional ◊ *unconditional branch instruction*.

transfluxor A type of magnetic storage element, in which a small piece of perforated ferromagnetic material is used, which provides a *non-volatile memory*.

transform To convert data to another form without changing the information content, e.g. to *normalize* a *floating point number*.

transient As in 'transient fault', a rapid disturbance of a signal or circuit which then swiftly reverts to a stable or normal condition.

transistor A small solid-state semiconductor which can operate as an *amplifier* or as a switching device. Transistors are usually constructed of silicon or germanium; they are small and light and have very fast switching speeds.

transition 1. A change in a circuit from one operating condition to another. 2. Also known as *bridging*. ◊ general article on *Transition*.

transition As computer systems become larger and more complex so the *software* associated with such systems increases in complexity. A typical software system on a larger machine will consist of an interlocking set of user-programs and manufacturers' software under the overall control of a larger *operating system*, possibly also making use of a sophisticated *data base management system*.

Transition is the term given to the problem of transferring such a system from one $range^2$ of equipment to another. This problem has a different order of magnitude to the associated but much simpler problem of transferring an individual program from one machine to another.

In the latter case, procedures are relatively straightforward. If the program is written in a *high-level language* such as $C\,O\,B\,O\,L$ or $F\,O\,R\,T\,R\,A\,N$, the *source program* can be *recompiled* on the new machine. Usually this is sufficient to produce a version of the program which will run adequately, possibly with some minor amendments to cater for any differences of *configuration* or idiosyncrasies of *compiler*. Even in the simple case, some problems arise in transferring *data files* to the new system. Hardware conventions may mean differences in internal format of data fields,

415

differences in the *labelling* of files and so on. Some method of transferring simple data files from one convention to another is required. This usually takes the form of a special program which will read a file in one format and convert the data formats, labels etc. into the new format. This process is known as *conversion*[2].

As systems become more complex so the transfer from one range to another becomes more complex. The task cannot be accomplished effectively by simply *recompiling* all programs and converting all files as in the simple situation outlined above. Where many hundreds of programs are involved, and the programs themselves are interrelated with each other and with the overall operating system and data base system, individual recompilation will certainly result in an incompatible set of new software.

One solution to this problem is known as *emulation*. This solution cuts the Gordian knot by making the new machine act as though it were the old machine.

This feat is performed either by special hardware, or special software, or a combination of both. The entire system: programs, operating system, data files, is taken on to the new machine in machine readable form, and the emulation process converts each instruction or data item into the new machine's version, executes it, and re-interprets the result in the old format.

In practice of course life is not quite so straightforward. No emulator is capable of behaving precisely as the old machine: some adjustment to software and data formats is necessary to ensure that the old system behaves exactly as before on the new machine. The more sophisticated the transition software, the less has to be done to change the old system to enable it to run on the new machine. Clearly, using this process does provide a considerable saving in the time and effort needed to convert each individual program and data file.

Using this type of software does however have a penalty. Interposing emulating software between the old system and the new machine means a loss of efficiency. To a certain extent the power and speed of the new hardware will compensate for this, and the system will be expected to run more efficiently than before. However, to exploit a new and more powerful machine fully, means that in the end an entirely new version of the system must be developed to make maximum use of more advanced facilities. Transition provides a bridge to the new machine, and allows the user time to develop more advanced systems while continuing to run his existing systems with minimum interruption.

transition card A *punched* card used to indicate the end of a *pack* of *program* cards. Thus, when the program pack is read into the computer, the transition card terminates the *loading* phase and initiates the execution of the program.

translate To change data expressed in one form into another form without loss of meaning. For example, to convert automatically from a *source language program* to an *object program*.

translater ◊ *translator*.

translation An operation which converts data from one format to another without changing the meaning of the information.

translator A *program* which converts statements written in one *programming language* to the format of another programming language, e.g. from a *source language* to *machine code*.

transmission The transfer of *data* from one location to another by means of electromagnetic waves; e.g. by radio waves or over telephone or telegraph circuits. ◊ *data transmission*.

transmission control character A character forming part of a message, specifically included to control the routing of that signal to its required destination.

transmission interface converter A device which converts data to or from a format suitable for transfer over a *data transmission channel*.

transmission loss Synonymous with *attenuation*.

transmission, parallel ◊ *parallel transfer*.

transmission, serial ◊ *serial transfer*.

transmission speed The speed at which data may be transmitted from a particular device or over a particular type of circuit. Measured as the number of data units transmitted over a unit of time; e.g. 10 *characters* per second, 2,000 *bits* per second.

transmit 1. To send data from one geographical location to another via a *data transmission* circuit. 2. To *transfer* information from one *memory location* to another, *overwriting* any *data* previously *stored* in the new location.

transparency A characteristic of *data management software* which allows *application programs* to use *files* while remaining unaware of, and independent of, the structure of the *physical files*. The programs regard the data and file organization as those which have been stated in the program's requirements. ◊ general article on *Data Base Management Systems*.

transport delay unit Pertaining to *analog* computing equipment, a device which outputs a signal as a delayed form of an input signal. Also known as transport unit and delay unit.

transport mechanism, tape ◊ *tape transport mechanism.*
transport unit 1. ◊ *magnetic tape transport.* 2. ◊ *transport delay unit.*

trap A *branch* operation initiated automatically by *hardware* on the detection of some unusual condition during the running of a *program*. Usually traps are associated with some *operating system* or *monitor program* which automatically assumes control and corrects the condition or notes the cause of failure. Trapping is a feature of certain *diagnostic routines*, but can also be used in processing routines, e.g. to recover from *arithmetic overflow* or unusual *input/output* conditions.

trapezoidal integration A process of integration in which it is assumed that y, an input variable, is subject to a constant rate of change during a step. ◊ *digital integrator.*

trapping A feature of *monitor programs* in which automatic checks are made upon the performance of other programs. A *trap* is designed to detect unusual incidents during the running of a program and will initiate an *unconditional branch* to some *diagnostic program* or recovery routine.

trap setting A *trap* is usually activated as the result of a condition detected in the running of a *program*. The program is automatically interrupted and a *hardware* or *software* device *transfers control* to a *routine* forming part of the overall *operating system* for the computer. Usually the *operator* has the power to determine the traps to be set for any particular *run*; this is achieved by the setting of manual controls on the *console*. Thus several traps may be associated with particular conditions but the operator can determine which of these are to be allowed to *interrupt* a program.

tree A type of *decoder* in which the graphical representation of the input and output lines resembles a tree.

triad A group of three *characters* or three *bits*; a unit of data forming part of a *message* or *record*.

tributary circuit A branch circuit that connects to a main communications switching network.

trigger 1. An electronic device which can be activated to adopt a particular stable condition. A switching device used in the logic circuits of a *central processor* or its *peripheral units*. 2. To trigger, to activate a machine or a *program* automatically; e.g. to *branch* automatically to the *entry point* of a program in *memory* after *loading* the program. Also known as initiate.

trigger circuit, bistable ◊ *bistable circuit.*
trigger circuit, monostable ◊ *monostable device.*

trigger circuit, stable   Synonymous with *bistable circuit*.

trigger pair   Synonymous with *bistable circuit*.

triple-length working   Performing arithmetic operations on numbers which require three *words* in order to develop the necessary precision for the *result*.

trouble shooting   Searching for errors in a *program* or for the cause of some machine failure. Identifying and eliminating errors in a *routine*. Also known as *Debugging*, on which there is a general article.

true complement   ◊ *radix complement*.

true-time operation   1. An *analog* system that operates coincidentally with the physical system being simulated. 2. Sometimes used as a synonym for *real time* working.

truncate   To suppress those digits of a number which are not significant according to some predetermined requirement for accuracy in a result.

truncation error   An error arising from inaccuracy in truncating a result.

trunk   1. Sometimes used to describe an *interface* channel between a *peripheral unit* and a *central processor*. 2. Synonymous with *highway*.

trunk circuit   A channel connecting two telephone or telegraph switching centres.

trunk link   An interface which allows *peripheral units* to *access* the *main store*.

truth table   A *Boolean operation table* in which the values 0 and 1 given to the variables are interpreted as measuring 'true' and 'false'. ◊ *Boolean algebra*.

tube   An abbreviation for *cathode ray tube display unit*.

turn around document   A document produced as output from a computer system, circulated to initiate some clerical transaction external to the computer procedures and then re-input to the system to *update* computer *files*. Such documents are often found in systems that employ *optical character recognition* for data input. Documents printed by the computer are circulated, other data is then added and an O C R reader accepts data from the document into the computer once more.

turn around time   The time required to complete a task; e.g. to collect data, transcribe it for processing, carry out computation and provide results to the user. ◊ *response time*.

twelve punch   A term once used to denote a hole in the topmost *punching position* of a *card column,* now commonly known as the 10 or Y-position. But ◊ *Y-position.*

twenty-nine feature A device used on *punched card* machines to enable values up to a maximum of 29 to be recorded in a single *card column,* the *punching positions* 11 and 10 being used to represent 10 and 20.

twin check Any checking method in which an operation is performed twice; e.g. to *read* data twice and perform an automatic comparison.

two address instruction An *instruction* in which the *addresses* of two *operands* are specified as part of the *instruction format.* When arithmetic operations are to be performed one of the *locations* addressed will be used to hold the *result* after the instruction has been executed.

two-core-per-bit store Descriptive of a *memory* in which each *binary digit* is represented by two *magnetic cores.*

two-dimensional storage Related to *direct access* devices; in which an area allocated to a particular *file* need not be a series of physically contiguous *locations* but instead will be specified as a number of *buckets* drawn from one or more *seek areas.*

two gap head ◊ *magnetic tape head.*

two input adder A *logic element* which performs *addition* by accepting two digital input signals (a digit of a number and an *addend* or a *carry*) and which provides two output signals (a carry digit and a digit for the sum).

two input subtracter A *logic element* used to effect the operation of *subtraction.* It accepts two input signals (a digit of a number, and a *borrow* digit or one representing the *subtrahend*) and produces two digital outputs, a borrow digit and one for the *difference.*

two-level subroutine A *subroutine* containing another subroutine within its own structure.

two-out-of-five code A coding system in which *characters* or *digits* are represented by groups of five *binary digits,* any two of which may be set to 'one' while the other three are 'zero'.

two-plus-one address Pertaining to an *instruction format* in which two *addresses* are employed to specify separate *operands,* while a third address is employed to indicate the *location* for the *result.*

twos complement A *radix complement* for the *binary notation* system.

two state variable A variable that can be a value from a set containing two elements only.

two-valued variable Synonymous with *binary variable.*

two-wire channel   A circuit which can either transmit or receive along two paths.

T W X   A communications system providing two-way transmission for telegraphic communication over the switched telephone network.

type bar   A *print member* embossed with a range of *characters* or *symbols*, e.g. forming part of the *print unit* for a *punched card tabulator*.

type bar, interchangeable   ⋄ *interchangeable type bar.*

type drum   A barrel-shaped drum used on a *line printer* and containing a number of *print positions* each consisting of a band of about fifty characters embossed around the drum's circumference. A typical drum might contain 160 print positions. ⋄ *Output Devices.*

type face   The design of the characters printed by a particular *printer*.

type fount, optical   ⋄ *optical type fount.*

typewriter   ⋄ *console typewriter, interrogating typewriter, on-line typewriter.*

U

ultrasonics Supersonics: the study of pressure waves with frequencies which are above the audible limit (20 kilocycles per second), but which are of the same nature as sound waves.

unary operation Synonymous with *monadic operation*.

unattended time Time when a computer is switched off but not subject to maintenance work.

unconditional branch instruction A *branch instruction* which results in control being transferred to another part of a *program*. This transfer is independent of any previous conditions or states of the program.

Also known as unconditional jump instruction and unconditional transfer instruction. Contrasts with *conditional branch*.

unconditional jump instruction Synonymous with *unconditional branch instruction*.

unconditional transfer instruction Synonymous with *unconditional branch instruction*.

underflow The generation of a result whose value is too small for the range of the number representation being used. Contrasted with *overflow*.

underpunch A hole punched in any of the *rows* in a *punched card* except those used for *zone* punching. That is, a hole punched in the lower nine rows of an 80-column card of twelve rows where the top three rows have zone significance.

undisturbed one output signal The output from a *store* previously set to one when it is subjected to a full *read* pulse.

undisturbed output signal The output from a *store* – previously set to one or zero – when it is subjected to a full read pulse with no intervening partial pulses. Related to *undisturbed one output signal* and *undisturbed zero output signal*.

Also known as undisturbed response voltage.

undisturbed response voltage Synonymous with *undisturbed output signal*.

undisturbed zero output signal The output from a *store* previously set to *zero* when it is subjected to a full read pulse.

unexpected halt A *halt* in a *program* not due to an *interrupt* or *halt instruction*; usually the result of a program error or *hardware* failure.

Also known as hang-up. Contrasted with *programmed halt*.

uniformly accessible store Synonymous with *random access store*.

union Synonymous with *inclusive-or operation*.

union catalogue A compilation of the listings of two or more catalogues (of libraries, for example).

unipolar An input signal is defined as unipolar if the same electrical voltage polarity is used to represent different logical states. Contrasts with *bipolar*.

unipunch Synonymous with *spot punch*.

unit, anti-coincidence ◊ *anti-coincidence element*.

unit, card punch ◊ *card punch*.

unit, card reader ◊ *card reader*.

unit, central processing ◊ *central processor*.

uniterm system An *information retrieval* system which makes use of cards distinguished from each other by a word, symbol or number which is unique and in some way describes the content of the card. The descriptors used are often designed on a coordinate indexing basis.

unit, magnetic tape ◊ *magnetic tape unit*.

unit, manual input ◊ *manual input unit*.

unit, manual word ◊ *manual word generator*.

unit, output ◊ *output devices*.

unit record A storage medium, e.g. a *punched card*, containing one complete *record* formed of several *data elements*. For example all data relevant to one staff number contained in one punched card.

unit string A *string* with only one member.

unmodified instruction Synonymous with *basic instruction*.

unpack To recover original data from a storage location in which it has been packed along with other data. Contrasts with *pack* [2].

unpaged segment A *segment* which is not divided into *pages* and is thus transferred as a complete unit between *main store* and *virtual store*.

unset Synonymous with *reset*.

unused time Time during which equipment is switched off and is unattended.

unwind To show in full, without *modifiers* or *red-tape operations*, all the *instructions* used during a *loop* of instructions. Unwinding may be performed by a computer.

update To apply *transactions* to a data *file* in order to amend, add or delete records and thus ensure that the file reflects the latest situation. ◊ general article on *Updating and File Maintenance.*

updating and file maintenance In ordinary office procedure a file is a receptacle for holding documents, usually partitioned into sections which are indexed in some way to help both the filing and retrieval of documents. Computer files are like this in that they are used to store information and they are indexed, but their outward form is different and information is coded, not stored as pieces of paper. Moreover computer files are not widely used at present to store lengthy items of text such as correspondence, but more usually for numeric information, and in this respect are more like office ledgers containing accounting transactions. This file needs to be updated and maintained, updating being the reflection of actual events changing the information and maintenance being the adding, deleting or correcting of material to ensure that the information properly reflects the real situation. For example, consider a computer file containing customer accounts, showing, for each customer, the account number, name and address, outstanding balance and credit limit. The customer may order items from the firm holding the file, in which case his account must be debited with the price, and he will make payments in which case his account will be credited: the original statement is updated to take account of these transactions. The maintenance of the file described might involve correcting an account that was showing a false balance, adding new customers or removing records of customers who are no longer doing business with the firm.

The file described above consisted of a number of accounts. Files might also contain quantities and descriptions of a number of stock items, or a list of the firm's employees with personnel details. The items different files might contain are commonly known as *records* and files are said to be composed of a number of records each of which breaks down into a number of *fields*. One of the fields within a record is known as the *key*: this is different for each record and will be used to identify it during computer processing. Examples of record keys are account numbers, works numbers and part numbers. Each file in a computer installation is given a name which enables the computer to identify it, such as 'Customer File', 'Personnel File' and so on.

To understand how computer files are updated and maintained it is necessary to appreciate the characteristics of the storage media used for files. Files are typically held on *magnetic tape, magnetic disks, magnetic drums* or *magnetic cards*; this type of medium is collectively known as *backing store*, as distinct from *main store*, which is the working *memory* of the computer and not used for storing permanent data. All data on backing store is recorded as a series of flux changes in a magnetic recording surface. Each flux change is regarded as a change of state from 0 to 1 or vice versa, i.e. a *binary* code is used to represent numbers or letters of the alphabet. Data is written to backing store by an output from main store, and subsequently read by an input to main store.

Magnetic tape is a *serial* recording medium, differing from magnetic disks, drums and cards which are *direct access* media. Serial files can only be updated serially, by copying from one file to another. Direct access files can be updated serially, but also randomly and *selective-sequentially*.

The characteristics of serial updating are as follows. Records are stored in sequential order according to the record keys. Sorted transactions and file records are each read in turn and the keys examined for a match. If a transaction does not apply the record is written unchanged to a new file. If a transaction does apply the record is updated and similarly written to the new file. Eventually a completely new updated file will have been created. The old file is usually retained for a while in case mistakes have been made during the updating, and usually several *generations* of a file are preserved, all at successive stages of updating. All these generations of a file will have the same file name, and to distinguish between them, each is given a unique number (known as a *generation number*).

The main features of serial updating are that the input transactions with which the file is to be updated are collected into a sizeable batch and sorted into record key order, and every record on the file has to be read and written to a new file whether or not it has been updated. The closer the batch size approaches the file size the fewer will be the number of unwanted records read and rewritten. Magnetic tape files, therefore, are most suitable when large volumes of data are being presented during the updating run. Magnetic tape is the most common method of storing files because of its relatively low cost; the extra flexibility of direct access processing, however, frequently justifies the higher price of the equipment.

The characteristic of direct access files is that *addresses* within the file can be specified, not necessarily in sequence. This permits selective-sequential or random updating. For selective-sequential processing the records within the file are held in key order and input transactions are sorted to this order, as with serial processing. Only those records for which there are transactions, however, are read from the file and, when updated, the records are written back to where they came from. Thus, unwanted records are not *accessed*, with a consequent saving in time, and the file is updated in situ, without copying. This increased efficiency brings with it two problems. First, updated records may not fit back into the file if they have been expanded and there may be no room for new records. Secondly, since past generations of the file are not preserved an alternative system of file security must be devised. The first problem is known as *overflow* and is catered for by having files bigger than they presently need to be. File security is dealt with by keeping copies of files, or copies of the parts that have changed.

Random updating of direct access files eliminates the need for batching and sorting the input transactions, which can be dealt with as they occur. There is no difference in principle from selective-sequential updating, but this implies an orderly progression through the file, while random access involves the need to access any part of the file at any particular instant and is most suitable for low volumes of data. Where response time is critical in file updating, however, for example in airline flight booking, random access is essential.

upper curtate Those *punching positions* of a *punched card* which have *zone* significance and which are usually grouped at the top of a card. Contrasted with *lower curtate*.

up time Synonymous with *serviceable time*.

user 1. A general term for any individual or group ultimately making use of the *output* from a computer system. 2. In an *operating system* an individual exercising control over, or using, a particular *resource*.

user group A group of users of a particular manufacturer's equipment. The group meets to discuss problems, exchange *programs* and generally exchange knowledge gained in installing and developing systems.

user hook A facility provided by suppliers of *software* enabling users to alter, replace or bypass parts of the software.

utility programs Utility programs are part of the *software* of a system, devised to perform operations on *files* of data. Utility programs are not concerned with the specific contents of any file, but operate on whole files treated as units, transferring them from one medium of store to another, making copies of files and re-organizing their sequence.

Utility programs used for transferring data from one storage

426

medium to another include *punched cards* to *magnetic tape* and *paper tape* to magnetic tape programs, magnetic tape to *direct access* storage, and *routines* for printing contents of *storage devices* on a *printer*. The purpose of transferring data from one type of medium to another is usually to place data required for subsequent processing onto a faster storage medium. Thus, for example, a punched card file may be transferred initially to magnetic tape. Once on tape, the file can conveniently be sorted into any required sequence and the data processed by several routines by being read from the magnetic tape. Such *file conversion* routines may also perform *editing* and validation on the basic data, ensuring that the formats on the new storage medium conform to the requirements for subsequent processing. The listing of contents of storage devices on a printer is usually performed for *debugging* purposes, or in the course of program testing, in order to provide a programmer with full details of the file contents. Such routines are seldom used as part of a normal production run, since although the output gives full details of the file content, the format will usually be inconvenient from a user's point of view.

Conversion routines are also usually provided for transferring data from a fast to a slow peripheral, e.g. magnetic tape to cards. Such a transfer would be performed if, for example, it were necessary to convert a data file from one type of magnetic tape to another, incompatible with the former. In this case, the cards punched from the first tape would be read again and converted onto the second tape. In the case of direct access storage devices, it is usual to place the contents of storage onto magnetic tape or some other storage device from time to time, so that if the contents of the direct access file were destroyed in any way, the file may be re-created. This problem arises because with direct access storage updating a file may cause previous information to be *overwritten*, whereas with magnetic tape the original file is not altered in any way.

Utility programs are also produced for making copies of files on the same type of storage device: keeping copies of data files is an essential part of the security of a data processing system, particularly if the organization of the system does not permit re-creation of files through a *generation* system of updating or through *restart* procedures. Copies of files may also be made for use on other machines or by other users.

Programs for re-organizing the sequence of data files form an important section of utility programs. *Sorting* of files, either on magnetic tape or on direct access storage devices, enables the data items in the file to be placed in any required sequence, for subsequent processing. File re-organization also forms an important part of the techniques of storing data in direct access devices, where data is not held in a serial sequence as, for example, on magnetic tape. Using the technique of storing data in *buckets*, whose address is derived from the *key* of the data item being stored, means that the buckets become full up and additional data items have to be stored in other buckets, access being achieved by means of storing the new bucket address in the original bucket. As more and more bucket overflow occurs, the storage device holds more and more addresses as well as data. Thus, in order to release the space taken up by addresses, re-organization of data must take place from time to time.

Other utility programs prepare storage devices to accept data files and check their performance and accuracy. Such programs give *labels* to files, remove labels from files which are no longer required, and can be used, for example, to check magnetic tapes for *parity* errors or direct access devices for flaws in bucket areas.

Utility programs are also used for handling files which hold details of programs and for transferring programs from one type of storage device to another. Such programs operate in the same way as data file utility programs, but also include programs to create and update program *libraries*. Programs for debugging purposes, such as *trace* programs, are also sometimes referred to as utility programs, but since such programs are more specialized than normal utility software the term should not strictly be applied to them.

⇨ articles on *Software, Debugging, Sorting.*

utility routines Synonymous with *Utility Programs.*

utilization ratio The ratio of *effective time* of an *automatic data processing* system to the *serviceable time*, i.e. the ratio of the time spent on productive work, *program* development and incidentals, to the total time during which the system is in a state where it can operate normally.

V

validity check A check to ensure that data falls within certain prescribed limits, e.g. that numerals do not appear in a *field* which should have alphabetic characters only, that a field for days of the month does not contain a number over 31, etc.

variable address Synonymous with *indexed address*.

variable block A *block* whose size is not fixed but varies (within certain limits) according to the data requirements. ⟡ *block mark*. Contrasted with *fixed block length*.

variable connector A *connector* which may be connected to more than one point in a *flowchart* depending on the path taken from a *decision box*.

variable field A field whose length may vary within certain prescribed limits according to the requirements of data. The end of the field is indicated by a *terminal symbol*.

variable length ⟡ *variable field*.

variable, two-valued ⟡ *binary variable*.

V D U Acronym of *visual display unit*.

vector mode display A method for presenting data on a *cathode ray tube visual display unit* in which vectors are displayed as straight lines between points on the screen.

verge-perforated card Synonymous with *margin-punched card*.

verification The process of checking the original punching of data into *punched cards* or *paper tape*. ⟡ the general article on *Data Preparation*.

verifier A *keyboard* operated device used to check the original punching of data in *punched cards* or *paper tape*. ⟡ *punched card verifier, paper tape verifier*. ⟡ the general article on *Data Preparation*.

vertical feed The feed mechanism in which a *punched card* is placed in a *hopper* and passes through a *card track*, all in a vertical position. Contrasted with *horizontal feed*.

video A term generally used for a visual displayment. ⟡ *visual display unit*.

virgin medium A medium completely devoid of any information, e.g. a coil of *paper tape* with no punching, not even feed holes. Contrasted with *empty medium*.

virtual address   An address referring to a *store location* but which must be converted by *address mapping* to obtain a *real address* referring to a specific *main store* location. Has a meaning similar to *relative address* but is applied to computers providing *virtual storage* facilities.

virtual machine   The environment in which all *code* and *data* required to carry out a particular function is executed. ◊ general article on *Virtual Machine Environment.*

virtual machine environment   An environment in which several different users are able to operate their *applications* within a computer system in such a way that there is considerable sharing of *hardware* and *software* facilities. However, each user application is unaware of the existence of other applications, and is developed as though it alone occupied the computer.

In a virtual machine environment each user regards his program as consisting of a series of *instructions* to solve his particular application program. When the program is *compiled*, additional instructions are added to provide an interface with standard *system software* or *middleware* e.g. input/output routines, or file handling routines. During the compiling process, a program is also allocated hardware *resources* including *peripheral devices*.

To the user, the various items of system software which operate in conjunction with his program are not thought of as forming his program – indeed, they will reside in a separate part of the main store and be shared by several other application programs.

The importance of a virtual machine environment is that hardware and software resources are efficiently shared by all users without them being conscious of the fact and with full *security* and privacy for individual programs. Each user's virtual machine thus has protection from interference although it may co-exist with several other virtual machines each operating independently.

Each virtual machine contains a hardware and software mechanism to handle all requests for system software facilities and to pass control to relevant routines. The interaction of all co-existing virtual machines is governed by the *kernel* which is usually that central part of an operating system which interfaces directly with the hardware, and provides mutual synchronization and protection to processes active within the computer. The kernel is instrumental in *mapping* individual virtual machines on to the hardware, and controls the transfer of *segments* between main store and backing store. The kernel monitors virtual machines and their dependence upon events – e.g. the termination of a peripheral transfer – and controls the activation of virtual machines accordingly. It schedules processing time between active virtual machines, and manages peripheral transfers and interrupts within the system.

For the *virtual machine* concept to be effective it must be supported by hardware *architecture* which offers a comprehensive system of protection to all processes active within the system. Such a system provides protection for code and data within a virtual machine from errors internal to that machine, and from the effects of errors occurring in other vitual machines.

A virtual machine environment is one which enables each user application within a computer system to operate independently without interference with other user applications with which it must co-exist, the computer system being designed so that all user applications can efficiently share the resources of processing time, main storage, and system software.

virtual storage A *store* management system in which a user is able to use the storage resources of a computer without regard to constraints imposed by a limited *main store*, and the requirements of other *applications* which may be using the system.

In a computer capable of *multiprogramming*, several application programs may operate at the same time, and must share the resources of the computer. The resources will include main store and *backing store*. This usually means that the programmer responsible for writing the application has to observe constraints on the amount of main store that he uses, and where a program exceeds a specified allocation of main store the programmer must arrange for *overlays* to be organized.

In more advanced computers, hardware and software mechanisms are used to relieve the programmer of the need to observe the constraints of a limited main store. The users of the system are able to assume that the main store is of infinite size. (In practice a program and its data are automatically considered to consist of *segments*, a limited number of the segments will reside in *main store* and the remainder will exist on a fast backing store device.) The maximum amount of storage allowed to any program is of such size as to present no practical constraint to the user. This facility can be provided only by computers with a large enough capacity of main store and backing store, and with an advanced *operating system* to handle the management of storage facilities and the *interrupts* which must occur to ensure that programs are provided with the application code and data from backing store when required.

visual display unit

One method of handling the management of storage in a virtual storage system is *paging*. The object of paging is to ensure that the physical storage capacity is efficiently allocated, particularly the main store. The paging system handles the moving in and out of segments to and from main store. The system operates in such a way that segments currently required for application programs are kept in main store, new segments are brought in as required and inactive segments are transferred to backing store to make room as necessary.

A segment is a large unit of data: segments may be of variable length but each occupying several thousand *words* or *bytes* of storage. They are necessarily so, in order to ensure efficient transfers between main store and backing store; it would be very inefficient to call continually for smaller amounts of information from backing store. However, because the segment is a relatively large unit of store, it cannot readily be accommodated in odd areas of main store which may remain unused at any moment in time. To overcome this problem, segments are considered to consist of smaller units known as pages which can be handled by allocation to small unused areas of storage. A page may be about one thousand words or bytes in size.

Wastage of storage allocated in this way is sometimes referred to as *fragmentation*; a certain degree of main store fragmentation occurs in a paging system but it is much less significant than in a system in which segmentation alone is used.

It follows that if the pages of a particular segment are distributed over a number of areas of the main store, the system used to manage the store must be capable of handling pages so that to all intents and purposes they appear to the user as existing in contiguous areas of storage. A virtual storage system has to ensure that there is complete *security* and a lack of interference between segments and pages used by the different application programs. The principles of *virtual storage* systems can be extended further to the concept of a *virtual machine environment*.

visual display unit A display unit that consists of a *cathode ray tube* which is used to display characters or graphs representing data read from the *main memory* of a computer. A visual display unit also incorporates facilities to key in inquiries so that computer *files* can be interrogated from remote locations.

voice-grade channel A *channel* capable of transmitting speech quality signals.

volatile memory Memory which does not retain stored data when power is cut off. Contrasted with *non-volatile memory*.

volume A unit of magnetic *storage* which can be connected to a computer system; e.g. a reel of *magnetic tape* or a *disk pack*.

W

waiting time The waiting time of a computer *store* is the interval between the moment a *control unit* calls for a *transfer* of data to or from the store and the moment the transfer begins.
Also known as latency.

walk down Successive *partial drive pulses* or *digit pulses* in an incorrectly operating *store* will cause a progressive *irreversible magnetic process* in a magnetic cell. Such a process is known as walk down or *loss of information*. In a correctly operating store, a *steady state condition* (where only *reversible processes* occur) is reached after the application of relatively few partial drive or digit pulses.

warm restart ⋄ *restart.*

waste instruction Synonymous with *do nothing instruction.*

wheel printer A *printer* which prints characters from the rim of a *print wheel*. The available characters are placed round the rim of each wheel and there is a wheel for each printing position.

Williams tube An electrostatic storage *cathode ray tube* which uses a cathode ray tube with only one gun assembly. The device was developed by F. C. Williams of the University of Manchester and was a significant advance in the development of digital representation.

Williams tube storage A method of storage using a *Williams tube.*

wire printer Synonymous with *stylus printer.*

word A basic unit of data in a computer *memory*; the unit will consist of a predetermined number of *characters* or *bits* to be processed as an entity; i.e. a *program instruction* or an element of data. In many digital computers a *fixed word length* is used, but in other machines characters may be grouped to form words of variable length according to the requirements of the particular instructions to be performed.

word length The size of a *word*, measured by the number of *digits* it contains, e.g. a 24-*bit* word will be able to hold numbers in the range -2^{23} to $+2^{23} - 1$.

word oriented A computer is said to be word oriented if the basic

434

element of data which can be individually *addressed* in *store* is a *word*. The individual *bits* or *characters* within the word may be *accessed* by the use of certain *instructions* if required.
Contrasted with *character oriented*.

word time The time required to process one *word* of information in *memory*.

work area An area within *memory* in which items of data are stored temporarily during processing. Also known as working storage, *intermediate storage*.

work assembly The clerical function concerned with the assembly of the data *files* and materials necessary to run a *program* or *suite* of programs. The general coordination of data passing to and from a computer system, including perhaps the maintenance of *manual control routines* to validate the quality of the data received and/or generated by the system.

working, double-length ◊ *double-precision arithmetic*.

working, off-line ◊ *off-line*.

working, on-line ◊ *on-line*.

working, real time ◊ *real time*.

working storage Synonymous with *work area*.

work measurement The use of certain techniques to establish the time a worker should take to carry out a job. ◊ *Time Study*.

work tape A *magnetic tape* retained in the computer room for general use during processing; e.g. available for intermediate *passes* of a *sort program* or for use in program testing. An expired master file might be used as a work tape, or a set of tapes may be assigned a permanent role as work tapes. Compare with *scratch tape*.

work time, machine-spoilt ◊ *machine-spoilt work time*.

wrap round Because the screen of a *visual display unit* cannot always present all the information called for, the wrap round technique allows further data to be displayed at the start of the top line of the screen, overwriting existing data. The rest of the existing data is then successively overwritten until the bottom line is again completed and the process is repeated. Compare with *rack-up*.

wreck Synonymous with *jam*.

write To transcribe data onto a form of *store* from another form of store, e.g. transcribing data onto a *magnetic tape* from the *main memory* of a computer. Data is 'written to' tape rather than 'written on' tape. Contrasted with *read*.

write head An electromagnet used to write on a magnetic medium such as *magnetic tape, magnetic disk*, or *magnetic drum*.
Also known as recording head or writing head.

write inhibit ring   A *file protection ring* which is attached to the *hub* of a *magnetic tape reel* in such a way that it physically prevents any *writing* from occurring on the reel. Contrasted with *write permit ring*.

write permit ring   A *file protection ring* which is attached to the *hub* of a *magnetic tape reel* in order physically to allow data to be *written* to the reel.

Also known as write ring. Contrasted with *write inhibit ring*.

write pulse   A *drive pulse* which either sets the *one condition* of a magnetic cell or writes into the cell.

write ring   Synonymous with *write permit ring*.

write time   The time interval between the instant transcription to a *storage device* begins and the instant it is completed. The write time is therefore the *access time* less the *waiting time*. Related to *read time*.

writing head   ⇨ *write head*.

X

xerographic printer A *page printer* (i.e. a printer in which the character pattern is set for a whole page before printing) using the principle of *xerography*.

xerography A dry copying process: the image to be copied is projected onto a plate causing an electrostatic charge to be discharged where the light falls and retained where the image is black. Resinous powder is then tumbled over the plate, adhering only to the uncharged areas. The resin is transferred to paper or other medium for use as a printing master.

X-position Usually the *punching positions* in the second *row* of a *punched card* starting from the top, also known as the 11-position; the top row is Y or 10, the second X or 11, the third 0 and the rest 1–9. Sometimes however, the notations X and Y are reversed, and it is as well to take great care when making reference to these positions.

X-punch A hole punched in the X-position of a *punched card* (usually the second *row* starting from the top, but ◊ *X-position*).

X-Y plotter ◊ *data plotter*.

Y

Y-edge leading As the top *row* of a *punched card* is known as the Y-row, a card fed long edge first (*parallel feed*), with the top row nearest the read mechanism, is said to be fed 'Y-edge leading'. This contrasts with '*9-edge leading*'; '*serial feed*, column 1 leading'; and, in an 80-column card, 'serial feed, column 80 leading'.

Y-position Usually the *punching positions* in the top *row* of a *punched card*, also known as the ten position; the second row is then X or 11, the third 0 and the rest 1–9. Sometimes, however, the notations X and Y (10 and 11) are reversed, and it is as well to take great care when making reference to these positions.

Y-punch A hole punched in the Y-position of a card (usually the top *row*, but ◊ *Y-position*).

Z

zero 1. Nothing. 2. A numeral denoting zero magnitude. 3. The condition of codes recognized by a computer as zero, such *bit* structures often being different for positive and negative zero.

zero access storage This phrase was once in frequent use for describing storage with a very short *waiting time* or *latency*. A waiting time of zero, however, is not strictly possible, and the phrase has now fallen into disrepute.

zero address instruction format An *instruction format* with no *address* part. Such a format is used when no address is required, e.g. when an instruction refers automatically to another *location*, as in *repetitive addressing*.
Also known as addressless instruction format.

zero balance The result of a technique of balancing if details and totals are both correct: when both details and totals are processed together, with details as negative and the totals as positive, a balance of zero will be obtained if both accumulations are correct.

zero condition The state of a *magnetic cell* when it represents zero.
Also known as zero state and nought state.

zero elimination Synonymous with *zero suppression*.

zero fill To replace all data in a *store* or group of *locations* with the repeated representation of *zero*.

zeroize 1. To reset a mechanical register to its *zero* position. 2. To replace the contents of a *storage area* by pulses representing zero.

zero-level address Synonymous with *immediate address*.

zero output ◇ *zero output signal*.

zero output signal The output given by a *magnetic cell* in the *zero condition* when a *read* pulse is applied.

zero output signal, undisturbed ◇ *undisturbed zero output signal*.

zero state Synonymous with *zero condition*.

zero suppression The elimination before printing of non-significant *zeros*, e.g. those to the left of significant digits. The suppression is a function of editing.
Also known as zero elimination.

zone 1. That area of, for example, a *punched card* in which *zone* *digits* are punched. 2. Part of a *magnetic disk* with a *transfer rate* which differs from the transfer rate of other areas on the same disk; this allows optimum utilization of the surface area. 3. A part of *main memory* allocated for a predetermined function.

zone bit   For example, where six *bits* denote each *character*, the two most significant bits may be used in conjunction with the numeric bits to represent alphabetic and special characters. (✧ *zone, zone digit*.)

zone digit   The numerical key to a section of a *code*; e.g., where a hole is punched in the *X-position* of a *column* of a *punched card* it will give a value to a hole punched in the 2-position of the same column of that card. If a hole were punched in the *Y-position* instead of the X-position, a different value would attach to the hole in the 2-position, and the X-, Y- and (if appropriate) 0 *punching positions* are thus zone digits. Zone digits may be used independently of other punchings for control significance, etc.

zone punch   Synonymous wth *zone digit*.

MORE ABOUT PENGUINS
AND PELICANS

For further information about books available from Penguins please write to Dept EP, Penguin Books Ltd, Harmondsworth, Middlesex UB7 0DA.

In the U.S.A.: For a complete list of books available from Penguins in the United States write to Dept CS, Penguin Books, 625 Madison Avenue, New York, New York 10022.

In Canada: For a complete list of books available from Penguins in Canada write to Penguin Books Canada Ltd, 2801 John Street, Markham, Ontario L3R 1B4.

In Australia: For a complete list of books available from Penguins in Australia write to the Marketing Department, Penguin Books Australia Ltd, P.O. Box 257, Ringwood, Victoria 3134.

In New Zealand: For a complete list of books available from Penguins in New Zealand write to the Marketing Department, Penguin Books (N.Z.) Ltd, P.O. Box 4019, Auckland 10.

Penguin Reference Books

Containing more than 50 titles, the series caters for a diverse readership and covers an extensive range of subjects: from architecture and the arts, to history and archaeology, literature and language, business and economics, geography and the natural, physical and social sciences.

The Penguin Dictionary of Science

E. B. Uvarov and D. R. Chapman, revised by Alan Isaacs

Completely revised and enlarged to include many new words and tables. This dictionary provides reliable definitions and clear explanations of the basic terms used in astronomy, chemistry, mathematics and physics, with a smattering of the words used in biochemistry, biophysics and molecular biology. Notes are also included on all the chemical elements and most of their important compounds.

The Penguin Dictionary of Physics

Edited by Valerie H. Pitt

An abridgement of the latest thoroughly revised version of Grey and Isaacs's *A New Dictionary of Physics*. Includes information gleaned from the latest research, and is intended to provide a concise, accurate guide to the terminology of physics and related disciplines. SI Units used throughout.

The New Penguin Dictionary of Electronics

E. C. Young

Students, teachers, technicians and technologists in the field of electronics will find this an invaluable source of authoritative descriptions and definitions. Emphasis has been given to explaining the action of solid-state devices and circuits, as well as the major techniques used in their fabrication. SI Units used throughout.

Penguin Reference Books

The Penguin Dictionary of Psychology
James Drever

A guide for the student and the layman to the technical vocabulary used by psychologists. Includes recent developments in psychometrics, social psychology, psychopathology and industrial psychology.

The Penguin Medical Encyclopedia
Peter Wingate

This encyclopedia, which has been revised and updated, is addressed to anyone who is concerned with the care of sick people, and in particular to the patient himself, without being a 'do-it-yourself' medical manual. Hundreds of entries deal with the body and mind in health and sickness, with drugs and surgery, with the history, institutions and vocabulary of the profession and with many other aspects of medical science.

The Penguin Dictionary of Biology
M. Abercrombie, C. J. Hickman and M. L. Johnson

Provides basic and invaluable information about more than 1,000 terms which may be encountered by laymen reading scientific literature, students embarking on a science career and qualified biologists reading outside their own field.

The Penguin Dictionary of Economics
Graham Bannock, R. E. Baxter and Ray Rees
(Second edition 1978)

Over 1,600 entries on economic terms and theory, the history of economics, and individual economists where they have made a definite contribution to economic thought. In this revised edition the authors have completely updated the text, incorporating new material where necessary and adding more than 100 new entries.

Penguin Reference Books

The New Penguin World Atlas

Edited by Peter Hall

A completely new edition of *The Penguin World Atlas* – revised and re-designed throughout to make it clearer and simpler for easy reference and to give greater coverage to the Middle East and southern Africa. There are 72 pages of full colour maps in a variety of scales and with an ABC:123 grid system, plus an invaluable 32-page gazetteer.

The Penguin Dictionary of Geography

W. G. Moore

Now revised and enlarged, this dictionary concentrates on physical geography, but includes climatological and meteorological terms, and a number of unclassifiable terms which might be met during a study of physical geography.

The Penguin Dictionary of Geology

D. G. A. Whitten with J. R. V. Brooks

Invaluable for the student as a supplement to the textbook, but also useful to scientists in other fields and to amateurs. Defines and discusses about 3,500 of the most commonly used geological, mineralogical and palaeontological terms. There are 161 text figures which are simple and clear, while a tabular appendix gives technical data for all the minerals which appear in the dictionary.

The Penguin Dictionary of Building

John S. Scott

Explanations and descriptions which are likely to be useful on the job, for the professional builder and the 'do-it-yourself' handyman. The entries range from foundations and footing, to tiling and bricklaying, joinery, plastering, plumbing and lightweight concrete work, among explanations of a host of other processes, tools and materials.

Penguin Reference Books

The Penguin Dictionary of Quotations

J. M. and M. J. Cohen

The reader, the writer, the after-dinner speaker, the crossword-solver and the browser will find what they want among the 12,000 or so quotations which include immortal lines from Shakespeare, *The Bible* or *Paradise Lost* side by side with remarks and stray lines by almost unknown writers.

The Penguin Dictionary of Modern Quotations

J. M. and M. J. Cohen

This companion to *The Penguin Dictionary of Quotations* ranges from the wit of the Goon Show to the declarations of statesmen and the most memorable sayings of the famous and infamous.

The Penguin Dictionary of Twentieth Century History

Alan Palmer

The Penguin Dictionary of Twentieth Century History is designed as a companion volume to the author's earlier book, *The Penguin Dictionary of Modern History, 1789–1945*, and provides a compact reference guide to the political, diplomatic, military, social, economic and religious affairs of the present century.

Mathematician's Delight

W. W. Sawyer

This volume is designed to convince the general reader that mathematics is not a forbidding science but an attractive mental exercise. Its success in this intention is confirmed by some of the reviews it received on its first appearance:

'It may be recommended with confidence for the light it throws upon the discovery and application of many common mathematical operations' – *The Times Literary Supplement*

'It jumps to life from the start, and sets the reader off with his mind working intelligently and with interest. It relates mathematics to life and thought and points out the value of the practical approach by reminding us that the Pyramids were built on Euclid's principles three thousand years before Euclid thought of them' – *John O'London's*

Playing Politics

Michael Laver

For anyone who wants to be a politician, conduct elections, overthrow governments, seize power, make money, or simply learn how to come out on top, this original collection of seven card games illustrates the essential dynamics of the political process. These games, which are perfect for the classroom as well as informal fun, can be played by any number of people and require calculated interaction on the part of the players. Choose among master game plans that include: the establishment of the political system, the development of the electoral process, the forming of parties and coalitions, and the wheeling, dealing, and agenda-controlling of committee politics. To set the stage for classroom discussion, Michael Laver follows the description of how each game is played with a thorough analysis of its relationship to 'real-life' politics.

Burger's Daughter
Nadine Gordimer

'The book has a passionate urgency and suspense, rich, intimate, even confessional . . . a beautifully manipulated work of art, moving towards a tragic and triumphant resolution' – Anthony Thwaite in the *Observer*

In this brilliantly realized work Nadine Gordimer unfolds the story of a young woman's slowly evolving identity in the turbulent political environment of present-day South Africa. The prison death of her father Lionel leaves Rosa Burger alone to explore the intricacies of what it really means to be Burger's daughter. Moving through sensuously described landscapes in Europe and South Africa, through painful love affairs and an overwhelming flood of memories that will not release her, she arrives at last at an understanding of a life bounded on all sides by forces not of her own choosing.

Lovers of Their Time and Other Stories
William Trevor

'I enjoyed and admired every page of it' – John Fowles
With the lightness, grace and wit that characterizes his work, William Trevor has once again produced a masterly collection of stories that will stir and haunt the imagination.

'Polished, pared, precise, delicate stories that make the ordinary and humdrum fascinating, and, as always, beautifully understated and exactly right' – *Sunday Express*

'Uniformly excellent – funny, and sad, and beautifully evocative of time and place, whether the setting is England or Ireland' – *Observer*

DEFIAN

DEFIANCE

C.J. REDWINE

www.atombooks.net

ATOM

First published in the United States in 2012 by Balzer + Bray,
an imprint of HarperCollins
First published in Great Britain in 2012 by Atom

A CIP catalogue record for this book
is available from the British Library.

ISBN 978-1-907411-33-5

Printed and bound in Great Britain by
Clays Ltd, St Ives plc

Papers used by Atom are from well-managed forests
and other responsible sources.

MIX
Paper from
responsible sources
FSC
www.fsc.org   FSC® C104740

Atom
An imprint of
Little, Brown Book Group
100 Victoria Embankment
London EC4Y 0DY

An Hachette UK Company
www.hachette.co.uk

www.atombooks.net

For Clint, who cheerfully sacrificed his free time to support my dreams. Thank you for believing in me. I love you.

CHAPTER ONE

The weight of their pity is like a stone tied about my neck. I feel it in the little side glances, the puckered skin between frowning brows, the hushed whispers that carry across the purple-gray dusk of twilight like tiny daggers drawing blood.

He isn't coming home.

It's hard to ignore the few citizens still milling about the gate leading out into the Wasteland, the guards who flank the opening, and Oliver's solid, reassuring bulk by my side, but I have to. I can't bear to let one sliver of doubt cut into me.

Peering out into the forest that presses against the fifty-yard perimeter of scorched ground that we keep around the city to prevent any threats from approaching our Wall undetected, I look for movement. The Wasteland is a tangle of trees, undergrowth, and the husks of the cities that once were, all coated in the bright, slippery green growth of early spring and the drifting piles of silvery ash that remind us of our fragility. Somewhere in its depths, bands of lawless highwaymen pillage for goods they

1

can trade at the city-states. Somewhere beneath it, the Cursed One roams, seeking to devour what little remains of a once great civilization.

I don't care about any of that. I just want Dad to make it home in time.

"Rachel-girl," Oliver says, his brown, flour-stained fingers wrapping gently around my arm as if to prepare me for what he wants to say.

"He's coming."

"I don't think—"

"He *is*." I dig my nails into my palms and strain to see movement in the thickening twilight, as if by the force of my will I can bring him home.

Oliver squeezes my arm, but says nothing. I know he thinks Dad is dead. Everyone thinks so. Everyone but me. The thought that I stand alone in my conviction sends a bright, hard shaft of pain through me, and suddenly I need Oliver to understand.

To agree.

"He's not just a courier, you know." I glance at Oliver's broad shoulders, which carve a deep shadow into the ground beneath him, and wish for the days when I was little enough to perch on his back, feeling the rumble of his voice through my skin as we walked to the gate to meet Dad after yet another successful trip. "He's also a tracker. The Commander's best. There's no way he got caught unaware in the Wasteland."

Oliver's voice is steady as he says, "He is good at his job, Rachel-girl. But something must have . . . held him up. He isn't coming home in time."

I turn away, trying to see where the perimeter ends and the

Wasteland begins, but the sun is nothing but a fiery mirage below the tree line now, and the shadows have taken over.

"Last call!" one of the guards shouts, his shoulders flexing beneath the dark blue of his uniform as he reaches for the iron handle beside him and begins tugging the gate inward. I flinch as it slams shut with a harsh metallic clang. The guards weave thick, gleaming chains through the frame, securing it until the guards on the morning shift return with the key.

For a moment, we stand staring at the now-closed gate. Then Oliver wraps an arm around me and says, "It's time."

Tears sting my eyes, and I clench my jaw so hard my teeth grind together. I'm not going to cry. Not now. Later, after Dad has been officially declared dead, and my Protectorship has transferred to Oliver, I'll let myself feel the pain of being the only one left who's willing to believe that Jared Adams, Baalboden's best tracker, is still alive.

I use the wooden step box to climb into the wagon that waits for us, and reach a hand back to help Oliver hoist himself up as well.

As the wagon sways and lurches over the cobblestone streets to the Commander's compound, I wrap my fists in my cloak and try to ignore the way my stomach burns with every rotation of the wheels. Oliver reaches out and unravels my cloak from my right hand. His palm swallows mine, his skin warm, the maple-raisin scent of his baking comforting me. I lean into him, pressing my cheek against the scratchy linen of his tunic.

"I'm sorry," he says softly.

For a moment, I want to burrow in. Soak up the comfort he offers and pretend he can make it better. Instead, I sit up, back straight, just the way Dad taught me. "He didn't come back today, but that doesn't mean he won't come home at all. If anyone knows how to survive the Wasteland, it's Dad." My voice catches on a sudden surge of grief—a dark, secret fear that my faith in Dad's skills will be proven wrong, and I'll be left alone. "It isn't fair that he has to be declared dead."

"It's probably my job to tell you life isn't fair, but I figure you already know that." His voice is steady, but his eyes look sad. "So instead, I'll tell you that hope is precious, and you're right not to give it up."

I look him in the eye, daring him to feed me a lie and tell me he still believes. "Even when it looks like everyone else already has?"

"Especially when it looks like everyone else already has." He pats my hand as the wagon grinds to a halt, its bed swaying long after the wheels have stopped.

The driver hops down, walks toward the back of the wagon, and jerks the canvas flap aside. I climb down and watch anxiously as Oliver follows. Though only faint creases mar the brown skin of his face, his hair is more gray than black, and he moves with the careful precision of age. Reaching for him, I slide my arm through his as he navigates his way off the heavy wooden step box. Together, we turn to face the compound.

Like the Wall surrounding the city of Baalboden, the compound is a massive expanse of weather-stained gray stone bolstered by ribbons of steel. Darkened windows are cut into the bulky exterior like lidless, unblinking eyes, and the roof holds several turrets manned with guards whose sole job it is to cut down any intruders before they've gone twenty paces.

Not that any citizen of Baalboden would be stupid enough to defy the man who rules us with a ferocity rivaled only by what waits for us out in the Wasteland.

Before the guard manning the spiked iron gate can open it, another wagon rumbles to a stop behind ours. I glance over my shoulder and heat stings my cheeks as Logan McEntire strides toward us, the dying sun painting his dark-blond hair gold.

I will my pale skin not to betray me and do my best to pretend I don't see him. I've spent so much time today hoping Dad would finally return from the Wasteland, I neglected to consider that any reading of his will would naturally include his apprentice.

Which is fine. As long as I don't have to speak to him.

"Oliver. Rachel," Logan says as he comes to stand beside us. His voice is its usual calm, I-bet-I-can-find-an-algorithm-to-fix-this tone, and I have a sudden desire to pick a fight with him.

Except that would make it look like I care that he's here.

And I *don't*.

His presence won't change anything. My Protectorship will be given to Oliver, Logan will take over Dad's courier duties, and I'll keep checking off the days until Dad comes home again, and life can go back to normal.

Oliver reaches out to clap his free hand on Logan's shoulder. "Good of you to come," he says. As if Logan had a choice. As if any of us have a choice.

"It feels too soon," Logan says softly as the guard opens the gate and waves us forward. "Jared's tough. We should give him more than sixty days past his return date before we're forced to declare him dead."

I glance at Logan in surprise, and find his dark blue eyes on mine, the fierce conviction in them a perfect match for what burns in me. My lips curve into a small smile before I remember I'm not going to act like I care about him.

I've had enough firsthand experience with caring about Logan McEntire to last me a lifetime.

I look away and walk into the compound without another word.

Oliver and Logan follow on my heels. A steward, dressed in black, leads us into a box of a room and quietly excuses himself, shutting the door behind him.

Straight-back wooden chairs surround a long polished table, and six torches rest in black iron brackets against stark white walls. The air feels smoky and closed off, but I don't know if the choked feeling in my throat is from lack of oxygen or from the fact that facing us at the end of the table is Commander Jason Chase, ruler of Baalboden.

The torchlight skims the gold braid on his crisp blue military jacket, scrapes over the twin furrows of the scar that twists a path from his left temple to his mouth, and dies in the unremitting darkness of his eyes.

"Sit," he says.

We obey. Our chairs drag against the stone floor, a high-pitched squeal of distress. Two men sit on either side of the Commander's chair. One worries a stack of parchment lying in front of him with nervous fingers. The other wears a studious expression on the doughy folds of his face and holds a quill poised over an inkwell, a sheet of blank parchment unfurled before him.

The Commander examines each of us in turn before sitting in his chair, his spine held at rigid attention. Without sparing a glance for the two men beside him, he says, "Oliver James Reece, Logan McEntire, and Rachel Elizabeth Adams, you have been called here today to deal with the matter of the death of Jared Nathaniel Adams."

I jerk forward at his words, leaning past Oliver on my left so I can meet the Commander's gaze, but Logan grips my right arm and pulls me back.

"Shh," he breathes against my ear.

I yank my arm from his grasp and swallow the protest begging to be unleashed. We aren't here because Dad is dead. We're here because the Commander won't allow more time for us to prove he's alive. Anger hums beneath my skin.

The Commander continues. "Upon his failure to return from his courier mission to the city-state of Carrington, I invoked the sixty-day grace period for return. Those sixty days are now over."

The round man scratches furiously on the parchment without spilling a spare drop of ink from his quill. I want to speak. To make him record my protest. Anything could have gone wrong in the Wasteland. Dad could've taken sick. Been kidnapped by highwaymen. Been driven off course by the Cursed One. None of those events are necessarily fatal. We just need to give him more time. My body vibrates, tension coiling within me until I have to clamp my jaw tight to keep from interrupting.

"Therefore, by right as ruler and upholder of law in Baalboden, I now pronounce Jared Nathaniel Adams dead."

The small, nervous-fingered man gathers the stack of papers in front of him, clears his throat, and begins to read Dad's will.

I let his words slide past me, willing him to hurry up so we can leave. But when he suddenly falls silent and frowns, I start paying attention.

"Is there a problem?" the Commander asks in a tone meant to convey that there'd better not be.

"It's, ah, just a bit irregular. Highly irregular." The man's fingers clench the parchment, curling the edges until they begin to crumble.

"Continue," the Commander says to him.

A hard knot forms in the pit of my stomach.

"'In the matter of the Protectorship of my daughter, Rachel Elizabeth Adams, I do hereby appoint as her Protector . . . '" Another clearing of his throat. A swift glance in my direction.

No, not in my direction. In *Logan's*.

I grip the table's edge with clammy fingers and feel the bottom drop out of my world as the man says, "'I do hereby appoint as her Protector, until such a day as she is legally Claimed, my apprentice, Logan McEntire.'"

CHAPTER TWO

LOGAN

It takes a second for the news to sink in. For me to realize he said *my* name. Not Oliver's. Mine.

Even as I absorb the sucker punch of panic to my gut, I'm scrambling for a plan. Something we can all agree on as reasonable and just. A Protector is an older male family member or a husband. Not a nineteen-year-old orphan who carved his way out of poverty and desperation to become the apprentice to Baalboden's best tracker.

Maybe the Commander will intervene and tell us how preposterous this is. Acknowledge that I can't possibly be expected to take on a sixteen-year-old ward. Not when a man of Oliver's age and reputation is willing and able.

Instead, the Commander looks across the long expanse of table between us and smiles, a small tightening of his mouth that does nothing to mitigate the predatory challenge in his eyes.

He won't step in without seeing me beg him for it first. I press my lips closed, a thin line of defiance. I'd rather combine every element on the Periodic Table and take my chances with the outcome than humble myself before the Commander. Even for the worthy cause of giving both Rachel and Oliver what I know they want. I'll have to come up with another way to put Oliver in charge of Rachel. Maybe as her new Protector, it's within my rights to assign her to another?

Before I can pursue this line of thinking, Rachel leaps to her feet and says, "No!"

Oliver grabs for her, tugging her toward her chair, but she shakes him off.

"No?" The Commander draws the word out with deliberate intent, looking at her properly for the first time since we entered the room. Dread sinks into me at the way his eyes scrape over her like he'd enjoy teaching her how to keep her mouth shut.

I've seen that expression on the kind of men who frequent the back alleys of South Edge. It never bodes well for the woman they've selected as their prey.

Rachel's voice shakes. "He's not . . . I can't be. . . . This is crazy."

I snatch her arm and forcibly seat her again before she says something that gets her in the kind of trouble I can't save her from. "What she means is that this is very unexpected."

"What I *mean* is there is no way in this lifetime that I'll ever willingly answer to you." She glares at me, but her words are laced with panic.

I understand the feeling. I don't know how to be a Protector. Especially Rachel's Protector. And I don't know what words to say that would make her despise the situation less.

"You dare argue against your father's wishes?" The

Commander leans forward, placing each palm flat against the table.

"No, she doesn't."

"Yes, I—"

"You *don't*." I meet her eyes and try to convey with my expression that she should be quiet and let me handle this. Not that I've ever known Jared's headstrong daughter to be quiet about anything. But the thought of what the Commander could do to her if she angers him makes me sick with fear.

She throws me a look of absolute loathing, then pulls her arm free and turns to the Commander. "He's only nineteen. Wouldn't a man of Oliver's years and experience be a better choice?"

Her words hurt, a sudden sharp ache that takes me by surprise. The fact that I was about to suggest the same does nothing to lessen the sting.

"Your father didn't think so," the Commander says dismissively, turning his gaze from her as if she couldn't possibly have anything more to say.

"But . . . I'm nearly Claiming age. Just three months away. Surely I'm old enough not to need to stay under the roof of my official Protector—"

The Commander straightens abruptly and glares Rachel into silence. "First, you question your father's wisdom over you. Now, you question the Protectorship laws of Baalboden itself?"

"Sir, she's just a bit off balance right now. It's been a difficult day for her." The calm in Oliver's voice is strained around the edges.

The expression on the Commander's face turns the dread coursing through me into stone. Oliver can't defuse him. Rachel can't either, not that she'd try. That leaves me. Standing between the leader who's hated me for most of my life and the girl who thinks she hates me too.

"To argue against the law of Baalboden is to argue against me." The Commander chops each word into a sharp-edged weapon. "Are you absolutely sure you wish to take me on, girl?"

Stepping away from his chair, he marches toward us with slow deliberation. The torches paint grotesque shadows on his face as he passes them, and I brace myself.

Best Case Scenario: All he intends is to give Rachel a lecture, and I can wait until it's over before quietly insisting, as her Protector, that we take her home.

Worst Case Scenario: He intends to punish her physically for having the gall to argue with him, and I'll have to step in. Promise to do the job myself when I get her home. Transfer his attention from her to me. It's what a true Protector would do.

I no longer harbor false hope that I can somehow delegate the job to Oliver. The Commander won't allow it, not after this. Jared trusted *me* with the person he loved most. Not Oliver, her surrogate grandfather. Not Roderigo Angeles, her best friend's father. Me. The orphaned apprentice she once said she loved. I don't understand why Jared felt this was best for her, but I don't have to. He offered an outcast street rat a place at his table. Not just as an employee, but as a friend. I owe it to him to do my best for Rachel.

And because I understand how it feels to have the foundation you built your life on get ripped away from you, I owe it to Rachel, too.

The Commander now stands behind Rachel's chair, gripping

its back with bloodless fingers. He's beginning to look close to his seventy-odd years. His skin is worn and thin, and wrinkles score the backs of his hands. Still, his frame is muscular, and he moves with the steady grace of an experienced fighter. Only a fool would underestimate him.

"If not for *me*, the survivors of the Cursed One's first attacks fifty years ago would be scattered across the ruins of their cities. Leaderless. Hopeless. Or do you forget that while the monster might lay waste to others, it never comes within Baalboden's Wall?"

The Commander leans closer, the torchlight flickering across his skin to gild Rachel's hair with flame. His words are brittle slaps against the air.

"If not for *me*, the Cursed One would have burned this city to the ground decades ago." His voice is rising, his fingers clenched against the back of her chair like he means to snap it in two.

"I will not tolerate dissension. I will not tolerate disobedience."

He grabs a handful of her hair and twists her around to face him. I clench my fists and prepare to defend her if he takes it any further. She hisses a quick gasp of pain, but meets his eyes without flinching.

"And I will not tolerate a mere girl speaking to me as if she was my equal. You live because I allow it. Never forget that."

Deliberately unclenching my fists, I open my mouth to offer the Commander whatever assurances it takes to get him to calm down, but Rachel beats me to it.

"I won't forget it."

She sounds appropriately frightened and humbled, though

knowing her it's possible she's simply figured out how to show him what he expects to see. He uncurls his fingers from her hair, wipes his hand against his pant leg as if he's touched something filthy, and abruptly turns to me.

"Let that be a lesson to you in how to control your ward. It appears Jared was somewhat remiss in her education."

He has no idea just how remiss Jared's been about instilling in Rachel the docile, meek obedience expected from a woman in Baalboden. I manage a single nod, as if grateful for the tutelage.

"I should take her home now," I say, making every effort to sound as if I feel nothing about the entire proceeding.

"Indeed," Oliver says, reaching out to engulf Rachel's hand in his. His voice is just as unruffled as mine. We both know better than to show emotion to the Commander. "We'll need to pack her belongings. Or are you planning to move into Jared's house?"

It's going to be hard enough to adjust to living under the same roof as Rachel. I don't think I can bear it if I also have to adjust to leaving the solitude of my little cottage behind as well.

"She'll move to my house."

Rachel jerks as if I've slapped her. It suddenly occurs to me that maybe she can't bear the thought of leaving her home either, but it's too late to take it back. To show indecisiveness in front of the Commander is foolish in the extreme. Regret over my words mixes with anger at being forced into a position where my only choices are to give up everything or expect Rachel to instead. There's no right answer, no easy solution that will somehow make this bearable for either of us. The weight of my new responsibility feels heavy enough to crush me.

"May we leave?" Oliver asks the Commander.

His dark eyes gleaming, the Commander says, "You may." But as we push our chairs away from the table and get to our feet, he steps closer to Rachel and glances at me, malice glittering in his eyes. "Tell me, girl, why do you despise your new Protector so much? And don't bother trying to lie." His eyes slide off of me and onto her. "I'd only have to punish you." He doesn't sound sorry about this.

Rachel throws me one quick look, her blue eyes pleading. It's the same look I saw two years ago, the morning of her fifteenth birthday, when everything changed between us. I'd just won the apprenticeship to Jared, and he was out on a courier mission to Carrington, a city-state several days' journey to the east of us. Oliver was staying at the house as he always did when Jared was away, and he was busy in the kitchen baking Rachel's favorite lemon cake for her birthday treat. I'd joined Rachel on the back porch at her request. I thought she simply wanted to talk about missing Jared, or missing her mother, something we both had in common.

Instead, she sat beside me, her cheeks flushing, her eyes refusing to meet mine, and told me she was in love with me. I heard the vibrant hope in her words, heard the way her breath caught in her throat when I took too long to answer, and felt clumsy and foolish.

She looked at me as I sat, baking in the early summer sunshine, scrambling for something to say that wouldn't hurt her but wouldn't encourage the impossible. I tried to explain. To tell her I couldn't think about romance when I had so much to prove. To make her see how fast Jared would terminate my apprenticeship if he thought there was anything improper between us. To assure her she was young, and there would be others.

The words were awkward and stilted, and I couldn't figure out what to do with my hands as the hope in her eyes slowly turned to pleading and finally subsided behind a cold wall of anger. I reached out, bridging the distance between us like I could somehow erase the damage, but she jumped to her feet and left me sitting there with nothing but the echo of my promise that she'd get over me.

She's spent every second since proving me right. I haven't had a glimpse of anything beneath the fierce independence she wears like a second skin until now. Now, with the Commander demanding to be privy to details that I know humiliated her, she turns to me. I don't intend to let her down.

"I'm afraid I've behaved rather poorly toward Miss Adams in the past," I say, stepping slightly in front of Rachel so the Commander has to either deal with me or be the first to step back. "I can't blame her for hoping a good man like Oliver would be her father's choice."

He studies me with a smirk. "Either Jared didn't care about this poor behavior of yours, or he never knew about it."

I nod toward the Commander with the barest pretense of respect before turning to face Rachel. "Shall we go get your things packed?"

Her face is dead white. Even the torchlight refuses to lend her any color. Straightening her spine, she slides her shield of fierce independence back in place and says, "Fine. But only until Dad returns." Then she walks out of the room.

I move to follow her, but the Commander's hand snakes out and digs into my shoulder. "And when is Jared planning to return?" he asks.

"I beg your pardon?"

His tone is vicious. "She said 'until he returns.' When do you expect his return?" His other hand rests on the hilt of his sword, and his fingers bite into my cloak like he wishes he could draw blood.

"We don't expect his return," I say calmly, though my mind is racing. If the Commander really thinks Jared simply died while traveling the Wasteland, why the sharp interest in Rachel's belief Jared will return? "Rachel only wishes things were different."

"If you know something more about Jared's recent failure to return, tell me now."

"I don't know anything."

"Don't even think about lying to me," the Commander says, malice dripping from every word.

The silence between us is thick with tension, and my thoughts race. The Commander doesn't think Jared ran into trouble on his last mission. And he certainly doesn't think Jared's dead. I'm not sure what's going on, but I know with terrible certainty that Jared is in more danger from his leader than he could ever be from the Wasteland.

"I'm not lying," I say.

The Commander leans forward, chopping off his words like he'd spit them in my face if he could. "If I find out otherwise, I'll punish the girl first. You, of all people, should understand that."

The sudden memory of my mother's broken body lying lifeless at the Commander's feet makes it nearly impossible to say, "I understand."

He releases my shoulder slowly, and I turn to leave the room, keeping my head held high. My back straight. My face schooled into an expressionless mask as if the twin fuels of panic and anger haven't been ignited deep where the Commander never thinks to look.

Jared's in trouble. I have to come up with a solution—something I can use to track him down before the Commander does. And I have to do it before the Commander decides we know more than we're telling. As I stride out of the compound, following Oliver and Rachel toward the waiting wagons, I begin to plan.

CHAPTER THREE

RACHEL

Oliver and I take a wagon to my house while Logan decides to walk the considerable distance from the compound to his little cottage in the southwest corner of town. I imagine he wants time to assess the problem of being my Protector and come up with a plan for how to handle it.

Except there is no plan that will make living under the same roof as Logan easy to bear. And there is no plan that will make me accept having Dad declared dead. This isn't one of Logan's precious piles of wire and gears. He can't fix this.

We enter my house, greeted by the lingering aroma of the sticky buns Oliver made for breakfast. I guess he'll move back to his own house now, and this little yellow rectangle with its creaking floors and generous back porch will be home to no one at all.

I stand in the front room, wishing desperately I could over-turn Logan's edict and stay right here.

"Rachel-girl, it's full-on dark. If we don't leave soon, we won't make it out to Logan's tonight."

"Then we'll stay here."

"We can't." Oliver brushes a hand against my arm and nods toward the front window. I look and find two guards standing on our front lawn, waiting at the edges of the street torch's flickering light. "I guess the Commander had some doubts about you fulfilling your father's will."

I turn away from the window—and the proof that I have no power to change my situation—and say, "Let me take a minute to say good-bye."

"I'll put your clothes into a trunk while you do."

I wander through the house, touching pieces of my childhood and letting the memories swallow me whole.

The doorway where Dad gouged out a notch and carved in the date every year on my birthday to track my growth.

The sparring room with its racks of weapons where Dad taught me how to defend myself.

The kitchen table where Dad and I joked about his terrible cooking. I run my fingers across the heavy slab of wood. This is also the table where Logan first became a part of our lives, back when he was a skinny, dirty boy with hungry eyes hiding behind Oliver's cloak. I'd watched him as the years passed. Watched him soak up knowledge and skill like a dry blanket left out in a rain storm until eventually he turned himself into the kind of man who could command Dad's respect. And I'd foolishly thought myself in love with him.

The memory burns within me, a bed of live coals I swear I'll stop walking across. I don't want to think about Logan, about feeling soft and hopeful toward him once upon a time. Not when I'm saying good-bye because Logan couldn't be bothered to understand how hard it would be for me to lose both my dad and my home on the same night.

Grief rises, thick and hot, trying to suffocate me. My eyes sting, and I dig my nails into the tabletop as a single sob escapes me.

I will not break down.

I will *not*.

I refuse to walk into Logan's home with tear-stained eyes and trembling lips. Stifling the next sob that shakes me, I blink away the tears and clench my hands into fists. Dad would've returned by now if he could. I can't hold on to false hope any longer. He isn't coming home. Not without help.

My eyes slide toward the still-open door of the sparring room as an idea—a ridiculous, bold, almost impossible idea—takes root. Dad can't come home without help, and the Commander shows no inclination to send a search party. But Dad doesn't need a sanctioned search party. Not when he's spent years training me how to handle myself in the Wasteland, smuggling me out of Baalboden so I could go with him on his shorter missions and making sure I could defend myself against any threat.

And not when Logan knows how to track.

The memory of Logan's belief in Dad's survival skills is a tiny sliver of comfort I grab onto with desperate strength. It pains me to admit it, but Logan is better at planning than I am. If anyone can help me—if anyone in Baalboden would *want* to help me—it's Logan.

The grief subsides, sinking beneath cold, hard purpose. I walk into the sparring room, strap a leather sheath around my waist, and slide my knife into place.

I'm going to find a way over the Wall and bring Dad home. Logan can either help me, or get out of my way.

CHAPTER FOUR

LOGAN

She's been under my roof for twelve hours. One hour was spent trying to cook and eat a meal without accidentally brushing up against each other and without engaging in conversation. Mostly because she looked shocked and lost, and I had no words that would make it better.

Two-point-five hours were spent listening to her move around the tiny loft above me while I worked on a design for a tracking device and told myself no one should have that much power over my ability to concentrate.

The other eight-point-five hours, we slept. Or she did. I hope she did. I lay awake for more hours than I care to recall listening for a telltale catch in her breathing that would tell me how deeply she must be hurting. She remained silent, and I remained mostly sleepless.

Now the morning light feels harsh against my eyes, and my brain feels incapable of even the most rudimentary exercise in logic. Twelve hours into my role as her Protector and I'm sure of one thing: Moving Rachel into my little brick-and-mortar cottage wasn't one of my better ideas.

The small stipend I receive as Jared's apprentice is enough to pay for a house of my own with a bit left over for tech supplies and food. I have no idea how I'm going to make it stretch to cover Rachel's needs as well. However, considering the current state of our relationship, money is the least of my current difficulties.

I'm sitting on my patched leather couch when she climbs down from the loft, sunlight tangling in the red strands of her hair and shimmering like fire. Her face is pale and composed, at odds with the fierce glint in her eyes as she looks at everything but me.

I should say something.

Anything.

No, not just anything. She had a rough day yesterday. She probably needs words of comfort and compassion.

I should've invited Oliver to breakfast.

She wanders through the living room, bypassing stacks of books and running her finger along my mantel, leaving a flurry of dust in her wake.

Did I ever realize there was dust on the mantel?

The silence between us feels unwieldy. I clear my throat and try to think of the most conciliatory greeting I can compose. How are you? Did you enjoy sleeping in my tiny loft instead of the comfortable bed you've always known? It's somewhat cold outside. Did you bring your heavy cloak when you packed up all your belongings to move here because I didn't think fast enough on my feet to realize I should let you keep your home?

If those sound half as stupid coming out of my mouth as they do in my head, I can't say them. Maybe I should just offer her some breakfast.

Her shoulders are tense as she moves away from my mantel and toward the slab of pine I use as my kitchen table. Its surface is covered with papers, inkwells, wires, and bits of copper. In the center, beside a stack of carefully drawn designs, lie the beginnings of the invention I'm hoping will solve this entire situation.

Her lips are pressed tight, dipping down in the corners.

I can say I'm sorry. She'll hear the sincerity in my voice. I'll say I'm sorry and then—

She reaches her hand toward the delicately spliced wires of my new invention. I leap to my feet, scattering books across the floor, and say, "Don't touch that!"

She freezes and looks at me for the first time.

"I mean . . . it's still a work in progress and it needs . . . Did you sleep okay? Of course not. You have your cloak, right? Because the weather is . . . I'm just going to make you some breakfast."

I sound like an idiot. Being solely responsible for a girl—no, being solely responsible for *Rachel*—has apparently short-circuited my ability to form coherent speech. Partially because the only girl I've ever really talked to is Rachel, and we stopped talking two years ago. And partially because ever since she said she loved me, I've felt unbearably self-conscious around her.

She stares me down and then deliberately presses her finger against the half-finished device before her. Her expression dares me to pick a fight, and I could easily take her up on it. It might be a relief to get some of the uncomfortable, volatile emotions from yesterday out into the open.

But Rachel doesn't need to deal with my grief and anger. She needs an outlet for her own. Any other Baalboden girl would want sympathy and the cushion of her Protector keeping all hardship from her. But while other girls were raised to be dependent and obedient, Rachel was taught to think and act for herself. I know exactly how to help her.

"Want to spar?"

She frowns and slowly pulls her hand away from the wires. "Spar?"

"Yes."

She glances around as if looking for the trap. "Why?"

"Because it's been two and a half years since you last knocked me flat on my back. I figure I'm due." Not that I'm going to make it easy for her to beat me. She'd hate me if I did.

I smile as I walk toward her and nearly trip on a stack of haphazardly organized books.

Why don't I ever put things away around here?

She lifts her chin. "I only spar with—"

Jared. She only spars with Jared, but she can't make herself finish the sentence. Her lips tremble before she presses them back into an unyielding line.

"I'm sorry." I reach a hand toward her, but she doesn't look at it, and I let it fall. "I wish I could change things. I wish I hadn't made you move in here when I should've let you stay in your home. I wish Oliver had been named your Protector, so you'd feel comfortable. And I wish Jared . . ."

I can't say I wish he wasn't dead, because I don't think he is. The Commander doesn't think he's dead either. I'm hoping to be the first to prove that theory right. If I can't finish my invention and track Jared across the Wasteland before the Commander homes in on him, I'm afraid Jared will face the kind of brutal death only our leader is capable of dispensing.

Rachel's glare softens into something bright and fervent. "You don't think Dad's dead, do you?"

I shake my head.

"I knew it. I hoped I could count on you." Her cheeks flush faintly, and she leans closer. Warmth unfurls in my chest at her faith in me. If she can learn to trust me, maybe we can start over. Rebuild our friendship and figure out how to make this impossible situation work.

She says, "I've been thinking of ways we can get out of Baalboden so we can find him. If there's a sanctioned highwayman trading day, we could . . ."

The warmth within me turns to ice as she talks, one wild escape idea after another spilling from her mouth, a collection of dangerous pitfalls guaranteed to trap her beneath the merciless foot of the Commander. The memory of his whip falling in cruel precision across my mother's back slaps at me with a swift shock of pain.

Jared is counting on me to protect Rachel. Oliver is too. And with the Commander already suspicious that we know Jared's whereabouts, the risk of getting caught in an escape attempt is high.

Too high to allow her to come along.

She'll fight me on it. Probably hate me for it. But since she already despises me, I've got nothing to lose by standing in her way.

"We aren't leaving Baalboden to go looking for Jared," I say quietly.

The sudden silence between us is fraught with tension.

"But you said you think he's alive." She sounds baffled and hurt, and regret is a bitter taste in my mouth, but I can't allow her to risk everything. Jared wouldn't want his daughter to die trying to save him.

I don't want her to die either. She may not like me now, but I haven't forgotten that of all the citizens in Baalboden, only Oliver, Jared, and Rachel ever bothered to look at me like I was worth something.

"Logan?"

I make myself meet her eyes. Make myself memorize the way they look when they aren't filled with animosity or anger. Then I shove my regret into a corner and focus on the more important task: Keep Rachel safe until I can stash her with Oliver and go out into the Wasteland to find Jared myself. I don't know what Jared could've done to gain the Commander's merciless animosity, but he's become family to me. I can't stand back and do nothing.

"I do think he's alive," I say. "But we aren't going out looking for him. It's a suicide mission, one he'd never allow you to—"

"Don't tell me what Dad would allow me to do!"

"Rachel . . ."

Her face is dead white, her eyes a blaze of misery and fury. "So, you're content to just sit here in your little house, doing whatever it is you do all day, while somewhere out there Dad needs our help?"

No, I want to tell her. I'm about ten days out from finishing an invention I made specifically because I couldn't stand to sit here doing nothing while somewhere out there Jared is missing. But if I tell her that, it's tantamount to giving her permission to come along. And I'm not willing to do that.

I clench my jaw and say, "We aren't going."

Her lip curls, a scornful expression that seems to say I've just lived up to her lowest estimation of me, and she steps back. Her disappointment hurts, but I meet her gaze without flinching.

"I'm sorry, Rachel."

She turns and walks out of the house.

CHAPTER FIVE

RACHEL

Logan does *nothing* but spend hours hunched over his kitchen table fiddling with wires and bits of metal. I want to punch him every time I walk into the room. We barely look at each other. Barely speak. He won't change his mind, and I'm not about to beg. I don't need Logan to travel the Wasteland with me as I track Dad. All I need is a way over the Wall.

Three days after moving into Logan's house, I found his magnetic handgrips, perfect for sliding safely down the bulky steel ribs along the Wall. Three days after *that*, he unknowingly presented me with the perfect opportunity for escape.

Now I wrap my cloak around myself and push into the sparse crowds still drifting stall to stall in Lower Market, haggling over produce, rubbing linens between their fingers to check for quality, and whispering in my wake.

It's been thirteen years since a woman dared walk through the Market without her Protector. She paid for her actions with her life.

Flicking the hood of my cloak over my head, I make sure it hides every strand of the red hair that makes me so easily recognizable. I don't like the idea of risking my life by going through Market alone, but I'm desperate for the chance to do what no one else seems willing to do—search for Dad outside the Wall.

Lower Market is laid out like a man's back. The main road forms the spine and leads toward the North Tower, while smaller roads and alleys branch off like ribs running east and west. My heart pounds a little faster as I aim for the left side of the main road and start walking.

The first stall I reach is a trestle table laden with a few remaining crates of juicy pears and thick-skinned melons. A woman and her Protector squeeze the fruit between their fingers before loading up their sack, murmuring to each other as they weigh each choice. Ignoring them, I move on. A glance at the sky tells me I have about thirty minutes until twilight and the final closing of the gate.

Puddles gouge the gritty road, courtesy of an early-afternoon rain shower. I pass the butcher, already cleaning his knives and packing away the last of his mutton, and wrinkle my nose as the rusty scent of drying sheep's blood lies heavy on the air, mingling with the smell of mud.

Two more stalls down, I reach the candle maker's and the first of the west-running roads. I tuck my head down, hiding both my hair and my face beneath my hood. No one stops me as I make the left turn, though I feel the stares burning through the heavy leather of my cloak. Probably wondering what idiot of a Protector is fine with allowing his ward to walk unescorted through Lower Market.

31

Of course, Logan isn't fine with this. Or he won't be, once he finds out. Right now, though, I'm pretty sure he's talking tech with vendors far away from here, but still I tighten my cloak and try to look a little less . . . Rachel. Just in case.

A man on my left is hawking a collection of hunting knives with leather sheaths. Giving his wares a cursory glance, I slide my hand beneath my cloak and run my fingers along the sheath I wear strapped to my waist. His knives are nice.

Mine is better.

Leaving my knife alone, I keep walking. I've made the journey to Oliver's tent with Dad more times than I can count, and there are never any guards on the western side of Lower Market this late in the day. Still, I move briskly and keep to the sides, hoping to avoid attracting too much attention.

I'm nearly halfway to my destination when I reach an open wagon filled with bags of dried lentils, onions, and white beans. Three men lean against the side, watching in silence as the merchant's daughter scoops beans into burlap sacks. I sidestep them, but pull up short as one of the men whistles softly, a low thrice-note tune of warning that sends chills up my spine.

That warning whistle can only mean one thing: guards. In Lower Market at twilight.

I can't waste time wondering why guards are here, of all places, on the one day when I've decided to break the most sacred laws on the books. My heart pounds, a thunderous, uneven rhythm, and I start looking around for a way out.

I have no intention of allowing them to catch me.

CHAPTER SIX

LOGAN

"Copper tubing. Twenty-two gauge." Which I could get just about anywhere. "A spool of wire. Sixteen gauge." A little trickier to come by, especially since I'm picky about my wires, but still, not an over-the-top request. I take a second to steady my nerves before making my final request.

"That all?" the proprietor asks.

Hoping I don't sound like I'm concerned about the consequences of committing treason I say, "I'll also need a barrel of acid."

This is the moment when every other merchant I've visited today suddenly decided my money was no longer welcome. I'm scraping the bottom of Baalboden's list of possible vendors by coming here, but there aren't any others left to try unless I want to deal with the highwaymen selling their wares outside the gate.

I don't.

I'd rather not advertise to the guards patrolling the perimeter that I'm using unstable substances in my inventions.

The proprietor stares me down, his hands slowly working the tap on a large wooden barrel full of hazy golden ale. "Don't think I rightly heard you."

I keep my voice low and repeat my request as I lean against the far corner of the bar-top counter in Thom's Tankard. The wood, a dull dirt brown, is sticky with the residue of spilled drinks and fried potatoes, and I'd sooner swallow lye than eat anything on the menu, but I'm not here for food.

Thom slaps a heavy wooden mug filled with ale in front of me, though I haven't ordered a drink. "Ain't got none."

Sure he does. Or if he doesn't, he knows where to get some. There aren't any black-market vendors operating in Baalboden without Thom's knowledge.

"Where can I find it, then?"

He shrugs his massive shoulders and picks up a grimy rag to smear across the greasy countertop as if cleaning is suddenly a priority.

I'm sick of running into roadblocks. If I can't convince him to give me what I need, I won't be able to finish my current invention. If I don't finish my current invention, I can't head into the Wasteland to find Jared. And if I don't find Jared, Rachel and I are stuck together until next year's Claiming ceremony, when another hapless man can do his best to tame her strong will into something that won't get her tossed into the Commander's dungeon.

I wish him luck.

"How much for the supplies?" I ask Thom. Maybe if he sees that I refuse to go away, he'll deal with me. *Someone* has to deal with me. They can't all be afraid of the potential repercussions.

"Boy, you must be stupid."

I laugh, a short sound devoid of mirth. I'm a lot of things—Protector, orphan, inventor, outcast—but I'm not stupid.

I am, however, a little desperate.

By the look of the place, so is Thom. The grooved wooden floor is splintered and sagging. The walls are stained with soot from the torches he uses instead of lanterns. And his stock of ale behind the counter looks more than half depleted. I don't have the kind of money that will take care of the slow decline I see here.

But beneath the decline, I sense something else. In the darkened corners, in the tense, watchful eyes of the serving girl who glances repeatedly out the heavily shrouded windows, and in the huddled, quiet conversation of the six men sitting behind me—the only other patrons in the tavern—an undertone of secrecy wraps the room in deliberate seclusion.

What would Thom pay to protect those secrets from the prying eyes of the Commander and his guards? I pull a pair of small circular wooden objects from my cloak and set them on the counter. "You see these?"

He grunts and darts a look at the group in the corner. Interesting. I'm guessing he isn't their leader, or he wouldn't be looking to them for permission to continue our discussion. And they wouldn't be hiding in the corner if they were in good standing with the Commander. Which means all of us are on the same side.

I just need to make them see it.

Raising my voice only enough to reach the group's ears without sounding obvious, I say, "These are surveillance discs modified to alert you to the approach of a guard anywhere in a twenty-five-yard radius. You insert a battery in each"—I pull out a small battery from the batch I made last week and slap it on the counter—"and mount one to the outside of your building. It sends out a sonic pulse every thirty seconds and takes a reading of every citizen's wristmark in the immediate area. If any of those wristmarks carry the military code, the outside disc triggers an alarm built into the disc you keep behind the counter. A twenty-five-yard radius means you have at least a forty-second warning. More than enough time to modify any suspicious behavior before getting caught."

I sense more than hear the sudden quiet in the group behind me.

"I'm happy to give you a demonstration of their capabilities, but once I do, I expect my tubing, my wire, and my barrel of acid."

A deep voice speaks from behind me. "You're Logan McEntire, aren't you?"

Turning, I face the group and their speaker, a man with bushy black hair, a silver-shot beard, and dark eyes, assesses me with fierce concentration.

I nod slowly, trying without success to put a name with his face. "I am."

"Guess the fine merchants of North Hub didn't have what you need. Or if they did, you aren't exactly the person they want to be seen selling it to, are you?"

"No."

The silence thickens between us, broken only by the slow steady drip of ale leaking from the barrel behind Thom and the quiet movements of the serving girl, who takes another look out the window as if searching the street for something.

"You take a risk bringing tech like that out into the open." The man gestures toward the discs lying on the counter beside me. "If you're caught, it's the dungeon or worse for you."

"The guards leave me alone as much as the rest of you do."

"And how do you feel about that?"

"Am I supposed to feel something about it?"

His stare is unwavering. "If my mother was flogged to death for breaking the law, and I was declared a social outcast when I was but six years old, I think I'd feel something about it. Especially toward the man doing the flogging."

His words rake across a long-healed scar, drawing fresh blood. He's right. My mother broke the law and paid the price. And in a perpetual example of the consequences of disobedience, the Commander declared me an outcast, fit for nothing but life on the street until I came of age at seventeen. It's impossible to separate the law and its punishments from the Commander, since in Baalboden the two are one and the same, but I've tried. It's the only way I can live here without wanting to kill him.

"She shouldn't have broken the law," I say, though it's hard to sound like I mean it.

"Or maybe the law shouldn't demand a flogging for a woman caught walking the city streets without her Protector." The man watches me closely.

This is my test. The hoop I must jump through to convince them to allow Thom to do business with me. With the memory of my mother's last moments burning into my brain, I find it easy to agree. "Maybe it shouldn't."

"Bet you're wondering what we're doing meeting here discussing things that sound like treason."

"Bet you're wondering what I'm doing standing here asking for materials banned by law."

The man smiles, a wide crack of white in his black and silver beard. "I'm Drake. I've been looking forward to meeting you for some time."

I try to match his smile, but my mind is racing. Either Drake was a friend of my mother's and has waited until now to offer his friendship, or he thinks I'm an acceptable target to be recruited into what appears to be an anti-Commander group.

Which isn't going to happen. Not that I don't share their sentiments, but my mother is a prime example of how the price of dissent isn't worth the negligible payout.

Besides, I have an invention to finish, my mentor to track across the Wasteland, and a very independent ward to keep out of trouble. My plate is full.

"Any chance I can do business with your man here?" I nod toward Thom.

"Thom, get the man his supplies. Take the discs as payment."

Thom needs an extra day to procure the acid, so I agree to come back the following evening to complete the purchase. And because I'm not a fool, I take one of the surveillance discs with me as I go. He can have it once he delivers the rest of my order.

Setting out at a brisk pace toward the prosperous North Hub section of the city, where Rachel is spending the day with her best friend, Sylph, learning how to properly host a dinner party, I try to shake off the lingering image of my mother dying beneath the bite of the Commander's whip. I've had years of practice, and the picture fades before I've gone fifteen yards. The small spark of sedition ignited within me at the dingy tavern takes much longer to dissolve.

CHAPTER SEVEN

RACHEL

There shouldn't be guards this far west in Lower Market, but I don't doubt the warning whistle in the least. My pulse kicks up, pounding relentlessly against my ears, and I clench my fists to keep my hands steady. I refuse to be caught. Stopping beside the man who gave the warning, I turn and pretend to examine a sack of pearly-white onions while I sweep the area.

Men on their own or women with their Protectors continue to drift from stall to stall, but there's a jerkiness to their movements now. A prey's instinctive awareness of a predator.

My eyes scrape over canvas tents anchored to the ground with iron pegs, linger in the shadows between the rough-hewn stalls, and finally catch a diamond-bright shard of sunlight kissing the silver of a sword.

The guard is wedged in the narrow space between Madame Illiard's display of silk Claiming dresses and the painted green stall of Parsington's Herbal Remedies.

He isn't alone—they never are—but his partners aren't as

easy to spot. It takes a minute before I see them. Cloaked. Carrying sacks and baskets. Trying to look like they're just another group of citizens.

As if citizens ever spit-shine their boots and need enough space beneath their cloaks to accommodate a scabbard.

My heart is pounding so hard I worry the man beside me will hear it. I need a plan. One that keeps me out of the dungeon but still gets me to my destination in time.

The first guard raises his hand, and I spot the gleaming black oval Identidisc a split second before the green light flashes, sending a sonic pulse across a seventy-yard radius, scanning the unique wristmark every citizen has tattooed onto their left forearm at birth. My fingers want to creep to my wrist to worry the magnetic bracelet Logan insists I wear to block the disc's ability to read my wristmark, but I clench my fist and remain still.

As soon as the guard drops his gaze to the Identidisc's data, I move.

Sliding past the wagon, I duck into a tent half filled with sturdy cast-iron pots and watch for my opportunity. It doesn't take long. The citizens know better than to stand around staring at the guards. Crowds begin sluggishly moving along the street again, though conversations are muted, and most look like they want nothing more than to leave the Market behind.

I couldn't agree more. My heart is pounding like it wants out of my chest, and it's a struggle to force myself to think clearly, but I must. I have to plan. To find a solution that doesn't end with me trapped between two guards, trying to talk my way out of the kind of flogging that long ago cost Logan his mother.

Logan.

What would Logan do?

Logan wouldn't be in this position in the first place because he'd already have everything mapped out with the kind of meticulous precision he applies to everything—a trait that usually irritates me, but now suddenly seems more attractive. Not that I'd ever admit it to him. Still, thinking like Logan gives me an idea, and I start searching for what I need.

Before long, I see my way out. A man—single, older, stoop-shouldered—walks slowly by my hiding place. I step out, match his pace, and lower my eyes as though I've been taught to respect my betters.

The man doesn't seem to notice my presence, which saves me the trouble of trying to come up with a plausible explanation for pretending he's my Protector. When he stops to browse for new boots, I seamlessly transfer to the next single man walking west.

This one casts a quick glance in my direction, frowns, and whispers, "What are you doing? Where is your Protector?"

I widen my eyes and do my best to look surprised. "I'm sorry. From the back, you look so similar. I thought . . ." I gesture, a tiny fluttering of my hands that conveys both helplessness and distress. "He said to wait while he went to Oliver's, but there are guards, and I got scared." My voice trembles just a bit.

His frown deepens, and he steps closer. "He should know better than to leave you alone at all." He glances around the street. "There's something going on today."

I wring my hands together and consider producing a few tears. That seems to bring most men to their knees. Except for Logan, curse his stubborn soul. Not that I *wanted* Logan on his knees. Not anymore.

The man nods once, as if resolving some internal debate. "I'll take you to Oliver's. Stick close and keep your eyes down as is proper."

I nearly bite my tongue in half to keep from telling him, in great detail, where he can put his ideas of what's *proper*. Instead, I look carefully at my feet and follow my borrowed Protector as he slices through the rapidly dwindling crowds on his way to Oliver's.

Two left turns later, we're at the western edge of the Market. I sidestep a woman wrestling a plucked turkey into the woven basket strapped to her back, and approach Oliver's stall. The yeasty aroma of braided raisin loaves pierced by the sharp sweetness of orange buns wraps around me, and my stomach reminds me I haven't bothered to eat since early morning. Oliver stands alone amid wooden tables draped in crumb-coated white cotton and covered with trays holding the last of Oliver's baked goods.

Turning to me, my escort asks, "Where is your Protector, young lady?"

Oliver shakes his head, sending his chins swinging, and plucks a sticky bun from the stash he always keeps for the children who visit. He knows they're my favorite. "It's a bad day for you to be at Market, Rachel-girl."

"Rachel?" The man asks.

I shrug, and my hood slips a bit. The man catches a glimpse of my red hair and swears with admirable proficiency.

"Jared Adams's daughter?"

I nod, and snatch the sticky bun Oliver tosses in my direction.

"You lied to me." He doesn't make it sound like a compliment.

I tear off a chunk of bread. "I'm sorry about that. I needed to reach Oliver's without getting hassled by a guard."

"Hassled by a guard? *Hassled?*" The man's face turns red. "Didn't you see their uniforms? Double gold bars on the left shoulder with a talon patch directly below."

The warm, gooey sweetness of the sticky bun turns to sawdust in my mouth. Not just guards. Commander Chase's personal Brute Squad. A flogging would've been the least of my worries if I'd been caught.

Which I *wasn't*. Because I can think on my feet.

Turning away, I ignore Oliver's quiet thanks to him as the man takes his leave. I don't meet Oliver's soft brown eyes as I slip my bracelet from my wristmark and lean forward to slide the mark across his scanner.

He grabs my arm, the rich mahogany of his skin a startling contrast against the paleness of mine, and says softly, "Not today, Rachel-girl."

"How else can I pay you for the bun?"

"Put the bracelet on and leave it there. You're practically my own granddaughter. The bun was a gift."

I slide the bracelet back in place and lean into Oliver's massive chest as he opens his arms to me. The warm scent of his baking clings to him and fills me with memories of happier times when I could crawl into his lap, listen to his deep voice tell me a fairy tale, and feel my world settle back into near-perfect lines again.

"Why did you come here today?"

I shrug and wrap my arms around him. I want one last moment with him before I face the dangers of the Wasteland alone.

He hugs me back and says, "Is this about you and Logan? I'm sure it must be an . . . adjustment."

My laugh sounds more like a sob, and I choke it back. Two years ago, I would've jumped at the chance to have more time with Logan. My chest still burns whenever I let myself remember inviting him over for birthday cake, and then making sure I got him alone on the back porch so I could tell him I thought he was different. Special. A man like my father.

The kind of man I wanted to marry.

My humiliation at his exquisitely logical rejection is now coated with anger at his refusal to help me look for Dad, and every time I see him, I want to hurt him.

I give Oliver a tiny smile as I pull away. "It's fine. *I'm* fine, but thank you."

"If you're finpe, why take the risk of coming here?" His smile is gentle, but beneath it is the unyielding expectation that I will tell him the truth.

And because he's the closest thing to family I have left, I give him as much of the truth as I can without making him an accomplice.

"I need to say good-bye."

"To Jared?" He glances in the direction of the Wall, and I let him assume I've come to the edge of Baalboden to feel close to Dad one last time.

"Your dad wouldn't want you taking such risks." He raises a hand to my cheek, and love glows in his eyes, filling me with bittersweet warmth.

"My dad is the one who taught me how." I stand on tiptoes and press a kiss against his weathered cheek. I already ache with missing him, but I ache with missing Dad more. Moving away from Oliver, I circle behind a table and head toward the back tent flap, fumbling with my cloak fastenings so I won't have to look at him.

"Where do you think you're going?" Oliver asks. There's a bite of apprehension in his voice now.

"I'm going to the Wall."

"I can't allow this." He starts toward me.

"I'm going." I edge to the back of the tent.

"What am I supposed to tell Logan if I let you put yourself in danger?" Oliver asks, still moving toward me, though we both know he can't catch up.

That I'm sorry? That I no longer meant any of the things I'd said two years ago? That he brought this on us both by not listening to me and helping me search for Dad? I square my shoulders, flick my hood over my hair again, and pat the sheath strapped to my waist.

"Tell him he's too late," I say, stepping out of Oliver's tent and into the shadow of the Wall.

CHAPTER EIGHT

LOGAN

"I'm here to pick up Rachel," I say when Maria Angeles opens her front door. "I hope the girls enjoyed learning how to host a dinner party."

Actually, I'm hoping Rachel didn't shock the Angeles family by expressing her strong distaste for setting a table with more than one fork per person unless you were expecting to use the second fork as a weapon. My lips quirk, and I suppress a grin before I have to explain to the formidable figure of Mrs. Angeles what I find so amusing.

She opens her mouth, snaps it shut, and stares at me. "Rachel?" she asks, as if uncertain. As if I might be at her doorstep to pick up someone else.

Dread pools in my stomach, and a lick of anger chases it up my spine. "I dropped her off here two hours ago. She said . . . never mind what she said. Is she here?"

Mrs. Angeles shakes her head, turns, and calls over her shoulder, "Sylphia, come to the door, please."

Sylph obeys immediately, but when she sees me, she flinches and her steps falter. Mrs. Angeles's voice cracks like a whip. "Where is Rachel?"

"I don't know." Her voice trembles. She's a terrible liar. I'm grateful.

"Sylph, please. If Rachel gets caught—" The unbidden image of my mother lying broken and bloody on the cobblestone streets while a crowd of citizens slowly back away fills my head. The air is suddenly too thick to breathe.

Sylph looks at the floor. "She just wanted to spend the afternoon at Oliver's."

"I would have taken her there." My tone is harsher than Sylph deserves. She isn't the mastermind. Fear drives the anger that pounds through me now with every heartbeat. I couldn't protect my mother from the Commander's ruthless punishments. But I can protect Rachel. I have to. I can't bear the thought of adding that failure to my list.

"She wanted to spend time there without . . ." Sylph doesn't continue, but I can fill in the blanks on my own. Rachel wanted to see Oliver without having to worry about me looking over her shoulder, listening in, telling her when to leave and what road to take on our journey home.

I can't blame her for chafing at the restrictions placed on her by Baalboden law, but the proof that she'd rather risk a public flogging than spend time with me hurts more than I want to admit. Barely pausing to say good-bye to Sylph and her mother, I hurry through North Hub.

As I rush through Lower Market, I note the unusual number of guards present. A flash of double gold bars above a talon on one of the guard's uniforms catches my eye.

Brute Squad.

Suddenly panic claws at me, threatening to fill my head with useless noise, and I beat it back. Rachel is okay. She has to be. I'm going to get to her before the Brute Squad notices a girl walking without her Protector. And then I'm going to lock her in my loft for as long as it takes to finish working out my plan to go looking for Jared.

I reach Oliver's stall in record time, burst through the tent flap, and say, "Where is she?"

Oliver waves his hand impatiently at the back flap. "There you are! Took long enough. She left me in the dust fifteen minutes ago. She knows I can't keep up with her." He gestures at his considerable bulk, and then snaps, "Why are you still standing there? Brute Squad is out there!"

"Where did she go?"

"To the Wall."

I stride forward and yank the back flap of the tent aside. I should've known that in the face of my refusal to make a plan to escape Baalboden with her, she'd leap headfirst into a plan of her own.

The alley behind Oliver's tent cuts through the remaining stalls on the western edge of Lower Market before merging with one of the last paved streets on this side of the city. I keep to the side, head down, looking like I'm doing nothing more than hurrying home.

Dark clouds cover the sky, and a chilly breeze is blowing, carrying hints of the storm to come. I calculate no more than ten minutes before a fierce round of early spring rain hits, reducing visibility to nothing.

I pick up my pace. I can track her through the rain if I have to, but that isn't what worries me. A glance around the streets shows the number of guards has increased in just the last few minutes. I don't believe in coincidences, which means somehow Rachel tipped them off to her intentions. She's smart, resourceful, and knows her way around weapons, but she's no match for the Brute Squad.

I'd rather not be a match for the Brute Squad either, but I'm not about to fail her.

I exit the alley, turn right, and stride along the street, my cloak wrapped close, my expression neutral. There's a guard in the doorway of the feed merchant, another pair outside Jocey's Mug & Ale, and I'm certain I caught the glint of a sword on the roof above me as I make the left into the alley between the armory and an abandoned warehouse. Under the pretense of adjusting my cloak, I scan the street.

No one seems to be following me. That doesn't reassure me about the guard on the roof, but I have quick reflexes.

The alley twists away from the street and ends abruptly at the edge of an expanse of waist-high yellow grass about fifty yards wide. Beyond the field of grass, the Wall looms. Immense steel ribs joined by tons of concrete as thick as twelve men standing shoulder to shoulder wrap around the city, holding the Wasteland at bay and the citizens beneath the Commander's thumb. Every one hundred twenty yards, a turret rises. Guards assigned to the Wall spend most of their shift in their assigned turrets. But three times a day—at dawn, at noon, and at sunset—they turn off the motion detectors and leave their turret to do a detailed sweep of their section of the Wall.

I reach the edge of the field just as the first drops of rain slam into the ground, the sun sinks below the Wall, and the low hum of the motion detector stutters into silence. The guards in the turret closest to me step into the steady downpour, swords in hand, NightSeer masks in place, and walk north with measured precision.

Rachel rises from the center of the field. The panic I've kept at bay flares to life as she stays low to the ground and races across the field in spurts—sprint, drop, roll into a crouch, and repeat. Beneath the curtain of rain, aided by the swiftly falling darkness, she's nothing but a shadow.

If I can see her, so can the guard above me. In seconds, I hear the soft whoosh of a body plummeting to the ground and brace myself. He lands slightly to the right of me, all of his attention on Rachel. I leap forward, slam my fist into the side of his head, and drag his unconscious body back under the lip of the roof. A quick scan of the area confirms that no other guards are pursuing Rachel. If I can get to Rachel before she's seen by the turret guards, maybe I can avert disaster completely. I take off after her at a dead run.

She reaches the Wall before the faint glow of the guards' NightSeer masks has completely disappeared in the distance. I estimate just under ten minutes before the guards return. Just under ten minutes to capture her, subdue her inevitable argument, and get her back into the relative safety of the city before she puts both of us on the Commander's execution list.

The driving sheets of rain make it hard to be certain, but I'm pretty sure she just dropped her skirt to the ground and started up the ladder in a pair of skintight pants. Fury overtakes my panic and fuels me. If a guard sees her dressed like that, he won't hesitate to take what he thinks she's freely offering, and then I'll have to kill him.

She makes it to the top before I reach the base. The rain pounds into me, but I barely feel it. The rungs are slippery, so I wrap my hands in my leather cloak, grasp the metal, and climb as quickly as I can.

Best Case Scenario: She's foolishly setting herself up for a covert trip down the side of the Wall and into the Wasteland, and I get the unenviable task of standing in her way, but she hasn't been noticed by any guards.

Worst Case Scenario 1: The turret guards return early, and I talk our way out of it.

Worst Case Scenario 2: The Brute Squad finds her, and we fight our way out.

Worst Case Scenario 3: Commander Chase discovers her act of treason, tries to punish her for it, and I draw my weapon against the man who rules all of Baalboden with an iron fist of terror.

I climb swiftly and pray I'm not too late.

CHAPTER NINE

RACHEL

I scramble over the lip of the Wall and race into the rounded stone turret a few yards to my left. Rain pounds the walkway as I grab the magnetic handgrips I'd snatched from Logan's supply of inventions before leaving with him for Sylph's house. The metal circles feel cold against my skin, and I hurriedly strap them onto my palms. I don't have long before the guards return.

I wave my hand cautiously in front of the iron torch bracket beside the doorway, and the handgrip slams my arm to the bracket. It takes most of my strength to yank myself free. These will easily adhere to the steel ribbing on the outside of the Wall and hold my weight as I descend. It pains me to admit it, but Logan is a genius.

Not that I'd ever tell him that.

I drag my cloak closer to my body. The rain is falling in opaque sheets. I'll be lucky if I can see two yards in front of me. Which means the guards won't be able to see me either.

But it also means I can't see what waits for me in the

Wasteland. I'm not too worried about highwaymen or wild animals. What I can't kill, I can elude. Dad trained me well. Facing the Cursed One, however, is another matter.

We don't know how long the beast lurked in its lair beneath the surface, but we know what set it loose. A rich businessman searching for a new source of renewable fuel bought up land all over the globe, hired crews, and on one fateful day, had every crew drill down through a layer of metamorphic rock deep beneath the earth's crust. Instead of finding a new source of fuel, the crews woke immense, fire-breathing beasts who tracked their prey by sound. Driven wild by the noise of the civilizations living above them, or perhaps driven by nothing more than a feral instinct to destroy anything that might be able to destroy them, the beasts surfaced and laid waste to miles of densely populated areas each time they broke through the ground.

In the ensuing chaos, every military branch positioned their most experienced squadrons in densely populated areas with the plan to set traps for the beasts. It was a suicide mission. No one could predict when or where the creatures would surface, and any troops not perfectly in position were immediately destroyed. Several squadrons got lucky and blew a beast or two apart before they themselves were killed, but the military was shattered before they could kill them all.

As a last-ditch effort, the government on our continent sent all they had left—a team of young, inexperienced soldiers and a handful of geologists—down into the bowels of the earth to seal our beast back into its lair. The team, led by Commander Chase, failed, and when the surviving members returned to the surface, there was no government. No law and order. Nothing but panic, fire, and one surviving monster systematically killing the survivors.

The Commander and his team took charge, organizing food and relief efforts, and proving repeatedly that, for reasons they refused to share, the remaining Cursed One never attacked them or anyone around them. It didn't take long for the survivors to rally behind the protected men and proclaim them their new leaders. Within a decade, nine city-states led by the Commander and the other members of his team stretched across our continent, offering citizens shelter and protection in exchange for swearing allegiance to the leader of that city.

Leaving the protection of Baalboden behind meant risking an encounter with the beast, especially since the Commander built his city-state closer to the creature's den than any of the other leaders. One wrong move, and I'll never be heard from again.

Which means I can't make a mistake. My hands shake as I rehearse my plan.

Run out the doorway. Grab the edge of the Wall. Vault over. Slam my hands against the steel ribbing as I fall. Slide down and escape into the vast, treacherous darkness of the Wasteland with nothing but my wits and my knife.

It can work. It has to work.

I take a deep breath and sprint out the door.

I haven't gone more than three yards before I slam into a hard, unyielding obstacle. Strong fingers reach out to grab my arms, and I look up.

Commander Chase.

Terror rips a white-hot path through my body, and I can

barely breathe.

I'm dead.

He stares at me for an excruciating moment, then shoves me through the turret's arched doorway, two members of his Brute Squad on his heels. One of them strikes flint at the lantern resting on the room's table, and the sudden light stings. Fury burns in the Commander's dark eyes, and my knees threaten to collapse beneath me.

We take three steps into the room before he lets go of me with a shove that propels me backward toward the table. I stumble over the edge of my cloak and crumple to the floor, twisting my body in midair so I land with my back to him.

I need a second to tug Logan's magnetic hand grips off my palms and shove them into my inner cloak pocket. I might be going down, but I don't need to take Logan with me. Covering my actions by struggling to stand again, I feel a tiny rush of relief when the grips slide into my pocket without incident.

"You've been keeping secrets from me." There's no room in his tone for avoiding the inevitable. The two guards with him move to flank me, their hands already wrapped around the hilts of their swords.

I shake my head, my blood roaring in my ears.

He whips his right hand into the air, palm facing me, and the guards draw their swords.

"Tell me the truth, girl, or die. I don't care which you choose."

"I was trying to sneak over the Wall," I say in a voice that's parchment thin. "I want to find my father."

He nods once, and the guard beside me lays the edge of his sword against my neck. I raise my chin as the silver bites into my skin, but I refuse to beg for mercy. He should've sent a tracker when my father failed to return from his last mission. If he didn't have mercy for his best courier, he isn't going to find any to spare for me.

"I knew it." He spits the words at me. "On the day his will was read, I could see that you knew something about his whereabouts." The smile he gives me makes me feel sick. "It's nice to know the extra effort I've taken to have you followed since then is about to pay off. Now, where is he?"

"I don't know."

His smile stretches until it strains against the thick rope of scar tissue marring his face. "Of course you know where he is. He's probably supposed to meet you on the other side of the Wall. A girl doesn't go out into the Wasteland alone." His tone is full of contempt, his hand still raised as if at any moment he might fold it into a fist, giving the guard permission to kill me.

"Why not?" I ask, proud that my voice only shakes a little.

His smile dies slowly. "You're in desperate need of someone to teach you your proper place."

I bite my lip to keep it from trembling, and try to ignore the way the silver blade at my throat scrapes my skin raw.

"Where is he?" the Commander asks.

"I don't know."

He draws his own sword and steps close. The guard withdraws his blade from my neck but doesn't sheath it.

I can smell the warm, wet wool of the Commander's military jacket mixed with the dank, foul scent of his breath. My knees feel like liquid, and I have to clamp my teeth together to keep them from chattering as his dark eyes devour me.

"You're lying." His lip curls around the words as they fall like stones between us. "If you don't know where he is, how did you expect to find him?"

"I was going to track him."

"Track him?" The Commander steps back and turns to the guard beside me. "She was going to *track him*." They both laugh.

Anger straightens my spine. "I can do it."

"Look at you." The Commander flicks his sword at me, and I flinch as the tip slices the air beside my face. "Nothing but a girl who thinks she can track one of my best couriers into the Wasteland with only pants and a cloak for protection. Women like you are the entire reason we need the Protectorship protocol. We save ourselves from your foolishness."

"It isn't foolish. I know what I'm doing. My father saw to that."

In the sudden silence following my announcement, I hear the heavy patter of the rain outside the room as it bounces off the stone walkway. I also hear the low sound of men's voices just beyond the turret. Before I can do more than cast my eyes toward the door, Commander Chase wheels toward me, his expression reminding me of a predator about to pounce on his prey.

"Did he, now?"

I nod and force myself to swallow past the icy lump forming at the back of my throat. I have to convince him Dad is still alive, and I'm qualified to find him. My plan to sneak over the Wall might be dashed to pieces, but there was nothing to say I couldn't head into the Wasteland on a Commander-sanctioned mission. Even Logan wouldn't be able to argue against that.

Well, he'd argue. But he wouldn't be able to stop me.

"And how did he make sure you, a girl, knew how to survive the Wasteland?"

"He took me with him on some of his courier missions."

Something vicious flashes across his face, and he smiles, a horrible parody of mirth. I take a step back and bump against the table behind me.

More guards enter the room, pushing another man in front of them. I barely spare them a glance, but freeze when I see who it is they've caught.

Logan.

My heart clenches, a sudden pain that makes it hard to hold Logan's gaze as he stands to the left of the Commander, his hair plastered to his head, and his blue eyes locked on mine. I'm responsible for this. He's only here because he's trying to be a good Protector. No matter how angry I am at him for refusing to help me track Dad, he doesn't deserve to receive the brunt of the Commander's wrath.

Maybe if I keep the Commander distracted with what I can offer in the effort to track down Dad, he'll spare Logan whatever harsh consequence a Protector receives when his ward goes horribly astray.

Commander Chase doesn't bother turning around. Instead, he takes a step toward me, crowding me against the table. "Did your father take you with him on his second to last mission?"

I open my mouth, but Logan shakes his head frantically and says, "No."

The Commander tosses a glance over his shoulder. "Ah, the arrival of your Protector." He swings his sword until the tip digs into the soft skin beneath my chin. I grip the table with clammy hands and try to remain absolutely still. "Not another word, or she dies."

Logan's hands curl into fists, but he clenches his jaw and remains silent.

The Commander's sword remains steady as he says, "The truth, please. Did you go with your father on his second to last courier mission?"

"Yes." I breathe the word, but even that slight movement scrapes my skin across his blade. The pain is sharp and quick, and a hot trickle of blood slowly snakes its way down my neck.

"Where did you go?"

"Rowansmark." More pain. More blood.

Logan makes a sound that reminds me of a starving alley dog stalking his next meal.

The Commander smiles. "And here is where you give me either your secrets or your life." His sword tip digs into my chin, and tears sting my eyes. "Did anything unusual happen on the trip to Rowansmark?"

I glance at Logan. His face is white. I can read the plea for silence in his eyes as easily as if he'd begged aloud. But I believe the Commander's promise to kill me. And this is my only way out of Baalboden to track Dad. I have to tell the truth.

I try to tilt my chin away from the sword's tip and pray I'm not making the biggest mistake of my life. "Yes."

CHAPTER TEN

LOGAN

Blood runs down Rachel's neck and her body trembles. Something ugly fills my chest, begging to be unleashed. It was foolish of her to risk so much to go searching for Jared. It was also incredibly brave. I know she thinks she's ready to pay the price for this act of courage, but I can't stand the thought of watching another woman I care about die.

I should've seen this coming. If I had, she might not be trapped at the point of the Commander's sword. Scanning my surroundings, I start cataloging my options.

We've been joined by the turret's pair of guards, back from their sunset inspection of the Wall. The room feels cramped and the smell of warm bodies and rain-damp cloaks chokes the air.

"So, to the matter at hand." The Commander removes his sword from Rachel's throat, and the tightness constricting my chest eases a fraction. We have a chance. As long as he thinks we have something to offer, we have a chance.

Lantern light flickers along the blood-red stone the

Commander wears on the ring finger of his left hand. The gold dragon talon bisecting the stone glows softly, and I look away.

He's watching Rachel. "You say something unusual happened. What was it?"

She casts me a quick look, but there's nothing I can do to stop this. Not until I see what he really wants, and how to convince him that keeping us alive is his only chance at succeeding.

"Someone gave him a package. Not an official one, but after we were almost out of Rowansmark," she says.

His dark eyes gleam. "And did he open it?"

She hesitates for a fraction of a second before saying, "Of course not."

He steps closer to her, his fist gripping his sword handle until the veins in his hands bulge. "We've had peace with Rowansmark for nearly four decades. Do you know why?"

"Because neither of us has the technology to destroy the other?" Rachel asks, holding his gaze while she repeats a line I'd heard Jared say countless times. My stomach drops. Now is not the time to call the Commander on his actions. Those in the courier trade are well aware of the animosity between Commander Chase and his former major James Rowan. Most of the missions to Rowansmark are spy assignments disguised as ordinary trade negotiations. The Commander has made it his business to know everything James Rowan might be up to.

I have to wonder if Jared disappeared because Rowan has been busy doing the exact same thing to the Commander.

"Interesting theory," he says. "Did you hear that from your father after he opened the package?"

"He never opened it. At least, not in front of me."

"Where is it?"

"He hid it on the journey back."

"Because he planned to return it to Rowansmark?" His voice cracks the air, full of fury, and Rachel jumps.

"He would never do that! He's loyal to Baalboden."

"You have one chance to prove that to me. Where did he hide it?" His sword arm flexes as he raises the blade toward Rachel's face.

"I'm not sure. But I know where we went, and I know Dad's hiding places," she says, sounding so confident that I'm sure the Commander will believe he needs her to help find the package. Now, he needs to be convinced to send me with her. There's no way I'm letting Rachel travel the Wasteland alone with the Commander's Brute Squad.

"I know where it is," I say.

All eyes turn toward me. I find the Commander's dark gaze and hold it steadily.

"More secrets?" he asks softly, and pivots toward me, his sword pointing with unwavering accuracy toward my throat. The Brute Squad guards on either side of me tighten their grip on my arms, but I refuse to struggle. I'm not going to give the Commander that satisfaction.

"Rachel's right. She knows where they traveled and what safe houses they used on the journey. But Jared spoke to me about the package. Things he refused to share with Rachel."

The Commander's expression is tinged with malice, and the tension in the room coils within me like a living thing.

"Tell me what he told you," he says.

I can't. Revealing information now would cancel out my

usefulness and possibly Rachel's as well. Plus, I don't have any information to reveal. I'm betting he wants the package enough not to call my bluff. I don't want to consider the consequences if I'm wrong.

"I'm not sure I can accurately describe the locations he gave me. I believe I need to see it to know it," I say. "Rachel can guide me to the general location, and I'll take it from there."

He snarls at me. "Do you think you're that valuable to me, Logan McEntire?"

There's no right answer. If I say yes, I'll be killed to prove my words false. If I say no, any chance I have of accompanying Rachel will disappear, and I'll probably be killed for my interference.

"My value is for you to decide. Sir." I nearly choke on the *sir*.

The Commander slams the flat of his sword onto my shoulder, slicing into my skin. Rachel gasps and slides her hand beneath her cloak. I have a terrible suspicion there's a weapon hidden in there.

She's going to get herself killed defending me if I can't defuse this, but I don't know how. My stomach clenches as I frantically run scenarios and try to see a way out of this. There isn't one, unless the Commander believes we're both necessary to getting him what he wants.

Please let him believe we're necessary to getting him what he wants.

"Jared Adams has something I need," he says. "You and the girl will get it back for me."

Relief rushes through me. "I understand."

He spits his words at me. "You listen to me, inventor who

likes to play with words. You are replaceable. The girl is replaceable. I won't hesitate for a second to spill her blood and find another willing to take her place. Do you really think the life of any one citizen matters in comparison to what I decide Baalboden needs?"

Before I can do more than draw in a sharp, panicked gasp of air, he spins on his heel and lunges toward Rachel, his sword raised.

CHAPTER ELEVEN

RACHEL

"Rachel!" Logan throws himself forward, struggling to get free of the Brute Squad holding him in place.

My back slams against the table as the Commander's sword flashes by me and plunges deep into the chest of the guard beside me. The man makes a wet gurgling noise in the back of his throat and reaches one hand up to grasp the blade embedded in his chest. Blood pools beneath his palm and slides along the silver in a single, sinuous streak as he slowly crumples to the floor. His eyes lock on the Commander's until the knowledge within them hardens into the far-seeing gaze of the dead.

I can't remember how to move.

The Commander places one booted foot on the guard's shoulder, grabs the hilt of his sword with two hands, and tugs. The blade comes free with a damp, sucking sound, flinging stray droplets of blood into the air as the ring on the Commander's finger glistens wetly beneath the torchlight.

I gag, and the Commander holds his bloody sword to my

throat. My knife feels useless in my numb fingers. It was so much easier to imagine killing a man before I realized what that looked like.

"I warned you I'd teach you your place," the Commander says softly.

I can't speak around the sickness rising up the back of my throat. The metallic tang of blood swamps my senses. I hold my breath, but that just forces me to swallow blood-tainted air until I feel like screaming.

He smiles. Reaching out, he fingers a long strand of my hair. The spit dries in my mouth, and I feel foolish clutching my knife beneath my cloak as if it could possibly save me.

The Commander looks at Logan, letting my hair slide slowly through his fingers. "I was going to threaten her life to gain your complete cooperation, but I've changed my mind. It would be a shame to extinguish such spirit before one has had the opportunity to tame it, don't you think?"

Something desperate and dark awakens within me, biting through my stomach like bile. I want to slap his hand away from me, but with the sword still at my throat and Logan restrained by guards, I can't move.

Logan looks like he's going to be sick, but beneath his pallor I see something I never knew he was capable of: rage. If the Commander notices, he doesn't react. He's too busy looking at me like I'm his next meal. I shudder at the predatory gleam in his eye. I can't decide if he wants to kill me or Claim me as his own.

"Sir—" Logan begins.

"Instead, I've decided the terms of your service to me will be thus: Give me your word you'll return what belongs to me, and I'll let you live. Otherwise, the girl will need to be assigned another Protector while she retrieves my package for me." He reaches out and brushes a stray drop of blood from my cheek, and I shiver. "I'm sure I can find a man willing to take her on."

"That won't be necessary." Logan's voice shakes.

"Your word?"

"You have it."

"You may take a few days to gather your supplies and plan your trip. Notify me when you're ready to depart. I'll be sending guards to accompany you." Abruptly, the Commander turns from me, wipes his blade on the cloak of the dead man beside us, and strides toward the doorway. "Toss that mess into the Wasteland," he says to the remaining turret guard, and then he and his Brute Squad disappear into the night.

CHAPTER TWELVE

LOGAN

I can't speak past the anger flooding me as we leave the Wall behind and walk through the deserted streets of Lower Market. The image of the Commander eyeing Rachel in her skintight pants while rubbing the back of his hand against her bloodstained cheek fills my head, and I plow my fist into the wall of the wooden stall beside me.

Rachel jumps and gives me a sidelong look. She's only seen the man I made myself into after Oliver took an interest in me. She has no idea the kind of things I'm capable of when backed into a corner.

But I know, and punching a wall is the best option available to me unless I plan to do something far more destructive with my anger. Like draw my sword against the Commander.

"Feel better?" Rachel asks, and I punch the wall again just to keep from letting my anger loose on her. Not that she doesn't deserve some of it.

I shake out my hand and take hold of her arm as we leave

Lower Market behind. I have to calm down. *Think.* The Commander now knows for certain Jared received a package he didn't deliver. And he understands he's found a useful tool in Rachel's fervent belief that she can save her father.

And none of it would've happened if she hadn't tried to sneak over the Wall.

"You're hurting me," she says as she matches my pace through the torch-lit streets.

"You're lucky," I say.

"That you're hurting my arm?" Her voice is full of its usual sass, but I hear the unsteadiness beneath it.

"You're lucky I'm not wringing your neck."

She remains quiet, and I soften my grip.

We move past the ridiculous wealth of Center Square, where multistoried homes gleam beneath the warmth of lanterns hung at their doorways, and no one inside knows what it's like to go hungry. When I was a boy, lonely and wild, I used to walk Center Square at night, imagining the perfect lives of the families who lived inside such beauty and wishing I belonged with one of them. That was before Oliver and Jared reached out to me, and I learned that true family is found in those who choose you. Wealth has nothing to do with it.

Leaving Center Square behind, we move south. The houses grow smaller. With the street torches further apart, the alleys darken, and I scan the streets constantly, cataloging potential threats, discarding those I know we can handle with our eyes shut, and planning our escape route from those we might not be able to avoid.

"What were you thinking?" I ask her as we round the corner

into South Edge. Here the street torches disappear, and the only visible light hovers timidly behind windows boarded shut. I finally let go of her arm and reach for my sword even as she slides her knife free. Only a fool walks through South Edge unarmed.

"I was thinking Dad needs to be rescued," she says, her tone sharp.

Something moves in an alley to our left, and I pivot around her back and resume walking, putting my body and my sword between her and the yawning darkness of the alley's mouth.

"Let me get this straight." I bite off each word to keep from spitting them at her. "You want to rescue your dad, so you decide to sneak over the Wall alone? Do you have a death wish?"

"Don't be an idiot." She sounds like she's gritting her teeth. "I didn't know the Commander had his guards following us."

"Of course you didn't. Because you're so wrapped up in missing Jared, you refuse to look at anything else." I regret the words as soon as I say them. I hadn't realized we were being followed either, and as her Protector, it was my responsibility to see it.

I press my palm to the small of her back and guide her to the opposite side of the street. The heat from her skin seeps into mine and feels like comfort.

Which is proof my ability to think logically seems to be compromised. I'm beginning to worry being responsible for Rachel has somehow thrown me permanently off-kilter.

She steps away from my hand. "At least one of us is caught up in missing him."

"Who says I don't miss him?" A shadow moves out of a doorway behind us. A man. Taller than me by about two inches, but I have him by a good twenty pounds. Plus, he's limping. Still, I wrap my hand around her arm again and pull her through some-one's backyard, over a small fence, and onto the street running parallel to the one we were just on.

He doesn't follow us.

"Are you listening?" she asks, and I realize she's been talking the entire time.

"I am now."

"Typical. I was asking how you can say you miss him. All you do is sit around day after day, drawing pictures—"

"Pictures! They're intricately scaled plans for an invention—"

She waves her knife through the air as if she can slice through my words and draw blood instead. "Drawing pictures, piecing together your little toys—"

That takes it. "You didn't think so poorly of my little toys tonight when you planned to use my handgrips to sneak over the Wall, did you?" My voice is rising. My little *toys* are about to give us a way to find Jared and get off the Commander's radar.

Of course, I haven't actually shared that with her. I thought I was protecting her, but maybe if I'd trusted her in the first place, we wouldn't be in our current situation.

She raises a fist like she wants to punch me. "All the toys and plans and books in the world won't get us one step closer to rescuing Dad, and you just sit there like we aren't running out of time!" Her voice breaks, and I reach out to haul her close to me and out of the path of a mule-drawn wagon clip-clopping along the street.

"We *are* almost out of time. I can feel it. Can't you feel it?" Her voice is unsteady, and I'm shocked to see tears sliding down her face, chasing a trail of heat between the icy pellets of rain still plummeting from the heavens.

I've never seen her cry before. Not when she was a young girl training with a man's weapons, getting injured more often than not. Not when she was a budding woman facing me across her back porch and spilling her heart only to have me hand it back to her. Not even when it became clear Jared wasn't coming back. The fury in me sinks beneath a sudden, sharp ache, and I wish I knew how to have a civilized conversation with her.

We take the corner marking the line between South Edge and Country Low. I want to have the perfect words to comfort her, but I don't, so I walk in silence as the ramshackle houses become cozy little cottages, and the patches of dirty grass between them expand into gardens, farm fields, and small orchards. Though no street torches exist, the darkness is now friendly.

My house comes into view, and she pushes ahead of me to stalk up the stone walkway, reaching the iron-hinged wooden door first. Hanging her damp cloak on a hook beside the door, she enters the main part of the cottage while I light the pair of lanterns hanging in the entryway.

She's rummaging through the kitchen, her movements jerky with either anger or grief. Probably both. I make my way across the living room until I'm less than three yards from her.

"I know we're running out of time. But you have to trust me. I know what I'm doing."

She jumps at the sound of my voice so close behind her, and shoots a glare over her shoulder before moving toward the wooden box of a pantry resting in the corner. "I know what you're doing, too. You're going into the Wasteland with me. I'm sorry about that, by the way." She opens the pantry and rummages through it.

Sorry for what? Having to take me with her? Does she really despise me that much? The hurt that follows this thought is a slow, dull ache that takes me by surprise. My voice is sharp as I follow her and ask, "Are you really sorry?"

This time, she bangs her head when she jumps. Turning, she shoves a sack of mutton jerky into my arms and snaps, "Stop sneaking up on me."

I grab the sack before it falls, and frown. "Why are you removing food from my pantry?" I toss the jerky onto the table behind me as she pulls two dusty jars of fig paste from the back of the pantry, knocking over a bag of potatoes in the process.

"Packing, of course."

"Wait a minute."

She shoves the paste at me and rolls her eyes. "Fine. I'll finish apologizing. I didn't want you involved. I should've made it over the side before they caught you. Then this whole thing wouldn't be an issue."

I slam the paste onto the wooden table beside the jerky. "How can you say that?"

She fists her hands on her hips and ignores the potatoes rolling across her feet. "I would've been gone, Logan. Deep into the Wasteland. And if you'd kept quiet about your reasons for being at the Wall, nothing would have changed for you."

"Nothing . . ." My stomach drops as I realize how little she thinks of me.

"You'd be free to invent and read and make life better for the citizens here. Duty finished." She kicks a potato, sending it careening across the floor as something blazes to life within me.

I glare at her. "And what duty would that be? The one I swore to the memory of the man I consider my one true friend?" I lean toward her as my voice rises. "The one I swore to myself when I could see how lost you are without him?"

She takes a step back and bumps into the pantry. "I'm not lost."

"You're *lost*. And everyone knows it. Three months till Claiming age. Every available man in the city suddenly looking at you like you're . . ." I snap my mouth closed and turn my back before I say what I'm really thinking. What every man who stops to stare at the fiery beauty with the indomitable spirit and glorious red hair is thinking.

She's yelling now. "Like I'm what? Pathetic? A poor little girl who needs a man every time she leaves the house? I'm not like that. My father saw to that. You should've gone after him with me when I first asked you to. You should've gone!"

I whirl to face her, and step forward until the distance between us can be measured in breaths. She's trembling. I am too. She stares at me with wounded eyes, and I want to wipe all the ugliness out of our lives, but I don't know how.

"Rachel."

Her hair is drenched. Glistening drops of water slide effortlessly down her pale skin. I raise my hand slowly, but she doesn't flinch as I press my palm against her cheek, letting the water slide over us both. My fingertips are calloused and ink-stained, rough against the softness of her skin. She looks fragile and fierce, and I long for something more than the animosity between us.

"You're right." I say quietly. "I should've gone after him. Does it make it better to know that I always planned to go? "

"When?" she whispers.

"When I finish building the tracking device I want to use to find him."

Her skin warms beneath my hand as her anger fades into something tentative and soft.

"I should've told you what I was doing." My thumb traces a path across her cheekbone, catching another drip of water. "I should've trusted you. I'm sorry."

"No, I'm sorry. Sorry I misjudged you. Sorry I got us caught tonight." She sways closer to me.

My gaze wanders to her lips, and I can't see anything but a thin trail of water gliding over her skin, gathering at the corner of her mouth, and then slowly drifting toward her neck. She raises one shaky hand and presses her fingers against her lips. Her breath catches, a tiny sound that makes me realize how close I'm standing to her.

Warmth rushes through me, and I dip my face toward hers.

"Logan?" Her voice is soft, but the sound of my name slaps some sense into me.

I jerk back a step and swear.

CHAPTER THIRTEEN

LOGAN

"I'm sorry," I say and back up another step.

She looks away and crosses her arms over her chest. "For what? Swearing?"

"Yes. No. I mean, yes, but . . ." The haze of warmth sweeping my system drains away as cold reality sets in.

I almost *kissed* Rachel.

The realization isn't nearly as shocking as the fact that despite our differences, our current situation, and the impossibility of it all, I still ache to press her against the wall and taste her.

That thought does dangerous things to my self-control. I need something else to talk about—something else to *think* about—fast. Glancing around for inspiration, I spy the partially built invention on my table and say, "Do you see that?"

Of course she sees it. She isn't blind.

"Are we changing the subject?"

"Rachel . . ." Yes, we're changing the subject. I don't know what to say to explain my actions, and it's either talk about technology, or I'm going to go take a walk in the rain.

"Fine." She won't look at me. "What's so special about that"—she flicks a hand toward the table—"that simply must be discussed right this second?"

"It's going to lead us to your dad."

She raises her eyes to mine, her expression cautiously hopeful. "How?"

I'm grateful to be asked for an explanation I can readily give. "Your father's wristmark has a tracking device embedded in it. All wristmarks do. It's short range, just like all our tech. Designed to work within the Wall and nowhere else."

This isn't news to her. All tech is specific to the city-state where it's issued. Without a network of wires across the Wasteland, there's no way to send any kind of long-range signal. A tracking device is useful outside the Wall only if you can get within two hundred yards of someone. Without a fairly exact location for Jared, we could wander for years and never get a ping.

"The invention I'm working on is a tracker designed to pick up traces of your dad's signal, even if he's already moved on."

"How is that possible?" Cautious hope is edging toward enthusiasm in her voice.

"Sound navigation ranging. A courier's tracking signal uses active sonar, sending out sonic pulses that leave a unique echo in the environment. The guards can find a courier using an Identidisc to receive those echoes as they're sent."

"So why can't we just steal an Identidisc and use that to track Dad?"

I shake my head. "Because Identidiscs aren't designed to pick up a signal any older than two weeks."

"Why not?"

I grin. "Because I didn't design them. Besides, we aren't going to steal anything and risk showing the Commander what we're up to. The device I'm building uses passive sonar, which means it receives echoes without sending its own out. I'm tasking it to only receive the lingering echoes of Jared's unique signal."

"But if it's been months since he was in an area—"

"Sound never really disappears. I'm building a powerful battery for this, so if he's been in an area within the last six months, I'll catch his echo and we'll be able to find him."

She smiles, and genuine warmth fills her eyes. "You're a genius. Thank you."

Her words make me feel like I'm standing taller. "You're welcome."

She gestures at the half-finished invention. "Why did you apprentice yourself to Dad? It's clear inventing tech is what you love. Why train to be a courier?"

I meet her gaze for a moment, weighing the risks of telling her what I've held in secret all these years. We might not like each other half the time, and we might misunderstand each other regularly, but she's loyal to the core. Knowing I can trust her unlocks the words, and they rush from me as if they've been waiting for a chance to be heard.

"Because I *hate* living in Baalboden. Every time I look at the cobblestone streets, I see my mother dying. Every time I look at the Wall, I remember who killed her and branded me an outcast when I was just a child. If I have to stay here for the rest of my life, I might . . . I don't know if I can be the man I want to be while I live here."

She nods, her eyes remaining steadily on mine.

"I figured if I learned to be a courier, one day the Commander would send me out alone."

"And you could disappear?"

"Yes."

Her voice is sharp. "Did you think of what that would do to those of us who care about you?"

My throat feels tight as I say, "I didn't realize you would miss me. Besides, did you think of what your disappearing act tonight would've done to me?"

Her cheeks flush a delicate pink. "I didn't realize you would miss me, either."

I smile, and it takes a minute to realize my common sense is once again sliding into Kiss Rachel territory. This time, it's not because my body demands it, but because the affection in her voice beckons me.

Which clearly means I'm in dire need of another subject change.

"We don't have to worry about that now," I say. "We'll be leaving together. Give me one week, and the tracking device will be ready. We can leave the day after the Claiming ceremony."

I ignore the way her smile lights the room, and turn toward the table. "I should get to work."

"I should get some sleep." Her voice sounds breathless as she slips past me to head toward the loft.

I sit at the kitchen table and face the tracking device, shelving all distracting thoughts of Rachel. I hope the Commander is willing to give me a week to get ready for the trip. I need those seven days. Two days to finish Jared's tracking device. And five more to build one for Rachel.

I'm not going to be caught off guard again.

CHAPTER FOURTEEN

RACHEL

It's been three days since my disastrous escape attempt. Logan spends most of his time fiddling with circuitry and ink-stained plans. I spend most of my time sharpening weapons and practicing how to run a man through the heart while I do my best to forget the awful wet sucking sound a sword makes when it pulls free of a body. We have little to do with each other until the evenings when he sets aside his work, I put down the swords, and we sit on his tiny porch eating supper and watching the sun bleed itself out over the ramparts of the Wall.

We talk about Dad. Oliver. Sparring techniques. The fact that neither of us has a clue what's in the package and why Dad refused to deliver it. We talk about anything but the strange almost-kiss we shared the night I tried to go over the Wall. Its unspoken significance presses against my heart, making it hard to look at Logan without yearning for something I know neither of us really want.

Logan made it plain years ago that romance wasn't an option.

And I'm a different girl from the starry-eyed fifteen-year-old who thought she was in love. The almost-kiss was nothing more than too much emotion, too much tension, and a split second of dropping my guard. It won't happen again.

Over breakfast, Logan announces that we need to go into town for supplies. Ordinarily, he wouldn't require me to come along. But with guards watching the cottage day and night, leaving me home alone is a risk he isn't willing to take.

I don't bother arguing. I'm eager to get away from the small confines of Logan's house, and I'm surprised to realize I look forward to spending the day shopping for supplies with him. We've somehow worked our way into a tentative truce, and it feels nice to walk next to him down the pressed dirt road leading into town.

Logan's cottage is nestled in between his neighbor's apple orchard and a planting field owned by one of the wealthy merchants from Center Square. Last year, the merchant planted corn, and the broken stubs of the harvested plants still poke through the ground like jagged teeth. A guard rises up out of the cornfield as we pass, and another steps out of the orchard. I mutter something under my breath.

"Don't antagonize them," Logan says, nudging me with his shoulder.

"Maybe they should worry about antagonizing us."

He laughs, and the sound makes my skin tingle. I'm suddenly aware of how his shoulders fill his cloak. How his hair glows like honey in the morning sunlight. The tingle racing along my skin becomes an almost painful need I don't know how to fill.

"You have no idea how to be diplomatic, do you?" he asks,

but there's no judgment in his voice.

"What's the use in being diplomatic? I'd rather just pull my weapon and wing it." I nudge his shoulder back, and warmth spreads through me as he winks and leaves his arm pressed against mine as we walk.

We leave the cornfield behind, the guard from the orchard trailing us by about twenty yards. I'd like to turn around and tell him exactly what I think about his stupid job and his stupid boss.

Logan seems to sense my intentions because he slides his hand onto the small of my back, presses gently, and says, "Remember, sometimes diplomacy is the better side of warfare."

The heat of his hand feels like tiny sparks racing through me. "Diplomacy is a lot easier to accomplish if you've got your foe on his knees hoping you don't lop off his head."

"Do you really have to go into every situation with nothing but your wits and your knife?" he asks.

"Do you really have to go into every situation with more caution than a grandmother crossing Market Square?"

"It's called a well-reasoned plan." His hand slides away, and I shiver.

The dirt road gives way to the mud-caked cobblestones of South Edge. The fetid, rotting smell of trash heaps lies ripe on the morning air, and the few people who are outside of their miserable dwellings scuttle along the street with their eyes on their feet. Another guard steps out from behind a weather-worn house, his hand on the hilt of his sword as he watches us pass.

Clearly, the Commander expects us to run. To somehow sneak over the Wall without his knowledge, take his precious missing property, and disappear. It's not a half bad idea. If Dad thought the package was something the Commander shouldn't have, I'm not about to bring it back to Baalboden. Keeping my voice low, I say, "Maybe we should sneak out of the city."

Logan makes a choked noise. "No."

"But I don't like the idea of traveling with the guards."

"And I don't like the idea of getting caught committing treason."

I slide my knife free and hold it beneath my cloak as we enter the main stretch of South Edge. Not that I expect danger in broad daylight, especially with the obvious presence of guards at our backs, but I'm not going to risk it. Logan's hand is on his sword hilt, his eyes constantly scraping over our surroundings, looking for threats. We both know the real threat resides in the stone-and-steel compound rising out of the northern edge of the city.

"We need to travel without guards. Dad risked everything to keep that package from the Commander. We can't bring it back," I say quietly.

"No, we can't. But we can't go over the Wall. Or through the gate. The Commander will be expecting both. And there isn't another way out."

"Then maybe you need to look at other options."

He gets the faraway look in his eye that I now associate with hours of scribbling incomprehensible sketches while muttering to himself like a crazy man. I snap my fingers in front of his face. He jerks to attention and says, "You're right. I need other options. Which means I have to extend today's trip a bit."

"No problem."

He smiles at me, and our eyes linger one each other for a moment before I look away, pleased that he trusts me as an equal.

The guards behind us melt away as we swing into Lower Market, but it isn't long before I realize a tall cloaked man is stalking us. I point him out to Logan as we take the main road running west, stepping around a woman and her children who shoo chickens into a crate held by their Protector.

"I see him," Logan says. "Looks like Melkin. I guess this close to the gate, the Commander feels he needs a tracker following us. Just in case."

I glance at Melkin's scarecrow-thin form. "He doesn't look like much."

"With your dad out in the Wasteland, Melkin is the best tracker at the Commander's disposal."

"I guess we should take that as a compliment."

He laughs and grabs my elbow as a fast-moving wagon lumbers by, forcing us to quickly step aside.

"So, what's the plan today?" I ask.

"The plan is you stay with Oliver while I evade our followers and gather supplies."

I yank my elbow free. "I don't think so."

"I'm leaving you with Oliver for the day, Rachel. We have nothing more to discuss."

"We have plenty to discuss," I say. "I don't want to be stuck inside Oliver's tent all day. I'm an equal part in this whole thing, and I want to help you find supplies."

"Well, you can't."

I feel my face settle into mutinous lines. Does he really think telling me I can't do something is going to stop me? When I remain silent, Logan glances at me and frowns.

"Listen," he says. "The things I need to find aren't at respectable establishments."

I lift my chin and stare him down. "You're acting like poor, delicate Rachel must be kept away from even a hint of danger."

He laughs, tries to choke it back when he sees my face, and then laughs some more.

"Delicate? You could wipe the cobblestones with just about anyone in Baalboden. I'd hardly call that delicate."

"What do you mean, *just about*?" I've worked far too hard on my sparring skills to take that kind of insult lying down. "I can get the best of anyone who comes at me."

"You can't get the best of me."

"Try me, and you'll be singing a different tune. If I let you keep your lungs."

His smile is a slow journey of warmth that lights up his face and lingers in his eyes. "I'm going to take you up on that."

My stupid traitorous mouth smiles back before I remember I'm mad at him. Quickly wiping all expression from my face, I tap my foot on the cobblestones.

He leans closer and says, "I don't undervalue you, Rachel."

"Then why not take me with you?"

"Because I need the kind of supplies an upstanding merchant won't sell me. And the place I'm going to is also home to some people who sound like they might be plotting against the Commander."

"Really?" I bounce on my toes as I think of what a group like that might do for us if we decide to escape early.

He whips his hand into the air and says sternly, "I'm not

getting involved with them, and neither are you. Getting caught up in that is a good way to ensure neither of us ever gets to leave Baalboden to search for your dad."

"Good point. But still—"

"I'm already on this group's radar, but you don't have to be."

"Fine. But I still think—"

"If we get caught, who goes looking for Jared?" He reaches out and takes my hand. I slide my fingers between his without thinking, press his calloused palm against my own and study the fierce purpose burning in his eyes. "If I get seen doing business with traitors, I alone will take the blame. You'll still be able to leave."

My lingering irritation dissolves, replaced by gratitude and something deeper. Something that tightens my chest and makes my heart hurt. I've misjudged him. Badly. His protectiveness toward Dad is eclipsed only by his unwavering commitment to protect me.

I don't deserve it. I don't, but he can't see that. He takes his responsibilities seriously, and now that I'm part of his burden, he'd face the dungeons rather than let me down.

The heat between our palms seems to scorch me, and staring into his eyes makes me feel like all my secrets are slowly rising to the surface, whispering my truth without my permission.

Pulling my hand free, I step back and look down. "Thank you." The words are inadequate, but if I open my mouth again, I'm afraid of what I'll say. Instead, I quietly follow him to Oliver's tent, the imprint of his palm on mine lingering long after the heat of his skin fades away.

CHAPTER FIFTEEN

RACHEL

I've been cooped up in Oliver's tent for hours helping him sell his baked goods when he finally says, "Why don't we take a walk?"

He doesn't have to ask me twice. I grab both our cloaks and hold the front tent flap open for him. He eases through and tosses his cloak across his shoulders to ward off the brisk afternoon breeze.

Sliding my arm through his, I drag in a deep breath of air layered with the scents of the Market—candle wax, leather cloaks, mutton, sun-warmed produce, dirt.

"Ready?" I tug his arm, and he laughs as we set off through the Market.

We circle a small cluster of men haggling over a small gray donkey with drooping ears, our steps slow enough to accommodate Oliver's measured tread.

"I'm glad you've made your peace with your Dad's . . . absence," he says.

I flinch and look at my feet. I haven't made my peace with that, but I don't want to tell Oliver our plans until just before we leave. Maybe it's selfish of me, but I can't bear to put the shadow of an imminent good-bye over our day.

He pulls me to a stop in front of a stall selling steaming hot skewers of beef and onions. "Two, please."

"It's too expensive," I whisper to him, even though I know he won't listen.

He treats me to one of his wide, gentle smiles, his dark eyes shining. "Who else am I going to spend my money on? I already know you won't let me buy you any of the pretty, frilly things girls your age like to have, and I'm not about to purchase another weapon to add to your collection."

"Because I don't like pretty, frilly things. And there's nothing wrong with having a nice collection of weapons."

His smile looks sad around the edges. "That may be my fault. Jared didn't know how to raise a girl, and when he hired me to look after you in his absences, I didn't do any better."

I frown as I take my beef skewer, the juices running down the stick to sear my fingertips. "Or maybe that's just the way I am. There's nothing wrong with me."

He wraps his arm around me. "I didn't say there was. You're a wonderful girl. I just worry I didn't do enough to make up for you not having your mama alive to raise you."

I lean my head against his shoulder, and then take a bite of the delicious beef. "You and Dad are all I ever needed."

"And now Logan."

Do I need Logan? We've fumbled our way into what feels like the beginnings of a solid friendship, but I'm still constantly looking to avoid awkward moments in our conversations. Moments where he remembers I once said I loved him, and he once said I'd get over it. The memory of his palm pressed to mine makes my heart beat a little faster, and I tug Oliver away from the food stand.

Oliver clears his throat loudly. "With your dad gone, and your mama dead, I guess it falls to me to explain the way things, um, work between a man and a woman."

"What? No." I shake my head violently. *Nothing* could be more awkward than Oliver giving me the here's-where-babies-come-from talk.

"Unless you'd rather have this conversation with Logan."

I stand corrected. "Stop right now."

We turn the corner by the alchemist's and move toward the gate, still choked with citizens coming to trade with the band of highwaymen who've set up temporary camp at the edge of Baalboden's perimeter. The sun hangs in the sky like a ripe orange, though the breeze still carries the last remnants of winter's chill.

"You're nearly of Claiming age. Soon, men will look at you in a certain way. Even Logan might look at you differently."

I remember the intensity in Logan's eyes as we leaned close to each other in his kitchen. The way his hand felt pressed against my skin. The moment I realized I'd misjudged his intentions and his courage. I don't know if Logan is looking at me differently now, but I feel like I can see him clearly for the first time in all the years I've known him. The new understanding I have of him makes my heart ache just a little for the two years of lost friendship my wounded pride demanded.

"I don't want you to accept a Claim by just any man who

looks half decent and has a roof to offer. You're worth more than this entire town put together, Rachel-girl. Don't you forget it."

"You're biased."

He laughs, a warm, rich sound that vibrates through my cheek as I press against him. "Maybe I am. But when the time comes, don't settle. Make sure the man you choose sees you as you truly are and loves you for it."

"I will."

"Sure is going to be a proud day for me when I see you decked out in that finery on the Claiming stage. I just hope I live long enough to be a great-granddaddy to your children." He finishes his meat and tosses his stick aside.

"Of course you will." A sharp pain slices into me as I realize if Logan and I disappear into the Wasteland with Dad, Oliver will miss seeing me Claimed, and he'll never be a great-granddaddy to my future children. I glance at a passing guard, resplendent in his military uniform, and my steps falter as the full impact of our plan hits me. Not only will Oliver miss those important moments in my life, he'll be the only one left here to pay the price for our deception. I have no doubt the Commander will torture and kill Oliver as a lasting example of the price of disobedience and disloyalty.

I tighten my hand around Oliver's arm and make a decision. Logan will just have to figure out a way to smuggle Oliver out with us. I refuse to leave him behind.

We're nearly past the gate when the ground beneath us trembles. Little pebbles and loose grains of sand skip and slide across the cobblestones. Outside the gate, someone screams.

I lock eyes with Oliver, and he pushes me off the road as the citizens nearest the gate panic. Knocking each other down, Protectors half-dragging their women, they race past us. I stumble off the cobblestones and onto the uneven space of grass between the gate and the Market road. Oliver is right behind me.

The vibrations beneath us increase in strength, and I dig my fingers into Oliver's arm.

"It will surface outside the Wall," he says. His voice sounds like he's carrying a weight he can't bear to shoulder.

I look through the still-open gate and my stomach sinks. Baalboden citizens are out there. They left for the sanctioned highwaymen trading day, and they won't have time to cross the perimeter of scorched earth to get back inside the Wall before the Cursed One arrives.

Even as I finish the thought, several citizens break free of the frightened, milling pack at the edge of the Wasteland and sprint toward the safety of the gate. Others scramble to climb trees or get in the highwaymen's wagons, though I can't see how that will help. A guard leaves the gatehouse and races past us on horseback, no doubt heading toward the Commander's compound.

"Get back. Rachel, get back!" Oliver pulls at me as another wave of terrified citizens fight to get out of harm's way and back into Lower Market.

I take an elbow to the chest from a husky man in a tattered cloak, and spin out of the way before the mule rider behind him can crush me beneath his steed's hooves.

"Rachel!" Oliver yells as the same husky man gets knocked off the road by the mule and slams into Oliver, sending them both sprawling. The ground shakes so much it's hard to find my footing, but I claw my way over to them, grab the man's arm, and wrestle him off Oliver.

Behind me, the screams are eclipsed by a raw, primal roar of fury, and I whip my head around to see the glistening black length of the Cursed One burst through the ground. It's huge, nearly half the height of the Wall, and just as thick. It's my first actual sighting of the beast, and every instinct in me screams to run, but I can't look away. Besides, running means leaving Oliver behind, and I won't do that. I just have to hope the legend about the Cursed One never attacking inside Baalboden's Wall is true.

Lashing its serpentlike tail, the beast crushes two of the citizens running toward the gate, but its attention is on the horde of highwaymen and citizens in front of it. Horror trembles through me as the creature opens its mouth and strafes the closest wagons and people with fire.

"Rachel, leave!" Oliver is yelling at me, but I can barely hear him over the screams.

People are burning, throwing themselves on the ground and beating at the flames, but the beast just keeps spewing fire at anything that moves. Sickened, I turn and hang on to Oliver. I want to cry, to give voice to the rising shock and terror within me, but Dad taught me better than that. Losing your head in a crisis is a good way to *become* the crisis.

Instead, I loop my arm under Oliver's and tug. "Get up. We can't stay here."

The man with the tattered cloak still lies where I threw him, his eyes fastened on the destruction outside the gate. I punch him in the shoulder. "Hey! Help me get him up."

He rips his gaze away from the carnage and barely glances at me. "Help him yourself," he says, and shoves himself to his feet. He's gone before I can tell him what a filthy coward he is.

I swear and plant my feet so I can leverage Oliver off the ground. Behind me, the creature roars, people wail, and fire snaps viciously. I refuse to look. As I finish hauling Oliver to his feet, hoofbeats pound the cobblestones. I look up. The Commander now sits astride the guard's horse and is galloping straight for the gate, his whip flashing as he urges the terrified animal toward a certain doom.

Oliver wraps his arm around my waist as the Commander reaches the gate, which is choked with desperate citizens fleeing the attack. He never slows. Instead, he slashes with the whip, driving people into the side of the Wall. One man can't move out of his way fast enough, and the Commander rides over the top of him. The man lies crumpled and still in the Commander's wake.

He's going to die. Be disintegrated right in front of us. Fear and bitter hope twine themselves together within me until I can't tell them apart. I don't want Baalboden to be thrown into leaderless chaos, but I can't pretend I'd mourn him.

The beast lashes its tail, narrowly missing the Commander. His horse shies and refuses to move closer, despite repeated lashes of the whip. Abandoning the horse, the Commander leaps to the ground and strides toward the creature. People still stagger in through the gate, burned and limping. In the Wasteland, little remains of the highwaymen and citizens trapped in the Cursed One's fire.

Before the Commander can reach the beast, it trembles, a shudder running the length of its monstrous black body. Pointing its snout into the air, it sniffs and shudders again. Then just as suddenly as it appeared, it dives back below the ground, leaving the Commander standing alone outside the gate.

"Why?" I look at Oliver. "Why did it leave like that?"

He stares at the flames, his expression haunted. "Some say the Commander has power over it."

"That's ridiculous. The Commander never even got that close to it," I say as the Commander ignores the victims of the beast's fire and strides back toward Baalboden.

"No one else showed the courage to face down the Cursed One in defense of our citizens," Oliver says quietly, like it pains him to admit it.

The Commander reaches the gate and steps over the body lying there without a downward glance. Fury bites at me, chasing the last of my terror away.

"Was it courage to whip people out of the way? To run a man down like his life was worth nothing?"

"Shh." Oliver shakes my arm as the Commander nears us. "Don't talk like that."

"Somebody has to."

Oliver's voice is low and fierce. "The Cursed One never attacks inside Baalboden's Wall. Living under the Commander's rule is the price we pay for our protection. In here, we're safe."

"Not safe enough." I meet the Commander's dark gaze as he strides past us. His stare is penetrating, and my hands grow clammy at the way his eyes slide from me to Oliver as if he's just remembered something important.

We stand on the grass until the Commander is long out of sight. I spend the entire time thinking of ways Logan and I can take Oliver with us when we go.

CHAPTER SIXTEEN

LOGAN

I step out of Thom's Tankard, pleased with my purchases, and walk straight into chaos. Citizens race up the roads from the western reaches of Lower Market, pushing and shoving to gain a better position over each other. Some are crying. Yelling. Screaming.

I whip my head toward Lower Market and see the black smudge of smoke on the horizon.

Rachel. Oliver.

All that still matters to me in this world is somewhere down in Lower Market.

The crush of people move in mindless panic. Those who hesitate or turn against the mob are flung to the side or trampled beneath pounding feet.

I dive into the edges of the throng and push against the flow. At first, it's easy to let the occasional citizen bounce off me, but as I leave South Edge and enter the Market proper, the crowds thicken and my progress slows.

I need another route to Oliver's. Ducking into the nearest stall, I reach into my boots and pull out my knives. Seconds later, I slip out the back and use them to climb my way to the roof. Drive the blade in, pull myself up, drive the other blade in, pull myself up, and then yank the first blade free so I can do it again.

Once I reach the rooftop, I can see that the smoke is coming from outside the Wall. Which means Oliver and Rachel should be safe inside his tent. He'd never try to move through this mob with Rachel by his side.

A deafening roar splits the air, and the truth hits me, a sickening blow. The Cursed One is out there. On a sanctioned highwayman trading day. Any citizen still outside the gate is as good as dead.

I've never known the beast to surface so close to Baalboden, and even though every citizen knows the Commander claims to be able to protect us, I don't trust him. The creature could enter the city limits at any second, and then Oliver and Rachel could die.

I don't think. I just *move*.

I'm running, gathering speed before I even realize what I'm doing. I reach the edge of the roof and leap. Nearly missing the next roof, I crash hard to my knees. The edge of one of my knives nicks my palm and blood flows warmly down my arm. I shove the blades back into their sheaths, push myself up, and start running again.

In the distance, screams mingle with the mindless roar of the beast. I tune them out and take a flying leap onto the side of a tent. The canvas sways precariously, and I snatch the metal pole that braces the corner closest to me. Swinging over the pole, I run and jump, slamming into the side of the next stall.

As I climb onto the roof, I hear hoofbeats pounding behind me and turn to see the Commander thundering down the road, heedless of the panicked people desperately trying to get out of his way. The gate is a mere thirty yards ahead. Oliver's tent is at least eighty yards to my left. I'm about to make the turn when a flash of brilliant red near the gate catches my eye. I strain to see past the running people, and for one second, I have a clear sight line.

Fear seizes my chest with icy fingers, and my feet move before my brain can finish telling me I'm looking at Rachel. Caught in the crush of panicked, screaming people at the gate. Close enough to the beast that if the Commander is wrong about his control over it, she'll be one of the first to die.

I hit the roof next to me, skid across it, and leap into the air without pausing for breath.

If Rachel is there, surely Oliver is with her. My heart pounds, a desperate rhythm driving me forward. I nearly fall on the next leap, and slide to the ground. Time to start fighting my way through the crowds.

The beast outside the Wall bellows and the ground shudders, nearly throwing me to my knees. Quiet descends, sharp and unnatural, punctuated only by the sound of sobs and the distant crackling of fire. I skirt two men who stand, cloaks still smoking, shining pink skin blistering along their arms. They've just come from outside, and now they stand frozen, looking around as if wondering where the beast will attack next.

I don't know if it will surface again, but I'm going to be

standing in front of Rachel and Oliver if it does.

I see her now. She's clinging to Oliver, and though her body trembles, she looks fierce and ready for battle. A handful of people pass between us, and when I see her again, she's staring at the gate with furious eyes. I follow her gaze, and see the Commander stepping over a man's prone body. He meets Rachel's eyes, and dread seizes me at the speculative look he gives Oliver.

He knows we love Oliver. If we don't leave on the Commander's schedule and bring the package back to him, he'll sentence Oliver to death for our crimes. My heart aches, sudden and fierce.

Oliver will just have to come with us. I have four days to figure out how. I hurry across the cobblestones as the Commander disappears into Lower Market and gather Rachel and Oliver to me. Oliver claps me on the back, and I see the relief in his eyes that both of his surrogate grandchildren are still alive.

Rachel leans into me, but the tension vibrating through her resonates with me as well. I pull her closer, and watch the flames eat through the remains of the highwaymen's wagons and gutter into nothing.

CHAPTER SEVENTEEN

RACHEL

We don't leave the cottage for another two days while Logan tinkers with his invention and works on a plan to smuggle Oliver safely out of Baalboden, and I brush up on my knife-wielding skills. When we talk, we focus on how to leave. How to deal with the Cursed One if he attacks while we're in the Wasteland. And what might be inside the package the Commander wants so badly. We leave alone both the topic of our almost-kiss and the way we clung to each other in the wake of the beast's attack, and I'm grateful. I don't know how I feel about any of it, and I don't want to be the one to ruin things by talking about it.

In addition to a pair of guards, the tracker Melkin haunts the orchard near the house at night, and another tracker watches the cottage during the day as well. We can't do anything about the constant surveillance, so Logan works harder on his gadget, and I move on from my knife to practice with Dad's Switch.

The Switch is one of Logan's more useful inventions. It looks like a solid wooden walking staff, but one end is weighted enough to crush a man's skull, and the other conceals a spring-loaded double-edged blade. It takes hours of work before I can balance the heavier end, swing it like a mallet, and knock Bob, our practice dummy, flying. Even so, I'm still off balance enough that if I have to deal with two foes at once, I'll find myself skewered at the end of a sword before I can regain my footing, and I've yet to manage springing the blade after the initial hit without getting knocked to the ground.

Bob is about Logan's height and weighs in at an even one hundred seventy pounds. He's got me by forty pounds and five inches. Dad always said if I could take out the dummy, I could handle any man who tried to give me trouble.

I doubt he was thinking of Commander Chase when he said it.

Last year, Logan strung a heavy wire between two trees and hooked Bob to it. The dummy slides, swings, and moves with my own momentum, and while it isn't the same as fighting something with intelligence, he keeps me on my toes. I can run him through with my knife, yank the blade free, duck, and spin around to bury my weapon in his back while he slides toward me. The Switch is another story. I slam the weighted end of it into Bob's side, but can't spin the blade side around before my sparring partner swings back and sends me sprawling.

After my fourth disastrous attempt, I let fly with the most creative swear word I ever heard my father say and toss the Switch onto the grass beside me. I can't master it. Can't swing it around in time to deliver the crucial blow that could mean the difference between life and death. I lay back on the grass, squint against the glare of the afternoon sun, and suddenly feel like crying.

With Dad by my side, I'd always felt invincible. Now I feel like a freshly shorn lamb, stripped bare of a shield I never thought I'd lose. Whatever was in that package he refused to deliver, whatever he's keeping from the Commander's grasp, I have to help him. And to help him, I have to be prepared to face anything the Wasteland has to offer. Which means that failing at the Switch isn't an option.

I slowly push myself to my feet. Grasp the Switch. Close my eyes. Take a deep breath that smells of grass, sun-warmed dirt, and the fresh buds slowly unfurling in the orchard next door. If I keep my eyes closed, I can imagine Dad, standing behind me, his arms wrapped around me, his hands covering mine and holding me in place.

I widen my stance, crouch, and remember the last time we sparred together.

"Drop your shoulders a bit. You'll need the room to move." He tightens his grip on my hands when they start to slide together. *"No, you don't. Nice, wide grip. Keep it loose. Gives you balance and control. There's my girl."*

I drop my shoulders, widen my grip, and keep my eyes closed.

"All right, now, you've got a weapon on either end. You'll only have seconds to decide which one to use." He lets go of my hands, and places calloused palms on my shoulders. *"Big man, sprinting toward you."*

"Weapon?"

"Doesn't matter, Rachel. He's twice your size and his speed will bring him in range within seconds. Which end do you use?" His fingers curl around my shoulders as if willing me to know the answer.

"Blade. No time to swing the weighted end." I slide the blade free and crouch, the afternoon sun painting crimson swirls against my closed eyelids.

"Very good." He squeezes my shoulders and walks around to face me. "Now, if you must engage an opponent who is bigger, stronger, and faster, what do you do?"

"Take him down. Make it so he can't get up and come after me."

"Yes. He won't expect a Baalboden girl to know how to stop him. You get one chance to surprise him. Make full use of that advantage. Where do you make the first cut?" His eyes are deep gray, like a sky before the rain falls, and the fierce determination in them fills me with the same.

I'm Jared Adams's daughter. I can do this.

"Let him come in, then spin and slash the inner thigh as I turn. Cut open the artery." I draw in a deep breath, imagine a man barreling toward me, let him come almost too close for comfort, and then spin and slash, planting my left foot to keep my balance for the next move.

"Good! He's bleeding, but the pain hasn't hit yet, and he doesn't realize how badly he's hurt. He'll try to come after you. How do you stop him?"

"Cut the Achilles tendon as he passes me, then get out of range." I spin and slash again, the Switch beginning to feel like an extension of my arm as I thrust, turn, and slice in tune with my father's voice in my head.

He's clapping, pride and love written on his face. "You did it. I knew you could. I always knew you could."

"But what if I can't?" I lower the Switch. "What if one day I don't know what to do?" My throat closes, and I have to force myself to whisper, "What if you're gone, and I have no one left to teach me?"

But the scene in my mind falls silent. I never asked him those questions last time we sparred together. I never knew I should. And now, when I desperately want to fill in the blanks, to hear his voice tell me how to escape Baalboden, how to find him, and how to keep the Commander from finding what Dad so desperately wanted kept hidden, he's gone.

"I can teach you," Logan says quietly, and my eyes snap open.

He's a few yards away, his face shadowed by the branches of the tree he stands under. As he steps forward, I swear if I see pity on his expression, I won't speak to him ever again. But when the sunlight brushes against his face, there's no pity in his eyes. Instead, they're steady and filled with the same determination I always saw in Dad's.

He walks toward me and reaches out to slide his hand along the weighted end of the Switch I still hold.

"I miss him," he says. "That unmovable assurance he always carried with him. Like he could shoulder the weight of the world, and it wouldn't break him." His fingers brush mine, but neither of us pulls away.

My voice is quiet. "I miss his laugh. Remember?"

He smiles. "He filled a room when he was in it, didn't he?"

I nod, and the raw ache of feeling so alone subsides a bit.

"I know I can't take his place, and I don't want to. But I know how to use a Switch. And you'll need it in the Wasteland. Will you let me teach you?"

I smile a little. "If you don't mind getting humiliated by a girl, tech head."

"You're going to eat those words."

I toss my hair out of my face. "Make me."

CHAPTER EIGHTEEN

LOGAN

She stands in front of me, wild red hair streaming in the wind, a fierce gleam in her eyes. I want to reach out and touch her. Let some of the brilliant light she carries spill over onto me. I stretch out my hand, but rational thought kicks in at the last second. I grab Jared's Switch instead.

"This is too big for you. I'll make one your size, and we'll train."

"But the tracking device—"

It takes me a second to realize she still thinks I need time to work on the device to find Jared. I don't. I simply need another day or two to finish the one I'm making to find *her*. Just in case the Commander gets away with whatever treachery I'm sure he's planning.

"I can do both," I say. "Listen to me, Rachel." I wait until her eyes meet mine. "I want you to promise me that if the Commander ever makes you feel threatened, you'll do exactly what Jared taught you. Strike him down, and get away."

"If I do that while we're still in Baalboden, everyone I love will pay the price. I can't." Her voice is firm, but her eyes look shadowed. She knows the kind of danger she's in, but she's determined, if it comes to it, to lay down her life for Oliver. For me.

As if I could ever let her do that. Anger licks at me, chased by a cold frisson of fear. She isn't my Protector. I'm *hers*. And I'm not dropping this until I get her promise.

"Yes, you can." When she shakes her head, I snap at her. "You *can*. He's just a man. A cruel tyrant who doesn't deserve the power he's been abusing." Pain pierces me, swelling on a tide of something almost feral as I remember the heat floating off the dusty cobblestones, the heavy smell of my mother's blood, the way her breathing hissed in and out slowly until suddenly it was gone. *She* was gone.

"But—"

"Do you know what happens to girls in Baalboden who cross the Commander, Rachel? Do you?" My voice cracks. "They *die*. He kills them. He'll kill you if he finds out what we're planning."

"Logan—"

"He'll kill you. Do you understand?"

She nods.

I look away. At the distant orchard where men crouch behind trees waiting for us to run. Where the idyllic picture of early spring is nothing but a mirage covering the bloody truth of life in Baalboden. I look, but I can't quite erase the sight of my mother's lifeless eyes staring at something far beyond anything I could imagine. Missing her is a constant ache I carry with me.

"Logan?"

I turn toward her, braced for the pity I'm sure I'll find, but she has none. Instead, she watches me with steady understanding.

"I never told you how much I admire your mother."

The ache in my chest eases. "Really?"

"Really. Dad told me how she was the only woman in Baalboden who wasn't allowed to go through the Claiming ceremony again after her husband passed on. I guess he died before you were born?"

I nod. Mom rarely spoke of my father. Instead, she'd hold me close and say she was lucky. She had me, and who needed anything else?

"Dad also told me the Commander assigned himself as her Protector, but he wouldn't check in on her for weeks at a time. Don't you find that strange? Why break the protocol for your mom and no one else?"

"I don't know." But I wish I did. Maybe if he hadn't kept her from being Claimed again, she'd still be alive.

She frowns, and says slowly, "It's almost like the Commander hated you from the very start. Dad said he, Oliver, and some of the other men would bring her food. See what she needed in between the Commander's visits."

"Until Oliver was sick. Jared was out on a mission. And no one else remembered us." The words are hard to say. The memories they evoke are worse. The bare cupboards. The desperation in Mom's eyes as days passed, and we slowly starved.

"She was a hero. It was unfair of the Commander to deny her real Protection. Unfair to treat her differently than any other woman here. It took courage to go to Market without permission. She did it for—"

"Me! She did it for me, and it cost her her life." I can't breathe past the sudden wave of guilt and grief tearing at me. "If I hadn't been hungry, she never would've risked it."

Rachel leans close until all I can see is her. "No. If you hadn't been there, she wouldn't have had anything left to live for at all. She loved you, and you were worth the risk. You still are."

We stare at each other as her words hang in the air between us. Then she steps back, looks at the ground, and says, "Are you going to make me a new Switch or not?"

Turning my attention back to the matter at hand is easy. Figuring out what to do with Rachel's words isn't. Setting them aside for now, I search for a stick heavy enough to turn into a Switch, and start working.

By late afternoon, I've finished making her Switch and have turned her loose on the dummy. The weighted end smacks into Bob with a satisfying crunch, and she spins the stick, releases the double-edged blade, and buries it into Bob's heart as he crashes back toward her.

She grins and yanks her weapon free. "For someone who spends his days hunched over boring old papers, you sure know how to create a nice killing stick."

Time to teach her who she's dealing with. "I didn't grow up in South Edge without learning a trick or two," I say as I pick up Jared's Switch. "Sheath your blade. We'll count a solid touch from the blade end as a strike."

She sends her blade back into its hiding place, widens her stance, and rolls to the balls of her feet. I walk toward her, the resolve I feel to protect her blazing into something hard and bright in the face of her courage.

"I spend my days hunched over boring old papers, do I?" My stick whistles through the air, and she leaps back to dodge the blow. Spinning, I tap her with the sheathed blade before she can raise her arms in defense.

"My point," I say, and don't bother hiding my smirk.

She circles me. "Lucky shot."

I lash out again, but she's ready. Blocking me with the middle of her Switch, she whirls beneath my outstretched arms and slams the weighted end into my thigh.

Pride keeps me from swearing at the pain. Instead, I sweep her feet out from under her. She flips in midair and rolls forward as she lands, coming up with her stick ready.

The controlled grace of her movements would make Jared proud. I decide the warm emotion sweeping through me must be pride too.

"You're fast. That's good," I say, advancing toward her.

"You're not bad for a tech head."

We block, parry, and break apart. She's strong and quick, but I worry she doesn't know how to anticipate the unexpected. I step back, inviting an attack, and she charges forward, swinging the weighted end of her stick like a butcher slicing the head from a sheep. I wait until the last second, then drop to the ground and ram her with my shoulder. Her forward momentum carries her over the top of me and she lands face-first in the grass.

She spits dry blades of grass from her mouth, and swears, but a new respect for me is in her eyes.

I laugh, and my fear for her eases into something I can use to focus on planning. She stares at me, a tiny smile flitting across her lips, and the affection on her face makes me feel like the richest man in the world.

"I was a fighter long before I was a tech head." I offer her a hand up. "You need to be ready for an opponent who does the unexpected."

She takes my outstretched hand, closing her soft fingers over mine without breaking my gaze. The sun blazes a golden path through her fiery hair, and my eyes slide over her pale skin and come to rest on her lips. Warmth pools in my stomach and spreads lazily through me as I tug her hand and pull her closer.

I'm not going to kiss her. That would be . . . I don't know what that would be. I can't seem to think straight. All I see is *Rachel*, filling up my empty spaces and making me into more than I ever could be on my own.

Maybe this is what family does for each other. She's my family now. Which is why, even as I lean toward her, unable to tear my gaze away from the softness of her mouth, I tell myself I'm not going to kiss her.

She steps toward me, face upturned. I lean in.

Behind us, someone clears his throat.

CHAPTER NINETEEN

LOGAN

I drop her hand and whip around, my Switch ready. Oliver stands on our back porch with the sternest expression he can manage aimed straight at me.

Rachel steps back and bends to pick up her weapon. I find I'm suddenly very interested in the exact position of the sun, and I take a moment to study the sky. When I look back at Oliver, his brow is raised.

"Going to invite an old man in? Or going to stand there pretending I didn't just see—"

"We were sparring." Rachel hefts her Switch to prove it.

"That's not what we called it in my day," Oliver says, and motions for us to come inside the house with him.

I can't look at Rachel as we walk inside. The room feels charged with awkwardness, and I have absolutely no idea how to defuse it without just addressing my sudden, inexplicable attraction to her head on. Which I might do, if I could explain it. And if Oliver wasn't in the room.

He claps me on the shoulder and uses his other arm to drag Rachel to his side. "It's nice to see the two of you putting aside your differences and discovering how much you really have in common. Rachel, would you mind getting me some water?"

As Rachel hurries toward the kitchen, Oliver looks me in the eye. "You're a good man, Logan McEntire. You're the son I never had. I know I can trust you with her."

The weight of his trust lands heavily on top of the trust already placed in me by Jared. "It won't happen again," I say, though I don't know if I mean it.

He grins. "Oh, I wouldn't go making promises you might not be able to keep. Just see that if you do decide she's the one for you, you handle it properly."

The one for me? I stare at Rachel as Oliver leaves my side and enters the kitchen, settling his bulk at my cluttered table. It was just an impulse. She's beautiful and strong in a way I appreciate. Of course I find her attractive. It doesn't mean I'm ready to Claim her. Or anyone else, for that matter.

Feeling unaccountably irritated by Oliver's assumption, I follow him into the kitchen. Rachel settles on the floor, leaning against Oliver's legs as he takes out a towel-wrapped bundle of sticky buns and hands it to her. I take the other chair. Time to set aside the baffling subject of my feelings for Rachel and concentrate on something far more straightforward: my plan to get Oliver out of Baalboden with us.

Before I can speak, though, Oliver says, "You two may be right. I think Jared's still alive."

"What?" I lean forward as Rachel's eyes meet mine, full of shock and eager anticipation.

"Why do you think that?" she asks, setting the sticky buns on the table.

"I talked with some folks who were out trading with that band of highwaymen that got themselves killed by the Cursed One the other day. Word among the city-states is that your father is the most wanted man in the Wasteland."

"Wanted for *what*?" I ask.

"For thievery and treason against the ruler of Rowansmark."

Rachel sits up straight. "That's a dirty lie! He never stole anything, and he wouldn't commit treason, either."

Oliver gives her shoulder a gentle squeeze. "I know that. Everyone who knows him knows that."

"He didn't steal that package from Rowansmark. Someone gave it to him," she says.

"I'm guessing whoever gave him that package is the one who committed treason," I say. "It's possible the Commander managed to bribe or coerce a citizen of Rowansmark into stealing it for him, intending to use Jared as the delivery person."

"Except Dad got suspicious, figured out what was inside—"

"And had the integrity and courage to keep it from the Commander," I say.

"But why not return it to Rowansmark if it belongs to them?" she asks.

Oliver shakes his head. "I don't know, but James Rowan is doing everything in his power to get it back. There's a reward posted. A year's supply of wheat, a head of cattle, and a lifetime appointment to Rowansmark's Military Council for whoever brings in your father. Alive."

Rachel and I are silent as the absurd generosity of the reward sinks in.

"No one's claimed the reward yet, so unless he got caught by the Cursed One, he's alive." Oliver gives Rachel's shoulder one more squeeze and heaves himself to his feet. "Thought I'd make a trip out here to tell you that." He picks up the water set before him and downs it in five long gulps. "Best be on my way. Don't want to get caught out after dark."

Rachel launches herself at his chest, clinging to him. "Not yet. We have something to tell you."

He looks at me.

"We're leaving the day after Claiming." I stand, wrapping my arm around his shoulders and hoping he understands that though I don't know how to show it, I understand I owe him my life. If he hadn't quietly defied the Commander's decree and befriended a dirty little street rat, I wouldn't be a man worthy of calling people like Jared, Rachel, and Oliver family. "We're traveling the Wasteland to find Jared. And we're bringing you with us."

"I'm too old for journeys across the Wasteland." Oliver wraps one arm around my middle as well. "I'm proud of you both. Jared would be too. Remember that, and stay alive."

"But you have to come with us!" Rachel's eyes are damp.

"We aren't coming back," I say. "We trust that Jared's reasons for not delivering the package to Baalboden are sound, so we won't be giving the Commander what he wants. When we don't come back, he'll take our treason out on you."

"How am I supposed to hike across all that wilderness looking for Jared? I'll just slow you down."

"There's another group of highwaymen scheduled to trade

tomorrow. You'll go out to trade as usual, but you won't come back."

"The guards sweep the area with Identidiscs," he says.

"I have tech that can block those. You usually bring a donkey out with you to carry supplies to and from the trading area, don't you?" I ask.

He nods.

"This time, beneath your baked goods, pack clothing, food, a torch, and a weapon. Trade only for items you can use in the Wasteland. At the guards' shift change, mingle with the highwaymen's wagons, hand out baked goods to deflect suspicion if you have to, and then just walk right into the Wasteland. We'll join you the next day."

"That's downright brazen." Oliver's smile is full of pride.

"It will work. It has to." I clamp my hand on his shoulder. "You'll be invisible on the Identidisc. You can ride the donkey across the Wasteland to make the journey easier. We'll leave you at one of the safe houses until we find Jared. Then we can all build a new life together somewhere else."

His dark eyes meet mine, calm and assessing. "Seems a lot of risk for you two to take just for one old man."

"You're family. We aren't leaving without you."

"If you stay, he'll kill you." Rachel's voice breaks, and Oliver hauls her close.

"Don't cry, Rachel-girl. I aim to be a great-granddaddy. If that takes riding an ass across a godforsaken wilderness, I guess that's what I'll do."

"Thank you." I slip a magnetic wrist cuff into his hand. "Wear that over your wristmark on trading day and the Identidisc won't be able to find you."

Oliver holds on to us both a moment longer, and then he's gone. The cottage feels empty without him.

CHAPTER TWENTY

LOGAN

The Claiming ceremony is tomorrow. By this point, Oliver should be mingling with the traders, getting close to disappearing into the Wasteland to wait for us. I finish the last piece of equipment I need to cover every conceivable contingency for our mission. Need to evade another tracker? Not a problem. Guards refuse to be left behind? I can handle that. Rachel and I get separated? I can find her anywhere. The Commander double-crosses us?

I almost hope he tries.

I have every avenue covered, every plan fleshed out, every piece of technology working as it should. The sense of triumph I feel at having an edge on the Commander and any other tracker he employs to go after Jared is a vicious light burning within me.

Rachel feels it too. I can tell by the battle light in her eyes as she double-checks our weapons while I make sure the list of last-minute provisions I want to purchase at Market today is in my inner cloak pocket.

We've avoided touching each other since our sparring match. I don't know her reasons, but mine are clear: I'm attracted to her. I've always found her beautiful, but now I see beneath that to the courageous, passionate girl who would go against any foe to fight for those she loves. She's . . . admirable.

But I'm not sure the craving I feel to run my hands through her hair and pull her to me can be accurately labeled admiration. Until I can get it under control, I keep my distance. I have to. I'm standing in Jared's place. He trusts me. *She* trusts me, a fragile development at once terrifying and immensely gratifying.

I'm not ready to discuss my irrational inner thoughts, but still I want to reach out to her with something more than battle plans and Worst Case Scenarios. With that in mind, I look up from my Market list and say quietly, "We leave day after tomorrow, and we won't be spending a lot of time together before then, so—"

"Why not?" She looks up from the weapons she's packing.

"I have some last-minute supplies and information to gather, and this is your last chance to see Sylph. I thought you'd like to spend the day with her."

Pain flashes across her face and she resumes packing the weapons.

"Anyway, I wanted to give you a compliment."

Her eyes widen, flash to mine, and then look down again. "Why?"

"Because I realize, even though it doesn't make logical sense given what I know of you, that you need softer words from me sometimes."

Now she's looking at me like I've suddenly sprouted two

heads, and I feel like an idiot.

"You're telling me you're going to give me a compliment even though I shouldn't logically need one?" Her voice doesn't sound pleased.

I pick back through my words, but don't see anything that could cause offense, so I nod. "Common sense would dictate a woman like you shouldn't be dependent upon—"

"What is that supposed to mean?" She throws the bow and arrow set she's holding onto the floor and stands, pink spots of color in her cheeks. "Why shouldn't I need a few compliments?"

I have no idea how this conversation went awry so quickly. I just want to tell her something nice. Does it have to be a ten-minute discussion about motives and semantics?

Maybe if I enunciate clearly, she'll understand. I lean toward her and say with exquisite clarity, "Because of the kind of woman you are."

Speaking slowly solved absolutely nothing. She looks like she might pick up one of the weapons and throw it at my head. I feel more than a little irritated myself.

She speaks around gritted teeth. "And what kind of woman do you think I am, Logan McEntire?"

I snap right back at her. "Confident. Strong. Capable. Stunning. An equal partner in this endeavor in every sense of the word."

The pink in her cheeks darkens, but instead of sparks, her eyes look soft and warm. I have no idea how a compliment delivered in anger can work that kind of magic with her, but I'm grateful.

"You think I'm stunning?" she asks, and suddenly I feel like the tunic laced at my throat is choking me.

"I didn't say that."

"Yes, you did," she says softly, a tiny smile on her lips even as she refuses to meet my gaze.

Did I? I scroll back through the words I threw at her and realize she's right. I did say *stunning*. Which, incidentally, isn't a crime. Anyone looking at her would think the same.

I shrug and make sure I sound casual when I say, "I guess I did. Ready?" I pull my cloak over my shoulders and wait for her to call me on my words. To demand an explanation I'm not ready to give.

Instead, she says, "Let's go." Her voice sounds stilted and unnatural, but I let it go. I have no idea what else to say.

The tension between us lingers as we walk the dusty road into town with nothing but the early-morning sounds of farm animals and birds to keep us company in our silence.

The torch boys have already extinguished the streetlights in Center Square, and we pass the stage as workers scrub the wood and set up booths in preparation for tomorrow's Claiming ceremony.

I'm grateful we'll be leaving Baalboden before Rachel reaches Claiming age. The thought of standing behind her on the stage while a group of eager townsmen try to convince me to give her over to them forever makes me want to knock their heads together. Not because I can't give Rachel to the right man for her. But I know every available bachelor in Baalboden, and while I've never really considered it before this moment, I'm quite confident none of them measure up to her.

We enter North Hub and arrive at Sylph's house. Rachel

barely says good-bye before heading inside. I plant myself on the road and wait until I see her enter the house before continuing on toward Lower Market.

Halfway there, I duck down a side street, take a short cut through an alley, and slide into the back entrance of the butcher's, where the first of my black-market contacts waits to give me the most current information on Rowansmark and the search for Jared.

I'm going into the Wasteland armed to the teeth with knowledge, technology, and the kind of fierce tenacity the Commander always assumes no one owns but him.

I can't wait to prove him wrong.

CHAPTER
TWENTY-ONE

RACHEL

Sylph, her mother, and her oldest brother are waiting for me in their main room. Sylph shoots me a quick grin as she puts on her cloak. "We're going to get my final fitting at Madam Illiard's North Hub shop. Can you believe the Claiming ceremony is tomorrow?"

She lingers over the word *tomorrow* as if her dreams are pinned to it. Maybe they are. I try to smile as she bounces next to me, chattering about her dress and the weather predictions for tomorrow's ceremony, but it's hard to pretend. Knowing I'm leaving day after tomorrow twists me up inside until I don't know how to feel.

I want to stop wasting time. Stop lingering while somewhere out there, Dad is alone in the Wasteland. I also want to savor every precious moment I have with Sylph in case I never get the chance to see her again.

Sylph doesn't notice my lack of response. We've fallen into step behind her mother and brother, and she's whispering about her secret hope that Smithson West will Claim her. I listen with half an ear, nod at the appropriate times, and try to memorize everything I love about her while grief swells within me and makes it hard to breathe.

We've been friends since we shared a table at Life Skills, the few years of schooling deemed appropriate for a girl in Baalboden. We learned things like cooking, bargaining, sewing, and proper etiquette when out in public with our Protectors.

The boys received six more years of schooling and learned things like math, reading, the history of the Wasteland, the differing laws and protocols of the other eight city-states, and Commander Chase's pivotal role in saving the citizens of Baalboden from the Cursed One.

I never thought it was fair that anatomy decided what my brain was fit for. Dad agreed, and I'd soaked up everything he could teach me. Once, I'd tried to teach Sylph the wonders of being able to open a book and understand the words inside, but she'd shrugged it off. She didn't need to read. She'd have a Protector for that.

Now I study her dark green eyes, lit with pleasure at the prospect of our day, her black curls that constantly mock her mother's attempts to conjure a ladylike style, and the excitement quivering through her softly rounded frame, and lean forward to give her a hug.

She hugs me back. We enter Madam Illiard's shop, where fancy Claiming dresses hang near the front window and bolts of fabric line the walls in a feast of color. Two tables are set up on either side of the shop. One has baskets of useless things like beads, buttons, and rolls of ribbon. The other is empty of anything but a measuring tape and two pairs of scissors.

I don't know how anyone can spend more than five minutes inside this place without going stark-raving mad. Sylph, however, bounces on her toes and hugs her mother as they examine the almost completed Claiming dress designed just for her. Seeing them pressed close to each other as they finger the fabric and admire a piece of lace sends an unwelcome shaft of longing through me.

I don't usually miss my mother. How can I? She died right after I was born, and I never knew her. But at moments like these, I miss what we might have had together. I imagine our hair would've been the same shade of red. Our eyes the same shade of blue. Maybe we would've both loved lemon cake and hated spinach. Or maybe we would've both thought the only truly useful items in Madam Illiard's shop were the scissors, because pointy things make excellent weapons.

I'll never know, and thinking about it won't help me escape Baalboden and find Dad, so I shove the longing away and follow Sylph into the windowless back room for her fitting.

Nearly two hours pass before Madam pronounces Sylph's dress perfect. The dark green velvet hugs her upper body and falls in graceful lines to her ankles. Black lace panels shimmer between the skirt's folds, and black ribbon laces up the back. When Madam Illiard and Sylph's mother leave the room to haggle over the final cost, Sylph twirls in front of me and asks, "Don't you love it?"

"It's beautiful."

"Do you think Smithson will like it?"

"I'm sure he will."

She grabs my arm, and looks at me properly for the first time. "What's wrong? You don't think Smithson is right for me?"

"I think he's a nice man," I say, because Sylph's heart is set on him, and because it's true. He's quiet, sturdy, and seems to want nothing more than a wife, a home, and a decent crop from his patch of farmland. "He's perfect for you."

She glows for a moment, but then her expression falls. "I wish you were in this year's ceremony with me."

"I'm not yet seventeen." I try to sound as if I'm disappointed too, though I'm not. I can't even think about wanting to parade across the stage in Center Square while one of the eligible townsmen decides I'd make a perfect wife. Besides, what do I know about being an obedient wife? There are much more important qualities to have than a docile disposition.

Logan seems to agree.

Warmth spreads through me at the thought of Logan's fumbling attempt at giving me a compliment today.

Stunning.

His words feel like a gift I want to keep reopening when no one else is looking. What would Sylph say if she knew I'd almost kissed Logan? If she knew I sometimes watch him while he's bent over his inventions and want to trace my fingers over the muscles in his shoulders for no apparent reason at all?

The secret trembles at the edge of my lips, but there are other secrets right behind it. Secrets about the Commander. Oliver. Treachery. Sylph can't know anything about that. It's the only protection I can offer her after I'm gone.

Sylph is still talking, rambling on about ways to get me into the Claiming ceremony with her. None of her ideas are plausible.

Finally, she slumps her shoulders and says, "You're so close to seventeen! If only your dad was still here, he could've petitioned for a special sanction . . ." Her eyes widen and fill with tears.

"Sylph—"

She runs to me and envelopes me in a cloud of velvet and lace. "I'm so sorry! I wasn't thinking."

I push her away gently. "I'm not mad. I know you didn't mean anything by it."

Her eyes brighten. "Maybe Logan could Claim you!"

My heart speeds up, but I shake my head. "Don't be silly."

She grabs my hands and dances in place. "Wouldn't that be romantic? I'd be Mrs. Smithson West. And you'd be Mrs. Logan McEntire. We could host dinner parties together, and go to Market together, and—"

I laugh a little desperately and link my fingers with hers. She twirls us around, and I let her spin me, let myself ignore the Wasteland, the bounty on my father's head, and the complications lying between Logan and me. She doesn't know it, but it will be our last time together. I want to leave her with nothing but happy memories.

We stumble and fall to the floor, doubled over in breathless laughter. I wrap my arms around her and squeeze. She hugs me back, but then her laughter chokes into the kind of silence she's rarely capable of. I turn my head to see the cause and feel my stomach lurch.

Commander Chase stands in the back doorway, his sword drawn and his dark eyes cold.

CHAPTER
TWENTY-TWO

RACHEL

Sylph's arms tighten around me, and I squeeze her back before slowly disengaging. My knees are shaking as I force myself to my feet, moving to stand between the Commander and my best friend.

"You're coming with me." He gestures toward the door behind him. The polished silver buttons on his crisp blue uniform catch the morning sunlight and wink like little diamonds. I look away.

It doesn't occur to me to argue, despite my promise that I would strike him down and get away if he threatened me when Logan wasn't around to help. Sylph is here. She'll pay the price for my actions just as surely as I will, and I'm not about to risk it. Besides, he still needs me.

I hope.

"Rachel!" Sylph whispers as I head toward the door. I toss one look at her and try to smile, though my lips are trembling. I step into the morning light, a light breeze playing with my hair as I face the trio of Brute Squad guards waiting for me on the cobblestone street.

Their swords are drawn too.

The Commander presses his palm against my back. Without my cloak, the heat from his body scorches mine.

"Get in," he says, and the Brute Squad steps aside to reveal a large mule-drawn covered wagon.

I glance around the street, but if anyone notices what's happening, they aren't stopping to stare. I can't blame them. Shrugging off the Commander's hand, I refuse the assistance of the guard closest to me and climb into the back of the wagon. The Commander and one of the three guards follow on my heels. In a moment, the wagon lurches forward and rumbles over the cobblestone street.

The heavy canvas covering dilutes the morning sun into something dim and gray, and my eyes struggle to adjust. It takes a few seconds to notice the cloth-covered lump leaning against the far wall of the wagon. Foreboding fills me, an oily poison that makes me queasy.

I don't know what's under the cloth, but it can't be good.

"Have a seat." The Commander moves past me, knocking me into the wooden bench lining the wagon wall behind me, and settles on the opposite bench, right beside the lump. His sword is still drawn.

The other guard braces himself against the back of the wagon and stands, sword drawn, blocking the exit. I want to scan my surroundings looking for possible escape routes, but I can't tear my eyes away from the lump. There's something horribly familiar about its shape, but I don't want to put it into words because it isn't possible.

It can't be possible.

"You and that inventor have been keeping secrets." The Commander's eyes are bright, hard orbs lighting the dim space with malice. "Did he really think I wouldn't know your every move before you do?"

I look at the cloth-covered lump and dread pools in my stomach. It's just the right size for a person.

Logan. The Commander's always hated Logan. He didn't want him to come with me. I look at the person shrouded in cloth and try to find my voice, though I have no idea what I'll say.

"Not going to tell me what you're up to?"

I open my mouth but nothing comes out.

"I see you need a bit of convincing." He smiles and drives his sword into the lump. Whoever is trapped beneath the cloth sucks in a raspy breath and moans. Blood blossoms beneath the cloth and spreads like a fast-blooming rose.

My breath leaves me as if I've been hit in the stomach. "Who is that?"

Oh please, oh please let it be a stranger. Another guard. Another object lesson. Please. Don't let it be Logan.

The Commander ignores me. "I don't trust Logan McEntire. I don't trust you, either, but you have a quality he lacks."

I can't look away from the blood, and I feel a scream clawing for freedom at the back of my throat.

"Do you know what that is?" He pulls his sword free, and the person beneath the cloth twitches. "It's loyalty."

I can't breathe. I try to stand, but my knees won't hold me, and I crumple to the splintery wagon floor.

Logan.

Ignoring the Commander, I crawl toward the person beneath the cloth. I'm nearly there when the Commander drives his sword into the wagon floor, inches from my face.

His voice is harsh as he bites each syllable into pieces. "Logan isn't loyal. He thinks he is, but if I put him to the test, he'd fail. His own agenda will always be more important to him than anyone else."

My breath catches on a shuddering sob, and I try to crawl around the sword. It nicks my shoulder as I pass, and the Commander laughs.

"You, on the other hand, are loyal to a fault. You won't scheme, manipulate, or betray. Not if it will cost you someone you love." He yanks his sword free of the floor and slides it into the blood-soaked lump again. "No, you'll go to the ends of the Wasteland, do everything that's asked of you, ignore your own ethics and instincts, as long as you get to save the one you love."

I've reached the cloth and am tearing at it with shaking hands while the person beneath it moans in agony.

"Please." I can't loosen the cloth. "Please!" I look at the Commander, and his scar twists his smile into a grotesque parody of mirth.

It will be a guard. A prisoner. Someone who means nothing to me. I can't bear to be wrong.

I can't bear to lose Logan.

"Allow me to help you," the Commander says in a voice filled with malice. Pulling his sword free again, he slices it through the cloth and splits it top to bottom.

I snatch at the pieces and yank them free. A scream builds in my chest as I stare.

Not Logan.

Not a stranger.

Oliver.

Oliver.

He's supposed to be outside the Wall now. Safe. He's supposed to be, but he isn't.

Oliver looks at me, sadness and pride mingling with the love he's always shown me, and then moans again. I come undone.

"No, no, no, no, no." I try to find the cuts, but there's so much blood. So much. It pours from his chest and covers my hands, and I can't stop it.

I can't stop it.

"You shouldn't have plotted behind my back," the Commander says, his voice as hard as the wagon floor beneath me. "You were disloyal, and now it's cost you."

"It's going to be okay," I tell Oliver. Tears burn my eyes, and I have to blink to see him. "It's going to be okay," I lie, because I don't know what else to do.

He tries to speak, but blood bubbles from his lips instead. I grab the cloth and press it against his chest with both hands.

"It's going to be okay," I say again, and press harder, though I don't know how to make my words true.

Oliver shakes his head slightly and tries to raise his arm. I grab his hand with mine and wrap our fingers together the way he used to when I was little and he was walking me through the Market. His hand still swallows mine, though now his skin is like ice.

"Save him," I say to the Commander. "Please. Get him to a

doctor. I'll do anything you want. Anything."

"Yes, you will," he says. "Because if you don't, I'll kill Logan in ways the citizens of Baalboden will remember for decades to come."

"Logan?" I look up, tears obscuring my view of the Commander's face. "I don't understand. This is Oliver. I want you to save *Oliver*!"

"Oh, it's far too late for him," he says and, with a flick of his wrist, drives his sword through Oliver's neck.

The scream inside me rips through my throat. I reach for the sword, but it's already gone. Throwing myself on Oliver, I shove the cloth against his neck and beg for him to look at me, though I know he can't.

He can't, and he never will again. Wild sobs choke me, and I can barely find the air to let them loose.

Rough hands grab my arms and pull me from Oliver. I scream and beat at the person behind me to no avail. The wagon stops, and the two more guards enter, scoop Oliver's body up inside the cloth, and haul him out. The guard holding me tosses me to the floor and exits as well, leaving me huddled at the Commander's feet.

He crouches to my level, Oliver's blood still glistening on his blade.

"You will be in the Claiming ceremony tomorrow."

I stare at his sword, cross my arms over my chest, and rock back and forth.

"Are you listening?" He grabs my chin with his hand, forcing me to meet his gaze. "Pay attention. Logan McEntire's life depends on it."

My teeth are chattering, and my body shudders, but I make myself nod. Logan is all I have left. Whatever it takes to get him off the Commander's kill list, so help me, I'll do it.

"You will be in the Claiming ceremony. I've seen the way Logan looks at you. I have no doubt he'll try to Claim you." His smile flickers at the edges. "You are going to turn him down."

I'm too numb to protest. To wonder what the Commander thinks he sees when Logan looks at me. To argue that no one's ever turned down an eligible man in the history of Baalboden's Claiming ceremonies.

"When you turn him down, I will declare you a ward of the state. Logan's influence will be legally severed, and you will then travel the Wasteland without him." His voice lowers. "You will show my tracker where your father hid the package he received at Rowansmark, and you will return it to me, or Logan will be tortured and killed."

He lets go of my chin and runs his palm across my cheek, tangling his fingers in my hair. "Do I make myself clear?"

I nod, a wobbly, uncertain movement, and watch the blood slide down his blade.

"Until tomorrow," he says, and then he's gone.

CHAPTER
TWENTY-THREE

RACHEL

The wagon lurches forward again, and it takes a moment to realize I'm not alone in the back. One of the guards is sitting on the bench behind me, holding a paper-wrapped package in one hand and a damp cloth in the other.

I scoot as far away from him as I can without touching the puddle of Oliver's blood seeping slowly into the floorboards. When he ignores me, I wrap my arms around my knees and try not to let the agonized wailing I hear inside my head leave my lips.

Oliver is dead.

Dead.

He'll never be a great-granddaddy. He'll never hand me another sticky bun, or call me Rachel-girl, or see me clear my father's name.

The truth is too harsh to touch, and I shy away from it before it sears itself into my brain and becomes real. Instead, I find a quiet place within myself where the Commander doesn't exist, my family is still intact, and I'm not covered in anyone's blood.

The harsh keening inside my head becomes muted—the grief of some other girl. Not mine.

I rock, holding myself as if I'll fly into a million little pieces if I let go.

The guard says something, but I can't hear him. If I listen to him, I might hear the grief-stricken wail of the girl who just lost something precious.

He slaps me, but I can't feel it. He says something else, then crouches down in front of me and scrubs my face with rough persistence. When he pulls back, the damp cloth in his hand is covered in bright red patches, like little crimson flowers decorating the fabric.

Bile rises at the back of my throat, and I tear my eyes away from the cloth.

He removes the string on the package he carries and tears off the paper. I don't look to see what he has. It might be covered in red too.

He's talking again, louder this time. His boots dig into the hard wooden floor beneath us as he stands. I catch a glimpse of crimson staining the edge of his right sole, and tuck my head toward my chest.

My chest is covered in rust-scented crimson.

Covered.

I beat at it. Tear at it with frantic fingers. I have to get it off me. I *have* to.

The guard helps. Rough hands unlace my tunic, and I claw my way free. I'm panting, harsh bursts of air that fill the wagon.

He attacks my skin with his red-flowered cloth again, and

I twist my body, trying to get away. I don't want him to touch me with that thing. I can't stand to have it touch me for another second.

He drops the cloth. In its place, he holds a new tunic that looks just like my old one used to look. Pure white. Crimson-free.

I let him slide it over my head. Let the rough linen threads scrape against my skin. Maybe if they scrape hard enough, I'll forget. About the crimson. About the awful wailing I still hear inside me.

About what I just lost.

The guard pulls me to my feet and fumbles with the laces on my skirt, but I don't help him. How can I? I'm not really there. I'm home, on our back porch, sipping lemonade while my family is close by, just out of sight.

He says something, but I don't hear him. I'm too busy listening to the deep rumble of men's voices coming from somewhere behind my back porch.

My skirt puddles around my feet, and he lifts me out of it.

The lemonade I sip is the perfect combination of tart and sweet. I want to share it with my family, but they stay just out of reach.

He pulls a new skirt over my head. Light blue, just like the one he removed.

Light blue like the summer sky I see from my porch.

I'm sitting on the wagon's bench.

No, I'm sitting on our rocker.

My shoes are gone.

It's summer. I don't need shoes.

Now, they're back again. A stranger is tying them. Which is silly, because I can tie my own shoes. If I want to. Which I don't, because the summer sun is hot, and I'm too tired.

I'm so tired.

I stop rocking on the porch. Or maybe the wagon stops.

I'm not in a wagon. I never was.

Hands lift me up and set me down on a cobblestone street. I stare at my boots. They're the same color and design as always, but the scuffs and creases are gone as if they never were.

Behind me, a wagon clip-clops away. I don't turn. I don't know where my porch is. Where the summer sun went. It's cold now. Cold and gray and the air feels damp against my skin.

Someone calls my name, and I look up to see Sylph, her dark eyes full of fear, beckoning from the doorway to my right. As I turn and walk toward her, I hear the faint wailing of the grief-stricken girl grow louder, and clamp my lips tight to hold it in.

CHAPTER
TWENTY-FOUR

LOGAN

I've met with contacts at the butcher's, the blacksmith's, and a corner table at Thom's Tankard. No one knows anything more about Rowansmark or Jared than Oliver already told me.

I need to know what Jared took from Rowansmark, who gave it to him, and why. I need to understand why he hid it instead of bringing it into Baalboden. Most of all, I need a clear picture of the Commander's role in all of this.

I might not be able to gain more information on what is happening outside our Wall, but I know how to get information on the Commander's activities. Wrapping my cloak around myself, I walk through South Edge in circuitous routes, ducking through alleys and backyards, making sure I lose my followers. Approaching my destination with caution, I knock and wait to be allowed entrance.

Monty runs his business out of his kitchen at a table that leans precariously toward the floor on one side. On one side of the room, stacks of goods rest in haphazard piles, evidence of a successful week in the information-for-hire trade. On the other, Monty leans back in a chair, a wicked-looking dagger lying across his lap, sipping a mug of ale and watching me with narrow dark eyes.

"Monty." I nod and settle into an open chair beside him.

He sets his mug on the table and lets his chair legs slam back onto the scuffed, dirty floor beneath him. "Logan McEntire. Haven't seen the likes of you in these parts for several years. Thought maybe you'd outgrown good old South Edge."

I don't take him up on his clever invitation to tell him what I've been doing and with whom. For one, he already knows I earned the apprenticeship with Jared. Everyone does. For another, in a room where information is part of the currency, I'm not about to part with mine for free.

Instead, I rest my elbows on the table, steeple my fingers, and look at him steadily over the top of my hands. "How many times in the past three years have you been forced to relocate before the guards arrested you or one of your clients? Five? Six? Help me out here, because I've lost track."

Monty's eyes harden, but his expression remains calm. "What is it you want, Logan?"

"It's what *you* want, Monty. What I can do for you."

He's silent for a moment, assessing me while he wipes beads of condensation from his mug of ale. Then he says, "What can you do for me?"

Reaching into my cloak, I pull out a copper circle about the size of a flat orange. It glows beneath the faint sunlight leaking in past the layer of filth on Monty's kitchen window.

"Shiny." Monty says, his tone noncommittal. "But I already

have plenty of shiny."

I place the disc on the table. "Still have that stolen Identidisc around here somewhere?"

He lifts his eye to mine, and his expression reminds me of a snake. Cold. Calculating. And dangerous if cornered. Finally, he nods. "Let's say I do have one of those. What does that have to do with this?"

"The last thing you need is a guard wandering through with an Identidisc and seeing a list of anyone you happen to be doing business with at the moment. It compromises your reputation, inhibits your ability to do business, and could easily land you in the dungeon. This"—I rub my thumb across the glowing copper surface—"blocks every wristmark within a thirty-yard radius. Basically, if you turn this on whenever you do business, everyone in your house will be dark to the guards."

He blinks once more and when his eyes meet mine, greed peeks out behind the cold calculation.

I have him.

"I want proof it works," he says, and gets up to rummage through his cupboards, his dagger still grasped in his hand. In seconds, he returns to the table carrying a black Identidisc. It's an older model, but a glance at it shows the battery still has enough juice left to take a reading. I remain still while he powers it up and sends out a sonic pulse.

Both of our names show up on the screen.

So does the name Anthony Ruiz.

I frown at Monty. "Who's Anthony Ruiz?"

Monty shrugs. "A boy who delivers messages through South Edge. Never mind him, turn on your device."

I comply and wait while the Identidisc sends out another pulse. This time the screen shows no list of citizens in the immediate area.

Monty sets down the Identidisc and looks at me. "How much?"

"I'm thinking it's fairly priceless."

"I can put a price on anything. What do you want?"

"Money would be nice," I say, and Monty's lips thin. "But I'll settle for useful information instead."

"What kind of information is worth a device like this?"

"I'd like to know what the Commander's been up to lately."

"That's a pretty vague request."

I nod. "Then I guess you'd better tell me everything you know about him, his activities, and anything unusual happening in the compound, and let me decide what's useful for my purposes and what isn't."

Monty shakes his head. "Too steep a price, Logan."

I shrug, scoop the copper disc off the table, and stand. "I'll be on my way, then." I'm halfway through the door when he calls me back.

"Fine. Sit down. Leave the disc. I'll tell you what I've heard."

I return to the table, set the disc in front of me, and listen while Monty tells me the few things he knows for sure about Commander Chase.

Fact 1: The Commander has a small object attached to a chain and wears it underneath his uniform. Most sources agree he never takes this pendant off.

I don't see how this is relevant or useful to me, but I file it away just in case. If nothing else, I can use the chain to choke him during hand-to-hand combat if it ever comes to that.

Fact 2: After Jared's disappearance, the Commander sent two couriers on missions, but neither of them were heading toward Rowansmark. They haven't returned yet, though the first is due any day.

This might be nothing more than the usual messages, negotiations, and trade between our city-state and another. But the fact that the Commander neglected to send any official message to Rowansmark in the wake of the accusations against his top courier is suspicious. Why not reach out to make peace? Offer to help bring Jared in? The only answer I can come up with is that the Commander needs to find Jared first.

Fact 3: This morning, every remaining tracker in the city except Melkin was sent out on a mission.

I've never heard of so many trackers being given missions at once. I can only assume they've been tasked to cover all four corners of the Wasteland in the search for Jared, even while Rachel and I look for the package. I don't like the fact that Melkin wasn't included in the mass send-off this morning. Either he's going to be part of our mission, or the Commander has a double-cross up his sleeve.

Let him try it. He isn't the only one who knows how to think three steps ahead.

I leave the house and a rail-thin boy with hungry eyes detaches from the surrounding shadows and approaches me. I'm guessing this is Anthony Ruiz, messenger boy.

"Logan McEntire?" He waits well out of sword range for my reply.

"Yes."

Someone bangs a door further down the street, and the boy tenses like he's ready to run. "Roderigo Angeles is looking for you. His wife needs you to return to Madam Illiard's shop in North Hub immediately."

Rachel. She snuck out again. And she's been caught. The image of my mother's body wavers and reforms into Rachel lying broken and bloody at the Commander's feet.

The boy says something else, but I can't hear anything beyond the pulse roaring in my ears. I toss him a coin for his trouble and hurry toward the main street, fear driving my steps.

CHAPTER
TWENTY-FIVE

LOGAN

She hasn't snuck out. Instead, she's huddled on the floor, pressed against the back wall of Madam Illiard's stock room.

I can't process this Rachel. I've never seen her like this.

Sylph is sitting near Rachel, watching her and crying. I ignore Mrs. Angeles and Madam Illiard in favor of heading straight for the girls. Sylph looks up and stands so I can take her place.

I crouch on the floor beside Rachel. She looks into my eyes, and there's nothing but glassy shock in hers. My heart sinks. "Rachel? What's wrong?"

She begins rocking as if she needs that simple rhythm to keep herself anchored.

"Can you tell me?" I ask, my mind racing. Maybe something happened to Jared, and my contacts hadn't heard of it. Maybe she's realized the magnitude of what it means to leave Baalboden forever, though I doubt that would cause this state of shock. Maybe a man hurt her. I don't know how, since she's been in the Angeleses' care the entire time, but I have to acknowledge the possibility.

If that's the case, I'm going to hunt down the perpetrator and kill him. In the most inhumane method I can possibly devise. And then I'll invent something I can use to reanimate him and kill him all over again.

Her lips tremble, and she clamps both hands across her mouth.

"Rachel?" I ask, but she isn't listening.

Mrs. Angeles approaches me. "The Commander showed up while Rachel and Sylph were in the fitting room. He took Rachel."

Panic erases all rational thought from my head. "Where did he take her?" I ask, trying to keep my voice calm for Rachel's sake, though I hear the edge beneath it.

"We don't know."

"How long was she gone?"

"Over an hour. When she returned, she was like this."

Fierce anger surges through me. I can't speak or I might release it on those who don't deserve it. Instead, I turn back to Rachel. I'm in over my head here. I can't fix this. Can't understand where to begin making it right if I don't have all the information. And she can't bear to tell me. She might tell Oliver, but he's already in the Wasteland.

"It's going to be okay," I whisper so no one else can hear me. "You can talk about it with Oliver soon. He can help."

She rocks faster, banging her head against the wall behind her. I lunge for her, wrap my arms around her, and pull her against me. Pressing my mouth against her ear, I whisper promises I don't know how to keep. She quiets into an unnatural stillness that scares me more than the rocking did.

"He left this for her when he dropped her off," Mrs. Angeles says, and hands me a parcel wrapped with blue ribbon.

I accept the parcel and help Rachel to her feet.

"She hasn't spoken since she returned," Sylph says.

I meet her tear-filled eyes and make another promise I don't know if I can keep. "I'll get her to speak to me. She just needs to go home now."

Tightening my arm around Rachel, I guide her from the shop and into weak afternoon sunlight shining through a haze of mist that makes visibility sketchy after twenty yards or so.

I almost hope someone tries attacking us. The rage within me begs for a target.

The fact that the real target is the most well-protected man in the city makes no difference to me. He's mine now. I don't know how I'll do it, but before my life is over, I'll end his.

"I'm taking you home," I say to her, though I don't expect a response. "Will it be too difficult to walk?"

She doesn't respond to that, either, so I watch her gait carefully. If she's been violated, she'll have trouble walking.

If she's been violated . . . I can't bear to think of it.

She walks with wooden steps, her eyes on the ground. Despite the evidence that physically she can handle the journey, I can't bear to put her through it. Instead, I decide to use what little coin I still have on me to purchase a wagon ride home.

I guide her to a stop in Center Square. She stands still, looking at our feet, and I whistle for a driver. She jerks away from me at the sound, and trembles.

My heart hurts as I gather her to me again and say, "It's okay,

Rachel."

She leans into me, closes her eyes, and breathes deeply. I press my lips to the crown of her head, and watch the driver ease his wagon to a stop in front of us.

I give my address to the driver and try to tug her toward the back of the wagon.

She digs her heels in and pulls against my arm.

"You don't need to walk. We'll take a ride home. It'll be easier on you this way," I say, and something within her breaks loose.

She twists free of my arm and takes off.

I race after her as she cuts through Center Square and flies into South Edge. I'm a fool. Of course he picked her up in a wagon. He wasn't going to hurt her on the streets where anyone could see and begin questioning why the Commander feels himself so far above the standard he sets for every other man in the city.

She turns a corner and slides into an alley. I follow just in time to see her stumble and fall toward the cobblestones. Lunging forward, I catch her, twisting my body so that I land on the street beneath her.

Her breath scrapes my ear in harsh pants, and she's shaking from head to toe. I gather her to my chest and say, "I'm sorry. I'm so sorry." My voice breaks, and I have to swallow hard to get the next words out. "I didn't know he had you in a wagon. I was trying to spare you the long walk home. I'm sorry."

She feels unbelievably fragile in my arms. I don't know how to get us home without hurting her further, but my options are limited.

A trio of men, swords drawn, block the mouth of the alley.

The middle one smiles wide enough to show gaps where his teeth should be, and says, "Give us yer money and no one gets hurt."

For one brief, blazing second, I imagine honing the rage blistering through me into something I can use to obliterate the sorry excuses for human beings who dare to threaten us now. It wouldn't be hard. They're drunkards. Already shaking with withdrawal. Desperate to have just enough money for their next jug.

As tempting as the idea is, the confrontation isn't worth it. I can toss a small handful of coin away from us and walk out of the alley as they scramble across the filthy cobblestones to snatch it.

Or I could if I didn't have to worry about getting Rachel home.

Looking up, she sees the men and freezes. I'm about to coach her on my exit strategy when she sucks in a raspy breath, and her expression goes from blank to feral in a heartbeat. She pushes against my chest and leaps to her feet. I stand as well, reaching out a cautionary hand to her.

"They just want money. I'll take care of it."

She isn't listening. Shoving my hand away from her, she curls her lip into a fierce snarl. Before I can stop her, she whips her knife out of its sheath, raises it above her head, and rushes toward the men.

"Rachel, no!" I grab for my sword as the men brace themselves for her attack. I race for her, but I'm too late.

Aiming for the man in the middle, she ducks beneath his raised sword arm and launches herself into him. They both slam into the street, but I don't have time to see if she's okay. The other two are attacking me.

I block, parry, thrust, and slice, but I can barely focus. Rachel is screaming, harsh bursts of sound that flay the air. I slam the butt of my sword into the man closest to me, whirl to block a blow from the other. Rachel rises from the inert body of the first man, her eyes desperate and wild, and races to jump on the back of the man I've just hit. She drives the tip of her knife into the soft tissue beneath his throat, and he raises his arm and drops his sword in surrender.

The man I'm fighting glances at them, and I take advantage of his distraction to lower my shoulder and body-slam him into the filthy brick wall beside us. I turn back to see the other man punch Rachel's knife hand away from his throat. The tip gouges his skin as it goes and a stream of blood arcs through the air. Rachel watches it and comes undone.

The man throws her to the ground, but she kicks his legs out from beneath him, and scrabbles across him, that terrible scream still ripping its way out of her throat as she punches, kicks, and tries to stab him with her knife.

I yell her name until my throat is hoarse, but she can't hear me, and the two of them are too tangled up for me to intervene without injuring her. I ready myself for the first available opportunity, and watch in horror. She takes his blows like they're nothing. Digging her nails into his skin as if it's a wall she has to climb, she claws her way up his body. She slams her knife hilt into his forehead, rendering him nearly senseless, and then flips her weapon around and drives the blade toward his throat.

I knock her off him from the side before the blade finds skin, and she sprawls on the cobblestones, her knife skittering across the alley.

She pushes herself up to her hands and knees and crawls toward it.

Leaping ahead of her, I reach it first. Grasping it, I turn and approach her carefully. Her eyes are that of a panicked animal cornered and fighting for her life. Her voice is nearly gone from screaming. She reaches for her knife, but I hold it away from her.

"Rachel." I breathe her name in a voice full of pain.

She looks at me, eyes still glassy from shock, and reaches for the knife again.

"They just wanted money," I say softly. "Just money. You don't need your knife."

She shakes her head and whimpers. I slowly extend the hand that doesn't hold her knife.

"I'm sorry." It's a hollow offering in the face of what she's been through, and I don't intend for it to be the best I can do. But for now, I just need to get her home. I can make a plan from there.

She doesn't respond.

"I don't know what he did to you, but killing someone else isn't going to make it better. I'm going to help you up. That's all I'm doing. Can I touch you?"

She looks down at herself and starts shaking again. I pull her to her feet, though I'm not sure she can stand on her own now. She's trembling uncontrollably, and I want to rip the Commander into tiny little pieces and light each of them on fire. I tuck her knife in my belt and scoop up the parcel Mrs. Angeles gave me.

"I'm taking you home," I say, though I no longer hope for a reply. "I'll figure out what to do once we get there."

And I will. I have to.

CHAPTER
TWENTY-SIX

RACHEL

My throat is raw from the screaming I unleashed at the men in the alley, and I can't stop shaking. I don't know what's happened to me, and I don't want to talk about it. Not yet. Logan doesn't seem inclined to talk either, or maybe he's realized I'm not going to answer. We walk side by side through Country Low while a breeze plucks at newborn leaves and tangles in my hair, and the shadow of the Wall slowly stretches east.

When we reach his cottage, I leave him standing in the living area while I lock myself in the bathroom, ignite the pitch-coated logs beneath the water pump, and strip out of my garments.

I don't light a lantern, though there's no window in this room. The glow from the logs is enough to for me to find my way around. I don't want to see.

The pump whistles softly to tell me the water is warm enough, and I release the handle to drain its contents into the carved stone tub resting in the center of the room. I slide into the bath and sink beneath its skin. It's quiet here, the outside noise muffled and distorted by the water around me. I pretend I'm in a cocoon, asleep, the world passing me by, and when I wake, all of this will have been a very bad dream.

The water is cooling when I finally decide to shampoo my hair and attack my skin with soap. I scrub until it hurts, but I'm still convinced the crimson stains me deep within where no soap will ever reach.

The memory of Oliver, holding my hand with icy fingers while his life spilled from his chest, is more than I can bear.

I comb through my water-heavy hair and it hangs down my back, sticking to my skin in damp strands. Pulling on a long yellow tunic and a pair of leggings to match, I open the door just in time to see Logan crumple up a thick piece of paper and throw it down. He slams his fist onto the kitchen table and swears viciously.

I cross my arms over my chest and move to curl up at the end of the couch. He meets my gaze with misery and fury in his eyes.

"Do you need anything?" he asks, and I know he's asking about more than food and water.

I shake my head, but he stands and brings me a cup of water and a plate of goat cheese, dried apple slices, and a hunk of oat bread as if I never responded. I take a bite of apple to please him, but I can't taste it.

He eases himself onto the couch, closer to me than to the other end, but still keeping a careful distance between us. He's moving slowly, as if afraid he'll spook me at any moment.

I want to tell him about Oliver. I want to open my mouth, let it all come gushing out, and find solace in weeping. But the words I need to rip Logan's world to pieces won't come. Instead,

I take a tiny bite of cheese and concentrate on chewing.

"I need to talk to you. It's okay if you don't want to respond, but I need to know you're listening," he says quietly, and waits.

I swallow the cheese, take a sip of water, and set it all on the floor at my feet. I owe him this.

I owed Oliver too.

The thought draws blood, and my eyes slowly fill with tears. I'm tired. So tired. I ache, inside and out, and nothing seems simple anymore. Nothing seems right.

"The Commander put you into the Claiming ceremony tomorrow," Logan says, waving his hand toward the crumpled up paper. His voice is hard. "You don't need to worry, Rachel. I'm going to Claim you. I won't leave your side. He'll never get a chance to touch you again."

His expression is haunted, and I know he blames himself for today. I don't know how to comfort him when nothing soft and conciliatory lives inside me anymore.

Something catches my eye, and I turn to see a deep-blue silk dress encrusted with glittering diamonds hanging beside the fireplace. Logan follows my gaze.

"Along with a letter demanding your presence on the Claiming stage tomorrow, he sent a dress. They were both in the parcel Mrs. Angeles gave me." His fingers curl into a fist.

Beneath my grief, uncushioned by my shock, a hard kernel of anger takes root and burrows in. I failed Oliver today, yes. But I don't have to fail him again. A debt is owed for his life, and I intend to pay it.

I glance around the cottage and find my knife, cleaned and polished, lying on the kitchen table, inches from the paper announcing my new status as a participant in the Claiming. I want to hold the weapon, to feel like I have some way to keep the promises I've made to myself, but I don't know how Logan feels about giving it to me.

"You can't attack everyone who pulls a weapon," he says when he sees me gazing at my knife.

He's wrong. If you don't attack first, you lose everything.

Everything.

"You scared me today," he says softly, and I look away from the knife. "They'd already demanded our money. The swords were just to intimidate us into giving them a way to buy their next drink. It was a situation you could've talked your way out of with your eyes shut. Instead, you tried to kill them."

I can't look away from the worry on his face, even though I want to tell him I've learned my lesson. The lesson he tried to teach me when he made me promise to strike down the Commander if he ever threatened me. It's branded deep into the fibers of my being now, and I don't plan to act like it isn't.

"How can I trust you to carry your weapons if you don't know who deserves a death sentence and who doesn't?" he asks, and slides closer to me, wrapping his arms around me and pulling me against his chest. "Rachel. I should've been with you today. I'm so sorry."

It's not his fault.

I should've killed the Commander.

I should've entered the wagon and attacked without hesitation.

I should've kept my promise to Logan. If I had, Oliver would still be alive.

A small whimper escapes me, and tears spill down my cheeks. I try to tell him. To make the words come, but sobs choke me instead. My fingers are icy, trembling, as Logan pulls me down beside him on the couch. I stare out his window, watching the sky darken as tiny stars tear holes in its velvet surface until I cry myself to sleep.

CHAPTER
TWENTY-SEVEN

RACHEL

I wake lying next to Logan on the couch beneath his heavy wool blanket. His arm is still wrapped around my waist, his cheek pressed against the crown of my head. I keep still, letting the warmth and the solidity of his body imprint itself to mine. I want to memorize this moment, a tiny piece of what I once wanted, to hold with me while I face what comes next.

"Are you awake?" His voice is a low rumble against my ear.

I nod, though I don't want to.

"I've been thinking. About yesterday."

Oliver. I have to tell him. Now.

I struggle to sit up, but his arm tightens. "Please. Just listen for a minute."

I stop struggling, but tension coils within me.

"I don't know what happened. But I need to tell you, to convince you, that if he . . . if there was anything . . . if he hurt you in the way a man can hurt a woman, it wouldn't change how I see you. He can't break us, Rachel, unless we let him."

"I also want to make a promise to you. Will you look at me?"

I roll over, the leather squeaking in protest beneath me, and tilt my head back to stare into his dark blue eyes. He raises his hand and strokes the side of my face. His touch is far gentler than his words.

"I'm going to make the Commander pay for what he did, Rachel. I swear it. And if he dares lay hands on you today, I won't stop until he's dead."

This kind of response will ruin everything. All the Commander needs is one tiny excuse to take Logan from me forever. And I'm about to tell him something that will make his anger so much worse.

Suddenly I realize this is what the Commander is banking on. Logan will try to Claim me to protect me from the Commander's machinations, and I'll blindside him with the Commander's plan. The only one who benefits is the Commander.

Unless Logan *knows*.

The shadows of grief and loss can't obscure the startling clarity of this thought. I feel like I've emerged from a long slumber, awake and ready to act.

I'd be a fool to take the Commander at his word. I have to protect Logan, and the only way to do it is to trust him the way I promised I would. Logan won't lose it at the Claiming ceremony and give the Commander an excuse to hurt him if he's prepared to have me turn him down.

And he won't try to exact unthinking, furious revenge for Oliver if he has a chance to grieve and then formulate a plan.

My voice is still hoarse from the screaming I did yesterday as I look Logan in the eye and say, "I already knew about the

Claiming ceremony. He told me when he—"

My throat closes as the memories hit. Being inside the wagon. Oliver. Crimson everywhere.

Logan reaches up to cup my face with his palm, and I smell him—ink, fresh paper, and musk. "Listen to me, Rachel. You can take this one piece at a time. I'm in no hurry. Tell me about the Claiming ceremony. We'll start there."

"He says you'll try to Claim me."

"I will."

"But that's what he wants. What he expects."

Logan frowns, and I can almost hear the gears of his mind working, analyzing, and plotting.

"He wants me to turn you down."

"You don't legally have that right. Only your Protector does."

"You're my Protector."

"Which is what he's going to use against me," Logan says in his I-have-a-puzzle-to-solve voice. "He's going to say as your Protector, I can't both Claim you and speak for you. But why bother? What does he stand to gain? He doesn't want you Claimed by someone else because he's planning to send you into the Wasteland . . ."

I can see the answer written in his eyes even as I say it. "He'll publicly renounce your Protectorship so you can't legally stop him. He wants us separated because you aren't going with me."

"The hell I'm not." His face is hard and bright.

"He said . . ." Grief surges through my chest, burning a path to my throat.

"Tell me."

"He's going to kill you." Suddenly the words are there,

tumbling over themselves in a rush to be heard. "He said I'm loyal to a fault, and I'll do anything to avoid having him kill someone else I love."

The wagon bed. The cloth-covered lump. Crimson everywhere.

I can't breathe as the blood-soaked image of Oliver burns itself into my brain and *stays*. Pushing away from Logan, I rush to the back door, wrench it open, race across the porch and fall onto the grass, retching.

He's behind me in seconds, holding my hair back.

When my stomach is empty, he helps me sit on the bottom porch step, goes into the house, and returns with a glass of cold water and a sprig of mint.

I chew the mint and sip the water in grateful silence, but it's a brief reprieve. He needs the rest of the story, and I have to find a way to give it to him.

He sits beside me, his shoulder touching mine, and says quietly, "Did he claim to have killed Jared?"

I shake my head, and set the glass down before my shaking hands drop it on their own. "He took me. In a wagon. There was a cloth-covered lump. And he said we were plotting behind his back." My voice rises as I rush to get through it all. "I thought it was you. I thought he'd taken you, and I prayed it would be a stranger. Another guard like the one in the tower. But it wasn't."

My voice trembles. "He stabbed the person beneath the cloth, and there was blood everywhere, and I tried to reach him, but I couldn't." I reach a hand out to Logan, for absolution or for comfort, I don't know. "I couldn't save him. I thought he was safe, waiting for us in the Wasteland, and I didn't save him. I'm so sorry!"

My voice breaks, and I drop my hand as terrible awareness comes into Logan's eyes. "Oliver?" he asks in a voice that begs me to lie. To make the truth something he can still fix.

I nod.

He stares at me, eyes glassy with shock, then jumps to his feet and strides across the yard. When he reaches the sparring area, he takes a vicious swing and sends Bob flying along his wire. Minutes pass as Logan pounds his fists into Bob as if by obliterating the dummy, he can obliterate the truth.

Finally, his arms fall to his sides and he drops to his knees on the grass. I go to him and lay a hand on his shoulder. Turning into me, he wraps his arms around me and drags me against him. I hold him and vow I will make the Commander hurt for what he's done to us. When Logan finally lifts his face to me, I can see he feels the same. His eyes are haunted, his expression hard.

"I'm sorry." My voice is small against the weight of our loss, but it's all I have to give.

"I can't believe he's gone." His voice chokes on the last word, and he scrubs his hands over his face. "Where is he?"

"I don't know."

"They took him away in the wagon?"

"Guards came in and took him." I can't look at him. I can't bear to see the shadows in his eyes. "They just . . . dragged him away."

"I want to see him. I want to . . ."

Say good-bye. Say the things he now wishes he'd said the last time he saw Oliver. I don't know if it would make it easier, but

I know he needs it. I do too, but we aren't going to get it. We aren't going to get another word to say on the matter that doesn't involve the sharp end of a sword.

"He should have a proper burial."

"Yes. But he isn't going to get it." The words taste like ashes. We'll never lay Oliver to rest. Never say the words he deserved to hear. Never bring flowers to a sacred patch of ground set aside for Oliver alone. "He isn't going to get it. But he can have *justice*. If we work together."

I make sure Logan meets my eyes and say, "You can't Claim me today, or the Commander will turn it against you and separate us."

Logan looks fierce. "We're going to turn his plan against him instead. I'm going as your Protector. We'll hide our travel bags before we get to the Square. Someone will try to Claim you, and I'll agree to it, but it won't matter. When everyone is dancing and celebrating, you and I will sneak away, grab our bags, and be gone before he even realizes he's lost the game."

Suddenly, his arms are around me again, and I'm against the hard wall of his chest. "Rachel, I'm sorry you had to see Oliver die."

"No, I'm sorry. If I'd just stabbed the Commander like you said—"

"This wasn't your fault. It wasn't mine. It was the Commander's. And one day, I'll make him pay for it in full."

"No, one day *we'll* make him pay for it in full," I say.

"Yes," he says, holding my gaze. "We will. Starting today."

CHAPTER
TWENTY-EIGHT

LOGAN

Rachel doesn't want breakfast, but agrees to eat something when I point out she can't execute our plan on an empty stomach. I don't want breakfast either. The knowledge that I've lost the only father I've ever known burns within me.

My heart aches, a constant pain that makes it hard to breathe. Losing Oliver is like losing the best part of me. The part that believed I could rise above. The part that said I was worth something even before I proved him right.

I don't know how to move forward without him, but I have to. I have to put our plan in motion. Get Rachel away from here. Find the package. Find Jared before a Rowansmark or Baalboden tracker finds him first. And return to Baalboden with a foolproof plan for destroying the Commander and avenging us all.

I don't have solid plans in place for all of it, and I'm worried the grief that tears at me with bitter fingers will compromise my ability to think, but I do know how to get us through the

Claiming ceremony and into the Wasteland, so I decide to focus on that alone. There will be time for both grief and planning later.

Rachel dresses in the bathroom, and when she enters the living room, I take one look at her and feel as though all the oxygen has been suddenly sucked out of the air.

The dress *fits* her. The neckline dips down and curves over breasts I didn't realize until just this minute were so . . . substantial. I force my eyes to scrape over her trim waist, but in seconds I'm staring once more at the way the glittering line of thread along her neckline barely contains her.

Every man who sees her will be paying attention.

Me included.

I don't want to admit my attraction to her is strong enough to rise above my grief and my sense of responsibility, but they're *breasts*. And they're nearly spilling out the top of her dress. I look around for a scarf or some other piece of cloth to cover her up, but all I have is a scrap of a kitchen towel, and I already know she'd never agree to it.

Which settles it. I'll have to stand in front of her the entire time.

The deep blue of the dress brings out the blue in her eyes, and the diamonds sewn into the bodice sparkle in the light.

Which draws the eye straight to her breasts.

She's wearing the dish towel. I don't care what she says.

"Acceptable?" she asks, and bends to look down at her full skirt. I want to tell her to straighten up and never bend down again, but my mouth has unaccountably gone dry.

Acceptable? She's breathtaking.

I nod, but when she slides her skirt up her leg to strap her knife sheath to her thigh, I turn around and begin rummaging aimlessly through the papers on the kitchen table.

"How am I going to reach this in a fight?" she asks, and I make the incredibly foolish mistake of turning around while her pale leg is still completely exposed.

I turn back around and address my comment to the table in front of me. "Make a slit in the silk and that stiff, crinkly stuff beneath it. You can hide the slit with your arm while you're on the stage, but you'll be able to reach your weapon if you need it."

I wait until I'm sure she's had enough time to cover herself again before turning. Her leg isn't showing anymore, but she's bending over her travel bag, packing a box of flint.

What kind of man looks at his ward like she's a temptation? Especially on the heels of such trauma and grief?

I instruct myself to regain my common sense and focus on getting ready for the day. Closing my eyes helps. First order of business: Make sure Rachel isn't in danger of going into a homicidal rage at the wrong person again.

"Be sure you know if the person you're drawing on deserves what you're about to give him," I tell her. I have to trust that she's found enough of her equilibrium to handle herself. There's no way I'm sending her into Center Square today without a weapon.

Second order of business: Make sure we have everything we need. "Let's do a last bag check," I say, and realize I can't do my end of it with my eyes shut.

Which isn't a problem because I can just look at my bag. I don't have to look at her and see her double-check the contents of her pack—fuel, clothing, Switch, dagger, and a bow with arrows.

I don't have to see the way the sunlight plays with the red-gold strands of hair she's left unbound.

She ought to look girlish with her hair down below her shoulders. Instead, the wild strands make her look both fierce and feminine, a combination I'm confident every single man signed up to Claim today will find irresistible.

When I realize I'm staring again, I look down at my bag and carefully go through it without once looking up. Everything is there, and I feel a sense of accomplishment for breaking whatever strange hold Rachel's had over me since the moment she came out wearing that cursed dress.

"I'm ready," she says, and I look at her, standing in the sunshine, grieving and beautiful, her boots peeking out from beneath her silk skirt, her eyes hard with something I've never seen there before.

I look, and I'm afraid.

That he's taken her innocence. That something will blow up in our faces today, and this will be our last moment of peace together.

That somehow I'll fail her. Oliver. Jared. Myself.

"I've made a new magnetic bracelet for you," I say, and scoop it off the table. It's a cuff of battered copper that covers the tracking device I've worked so hard to perfect. I've burned the outline of a Celtic knot into the center and filled it with brilliant sapphire wires, each attached to an inner gear that, unbeknownst to her, can turn this tracking device into a weapon.

I'm hoping I never have to activate it. But it's better to be prepared than dead.

She takes the cuff, runs her fingers over the wires, and then tugs it over her arm. "Why do I need a new magnetic bracelet if I'm going to be in the Wasteland?"

"I hid the tracking device inside of it."

"How will we know if it's working?"

"You'll feel a gentle buzz against your skin, and the wires will start to glow. They'll glow brighter the closer we come to him."

I don't tell her I've embedded a tracking device inside the cuff that will lead me to her as well. Just in case.

"Then we're ready," she says, and the hardness in her eyes makes me ache.

I want to give her something more valuable than just another one of my inventions. Something that will remind her of love. Family.

Me.

I reach into my front pocket and close my fist around the leather pouch I've carried since the day my mother died. "I want to give you something else," I say as I pull the pouch out into the open.

"What is it?" She glances at her bag as if wondering what else she can possibly add to the pile.

"No, not a weapon. Something more . . . feminine."

Which sounds incredibly stupid, but I don't know how to do this.

She frowns and looks down at herself. "I think I'm already feminine overkill."

"Yes," I say in fervent agreement, and she raises puzzled eyes to mine. But I have no intention of explaining myself. Instead, I say, "I have a gift for you. It would mean a lot to me if you'd accept it."

She holds out her hand, and I press the soft, time-worn bag into her palm while making sure to look at the wall behind her. She tugs open the brown drawstring and dumps the contents into her hand.

It's an intricately designed silver pendant made of a dozen interlocked circles with a glowing blue-black stone in the center of it. The necklace hangs on a glittering silver chain. It's the one thing of beauty I can call my own.

"It was my mother's. The only thing I have left of hers," I say, and hope she understands that this means she's my family now.

She clenches her fingers around it, and then slowly reaches out to hand it back to me. "I can't accept this."

I close my fingers around hers, the necklace still resting in her palm, meet her eyes, and say what Oliver once said to me.

"You're worth so much more than anything I can give you. If you can't believe that right now, believe in me."

She stares at me, and I hold her gaze. I don't know what she sees in my face, but she turns, lifts up her hair, and waits for me to fasten the chain against the back of her neck.

When she turns back, the pendant rests against her chest, glowing like it was always meant to be hers. I can't tell what she's thinking. She still looks fierce, running on rage and grief. But one day, maybe, she'll look at the necklace and realize I see much more inside her than the tangled mess she feels now.

"It's a Celtic knot. The same design I burned into the cuff I just gave you. It symbolizes eternity. The stone is a black sapphire, which symbolizes faithfulness." I reach out and trace my finger over the pendant.

She looks at my finger, and then back at me, and a tiny

tremble goes through her.

"It means"—I lean closer and will my words to take root within her—"I will always find you. I will always protect you. I won't let you down. I promise."

Something softens the fierceness of her gaze. It's a small shift, but I catch it. "Do you remember the first time we met?" I ask, closing my hand around the pendant, her skin warm against mine. "Reuben Little stole bread from Oliver, and you chased him through the Market, cornered him in an alley, and were pelting him with items from the trash heap."

"Oliver sent you to find me, so he wouldn't have to tell my dad I'd run off into the Market on my own again. I was eight," she says, and grief shivers through her voice at the memory.

It shivers through me, too, and I welcome it. It's my last connection to Oliver.

I lean a little closer, until the space between us can be measured in breaths. "You were this wild girl with spirit, brains, and so much beauty it almost hurt to look at you. I was this penniless orphan, spurned by our leader and scrounging in trash heaps for my dinner. I never thought I'd be in a position to offer you protection, but I am. And nothing is going to stop me."

"Nothing is going to stop me, either," she says, and I hear the warrior she's becoming coat her grief with purpose.

I lean my forehead to hers, our breath mingling for a moment, while my hand still clenches around the pendant and every rise and fall of her chest scrapes against my skin and makes me feel alive in a way I've never felt before.

Then she steps back, picks up her bag, and feels for the weight of her knife sheath beneath her skirt. I strap on my sword, heft my bag, and meet her gaze.

"Ready?"

Her smile is vicious as she holds her hand out to me. "Time to start paying our debt to the Commander."

I match her smile with one of my own, lock fingers with hers, and together we walk out the door.

CHAPTER
TWENTY-NINE

LOGAN

A s we walk hand in hand through Country Low, I realize it's the last time I'll see the fields stretching between the orchards and offering the space to breathe. The last time I'll come around this bend and see the city laid out before me. I should probably feel a sense of loss, but with Oliver dead, Jared somewhere in the Wasteland, and Rachel leaving with me, I find I have nothing left to tie me to this place but a burning hatred for the Commander.

We enter South Edge and Melkin steps out from behind a building. If he wonders why we're bringing travel bags to the Claiming ceremony, he doesn't show it. Instead, he follows us as we head toward Center Square. As soon as we turn north, he falls back, apparently satisfied that we're obeying the Commander's orders. I scan the street for any guards who might be following us as well, but see no one.

The Commander thinks he's broken Rachel so badly he's already won. I can't wait to prove him wrong.

The streets bustle today, full of people heading to the Square for the ceremony. Most of Baalboden's citizens will attend. Some because of the ceremony itself. Some because the Commander provides a banquet and dancing afterward.

The deserted shops work to our advantage. I pull Rachel into a side street a block from Center Square, and we hide our bags behind the bushes at the back of the mercantile. It's closed for the day, and if we duck out of the festivities early enough, we should have no problem reclaiming our belongings.

"That's good," I say as she pulls at the branches of a bush until it covers any sign of the bag hidden behind it. We slide back into the crowds heading toward the ceremony. The closer we come to the stage, the more color Rachel loses. We're nearly to Center Square when I stop and squeeze her hand gently.

"Look at me when you're on the stage," I say. "Look at me, no matter what he says. I won't let him hurt you."

She nods, but she's trembling. I don't know if it's from anger, trauma, or nerves. Most likely a combination of the three.

By the time we arrive, citizens have filled Center Square. Girls in brilliant jewel-toned dresses cluster together, whispering and giggling as they eye the group of eligible townsmen lined up near the platform, each looking tremendously uncomfortable. The wooden stage, the same one used to carry out Commander-sanctioned executions, is scrubbed clean and draped with red ribbon.

Sylph is here, glowing in her emerald and black dress, her hair somehow tamed into the intricate updo favored by most girls on Claiming day. A quick glance at those assembled shows Rachel is the only one who left her hair unbound. She's also the only one with a dress cut low enough to attract the notice of every male mingling at the edge of the stage. I see the moment they realize she's going to be part of the ceremony, and have to stop myself from reaching for my sword just to give them something else to think about.

I wonder which of them will have the nerve to stand up and Claim her. Mitch Patterson? I can't agree to that. I once saw his left eye twitch for an entire hour. That has to be a sign of mental instability. Wendall Freeman? He can't hold his liquor. And he tells terrible jokes. Peter Carmine? He's . . . I search for the fault I know is there and finally decide he's too short for her. Too short and too stupid.

I don't actually have proof that Peter Carmine is stupid, but he looks like he could be, and that's enough in my book.

Which just goes to show I'm the one who should be worried about mental instability and rampant stupidity. It doesn't matter who steps forward to Claim her. She isn't going to be here long enough for them to make good on their offer.

We stick to our plan. Foil the Commander on his own stage. And leave.

I have backup travel bags stashed where the Commander would never think to look, just in case the bags hidden behind the mercantile are inaccessible when we need them. I know where to hide in South Edge and how to block our wristmarks so the guards can't find us as we figure out a new way across the Wall.

And I have an alternate plan of my own ready for anything the Commander might pull.

We're as ready as we can be. I step in front of Rachel to block the ogling idiots at the stage, and a bell, sonorous and deep, echoes across the Square. The crowd stirs and whispers as the girls line up to the side of the stage, a bewildering display of color, jewels, and anxious smiles. Sylph sees us, eyes widening at the sight of Rachel in a Claiming dress, and gives a tiny, hesitant wave.

Rachel doesn't wave back. I'm not sure she even realizes Sylph is there. I don't think she sees anything but the stage, and the fact that she'll have to stand next to the Commander while she gives the performance of her life.

The girls begin mounting the stairs, taking dainty steps to avoid tripping over their long skirts. Their Protectors file up the stairs after them. The eligible townsmen yank at their collars as if they're in danger of choking, and the bell peals three long notes.

The Commander is here.

It's time.

I pull Rachel to me, inhale the midnight citrus scent of her, and then I let go, and we move to take our place on the stage.

CHAPTER THIRTY

<u>RACHEL</u>

Armed guards enter the Square and fan out, stationing themselves at three-yard intervals along the edges. Behind them, the twelve members of the Brute Squad march through the Square, two by two. The lead pair reaches the stage, halts, and pivots to face each other. Each subsequent pair also stops and faces each other until they've formed a tight, citizen-free aisle between them.

Another three long peals from the bell and every guard in the Square snaps his right forearm up to his forehead in a rigid salute. Silence, dense and absolute, falls across the Square as the Commander strides down the aisle toward the stage.

My mouth goes dry, my pulse pounds against my skin, and my vision narrows until all I see is him. I press my arm against my side and feel the outline of my knife sheath beneath my skirt as he approaches the steps.

I'm the last in the line of girls across the stage. As he walks up the steps, he meets my gaze and smiles as if only the two of us exist.

My skin crawls, and something hot and sharp seeps out of my grief and begs for his blood.

I reach for the slit in the side of my skirt, but he's already past me, greeting the Protectors who stand behind their daughters, and turning to face the assembled crowd.

"No weapons," Logan breathes against my ear. "Don't give him a reason."

He's right, but I don't take my hand away from the outline of my knife.

The Commander greets his citizens, says a few words about the honorable tradition of Claiming and how protecting the innocent among us keeps us strong, and gestures toward a girl on his left. Her Protector brings her forward, and a young man steps to the stage to Claim her.

My hands shake, but my thoughts are clear.

The girl's Protector accepts the young man's claim and hands over his daughter.

The Commander expects Logan to defy tradition and Claim me even though he's also my Protector.

The girl places her hand into that of her new Protector and recites her vow of obedience while her mother dabs her eyes and her new Protector looks slightly stunned by his good fortune.

He expects me to turn Logan down and ask to be a ward of the state.

Another girl is called. Another man steps forward. Another vow of obedience.

Another step closer to sealing my fate.

I can't make this look like I'm defying the Commander's

direct orders. Instead, I have to make it look like I'm just another girl, excited to see her dream of being Claimed come true, while Logan makes it look like he's clueless about the Commander's plan. The Commander can't alter the Claiming ceremony for me in front of all these people without raising serious questions. He'll have to accept the turn of events, at least publicly. We just need to get out of his reach before he finds an opportunity to deal with us privately.

Sylph's name is called, and she hurries to center stage, casting one anxious glance my way as she goes.

I don't know if she's anxious for me or for herself, but I can't afford to think about it. Not when I'm about to commit treason while making it look like I have no idea what I'm doing.

Smithson West steps forward to Claim her, but so does Rowan Hughes. The Commander turns the choice over to Sylph's father as is proper, and he doesn't even glance at Sylph as he chooses Smithson West. Sylph laughs and hugs her father, before remembering the requirements of decorum and subsiding into respectful silence.

She is repeating her vow when I look up to see the Commander's fierce dark eyes locked on mine.

I'm next.

The Brute Squad breaks formation and circles the stage. They expect trouble. They expect Logan to draw his sword against the Commander and give them a reason to act.

I'm grateful Logan is prepared to play his part.

I look back at the Commander, at the sly, feral smile twisting his scar as he calls my name, and wish for it to be over quickly. The ribbons behind him glow crimson in the sunlight, and as

I walk toward the Commander on legs that feel like saplings in a storm, the poisonous anger within me spreads. Logan walks behind me, his hand resting lightly on the small of my back.

"Rachel Adams, you are here without your true Protector." The Commander's voice booms across the Square.

This is the man who shattered my life.

The man who covered me in crimson.

"I am her assigned Protector," Logan says, his voice calm.

"And are you willing to give answer to any who wish to Claim her?" The Commander's tone mocks him, and I struggle to breathe.

This is the man who took my father. Oliver. And wants to take Logan, too.

"I am," Logan says, and the group of eligible townsmen murmur amongst themselves.

I doubt any of them will step forward to claim me. I'd hardly make a suitable wife.

The Commander laughs, a hideous parody of mirth, and shakes his head. Turning to the group of men below him, he asks, "Who will step forward to Claim this woman?"

He expects Logan to see this as an opening. A way to negotiate my safety. Instead, Logan waits quietly like any other Protector would do. The only sign of tension he gives is the slight increase in the pressure of his hand against my back.

Peter Carmine steps forward. "I will Claim her."

Logan's fist clenches a handful of my dress.

The Commander frowns at Peter and turns to face Logan. "And do you accept this man's Claim?"

Logan doesn't hesitate. "I do."

If he pulls on the back of my dress any harder, it's going to rip.

The Commander looks from me to Logan, and the cold calculation on his face chills me. I press my arm against my side, feeling the weight of my knife bite into my hip. Behind me, I sense Logan change his stance, rolling to the balls of his feet.

The Commander pins me with his dark eyes. "In the absence of your father, I feel I should ask you, Rachel Adams, if you want to be Claimed." He wraps his hand over my arm and squeezes.

Heat sears a path through my brain, and I shake off his hand before I think better of it. This isn't the way it's supposed to go. He isn't supposed to deviate from the Claiming ceremony script in front of all these witnesses. I can't say I want to be Claimed without the Commander realizing I'm going against his orders. I can't say I don't want to be Claimed without giving him the leverage he needs to separate me from Logan since Logan has already given his permission.

I hope Logan thought of a plan for this scenario.

Logan's voice rings out across the Square. "As is proper, Rachel will not choose whether she gets Claimed. I choose for her."

There's no arguing with the protocol Logan has invoked unless the Commander wants to set an ugly precedent with the rest of the citizens. I see the moment this realization hits the Commander. He looks from me to Logan, and my stomach sinks.

He isn't going to let this happen.

"You have one last chance to speak," he says with quiet menace and lays his hand on me again, digging his nails into the soft tissue of my forearm. "Do you want to be Claimed?"

The only choice I have is to stick with the prescribed Claiming script and hope the Commander refuses to make a scene in front of the citizens for fear more of them might rise up and demand the opportunity to choose their own destiny as well.

"I bow to the wishes of my Protector," I say, and fury explodes across the Commander's face.

He twists my arm and yanks me forward, breaking Logan's hold on my dress. "You realize what this means?" he asks me in a voice only I can hear. "I will kill him for your betrayal, Rachel. Renounce this Claiming and leave as planned, or I will leave you with nothing."

"Let go of her." Logan's voice, laced with terrible purpose, rings out across the Square.

The crowd erupts into a frenzy of hushed conversation, and the Commander twists my arm until I'm sure he means to wrench it from its socket. Pain is a living thing clawing at me, and I turn my face to look at Logan.

I need to know the plan. How to keep Logan alive and avoid being separated from him. I expect to see steady calculation in Logan's eyes. Instead, I see blind fury. His hand is already reaching for his sword as the Commander drives me to my knees.

He's going to attack the Commander. Try to kill him. And the Commander will stab a sword through him the way he stabbed a sword through Oliver and then laugh while I sit in silence, soaking up every drop of blood until my skin is flushed crimson with the shame of my impotence.

The brilliant rage surging within me coalesces into one fierce purpose.

Save Logan.

"I don't want to be Claimed," I say, and each word drops to the ground like a stone. I pray Logan will understand.

"You deny your current Protector's authority over you?" The Commander asks, his voice steeped in vicious triumph.

"I do."

Logan isn't looking at me. He's locked on the Commander, who still has my arm twisted above me, pinning me in a supplicant's position below him. His hand grips the hilt of his sword, his knuckles white.

If he loses control, the Commander wins.

And with the Brute Squad cutting off all escape routes, Logan doesn't stand a chance.

"What do you say to that, Logan McEntire?" The Commander looks at Logan, while the crowd moves uneasily, backing away from the stage.

I don't give Logan a chance to answer. With our plan in shambles, and my back against the wall, I say the only thing that could possibly keep him safe. "It doesn't matter what he says. He isn't my true Protector. I petition to be a ward of the state."

The Commander doesn't spare me a glance, so I raise my voice. "Do you accept me as a ward of the state?"

Some of my fury leaks into my tone, and I raise my chin. I don't care. Let him know I'm angry. Let him see the bloodlust on my face. Let him look into my eyes and discover the girl he thought he understood is gone and in her place stands a weapon of his own creation.

He turns his head slowly to stare at me, his scar pulling his lip into a snarl, and lets go of my arm to backhand me across the face.

I tumble to the floor and see Logan, sword raised, face ablaze, charge the Commander.

CHAPTER
THIRTY-ONE

RACHEL

"**N**o!"

I'm screaming, but it's too late. The girls on the stage scatter, their fathers dragging them to safety as the Brute Squad swarms onto the platform, coming between Logan and the Commander. Logan drives his shoulder into the first guard who reaches him, sends the man flying off the stage, and whirls to block the sword thrust of another.

The Commander stands above me and laughs.

I slide my hand into the slit I cut in the side of my skirt, find my sheath, and pull my knife free.

Someone calls my name, and I see Sylph break away from Smithson's hold and rush toward the stage.

"Go back!" I yell and struggle to my feet, my knife ready.

Smithson catches her around the waist before she can reach me, and she slaps at him. I turn away, praying Logan isn't already dead.

He isn't. He fights like a man possessed—swinging, thrusting, and attacking with terrifying speed and force, disarming and disabling every opponent who comes at him. I had no idea he had this in him, and it's clear I'm not the only one.

The Commander stops laughing and draws his own sword.

Raising my knife, I calculate the angle I'll need to drive the blade through his back and into his heart. Before I can thrust the weapon forward, I'm body slammed from the side and sent sailing off the platform and into the crowd of eligible townsmen still milling at the base of the stage, unsure what their role in this unprecedented display of violence should be.

Hands reach for me, steady me, and try to hold me back. I punch, kick, and swing my knife until they back away. I can't save Logan unless I'm on the stage. Anyone standing between me and him is dead.

I race toward the steps, beating away the few that still reach for me, but before I can mount the stage, a guard jumps in front of me. I drive my knife through his stomach, twist it to the right, and yank it free while he's still in the act of telling me to halt.

Crimson splashes onto my pretty blue skirt. I look away from it and concentrate on reaching Logan. I'm on the stage driving my knife into the back of the guard blocking that exit before he even knows what hit him. Not stopping to see if he's dead, I vault over his body and try to see Logan.

He's trapped center stage. Eight Brute Squad. Another dozen guards. And in the center of it, the Commander.

I race forward, and the Commander screams for his guards to fall back. Logan is bruised, battered, and bleeding, but holds his sword steady. Not that it will help him now. There are too many. He can't take them all.

I can't either.

I look to the crowd, hoping for swords and friendly faces, but there's nothing but mass confusion and panic. Logan is a dead man walking, and so am I.

Except I'm not. Because I alone know where to find the Commander's precious package. Maybe he forgot that in the heat of the moment. Maybe he figured there would be others he could hurt to make me bend to his will. Maybe he's arrogant enough to think I'll be too frightened of him to disobey, even without the threat of Logan's death hanging over my head. Maybe the lives of others mean so little to him that he can't imagine a single death that could significantly alter his plans.

He's wrong.

Logan and the Commander circle each other as the guards fall back.

I creep behind the guards, looking for an opening.

The Commander thrusts. Logan blocks, but it's clear he's been injured and lacks the strength to keep up the fight for long.

He won't have to. I know how to change the game. How to take away the one advantage the Commander is banking on.

Logan whirls and swings, flinging drops of blood. His sword goes wide, and the Commander steps into the gap, using Logan's momentum against him. In seconds, he has his sword against Logan's neck, and his vicious smile twists his scar into an ugly, knotted ball of prickled flesh. The guards behind Logan grab his arms, fling his sword to the floor, and pin him in place for the Commander.

"You drew a weapon against your leader. Killed multiple guards." The Commander's voice shakes the Square as he chops each syllable into jagged shards.

I see my opportunity and slide into the circle. Logan meets my eyes, and his expression begs me to leave. Run. Escape this hell of a city and never look back.

"The penalty for this is death." The Commander turns to Logan.

"And what is the penalty for killing innocent citizens? For terrorizing a young woman? Who holds *you* accountable?" Logan is shouting, the same brilliant rage that burns through me spilling out of him.

The Commander's smile dies slowly, extinguished by the look of pure hatred he gives Logan. "*I* am the law. *I* am justice." He's spitting the words in Logan's face. "*I* am the one thing that keeps this city safe. You dare question me?"

"You aren't justice. You're a misbegotten monster too drunk on his own power to be trusted with it anymore."

Purple flushes the Commander's face, and he raises his sword arm.

"I, Commander Jason Chase, for the crime of treason and murder, do hereby sentence you to death," he says, and aims his blade at Logan's throat.

"Wait!" My voice carries across the Square and freezes everyone in place for the split second it takes me to fall to my knees where the Commander can see me, but no guard can reach me in time.

The Commander laughs. "Come to beg me to save him?"

My smile feels just as vicious as his. "He isn't the one who needs saving."

"Rachel, no," Logan breathes.

I ignore him.

"What are you going to do, girl? Kill me?" The Commander's voice is full of malice.

"No," I say. Raising my knife, I aim it at the soft spot just below my sternum and take a deep breath.

The Commander's sword, still pointed at Logan's throat, wavers. "What are you doing?"

"Taking away the one thing you really want." I say and dig the tip of the knife into my flesh, feeling a flash of pain and then the warmth of blood running down my skin.

Guards surge forward, and I scream, "Stop, or I'll do it!"

The Commander sweeps his hand up, palm out, and the guards stop.

"Rachel, please," Logan says softly. "Not this."

I don't look away from the Commander. "You want what only I know how to get. If you or anyone else in this city lays another hand on Logan, I'll kill myself and you'll never find the package."

His jaw is clenched, pulling his scar taut. "Yesterday, I wouldn't have said you had this in you."

"The girl you dealt with yesterday is gone." My voice is cold, my words rising from the terrible grief he carved into me with Oliver's death. "Give me your word before all these citizens that Logan will remain unharmed for the duration of my journey, or the knowledge of where to find the package dies with me."

His eyes are fierce pits of hatred as he slowly lowers his sword. "He will be unharmed as long as you return with what I need." He makes a gesture to the guards holding Logan, and they begin dragging him from the stage.

"Wait!" I leap to my feet. "Where are you taking him?"

"You didn't honestly think I would let my insurance policy wander around freely while you were gone, did you?" The Commander smiles. "He'll be in the dungeon until you return."

I lock eyes with Logan as the guards pull him past me, and I reach up to wrap my hand around his mother's necklace.

He says softly, "Remember my promise, Rachel."

I reach a hand toward him, but he's already off the stage, being pulled through the crowd, which parts like water around him.

"You leave at dawn. Melkin goes with you." The Commander is next to me, his sword still grasped in his hand. "I suggest you hurry. I doubt even a young man like Logan can withstand the hospitality of my dungeon for long."

For one brief, glorious moment, I imagine turning, thrusting my knife through the Commander's crisp blue military uniform, and watching with pleasure as he learns just how vulnerable a flesh-and-bone man really is.

But I'd never get to Logan before the guards deliver the death sentence I would've caused. I let the moment pass and turn to stare straight into the Commander's dark eyes as I silently promise myself I'll retrieve the package, secure Logan's freedom, and deliver justice before the Commander realizes the girl whose loyalty he purchased in blood will be his final undoing.

CHAPTER
THIRTY-TWO

LOGAN

Rachel is alone. I've failed her. Bitter regret swamps me, a twin to my awful grief over Oliver, but I can't give in to it. I have to pay attention and figure out how to get out of this.

The dungeon is a dank, smelly pit carved out of the stone foundation of the Commander's compound. Individual cells are simply hollowed-out husks within the stone. The walls are slimy with moisture, iron bars block the doorways, and a few half-hearted torches burn along the aisle between cells.

I'm dragged past five cells before the guards reach the one set aside for me. Two of the cells I pass are empty. One holds a gaunt man in filthy clothing huddled on a thin straw palette. One holds a younger man shackled to the back wall. The cell across from mine holds a young pregnant woman wrapped in a coarse brown blanket. She doesn't look at me.

I wonder which of them is the spy planted here to gain my trust.

After pulling me into my cell, the guards fasten heavy iron

cuffs around my wrists, and take my sword, the dagger in my left boot, and my scabbard. While one guard pats me down, looking for additional blades, the other yanks on the heavy, rusted chains attached to the cuffs at my wrists, testing them for weakness. The chains loop through iron circles welded onto the back wall of the cell and restrict my ability to go more than halfway toward the doorway. I ignore them in favor of scanning the ceiling for surveillance devices. I can't find any, but decide the smartest move is to act like I'm being watched at all times.

If I'm going to escape, I can't afford a single misstep.

Satisfied I'm weaponless, the guards take my cloak and toss it just out of my reach, leaving me to the mercy of the dungeon's chill. They laugh as they slam my cage door shut and leave.

Lucky for me, they're too shortsighted to understand a man's true weapon isn't something that slides into a scabbard.

A few strong pulls assure me my chains aren't coming out of the wall without help. Which means I can't reach my cloak. Which limits my options.

Fear for Rachel is a constant hum in the background of my thoughts, but I can't give in to it. The only way I can be useful to her now is to keep a clear head and apply logic to my current circumstances.

I have my boots. My belt buckle. My empty knife sheath. Not enough to stage an escape attempt. I need my cloak, but I refuse to reach for it. I refuse to even glance at it. If I'm being watched, the fastest way to ensure I never see my cloak again is to look like I want it.

My cell has a thin, water-stained palette lying on the stone floor, and a half-rotted wooden bucket shoved into the corner closest to me. Neither seems particularly useful in an escape effort, but you never know what might come in handy.

The shackles bite into my wrists as I stand and slowly pace the back wall, counting the measurements and feeling for drafts so I can calculate how close I am to the outside wall of the dungeon.

Heavy footsteps sound at the main entrance, and I look up to see two guards, blazing torches in hand, precede the Commander into the miserable space.

I move closer to the bucket, putting enough space between me and the door of my cell that he'll have to come all the way inside if he wants to hurt me.

He doesn't come to my cell, though. He stops in front of the cell containing the pregnant woman huddled in a blanket.

"Warm enough, Eloise?" he asks without a hint of concern in his voice.

She doesn't respond.

"I thought you should know your husband has agreed to the terms I set before him." He looks across at me. "Once he understood your life and the life of his unborn child were at stake, Melkin was quite willing to do everything I asked."

I keep my expression neutral as a tight band wraps around my chest. Melkin is the only tracker still in the city. Rachel is leaving to hunt down the missing package. It isn't hard to reach the conclusion that Melkin will be Rachel's escort in my place.

Why would the Commander need to threaten the lives of Melkin's family to get him to do his job?

I put the fact that Melkin is being asked to do something he was originally unwilling to do together with the fact that the

Commander wants me to know about it, and the band around my chest tightens further.

Rachel. It has something to do with Rachel. Nothing else makes sense. I don't need the specifics of his plan to know she's in danger.

Melkin's wife doesn't look up at the Commander as she pulls her thin blanket closer to her body, but it doesn't matter. He never expected a response. This show was for me alone.

His laugh is an ugly thing filling up the space between us as he crosses the aisle and gestures for the guards to open the door to my cell.

I back up until I have several lengths of loose chain at my disposal.

The Commander steps into my cell. The flickering torchlight lights his scar, throwing the rest of his face in shadow.

"You thought you could outsmart me, didn't you?" He flexes his right hand into a fist. The light slides along the golden circle of his ring, glowing within the olive-sized red stone and highlighting the wicked ridge of the raised talon through its center.

I brace myself and gather up a length of chain as quietly as I can, ignoring how bruised and battered I feel from the sword-fight on the Claiming stage.

"You were always so sure of yourself. So convinced no one could outwit the great Logan McEntire." His lip curls as he spits my name at me.

Maybe I shouldn't engage him. Maybe I should keep my silence and let him talk, hoping to pick up nuggets of information along the way.

Or maybe pushing him to his limits is the best way to peel

back the mask and see what I'm truly dealing with.

"How would you know?" I ask. "You've never bothered to have a proper conversation with me."

His fist plows into my gut, slamming me back against the wall. I double over and take the opportunity to gather more lengths of chain while catching my breath.

"I don't have proper conversations with the sons of those who've been disloyal." He kicks my feet out from under me.

I hit the floor hard, and nearly lose my grip on the chain I'm holding like a rope. Pushing myself back to my feet, I say, "My mother wasn't disloyal."

His fist slams into my shoulder, spinning me to the side. I narrowly keep from hitting the wall with my face.

"I wasn't speaking of your mother." His breath is a harsh pant against my ear.

I take a deliberate step away from him. He's playing games with me. He knows I have no idea who my father was, and he's using it against me. Still, part of me wants to ask, just to finally have that gap in my past filled in.

"You knew my father."

He laughs. "You're just like him. Two men cut from the same cloth."

"And what cloth would that be?"

His face, bathed in shadow and firelight, is lit with malice. "Unworthy. Disloyal. Without honor."

I straighten and brace my feet. "You wouldn't understand honor if it was branded into your skin."

He lunges for me, but I duck back. Swinging the chains up, I wrap them around his arm. One swift jerk and I fling him onto the filthy floor of the cell. He lands hard, and I drive my knee into his back, but the guards outside the cell are already on me.

They pull me from him, toss me to the ground, and attack. I swing the chains, brutally slashing one guard's face and knocking out another's tooth. One draws his sword, but I duck out of the way. Looping the chains around the sword's hilt as I go, I yank back hard. The sword goes skidding across the cell.

Two more guards arrive, and I'm fighting for my life. Dodging blades, absorbing blows, and doing as much lethal damage as I can with the lengths of chains in my hands.

It's four on one, and I know I can't keep it up much longer. I'm hoping I won't have to.

The Commander rises from the floor and screams at his guards to stop. They back away, bleeding and cursing.

I'm bleeding and cursing too, but I hold my head high as he approaches me. I have to make his next actions seem like his idea.

"Go ahead and kill me, if you can," I say, rattling the chains in my hands as if I'm ready to go another round with the guards. "You've given me all the weapon I need."

He spews venom at me. "The second I no longer need you to ensure the girl's cooperation, you're dead." He closes the distance between us, stopping just out of range of the chains. "She'll die thinking she saved you. Melkin will see to that. But *you*, you get to live long enough to know you haven't saved anyone."

I've got the answer I needed about Melkin's arrangement with the Commander. Ignoring my anger at the thought of Rachel traveling the Wasteland in the company of a man tasked to assassinate her once her usefulness is finished, I focus on getting the second thing I need.

I rattle the chains as if I still have the energy to use them. The Commander gestures at the closest guard. "Get those things off him and remove them from his cell."

I put up a fight, make it look like I mean it, and it takes three of them to get the shackles off me. The instant I'm free, I back into a corner like I know I've been beaten at my own game.

The Commander laughs and waves at his least-injured guards. "Teach him a lesson. Just make sure you leave him alive."

Two guards advance, fists raised. I parry the first punch and absorb the second as it plows into my shoulder, but see stars as one guard's booted foot slams into my ribcage and sends me sprawling. Pain flares to life within me, and it's all I can do to curl up in a ball and endure as the guards use me as their punching bag.

I've lost track of time when the Commander calls them off. I'm bleeding from my nose and mouth, my body feels like I've been run over by a wagon, and a rib on my right side feels like someone is skewering me with a lit torch every time I breathe.

The Commander strides over to me, grabs a handful of my hair, and wrenches my face around to his. "You've lost your little game. And everyone you love will die because of it." He gestures to a guard, and I hear something sizzle and spit in the flames of the nearest torch. I can't crane my head to look because the Commander holds my hair in a vicious grip.

A guard steps closer, a long pole in his hands. At the end of the pole, the metal insignia of the Brute Squad—a curved talon beneath two slash marks—glows red-hot.

I twist away from the Commander, but he settles his knee

on my side, turning my aching rib into a breath-stealing howl of agony, and holds my face steady with both his hands.

"I beat you," the Commander says, "and every time I look at you, I'll know it."

The guard presses the blazing-hot metal into the side of my neck, and I scream.

The smell of scorched skin fills the air, and I retch as brilliant spots dance in front of my eyes. I drag in a deep breath and try to ride out the worst of the agony, but it refuses to abate.

Letting go of me, the Commander rises and says to the dungeon guard. "Water only. Don't bother offering this one any food. We won't need to keep him alive long enough to warrant it."

Leaving me huddled on the floor, burned and bleeding, the Commander and his guards leave, slamming the cell bars closed in their wake.

I wait until I hear their footsteps fade. Until the door at the entrance closes. Until I've silently recounted everything I know about the Pythagorean Theorem. The conductive properties of copper. The relationship between negative mass and negative energy.

Only when I'm certain I've spent enough time looking defeated and broken that anyone watching me wouldn't question my need for warmth, do I slowly crawl across the floor.

Every inch is torture. I clench my teeth and tell myself pain is just a state of mind. I can rise above it. My body doesn't agree with my theory, so I force myself to recite the Periodic Table to give myself something productive to focus on.

I'm shaking by the time I reach my destination, but furious

triumph warms me from the inside as I lay hands on the one thing I wanted all along. The thing that will make inciting the Commander to remove my chains and beat me nearly senseless worth it. The thing that will make escape possible.

My cloak.

CHAPTER
THIRTY-THREE

Dawn is a whisper in the cold morning air as I tighten the leather fastenings on my cloak, wrap it around the tunic and pants I wear, adjust my travel pack until it fits smoothly against my spine, and face the gate leading out into the Wasteland.

I'm taking my own bag with me. The Commander instructed two of his guards to accompany me home so I could pack, and neither of them batted an eye when I headed into a side street off Center Square. If they wondered why I kept a bag hidden in the bushes near a mercantile, they never asked. Instead, they kept one hand on me and one on their weapons at all times. I'm betting they thought I might try to escape.

I would have, if I didn't have to reclaim the missing package so I can ransom Logan's life. Not that the Commander is the kind of man who'll keep his word to me once he holds the package in his hands.

Which is fine. I'm no longer the kind of girl who'll keep my word to him, either.

Shelving the need to plan a way to free Logan without giving the Commander what he wants, I study my travel companion while pretending to watch the guards unchain the gate.

Melkin is tall, about Logan's height, though he doesn't have Logan's muscle. Instead, his frame is all bones and angles, his skin stretched painfully thin. With deep-set dark eyes, a nose resembling a cloak hook, and a sparse coating of mud-brown hair hanging down his back, he resembles a starving hawk.

He clutches his cloak with long, skinny fingers and darts a glance at me. "Hope you know what you're doing. I don't figure on having to rescue you every time I turn around."

I simply stare at him. I don't know him. Dad kept me, and the fact that he'd trained me, separate from the others who ran courier or tracking missions for Baalboden. I don't know Melkin, but that doesn't stop the rage inside of me from begging to lash out at him. He works for the Commander. That's justification enough.

Whatever he sees on my face causes him to blink twice, tighten his hold on his cloak, and look away as the massive stone gate swings open with a high-pitched groan.

Four guards line up on either side of the gate, ready to let us out and remain behind to stand watch throughout the day in case there are those who want in. Melkin places a hand on my shoulder and presses me forward.

I snatch his hand, crush his fingers in mine, and spin until his arm is pinned behind his back.

"Don't. Touch. Me."

He doesn't respond, but when I release his hand, he watches me closely and follows me down the gritty cobblestone road past the guards, beneath the steel arch with the Commander's talon-and-double-slash insignia burned into the center of its smooth surface, and leave the city behind.

The road leads away from the Wall through the scorched ground that makes up Baalboden's perimeter and ends at the charred remains of the highwaymen's wagons. We walk it in silence until we reach the point where the road ends and the wild tangle of the Wasteland begins. Stopping, we open our packs and pull out our weapons.

Melkin straps a double-bladed leather glove to his right hand, and the six-inch blades of silver protruding from both his index and ring knuckles sparkle beneath the hesitant touch of the early morning sun. I recognize the glove as one of Logan's inventions, and it tells me plenty about Melkin.

He likes his prey close and thinks the abnormally long range of his arms will be advantage enough to keep him safe. When he straps a sword around his waist, I acknowledge that he must be proficient with his left hand as well. He takes out a thick walking stick and extends it to its full length. The black metallic surface swallows stray rays of sunlight whole.

He sees me staring and mutters, "It was a gift."

"I've never seen anything like it at any of the weapons vendors in the city."

"Because it isn't from this city. Now, you got any weapons, or am I going to be responsible for keeping the both of us alive on this trip?"

I unclasp my own bag. Minutes later, the bow and arrows are strapped across the outside of my pack, where I can easily reach back and grasp them; my knife rests against my hip; and my

Switch is in my hand.

"Where are we heading?" he asks.

"Somewhere in the vicinity of Rowansmark."

"Care to be more specific?"

"No."

He shrugs, and we pause for a moment, listening, but the Wasteland offers nothing beyond the sound of birds chirping over their morning meals. Which doesn't mean there aren't highwaymen lying in wait, but at least we don't have to worry about fending off the Cursed One at the moment.

Melkin steps off the cobblestones and slides into the dark tangle of trees, vines, and undergrowth waiting for us. I follow on his heels, my Switch ready in case of trouble.

The smell hits me first. Wet moss, crisp leaves, and the soft, musky scent of tree bark. If I close my eyes, I can imagine I'm standing next to Dad, listening to the deep, reassuring rumble of his voice quietly instruct me how to listen. How to walk without leaving an obvious trail. And how to survive anything the world throws my way.

I ache for him, a sharp, sudden longing that reminds me that missing him is how I started this entire nightmare. I draw in another breath, savor it against my tongue, and let myself feel a tiny sliver of raw hope. Maybe Dad is with the package. Maybe, by searching for it, I'll find him too. Maybe if I find him, he'll know how to make everything right again.

"You coming? Or you planning on sniffing trees all day?"

I ignore Melkin and start walking. The Wasteland is a strange mix of overgrown forests, bogs, and fields and the ruins of the sky-climbing cities destroyed or abandoned over five decades ago when the Cursed One was first released.

"Mind the thorns," Melkin says quietly, swinging his walking stick in the direction of a patch of pretty green undergrowth adorned with needle-sharp thorns.

I skirt the plants and use my Switch to swipe hanging vines out of my way as I walk. Melkin stops to listen, and I halt as well, though my ears don't pick up anything beyond the usual whisper of bug wings and breeze that mark the forested area of the Wasteland closest to Baalboden.

"Hear that?" he asks in a voice designed to carry no more than a few feet.

I listen harder and finally catch it—a faint *shush* of sound that could be an animal foraging for food, or could be the slide of a boot against the branch of a tree. I release the Switch's blade with a muted snick, and catch Melkin's slight frown as my walking stick becomes a weapon.

I don't hear the sound again, but I don't make the mistake of assuming a threat doesn't exist. Clutching my Switch closer, I rest my other hand on my knife sheath.

We walk as silently as possible, but don't hear sounds of pursuit again. I see the moment Melkin decides it was nothing but an animal. His shoulders drop, and the hand curled inside his bladed glove relaxes.

I don't sheath the Switch's blade, though. Better to be ready to deal violently with others than to be caught off guard.

Rowansmark is an eight-day journey southwest. Ten if the weather is foul or we have to go around a gang of highwaymen. I pace our progress by the familiar markers we pass—the lightning-struck oak, the creek with the stepping-stone bridge, and the swaying once-white cottage almost completely covered by kudzu. We're making good time, in part due to Melkin's pace. His long legs eat up the terrain, but I have no trouble keeping up. Fear for Logan's life demands nothing less. And the anger I feel toward the Commander refuses to let me rest.

I'm going to retrace Dad's route to his Rowansmark safe house and find the package. Once I find it, I'll figure out a way to secure Logan's safety while making the Commander pay for what he's done.

A tiny inner voice whispers that if I find Dad with the package, I won't have to figure it out alone. I tamp down the buoyant sense of hope that wants to blossom within me. The tracking device on my arm is silent, the wires cold. I have no reason yet to hope for anything.

The sun melts lazily across the sky, turning the forest we walk though into a damp, humid jungle. It's too early in the spring for mosquitoes, but beetles and gnats swarm the trees, and I keep my cloak on despite the warmth.

Twice more, we hear a rustle of sound behind us, but when Melkin circles back, he finds nothing. As we're sharing the Wasteland with a host of wild animals, hearing noises isn't unusual. Still, the lessons I learned about the Commander's lack of honor are carved into me with deep, crimson letters, and I'm not reassured.

When the sun reaches the middle of the sky, Melkin drops to a crouch against the thick trunk of an ancient oak, opens his pack, and offers me a flask of water and a hunk of oat bread. I take them and find my own trunk to rest against, keeping him well within my sights while I listen closely for sounds of human pursuit.

We eat in silence until Melkin looks up, wipes his mouth with the sleeve of his faded blue tunic, and says, "Your daddy taught you well."

I stare at him. "How do you know he's the one who taught me?"

"The Commander told me. I didn't fancy on taking a helpless little girl across the Wasteland with me, but you know how to move quietly. You keep your head up, eyes open. Looks like you know what to do with that stick you carry too."

I look away.

"Sure are a quiet one, aren't you?" he asks, and caps his flask of water. "Always thought of you as a girl with spunk and guts. Never realized you were afraid to open your mouth."

The bitterness festering in me bubbles up.

"How much spunk and guts does it take to chatter nonstop about nothing of importance?" I stand and stow my flask in my bag. "I have bigger things on my mind than discussing my skills. If you want conversation, choose a better topic."

He stands as well, irritation on his face, and drives the bottom quarter of his ebony walking stick into the forest floor. I imagine I can feel the ground beneath me tremble with the force of it.

"Nobody appreciates a woman with vinegar in her soul."

I slide my pack into place and stalk toward him, a distant roaring filling my ears as the anger inside me locks on to a handy target.

"Vinegar in my soul?" I'm closing in on him, and his hand tightens within the bladed glove he wears. "Is that what they call betrayal these days?"

My voice is louder than it should be, but I can't seem to find the air I need to calm down. "You stand there and pass judgment on me like you've earned the right. What have you lost?" I'm yelling, my fist raised as if I'll hit him. "What have you lost, Melkin?"

I need to hurt him. To lash out and hope that if he bleeds, it will somehow erase the specter of Oliver's blood washing me with crimson.

"Almost everything," he says, and pulls his walking stick free of the ground, raising both hands as if to show me he means me no harm. "I've lost almost everything."

I don't know what to say to this. I can't tell if he's lying. Before I can study his eyes to see if he understands the sense of overwhelming loss howling within me, the ground beneath us rumbles slightly, and something that sounds like thunder, muted and distant, comes closer.

I meet Melkin's eyes and we leap into motion. Shoving my Switch into the strap sewn on the side of my pack for this purpose, I grab the nearest low-hanging tree branch and start climbing. Melkin lunges for the tree as well, wrapping his long arms and legs around the trunk and shimmying up its length until he finds a branch thick enough to support him.

The rumble becomes a roar, and the ground below us begins to crack.

I'm one quarter of the way up the tree. The crack runs directly below me.

"Jump!" Melkin yells.

Frantically, I scan the branches around me until I find one

that reaches into the heart of the tree beside it and is thick enough to support my weight. I scramble along its length and leap for the next tree. My feet skid along the branch as I land, and I start running, grabbing branches for balance, swinging my body into the upper reaches of the tree, and then leaping for the next. Melkin is tree-leaping as well, though I'm too focused on my own survival to worry about him now.

I've put seven trees between me and my starting point when the roar becomes a deafening bellow, the ground we stood upon just a moment ago dissolves into nothing, and the Cursed One explodes out of the ground.

CHAPTER
THIRTY-FOUR

RACHEL

I freeze. I'm about seventeen yards from the monstrous beast slithering its way into the open. I don't think it's enough. At the very least, I need to move higher, but I can't without alerting it to my exact location.

The Cursed One coils its body along the ground and pulls itself from the hole it created. Up close, it looks like a giant wingless dragon covered in thick interlocking black scales with a tail the length of two grown men lying end to end and a ridge of webbed spikes running along its back. Thick yellow claws protrude from its muscled limbs.

Our weapons are useless. Swords break against its scales, arrows glance off, and the only area of weakness seems to be its sightless milky yellow eyes, but to get close enough to stab the eye is to court a fiery death from its mouth.

Besides, stabbing it in the eye is pointless. Nothing dies from losing an eye.

The only escape is to stay off its radar. It tracks by sound and smell, and when it stops and swings its head slowly side to side, huffing smoky little breaths, I don't dare move a muscle. I'm grateful I don't have the food in my pack. It would only add to my human scent and make me a bigger target.

Melkin isn't as fortunate. I slant my eyes to the side and see him clinging to the upper branches of the tree beside mine, but his pack is nowhere to be seen. I guess he had the presence of mind to drop it.

The Cursed One puffs its breath out, and small flames jet through its nostrils, scorching the earth in front of it. The burned dirt seems to infuriate it, and it shakes its head, puffing increasingly large flames from its snout.

If we're quiet, absolutely silent, it will leave. I focus on breathing in and out with slow precision, though my lungs scream at me to drag air in as quickly as possible so I can flee or fight.

I won't have to do either, though. I just have to be still.

Suddenly, it jerks its head up and points its sightless eyes straight at me.

My stomach lurches, and as I glance around for a way out, I catch sight of Melkin's pack hanging on a branch several feet below me. I didn't realize he'd climbed up behind me before switching trees, dropping his pack along the way. I'm about to pay the price.

Abandoning my efforts at controlled, silent breathing, I give in to my body's demands, dragging in a huge gulp of air while I tense my muscles for action.

The beast sniffs again, its body coiling like a snake about to strike.

If I don't move, I'm dead.

I have to time it just right. Leap as it attacks and hope the noise of the fireball it spews covers the sound of me landing in another tree. Glancing at Melkin's position, I judge the distance between my tree and his. He catches my eye and jerks his chin toward the branch below him.

I brace myself and watch for my moment.

I don't have to wait long. In seconds, the beast's agitation reaches a boiling point and it rears up, takes aim, and roars a giant ball of fire straight at my tree.

I run along the branch and leap for Melkin's tree as the trunk behind me explodes into flame. I land hard, slip, and nearly fall, but Melkin's unnaturally long arm snakes down and catches me.

I dangle against the tree, my feet struggling to find purchase on the branch below me, while the Cursed One roars its fury and swings its head from side to side, obliterating everything in its path.

Panic blazes through me, sharp and absolute. I'm not going to die. Not like this. I have too many promises to keep.

My feet find the branch, and I steady myself by holding on to the trunk below Melkin. He keeps his hand on my pack, and we freeze as the Cursed One slithers around the trees, sniffing and listening.

I don't know what called it here. Maybe it was close enough to hear me yelling. Maybe we were just in the wrong place at the wrong time, though I've never been a big believer in coincidence. Whatever caught the Cursed One's attention, we're in its sights now.

Any gratitude I feel at being high enough to avoid letting it sniff out our location disappears when it bellows, a throaty roar of fury, and strafes the trees in front of it with fire. The trunk below us bursts into flame, and heat licks at my toes.

Smoke billows up, choking me, and the flames crawl steadily toward us. My lungs scream for air, my muscles shake with the need to run, and my skin feels dry and parched, but switching trees now would be my death sentence. I hold my breath to keep from coughing, and focus on remaining still.

It works. The Cursed One swings its head back and forth for another interminable minute, then curls back around, black scales glistening in the flickering light of the flames it created, and slithers its way into the gaping hole it made in the ground.

We remain still until the last trace of it disappears. Then we explode into motion. Scrambling up the trunk, we run along the length of the thickest branch we can find and tree-leap only to do the whole thing all over again.

Fire spreads quickly in the packed density of the Wasteland, but I know there's a river less than one hundred fifty yards to the west. Melkin knows it too, and we head for it in unspoken agreement.

Behind us, a wall of fire chews through the forest, spitting sparks and embers toward the sky and gushing a cloud of black smoke in our wake. We leap, climb, run, leap, and at some point, Melkin's hand reaches out and takes my heavy pack off my shoulders so I can keep up.

In the distance, I see the deep blue-black surface of the river glittering beneath the afternoon sun. My lungs burn, and my hands are raw from snatching at rough bark for balance, but I increase my pace as the wall of heat behind me whispers along my skin.

Melkin reaches the river first, but doesn't jump. Instead, he waits, reaching a skinny hand back for me as I make my final leap and skid along the branch toward him. He catches me, grabs my hand, and together we dive out of the trees and into the crisp, cold water.

CHAPTER THIRTY-FIVE

LOGAN

I no longer know what time it is. I've been lying on the damp, gritty floor of this cell for hours. Maybe a day. Maybe more. Without a way to track the sun, I can't be sure.

Pain is my constant companion—stabbing me with every breath and making a mockery of my attempts at sleep. At least one rib is broken, my arms and legs ache fiercely with bone-deep bruises, and my eyes are nearly swollen shut.

But worse than all of that is the burn on my neck. Every throb of agony from my seared flesh is a reminder of the Commander's power over me. I want to use the pain to focus on a plan to remove that power from him permanently, but my thoughts are fuzzy and vague, and the pain seems so much more important.

A chill seeps into me from the stone floor I lay on, and even with my cloak, I'm shivering. I should force myself to stand up and walk. Loosen the muscles. Promote faster healing.

I inhale slowly, trying to keep from pressing my lungs against my rib cage with too much force, and place my palms flat on the floor in front of me.

My body shakes as I slowly push myself to my hands and knees, inch by torturous inch. Gray dots swirl in front of my limited vision, and my empty stomach rebels against the waves of dizziness swamping me.

I may have gained my cloak, but I'm in no shape to gain my freedom.

It's a devastating thought, but I can't hang on to it for long. Heat is eating away at my brain, blurring the edges of reality until I can't tell if the contents of my head are memories, dreams, or wisps of things not worth the effort it takes to force them into something that makes sense.

I can't stand without help. Crawling toward the wall is a slow, agonizing process, and I stop frequently to rest, laying my face against the filthy stone floor and shivering both from external cold and the internal heat that blazes through my head but refuses to warm my body.

How does one cure a fever? I can't remember. My body shakes as I force myself to keep crawling. Keep moving. Keep pushing my muscles to work through the bruises because *he'll* come back. And I refuse to let him kill me.

I reach the wall sometime later and discover my nose is bleeding. I don't know how long that's been going on, and I decide I don't care.

From a distance, I hear the main dungeon door open, and I know I should be afraid, but that takes too much effort. Instead, I dig my fingers into the rugged texture of the wall beside me, and pull myself to my feet.

The room spins in slow, sickening circles. I try to breathe

through the nausea this creates, but dragging air into my lungs ignites the terrible pain in my side.

Someone is walking along the row between cells. I don't know who it is. I can't seem to turn my head to look. Instead, I lean my forehead against the cold stone of the wall and shake uncontrollably.

Rachel is out there. Somewhere. I know I should remember something important about her situation, but with fire eating at my brain, all I can think about is her hair in the sunlight. Like flames. Like the flames pounding at the inside of my skull.

I bang my head against the wall to put out the flames, but they just multiply.

Move.

I have to move.

If I don't, he'll kill me before I can escape.

I slide one foot in front of me, but it wobbles, and I have to hang on to the wall to keep from falling over.

Someone opens the door to my cell. The noise explodes inside my head, sending brutal hammers of pain into my temples. I let go of the wall to cover my ears, and pitch forward onto the unforgiving stone floor.

Footsteps hurry my way, and I reach for my sword. It isn't there, and the motion triggers the pain in my side until I'm gasping air in quick, shallow breaths.

The owner of the footsteps reaches me and crouches down. I can't see who it is, but the soft scent of lavender seeps through the stench of my cell and makes me want to close my eyes and pretend I'm in a field. Safe. Free. Lying on a bed of crushed lavender while the pain in my body subsides into nothing but memory, and those I love are still alive and well.

"Oh," a girl's voice exclaims in a whisper. A cool hand presses against my forehead.

I'm dreaming. I must be. There aren't any girls walking freely through the dungeon. My brain has cooked up a fantasy, and if I don't snap out of it, whoever is truly inside my cell with me will kill me before I can keep my promise to Rachel.

Rachel.

Rachel doesn't smell like lavender. She smells like citrus and midnight jasmine, and I wish the lavender would disappear and become Rachel's scent instead.

It doesn't.

Instead, the same cool hands that were pressed to my forehead are busy pushing something into the pocket of my cloak.

"Food," she whispers against my ear. "I'm putting medicine for your fever in the water. When the fever goes down, eat."

A cup tips against my lips and a trickle of bitter-tasting water dribbles into my mouth. I swallow reflexively, though part of me is screaming that this is a trick. A trap. Another wicked ploy of the Commander's to torture me. Maybe it's poison. Maybe it's something that will scrape me raw inside, doubling the pain until I want to kill myself just to make it end.

I turn my face and let another mouthful of water leak out onto the floor.

A girl lays her face next to mine, her outline blurry through the swollen slits of my eyelids. "Swallow," she says softly. "We're trying to help you."

I want to ask her who she means. No one helps you once you're in the dungeon. No one has ever helped me outside the dungeon either, except for Oliver, Jared, and Rachel.

The hard, brisk steps of a guard echo down the row, coming swiftly toward my cell.

"Hurry!" she whispers and presses the cup to my lips.

The water feels good, even if it tastes vile, and I swallow. It might be a trick. It might make things worse, but the heat beating at my brain won't allow me the luxury of thinking through my options, and I'm desperately thirsty.

"What are you doing, girl?" the guard demands.

"Watering the prisoner as you asked," she says, her tone low and respectful.

"He's had enough. Get out of there."

She stands immediately and exits the cell, her steps hurried. The guard laughs as he looks at me lying on the floor, shivering while blood slowly seeps out of my nose.

I close my eyes and wish for a world where Rachel and Jared are safe and Oliver is alive.

CHAPTER
THIRTY-SIX

RACHEL

The water snatches me with icy arms as I plunge beneath its surface. The sound of the fire becomes muted, a distant roaring that can't compete with the swift rush of the river's current. I lose my grip on Melkin's hand as I'm flung downstream. I can't stop spinning. Can't break free of the current. Can't get to the surface.

My lungs burn, and my brain screams at me to take a breath, but I've spun so many times in the dark embrace of the river, I no longer know which way is up. I kick out, lash with my arms, and fight against the water.

It's useless.

My ears roar, and a strange hum grows louder within my brain as my chest convulses and I cough, sucking in a mouthful of water in exchange.

The water burns my lungs, and I cough again.

More water. More coughing. More pain.

And then it's gone. The pain recedes. My chest relaxes. My

lungs stop demanding air. I'm at peace.

I let the current spin me as the world darkens into nothing, but something wraps around me, hauls me through the water, and I break the surface.

I cough feebly, but my lungs are used to water now. They don't know what to do with air. And I don't care. I want to close my eyes and let the water take me. Let the tiny sliver of peace I felt swallow me whole.

But I can't. Because whatever is holding me won't let me slide under the surface again. By the time we reach the shore, my lungs are burning for air, and the peace I felt is gone.

I'm tossed onto the shore, flipped over on my back, and Melkin looms over me like a giant wet twig. He puts his hands together, one over the other, and slams them into my chest.

Water gushes up my throat, burning and suffocating, and fills my mouth and nose. He reaches forward and turns my head to the side as I spew the water onto the sand. Twice more, he hits my chest and I have to spit out mouthfuls of water. When he raises his hands a fourth time, my lungs contract, and I start coughing on my own. He lowers his hands, turns me to my side so any water I cough up can dribble onto the ground, and collapses next to me, his breathing harsh.

I don't know how much time passes before he turns over on his side to face me.

"You gonna live?" he asks, and I see my pack is still strapped to his back.

My throat burns as I answer. "I'm fine."

I should thank him. Between this and catching me before I fell from the branch below him during the Cursed One's attack, he's saved my life twice today. I should, but I don't. Because even though he's saved me, even though he claims to have lost almost everything, he works for the Commander. I don't need anything else to justify the slow burn of anger I feel every time I look at him.

It should be Logan who caught me. Logan who saved me from drowning. Logan who asks if I'm okay.

"I'm sorry for what I said back there," Melkin says.

I frown. I don't know what he means.

"I know your daddy's been missing for months. I saw what happened during the Claiming ceremony. If anyone has a right to bitterness, I guess it's you." His dark eyes wander away from mine, and he heaves himself into a sitting position, my pack dripping water, creating tiny streams on the riverbank.

I wish he wouldn't apologize. Wouldn't sit there like he understands and ask for nothing in return. It makes it hard to aim my anger at him.

I sit up as well, digging my fingers into the wet sand beneath me as my head spins slowly, and look around us. Nothing is familiar. We've traveled so far down the river, I've lost any place markers to show me where we are. The distant horizon is free of smoke, a clear indication we traveled for miles in the swift embrace of the water.

"Where are we?" I ask, and wish for the hot, syrupy drink Oliver always gave me to cure a sore throat.

The memory of Oliver stabs into me, and I force myself to breathe through it.

"About past the king's city," Melkin says, raising one bony arm to point to the bank above us to the left.

I turn to see a huge metal rectangle, its legs long ago turned into twisted wreckage, leaning against the top of the bank, one corner deeply entrenched in the ground. A man with jet-black hair and a smirk on his lips peers at us from the middle of the rectangle, his image sun-worn, the paint falling away in long strips. Vines twine around the top, obscuring the upper left corner, and tall grasses hide the base, but the word KING stretches across the center in faded, peeling red letters.

"How many days between this and Rowansmark?" I need familiar markers. A road I can remember. Something to help me find Dad's safe house. Every courier establishes his own off-the-main-path places to stock with essentials and use on their journeys. To share the location with others is to invite robbery and maybe even torture by those who would lie in wait hoping to extract any secrets they know.

"Maybe fifteen. We've been pushed off course by about five or six days," Melkin says, and stands, adjusting the weight of the pack on his back.

My pack. With my weapons.

I stand too, and though my knees wobble and my legs shake, I have no trouble remaining upright. A glance at the sky tells me we still have four hours until sunset. More than enough time to get past the King's City and find a safe place to camp. I unfasten my cloak, my fingers fumbling with the soggy leather bindings, and take it off. The damp garment is a dead weight against my shoulders, and I need the sun to dry my tunic and leggings as we walk. The copper cuff Logan gave me stands out in sharp relief beneath the wet material of my tunic. I hope Logan had the good sense to make the tracking device waterproof.

Melkin reaches a hand out for my cloak, and I jerk it toward my chest.

He frowns. "It's heavy. I'll carry it until you're feeling a bit stronger."

"It's mine. So is the pack." I reach for it.

He backs away. "You're in no shape to carry it."

My hands curl into fists. He has my Switch. My bow and arrows. Does he think if he takes most of my weapons, he'll have me at a disadvantage? I reach for the knife sheath strapped to my waist.

He holds his hands up, and I can't read the expression on his face. "You're a stubborn, suspicious one, aren't you?"

"With good reason." The knife slides free and I palm the hilt. "I want my weapons. You can carry the pack if you insist, but I carry my own weapons."

Never again will I be caught unaware. Unable to act.

He shrugs, but watches me closely as he slides my Switch free of its sleeve and hands it to me. The bow and arrows follow, and I see I'm down to three arrows from the original twelve. The rest must be swirling along the bottom of the river.

I strap the bow and arrows to my back, return the knife to its sheath, and hold the Switch with my right hand.

"Better?" Melkin asks softly.

"I don't need your pity." I snatch up my cloak with my left hand.

"What do you need, then?" he asks, and it sounds like he really wants to know.

Oliver, alive and unharmed. Logan, by my side. Dad, waiting for me with the package, able to help me figure out what to do next. The Commander, dead at my feet.

That's what I need, but I can't tell Melkin that. He works for the Commander, and he's only interested in the package.

"Rachel? What do you need?"

I remember Melkin saying he'd lost almost everything, the weight of unspoken grief hanging over his words, and wonder if giving him one piece of the truth might work in my favor. Especially if what I need is something he might secretly want as well. Looking him in the eye, I say, "Revenge. I need revenge."

His eyes darken and slide away from mine as he hefts the pack against his back. "Try not to harshly judge those of us with more than that left to live for," he says, and starts up the bank without looking to see if I'll follow.

Does he think I have so little left to live for? I have Logan. I have Dad. And I have a score to settle. None of those can be taken lightly. I clench my teeth around the words that want to burst free and scorch the air around me. Arguing would only give him more information than he needs to know. Instead, I dig my Switch into the soft sand beneath me for balance, and start the climb toward the King's City.

CHAPTER
THIRTY-SEVEN

RACHEL

We stop for the night in the shelter of a concrete box of a building with only two sides still standing against the ravages of time and weather. We left the King's City behind two hours ago, and I'm grateful. The twisted metal remains of buildings that once housed a vibrant civilization are now blackened husks coated in ash and wrapped with kudzu. Walking among them makes me nervous. A harsh reminder of what the Cursed One is capable of doing to us if we don't remain with those who've proven their ability to protect us.

Since I have no intention of remaining beneath anyone's authority again, I turn my back on the ruins of the city and refuse to consider the idea that I may have just glimpsed my future.

Melkin hasn't spoken to me since our words on the riverbank, and that's fine with me. I have nothing left to say. I just want this leg of the journey over with.

Thankfully, I have flint and fuel in my pack, so we don't have to worry about keeping ourselves warm or keeping wild animals at bay. I work with Melkin to gather firewood and stack it in the center of the makeshift shelter. I also still have my flask of fresh water, and I offer it to him.

He raises a brow at me, but accepts it and swallows three times before handing it back. I lay my pack against one of the still-standing walls of our shelter and grab my bow and arrows.

"Where are you going?" he asks as I stride out of the shelter.

"To catch dinner."

"I'll come with you."

I toss a glance over my shoulder. "I can handle this. You get the fire going, and stop worrying that I need a babysitter."

Which might not be fair, considering I needed his help twice today. But I can handle hunting, and I need some time alone without his watchful eyes tracking my every move. Without the strain of trying to appear like I don't want to scream in frustration when we've traveled for hours, and I still don't know where we are.

He doesn't follow me, though he moves to the edge of the ruined building and watches me as I go.

Our shelter is settled against a soft swell of land covered in tall grass already gone to seed. Beyond the hill, the broken remains of an old road wind through the grass and disappear for yards at a time. On the other side of the road, a copse of trees stretches as far as I can see.

The sun is drowning beneath the weight of a purple twilight as I enter the trees, walk twenty yards into the middle of them, their skinny trunks and thin, graceful branches reaching for the heavens as if hoping to scrape against the stars, and find what

I'm looking for.

A bush hugs the base of a tree, its branches curving like a bell, its leaves brushing the ground. Beneath it, a small, hollow space rests, and I crawl inside, string an arrow, and wait.

Night has nearly reclaimed the sky when I finally catch a glimpse of movement. I tense, hardly daring to breathe. My patience is rewarded as a creature about the size of a small sheep wanders close, nose to ground, snuffling. I draw in a slow, deep breath, rehearse each step in my mind, and then whip the bow up, close one eye to sight down the center, and release the arrow.

It flies true, striking the side of the animal, and I leap from cover as my quarry jerks around and starts to run with faltering steps. Crossing the distance between us in seconds, I yank my knife free, leap on the animal's back, and swing my arm beneath its neck to slice open its throat.

It dies instantly, and I wipe my knife clean on the ground beside it. Retrieving my arrow, I clean it as well and pack my weapons away. Flipping the animal over, I see I've caught a boar. A young one, by the size of its tusks.

I can't easily lift it, plus I refuse to get its blood all over me. The thought makes bile surge up my throat, and I cough, gag, and spit on the forest floor. I solve the problem by grabbing its hind legs and dragging it to the edge of the trees. I don't want to drag it across the grass and broken pieces of road to our shelter because the trail of blood could lead a wild animal straight to us while we sleep.

I don't have to.

Melkin is standing on the road, watching the tree line, his knife in his hands.

He doesn't see me at first, and I'm struck by the harsh, predatory silhouette he makes, caught in the moment before the sun's final death and the moon's rise. Before I can continue this line of thinking, he notices me and approaches, his long stride eating the distance like it's nothing.

"Nice," he says as he sees the boar.

I shrug, though his continued attitude of tolerant courtesy toward me is starting to make me feel uncomfortable in my own skin.

He lifts the boar with a grunt and turns back toward our camp. I follow and list the reasons I have for keeping my distance from him. For being angry with him.

It all boils down to the fact that he's in the Commander's pocket.

Of course, he could think the same of me.

I mull this over as Melkin carves the boar, separating muscle from bone with swift hacking motions, and tosses choice pieces of meat onto the flames to sizzle and snap. Maybe I'm supposed to feel enmity toward him. Maybe the Commander knew anyone he used to replace Logan would be a target for my mistrust. Maybe we aren't supposed to be a team working toward the same goal, because if we begin to think for ourselves, the Commander could be in danger.

The idea warms me with something more than fury.

Something that feels like another tiny fragment of hope.

I lay my damp cloak out to dry near the flames, and take a seat beside Melkin. Far enough away that I can draw my knife before his long arms could reach me, but close enough to indicate I'm not trying to shut him out.

He glances at me, but says nothing.

I force myself to say the words I know he deserves to hear. "Thank you."

He uses a stick to nudge the meat and flip it over. The scent fills the air and makes my mouth water.

"For what?" he asks.

"For saving my life. Twice. For carrying the boar. And for"—here I choke on the words and have to push them past my lips, their inflection sounding wooden and insincere—"understanding my attitude."

He stays silent for the time it takes to skewer three large pieces of meat on a stick and hand it to me. Then he says, "Didn't think I'd hear that from you."

I shrug and bite into the meat, which burns my lips but explodes against my tongue with glorious flavor. I watch him skewer his own before answering. "You work for the Commander."

"So do you."

"Not by choice."

"And you think I do?" He looks at me, and I'm struck by the depth of misery etched into his too-thin face.

I feel my way carefully through my next words. "You're a tracker. You've worked for the Commander for years. I figured this was just another assignment to you."

He looks into the fire. "You figured wrong."

I'm not sure I have. I have only my instincts to rely on, and my instincts tell me that Melkin doesn't wish me harm, and that he carries an inner grief of his own. If I can soften him toward my cause, maybe we can be a team against the Commander.

"Maybe I'm wrong," I say. "But how am I to know for sure?"

He laughs, a small, brittle sound, and looks at me. "How can either of us know anything for sure? We've been backed into a corner, threatened with losing everything, and then set loose to circle each other like South Edge dogs afraid to lose a prize bone."

I stare at him, my mind racing. Is he really in the same situation as me? Or has he been coached to say this so I'll trust him?

He shakes his head. "One of us has to tell the truth here. I'll start. You can do with it what you will."

I say nothing, but watch him carefully for signs he might be lying.

"It's true I've worked for the Commander for eleven years now. And it's true that he assigned me to accompany you."

"Why?"

"Apparently, he thought you might need the help. You're just a girl, after all." A ghost of a smile flits across his face. "A girl who knows how to keep her head in the face of the Cursed One, who can nearly drown and still trek for four hours, and who has the skill to bring down a boar. Bet the Commander has no idea how far he's underestimated you."

I bet the Commander hasn't underestimated me at all, and Melkin's true role is to make sure I don't commit treachery. Which means Melkin could make it look like we're on the same side when all he's trying to do is buy my confidence. Calculating the odds makes me ache for Logan, who could assess the options, list the worst-case scenarios, and come up with plans to address it all in half the time it will take me to decide if I should just sneak away from Melkin in the middle of the night and do my best to survive the Wasteland alone.

"So why do you say you didn't take this assignment willingly?" I ask, and Melkin swallows hard, his Adam's apple bobbing in his throat like a cork.

He's quiet so long, I begin to think he won't answer the question. When he finally speaks, he addresses his words to the flames in a voice so low, I have to strain to hear him.

"I would have. I would've tracked the package with you and returned it, just like I've done with every other assignment he's given me. But he didn't give me a chance to prove my loyalty." He looks at me suddenly, desperate grief in his eyes. "He threw my wife in the dungeon. She's due to give birth in a few weeks, and he threw her in the dungeon."

I don't doubt him for a second. The raw, aching pain in his voice reminds me of my own loss, and I want to stuff my fingers in my ears and pretend I can't hear him. His emotions are real, but that still doesn't mean I can trust his words.

"What do you have to do to get her out?" I ask quietly, because here is the crux of the issue. If he tells me the truth, perhaps we can work our way toward trusting each other. But if he lies . . . if I even *think* he's lying, then I'll have to think like Logan and start planning for worst-case scenarios.

He scrubs a hand over his face, breaking eye contact with me and looking at the fire again. "I have to deliver the package. Whether you agree or not." He looks at me. "I can't allow any obstacles to stand in my way."

And there it is. If I plan treachery against the Commander, he's the one tasked to stand in my way. No matter what it takes. And he will. Because his wife and unborn child are at stake.

I can't blame him for doing exactly what I would do myself.

And I can't help feeling empathy for his position. I know what it's like to have the Commander hold my loved ones over my head at the point of a sword. The difference is that I no longer believe the Commander's promises.

I don't share my conviction with Melkin, though. It wouldn't change the danger his wife is in. It would only wound him further. Or turn him against me.

Instead, I slide a little closer to him and say softly, "I have to deliver the package too. Or I lose someone I care for."

"And your chance at revenge?" he asks, and captures my gaze with his as if the fate of the world hinges on my answer.

Maybe it does. Maybe he needs to know someone is willing to take a stand against the Commander, and his current suffering won't be swept under a rug.

"Yes. I need to deliver the package so I can rescue Logan. And so I can get my revenge." The words sting the air between us.

Melkin nods once as though he's gained the answer he sought, and turns back to the fire to take first watch. I curl up on my still-drying cloak, my back to the fire, my face toward Melkin.

We might have reached a new accord between us. We might be working toward the same goal. But my knife is a comforting weight in my hand as I quietly pull it from its sheath and hold it, blade out, where I can strike anything that comes for me.

Just in case I'm wrong.

CHAPTER
THIRTY-EIGHT

<u>LOGAN</u>

She didn't kill me. Whatever the lavender-scented girl put in my water, it soothed my feverish thinking and kept the pain somewhat at bay. I'm able to wrap myself in my cloak, lean against the wall, and sleep until the next guard makes his rounds.

By the time he reaches my cell, I've slumped to the floor and I huddle there, shivering. It isn't hard to do. The stones beneath me radiate cold. He studies me for a moment, then makes the trek back to the main door, locks it behind him, and leaves the dungeon in silence again.

I wait a few moments longer to make sure he's truly gone, and then slowly sit up, making it look like it's a struggle to do so. That isn't hard either. My muscles protest the slightest movement, the scorched skin on the side of my neck throbs, and my broken rib aches fiercely.

But my fever is gone, and I can think clearly again.

Along with the return of reason comes the knowledge that I've wasted precious time succumbing to my injuries. I don't know what day it is, or how long Rachel's been gone. My body is weak from lack of food and lack of movement. And the Commander is probably due to arrive at any moment to toy with me.

I can't fix it all at once. I have to prioritize and determine an appropriate course of action. Whatever I choose, it has to be something I can do without raising suspicion if I'm being watched by more than just the occasional guard.

Food is the first order of business. I double over as if in excruciating pain and feel within my cloak pockets until I find the wrapped lump the girl left for me. Inside the cloth is a chunk of oat bread with cheese and dried apples inside. I take small bites, rocking back and forth to simulate pain so I can hide what I'm doing. My stomach has been without food for hours, maybe days. I need to take it easy.

One third of the way through the food, I stop eating. It's enough to get my system working again, and I need to conserve what I have left. I don't know when I'll be getting more.

I settle against the wall again as exhaustion overtakes me. I'd hoped to get up and walk a bit, but my head is already spinning, and I can't risk another fall. Instead, I slowly stretch each limb and tighten my muscles for the length of time it takes to recite the Periodic Table. By the time I'm done, I'm shaking and slightly nauseous.

Water would be nice, but that's one problem I'm helpless to address.

Through it all, the knowledge that Oliver is gone aches within me, a constant source of pain I rub against with every thought. For just a moment, the image of my mother's smile, the feel of Oliver's arm around my shoulders, and the warmth of Rachel's trust in me bleed together into one gaping pit of loss. I'm hollowed out. Empty of everything that once gave me reasons to live.

Grief is a deep pool of darkness, and I huddle against the damp, cold wall as it sucks me under. I had something worth losing, and now that's it's gone, now that *they're* gone, I'm realizing the life of solitude I always thought I wanted isn't good enough anymore.

I don't want to be alone.

I don't want to have only the cold comfort of my inventions to keep me company.

I want my family.

I want *Rachel*.

Not because she's beautiful. Not because she's my responsibility. I want her because she makes me laugh. Makes me think. Inspires me to be the kind of man I always hoped I'd be.

I want Rachel because the thought of a life without her is more than I can bear.

The grief recedes. It won't help me plan. I haven't lost Rachel. Not yet. I lean my head against the wall, careful not to rub my burned skin against the damp stone, and consider my options. Movement catches my eye, and I turn to see Melkin's wife, Eloise, staring at me.

I don't greet her. I don't need to announce to anyone that I'm capable of that. But I hold her gaze, trying to assess what I see there.

Best Case Scenario: She's an innocent caught up in all of this and means me no harm.

Worst Case Scenario 1: She means me no harm but will

unwittingly gather information she'll later deliver to the Commander under duress.

Worst Case Scenario 2: She's cunning enough to realize she might leverage her way out of here by providing the Commander with secrets about me.

Worst Case Scenario 3: She's his spy dressed up to look helpless and pregnant. Hoping I'll pity her. Hoping to play on the sense of honor the Commander swears I don't have.

The answer to every scenario is the same. Give nothing away and set in motion my plan for escape before anyone realizes I'm well enough to do so.

She's still looking at me, but I close my eyes and turn away. It's easy to look exhausted and sick. I don't even have to feign it. Let her report my weakness. The fact that I can't even stand. Let her tell them the Commander has me beaten.

By the time he realizes the truth, I'll be gone.

"Stop him," someone whispers, a mere breath of sound I barely catch.

I open my eyes a fraction, and she's still watching me, her eyes pleading. Stop whom? The Commander? Melkin?

This is exactly the kind of conversation I need to avoid. I close my eyes again, and keep my silence.

"Please."

Another breathy whisper. I tamp down on the surge of irritation that wants to snap my eyes open so I can glare her into silence. Does she think I'm so easily led that I'll fall for this?

Does she really think I have the power at the moment to stop anyone?

"He isn't a killer. He isn't . . ." Her whisper chokes off into stillness as the dungeon door opens with a clang.

If "he" isn't a killer, she can only be discussing Melkin. But how she thinks I'll ever be able to reach him in time while I'm lying indisposed in a dungeon of stone is a mystery.

Not that I don't have a plan for it, of course. But she has no way of knowing that, and her misplaced faith in me rings false.

Another sign I need to be careful what I allow her to see.

The footsteps traveling the aisle are light. They stop at the first occupied cell and a door slides open with a high-pitched squeal. A girl's voice, light and calm, murmurs through the air, and my stomach tightens.

This must be my secret savior. The one who gave me hope that someone on the outside is interested in helping me. I need more information, but I have to hide the transaction from Eloise.

I slide down to the floor and curl into a ball with my back facing the cell door. The girl is talking to every prisoner she encounters. Seeing her talk to me will raise no alarms, while seeing me question her will give more away than I can afford.

She moves to the cell with the young man in chains, and her voice is clearer now. I listen to her offer him food and water and then quietly suggest he put the paste she's placed in his tin of food on his abraded wrists rather than in his mouth.

She could be arrested for that alone.

I marvel at her courage, even while I tense for the appearance of a guard. No one comes, though, and she moves on to Melkin's wife. I strain to hear their conversation and catch snippets of admonitions to eat everything in front of her and drink her water slowly. Then there's the sound of fabric hitting the floor.

"You can't give me your cloak," Melkin's wife whispers.

Because apparently she is incapable of realizing the best way to punish a good deed is to announce it to everyone else. Or because she thinks turning in the girl will somehow grant her favor with the Commander.

Her mistake could simply be one of youth and ignorance, but I have precious little sympathy for either at the moment. Rachel is young too, and she'd be far too smart to make such a stupid mistake.

The door to my cell creaks open, and I'm swamped with the delicate scent of lavender a second before she drops to the floor beside me, clutching a tin water pail and a cup.

The concern on her face doesn't falter, even as she takes in my steady, fever-free gaze. She's tall, thin in a lithe, graceful way, and the torchlight flickers beautifully against her dusky skin. The cloud of dark hair hanging down her back throws off the lavender scent every time she moves.

She seems familiar, and I try to recall where I've seen her before. One of the stalls in Lower Market? A merchant's place in North Hub? Neither of those locations fit.

She scoops a cup of water out of the pail and leans toward me.

"Day?" I mouth silently before accepting a few swallows. The water is tepid and tastes of tin. It's the most refreshing drink I've ever had.

She frowns as if I've spilled the water out my mouth and fishes around in her skirt pocket for a scrap of cloth. Bending down, she pretends to mop my face with the cloth and keeps her face level with mine, her hair obscuring her features from anyone outside my cell.

"Tuesday." She says, and presses a small, paper-wrapped

packet into my hand. "For the pain."

Tuesday. The Claiming ceremony was Saturday. I've lost three days.

She sits up and scoops more water into her cup. I drink obediently, and watch her calm, competent movements. I've seen those movements before, but my brain still refuses to make the connection, and I let it go. I have more important things to think about. She's risked death today, not just for me, but for each of the prisoners here. I can't quite understand it.

"Why help?" I mouth to her, though I feel the answer may be too lengthy to share like this.

She dips her cloth in the remaining water and scrubs gently at my face, using her hair once more as a cloak to mask her face from any observers.

"Things must change," she says so softly, I barely catch it. "Someone needs to lead that change. We think it will be you."

I'm stunned into silence, and wait a beat too long to ask her the other questions that burn within me. She's already leaving, shutting my door behind her as if she hasn't just ignited a firestorm of speculation within me, when I remember where I've seen her.

Thom's Tankard. Wiping down tables while acting as a lookout for Drake and his men.

Drake's group has moved from trying to recruit me as a member to nominating me as a leader? I'd laugh if it wouldn't hurt my ribcage. I'm injured, locked in a dungeon, and the only people I still care about are far away from Baalboden. What part of that description makes me fit to lead a revolution here?

Not that I'm not sympathetic to their cause. The citizens of

Baalboden desperately need change. I'd been wrong to think my mother's death meant the price of dissent was too high to pay. Silent acquiescence in the face of tyranny is no better than outright agreement. My mother knew that. Now, so do I.

But revolution and change must wait their turn.

Rachel needs me.

Melkin needs to be stopped.

Jared needs to be found.

And the Commander needs to be brought to justice.

If I have to lead a revolution to accomplish that, so be it.

CHAPTER
THIRTY-NINE

RACHEL

We've been traveling the Wasteland for a week now. Four days ago, we skirted a Tree People village without incident. Not that I've ever known Tree People to get involved with the affairs of those who leave them alone, but we can't take any chances. I never used to understand why people would choose to build houses in the trees in hopes of avoiding the Cursed One rather than live beneath the protection of a city-state. Now, I know that sometimes the protection of a city-state comes at too high a cost.

Two days ago, I began recognizing markers along the way and knew we were back on the path to Rowansmark. The forest has changed and thickened, easing out of pin oak trees and into silver maples interspersed with pine. The morning dew hangs just as heavy in the air as it does on the ground, and large fields of waist-high grass ripple sluggishly beneath a half-hearted breeze.

Melkin and I have fallen into a rhythm. He leads, beating back the worst of the undergrowth, and I sweep the ground behind us to cover our tracks. I hunt for our dinner each night, and he makes the fire and handles the cooking. We speak only when necessary during the day, but at night, as we eat rabbit, boar, or turkey, we talk. Though we rarely discuss anything personal, it's beginning to feel like I'm traveling with a friend.

Though I never forget that our friendship could be his way of trying to hold me to the Commander's orders, and when I catch him watching me with something dark and brooding in his eyes, I know he feels the same.

As we make camp again for the night, I can see he misses his wife. It's carved in miserable lines on his face, bracketing his mouth with tension that refuses to ease.

I miss Logan, too. More than I thought I would.

The slap of humiliation I once felt every time I thought of him is gone. In its place, I see Logan sacrificing sleep so he could finish the tracking device. Offering to teach me to use the Switch and helping me hold on to the good memories I have of Dad. Drawing his sword against the Commander, despite overwhelming odds, to protect me. Logan is the lodestone I cling to when grief over Oliver and fear for Dad threaten to rob me of what little hope I have left.

Something in me has awakened and responds only to Logan. I lie sleepless long after Melkin begins to snore and press my fingers to my lips as I remember Logan leaning in, his breath fanning my face, his eyes locked on my mouth. A delicious ache pulses through me. I feel like a stranger waking up in my own skin—aware of every inch. Heat runs through my veins, both exhilarating and terrifying.

Exhilarating because every part of me tingles with life.

But terrifying because beneath the longing lies an inescapable truth: If he is my lodestone, it's because somehow in the last few weeks I've started to rely on him. Lean on him. Need him. My heart pounds a little faster as the realization sinks in.

I need Logan.

Not because I need saving. Not because he could plan our way out of this. But because on some basic, soul-deep level within me, he is the solid ground beneath my feet. The one who will move mountains to keep his promises. The one who looks at me and *sees*.

I can't imagine my life without him.

Everywhere I look, he's there. A constant thread binding my past, my present, and the future I want so badly to have with him.

With *him*.

My eyes fly open.

I'm in love with Logan.

Not the way I thought I was two years ago, when I offered him my heart. That love was uncomplicated and innocent, designed for a simple life. The love consuming me now is fierce and absolute—forged in a crucible of loss and united by our shared strength.

I love Logan. A laugh bubbles up, even as tears sting my eyes. I reach up to clasp his mother's necklace, the symbol of his promise to me, and hold the tender, vibrant thought of him close as the stars chase each other across the sky.

Halfway through the next day's journey, we approach the clearing where Dad and I always stopped for a meal, and the ache of missing him throbs in time with the ache of missing Oliver. If I can find him now, the fierce edge of my grief will lessen. He'll know how to save Logan without giving the package to the Commander. He'll take the burden of this awful responsibility off my shoulders.

I don't realize how much I want him to be waiting for me as we move past a thin line of maples and into the small field of yellow-green grass until I see he isn't there.

He isn't here.

I know it isn't logical to feel so hopeless when I had no real reason to think he'd be camped at the edge of the clearing waiting for me, but I can't help the tears that stream down my face. Loneliness eats at me, and for the millionth time since I left Baalboden, I wish Logan was with me.

Quickly swiping my palms across my cheeks before Melkin catches me crying, I start to turn away when movement catches my eye. A slice of deep purple shimmers gently against a tree trunk on the far side of the field. Veering off course without saying a word, I move toward it, my heart suddenly knocking against my chest like it wants its freedom.

"What are you doing?" Melkin asks behind me.

I ignore him and hurry, the crisp stalks of grass parting before me and *shushing* closed in my wake. The purple is a ribbon, wind torn and water ravaged, tied around the base of the lowest branch. The initials *S. A.* are embroidered in the corner.

I know this ribbon. It's one of a handful that belonged to my mother. Dad always carried them with him when he went into the Wasteland.

I want to laugh. To dance. To open my mouth and let the fierce joy singing through me echo from the treetops.

He was here.

And he wanted me to know it.

CHAPTER FORTY

RACHEL

As if connected to my thoughts, the cuff around my left arm vibrates gently, and I glance down to see the blue wires begin to glow—a hesitant, flickering light that fills me with wild, buoyant hope.

Dad.

I can find him.

He can fix this.

I just have to hold on a little longer.

"What does this mean?"

Melkin stands to my right, watching me closely, and I scramble to find something to say. I can't tell him I think we're closing in on Dad. I don't know how he'd react, and it's best not to introduce any new elements into our precarious partnership until it's already accomplished.

"It means we're on the right track."

His skinny brows crawl toward the center of his forehead. "I thought we already knew that."

I shrug and step forward, as much to tug the ribbon free as to hide my face from his prying eyes.

"You mean this is a sign?"

When I don't answer, he shifts his weight forward, his shadow swallowing me from behind, and says in a voice I scarcely recognize as the mild, courteous Melkin I've been with for a week, "Who's working with you? Better come clean now, girl, or you'll not get a second chance."

I fold the ribbon carefully and stow it in an inner cloak pocket before turning to face him. He looms above me, all sharp angles and seething suspicion, his hand resting on his knife hilt.

"Calm down. No one's working with me, but you had to know we're following my dad's trail since he's the one who hid the package. You should be relieved I recognize his signs."

Not that he had ever once deliberately left a sign before. But he'd never left without planning to return either. I give him kudos for knowing I'd follow him, and for knowing what would show me I'm on the right track.

Melkin's hand slides off his knife and he steps back, though his eyes still look troubled. I turn from him and plunge into the trees again. I can't bear to waste time. He follows me, and in a few moments, shoulders his way past me to resume the lead, his expression once more a sea of calm.

I'm not fooled. He's afraid. Of the consequences if he fails his mission, yes. But also of me and any tricks I might pull. I want to tell him he has nothing to fear from me or my dad as long as he doesn't stand between the Commander and justice, but I don't think he'd believe me. Not completely. It's hard for him to fathom the Commander falling hard enough to lose the power to ruin lives, and Melkin has two other lives at stake beside his own.

We break for a lunch of cold rabbit leftovers, creek water, and silence thick enough to cut with a knife. Finally, I look him in the eye and say, "What's the problem?"

He chews a bite of rabbit slowly, the bones of his jaw swiveling like a set of Logan's gears. "I don't like this whole situation."

"That makes two of us."

"What if we're being led into a trap?"

I squint at him through a shaft of blinding afternoon sun. "Who do you think is leading us into a trap?"

"Someone who wants whatever is in that package."

Which could be anyone. Trackers from Rowansmark. Others working for the Commander. Highwaymen who've heard of its existence. If I wasn't absolutely sure the signal came from Dad, I'd be thinking the same thing.

I pull the ribbon from my pocket, smooth it over my knee for a moment, my fingers slowly tracing the silvery *S. A.* stitched into the corner, and then hand it to Melkin. His fingers are cold as they brush against mine.

"*S. A.*?"

"Sarabeth Adams. My mother."

Quiet falls between us, though the Wasteland is quick to fill it up with the warbling chirps of birds and the drowsy buzzing of insects. Beneath the chirping and buzzing, I catch what sounds like the faint snap of a twig.

I freeze and look at Melkin, but he's staring at the ribbon and seems oblivious. Turning, I scan the area around us, but can't see anything amiss.

I'm not reassured.

"Do you miss her?"

I snap back around to Melkin. "Not really. She died right after I was born."

I don't have time to give him more than that. Someone is behind us. I'm sure of it. I toss the rest of the rabbit meat away from me, slide my arms into my pack, and remove my knife from its sheath.

"I bet Jared does."

"I guess," I say, keeping my voice low. "Come on. We need to go."

He looks at me, the ribbon threaded through his fingers like a bedraggled set of rings. "I can't lose Eloise. She's . . ." He chokes, clears his throat, and says, "Do you think the Commander will keep his promise to set her free if I . . ."

"If you what?" I can barely focus on him. I'm standing now, my Switch in my hand, scanning the trees.

He stands as well, towering over me again, his eyes suddenly reminding me of the dark, depthless holes carved into the ground by the Cursed One. "If I do what was asked of me. Will he keep his promise if I do what he asked of me?"

His knife is out too. That's good. At least he isn't completely immune to the signals I'm sending out. My voice is little more than a breath of air as I tell him, "I think someone is tracking us. Coming for us. I heard a branch."

He palms the knife.

"To the right. About thirty yards. Maybe more. I haven't heard anything since, but either we leave now or find a place to set up an ambush and wait." I look up at him, expecting a decision, and see the endless dark of his eyes still pinned on me.

"You didn't answer my question."

I glare and consider whacking him with my Switch, except I don't want to make the noise. "We're in danger, Melkin. Get moving."

His arm snakes out and snags the front of my cloak as I try to pass him, and I stare at him in disbelief.

Does he want us to die?

"Do you think the Commander will free Eloise if I do what he asked of me?"

The idiot isn't going to move until he hears what he wants to hear. Is the Commander going to keep his word? Not unless it somehow benefits him to do so. But I'm not about to open up that can of worms while someone is bearing down on us, and Melkin's common sense has taking a flying leap to parts unknown.

"Yes," I say with as much conviction as I can manage in a whisper. "Yes, I'm sure he will. Keep your end of the bargain, and she'll be fine. Now, let's go."

He releases my cloak. Pressing his lips into a thin line, he uses his knife to gesture toward a dense line of trees to our left.

"You first."

I don't need a second invitation. Brushing past him, I slip into the trees, moving like a shadow, while Melkin slides in after me, his knife glittering beneath a stray ray of sunlight.

CHAPTER FORTY-ONE

LOGAN

I think it's Saturday now, which would mean I've been a guest in the Commander's dungeon for a week. The girl from Thom's Tankard hasn't been back since she slipped me a paper-wrapped package of medicinal powder on Tuesday. Instead, a plump, stoop-shouldered woman old enough to be my grandmother has cared for the prisoners in silence.

I decide it's a good thing I haven't seen the girl again. Thinking about revolution might distract me from the pressing issues already on my plate. The most important of those is escape, but I'm not sure I'm well enough to outrun any pursuing guards as I sprint toward the Wall. I estimate another two to three days before my broken rib will allow me to run without doubling me over in pain.

Less if I can find a cloth to bind my chest.

I suppose I could use the shirt off my back, but I'd prefer not to be so obvious. Especially when Eloise in the cell across the aisle watches me every second of the day like a desperate baby bird hoping for a worm.

The Commander hasn't visited again, and the anticipation stretches my nerves until I want something to happen just to get it over with. I'd think he'd relish the opportunity to taunt me. Hurt me. Make sure I know he's won. I decide to take his absence as a sign Melkin still hasn't succeeded in killing Rachel, and focus on readying my body for my escape. Still, waiting for the inevitable festers in the back of my mind like an infection.

I've spent the last few days sitting or lying on the dungeon floor, doing my best to look hopelessly injured while I tighten and hold my muscles until they shake from the exertion. I've also done my best to honor the grief I feel for Oliver with a solid plan of action I think would make him proud.

But mostly, I've spent my time thinking of Rachel. The way her laugh makes me want to join her before I even know why she's laughing. The light in her eyes when she stares me down and challenges my opinions. The curve of her hip in the torchlight as she climbs the ladder to my loft.

I used to feel awkward and uncomfortable with the single-minded intensity she aims at anything in front of her, and distancing myself from her gave me peace. Now, the distance between us opens a hollow space inside me that can only be filled by *her*. I don't know how to explain it, and I don't bother trying. It's enough to know I need her like I've never needed anyone else. Once I find her, I'll take the time to figure out the rest.

I promise myself it won't be much longer before I'm ready to escape this hellhole and track her down.

My food ran out this morning, but I'm not worried. I won't be locked inside this cell much longer. Still, when the dungeon door creaks open, I hope it's the girl because more food means more strength.

But instead of the girl's light tread, or the dogged shuffling of the older woman, I hear crisp, purposeful boot steps striding toward my cell.

The Commander.

The next confrontation is upon me, and I need two things from it—information and a reprieve from further injury. I flip around to put my injured rib against the wall, out of reach of the Commander's boot, and begin planning as he orders a guard to open my cell door.

He enters my cell, his scar catching and releasing the flickering torchlight like some macabre game of cat and mouse. I pretend I can barely lift my head to see him. I've been pretending this sort of weakness since I woke up cured of my fever, so if he's had me watched, this won't raise any alarms.

He laughs, a vulgar, ugly sound full of arrogance. "Look at you." In three long steps, he's at my side. "What a pathetic excuse for a man."

I let my head roll to the side a bit and peer up at him.

"I leave you alone in this dungeon for a week. The great inventor Logan McEntire. The man who always has a plan." His boot lashes out, connects with my shoulder, and sends me sprawling onto the cell floor.

It hurts, but not nearly as much as I pretend it does. He needs to feel I'm already beaten, or he'll never give me what I need.

"And here you sit. Still locked up. Still unable to make good on your promises." His smile is vicious as he plants his boot on the throbbing burned skin of my neck and leans down.

I don't have to fake the pain this time. Waves of agony roll along my jaw and send dazzling lights exploding through my brain.

"You haven't beaten her," I say, pushing the words through teeth clenched tight against the raw, unending anguish eating at me.

He leans closer, grinding his boot into my neck. "What did you say to me, you worthless cur?"

"Rachel. You haven't beaten her." I draw in a shaky breath, tasting the leather and steel of his boot on the dungeon's fetid air. "She's stronger than you think."

"She's a girl alone in the Wasteland with a man who is both stronger than her and has more motivation to do as he's told."

His voice oozes his special brand of pride—two parts power, one part blind ego.

Perfect.

"She can take him. She's smarter than you give her credit for."

He snorts, but I can almost hear the doubt slipping in.

"You won't know if you're right until it's too late to make adjustments," I say.

"You'd like me to think that. But when Melkin sends the signal, inventor, you can bet your life he'll be alone." He laughs again. "And you are betting your life, aren't you? Because the second I have what I want, you're dead."

He isn't going to tell me what I need to know. He's too smart for that. I either need to find another source of information, or wing it once I get out into the Wasteland.

He stands abruptly, his boot sliding across my burned skin like a dozen razors. I breathe heavily, trying to control the waves of pain wracking me, and see Eloise staring at me with horror on her face.

Which is interesting.

She doesn't want me hurt. Because she can't stand to see another suffer? Or because she somehow thinks I can stop her husband from becoming a killer?

If I can't get the Commander to give me what I need, maybe I can force him to convince Eloise to do so instead.

"When the signal comes, I'd look long and hard at whoever sent it." I curl up on the floor in case he decides to kick any of my vital organs. "Because I'll happily bet my life that Rachel will kill Melkin when he attacks her."

"She's a girl." The Commander's voice is dismissive as he walks toward my cell door.

Time to play the big card. The one I hope will scare Eloise into spilling her guts.

"Every other girl in the city was raised with dolls and tea sets and proper etiquette. Rachel was sword fighting, clubbing our practice dummy, and learning how to eviscerate a man at close range with her knife."

Eloise worries her blanket with nervous fingers.

"Melkin won't even know what hit him. You've sent the man to his death."

The Commander shakes his head and walks out of my cell. "Do you really think I care which of them makes it back alive as long as I get what I want?"

The cell door slams shut. "Next time I see you, inventor, it will be at your execution." He leaves, taking his guards with him, and the silence in his wake is punctuated by sharp, gut-wrenching sobs from Eloise.

I wait, willing her to look at me, and finally get my wish. My voice is a thin whisper of sound as I say, "I can stop her. I can get to them in time."

She frowns but inches closer to the bars on her door. "How? I thought you could get out somehow. The girl said you could. But you haven't. You just lie there." Her voice is a faint breath of sound nearly lost beneath the sizzle of the torches lining the corridor. I have to hope the snapping flames and heavy stone walls are enough to keep the other prisoners from overhearing this.

I sit up and face her, careful not to look like I can move with ease. "Of course I haven't made it look like I'm anything but badly injured. You think they need that information?"

She chews her lower lip.

"I'm telling the truth about Rachel. She's a fierce warrior. And she went out there already angry and hoping for blood. Melkin isn't coming back unless I get out in time."

"Then *leave*."

"I will. But I need one more piece of information first. A piece I hope you have for me."

"What is it?"

There's no resistance in her tone. She believes me. Believes I can save her husband from becoming a killer, or worse, getting killed himself. I dislike the sudden weight of responsibility I feel in the face of her trust.

"I need to know the signal Melkin is supposed to give the Commander when he returns."

A frown puckers her face. "Why do you need to know that? Melkin will give the signal."

"Things happen in the Wasteland. It's a dangerous place. I give you my word I will do all I can to save both Melkin and Rachel, but if I fail, don't you want me to have the means to draw the Commander out of the city so I can deliver the justice he deserves?"

"I don't know."

"He said it himself. He doesn't care which of them comes back alive as long as he gets what he wants."

"If Melkin . . . if you're too late, why would you ever come back here?"

"Because Rachel and I aren't leaving you here. Any of you." The words roll easily off my tongue, and I wonder how long they've been breeding in the back of my mind. Probably from the moment I saw life leave my mother's eyes at the whim of our leader. I can't stomach the thought of one more innocent victim crushed beneath the bloody boot of Baalboden. "It's time for change, and we're going to deliver it."

She's silent for a moment, her hands tearing at the blanket, and then says, "He's to light a torch in the eastern oak at daybreak."

The eastern oak is a mammoth tree marking the edge between Baalboden's perimeter and the Wasteland, in direct line of sight of the far eastern turret, on the opposite side of the gate. I give the Commander credit for coming up with a signal I wouldn't have guessed on my best day, and nod to Eloise.

"I'll do my best to reach them in time, but either way, I'll come back for you."

Then I wait until snores tell me the other prisoners are all asleep before struggling to my feet for the first time in a week.

Tearing my shirt into a long strip of fabric, I wrap my chest tightly and drizzle a pinch of medicine on my tongue. I need to be able to run and fight without the interference of pain. I have the information I need, and if any guard happens to be watching, the Commander could right now be learning of my lengthy conversation with Eloise.

It's time to escape.

CHAPTER FORTY-TWO

RACHEL

While the Cursed One laid waste to every densely populated area across the land, many of the individual houses built far outside a city's limits were left standing. Some of those houses are uninhabitable due to time, weather, and neglect. But some are still safe enough to use as stopping points along our journey through the Wasteland. Every courier has found his own safe houses, stocked them with supplies, and hopes the outside still looks rundown enough to avoid catching the interest of a passing band of highwaymen.

We reach Dad's first safe house as dusk is falling. The itch on the back of my neck warning me we're being followed hasn't abated, though Melkin insists he senses nothing.

I'm not sure Melkin's mind is on the matter at hand, though, so I don't trust his instincts. He's been unapproachable since lunch, and I can't read his expression. However, he does take me seriously enough to keep his knife unsheathed for the rest of the journey.

The safe house is a two-story brick house with a wide, wrap-around porch and a line of stately columns across the front that used to be white until a century of sun faded them into something that resembles grayish clay. Ivy clings to the bricks, wraps itself around windows, and hangs down from the roof like glossy green drapes.

The front yard may have been a perfectly manicured gem once upon a time, but now the grass stretches past my thighs, wild and thick, and the trees behind the house creep closer with every passing year. Still, the house's location affords decent visibility for the entire circumference of the structure, a quality Dad insisted on in a safe house.

The wires on my arm cuff glow without flickering now, though the light is faint enough that I doubt he's still here. I don't care. It's enough to keep the wild, restless hope within me alive.

"This where he hid the package?"

"No."

"Then why're we stopping?"

I brush past him and mount the sagging front steps, making sure to skip the second from the top, where the wood is rotted to the consistency of fig pudding. "Because it's almost dark. And someone is following us. I want the protection of four walls around me."

Plus Dad might have left another sign for me inside.

Besides, Melkin looks wound tight enough to snap. He needs a break from fireside watches too.

A large padlock with a keypad on the front—another of Logan's inventions—bars the door. Dad made sure both Logan and I knew the codes to each of his safe houses. I type in the code, blocking the keypad from Melkin's view as he carefully climbs the steps behind me, and the lock opens with the barely audible snick of metal releasing metal.

The air inside is musty and heavy with mildew, and dust lies across every visible surface like a layer of gray snow. I move past the entryway and see it—footprints, faint outlines coated with less dust than the rest of the house.

He was here.

The hope inside me burns so fiercely I'm almost afraid to touch it.

Melkin shuts the door behind him, slides the bolt into place, and turns. His knife is still out.

"You can put that away now."

"What if someone's already using this place? I don't figure on surprising anyone unless I've got a weapon in my hand."

"If someone was here, they'd leave footprints in all this dust. See?" I point to the fading steps left sometime in the last few months by Dad.

Melkin grunts, but keeps his knife out as he moves further into the house, taking in the faded floral wallpaper with clusters of black mold spreading along the ceiling and the once-blue couch that has since become a muted gray. "Not if they came in through a window."

All the windows are sealed shut. Dad saw to that when he first chose this house. I don't bother telling Melkin, however. He needs to feel like he's done all he can to secure our safety, so I let him prowl the house, beating at curtains and checking under furniture until he looks every bit as grimy as the house itself.

I leave him to it and move carefully along the floor-to-ceiling windows lining the front of the house, keeping far enough back from the gauzy yellowed drapes that no one approaching the edge of the property can see me.

Someone is out there. I can't see them yet, and they might be expert enough to stay just out of range, but I know we're being followed.

The question is, by whom?

Someone who knew to pick up our trail on the road to Rowansmark? It could be guards assigned to follow us, which would mean the Commander intends to break his word much earlier than I'd assumed. Highwaymen who think they've spotted easy prey? That would be the last mistake they ever made. Trackers from Rowansmark tasked to keep watch over the paths couriers take in case one of them leads straight to the package?

That's a risk I can't afford to take.

We'll have to either flush our followers out into the open, or circle behind them and spring a trap. Which means Melkin is going to have to pull it together and help me.

"You're sure it isn't hidden here?" he asks directly behind me, and I whirl around, my hand reaching for my knife before sense overrides my instinctive panic.

"Sneak up behind me again, and I'll gut you like a sheep."

His eyes, black pits of something that looks like bitterness, capture mine. "Are you sure it isn't hidden here?"

"Yes. It's near the next safe house."

"He could've moved it."

"Really? With the Commander and Rowansmark already combing the Wasteland for him and for the package? He knew when he left Baalboden for the last time that he would be followed. He's too smart to lead them right to it."

He nods, a sharp movement that severs whatever line of tension he's been teetering on since lunch, and sheaths his knife. In his other hand, he holds a scrap of yellow.

"Found this tied around the doorknob in the kitchen."

It's another of my mother's ribbons. I take it from him, rub my fingers over the embroidered *S. A.* at the end, and tuck it into the same pocket that houses the purple one. I don't need the signs to know I'm closing in—Logan's tracker sees to that— but having this tangible connection to Dad soothes some of the ache within me. Having Logan by my side would go a long way toward soothing the rest.

"I saw our followers. Come up to the attic, and you can see them too. Mind the stairs, though. Half of them are rotted through."

I follow him, skirting spots of obvious rot and doing my best not to rub up against too much dust. The attic is a stale, cluttered box of a room with two grimy windows, one at each end. We head for the front window, and I scan the grass, raise my eyes to the tree line, and find them in less than a minute.

Standing two trees in, watching the front door, and moving restlessly beneath the fading rays of the early evening sun.

Amateurs.

Which means they're guards. Highwaymen and trackers are far too experienced to be so obvious. I say as much to Melkin.

"I thought the same. Can't figure why the Commander thinks we need extra protection."

"Please tell me you aren't that stupid."

He frowns at me.

"They aren't here for our protection, Melkin. If they were, they would've traveled with us from the start. They're here to pounce once we have the package."

"But we're going to bring it back. We have to. I'm not going to lose Eloise. You said you thought if I did what he asked, he'd keep his word."

I lied. But looking into the misery on his face, I can't find the cruelty to give him the truth. "Maybe they're insurance in case we decide we want whatever's in the package more than we want Eloise and Logan's safety."

"There's nothing more important than her safety."

"To *you*. But the Commander doesn't place the same value on human life as you do."

We're silent for a moment, staring at the two guards as the day subsides and the first stars of the night glitter like shards of silver in the darkening sky.

"What if they want the package for themselves?" he asks, the darkness he harbored earlier back in his voice.

"Then they'll try to kill us once we find it."

"Not if we kill them first."

Crimson. Sliding down silver blades. Covering me in guilt that won't ever wash clean.

I shake the morbid thoughts away. It's ridiculous to think I'd feel guilty shedding the blood of a guard. Especially one who is here with the express purpose of shedding mine.

But if I do this—if I deliberately ambush and kill without provocation—will I lose something I need? Something that keeps me from becoming like the Commander? Will it harden me toward violence the way repeatedly holding my knife builds calluses into the skin of my palm?

Or will it strengthen me into the kind of weapon I need to be to bring the Commander down?

"I'll go out the back and circle around. I've already checked through the window at the opposite end. There's no one watching us from behind. Give me at least an hour to work my way to them without being noticed. Then sneak out of the house as if you're going looking for the package. While they're focused on you, I'll kill them."

His voice is cold, empty, and more than a little scary. Gone is the courteous, understanding Melkin I've been traveling with for a week. In his place stands a fierce predator willing to do whatever he must to obliterate anyone who stands between him and Eloise.

I wonder if I'm catching a glimpse of who I'm becoming as well.

Banishing that unwelcome thought before it can take root, I nod my acceptance of his plan and follow him back downstairs. He leaves out the back door, and I mark time by lighting candles in the kitchen and assembling dinner from the supplies Dad keeps here. I eat my fill, leave plenty on the table for Melkin, and pack a spare travel sack with food supplies from the cupboards.

My hour is up. Checking that my knife slides easily from its sheath, I light a small torch, the better to make myself seen, and open the front door. The loamy scent of the sun-warmed ground is fading into the crisp chill of night. I creep along the length of the porch, peering beneath the boards as if I expect to find something.

My skin prickles with awareness. I'm being watched.

Which is exactly the point of this entire charade, but it doesn't make me feel any better.

When Melkin doesn't appear within the first few minutes, I leave the porch and wander to the side, still in full view of the guards at the tree line. I feel exposed with my brilliant little torch ablaze amidst the overgrown grass and the distant icy stars. The tingle of awareness becomes a full-fledged, adrenalin-fueled need to draw a weapon and be ready for anything.

I don't ignore it.

Instead, I drop down, shove the lit end of the torch deep into the soft soil at my feet to extinguish it, and run as silently as I can away from the spot where I was last seen. In seconds, I hear someone crashing through the grass behind me.

I dodge to my left, drop to a crouch, and freeze. The darkness will cover me. The person following me doesn't have a NightSeer mask, or I'd see its green glow.

He also doesn't have the sense to stop moving once he no longer hears me. Soft footsteps creep toward the spot I just vacated. I slide my knife free without a sound, and ready myself.

The fear I felt earlier at the thought of shedding someone's blood without giving them fair notice is gone. In its place is cold determination.

I'm not going to die. Not until the Commander lies in a pool of his own blood at my feet.

My pursuer is close enough that I can hear him breathe now, rough, uneven pants that speak of someone without the proper training to control his breathing when it matters most. I wait until he's a mere three yards from me, and tense for my attack.

A hand snakes out from behind me and wraps around my mouth while a second hand grabs my knife hand before I can swing it back.

"Wait," Melkin breathes against my ear, and I hold still.

My follower moves forward, making enough noise to announce his presence to any but an inexperienced fool, but I trust Melkin and wait.

By the time the man moves out of range, my muscles are stiff, and I can't feel my lower legs. I turn to look at Melkin, his gaunt frame a black smudge against the starry sky.

"Who?" My voice is little more than a whisper.

"Rowansmark tracker."

That doesn't make sense. Any tracker worth his weight would've been on me before I ever knew what hit me. And if by some chance I managed to elude him, he wouldn't have chased me in such a noisy, clumsy fashion.

"Are you sure?"

"Yes. He killed the guards before I got there. Saw his handi-work. He's an expert."

"Then why act like an amateur?"

He looks at me, and the answer hits me. Because the tracker didn't want to kill me. He wanted to flush me out so he could capture me and force me to reveal the location of the package to him. The realization adds fuel to the adrenalin already pounding through me. The cruelty of Rowansmark trackers is legendary. Some say they carve off pieces of their victims and feed it to the vultures bit by bit while the person bleeds and begs. Some say they know how to kill their victims with a single, deadly touch.

On our second-to-last trip to Rowansmark, we entered the

city through an aisle of half-rotted human heads skewered on stakes. Five on one side. Six on another. An entire band of highwaymen who'd had the stupidity to try cheating Rowansmark merchants out of their coin.

What would a tracker do to me to get the location of the package stolen from his leader? My skin is icy as I turn to Melkin.

"We need to leave."

Melkin nods, and together we slowly circle back to the house. I crouch in the shadow of a tree, my knife ready, while Melkin slips inside and snatches up my pack, my Switch, and the bag of food supplies. When he returns, we melt silently into the tree line behind the house and make our way south, our weapons out, our ears straining to catch the sound of pursuit.

CHAPTER
FORTY-THREE

<u>LOGAN</u>

I pace my cell, willing the blood to flow into my legs fast enough for me to leave before a guard decides to investigate my conversation with Eloise. The dungeon is full of the sounds of dripping water and heavy sleep. I'm chilled without my shirt, but I can't yet put on my cloak.

I need to dismantle it first.

My legs still tingle, but they'll hold me when I need to run. Approaching the far right corner of my cell, the one with the draft seeping in through the cracks, I run my fingers along the damp, craggy stone, judging distances and looking for a weakness I'm not convinced is there.

It doesn't matter. I'm about to obliterate the whole thing, weakness or not.

Turning to my cloak, I remove the five buttons lining the front flap. They come loose with a soft pop and reveal the plain steel fastenings underneath. Ignoring those, I flip the face of the buttons over and smile. The back of each holds one of my most destructive inventions to date—the gears of an ancient pocket watch attached to two tiny vials of liquid. One holds acid. The other holds glycerin. All my experiments have proven the combination to be explosive.

I hope it's enough to turn the back half of my cell into rubble.

I slide my fingers along the bottom of my coat until I feel a tiny knot of thread. Pulling on it, I rip out the extra seam I painstakingly installed just days before the Claiming ceremony and remove a length of wire already spliced into five pieces at one end. Finally, I sit down, tug my left boot free, jiggle the sole until it comes loose, and remove a tiny, copper-sheathed detonator.

The buttons attach to the wall with ease, the same gluey substance that stuck them to the plain steel fastenings on my cloak easily clinging to the wall like a second skin. I carefully wrap the loose wire ends around the central gear in each button, and then back away to the cell door, taking the thin straw palette of a bed with me.

Pulling my cloak over my shoulders, I fasten the toggles, flip the hood over my head, and crouch beneath the palette, my back to the wall. With steady fingers, I wrap the other end of the wire around the coils on the detonator and take a deep breath.

Time to show the Commander which of us can truly outwit the other.

I press the trigger on the detonator and hear a faint clicking sound as the pocket watch gears engage and set the vials on a collision course with each other. Then the entire dungeon shakes with the force of the explosion at my back.

I don't give the debris time to stop falling. I can't. The main door at the end of the row is already opening, and a guard is shouting an alarm. Keeping the palette over my head to protect myself from the worst of it, I stand and face the destruction of my cell.

The back corner is nothing but crumbled bits of stone and dust. A slippery pile of dirt is sliding in through the hole, but above that pile, the night sky beckons. I race forward, scramble over the debris, and dive through the hole as someone rattles a key in the door of my cell.

The straw palette wedges against the opening as I go through it, and I push as much dirt as possible against the back side of the hole while climbing my way toward level ground.

From the main compound, an alarm bell peals, disturbing the darkness with its insistent clamor. I scan my surroundings, take in the distance between me and the iron fence surrounding the compound, and start running.

I'm still ten yards from the fence when someone shouts behind me. I don't bother looking. It would just slow me down. Instead, I reach inside my inner cloak pocket and remove what look like two slightly thick Baalboden coins. A quick toggle of the tiny switch embedded in the ridges of the coins releases the spring-loaded mechanism inside, and they become a smaller version of the handgrips Rachel tried to use on her disastrous escape attempt.

More shouts echo across the yard, and I catch guards with NightSeer masks running along the fence line, primed to intersect with me if it takes me longer than twenty seconds to scale the iron poles.

I lunge forward, slam my hands onto the metal, feel the magnets latch onto the iron like they're soldered to it, and start climbing.

My rib screams at me, even through the pain medicine I took, but I ignore it. I won't get a second chance at this, and I refuse to fail.

The top seems impossibly high, and my arms tremble with the effort of ignoring the weakness on my right side, but I reach it just as the guards converge below me. One grabs at my foot, but I slam my boot into his forehead, wrap my hands around the top of the fence, and vault over to the other side.

I don't wait to see who's following me.

The compound is located in the eastern quarter of the city. I turn north and run, hoping the guards take note of my direction and report it back to the Commander. Let him fortify the North Wall. Let him comb the city streets. I won't be there.

Once I'm sure I'm out of sight, I change my trajectory and head southwest, trusting the magnetic field of my hand grips to block my wristmark from any Identidiscs being used to find me.

The only way out of the city is over the Wall or through the gate. Over the past week, thanks to Rachel's prodding, I've spent an inordinate amount of time thinking of another way to escape.

Most of the ideas I came up with had one fatal flaw: They were obvious choices, and the Commander isn't a fool. I discarded them all and decided the perfect solution is the one no one would be crazy enough to try. The one that could end with me accidentally calling the Cursed One to devour me in a single, fiery gulp.

I'm going out under the Wall.

I enter North Hub, avoiding the street torches by using backyards and alleys, and circle Center Square in favor of moving west. When I've gone far enough to be sure I won't be seen by any upstanding citizens, I cut south and hurry toward Lower Market.

I'm sure the travel bag I left behind in Center Square is long gone. I'm equally sure the bag I always keep at Oliver's has been confiscated too. If the Commander thinks he's backed me into a corner where my only two choices are heading home for more supplies or hitting up merchants who've undoubtedly been warned that the penalty for doing business with me is death, he's wrong.

I have Rachel to thank for it. When I chased her to the Wall, I went through the alley between the armory and the deserted building at the base of Lower Market, and realized it was the perfect place to hide a backup escape plan. No one ever goes into the abandoned building. And as I have no ties to the place, the Commander would never suspect it as a base of operations for me.

It takes me nearly an hour to reach it. I stick to the shadows, sometimes sacrificing speed for stealth, but I never see any signs of pursuit. Either the bulk of the guards are converging on the North Wall, or the guards in the western edge of the city have the brains to keep silent about their search.

It doesn't matter which is true. All that matters is that I've reached the building. I duck inside and use the faint moonlight streaming in through a broken window to sort through my stash.

Tossing the handgrips into my pack, I don a new tunic and pants and hastily chew on some mutton jerky to replenish my flagging strength. The leather of my cloak chafes the burn on my neck, so I take a minute to snatch salve and gauze from my first aid kit and secure a bandage in place. Then I strap on a sword, slide a sheathed dagger into my boot, wrap my cloak around myself again, and pick up my travel pack, ignoring the way my rib aches against the weight.

The distance between the building and the Wall is relatively short, but it takes me nearly twenty minutes because I'm constantly checking for guards. I aim for the curve of the Wall nearly at the halfway point between the two closest turrets. When another scan of my surroundings shows no glowing NightSeer masks, I drop to my knees at the base of the Wall, open my pack, slide on a mask to protect my eyes and filter the air I breathe, tug on a pair of heavy leather gloves, and remove a machine that looks like a metal crossbow with a thick spiral-shaped steel drill jutting out the front. Fastening my pack to my back securely, I slide my arms into the straps for the device, secure another strap around my waist, and flip the switch on the battery pack I built beneath the spiral drill. It comes to life with a muted whine.

Bending forward, I apply the spinning metal drill to the ground at the base of the Wall and it chews through the dirt, flinging debris to the sides. The vibrations send sharp jabs of agony into my ribcage, and I have to constantly remind myself to breathe through the pain. When the hole is large enough to accommodate me, I slide forward and switch my goggles to NightSeer, trusting the green glow to illuminate my path even as I quickly calculate angles, trajectory, and all the possibilities for failure.

Except that failure isn't a possibility.

Not when so many depend on me.

The drill eats through the ground, and I aim deep. Deep

enough to bypass the Wall's foundations. Deep enough to avoid causing any trembles through the tons of stone and steel resting above me. Deep enough that calling the Cursed One is a real possibility.

My mask lights the dirt around me a few measly feet at a time, and the air feels damp and cloying as it brushes against my skin. Every breath ignites a fierce agony around my broken rib as if I never took any pain medicine. The need for space crushes me, whispering that I'll go crazy if I don't get back into the open *now*.

I ignore it. Mind over matter. I have plenty of other things to think about. There are math equations to solve. Minute adjustments to make. And beneath it all, a terrible grief for Oliver mixes with a desperate worry for Rachel until I can hardly tell the difference between the two.

I will not be too late.

I will *not*.

When I calculate that I've traveled well beyond the width of the Wall, I begin slowly tunneling my way back to the surface, making sure to continue my trajectory until I'm beyond the circumference of Baalboden's perimeter. I break the surface with caution, instantly shutting off the machine so I can listen for threats.

I've come up between two ancient pin oaks. Keeping my NightSeer mask on, I scan the area. I'm far enough into the Wasteland that Baalboden is a distant, looming bulk on the eastern horizon. The western Wall appears quiet.

Best Case Scenario: No one discovers my true escape point until daylight.

Worst Case Scenario: The Commander realizes my flight north was a false trail and orders a search of the entire Wall.

The answer to both is the same: Run.

I close the machine, slip off the mask because I'd rather let my eyes adjust to the dark than announce my presence to others with the mask's glow, and pack them both away. Then I slide a copper cuff from my bag, the gears on it lined with the same blue wire I used for Rachel's, and pull it over my arm.

The wires glow faintly, but they'll light up like a torch the closer I get to her. By my best guess, she should still have a week's worth of travel before she hits Jared's Rowansmark safe house. I take a moment to mentally review the map Jared once had me commit to memory for the day when the Commander would allow me to leave Baalboden on my first courier mission. If I push myself, using dangerous shortcuts Jared would never have used while on a journey with Rachel, I can cut the distance between us in half in just four days. Three if I don't sleep much.

I have to hope Melkin didn't want to risk bringing Rachel through highwaymen-infested trails either. If Rachel was spotted, she and Melkin would be viciously attacked within hours. Melkin would never make it out alive, and Rachel would wish she'd died too.

Shoving that thought aside before it takes root, I settle my pack between my shoulders and brace my arm against my aching side. Then I turn my face to the south and disappear into the Wasteland.

CHAPTER
FORTY-FOUR

RACHEL

We've barely slept in the five days since we left the first safe house. The maples have turned back into oaks, and huge gnarled roots rip their way through the moss-covered ground. Traveling by day and catching naps at night while one of us remains alert for the presence of the Rowansmark tracker, we run ourselves ragged.

Melkin feels it more than I do. Lines of strain take up permanent residence on his face, digging bitter furrows across his brow. I think he worries someone will destroy his plan to return the package and ransom his wife. I can't be sure because he'll barely speak to me. The closer we come to the second safe house, the more he shuts down.

It doesn't matter. The wires on my arm cuff are glowing brighter with each passing day. Soon, it will be over. Soon, I'll find Dad, and we'll go rescue Logan.

We're less than a full day's journey from the safe house when I sense we're no longer alone. Melkin is ahead of me, using his staff to brush aside the moss that drapes across the branches around us like ribbon. I slow as if examining a mark on the ground, and whirl around, expecting to see a Rowansmark tracker.

An olive-skinned face stares at me from a branch in a tree I passed not thirty seconds ago. We lock eyes, blink, and in a flash of black hair and graceful limbs, she's gone.

It was a girl. I'm sure of it. Which means she isn't a tracker, a guard, or a member of a highwaymen gang. She must be Tree People.

I'm not threatened by her presence—it's natural for Tree People to be curious about the outsiders wandering through their area of the Wasteland—but there aren't any Tree People villages in these parts except for the one near the second safe house, and that's still hours away. It's unusual to see a Tree Girl so far from home. I file it away for further thought if necessary, and forget about her until we stop for lunch two hours later and I see her again.

This time, she doesn't pull back when I catch a glimpse of her peering out at me from the branches of a tree several yards back from where we sit. Instead, we stare at each other as I let my cloak hood drop, and she leans out of her tree enough for me to see we're about the same age. A quiver of arrows is slung over one shoulder, and she holds the bow in one hand. A long black feather dangles from an intricately swirled silver ear cuff wrapped around her left ear. Her dark eyes are full of aloof confidence.

I can't explain her, and I don't like what I can't explain. She shouldn't still be following us. I'm about to draw Melkin's attention to her when she pulls back into the tree and disappears.

I watch for her as I finish a cold lunch of turkey leftovers and the potted plums I took with us from the first safe house. Watch for her as Melkin barks at me to keep up. And watch for her as the shadows slowly lengthen into pools of darkness beneath the dying sun.

She never reappears.

Instead, the blue wires glow brightly, and I forget to be concerned about the insignificant wanderings of a Tree Girl. It will hurt to tell Dad about Oliver. It will also hurt to tell him I had to leave Logan behind, but Dad will know how to fix it.

I still haven't told Melkin we're about to find Dad. Five days ago, I would have. Five days ago, he seemed approachable, concerned only with saving his wife, and determined to protect me.

Now, he's a cold, silent ghost of the man I thought I knew. The closer we come to the package, the more he turns inward, until I catch myself shivering a little when he turns the miserable darkness of his eyes toward me.

Maybe he's finally realizing the Commander isn't a man of his word. Maybe he's beginning to understand that if we give our only leverage over to him, those we love are dead.

Maybe he's bracing himself for the worst.

We emerge from the forest, and I recognize the line of ancient oaks, their trunks as thick as one of the steel beams supporting Baalboden's Wall, their branches arching over a moss-covered path as if offering protection.

We're almost there.

I push ahead of Melkin, who offers no protest. The column of trees seems to go on forever as I hurry forward.

Almost there.

The cuff against my arm glows like the noonday sun.

Almost there.

At the end of the row of trees, a graying one-story farmhouse with once-red shutters faded to pink will be standing, and he'll be waiting. His big arms will open wide, his gray eyes will glow with pride, and I'll be home at last.

I skid on the moss as I reach the last tree, and grab on to the trunk for balance. And then I hang on to the trunk for one long desperate second, fighting vertigo as my eyes take in the impossible.

The farmhouse is gone.

Nothing remains but a sweeping patch of scorched dirt and a gaping hole where the Cursed One slid back to his lair.

I look around wildly, searching. My cuff is lit up like a torch. He's here.

He's *here.*

But he isn't. I can't see him. All I see is destruction.

"Oh," Melkin says behind me as he takes in the sight.

That tiny little word makes me want to hurt him, so I leave the shelter of the trees and walk toward the debris on shaking legs.

My cuff still glows. I scan the treetops. He could be there. Waiting for me. Staying hidden from trackers.

The soil beneath me turns to ash. Cold black flakes that cling to my boots as if trying to hold me back.

Where is he?

Something moves in the trees across from me, and the Tree Girl steps out, followed by a boy who looks about Logan's age. Both of them have dusky skin and straight black hair. The girl wears hers in a long braid. The boy lets his fall loose to his shoulders. He moves, and my eyes are drawn to a white paper-wrapped package the size of a raisin loaf in his hands.

"Who are they?" Melkin whispers.

"Rachel Adams?" The boy's dark brown eyes lock onto mine, making my stomach clench. There's sympathy in his gaze. I don't want sympathy.

I just want Dad.

"Yes." My voice is nothing but a wisp. The breeze snatches it and whisks it away. I try again. "Yes."

The girl beckons me, her slim hand waving me toward her.

Maybe Dad is with them. Hiding in their village. Staying off the usual path of trackers and couriers. Maybe that's why she followed us earlier. Maybe he sent her to watch for me, knowing one day I'd come.

My boots grind the sooty embers beneath me to dust as I cross the scorched ground. The foundation of the house is still there, buried beneath the ash, a jumbled mound of broken concrete I have to climb up and over. My feet skid as I reach the top, sending me sliding down the other side. When I reach the bottom, I look up at the Tree People, but stop when I catch sight of something else.

Just beyond the edge of the destruction, where the ash bleeds gently into soil again, a soft swell in the ground is marked by a small wooden cross painted white.

I can't breathe. My ears roar, and someone says something, but I can't understand the words because I'm walking toward the grave and the wires on my cuff are glowing like brilliant blue stars.

The boy steps to the side of the grave, and holds out his hand to me. I take it without thinking, but I can't feel him. I can't even feel myself, and I don't want to. Let this be some other girl standing here, holding a stranger's hand while the rest of her world comes crumbling down.

Please.

"He died a hero, Rachel. The Cursed One would've killed my sister and me, but he led it away from us. He saved our lives." His voice catches as if he's struggling with tears. "I'm sorry."

I pull my hand free. The cross is beautifully carved and someone has painted the words *Jared Adams* in the center.

Grief is a yawning pit of darkness blooming at my core. I can hardly stand beneath its weight. The sharp edges of Oliver's death collide with the unthinkable sight before me, and something inside me shatters as I fall to my knees.

I can't bear this. I can't.

The hope that blazed within me floats like ash into the darkness.

He's here, but not here.

I want to die too. Just stop breathing and hope I find him on the other side.

He's not here.

I sink down to lie on top of the dirt.

He's nowhere.

I'm bleeding inside where no one will see. Where no one will ever know to look.

He's gone.

He's *gone*.

CHAPTER
FORTY-FIVE

LOGAN

I reach the first safe house in just over three days.

I'm cutting through known highwaymen territory, running on adrenalin rather than sleep. My entire body feels battered, and my rib throbs incessantly no matter how tightly I wrap it. Every few miles, I have to stop, drag in some much needed deep breaths, and focus on getting the pain under control so I can continue. Twice, I've slept for a handful of hours, only to wake on the heels of terrifying dreams with a sense of dread churning through my system.

The pain refuses to relinquish its hold on me even during sleep, but I can't afford to give in to it. Guards will be on my trail. Maybe trackers as well, if any of them have returned to Baalboden since I left. The Commander won't sit idly by and wait for Melkin to succeed. He'll have an insurance policy in the works.

I just have to stay one step ahead.

I skirt the safe house, an ivy-covered once-white structure, and search for signs of life before leaving the cover of the trees. I don't find life, but death is waiting for me near the edge of the property. Two guards lie on the ground, the bones of their faces nearly picked clean by scavengers but the mark of Baalboden still clear on their uniforms. A small puncture wound rests over their hearts.

They were murdered efficiently, and the ramifications chill me to the core. A professional did this. Someone who knew how to kill with neat, deadly precision.

This isn't Melkin's handiwork. He's a tracker, but, as Eloise so desperately pointed out, he isn't a killer. He wouldn't know how to drop a man before he had a chance to see death approach.

It isn't Rachel's handiwork either. I'm not sure if she's become a killer yet. But rage fuels her and these kills contain less emotion than the soil on which the men fell.

Someone else is tracking the package. Closing in on Rachel and Melkin. Once he reaches his objective, their lives won't be worth more than those of the two poor souls lying at my feet.

Panic eats at me when I consider the possibility that the tracker has already found Rachel and Melkin, and their bodies wait somewhere on the forest floor for me to stumble upon as well.

Scrapping my plan to take a few hours of rest, I approach the house and type in the code for the padlock. Just inside the door, recent footsteps mar the dust. I bend to examine them. One of the boot prints is Rachel's. One is large enough to be Melkin's. And one, already coated in a thin sheen of dust, is Jared's. If Jared was here within the last few weeks, it's possible he's waiting for Rachel at the second safe house. If so, he'll protect her from

Melkin until I get there.

The possibility is real, but the weight of responsibility refuses to lift from my shoulders. I can't put any hope in possibilities. I have to contend with reality, and the reality is that even if Melkin doesn't try to kill Rachel, they have an assassin on their trail, and he won't hesitate to murder them both once they have the package.

As I leave the footsteps behind and enter the kitchen to restock on fuel and food, fear wraps itself around me, whispering terrible things.

You're too late.

Rachel can't beat an assassin. He'll stab her through the heart and leave her like she's nothing. Less than nothing.

Unless Melkin kills her first.

You've lost all the family you ever had because you're too late.

Too late.

The kitchen is a mess. Supplies are ripped out of cupboards and strewn across grimy countertops. The remains of a mostly uneaten dinner lie on the kitchen table. Fear sinks into my heart and refuses to let go.

They left in a hurry. They left on the run.

I have to believe they've continued to outwit the assassin on their trail. Any other thought threatens to compromise my ability to plan ahead. Forcing the fear into a distant corner of my mind, I rewrap my ribcage and stuff additional supplies in my pack.

I need to rest, but I can't. Every second I lose is another second Rachel comes closer to death.

Instead, I quickly eat a decent meal, drink my fill of water, and swallow a small pinch of pain medicine. Locking the house behind me, I head south again, looking closely for a sign of someone following Melkin and Rachel.

It takes nearly four hours to find it, but I do. Near a small clearing where they stopped to eat, a man hunched down behind the thick cover of a flowering azalea bush. His boots dug into the dirt in a way that suggests he was leaning forward on his toes. I can't distinguish enough of the sole to judge his height and weight, but the maker's mark on the tip of his boot tells me one very important fact.

He's from Rowansmark.

Once Rachel retrieves the package, she's dead. If Melkin fails to kill her, this man will.

My body screams for rest. My head feels heavy and off-kilter. I draw in a deep breath, brace myself for the pain, and start running.

Mind over matter.

I can't afford to let my body rule me now. I have an assassin to kill.

CHAPTER FORTY-SIX

RACHEL

Voices float above me as I lie on the cold, unyielding ground. I imagine sinking below it. Letting it take me under.

Finding peace.

The piercing pain of loss is a double-edged blade I can't bear to touch. How can I grieve for him? Cry for him? Bleed for him inside when it won't change anything?

It won't change anything.

He's *gone*.

All the words I never found time to say. All the things we never found time to do. Ripped from me with merciless finality.

Gone.

But I'm not gone. I'm still here—miles from home, surrounded by scorched earth and strangers, facedown on my father's grave.

Here.

Somewhere inside me, I hear an anguished wailing—the

wordless keening of unbearable grief. I can't stand to hear it. To feel it. To let it live.

A yawning darkness within me opens wide, whispering promises to take the pain. Swallow the loss. Make it possible to draw a breath without choking on the shattered pieces no one will ever fix.

I dig my fingers into his grave and flinch as the images of Dad and Oliver sear themselves into my brain. I will choke on this grief. Lie here impotent, unable to avenge them. Loss is a gaping hole with jagged teeth, and I can't *bear* it.

I push the images away, scramble back from the edge of that gaping hole, and let the darkness within me swallow it all. The wail of grief inside me slowly subsides into a well of icy silence—deafening and absolute. The silence rips me in two, cutting me off from everything I can't stand to face. I don't try to stop it. If I feel the loss, it will break me.

And I can't break until the Commander is dead.

Because Dad's gone. And I'm still here.

And before I follow him, I have a debt to pay.

My fingers clench into fists, my nails breaking as I shove them through hard-packed dirt. Fury is a welcome companion, warming me with something that almost feels like comfort.

It's the Commander's fault Dad was ever given the package in the first place. His fault I'll never see Oliver again. His fault Logan languishes in a dungeon.

His fault Dad is dead.

I owe him for all of it.

I can't find my grief for Oliver. My fear for Logan. My agony over losing Dad forever. I can't, and I don't care.

Feeling nothing but rage and resolve makes me stronger.

One day soon the Commander will realize just how strong he's made me.

CHAPTER
FORTY-SEVEN

LOGAN

When I stumble for the fourth time in ten minutes, I realize mind over matter isn't going to cut it. I need rest. If I keep going in my current state of exhaustion, I run the risk of missing a critical piece of information, blundering into highwaymen, or losing Rachel and Melkin's trail.

Plus, the pain in my side is making it difficult to think straight.

I can think of a hundred Worst Case Scenarios, but the solutions feel vague and prone to failure.

The need to reach Rachel is a constant pressure against my chest. I meant what I said to the Commander. If Melkin attacks Rachel openly, she'll drop him like a stone.

But Melkin isn't stupid. He's been traveling with her for over a week. Any misconceptions he had about her formidability as a foe must have been put to rest by now.

I find a large oak, its thick branches forming a cradle several yards off the ground, and I climb carefully, my rib screaming at me the entire way. Wrapping my cloak around me to better blend in with my surroundings, I settle my head against my knees and admit Melkin isn't Rachel's biggest problem.

The tracker will torture her before he kills her.

I shake my head and force that thought away. She won't die. I won't allow it. I'll come up with a plan. I'll find a way to reach her in time.

I will.

Closing my eyes, I give myself permission to take one hour of sleep before I move again. I conjure up the memory of Rachel's face and cling to it like a lifeline as I allow my weary eyes to close.

CHAPTER
FORTY-EIGHT

RACHEL

My fingers ache with stiffness. I've been lying face-first on my father's grave for hours, clutching fistfuls of dirt as if by touching what covers him now, I can somehow touch him.

At some point, I realize the Tree Boy is sitting quietly beside me as if to let me know I'm not alone.

He's wrong.

I've never been more alone.

I turn my face to look at him and realize darkness is falling, obscuring the tree line and hiding the ugly remains of the safe house. He sits cross-legged, the package resting on his lap, his wide palms braced against his knees. His dark eyes seem to penetrate the emptiness inside me with something that looks like regret.

He can keep his regret. His sympathy. His quiet understanding.

I don't want it.

I don't need it.

All I need is the Commander's blood on my hands.

I'm still staring at him, and he slowly offers me his hand as if afraid I'll shy away at any sudden movements.

"Willow made dinner," he says as if this should make sense to me.

I ignore his hand. I'm not hungry.

"Willow's my sister." He turns to look over his shoulder. I follow his line of sight and see the Tree Girl bending over a pot on a small fire. Melkin hunches down on the opposite side of the pot, watching me. "She made stew."

Doesn't he know I don't care? I turn my face away, letting the ground scrape against my cheek. The pain feels good. Real. A tiny piece of what I should be feeling but can't now that the silence inside me has swallowed everything but rage.

"I'm Quinn."

I can't make small talk. If I open my mouth now, all the hate and fury bubbling just below the surface will spill out and consume him.

His voice is husky with something that sounds like grief. "Your father was a good man. I'm very sorry."

I look at my arm. The cuff is still glowing, confident that it's reached its intended target, and I'm suddenly, illogically, angry at Logan for inventing it in the first place.

For giving me something as cruel as hope.

"You can't stay here." The boy is still speaking, though I show no indication of listening. "There are men from Rowansmark moving through the forest to the northwest searching for what's in this package. Your dad said if anything happened to him, I was to retrieve this from its hiding place and give it to you or to a man named Logan McEntire." He sounds urgent, and I'm surprised to see genuine grief and worry in his eyes.

I can't leave. What will be left to me if I walk away from this spot?

He leans forward, his eyes looking so much older than the rest of him. "I'm sorry, Rachel. I wish you had more time, but you don't. If you get caught, everything Jared did to keep this out of the wrong hands will be in vain."

His words find their mark. If I'm caught, Dad died for nothing, and I lose my leverage against the man I hold responsible. I sit up slowly, still clutching fistfuls of grave dirt. I can't bear to let it go.

He looks at my hands, a tiny frown creasing the skin between his eyes, and then digs into the front pocket of the leather vest he wears. "Here." Stretching out his hand, he offers me a small pouch.

I take it. The dirt slides into the pouch with a whisper of sound, and I pull it closed. The strings are long enough to tie behind my neck. I knot them securely and let the final piece of my father rest over my heart, just below the necklace Logan gave to me.

"Come eat. You'll need your strength."

He's right. I can't travel back to Baalboden and destroy the Commander on an empty stomach. I stand and follow him to where Willow is now using dirt to smother her cooking fire before the flames alert someone to our presence in the gathering gloom.

My body moves just like it always has. My feet follow one after the other. My nostrils capture the scent of wood smoke and meat, and my ears note the creaking of branches and the crunch of ash-coated debris beneath me. But it's all meaningless. I'm a stranger beneath my skin. I wear armor on the inside, a metal forged of fury and silence, cutting me off from myself.

I'm no longer a daughter.

No longer a granddaughter.

No longer a girl with dreams. With hope.

I'm a weapon, now.

I embrace my rage. Let it sink into my secret spaces and make me its own as I sit down beside the ruins of the fire, accept a bowl of stew, and begin to plan.

CHAPTER
FORTY-NINE

LOGAN

I overslept.

It's already dark when I wake, and even while I curse my stupidity, I can tell the sleep helped. My body aches, but the overwhelming fatigue is gone. Best of all, my thoughts are clear again.

I'm two days' hard travel from the second safe house if I use short cuts and only stop twice more for brief rests. A check of my arm cuff shows the wires glowing steadily, though the light is too dim for her to be close yet. Still, I'm reading the remnants of her signature and it's getting stronger the further south I go. I'm on the right trail.

But someone else is too.

Taking a few minutes to eat and rewrap my rib, I think through my options.

I can continue with my current trajectory and hope to intercept Rachel near the second safe house before she finds the package and her whole world goes to hell. Or I can pick up the

Rowansmark tracker's trail and try to reach him before he acts against her.

I might be giving a slight advantage to the tracker by alerting him to my presence as I join Rachel, but his advantage is mitigated by my knowledge of his agenda.

And I can't bear to break the promise I made to Eloise. I might not be able to stop Melkin from following through on the Commander's orders, but I'm honor-bound to try.

Climbing down the tree starts a fire in my ribcage. I gently shake out my cloak, readjust my weapons, and put a tiny pinch of pain medicine beneath my tongue. Then I take a moment to assess the quality of the silence around me.

Owls hoot mournfully in the tree tops. The whispery rustle of an evening breeze slides across leaves. And the occasional animal pads quietly across the moss-covered ground.

I'm reassured. If the animals feel safe, I'm safe too.

Best Case Scenario: I make good progress and don't run into anyone.

Worst Case Scenarios 1–3: I stumble onto a gang of highwaymen as I cut across their favored trails; I lose my footing in the dark and injure my rib further, making speed difficult; or I cross paths with the tracker.

The answer to each is caution, but too much caution on my part may cost Rachel her life. Hoping to strike a balance between good sense and quick progress, I pick up my pace and strain to hear any change in the cadence of the forest around me as I enter highwaymen territory, my hand on the hilt of my sword.

CHAPTER FIFTY

RACHEL

The stew tastes like ashes in my mouth, but I chew with dogged determination. It takes everything I have to force myself to swallow when I'd rather gag, but I do it.

Revenge takes energy.

Melkin doesn't eat. Instead, he sits hunched forward like a giant praying mantis, digging the tip of his knife in the sand, while he watches the rest of us in brooding silence.

The package rests beside me on the ground, a lifeless reminder of everything I've lost. What could be worth such bloodshed? Such single-minded greed from both Rowansmark and the Commander?

Setting aside my stew bowl, I reach for it.

"Don't open it."

I meet Melkin's dark stare in silence, my fingers still tugging at the bindings holding the thick paper in place.

"*Don't.*"

I unknot the bindings and rip the paper off. Beneath the

paper, a heavy black cloth is rolled up like a log. Laying it in my lap, I carefully unroll the cloth until I see what rests at its center.

A slim wand of smoke-gray metal with a hole at one end, like a flute but with only three raised finger pads along its length, gleams dully beneath the flickering light of the single torch that Melkin has allowed us.

"What is this?" I look up, first at Quinn, who shows no inclination to answer me, and then at Willow.

Her brown eyes are alive with excitement as she leans forward and says, "It's tech from Rowansmark. See the three finger pads?"

I nod, and Melkin shifts closer to me, his eyes on the wand.

"There are symbols on each pad."

I run my finger across the circles and discover a different raised design on each. "What do they mean?"

"Willow." Quinn's voice is gentle, but his sister darts a quick glance at Melkin and subsides.

I can't read the subtext of their communication, and I don't want to. I just want to understand what I'm holding so I can see the Commander's endgame and thwart it.

I need Logan. He'd know how to figure this out. How to get the information from them and make a plan.

And I need Logan because he'd understand that something inside me is broken. Something I have no idea how to mend. He'd understand, and if he didn't know how to fix it, he'd dedicate himself to learning how.

I need him, but he needs me more. He needs me calm. Focused. He needs me to get the information, make the plan, and rescue him. I'm not going to let him down.

Turning to Quinn, I speak in a voice as hard as the packed dirt beneath us. "I need to know what they mean. You told me men are looking for this. Clearly my father didn't want them to have it, or he would've just returned it. The leader of my city is looking for it too."

"Rachel, that's enough." Melkin's voice is low and furious.

I ignore him.

"If you don't tell me everything I need to know, people may die. I might die. And you said yourself, you didn't want my father's . . ." Death? Sacrifice? I can't put his loss into words. There aren't any terrible enough to convey how empty I am without him. My hand creeps up to clutch the leather pouch I wear around my neck, and Quinn's eyes are sympathetic.

I hate him for it.

"You said Dad was a hero." I throw the words at him. "You said he died saving you."

"Yes."

"I'm not asking you to die. I'm not asking you to risk anything but the truth. You can be a hero if you just tell me the truth."

"Your father didn't want you to use that." He looks at the wand.

"You have no idea what my father wanted."

He looks wounded, and the fury inside me lashes out. I grab the wand and wave it in his face. "What does this do? Tell me!"

"Stop!" Willow shoves herself between us. "Leave him alone."

"Then you tell me."

She darts a glance at her brother. "We've already done more than we feel comfortable doing, but we owed Jared."

"And you aren't done paying your debt."

"Rachel!" Melkin's voice is harsh, but I keep staring at Quinn and Willow.

"How am I supposed to keep this safe if I don't understand it?"

Melkin makes a choked noise at the back of his throat, but I don't break eye contact with Willow. She's going to tell me. I can see it.

"Wrap it up and hide it," she says.

"Not if I don't know what it does." I lean past her to look Quinn in the face. "If you don't tell me, if I don't understand, I could trust the wrong person. Are you really okay with that?"

"Are you really planning to simply keep it safe?" he asks. I look in his eyes and realize he *knows*. He knows I'm going to use it. Knows I'm capable of it.

My chin rises. "If by keeping it safe, you mean not letting it fall into the wrong hands, then yes. I am."

"Jared didn't want you to use it. He wanted it given to Logan McEntire to be destroyed."

"Logan is in Baalboden's dungeon. To get him out, I'm supposed to give this"—I gesture toward the wand—"to our leader."

"You can't!" Willow says, and reaches as if she'll take the wand from me.

I hold the wand out of reach, and stare her down. "Then tell me what it does. I have nothing left to lose. Tell me what this does, or I'll start pushing buttons and figure it out myself."

She looks at Quinn.

"It's her decision," he says quietly. Something in the weight of his words makes me feel like he thinks the consequences will be more than I can bear.

He's wrong.

Willow slowly lowers her hands. "Fine. The finger pads create individual sound waves on a frequency humans can't hear."

"What good is that?"

"Humans can't hear it. But the Cursed One can."

I immediately slide my fingers away from the circles.

"You mean this—"

"Is a device designed to call and control the Cursed One."

A vicious sense of power blooms inside me. I cradle the device to my chest and feel unstoppable.

CHAPTER FIFTY-ONE

LOGAN

I've been on the move for at least two hours now, maybe three, and the burst of energy I felt after sleeping is long gone. So is the small dose of pain medicine I took. I can't afford to stop for rest yet, despite the pain and exhaustion, so I force myself to catalogue the foliage I pass and come up with its scientific name. Mind over matter. Reason over pain.

The darkness obscures all but the smell and the most obvious of shapes, which adds an extra challenge that keeps me thinking of something other than the fire in my ribcage and my fear for Rachel.

I'm passing through a patch of pines. Sharp scent. Knobby branches. Widely spaced thin needles. Shortleaf pine. *Pinus echinata*.

What will I do if after I find her, Melkin still tries to carry out his assignment?

The low-pitched call of a great horned owl echoes from somewhere to my left. *Bubo virginianus*.

How can I look Eloise in the eye if I have to kill her husband?

The moss beneath my boots grows in spongy clusters that spring back easily after I lift my foot. *Bryum argenteum*.

Logic could work. Melkin might listen to me. Understand the only way to rescue his wife is to take up arms against his leader.

He might not.

I have to come to terms with the idea of either killing him or finding a way to leave him behind in the Wasteland so Rachel and I can get to Baalboden before him.

Sliding silently through a few loosely spaced pines, I brush up against a wide, glossy leaf adorning a tree whose thick spread of branches blocks my view for a moment. *Magnolia grandiflora*.

The low hooting of the owl suddenly subsides as I skirt the tree and nearly run into a man standing on the other side. The fact that his back is to me saves my life.

He hears my footfalls and turns, his weapon drawn, and I drop to my knees, grab the dagger in my boot, and thrust it up as his momentum drives his abdomen onto my blade.

Before he has a chance to do more than hiss out a breath, I lunge to my feet, grab his head with both hands, and wrench it to the side. His neck grinds and pops, his body goes slack, and I lower him as quietly as possible to the forest floor.

It isn't quiet enough. If anyone else is nearby, they'll have heard something. Even if they didn't, the sudden lack of bird or animal cries around us creates an alarm just as deafening as if he'd called out to the rest of his battalion.

And it is a battalion. I can just make out the burnished dragon scale adorning the front right pocket of his uniform. He's

Rowansmark military.

I'm in deeper trouble than I thought. So are Rachel and Melkin. Being hunted by Rowansmark trackers is dangerous enough. Being hunted by an entire Rowansmark battalion turns the odds against us so completely, I feel staggered at the thought of trying to plan our way out of it. Whatever is in the package, James Rowan will clearly stop at nothing to get it back.

I pull my dagger free of the soldier, wipe it clean on his pants, and slide it back into its sheath. No highwayman would be stupid enough to attack a military encampment's night guard. I've just announced my presence to the entire battalion.

Best Case Scenario: I make good time, masking my trail by using the trees, and create a significant lead time before this man's body is discovered at watch change.

Worst Case Scenario: I bring the entire Rowansmark military down around our heads before I've even had a chance to deal with Melkin or the tracker.

I lean down and measure the dead man's foot. Slightly bigger than mine, but it will do. Tugging his boots off ignites an unending stream of agony through my chest, but I don't have time for pain medicine now. Several minutes pass while I switch our boots and wipe the ground around him so no one can see what I've just done.

It takes everything I have to walk away without limping and giving myself away to every half-decent tracker stationed with the battalion. I wander a bit, brushing away my tracks, until I find what I'm looking for: the edge of the military encampment.

Now my boot marks won't stand out. With any luck, no one will even bother to look for me so close to the heart of the battalion. And if they did, all they'd find is the curious footprint of a Rowansmark man who stretched up to his tiptoes for a moment in the middle of the forest floor.

It's going to hurt like hell. I grab a twig from the ground and wedge it in between my teeth so I can bite down against the pain without making a sound. Then I look at the low-hanging branch skimming the air a foot above me, gather myself, and leap.

CHAPTER FIFTY-TWO

RACHEL

"We're bringing that back to Baalboden."

Melkin hasn't moved from his original seat by the fire's remains, though Quinn and Willow left a while ago to weave branches, vines, and moss together into a treetop cradle they can sleep in for the night. I've been sitting by the torchlight examining the symbols on the wand, trying to figure out what they mean.

"Yes. We are." Though I'm not about to willingly hand the Commander a weapon capable of destroying everything in our world.

"I have to give it to the Commander. Alone. I have to do that, Rachel. For Eloise." His voice sounds desperate and dark, but where once I felt compassion, now I feel nothing.

"No." I lay the device in its cloth and begin carefully rolling it back up.

"For Eloise."

"Not even Eloise is worth giving the Commander the power

to obliterate anyone who stands up to him."

He curses and crawls toward me. I jerk the device toward my chest and slide my knife free.

"What about Logan? What about rescuing him? He's all you have left!"

I hear the accusation beneath his words. He thought we were the same. Willing to do anything, no matter how unthinkable, if it would save us from loss. The Commander thought we were the same too.

They're both wrong.

"Eloise and Logan are dead unless we destroy the Commander."

"No." He shakes his head, fury leaping into his eyes.

I'll see his fury and double it. "Yes! Get your head out of the sand, Melkin. You work for a treacherous monster who never keeps his word. Never. The second he has what he wants from you, he'll kill you. He'll probably kill Eloise in front of you first, just because he *can*. And then you'll have done nothing with your life but hand the worst man in the world the power to rule it."

"Stop it!" He screams at me, spit flying from his mouth, his hand curled around his knife as if he needs a target.

"I won't stop. Not until he's dead. And now I have the means to do it." I push the cloth-wrapped device into the inner pocket of my cloak. "Either you go along with my plan, or you get out of my way. I don't care which you choose."

He drives his knife into the ground at his feet, and looks at me with the kind of loathing that once would have made my skin crawl. Now, his opinion of me means just as little as his foolish desire to sacrifice the rest of the world for one more moment with his doomed wife.

My father did not die in vain. I'm going to make sure of it.

God help Melkin if he tries to stop me.

CHAPTER FIFTY-THREE

LOGAN

I tree-leap as quietly as possible. Taking my time. Edging along the branches and biting on my twig hard as I use my knees to cushion each landing.

I was right. It hurts like hell. Every leap strains my ribcage. Every landing rattles it until I want to curl up, swallow enough medicine to obliterate the pain, and sleep for hours.

But I don't dare stop. Any second now, someone will find the dead guard and raise the alarm. I probably should've dragged his body into the woods, hidden it, and then doubled back to hide the trail, but the pain and weakness in my ribcage would've made that too time intensive. Better to flee as quickly as possible.

I'm maybe sixty yards from the encampment when I hear a shout go up. They've found him. And I can't leap quietly enough while I have Rowansmark military combing the woods for me. Quickly assessing the trees around me, I choose a tall silver maple with plenty of leafy coverage but no low-hanging branches and make the three leaps it takes to reach it.

Pain clouds my thoughts and dulls my instincts as I climb into the upper reaches of the tree. About two thirds of the way up, I find what I need and settle into a secure cradle of branches. Two of the limbs are thick enough to hold me should I need to leap, and both reach into the surrounding trees. I'm high enough that no one from the ground can look up and see me through all the foliage.

It's the best I'm going to get for the moment.

Quietly pulling my bag around, I take out the half-gone pack of medicinal powder and a Rowansmark-made cloaking device I once traded for with the highwaymen outside Baalboden.

A quick pinch of powder takes the worst edge off the pain, and I clip the cloaking device, which looks like a small oval disc, to the front of my tunic. When I flick the tiny switch on the side of the device, it vibrates once. I hope the blocking system contained within it is strong enough to withstand the technological might of Rowansmark's military.

CHAPTER FIFTY-FOUR

RACHEL

Melkin and I haven't spoken since I demanded he choose a course of action. I've decided to take his silence as compliance, though it doesn't matter to me one way or the other. My purpose is set. If he wants to give this device to the Commander, he'll have to do it over my dead body.

Quinn and Willow are sleeping in the trees close by. I suppose in the morning they'll return to wherever it is they live. That doesn't matter to me either.

All that matters is that I finally have a way to force the Commander to pay for everything he's done. The rage within me is viciously triumphant at the thought.

Leaving Melkin to keep the first watch, I unroll my travel mat over my father's grave and lie down with my face beside the carved wooden cross. Moonlight gleams on its surface, gilding his name with a beauty that should wound me. I reach out and grasp the wood with my bare hand, holding it tight as slivers gouge my palm.

It's a welcome pain, but it isn't enough to relieve the silent weight crushing me from within. Letting go, I turn my face away from the cross, away from Melkin, away from everyone, and close my eyes.

The wind sighs along the treetops and whispers over my skin like a lullaby, but I can't sleep. Soon, I'll have justice. A life for a life. It won't be enough to seal up the edges of everything that's undone within me. It won't be enough to shatter the silence and let me grieve in peace.

It won't be enough, but it's all I have, and I cling to it with desperate strength.

The wind dies down, and I hear a soft *crunch* on ash behind me. Tensing, I try to listen for it again, but I can't hear anything beyond the sudden roar of fury-laced adrenalin screaming through me.

My knife slides free of its sheath without a sound, and I brace my left elbow beneath me, flip the knife blade-side out, and shove off the ground.

Melkin stands behind me, his knife down at his side, his eyes pits of rage and misery.

He means to take the device from me. Destroy any chance of justice. Make my Dad's sacrifice worth *nothing*.

I raise my weapon. "Get back." I snarl at him in a voice I barely recognize. Cold. Empty.

"You said he'd keep his word if I just did what he asked."

His voice is cold and empty too.

"I lied."

His face contorts, his body shakes, his legs tense.

"Get. Back," I say.

He watches me, his knife hand trembling so badly that he'll never be able to stab me with it before I disarm him, tie him up, and leave him for Quinn and Willow to deal with. Rolling to the balls of my feet, I lunge for his right arm.

His left flashes out, silver streaking through the moonlight, and I remember his ambidextrous sword work a millisecond before he can slice into me. Spinning to the side, I drop and roll forward, coming up several yards away.

He isn't trying to take the device. He's trying to kill me.

I crouch, blade out. Something feral tears through me, obliterating Eloise, his unborn child, the kind of girl I once dreamed I'd be, and every cautious word Logan ever spoke, leaving nothing but pure, scorching bloodlust in their wake.

Melkin swings his sword in dizzying circles and rushes at me. I wait until he's almost on me, and then dive forward, low to the ground, crashing into his legs and sending him flying over the top of me. His blade nicks me as it goes by, but I can't feel the pain, and he drops his sword as he lands on his side.

I'm screaming now. Raw, agonized wails that flay the air with their fury. Out of the corner of my eye I see Quinn and Willow hurrying toward us, but I have no time for them. Whirling, I lunge forward while Melkin is still reaching for his sword. He sees me and slashes out with his knife instead. The blade catches my cloak and tears into it, but I don't slow down.

I can't.

Driving my boot onto his wrist, I grind the small bones together. He yells and drops his knife.

I slam my knees onto his diaphragm and feel the air leave his lungs.

He whips his left arm up and punches me in the face, and I land in a pile of ash on my back. He's already on his feet. Already coming for me. I can't see his weapons. I don't know which hand he'll use. And I don't have time to get up.

He's in the air, long legs dropping down, his face a mask of murderous intent.

I broke his right wrist. The weapon must be in his left hand. I roll to his right as he lands beside me, his left arm already swinging forward. Flipping my blade around, I push myself off the ground and bury my knife deep into his chest.

He sags, deflating slowly onto the ash beside me, and reaches for the knife with his empty left hand.

He isn't holding his sword. I scan the area and see it gleaming yards away from us. His knife lies beside it.

"I wanted to take it." His eyes stare into mine like a child trying to understand what he'd done wrong. "That's all."

"You were trying to kill me!"

He was. I know it. I had to have known it. I didn't just fatally wound an unarmed man who wanted nothing more than to steal from me.

His blood seeps along the knife hilt, thick and warm, and coats my hands.

"You tried to kill me." My voice shakes.

"Disarm. To take it." He coughs, a horrible wet sound that sprays me with blood.

"No. No." I pull the knife free as he slides onto the ground. "No."

My hands can't stop the bleeding, but I try. Pressing against his wound, I try to make sense of him. Of myself. Of what we've done.

What I've done.

He raises a hand, long fingers gleaming white in the moonlight. "Eloise?"

I can't look at him. I can't. But I've lied to him before, and I can lie once more. "Yes."

"Can't save you." His voice is nothing but a whisper straining against the blood filling up his throat.

"You just did." I can barely speak past the suffocating guilt choking me. I *killed* him. A desperate man. A pawn of the Commander's who wanted nothing more than to save his beloved wife.

He doesn't speak again, and I cover his wound with my blood-stained hands until his chest falls quiet.

CHAPTER FIFTY-FIVE

LOGAN

I hear the Rowansmark battalion before I see them. No need to use stealth when you have sheer numbers on your side, I guess. They swarm out of the trees, carrying swords and torches. Quickly, I close my eyes before the firelight costs me my night vision. I can track their movements with my ears instead.

It's immediately obvious they aren't tracking. They're hunting. Trying to flush out their prey. Walking with less than five yards between each soldier, beating at the underbrush with their swords, peering up into the trees they pass with the help of their torches.

I'll be fine. I'm up high enough that the torchlight can't reach me. I settle against the branches and wait while they spread along the Wasteland beneath me, calling to each other, swinging their swords, and making enough noise to announce their presence to anyone within two hundred yards of us.

Before long, they're gone. I wait until I can no longer hear them beating the bushes, until their yells fade into silence, and expect the normal noises of night in the Wasteland to resume.

They don't.

Which means I'm not as alone as someone wants me to think. Tension coils within me, and I slowly draw my knife.

It's a smart plan. Use loud, obvious hunters and hope that once the prey eludes them, he'll feel comfortable and give himself away. I'd have done the same myself.

Settling slowly against the tree, I hold myself absolutely still, ignoring the pain in my side demanding I readjust in an effort to find a more comfortable position.

It takes almost an hour, but then I hear him. A faint whisper of sound that could almost be mistaken for the breeze. Almost. But the birds are still silent, and the forest feels like it's holding its breath.

I don't try to look for him. If he's tree-leaping, I'll feel it if he lands in mine. But if I move to a position where I have better visibility, he'll catch the movement. And if he doesn't, he'll certainly catch the noise.

Instead, I wait. I don't hear him again, but eventually the birds hoot, coo, and chirp, and I hear the nocturnal ramblings of raccoons on the ground below.

He's gone.

But he and a battalion of Rowansmark military men are now between me and the safe house.

The only recourse I have is to move with extreme caution and come up with a plan as I travel. I can't single-handedly overwhelm an entire battalion. I have to hope I can outwit them.

CHAPTER FIFTY-SIX

RACHEL

I sit by Melkin's body until dawn bleeds across the sky. Quinn sits with me while Willow remains on guard somewhere in the trees.

I didn't ask him to sit with me. But somehow having him there, quietly present without offering judgment, makes the ragged edges in me settle just a bit. I haven't spoken since my final words to Melkin, but as the gloom around us lifts, I raise my eyes to Quinn's.

"I killed him."

He nods.

"I thought he was going to kill me first. He attacked me. He had his weapons out. I was sure he was going to kill me." I *was* sure, but now I'm not. Now, I'm looking back and remembering I jumped up from my travel mat with my knife already raised for battle while his was still trained at the ground. I lunged at him, blade out, before he ever raised his sword.

He was trying to disarm me and defend himself. And I killed

him.

I struggle to my feet and run to the edge of the trees, where I fall to my knees and retch.

I killed him.

My stomach is empty, but I keep heaving.

I *killed* him.

I'm shaking, my teeth clattering against each other violently, when Quinn's solid arms wrap around me from behind and hold me against his warm chest.

"You thought you were defending yourself."

I did think that, but it doesn't comfort me now, and it won't comfort Eloise.

"It happened fast. Did you make the best decision you could given the information you had?"

I twist around to look at him, his warm brown eyes steady on mine, his straight black hair haloed by the early morning light. "I don't want absolution."

"I'm not offering any. Take the blame that belongs to you, and nothing else. I'm asking you to look it in the eye and face it for what it is."

But I can't face it. Not really. If I do, if I let it cut me like I deserve, everything else will spill out too. Oliver. Dad. Melkin. Logan at the Commander's mercy in a dungeon. It's all one gaping pit of loss, destruction, and grief, and if I feel it, I'll never be able to protect the device and deliver judgment.

I don't even have to ask the silence to take it from me. It's already gone. Slipping into the emptiness before I make the conscious choice to send it there, and leaving me numb.

I push away from Quinn, and he lets me. Why shouldn't he?

I mean nothing to him. I'm just a broken girl who lost her father and then killed a man. And I'm about to go kill another.

Gathering my belongings, I stow them in my pack and then turn to find Quinn and Willow packed as well, standing by Melkin's body.

I can't abandon him for the forest animals to eat. Leaving my pack beside Dad's grave, I use my knife to start digging a new one a few yards away. Soon, Quinn and Willow drop down beside me and dig as well.

"I'll do it." I don't want their help. I need to do this for Melkin. Alone. A small piece of atonement in the lifetime of penance I'm going to serve for my crime.

"We can help. It will get done much faster," Willow says, but Quinn lays a hand on her arm, and they pull back.

It takes me almost an hour. I use my knife and then scoop dirt out with my bare hands, letting the dust of his grave mingle with the stains of his blood on my skin. Then the three of us lift him and lay him gently down. When Willow picks up his walking stick to lay across his chest, I hold out my hand for it.

On our first day in the Wasteland, the Cursed One incinerated everything but Melkin's weapons. His sword is far too long and heavy for me to carry across the Wasteland, but I can bring this back. A reminder of what I'm capable of. A faint comfort for the wife he left behind.

Together, we push the soil back into place until all that remains is a little hill of dirt. Quinn stands beside me, a solid, reassuring presence I refuse to lean on. Willow stands across from us, scanning the surrounding trees, her bow already in her hand. I should say something. A eulogy. A good-bye. But Melkin deserves to be memorialized by someone other than the girl who took his life, and I don't know how to put into words the cost of what I've done.

I turn away. I have a mission to complete. When it's over, I'll look for absolution. When it's over, I'll find what comfort is left to me.

I refuse to brush the dirt from my hands. Scooping up my pack, I arrange it against my back and slide my Switch into its slot so I can carry Melkin's ebony walking stick instead. When Quinn and Willow pick up their packs too, I frown at them.

"You don't need to come. I can find my way back on my own."

"Can you?" Quinn asks.

"I can find what I need to find."

"We'll go with you."

"Why? You don't even know me."

"I knew your father." His voice is steady, but pain runs beneath it. "And you were right when you said we still owe him a debt. I'd like to pay that debt by escorting you through the Wasteland."

There's a quiet insistence in his voice, and I'm too tired to argue. Besides, what do I care if two Tree People tag along? It isn't going to slow me down or change my plans.

"Fine. But remember how you insisted on coming with me when you find I've landed you right in the middle of a war."

CHAPTER
FIFTY-SEVEN

LOGAN

I've been traveling hard for three and a half days. Tree-leaping. Sleeping in the wide crook of an oak curtained by Spanish moss. Watching the wires on my tracking cuff get brighter by the hour as I cut across the safer trails Rachel would use and shave time off my journey.

I'm closing in.

So is the Rowansmark battalion. I've seen their signs. Heard thin snatches of conversation floating back to me. I don't know how close I am to them, but they're still between Rachel, Melkin, and me.

I haven't seen any sign of the tracker, and that worries me. He could've circled behind me. Gone ahead of the battalion to find the safe house. Caught up with Rachel and Melkin.

The scenarios are endless, and they all spell disaster.

Stopping to rest in another oak tree as the sun climbs toward noon, I assess my strategy. Following the battalion isn't getting me anywhere. I need to flank them. Get ahead of them. Intersect with Rachel and Melkin before they run into them.

Moving with care, I open my pack. I'm running low on food since I haven't been able to go to ground and hunt, but I still have a few jars of preserved fruit and some sheep jerky I took from the safe-house pantry. Choosing a small ration of each, I eat quickly and then grudgingly use a small bit of pain medicine.

I'm going to have to move fast. I can't afford to feel the full effects of my journey until later.

After packing my bag and assessing the noises around me to gauge the relative safety of moving forward, I aim southeast and start tree-leaping. Within twenty minutes, all sounds of the battalion are gone, and I'm deep in the Spanish moss–draped forest of the southern Wasteland, surrounded only by birds, bugs, and the occasional rabbit or squirrel.

When I judge I've traveled far enough south to risk cutting back toward the west without running into the battalion, I take another short rest, refuel on water and some jerky, and start leaping again.

The sun is sinking toward the west, about three hours from sunset, when I glance down at the tracker cuff I wear and freeze. The wires glow at one hundred percent. My heart pounds, and I have to remind myself to breathe.

I've found her.

Somewhere in a thirty-yard radius around me, Rachel is traveling the Wasteland. I'm not too late. I'm busy scoping out my surroundings, trying to determine the best direction to take, when I hear her approach.

She's arguing with someone. Melkin, most likely. I frown

as her voice carries clearly through the thick oaks and mossy undergrowth. It's not like her to forget how to move quietly.

Her oversight works to my advantage, though, and I brace myself for the climb down when she and a young man about my age enter the small clearing at my feet. He walks close to her, his left hand hovering behind her back as if he wants to touch her but isn't sure of his welcome. I assess him quickly. About six feet. Ropy muscles on a lithe frame. Olive skin, dark eyes and hair, leather laces holding his tunic and pants in place. A Tree Person. I don't know how he came to be with Rachel, but the way his eyes watch her with interest and concern make me want to send him back to his village.

Immediately.

Melkin isn't with her. Either he succumbed to one of the dangers in the Wasteland, or he tried to fulfill his assignment, and Rachel killed him.

I study Rachel next, and shock punches a little frisson of panic through me. Her pale skin is smudged with what looks like ash. Her cloak is torn and battered. And her *hands*. Her hands are covered in dirt and dried blood, and she clutches a long black metal walking stick like it's going to disappear if she lets go.

But worst of all is the look on her face. Cold. Fierce. Empty. Like someone snuffed out the Rachel I knew and sent out a hollow shell in her place. I hang on to the branch for another moment, trying to adjust to this new Rachel before I have to drop down and show her the shock written across my face.

"We need rest," her companion says.

"Then rest. I'm going on."

"You haven't eaten today. You've barely slept. If you keep this up, you'll collapse, and then what good will all this progress do you?" He asks, but his tone sounds genuinely curious instead of worried or upset. Like he's fine with allowing her the freedom to destroy herself as long as she's given the matter proper thought. In light of the facts he's just presented, my tone would've indicated a good shaking was in store for her if she didn't listen to common sense and take care of herself.

She doesn't respond to his invitation for self-reflection. Instead, she strides beneath my tree, her course set north, and acts like she can't hear him. He follows her. I let them both walk past me. My first meeting with this Tree Person isn't going to be me awkwardly trying to climb down a tree without hurting my rib. They're four trees up when I grasp the branch I'm on and ready myself for a painful landing.

A slight movement in the corner of my eye arrests my motion, and I hold myself still as a man in green and brown, a dagger in his fist, melts out of the shadows between the trees and silently follows Rachel and her companion.

The Rowansmark tracker.

Rachel must have the package. Or he thinks she does. And he's going to kill her to get it.

Except he didn't bargain on me.

He's approaching my tree. Five steps and he'll be here. I'll only have one chance to get it right.

Best Case Scenario: I kill him on my first try.

Worst Case Scenario: I miss, and never get another chance.

Best Case Scenario it is, then. Quickly assessing angles, momentum, and how much damage I can do without drawing my sword, I wait for him to walk directly below me, let go of my branch, and jump.

CHAPTER
FIFTY-EIGHT

LOGAN

He senses me and turns, but he's too late. I slam into him, wrap my hands around his throat, and drive both of us onto the ground.

Pain explodes through my ribcage on impact, and I nearly lose my grip. He whips his arms up and claps them against my ears, disorienting me. I'm dizzy, unable to draw a complete breath, and losing focus fast.

Digging my thumbs into his windpipe, I will myself to hang on. He bucks beneath me and catches me in the ribs with an elbow. Agony sears through me, and my hands slip. Knocking my hands away from his throat, he throws me onto the ground beside him, pulls a knife, and looms over me.

I can't breathe. Can barely move. I'm going to die if I don't figure out a way to get the upper hand. Fast.

His knife arm goes up, and his eyes lock on mine, but before I can react, an arrow sinks into the narrow space between his eyes with a soft *thud*. He shudders, his body sags, and I scoot to the side as he crashes to the ground.

Someone whistles softly from a tree behind me, a near-perfect imitation of a blackbird, but I can't look. I can't bear to move. I can hardly bear to breathe. Soft footsteps hit the forest floor and come toward me. In seconds, a girl about Rachel's age with olive skin and a long dark braid kneels beside me, a black bow in her hands.

"Did you get him?" Rachel asks from somewhere to my left, and now I understand why she was being unnecessarily loud.

It was a trap. A trap that worked. I want to give her kudos for planning ahead, but I can't seem to get enough air to speak.

"Two of them?" the man asks.

"This one jumped out of the tree and tried to kill the tracker. I decided not to shoot him."

I'm grateful. I hope she knows that. Pain sears my chest again, and I close my eyes, grit my teeth, and try to will it away.

"Who is he?" the man asks.

Another set of soft footsteps approaches, and someone drops to the ground next to me. "Logan?"

I open my eyes. Rachel crouches beside me, her glorious red hair lit with fire from the sun, her blood-stained hands hovering above me as if afraid to touch me, and her blue eyes so wounded, I want to hold her until some of her pain recedes. I lift my hand and press it against her cheek. She trembles.

"This is Logan?" The girl with the bow sounds surprised. "Rachel said you were locked in a dungeon."

My voice wheezes as I say, "I escaped."

"How?"

"Blew up a wall." My eyes are still locked on Rachel's.

"Nice." The girl grins at me. "I'd like to learn that trick."

"Logan." Rachel lays a hand on my shoulder as if testing to see if I'm really there.

"I told you I'd find you."

Her fingers clench around my shoulder, and she slowly curls toward me until she's laying facedown against my chest. Her weight hurts, but I don't complain. Instead, I cradle her to me and feel the missing pieces inside of me slide firmly back into place.

CHAPTER FIFTY-NINE

RACHEL

I lie against Logan's chest listening to him breathe and shake like I've been caught out in a snowstorm in nothing but a tunic. He's here. Alive. Warm and steady beneath me. I haven't lost everything.

And yet, with Melkin's blood still on my hands, I'm not convinced. The silence inside consumes me. I want to burrow into him and feel safe. Feel the grief, the anger, and most importantly the hope that I know hovers somewhere just out of reach within me. Digging my fingers into Logan's shoulder, I desperately try to feel *real* again.

Beside me the body of the tracker starts beeping, a high-pitched insistent tone that has Logan pushing me to get up.

"Get back!"

He can hardly obey his own instructions. Digging one hand into the ground, he groans as he tries to lift himself off the ground. Transferring Melkin's walking stick to my other hand, I reach down to help. Quinn joins me and together we scoop our hands under his arms and drag Logan away from the body.

The beeping speeds up.

"What's going on?" I ask Logan.

"Bomb," he wheezes, his face white with strain as we drag him into the trees. "Anatomical trigger looped on a closed circuit."

"Speak English," Willow says as she falls in step beside me and bends to help carry Logan.

"When his heart stopped, the device began its countdown."

"Why would anyone—"

The blast throws us to the ground and rains bits of dirt, twigs, and a fine mist I imagine was once the Rowansmark tracker all around us. I land partially on Logan's chest, and scramble off as he moans in pain.

"What's wrong with you?"

"Broken rib."

"We need to climb. Now." Willow is already moving, grasping the nearest branch and swinging into the tree, her bow strung behind her back. "If that explosion didn't call the Cursed One, it called every highwayman within one hundred fifty yards."

"Worse." Logan sounds like he can barely get enough air to speak. "Battalion. Rowansmark. Might have heard."

Quinn jumps up and circles to Logan's other side. "Can you get into a tree if we help?"

He nods, and we each take an arm and help him sit up. He sways, and it's clear that pride is all that keeps him from crying out at the pain. He's never going to be able to climb a tree. I see the moment he realizes it and decides to sacrifice himself for the rest of us.

"I'll stall them. You go," Logan says.

Quinn frowns and looks at me.

"Ignore him. He doesn't get to play the martyr today."

"Isn't that his choice?" Quinn asks.

"Not while I'm still breathing."

Logan jerks his arm away from Quinn. "Go."

"Absolutely not," I say.

"Rachel—"

"I love how you still think if you tell me to do something, I'll just check my brain at the door and do it." I try to infuse my voice with anger, but all I feel is fear. I can't bear to lose him.

"Hey! Idiots who want to argue while disaster is heading our way! Maybe you should shut up and get up a tree," Willow pokes her head out of a bower of leaves and glares at us.

"Listen." Quinn holds up his hand for quiet. We fall silent and realize there's no rumbling. No distant roar coming closer. The Cursed One must be terrorizing people on the other side of the continent or sleeping in its lair, because it isn't coming.

"Fine. The Cursed One isn't coming. But the battalion still could be, and I'm not going to watch you die just so these two can figure out who's in charge." Willow beckons to Quinn, but he looks at Logan again, and I can tell he doesn't want to leave him behind.

"Go. I'm fine. I'll stall them. Or hide." Logan looks around, and I resist the urge to punch him only because he's already injured.

"You're coming with us."

"No, I'm not."

"Then I'm staying too."

"I didn't travel all this way just to watch you die. Please, Rachel."

He's all I have left, and he sits there like today is the day he's going to die, and I should just be fine with it.

"Stop it!" I slam Melkin's walking stick into the ground. It sinks below the surface about six inches, and the earth beneath us trembles violently.

We freeze, and everyone stares at the ground and then at me.

"What did you just do?" Quinn asks, dread in his voice for the first time since I met him.

I'm shaking my head. "I don't know. I don't—I was mad. I hit the ground with the stick, and it just went right into it and then there was—"

"A sonic pulse," Logan says. "The Cursed One will have heard that."

"Oh, now you've done it." Willow starts climbing higher. "Get in the tree, Quinn!"

"I didn't mean to. I didn't know." I pull the stick from the ground as a faint thunder rumbles beneath our feet. "It's Melkin's stick . . ."

Melkin, who shoved the stick into the ground while I was busy yelling at him, and then saved me from the Cursed One moments later. Why? Why would he call the beast and put us both in danger like that? I remembered him saying his stick was a gift. Not from Baalboden. Was it possible he hadn't known what it could do?

I don't have the answers, and I don't have time to figure them out. The rumble is growing into a distant roar. We have less than a minute to get to safety.

"Get him up." I grab one of Logan's arms while Quinn grabs the other. Ignoring Logan's gasp of pain, we heave him to his feet.

He sways, and Quinn wraps an arm around him to steady him, but when we start moving toward the nearest tree, we discover Logan's slow progress is the least of our worries.

The Rowansmark battalion surrounds us, a tight circle of soldiers standing three deep and cutting off any escape from the Cursed One.

CHAPTER SIXTY

LOGAN

We're surrounded by Rowansmark's soldiers, their swords drawn as they establish a perimeter forty yards away from us, caging us in. We'll be destroyed, while they can stay relatively safe if they keep quiet after the Cursed One bursts through the ground in front of us.

We're going to die.

Willow drops out of the tree above us, swings her bow into position, and stands next to her brother like she doesn't want him to die without her.

I don't want to die without Rachel, either. I'm an idiot for not seeing it before. I didn't dream of her, worry for her, and push myself across the Wasteland for her to fulfill my responsibility to Jared. It took being thrown into a dungeon to realize I need her.

It takes facing imminent death to realize I love her.

I love her.

A fierce light consumes me from the inside out. It blazes through my body until I think there's no way I can contain it. I don't want to contain it. I want it to overtake me completely. It's illogical. Wonderful. Almost painful.

And I'm not going to die without telling her.

She moves against my side, and I turn to her, expecting her to fall into my arms and cling to me while fire consumes us. Instead, she shoves Melkin's walking stick into my fist and says, "Hold this."

She doesn't wait to see if I've complied. She's tugging a roll of black cloth from her cloak pocket, her expression fierce.

"Rachel, I—"

"You can save us," she says, and pulls a dark gray metallic flute with three finger pads down its center from the middle of the cloth. "Here."

She trades me the walking stick for the flute. Symbols decorate the top of each finger pad, but I don't know what they mean. The ground beneath us trembles violently, and the Rowansmark men step back, some of them furtively glancing up at the safety of the trees above them.

"I don't know—"

"It's a device to control the Cursed One through sound waves. Push the button to send it away."

"I don't know which button that is!"

The ground begins to crack, a jagged seam heading straight for us.

"Better figure it out, tech head, or we're dead." Willow hooks her arm through her brother's and drags them both backward, stopping about fifteen yards from the line of swords behind us.

"I can't read these symbols." Panic is beginning to claw at me.

"Experiment, then," Rachel says. "Deduce. Make connections.

Do what you do best." She grabs my face and looks at me with absolute trust. "I have faith in you."

The ground twenty yards in front of us explodes and spews the glistening black length of the Cursed One into the air. Its scales glitter beneath the sunlight, and its film-covered eyes swing in our direction as it sniffs the air, huffing puffs of smoke and rumbling in fury.

We're about to die. I don't know how to work this thing she's handed me. I can't understand the symbols on the finger pads. All the faith in the world won't change that. Still, I'm going to try. But not before I say what I need to say to her.

"I love you, Rachel."

Her eyes widen, but before she can say anything, I turn toward the beast and push a button with shaking fingers.

CHAPTER SIXTY-ONE

LOGAN

The beast roars and shakes its body, its scales rattling together like a thousand coins falling on a cobblestone street. Then it gathers itself, swings its muzzle toward us, and bellows. A brilliant crimson-orange fireball explodes out of its mouth and strafes the air above us.

We dive for the ground, and my ribcage screams at me as searing heat rolls over the top of us and sends the men behind us running.

Wrong button.

Panic is a relentless force inside me, erasing every logical thought from my mind. I take a deep breath and fumble with the device I hold.

The creature coils its body and digs its claws into the ground as it drags itself toward us, its milky yellow eyes glaring at nothing while it homes in on its prey. Desperately, I stab the second button.

Nothing happens.

"It's not working. It's not working!"

"It has to." Rachel reaches over and slams her fist on the top two buttons at the same time. The beast rears back, swings its head to the left, and strafes the line of Rowansmark soldiers with fire.

The flames incinerate most of them on the spot, but a few fall to the ground wailing in agony. The surrounding trees explode into flame, a deafening thunder of dry wood hissing and cracking.

Hope battles with the panic inside me, and I clench the device tight and hit the bottom two buttons simultaneously. The creature swings to the right and sends a fireball hurtling into the ranks of men standing there.

Chaos reigns. Men are screaming, running, swinging into trees and leaping for safety. There is no perimeter of swords around us anymore. What's left of the battalion is scattered, racing for safety while their fallen comrades disintegrate into ash and the lines of trees on either side of us burn fiercely. The Cursed One roars and coils itself to strike again.

"Send it back," Rachel says, as if I know what I'm doing.

I hit the top and bottom buttons at the same time and the beast slithers away from us, spitting fire. There aren't any combinations of buttons left except to push all three, and I'm afraid that will send it straight toward us. It's the only direction left for him to go.

I don't have much time left before the beast realizes we're the last remaining prey in the area. My hands still shake as fear pounds through me, but I grasp the device with white knuckles.

Pressing the first button alone seemed to antagonize the

creature. Logic would deduce that's the sound used to call it to the surface in the first place. The second button had no discernible effect unless used in conjunction with one of the other buttons.

That left the third as the most reasonable choice for driving the Cursed One back to his lair at the center of the Earth. I whisper a prayer and press it.

The beast shudders and lashes the forest with his enormous spiked tail, sending a hail of branches and corpses flying, then slides back toward the gaping hole in the ground. I hold my breath as it comes closer, my finger white with the strain of pressing against the third button. The beast never hesitates. It simply slithers back into the tunnel it created and slides once more toward the center of the earth. I keep my death grip on the device until I can no longer feel the vibrations of its movement beneath me.

All around us, sparks hiss and spit as fire chews through the ancient oaks, and the few surviving Rowansmark soldiers moan in pain on the forest floor. They don't have long before either the flames or the smoke put them out of their misery. The fire is spreading east to west, though that could change at the mercy of the wind. We have to put distance between ourselves and this spot. Not just because of the fire, but because as soon as they realize the Cursed One is gone, the last remnant of Rowansmark's battalion will return to finish their assignment.

"Help me up."

Rachel, Quinn, and Willow reach for me. My head swims from the pain in my side, and the scorched skin beneath the bandage on my neck throbs as the heat of the fire scrapes against it. I can't possibly put enough distance between myself and this place in this condition. I hand the device back to Rachel and reach for the packet of pain medicine. There isn't much left, and I don't know what else I'll have to face between here and Baalboden, but if I don't obliterate enough of the pain now, I'll never get the chance to find out. I tip the packet against my lips and let the rest of the powder slide onto my tongue. A moment later, Rachel has the device packed away in her cloak, and the worst of the pain is ebbing. I cast one more glance at the fire now burning between us and the surviving soldiers, then we disappear into the Wasteland, leaving the burning wreckage of Rowansmark's battalion in our wake.

CHAPTER SIXTY-TWO

RACHEL

We travel as fast as Logan's injury will allow us, and just before sunset set up camp in a small, sturdy log cabin we find hidden in a copse of overgrown fir trees. A steady rain falls from steel-gray clouds and slides against my skin with cool, soft fingers. The rain is an unexpected boon that will both douse the flames we left behind and obliterate our tracks.

Quinn and Willow are coming to Baalboden with us. Quinn because he feels honor-bound to pay his debt to my father by helping Logan with the arduous journey. Willow because she refuses to leave her brother's side, and because the prospect of seeing us try to bring down our leader fascinates her on a level I might find disturbing if I had the energy to care.

I don't. I just want to get moving so we can lay a trap for the Commander. We have the device. We understand how to use it. He doesn't stand a chance.

The cabin provides a welcome refuge from the rain, and Logan falls asleep almost as soon as we settle inside. I eat a cold dinner, wrap my cloak around me, and sit beside him. We haven't had a chance to talk privately since fleeing the fire, but his words keep blazing to life inside me with glorious persistence.

I love you, Rachel.

Once, I would've taken those words as a romantic, sugar-coated fairy tale and built a castle of dreams on them. Now, they're a hard-won promise forged in fire and loss by a man who means every word he says. I want to brand them into my skin as proof that I still have something left to fight for.

I wish I had the courage to give those words back to him, but the ugly brokenness inside me holds me back. I'm not the same girl Logan fell in love with. I'm not the same girl he fought to reach. I'm a hollow version of myself, and I have no right to grasp for happiness when I've caused so much misery. The thought slices into me, but the silence greedily swallows the pain before I can truly feel it.

I press close to him and study his face while he sleeps. Fading purple and yellow bruises blossom just beneath the skin of his left cheekbone, cuts run across his arms and hands, and a dirty gauze bandage covers a palm-sized area on his neck. I rummage through his pack, find his small first-aid kit, and gather the supplies I'll need to clean and re-bandage whatever lies beneath the gauze.

I pull the filthy tape away from his skin, remove the gauze, and immediately feel sick. The insignia of the Brute Squad is burned into the side of Logan's neck in a welt of blistered red skin turning black at the edges.

He's been branded. Marked for life by the man everything in me longs to destroy. Every time anyone looks at Logan, they'll know the Commander once had him at his mercy and proved to be stronger.

I dab antiseptic across the wound, sloughing away dead skin and trying not to gag at the sight. I want to torture the Commander before he dies. Hear him scream for mercy and know I have the power to deny him. The thought fills me with a heady sense of power, and my lips peel back from my teeth in a snarl as I gently cut away the blackened skin at the edge of the wound.

Logan stirs restlessly but doesn't wake as I spread salve over the burn and attach a fresh patch of gauze. I lie down, press myself against him, and ignore Quinn and Willow as they huddle in a corner, speaking in low voices.

I might not be able to torture the Commander. I might not be able to make him beg. Once the Cursed One is called, destruction is swift and certain. But I'll make sure the Commander's death is so horrific, so legendary, that for the rest of Logan's life whenever anyone sees the mark on his neck, they won't see a man who was once broken before his leader. They'll see the mark of a man who helped destroy the most powerful person in our world, and they'll tread with caution.

Holding this thought close, I close my eyes and drift to sleep as Logan breathes steadily beside me, Quinn and Willow fall silent in their corner, and the rain taps lightly against the cabin's moss-draped roof.

In the morning, after a quick breakfast of dried fruit, I help Logan pack his gear, and stuff half the contents of his pack into mine when he isn't looking. He doesn't want me to notice how much pain he's in, but I see it.

He reaches up, fingers the new patch of gauze on his neck,

and looks at me. "This is fresh."

"I changed it last night while you slept."

"Is it . . . did it look bad?"

"A little."

"It's probably permanent."

"It adds character." My smile feels wobbly at the edges, so I firm my lips before he notices.

"At least it takes the attention off my face." His smile doesn't wobble at all.

"What's wrong with your face?" I peer at it closely, looking for injuries I may have missed last night in the uncertain light of dusk.

"Nothing." He laughs a little. "It was a joke. You know, people won't have to look at my ugly face because they'll be too busy admiring the Commander's handiwork on my neck."

I scowl. "Your face is just as handsome as ever. And if we do this right, no one will look at your neck without shivering a little at the thought of the leader who went down in flames."

"You think I'm handsome?" A hesitant smile tugs at his lips.

"What? I don't know." I'm suddenly very interested in the state of his boots. Peering at them closely, I pray he'll change the subject. He doesn't.

"That's what you said."

Heat blazes across my face, and I turn away. "I also said we're going to take down the Commander. That's probably the more important part of that whole conversation."

"Not necessarily. Rachel, can we talk about what happened during the Cursed One's attack?"

I love you, Rachel.

The heat in my cheeks creeps down my neck, and when Willow and Quinn slide their leather packs against their backs and walk toward us, I'm grateful for the reprieve. A weak stream of sunlight slips in through the filthy window near the front door and sparkles against the silver ear cuff Willow wears. Her bow is already clutched in her left hand.

"Ready? Or do you two still need a minute?" She looks at my flushed face with something like amusement.

I bend over, pick up our packs, and hand Logan his. His fingers brush mine, and he says quietly, "We're going to have to talk about it sooner or later."

I know we are. But I want a few more moments to hold those four precious words close before he sees the kind of girl I've become. Without looking at him, I settle my pack against my back and lead the way out the front door.

CHAPTER SIXTY-THREE

RACHEL

We walk silently through the moss-draped oaks, Willow and Quinn preferring to travel through the trees above us. I can see Logan trying not to limp as each step jars his ribcage.

"Can you carry this for me?" I shove Melkin's walking stick toward him. If he leans on the end that doesn't slide into the ground, he can use it as a cane.

"Why?"

"Because I want to bring this back for Melkin's wife."

"You're doing an admirable job of carrying it yourself."

Stubborn, prideful man.

"But it was Melkin's. And I no longer want to touch it." I realize the words are true the moment they leave my mouth. I don't want his walking stick. I don't want to remember the bitter misery in his eyes as he asked me whether the Commander would spare his wife if he did as he was asked.

And I don't want to remember the way he kept his knife pointed at the ground while I attacked him.

Logan takes the stick and points the dangerous end toward the sky. "Are we going to talk about Melkin?"

"No."

"Let me rephrase that. What I meant to say is: We're going to talk about Melkin."

"No, we aren't."

We circle the base of a wide oak, its trunk gnarled and scarred, and head into a copse of pine trees. Willow tree-leaps ahead of us until she's nothing but a distant flash of movement in the stillness of the forest. Quinn stays behind us, the occasional rustle of leaves the only reminder of his presence. The air warms gently as we walk, though the shadows still cling to their predawn chill.

"What happened to Melkin?"

"What part of 'we aren't going to talk about this' is difficult to understand?"

His voice is gentle. "How can I help you, if you won't tell me what happened?"

What happened? I felt hope. Burning, brilliant hope that turned to ash beside my father's grave. I then killed my traveling companion for the crime of wanting desperately to save his wife. And I can't feel anything but icy silence for all of it.

We leave the sharp-scented pine behind and enter a field of deep green grass spiked with wildflowers. Willow is already in the center of the field, an arrow notched, her head constantly swiveling, searching for threats. The sun is a fierce, unblinking eye above us, and I feel flushed from its heat.

"I know he was sent into the Wasteland to kill you and return the package to the Commander. His wife had the cell across from mine. She's pregnant. That's enough motivation to sway almost any man into doing the unthinkable."

I can't stand the heat prickling against my skin and reach to unfasten my cloak.

"What happened to your hands?"

The fastening sticks, and I tug at it desperately. He reaches out and captures my fingers in his.

"You have bloodstains on your hands." His touch is gentle.

I want to slap his hand away and hear him condemn me. Tell me he's changed his mind. Tell me he doesn't love me now that he knows what I've done.

But he doesn't know. Because I haven't told him.

"Please," he says.

I take a deep breath, hold on to those four beautiful words for one more moment—*I love you, Rachel*—and then I tell him.

"I killed him." My voice sounds cold and empty as it echoes across the field of wildflowers. His hand tightens on mine.

"Why?" he asks. There's no censure in his voice.

"Because I thought he was attacking me."

"Then it was self-defense."

"No." Up ahead, water glitters beneath the morning sun, a piercing beauty that hurts my eyes. "No, it wasn't."

"Rachel, he was tasked with killing you once you found the package. It was self-defense."

"He wasn't going to kill me. I thought he was, but he wasn't. He was trying to disarm me. Steal the package and leave me behind. Alive." The words make me sick. I thought I'd feel relief to have it out in the open, but I don't.

He's quiet, though his fingers are still wrapped around mine as we approach the diamond-bright surface of a lake. Willow has tossed all but her undertunic aside and is wading into the water, her bow and arrow still clutched in her hands.

"If you thought he was trying to kill you, defending yourself is understandable, Rachel. I would've done the same."

"No, you would've stopped." I whirl to face him, suddenly desperate to make him see. "You'd have kept control. I know you."

Beneath the steadiness of his gaze, pain lingers. "Like I kept control when the Commander backhanded you during the Claiming ceremony?"

"That's not the same."

"I fail to see the difference." He steps close to me. "You were afraid. You knew you couldn't let him take the device and bring it to the Commander. Instinct kicked in, and you did what you had to do."

I shake my head. "You would've seen the signs, and stopped."

"Sweetheart, you haven't been reading people right since Oliver."

My voice is a rough whisper. "And Dad."

We're at the edge of the lake. Logan stops walking and faces me. "What about your dad?"

The words won't come. Maybe they don't exist. I strain to feel it. To let it cut me so I can cry. So I can share grief with the one person who will understand the depth of what I've lost.

"Please don't." His voice is quiet. Pained. His fingers curl around mine and force them open, and I realize I've clenched my fist so tight, my broken nails have gouged four crescents of crimson into my palm. My blood mixes with Melkin's, and I can't look away.

"He's dead, isn't he? Jared's dead."

I look at him.

"I'm so sorry." He drags me against him, and I lean into his shoulder.

"Why aren't you crying?" He pulls back and cups my face in his hands. Pain is carved into his face.

"I can't."

"Why not?" He's rubbing my cheeks with his thumbs as if he can transfer his living, breathing grief into my skin, shattering the icy silence within me into something he can understand.

I can't allow that. If I grieve now, how will I ever find my way out again in time to keep my promises?

"Because there will be nothing left of me if I do." I look at my hands, bleeding and bloodstained, the dirt from my father's grave mixing with the dirt from Melkin's in the creases. "And because I don't deserve it. I deserve to bleed."

I hold my hands up to him.

"I earned this. I did this. I deserve to be marked."

"No." He takes my hands in his. "You don't."

It's useless to argue. I know what I've become inside. If he can't see it now, it won't take long before he does.

I don't protest as he takes off my cloak and insists I strip down to my undertunic. He pulls off all but his pants, and I wince at the ugly purple and black bruises spreading like decaying blossoms across his chest. Then he lifts the leather pouch containing the dirt from my father's grave over my head, sets it aside, and leads me into the lake.

I don't want to let him wash my hands, but he pulls them beneath the water and carefully scrubs away the blood, the dirt, and the evidence of all that's been.

The crimson has seeped beneath my skin, entered my veins, and become a part of what's left of me. No amount of scrubbing can erase that.

"Yesterday, when the Cursed One came out of the ground, I said I loved you."

"I'm not ready to talk about it."

"Oh."

He sounds hurt. I don't want to hurt him. I just don't know how to obliterate the silence consuming me and find anything that feels like hope.

He clears his throat. "I didn't mean to . . . I guess I thought—"

"It's fine." From the corner of my eye, I see Quinn dive off a rock, slicing through the water with the barest hint of a splash.

"No, it's not *fine*."

I squint against the tiny pricks of light dancing over the surface of the water.

He sounds wounded. "I thought you'd at least be a little bit receptive."

I can't look at him. "I would've been. I *was*. Before."

"Before? Before what?"

I whip my head back to face him. "Before everything! Before I saw Oliver get murdered right in front of me. Before I knew Dad was . . . gone. Before Melkin. Before I became *this*." I gesture toward myself, wondering how he can think washing the blood off my hands makes it any less real.

He steps closer, his eyes glowing with fierce conviction. "You're still the same beautiful, stubborn, strong, fascinating Rachel you were before any of that happened."

My laugh sounds more like a sob, and I clamp my lips shut.

"Listen to me. I know it's bad for you. I see that. But shutting yourself off from something good because of all the bad is unfair. To both of us." His cheeks darken, and his eyes slide away from mine. "Unless you don't feel the same, and this is your way of trying to let me down easy, and I've just made a spectacular fool of myself."

He lets go of my hands, cramming damp fingers through his dark blond hair, and doesn't look at me. "I've just made a fool of myself, haven't I?"

"No."

"Yes, I have." He steps back. "What is it about you that makes rational behavior so difficult for me? Never mind. Forget I asked that. You're right. It's fine."

Hurt and embarrassment are written all over his face, and I realize the only one being a fool is me. He's offering me the one thing of beauty I can still claim as my own. I have to cling to it if I ever want to find my way back to the girl I used to be. And it isn't fair of me to deny him the truth just because I worry it means less coming from someone as broken as me.

"No, it isn't. It isn't fine at all," I say.

"We can stop this conversation right now."

"I don't want to."

His laugh is weary. "That makes one of us. At least now I know how you felt two years ago."

"I can do it again." The words are out before I give myself time to lose my nerve. I don't know how to do this. Love is a piercing ache that refuses to slide into the silence. I'm grateful to hold on to something real, but I don't know how to make him see it.

He stops backing away and looks at me. "Do what again?"

I mean to say something heartfelt and sincere like "give you my heart." Something that will erase his fears and leave us with one perfect moment in the midst of everything.

Instead, I step toward him, catch my foot against a rock on the lake bottom, and trip. Crashing into his chest, I plunge us both beneath the surface.

The water is crisp on top and murky below, where our feet kick up eddies of sand and rock. He catches me, his hands wrapped around my arms, as we plummet toward the bottom. My hair floats out to surround him, and he stares at me while above us the sun pierces the surface with golden darts.

Maybe this is better than words. Maybe this is all I need to show him he didn't offer his heart to me in vain.

He lets go, and I reach for him. Twining my fingers through his, I feel something soft warm the silence within me a little as he tangles his legs with mine until I can't tell where one of us ends and the other begins.

But it isn't enough. The ache within me pushes against my chest, tingles down my arms, and hurts the tips of my fingers. I need more. I need to disappear into what we are together.

I need *him*.

I pull him against me as we start floating back toward the surface, and he smiles.

We break the surface together, and the air feels alive in a way it didn't before. He smoothes my hair out of my eyes, and I impatiently shove his hands out of my way so I can reach him.

"Kiss me," I say, and I don't even have time to blush at the audacity of my words before he slides a hand into the hair at the nape of my neck and tugs me toward him.

Our noses bump, and his laugh sounds breathless. "Sorry."

"Don't be sorry. Hurry up and kiss me."

He tightens his arms around me and touches his lips to mine. His kiss is rough, tastes like lake water . . . and is the best thing I've ever felt. I press against him, consuming him like I'll never get enough, and when we break apart, my pulse pounds against my ear, and his chest rises and falls like he's been running.

"Done yet?" Willow calls from somewhere behind me. I hear Quinn shush her, but I don't care.

Because Logan is looking at me like I'm precious to him. And the silence inside me cracks open, just a little. Just enough to let a small piece of hope float to the surface. I grab on to it with desperate fingers.

He keeps one hand on the small of my back and uses the other to trace the Celtic knot on the necklace he gave me the day of the Claiming ceremony.

"I promised to always find you, remember?"

"I remember."

"I promised I would always protect you. You've been wounded badly because I failed to keep that promise."

I shake my head, and the tears spill over, scalding my cheeks with heat.

"But I won't fail you in this, Rachel. No matter what has happened. No matter what you've done. No matter what you will do. I will always love you. I swear it."

His hand clenches around the pendant, and he leans down to capture my gaze with his. "I will always love you."

His arms flex, pulling me against his chest, and his lips hover just above mine, our breath mingling in the dazzling morning air.

"I love you," he whispers and then he kisses me again, his lips rough against mine, his breathing ragged as he devours my fear and makes me long to feel this way forever.

CHAPTER
SIXTY-FOUR

LOGAN

We don't push ourselves on the return trip to Baalboden. I tell Rachel it's to let my rib heal, and I think she believes me. But really, I just want time with her. Time to lie next to her at night, holding her against me while I watch the rotation of the stars. Time to walk beside her during the day and try to draw her into conversation so we can get what has hurt her out into the open, where it can start to heal.

I ache to hear her tell me she loves me, but forcing her to put words to how she feels pushes her further into the silence she seems comfortable calling home now. I tell myself to be patient and understanding, but inside there's a longing only those words will fill, and it hurts to ignore it.

I'm restless. Hungry for something she keeps just out of my reach. It doesn't help that Quinn and Willow are traveling with us. As grateful as I am for their assistance, having others within earshot cuts down significantly on the things I'd like to share with Rachel. So, at the end of another day's journey, when

Willow announces she wants meat for dinner and is going hunting, I look Quinn straight in the eye and say, "You should go with her."

"Logan." Rachel puts her hand on my arm.

"I don't need help bringing down a rabbit," Willow says.

"But there might be highwaymen out there. Or more trackers from Rowansmark. It never hurts to be cautious." I look at Quinn. "You should *go*."

They all stare at me in silence for a second before Willow says, "Why don't you just come right out and say, 'Hey, I want private time with Rachel so I can kiss her senseless like I did at the lake'?"

"Willow!" Quinn frowns at her.

"That's not what he meant," Rachel says, refusing to look at me.

Willow laughs. "Yes, it is. He's itching to get his hands on you without an audience."

"That's *not* what he meant," Rachel says again, pink flushing her cheeks.

"Actually, I meant—" I start to say, but Willow cuts me off.

"What? It's true. He looks at you like he'd like to dip you in sugar and eat you up."

"Willow Runningbrook, that's enough." Quinn's eyes flash, and I catch a glimpse of something feral beneath his smooth exterior. It's gone as soon as I see it, submerged beneath the calm he wears like a second skin.

Willow tosses her hands into the air. "Apparently, honesty is a crime in this group. Look." She points at Rachel. "You're all, 'Revenge is all I want! I'll figure out my love life later!' and he"—she points to me—"is afraid revenge will kill you before he has a chance to really touch you—"

"No, he isn't."

I step forward. "Willow has a point."

"Willow needs to learn to share only those observations that others ask her to share." Quinn steps forward as well.

Willow shrugs and shoulders her bow. "I got tired of tiptoeing around the obvious." She winks at me. "How much time do you need to kiss her senseless?"

"He's not going to—"

"At least an hour," I say, dragging Rachel into my arms and kissing her before she can say another word.

I don't hear Willow leave or Quinn follow her. I can't hear anything beyond the wild pounding of my heart and the soft catch of Rachel's breath as I fist my hands in the back of her tunic and pull her against me like I can't stand to have a single sliver of air between us.

"Logan." Her voice is as shaky as the hand she puts on my chest, and I can't bear it. I can't bear to hear her tell me to stop. To pull back. I can't bear to be apart from her when she's all I have.

"Don't," I say, and she tilts her head back to look at me. "Don't keep me at a distance."

"Who said anything about keeping you at a distance?" Her smile lingers in her eyes.

But when she leans in to kiss me, I'm the one who pulls back because suddenly just being with her isn't enough. Not nearly enough.

"Logan?"

I close my eyes and reach for the courage to ask her to give me the words I need.

Her lips brush mine, sweet and hesitant, and I open my eyes. She's all I can see. All I can taste when I breathe in. Her body molds itself to mine like she was made for me, and I want her to feel it too. To acknowledge it.

To hope for it in the middle of so much hopelessness.

"Rachel, I need . . . " The words won't come. I don't know how to say that I need everything she is without making it sound like more than she can give.

Please don't let it be more than she can give.

"What do you need?" Her face is luminous beneath the golden fingers of the waning sun.

And suddenly the words are there, falling into place like I always knew the way to reach her. "I need to know what you need. What you want. Not from the device, not from the Commander, but from me."

She stiffens, shoulders lifting toward her jaw as if to protect herself from a blow she has to know I'll never deliver.

"Please." I can barely push the word out. "Please, Rachel. Look past the loss, the grief. Look at *me*."

She closes her eyes. I feel like I've been slashed open inside where no one will ever see me bleed. But then she takes a deep breath, relaxes her shoulders, and looks at me, tears filling her eyes.

"I need *you*, Logan. Just you."

I tighten my grip on her tunic. "Why?"

"Because I still love you." Her voice catches. "I never stopped. I thought I had. I wanted to. But somehow . . . it's like part of you lives inside the most important part of me, and I don't know how to separate the two." Tears spill over, tracing a glistening path down her cheeks. "I love you, Logan."

Joy surges through me, brilliant and wild. I cup her face in my hands and wipe away her tears. "I love you too, Rachel. Always." And then I do my best to use the full hour I've been given to kiss her senseless.

CHAPTER SIXTY-FIVE

<u>RACHEL</u>

I can't sleep. My lips are still swollen from Logan's kisses, and the ache I feel for him wants to spill out of my fragile skin, envelop me, and tempt me to forget everything that lies ahead.

But I can't. Beneath the ache, the silence lives within me, demanding justice for Dad. For Oliver. For all of us. Willow accused me of wanting nothing but revenge. She was wrong.

I want redemption.

I just don't think I can get it without exacting revenge first.

After tossing and turning on the soft bed of moss I made for us, I give up trying to sleep. I'm careful not to wake Logan as I get up. He looks peaceful beneath the pale light of the stars. I want to trace the lines of his face and memorize the way his skin feels beneath my fingertips, but I don't. He needs to rest until it's time for him to take the night watch shift from Quinn.

I walk a few paces away and sit with my back to a thick, silver-trunked oak. A few yards to my left, Willow sleeps in her tree cradle, her bow in hand. I don't see Quinn, but it doesn't matter.

I didn't get up for conversation. Besides, his calm stoicism is unnerving, and I never know what to say to him.

I sit in silence, listening to the distant hooting of an owl and the occasional whisper of a breeze as it tangles itself within the leaves above me. It's the first time in days that I haven't had someone talking to me, watching me, or expecting something from me. It doesn't take long for my thoughts to fill the void with violent images. Oliver's eyes growing distant as his blood spills onto me. Logan's mother lying at the Commander's feet, her back flayed raw, slipping away from her little boy until there's nothing left. Dad, risking everything to keep the Commander from gaining a weapon he could use to obliterate any opposition, and then giving his life to save Quinn and Willow and trusting Logan and me to finish his mission.

"Want company?" Quinn asks quietly. I have no idea how long he's been standing in front of me.

It's on the tip of my tongue to say no, but I was wrong. I do want conversation. Even with Quinn. Anything to save me from the overwhelming images in my head.

"Sure," I say, and he sits against the tree across from me, his long legs folded under him, his eyes scanning the area before coming back to rest on me.

"I hate it when people ask me how I'm doing," he says as if this conversational opener should make sense to me. And strangely, it does. Because the last thing I want to be asked right now is how I'm doing.

"I wasn't going to ask you that."

He smiles, a flash of white teeth against his dark skin. "I'll return the favor."

We sit in silence for a moment, then he says, "You're a lot like your dad, you know."

The words both hurt and heal, and I don't know how to respond.

"He always seemed so sure of himself, didn't he?" he asks.

"Because he always knew what to do."

Quinn smiles again, yet I swear I see sadness on his face. "No one always knows what to do, Rachel. We all just do the best we can with what we've got. Sometimes it works. Sometimes it ruins everything."

He looks away, and the breeze tugs at his black hair.

I say the words before I really think them through. "What did you do that ruined everything?"

"It's complicated."

I know the feeling. I'm about to back out of the conversation with the excuse of needing more sleep when he takes a deep breath and looks at me.

"I killed a man too. I thought I had to. I'm still not sure if I was right, but because of my actions, Willow and I were cast out of our village." His voice is low and steady, but sadness runs beneath it. He sits in silence for a moment, then says, "What's been done is done. I've had to learn how to live with what was left."

Shock robs me of speech for a moment. I lean closer to study his face, looking for the lie. For proof he's saying what he thinks I need to hear so he can gain my trust. The only thing I find in his expression is naked truth. I feel like an intruder. "I'm sorry. I didn't mean to pry."

He leans forward and traces patterns into the soil at his feet.

"You aren't prying. You asked because you know how it feels to think you've ruined everything. You're hoping if my story has a happy ending, there's hope for yours."

I shift uneasily against the tree trunk. I'm not sure I want to know, but I have to ask, "Does yours have a happy ending?"

His finger pauses, pressing into the dirt as he slowly raises his head to look at me. "I don't know. I haven't reached the end."

"Oh. I guess I thought . . . you seem so settled. So comfortable with yourself and others. I thought maybe you—"

"Had answers? I might." He shrugs. "But they're answers I had to find for myself. I don't think they'll work for anyone else."

I should probably feel awkward, sitting in the dirt across from a boy I barely know talking about the things that haunt us, but instead, I feel a tiny sliver of comfort. Here is someone who understands. Who knows what it feels like to have blood on his hands and not know if the guilt he feels should be his to bear alone. And he isn't broken. He's found a measure of peace, with himself and with others.

It gives me hope that someday, after I'm finished with the Commander, I might be able to shatter the silence inside me, grieve for those I've lost, and find a way to forgive myself for what I've caused. Someday, I might find my own measure of peace.

He leans back, and we sit in companionable silence while the tree branches creak and shiver in the wind and the stars slowly trek across the vast darkness of the sky above us.

CHAPTER SIXTY-SIX

LOGAN

"**A**bsolutely not." Quinn's tone discourages any argument.

"But they might need us." Willow stands, arms crossed over her chest, staring her brother down across the fire at our final camping spot before reaching Baalboden.

I couldn't care less about their argument. Whether they come with us or move on. I'm too busy running through tomorrow's plan of action, looking for weaknesses.

"You don't want to go into Baalboden with them because they might need you," Quinn says. "You want to go because you want to see if they can take out their leader."

"That's definitely a side benefit."

"Which is why I'm saying no."

She rolls her eyes. "You're no fun anymore, you know that?"

He freezes and something dark flashes through his eyes. That's the second time I've seen hints that what goes on beneath his surface doesn't always match the calm he wears on the outside. Which won't matter if he chooses to move on.

But if he stays in Baalboden once the Commander has been defeated, I'm going to have to keep an eye on him.

Willow slowly uncurls her arms and says, "I didn't mean to say that."

"I know." He turns away and begins gathering what he'll need to make a tree-cradle bed for her.

"Quinn." She hurries to him, wraps an arm around his shoulders.

"You think I don't know you're paying the price for my actions?" he asks quietly, and the pain in his voice seems to hit Willow hard. "Every moment of every day I carry the burden for causing you to be an outcast with me."

Definitely more going on beneath his surface than he wants us to know. I wonder what he did that caused the two of them to be punished like this.

Willow's lips tremble, and she steps in front of him to make him look at her. "I chose you. Do you hear me, Quinn Running-brook? You're all the family I need."

They walk to the edge of our campsite, talking in low tones. I give up speculating about what kind of crime would cause a Tree Village to cast out two of their own, and run through Worst Case Scenarios for tomorrow instead. In a few moments, Willow disappears up a tree, and Quinn returns, his face shadowed.

"We'll go no further. Our debt to Jared has been paid." His eyes seek out Rachel's and linger. "Be safe."

I slide my arm around her shoulders and pull her closer to me. "We will."

"Where will you go?" Rachel asks.

He shrugs. "We'll find another Tree Village to take us in.

Somewhere far from our first home."

"But the next closest Tree Village is a two-week journey east," she says, and turns to me. "They could live in Baalboden, couldn't they? Once the Commander is gone?"

I didn't realize she'd come to care for Quinn and Willow, and I wish she could let them go. I could lie and say it's because I can hardly guarantee any stability in Baalboden until after we succeed in restructuring the government, but the truth is I don't like the interest in Quinn's eyes when he looks at Rachel.

I can't tell her that, but I look at Quinn and make sure my expression doesn't match my words as I say, "Of course they can. But they might not feel comfortable living on the ground."

Quinn smiles. "We'll camp here for several days. See how it goes in Baalboden. We can decide what to do at the end of the week." His eyes are still on Rachel.

She smiles back. "Good. Once the Commander is gone, we'll see about finding you and Willow a place. There are plenty of trees in Baalboden."

My smile feels stretched thin as I say, "Thank you for helping Rachel and for assisting me. I won't forget it." I stand and shake Quinn's outstretched hand. His eyes flick toward me, and then he looks once more at Rachel, nods, and backs out of the clearing to take the first night watch.

I bank the fire and sit beside Rachel to talk though our plan one last time. I've barely started running scenarios when she interrupts.

"You're not tall enough to pass as Melkin."

It's the same argument she's been using for hours now.

"I'm tall enough. Plus, only Melkin knew the signal to give."

"Only Melkin and his *wife*. Who was next to you in the dungeon. You don't think the Commander might be expecting you to show up like this?"

She has a point, but since the only other recourse is to let her face the Commander herself, I keep arguing.

"It doesn't matter what he expects. He wants this"—I point to the device lying on a cloth between us—"too much to stay away. By the time he realizes it's me, he'll see I have the device and he'll start negotiating."

Her laugh is bitter. "He doesn't negotiate, Logan. He executes."

"Which is why I'll be the one taking the risk. Just in case."

"I can handle it."

Of course she can. But *I* can't handle it if it all goes wrong, and I have to watch her die.

"I need you to call the Cursed One for me. I need you to stay out of sight and use Melkin's staff to call the beast before the Commander takes the device from me."

"Oh, that's just perfect. We take revenge on the Commander, and all I get to do is shove a stick into the ground? No. I promised Oliver and Dad I would kill him. I'm not going back on that."

"And I promised I would always protect you. So—"

"So use Melkin's stick in time to call the Cursed One before—"

"No!"

"I have to kill him. I have to. It's the only way I'll have peace."

She's shaking. Maybe we both are. My emotions are running so high I can hardly think straight. I can't allow Rachel to take the risk, but if I don't, I'm not sure she'll ever forgive me.

Best Case Scenario: She evades any treachery on the Commander's part and remembers which combination of finger pads controls the Cursed One so she can turn the beast against him without dying herself.

Worst Case Scenario: Everything else.

Unless . . .

"I don't think the Commander knows what the device looks like."

"What makes you say that?" she asks.

"Did Melkin know exactly what he was looking for?"

She frowns and shakes her head. "I don't think so."

"I can guarantee if the Commander ever had the opportunity to see this thing in person, he'd already own it and the person who'd shown it to him would be dead."

"Agreed."

"So, at best, he only has a general idea of what it looks like."

Her smile looks more like a snarl. "So make a duplicate."

"And you can hold the real one while you hide. I'll keep Melkin's staff so my disguise looks more authentic."

"And when the Cursed One comes, I'll kill the Commander."

"Yes." I pull her to me so I won't have to see the vicious fury on her face and hope that by giving her what she so desperately wants, I haven't destroyed more of the girl I love.

We unstring Rachel's bow and use the lightweight black wood to mimic the design of the device. I still have copper wires hidden in the seams of my cloak, and after dismantling her Switch to get to the gears inside, I make a passable imitation of the Rowansmark tech. The wires are obvious, and it has gears instead of finger pads, but it looks like a piece of workable tech, and that's all we need.

We go over the plan, in detail, three more times until Rachel refuses to discuss it again. I don't push the issue. Pulling her against me, I wrap myself around her and listen to her breathe as the darkness hides the device, the terrible fury in her eyes, and the evidence that this may be our last night together.

Her breathing slows, an even cadence that comforts me. I brush my lips against her ear and whisper promises I'll die to keep.

CHAPTER
SIXTY-SEVEN

RACHEL

D awn is a faint, gray smudge on the horizon as we reach the ancient oak marking the line between Baalboden's eastern perimeter and the Wasteland. Logan hunches inside his cloak, his hood pulled forward to cover most of his face. The fake Rowansmark tech is in one hand and Melkin's staff is in the other.

I stay back several trees, the true device in my cloak pocket and a brilliant blaze of triumphant rage warming me from the inside out.

We've gone over the plan, the list of everything Logan worries can go wrong, and both of us are as ready as we can be. We might die. The whole thing might blow up in our faces, and we might fail. But it doesn't matter. What matters is that we're here. Standing against him. Committed to delivering justice, no matter what it costs.

Logan turns to look at me, his blue eyes lit with something I now recognize as uniquely mine. "Ready?"

"Yes."

The torch is embedded in the heart of the tree, far below the tall canopy of branches. He strikes flint at it, and fire blazes immediately, throwing shadows over his face as he waits.

I melt back into the forest a few yards, far enough that I can't be seen by anyone approaching Logan, but close enough that I can still see and hear what is going on, and climb into a tree. It takes two hours, but we finally see the Commander and the eight surviving members of his Brute Squad stride across the perimeter toward the tree.

It's too easy. Surely the Commander suspects treachery. He knows Logan escaped. He must wonder if Melkin could really carry out his assignment against me. And yet he walks toward us as if he doesn't have a care in the world.

The hair on the back of my neck rises, and seconds later, a team of guards slide out of the eastern Wasteland and converge on Logan.

No wonder it took two hours. The Commander needed time for his guards to exit the gate, enter the Wasteland, and circle around behind us. It's a trap, but we knew it would be. The Commander never meant to keep the one who delivered the package alive. We just never realized there would be *so many*. Logan thought the Brute Squad would be all the Commander deemed necessary to take down the one insignificant person delivering his precious package.

Logan turns, sweeps the ranks of guards behind him with a glance, and tightens his grip on the staff.

We'd planned for Logan to fall back during the confusion of the Cursed One's arrival, but there are too many guards behind him. He has nowhere to go. He can't call the Cursed One and survive unless he shimmies up the oak and starts tree-leaping. In our planning, that was a last resort, as there are too many ways that could end in disaster. The moment he diverts his attention to climbing the tree and avoiding the lit torch sticking out of its belly, the Commander could kill him. Any one of the guards could kill him. No, he'll need to talk his way out. Find a way to use the device for leverage. Maybe admit it's a fake and get the Commander to leave him alive because he knows where the real one is.

All of those are flimsy excuses for a plan. They won't work. Any of them. I can't think of a way out, but surely Logan can. He always can. I strain to see him past the three rows of uniform-clad backs between us.

The Commander reaches him, but stays several feet back. Logan is looking at the ground, but I see the moment he comes up with a plan. His shoulders straighten. He lifts his head, throws back his hood, and looks the Commander in the eye.

Then he slams the staff into the ground.

My fury at the Commander dissolves into terror for Logan. He hasn't made a new plan. He's called the Cursed One with almost no chance of escape, and now he's going to die in front of me.

My fingers shake as I snatch the device out of my cloak pocket.

The Commander laughs, a cruel sound smearing the morning air with malice. "Logan McEntire. I suppose you think I'm surprised to see you instead of Melkin."

First two buttons together turn the beast east. Bottom two buttons turn it west. I wish my hands would stop trembling.

Logan holds up the fake device. "I brought what you want. But it's going to cost you."

The Commander's smile is full of hate. "No. It's going to cost *you*." He waves the guards forward. Swords gleam, an impossibly thick row of sharp silver teeth reaching for Logan. "You've outlived your usefulness to me. To all of Baalboden. It's been nineteen years of waiting for my investment to pay off, and I can't wait to rid my city of the stench of you."

I forget the device for a moment as the Commander's words sink in, and Logan goes pale. What does he mean, he's been waiting for this? No one knew when Logan was born that one day he'd be in this position. A tremor runs through the earth. I can't think of the Commander's words right now. I have bigger problems.

My hands are clammy as I grip the device. Top and bottom buttons send it north. All three send it south.

The ground shakes. A distant roar surges closer. The guards stumble to a halt and look around, fear on their faces.

"You're going to die." Logan's voice rings out clearly.

The Commander's smile snags on his scar and morphs into a predatory mask. He lunges for Logan, snatches the fake tech from his hands, and backs away. The guards back away as well, their swords raised as if they can protect themselves from what's coming, but there are still too many of them between Logan and safety.

The ground cracks. The guards run. The Commander laughs. And Logan turns to leap into the oak tree as the Cursed One explodes into the air, black scales clinking together in deafening harmony, his mouth already spewing orange streams of fire.

Clumps of ground, roots, and branches fly through the air, a shower of debris that knocks a few guards flat on their backs. I check for the Commander's location, and try to breathe through the panic seizing my chest.

North. I need to send the beast north. My mind goes blank for a crucial second, and the creature roars at the oak tree, sending the entire thing up in flames.

"Logan!" I scream, racing along my branch toward where I last saw him.

He's already leaping clear. The guards behind him have abandoned their positions and are running for their lives. Logan races into the forest, sees me, and yells, "North! Send it north!"

My fingers find the top and bottom buttons before my brain can translate the thought. The beast surges toward the Commander as he flees toward the northern edge of the city's Wall. Fire leaps from the creature's mouth. Two members of the Brute Squad are incinerated and then crushed beneath the thing's monstrous length as it races forward. Now nothing stands between it and the Commander.

Reckless triumph surges through me. We've got him. There's no escape. No way to stop the Cursed One. Logan climbs onto the branch beside me and together we watch, ignoring the screams of the guards as they run into the Wasteland behind us. Ignoring the crackling flames as they eat through the ancient oak tree. We watch and wait for justice.

The Commander stops, holds out the fake tech, and tries to manipulate the gears wired to its surface.

I laugh, but choke on it when the Commander throws the fake device to the ground, rips open his uniform, and pulls out a heavy silver chain with what looks like a severed lizard foot dangling from it, its talons curved into wickedly sharp tips. It resembles a smaller version of the Cursed One's own limb.

The beast jerks to a stop and snorts, sucking in the air around it as if hunting for something.

"No." I press the bottom two buttons again. The Cursed One roars, but doesn't advance. "Why isn't it attacking?" I press the buttons repeatedly, and the beast coils in on itself, scales clanking. It shakes its head and blasts the ground beneath it with fire.

It will attack itself. But it won't attack the Commander.

"Logan—"

"Look at it. The beast is sniffing something—"

"It's always sniffing something. It tracks by scent. I can't get this to work!"

"No, it isn't tracking. It's shying away. Something about that lizard foot makes it unwilling to attack."

The Cursed One shudders as I press more buttons, willing it to get over whatever issue it has with the Commander's necklace and destroy him with fire. It shudders, giant ripples tearing along its frame, but it refuses to attack.

"The foot protects him. Where did he get it?" He mumbles beneath his breath, listing options, trying to make connections.

"Who cares where he got it? Let's go rip it off of him."

"He's had that necklace for as long as anyone can remember. In drawings of him protecting the first survivors fifty years ago, you can see the chain around his neck before the rest of it disappears beneath his coat. That was right after his team returned from the beast's den. It's a trophy. He must have killed another beast. The Cursed One's mate? Its children? No wonder it won't attack. The lingering pheromones must keep it at bay. What do you want to bet all the city-state leaders have necklaces just like this one?"

"I don't want to bet anything. I want the Commander to suffer and die. We have to kill him ourselves." I'm already reaching for my knife, but Logan stays my hand.

"Keep the Cursed One as close to him as you can to distract him." He throws off his cloak, drops to the forest floor and draws his sword. "I'm going after him."

"Wait!"

He looks at me, cold purpose on his face, his dark-blond hair turned red by the flames behind him, and says, "I know you want to be the one to kill him. But please don't ask me to send you against the Commander in the presence of the Cursed One with nothing but your knife."

I do want to be the one to kill him. But more than that, I want him *dead*. My knife is no match for the Commander. Logan has a much better chance.

"I wasn't going to argue."

"Then what were you going to do?"

The fire hisses and pops as the oak tree caves in on itself, and I jump down to the forest floor beside Logan. I regret all the things I never said to Dad and to Oliver. I'm not going to have regrets here, too.

I throw my arms around his neck. "I love you, Logan. Always."

A fierce smile lights his face for a moment, and he grabs the front of my tunic, hauls me against him, and kisses me. "I love you, too. Always." Then he's gone, and I'm pressing buttons with frantic fingers, trying to keep the Cursed One as close to the Commander as possible to give Logan a chance.

CHAPTER
SIXTY-EIGHT

I circle through the tree line to position myself behind the Commander. No one stops me. Every guard in the area is either running for his life or already dead.

The Cursed One roars, spitting fire in every direction, blackening the dirt perimeter that encircles Baalboden.

The Commander holds his severed lizard foot in front of him and laughs.

I heft my sword in the shelter of the trees twenty yards behind the Commander. All of my anger, pain, and loss coalesce into an unyielding sense of purpose.

He's mine. For Oliver. For Jared. For Rachel. For my mother. For the citizens of Baalboden who crave change.

For me.

My sword flashes in the sunlight as I step away from the trees and gauge my approach. I can sprint forward. Bury my blade in the back of his neck before he knows I'm there. And take the talisman that keeps the Cursed One at bay so I can hold off the creature's attack until Rachel sends it back to the depths of the Earth.

Raising my sword, I lower the point to the necessary trajectory, drag in a deep breath, and start running. I'm over halfway there when the entire plan falls to pieces.

The Cursed One jerks its head up as if it hears something and suddenly lunges west.

Straight for Baalboden.

The Commander yells, drops his talisman against his chest, and runs toward the city. Rachel bursts out of the trees, her face filled with desperate terror as she presses the bottom two buttons on the device. The ones that should turn the beast away from Baalboden.

The Cursed One never deviates.

Fire bursts from its mouth as it strafes the Wall. The stone is scorched black, but the Wall is too thick for even the Cursed One to destroy. Any relief I feel disappears in an instant as the beast rears up, plunges into the ground, and explodes into the air on the other side of the Wall in a shower of cobblestone, dirt, and flame.

"No!"

Rachel is screaming. Running toward the Wall. Slamming the third button. The one that *should* send the Cursed One back into the bowels of the Earth.

I race to join her as plumes of thick black smoke billow up from the city. The turret closest to us explodes into flame and slowly topples to the ground in a hail of sparks and fiery chunks of wood.

The Commander veers north, apparently thinking to run the

entire way around the Wall to get to the gate. He's a fool. By the time he reaches it, the city will be nothing but rubble.

"It isn't working. Help me!" Rachel thrusts the device into my hands, and I drop my sword so I can push the finger pads.

We're close enough to the Wall now that we can hear the screaming from inside. There's no way over the Wall. No gate unless we take the time to run all the way around the circumference of the city like the Commander. Rachel doesn't hesitate. We reach the jagged hole left by the Cursed One, and she leaps into it.

I follow. We slide down about fifteen yards before the tunnel turns upward again.

She's clawing her way toward the surface. I'm digging for footholds right behind her. Above us, the citizens in the East Quarter are screaming in agony.

We scramble through the crater left by the Cursed One, and my stomach sinks as I take in the chaos. Everything is burning. *Everything.* Brilliant gold and crimson flames chew through homes, spew thick black smoke toward the sky, and race blindly for the next piece of dry wood. Windows explode outward, sending hundreds of diamond-bright slivers of glass through the air. And through it all, the monstrous shape of the Cursed One coils, lashing out with its tail to crush wagons, buildings, and people. Strafing entire streets with blistering fire. Bellowing a hoarse, guttural cry that shakes the ground.

The few people still on their feet are running in a blind panic. As fire leaps from building to building, street to street, intent on destroying the entire East Quarter, the Cursed One abruptly heads toward North Hub, blasting anything that moves with flames.

"Make it stop, Logan! Make it go away."

I try. I push the button, and the creature pauses, shakes its head, and slams the ground with its spiked tail, shattering the cobblestones beneath it. Then it slides north again, spreading destruction and death in its wake.

Either our device is malfunctioning, or someone else is out there with another piece of tech capable of overriding this one. It doesn't matter which is true. The end result is the same. Baalboden's protective Wall has become a death trap for anyone left inside its embrace.

"We can't stop it."

She whirls toward me, her eyes full of tears. "We have to!"

"We *can't*. All we can do is rescue as many people as possible."

She doesn't argue as I pull her toward a side street that isn't yet on fire. It takes an agonizing three minutes to find what we need. In that time, the Cursed One turns North Hub into a blazing inferno. I pray the citizens there heard the screaming of their neighbors and had enough warning to start running.

The fourth backyard I check has a wagon and a panicked horse stomping in a double-stall animal shed. I hand the device to Rachel, and hitch the horse to the wagon as fast as I can. She stands beside me, staring at the wagon and shaking, but when I offer her a hand up to join me in the driver's seat, she doesn't hesitate.

We head down the alley and turn north. The sky is a haze of thick black smoke. Entire streets are nothing but sheets of flame. I crack the reins against the horse's back, and we thunder toward the destruction.

A few people still stagger about, and we stop to haul them into the wagon bed. Most of the East Quarter is in shambles, but set apart from the rest is the Commander's compound, untouched by fire. I calculate less than five minutes before the flames bridge the distance and begin destroying it. Which means Eloise and the other prisoners face a terrible death if I can't figure out a way to free them in time.

A man rides by us on a sturdy-looking donkey. I recognize him as one of Drake's companions from Thom's Tankard. "Hey!" I call out, and he turns.

"Logan? Logan McEntire?"

"The prisoners in the dungeon. They won't be able to escape without help. Can you—"

He turns his donkey toward the compound without waiting to hear the rest of my sentence.

"There should be a hole in the wall of the corner cell," I yell at his retreating back.

The northern roads are all impassable, so I turn the wagon and head south. The ground shakes as the Cursed One turns southwest and bellows, lashing at buildings with its tail. The streets in front of us are clogged with wagons, people on donkeys or horses, or families hurrying toward the gate on foot. At our backs, a wall of impossible heat precedes the flames that race toward us.

We've failed them. All of them. We thought to destroy the leader who tormented them, and instead, we've brought destruction down on their heads. Rachel sits beside me, her finger holding down the third button continuously. Her tears are gone. In their place is the white-faced shock I first saw when I picked her up at Madam Illiard's after Oliver's murder.

We inch our way through the streets, surrounded by sobbing, screaming people and the thunderous roar of Baalboden succumbing to its fiery death in our wake. The Cursed One is a black blur in the distance—twisting, lunging, and roaring its triumph as it consumes South Edge. The crowds grow dense, nearly impassable, as we head west, and when we reach the gate, I stare at it in disbelief.

The gate is closed. Locked. And the guards are nowhere to be seen.

Suddenly, a girl runs alongside the wagon, grabs the board beside me, and swings onto the platform. I glance at her and recognize my jail visitor. Her face is alive with purpose as she looks at me.

"Can you get us out?"

Is she crazy? A ton of concrete and steel stand in our way. How am I supposed to move that?

The ground beneath us shakes as the Cursed One explodes out of South Edge and into Lower Market, spewing fire.

We're next.

"Logan!" She snaps her fingers in front of me. "Can you get us out?"

A ton of concrete and steel. No way to get so many people over it. Or under it. We'll have to go through.

"I'll have to build a bomb."

"Tell me what you need."

"The abandoned warehouse beside the armory. There are two black metal barrels full of liquid. I need those and a supply of canning jars with lids. Can you help me get those?"

She cups her hands around her mouth and whistles, an ear-splitting note that momentarily silences those in our immediate vicinity.

"Logan can get us out. Dad"—she calls to my right, and I turn to see Drake standing there, soot stains on his patched tunic and part of his beard singed away—"get a team to the abandoned warehouse by the armory and bring back the metal barrels of liquid you find there."

He nods, grabs a hulking man wearing a tattered cloak, and they head toward the armory.

The girl looks at the crowd surrounding us. "The rest of you, go through the homes near here and bring me every jar and lid you find. Empty the contents if you must."

A few people immediately do her bidding, but most of them stare at us with nothing but confusion on their faces.

"Do you want to live?" She screams it at them, and more of them start moving. Before long, a line of people are dumping jars of every size into the back of the wagon.

North Hub and East Quarter are nothing but billowing clouds of black smoke. South Edge is a burning inferno behind us. Survivors of those three districts mingle with citizens from the western reaches of the city and jostle against the unyielding surface of the Wall like sheep penned in for a slaughter. I see Thom, his clothes still smoking, leading a donkey with Eloise perched on its back. He elbows his way toward us.

Another explosion rips through the air behind us, accompanied by a chorus of screams. The Cursed One is coming our way. I give it ten minutes before the beast reaches the gate and turns the citizens of Baalboden into nothing but a memory.

It'll be a miracle if we make it out alive.

"What's your name?" I ask the girl.

"Nola."

"Thank you, Nola." It's less than she deserves, but it's the best I can give.

Eight minutes left. Rachel is still holding down the button. I press a kiss against her head and say, "I love you."

She looks at me, tears gathering in her eyes. "I love you, too."

Six minutes. The ground beneath us trembles, violent shudders that send people to their knees. The flames are so close now, we can hear them crackling in the distance.

Five.

"Make way!" Drake and three other men stumble into the crowd, their clothing singed. Each pair holds a black barrel.

I let go of Rachel.

"Open the jars," I say to Nola, and yell to the people in front of me to clear out of my way as Drake and his helpers load the barrels onto the wagon bed.

People stumble to the side as my wagon pushes through. Rachel drops the device and climbs into the wagon bed to help open jars.

Four minutes.

Pulling the horse to a stop twenty yards from the gate, I look at Nola. "Get them away from the gate. Close enough that they can run through as soon as it's open, but far enough that they won't be injured by falling debris."

While Nola barks orders at the citizens filling the street, I leap into the wagon bed and point to Drake and one other. "Fill as many jars as you can with the liquid in your barrel. Be careful.

It's acid. It'll burn your skin."

"Better than being dead," Drake says, and starts his task.

"You two fill the rest of these jars with the liquid in your barrels. It's glycerin. Don't let it come in contact with the acid, whatever you do. It would kill us all."

"What can I do?" Rachel stands beside me. "Give me something to do."

"Press the button, sweetheart. Keep pressing it."

She climbs over the wagon seat and grabs the device again.

Three minutes.

Plumes of black smoke rise from the west now as the fires in North Hub eat through the city at a frightening speed. From the outside, it must look like the entire city is already up in flames.

I check the progress of the men in the back. Each team has about nine jars filled and capped now. Drake's hands are blistered raw, but he refuses to let his teammate dip for him.

Nine is good, but I don't know if it will be enough.

"Everyone who will listen to me is out of the danger zone." Nola appears beside the wagon. "Blow it up, Logan."

"Keep filling." I say to the men, and snatch the dagger from my boot so I can cut the horse free of the reins. He takes off running as soon as he's free, and I look at Rachel. "Come out of the wagon."

She scrambles down and stands beside me, still holding the device.

"We're going to flip the wagon over and use it as a shield."

Two minutes.

I call out a warning to the men, and they lift the filled jars and metal drums clear of the wagon bed. Then we flip the wagon to its side and crouch behind it. A quick count shows I have nearly twenty jars of each liquid now. Eighteen of acid. Nineteen of glycerin.

It will have to be enough.

Grabbing a jar of acid, I lob it at the gate. It explodes against the stone in a hail of glass and sizzling liquid. I bend down and pick up two more. Two of the men grab jars of acid too, and we throw all six of them against the gate. When they reach for more, I stop them.

"Save those. We'll need them."

One minute.

I scoop up two jars of glycerin. The men do the same. "Stay down," I say to Rachel and Nola, and then we throw the jars.

The glass missiles arc through the air, slam into the damp concrete, and shatter. The gate explodes in a brutal hail of concrete slabs, steel splinters, and suffocating dust. People scream as tons of debris come raining down around us. Some are crushed, others are knocked off their feet, still more are sliced open by the lethal barrage.

It's a sea of wreckage, blood, and chaos, but there's a hole in the gate big enough to fit three wagons side by side. Beyond the ruins, the Wasteland gleams like a jewel-green beacon of safety. Behind us, the roar of the beast is closing in.

"Get as many of them out as you can," I say to Nola, Drake, and the others. They hurry to comply, and I pick up another jar of each liquid as the Cursed One incinerates the last block of buildings between it and the gate and comes for us.

CHAPTER
SIXTY-NINE

RACHEL

I lean down beside Logan and pick up two jars as the beast comes closer. Grim determination anchors me to the ground as the flames eat through Lower Market and the cobblestones shake beneath the weight of the Cursed One's approach.

We did this. We brought it here. We have to do everything in our power to destroy it. It's the only chance the people outside the gate have of surviving.

"You should leave too," Logan says.

"Don't be an idiot. Whether we live or die, we'll do it together."

He doesn't argue.

We wait as the beast slithers its way over the cobblestone street toward us, its movements jerky, as if something beyond itself is driving it forward. We wait while it fills the grassy clearing between the gatehouse and the gate with fire. And we wait until we can see the milky yellow of its unseeing eyes.

I grip the jars with bloodless fingers, and ready myself.

"Now!" Logan yells.

We throw the jars and they explode against the impenetrable scales of the beast. The force knocks the creature to its back. It bellows, flips over, and comes for us.

"Again!"

The second round of explosions blows a section of its tail to pieces. Wild triumph surges through me.

We can beat it.

"It can be killed. Did you see that? It can be killed!" I reach down for two more jars, and the Cursed One jerks to a stop, shuddering as if held back by something. I lob the jars, and the beast bellows as they hit it in the side, sending a shower of ebony scales clattering to the ground and revealing a small patch of gray skin beneath.

"It's vulnerable!" I scream over the sound of flames and the roar of the beast.

Determination slides quickly into vicious purpose as I stare at the beast's exposed skin. I can't avenge Oliver. I can't stop the Commander. But I can destroy the creature that took Dad from me.

Logan would argue. Calculate angles and odds. Take a moment to plan. But if I do that, I could miss my chance. The fury inside me begs for vengeance. Promises that if I just obliterate the cause of my pain, I can find peace. I hold on to the bright, jagged edges of that idea and let it fill me up until I can't see anything else.

Then, as Logan bends down for more jars, I snatch my knife out of its sheath and charge straight for the Cursed One.

"Rachel!" Logan screams my name, but I keep running.

The beast bellows, a tortured sound full of pain and rage.

I skid on debris.

It whips its head in my direction.

I grip my knife with steady fingers.

It jerks its nose, sniffing the air.

Nine more yards. I raise my blade.

Its claws dig into the ground.

Eight yards.

"Rachel, no!" Logan screams again.

Seven.

The beast's tail slams into the ground.

Six.

It shudders and pins me with its sightless eyes.

Five.

I brace to launch myself forward. It lowers its snout and roars, blasting me with an unending stream of fire.

CHAPTER SEVENTY

LOGAN

"No!" I stumble, hit my knees against the pavement, and scream, "Rachel!"

One second she was there, running straight for the Cursed One, her knife raised above her head. The next second, there was nothing but flames.

I can't breathe. Can't think beyond the swelling tidal wave of unbearable grief rising up to suffocate me.

She's gone.

Gone.

Ripped from me, just like Oliver and Jared. Just like my mother.

"Rachel!" My breath sobs in and out of my lungs as I choke on her name. I dig my fingernails into the cobblestones beneath me as everything I'd built my world on turns to ash.

I have nothing left. Nothing but the merciless creature in front of me, still spewing the wall of flame that killed her. Nothing but the terrible need to take it with me as I die.

She'd promised we'd be together. Live or die. We'd do it together.

I'm going to make her keep her word.

And I'm going to take the Cursed One with me.

Pushing myself to my feet, I face the beast and raise the jars above my head. I'll ram them down the creature's throat and hope I find my family waiting for me after death swallows me.

Despair is nothing but cold, brittle determination driving me forward. One last plan. One last calculation. One last effort and my life will count for something as I join her.

Vaulting over a pile of broken steel, I brace myself to leap straight into the beast's mouth, but then I see the impossible.

Rachel.

She's sliding on her stomach beneath the wall of fire, her knife aiming straight for the monster's unprotected side. She's covered in soot, her clothing singed and torn.

She's the most beautiful sight I've ever seen.

The stream of fire exploding out of the beast's mouth sizzles into a puff of acrid smoke. It twists its head toward Rachel and sniffs the air.

I'm not about to let it kill her.

"Hey!" I yell and run forward. "Here! Look here!"

It ignores me.

Rachel's forward momentum slows as she hits the scales blown off the beast's side. She can't stab its side before it realizes she's there. She can't, unless I provide a distraction.

I calculate trajectories, pray I haven't misjudged the velocity needed, and hurl the jars I carry. They explode a few yards in front of the Cursed One and send me flying backward onto a pile of rubble.

The creature snaps its head toward the sound of the explosion and roars a stream of fire at the offending noise. Rachel belly-crawls over debris, pushes her left hand into the ground for balance, and raises her knife. The blade flashes crimson and gold in the light of the fire, and she buries it in the monster's side.

The Cursed One screams and spits fire as it coils in on itself. Rachel is trying to pull her knife free, but its tail knocks into her, sending her sprawling. I push off the wreckage and race to her. Grabbing her beneath her arms, I haul her backward as the beast screams again.

"Get a sword. Another knife. Let's finish it," she says.

But it's too late. The creature jerks its head up, trembling as if being held still against its will, then dives into the ground, scales and debris sliding in after it as it burrows toward its lair.

I pull Rachel to her feet and crush her to me. She wraps herself around me and holds on as if I'm all that is keeping her from drowning. My hands are shaking, and my throat feels raw from screaming, but in the midst of the flaming wreckage around us, all I can feel is gratitude that Rachel is still alive. I want to hold her until the shaking passes, until the terrible panic I felt when I thought she was engulfed in flames dies completely, but I can't. We're surrounded on three sides by fire.

"We have to get out of here," I say, and start leading her toward the shattered gate.

"I don't understand what just happened."

"I don't either. It left without trying to finish us off. It never leaves when it knows its prey is still alive."

Rachel stumbles over a slab of concrete and grabs for me. "It didn't look like it had a choice. It was behaving the same way it did when you controlled it out in the Wasteland."

"But if it wasn't obeying our device, then who was controlling it? Maybe Rowansmark has tech even stronger than the device the Commander tried to steal?"

She shakes her head. "I don't know." Looking at the carnage around us—the flames, the rubble, the bodies trapped in what would become their funeral pyre—she shudders. "It doesn't matter who was controlling it. We started this, Logan. We brought it here."

It does matter, because if the total annihilation of Baalboden was the goal, whoever was controlling the Cursed One can send it back to finish off the survivors. And it matters because I have no doubt the Commander and anyone else hungry for power will stop at nothing to get their hands on tech like that. We can't let that happen. Today is vivid proof.

But she's right. We called the Cursed One. We started this. And we'll need to live with that. I don't know how we'll do it. I'm weary, inside and out. I want to take her hand. Walk away from the destruction. Disappear into the Wasteland. We could travel for weeks. Months. Find a quiet place where there are no power-hungry leaders, no cities, no memories to reach out and slice into us when we least expect it.

We could, but then who would hunt down and destroy the tech that caused today's devastation? Who would honor the memory of Jared's sacrifice and exact justice for the Commander's actions? The weight of what must be done settles on my shoulders as I take Rachel's hand.

We climb over the debris, walk through the hole in the gate, and turn to face the city. She leans into me as I wrap my arms around her, and we watch Baalboden burn.

CHAPTER
SEVENTY-ONE

RACHEL

The city burns for three days. Most of its citizens never make it out. The ones who do are divided between worshipping the ground Logan and I walk on for rescuing them, and blaming us for bringing disaster upon everyone by rebelling against the Commander's protection.

We can't find the Commander. I don't see how he could've made it back into the city when we had to blow the gate to pieces to get out, but I suppose it's possible he's one of the charred bodies lying inside what used to be Baalboden.

I think it's much more likely that when he realized his city was doomed, he ran into the Wasteland with his guards like the coward he is. The thought sparks a weak flame of fury within me, but I'm too exhausted to keep it alive.

Sylph made it out, along with her new husband. I recognize a few other faces of girls I knew in Life Skills. Melkin's wife made it out too. I'm grateful, even though the sight of her fills me with suffocating dread.

When those who hate us leave to seek asylum in another city-state, I don't try to stop them. Neither does Logan.

The rest of them elect Logan as their new leader. Some of them simply because he rescued them by blowing up the gate. But most of them want him as their leader because he publicly stood up to the Commander at the Claiming ceremony, an unprecedented act of courage he then trumped by escaping from the dungeon.

There's talk of rebuilding elsewhere. Quinn and Willow join our group, and Willow quickly finds a kindred spirit in Nola. As Drake, Logan, Willow, and Nola organize teams of survivors to search the ruins for salvageable goods, I slip away and enter what's left of Baalboden.

The city is a carcass of bones and ash. Hollowed out. Every vestige of life burned into silence.

We understand each other.

The magnitude of what I've caused is a crushing weight I refuse to lift. Let it consume me. Let it drive me to my knees. It's less than I deserve.

I leave the rubble of the gate behind and walk the charred, twisted streets until I reach the ruins of the home I shared with Dad. The home where Logan first joined us as an apprentice. Where Oliver visited regularly with sticky buns and fairy tales.

The ash clings to me as I sink down to sit where our kitchen table used to be. If I close my eyes, it can all go back to the way it used to be. If I close my eyes, I can see Dad, his gray eyes shining with pride as I find my first target with a bow and arrow. Oliver opening his arms wide for me as he walks up to the front door.

If I close my eyes, I'm still whole.

But I can't close my eyes. I don't dare. I *need* to see this. To sear it into my brain so I never forget. When seeing isn't enough, I dig my fingers into the ash and let the silky texture cling to me like a scar I'll wear for the rest of my life.

"Rachel."

Logan drops down into the ash beside me and grabs a handful too.

"This is where I signed a contract with Jared. I had to work hard to look only at the paper and not get caught staring at his beautiful daughter." He looks to the right. "And that's where I suffered my first defeat in combat at the hands of a girl two years younger than me. You knocked my feet out from under me. I never saw it coming, because it never occurred to me a girl would know how to fight."

I follow his gaze and see us. Fighting. Laughing. Living.

There's no life here now.

"Someone else wanted this to happen. Someone else pushed the controls that sent the Cursed One into the city. It wasn't your fault," he says, and the silence within me shivers like pieces of broken glass.

"I started it all. Don't you see that? I tried to climb over the Wall and got caught, and look at the result." I fling my hand to encompass the blackened ruins around us. The wind tugs gently at the ash I hold and it floats away like bits of silver.

"No." He scoots closer to me, and takes my chin in between his thumb and forefinger. "You wouldn't have tried to get over the Wall if I'd told you what I was working on. I thought I was protecting you, but I should've trusted you."

His eyes are steady, and a world of pain and resolve lives

inside them.

"But beyond all that, none of this would've happened if the Commander hadn't tried to steal something that didn't belong to him. We aren't done, Rachel. He needs to be found and stopped. The other city-states need to be warned about the weapons Rowansmark has. If there is a master device out there capable of controlling the Cursed One, we need to find and destroy it. And there are people depending on us for leadership." He looks over his shoulder.

I follow his gaze and see Sylph, her face resolute, a new-found gravity carved into her by everything she's lost. Beside her, Smithson stands tall and steady, his arm curved around her shoulders. Nola, Willow, and Quinn are next to him, looking fierce and ready. Drake and Thom stand slightly behind them, their eyes trained on me, while behind them teams of survivors comb the wreckage for anything we can use to start over. I look at them and realize I see something I never thought I'd see again.

Hope.

They're broken, but they aren't beaten. They want to live. Not just breathe in and out, watching one day fade into the next. They want to *live*.

And they want us to help them do it.

I'm so tired. I want to lie down, sink beneath the ashes, let them slide gently into my lungs and carry me to Dad and Oliver. I want to, but I can't. Because Logan is right. We have to find the Commander. Warn the other leaders. And bring whoever invented the hellish device that started all of this to his knees.

My debts have yet to be paid.

Tugging at the leather pouch I wear, I let the ashes I hold

trickle inside to become one with the dirt from my father's grave. Logan reaches for me, and together we stand and walk toward the group waiting for us. Linking arms with Sylph on one side and Logan on the other, I lean my head against him in the ruins of what once was as the sun sets one last time on Baalboden.

ACKNOWLEDGEMENTS:

I have a deep fear that I'll thank the many, *many* people who have helped make this book possible and end up forgetting someone. My hubby assures me this won't happen. But we both know I'm the girl who constantly forgets to charge her cell phone and can never remember anyone's name. So . . . if you contributed to *Defiance* and I somehow forget you in this list of thanks, I humbly beg your pardon and promise you cookies and lemon bars to make up for it.

First, I have to thank God for giving me the ability to tell stories and for being the foundation beneath my feet.

And because dedicating the book to him isn't enough, I also want to thank my husband. Clint, thank you for letting me disappear for hours to write while you changed diapers, handled dinner, and made it possible for me to meet my deadlines. This book wouldn't have happened without your commitment to supporting my dreams. I love you.

Thanks also to Zach, Jordan, and Tyler for watching the baby so I could write, eagerly asking me about my story, and proudly announcing to everyone that your mom was going to publish a book. I'm also grateful to you, Johanna. Finally bringing you home from China gave me so much incentive to write the book I thought might be too big for me. You are amazing kids, and I'm so blessed to be your mom.

Thank you, Mom and Dad, for feeding my love of reading and for raising me to believe I could do anything I set my mind to.

I also owe a huge debt of gratitude to my awesome agent, Holly Root, for always believing in me and for being fiercely in my corner. You are a rock star in my world.

This book wouldn't be what it is today without the help of my incredible team of critique partners and beta readers. Not only did all of you help shape this book in different ways, you are all treasured friends. M. G. Buehrlen, thank you for reading, rereading, and rereading again. And for the conversation that helped me realize I needed to include Logan's POV. How many hours did we spend on the phone discussing this book? I'm grateful for them all! Myra McEntire, awkward kissing scenes FTW! Asking myself *What would Myra do?* is now my new go-to for all fictional romantic situations. Thanks also for being so excited for me every step of the way. K. B. Wagers, you've been by my side almost from the beginning. Thanks for being my weapons and sparring expert, my cheerleader, and my friend. Heather Palmquist, you are not only a fabulous beta reader, you are an even more fabulous sister. I'm so glad you were part of this journey with me. Sara McClung, you rock as a beta reader. Thanks for being so excited about this book. Shannon Messenger, thanks for reading scenes even while you were neck-deep in drafting, and for being unflinchingly honest. Jodi Meadows, thanks for helping me figure out what to call the Switch. And for being a huge fan of the almost-kissing scenes. Beth Revis, thanks for encouraging me as I neared my first deadline. Even though you did almost kill me with Nutella.

Tricia Bentley, even though you didn't read *Defiance* as I was writing it, you were my first ever reader (many moons ago) and while you keep assuring me I don't need to apologize for the mess of a novel you read, I really am grateful you were interested enough to keep asking me for more. You helped motivate me to finish writing my first book. Thank you.

A heartfelt thanks to the entire team at Balzer + Bray for embracing *Defiance* and making me feel so welcome. Kristin Daly Rens, I knew from our first conversation that you were the perfect editor for me. The llama simply confirmed my hunch. Your painstaking attention to detail and your unabashed enthusiasm for Rachel and Logan challenged me to push myself to do more than I thought I could do. Thank you. Sara Sargent, you are definitely a Ninja of many things! I appreciate you keeping me on track and making my interactions with B+B so much fun.

Thank you to Alison Klapthor and Alison Donalty for my gorgeous cover. You truly captured Rachel's fierce spirit along with all the key elements of the book. I nearly licked my monitor the first time I saw the cover. Thank you also to Emilie Polster and Stefanie Hoffman for your fabulous marketing efforts, and to Caroline Sun and Olivia deLeon for being my publicity gurus. I appreciate all of you.

Thanks to my amazing Pixie sisters. You've been my cheerleaders, my readers, my source of insight, and my friends since that wonderful summer in San Francisco in 2008. I can't imagine my publishing journey without you by my side.

While I was writing *Defiance*, I went on a writer's retreat with many members of the Music City Romance Writers' chapter. I wrote eleven thousand words that weekend, and just outside my bedroom I had the soundtrack of twenty-two women singing some pretty awesome karaoke. Whip it, MCRW! (And thank you for being a constant encouragement.)

A huge thanks to the talented Tashina Falene for designing the jewelry pieces from the book and for being so excited about the story. I also want to give a shout out to two book bloggers who have either read chapters for me or inspired me while I was drafting: Catie S. and Julie Daly. You make me want to write amazing stories. Thank you.

Finally, thank you to all of my blog readers, my Twitter followers, and my Facebook friends who got excited about this book and told a friend about it. From book bloggers to fellow writers to enthusiastic readers, you amaze me. I still have to pinch myself when I realize there are people outside of my immediate friends and family who love this book. I feel like the luckiest girl in the world.